C++ PROGRAM DESIGN

An Introduction to Programming and Object-Oriented Design

initial
6off
built in types at once nice
to assign

Erra P 180

Classes really don't come
particularly early - they are
used early through window API,
but actual creation can't
until after ref Parameter
Note: about when we introduce
There

functions, however, are lots capsuled
to when we introduce New,
working until after control

+ inheritance & templates at
End after pointers

Starts quite slow t ½ book to get
Maybe Procedure/ ref Parameter

+ classes early, however though
-- theory "windows" Class
- launches not as early as
   they might be -after
   (at least)
--- EZ windows PC Based

- cap first letter of
   var names and
   types names

- libraries in general
   not complete - only some
   shown

+ code in color makes
   easier to read

--- built ins are termed
   "object"

- most interesting example
   use "windows" class

-- first example of
   class of classes
   window API

+ numerous pictorial
   story var + menu
   usage with different
   concepts

C++ PROGRAM DESIGN

An Introduction to Programming and Object-Oriented Design

James P. Cohoon

Jack W. Davidson

both from
University of Virginia

IRWIN

Chicago • Bogotá • Boston • Buenos Aires • Caracas
London • Madrid • Mexico City • Sydney • Toronto

Irwin Book Team

Publisher*: Tom Casson*
Senior sponsoring editor: *Elizabeth A. Jones*
Senior developmental editor: *Kelley Butcher*
Project supervisor: *Beth Cigler*
Production supervisor: *Laurie Sander*
Designer: *Michael Warrell*
Director, Prepress Purchasing: *Kimberly Meriwether David*
Compositor: *Interactive Composition Corporation*
Typeface: *10/12 Times Roman*
Printer: *Times Mirror Higher Education Group, Inc., Print Group*

Library of Congress Cataloging-in-Publication Data
Cohoon, James P.
   C++ program design: an introduction to programming and object-oriented design/James P. Cohoon, Jack W. Davidson
      p.   cm.
   Includes index.
   ISBN   0-256-19744-X
   1. C++(Computer program language). 2. Object-oriented programming (Computer science). I. Davidson, Jack W. (Jack Winfred). II. Title.
QA76.73.C153.C653   1997
005.13'3—dc20   96-28420

Printed in the United States of America
 2 3 4 5 6 7 8 9 0 WCB 3 2 1 0 9 8 7

Dedicated to:

To Audrey and Joanne, our parents, families, and teachers from whom we have learned so much and owe our gratitude.

Preface

INTRODUCTION

It is an inescapable fact that the computer has become a fixture in our lives. Much like the automobile in the 1940s and 1950s, the computer has changed the way we live and do business. Computer systems are used increasingly to control complex systems such as telephone systems, air traffic control systems, and power plants that affect our everyday lives. It is truly amazing how far we have come in such a short time and how fast things are changing even today.

Because of the pervasive use of computers, we believe that everyone should have a basic working knowledge of how computers are programmed. This textbook is about the fundamentals of programming and software development using C++, a popular high-level programming language developed by Bjarne Stroustrup of AT&T Bell Laboratories. We chose C++ because it supports the development of software using the object-oriented approach. An advantage of object-oriented development is that it lets us build complex software systems employing many of the techniques that have been used for constructing complex physical systems, such as cars, airplanes, or buildings. This book is targeted for a first programming course, and it has been designed to be appropriate for people from all disciplines. We assume no prior programming skills and use mathematics and science at a level appropriate to first-year college students.

Some of the book's important features are:

- *Classes are introduced early.* Chapter 1 includes a gentle introduction to the object-oriented paradigm. Material is presented there to whet students' appetites. We believe that students must first be client users of objects before they can appreciate the difficulties of designing flexible, usable objects. All proficient designers started as users. The next several chapters introduce and use some standard stream class objects, such as cout and cin, and a limited number of objects derived from a graphical library developed for the textbook. This experience helps reinforce the concepts of encapsulation, software reuse, and the object-oriented programming paradigm. After this solid introduction to the use of objects, we design and develop over 25 classes and ADTs throughout the remainder of the book.

■ *We present the use of a graphical Application Programmer Interface (API) designed specifically for beginning programmers to develop interesting programs.* We provide a portable, object-oriented graphical library, named EzWindows, for the easy display of simple geometric, bitmap, and text objects. Using the API provides several important experiences for the student. First, students are client users of a software library. As mentioned earlier, using well-designed objects helps novice programmers begin to appreciate good object-oriented design. Their experience as users forms the basis for becoming designers. Second, using the API introduces students to the real-world practice of developing programs using an application-specific library. Third, using EzWindows to perform graphical input and output exposes the student to event-based programming and the dominant mode of input and output used in real applications, and it permits development of exciting and visually interesting programs. This experience motivates the students, and it provides a visually concrete set of objects that help students understand the object-oriented paradigm. EzWindows is simple enough that it allows even the first programming assignments to be graphical. Examples using EzWindows are sprinkled throughout the text. However, the presentation is done in a fashion that accommodates instructors who prefer to cover only ANSI materials.

■ *Software engineering design concepts are introduced via problem studies and software projects.* Besides containing numerous small examples for introducing C++ and object-oriented design concepts, each chapter considers one or more problems in detail. As appropriate, there is object-oriented analysis and design, algorithm development, and code to realize the design. There are also two chapters devoted to the principles of software project development using our EzWindows API (Chapters 11 and 16). These chapters are springboards for software reuse and for projects suitable for individual and group work.

■ *Programming and style tips are presented in boxes that clearly separate this material from the main text.* In addition to explaining C++ and object-oriented programming, we also give advice on how to be a better and more knowledgeable programmer and designer. For example, there are important tips on how to avoid common programming errors, writing readable code, the new directions the draft ANSI standard is taking, as well as tips on performance and software engineering. Boxes are also used to present one or two pages per chapter of historical information on computing.

■ *The C++ language as defined by the draft ANSI standard is given broad coverage.* Our original naive intent was to offer complete coverage of C++. However, such a presentation would be overwhelming for the beginning student. For example, the draft standard describes over 150 standard classes and libraries. Rather than being encyclopedic, we have adapted an educational paradigm used by our Computer Science department. This paradigm recognizes three levels of learning: exposure, familiarity, and mastery. We provide in-depth coverage of the materials that any reasonable introductory course would need, introduce much of the remaining matter, and give pointers to the rest. We have tracked the ANSI standardization effort and offer sections in the text that cover relatively new additions and modifications to the C++ language, such as type `bool`, and namespaces. The broad coverage provides flexibility for the instructor. For example, an instructor may choose not to cover inheritance, but instead to cover templates. For the students, the coverage allows advanced learners to go further in the language, and it makes the book valuable as a reference source.

CONTEXT

In 1991, with the support of the National Science Foundation, the department of Computer Science at the University of Virginia began developing a new Computer Science curriculum. We carefully examined our current curriculum and those of several other peer schools. What we found were curricula that emphasized:

- Use of a programming language that is rarely used outside of undergraduate courses.
- Construction of small programs, consisting of at most a few hundred lines.
- Use of text-based input/output interfaces.
- Development of programs "from scratch" for each assignment.
- Development in an environment lacking modern tools.
- Programming in isolation.
- The belief that if a program "works" it is acceptable.
- An informal development approach rather than one that is rigorous and requires analytical skills.

Comparing this with the situation in the real world, we saw considerable differences. Practicing computer professionals:

- Use programming languages designed for developing large applications.
- Deal with software systems that are often thousands or even millions of source lines long.
- Are involved most often in modifying and maintaining such systems rather than developing them.
- Work in teams, not as a single programmer.
- Do system development according to mandated specifications.
- Build systems that use graphical user interfaces to do input and output.
- Use existing libraries and tools to build systems.

To better prepare our students for real-world programming, we developed a course and this book.

Programming

Most of the important concepts and problems in computer science cannot be appreciated unless one has a good understanding of what a program is and how to write one. Unfortunately, learning to program is difficult. Programming well, like writing well, takes years of practice. In fact, teaching programming and writing are, in some respects, very similar.

Students are taught writing by reading examples of good prose, and by writing, writing, writing. In the process they learn the important skill of how to organize ideas so they can be presented effectively. As students develop their skills, they move from writing and editing a paragraph or several paragraphs on to larger pieces of prose, such as essays, short stories, and reports.

Our approach to teaching programming is similar to teaching writing, but with one very important addition. Throughout the text, we present and discuss many examples of both good and bad programming. Programming exercises give the student the opportunity to practice organizing and writing code. In addition, we offer examples that facilitate learning the practical skill of modifying existing code. This is done through the use of code that is specifically designed to be modified by the student. We have found this mechanism to be effective because it forces the student to read and understand the provided code. In the text, a disk icon signals that this code is on the floppy disk included with the book.

Why C++

As we began our new curriculum development, one of the first issues was choosing the programming language to use. Like many departments, we had been using Pascal. While it was unanimously decided that Pascal should be replaced, the choice of a replacement was the subject of much heated debate. Some of the languages we considered were C, C++, Modula-3, Scheme, and Smalltalk. A deciding factor was that we wanted to use a language that we ourselves use professionally. This narrowed the choices to C or C++. While the decision was not unanimous, we choose C++ based on the belief that the object-oriented paradigm would be the dominant programming paradigm of the future.

In hindsight, it appears that we made the correct choice. C++ has continued to grow in popularity, and many companies use it as their development language. Indeed, many of our graduates report that when they interview for a job, a question they are often asked is whether they know C++. We believe that we will see a continuing shift to C++ as the introductory programming language of choice. We have also been pleasantly surprised by the effect on our students. The students in our upper-level courses who have completed our software development sequence can tackle much larger and harder problems than the students who had completed the comparable sequence in our old curriculum. In addition, we have seen substantial migration of other disciplines to C++. For example, the commerce school at our university now has all of its students take a C++ course, and the engineering disciplines that had previously required an introductory Fortran course now either require or recommend our C++ course.

Objects early

Our experience of teaching C++ over the past five years shows that the object-oriented paradigm can be introduced to beginning programmers. In our initial course offerings, we introduced objects near the end of the course and did superficial coverage of objects, classes, overloading, and inheritance. Essentially we taught C using C++ syntax, and input and output mechanisms. This approach failed. It introduced a new concept too late in the course—students were not able to integrate the material. We revised our course to introduce objects earlier, and found this approach worked much better. Students now have time to absorb this material because it is used and reinforced throughout the course rather than just at the end. The objects early approach is reflected in this text. Students begin using standard objects in Chapter 2. Chapters 3 through 7 introduce the students to the use of graphical objects from the EzWindows API. After this solid introduction to using objects, Chapter 8 introduces classes and the design of objects, and it logically follows the chapters that introduce control structures, functions, and libraries (Chapters 4 through 7). We strongly believe that this is the proper sequencing of the material in an introductory textbook.

Software projects

As noted, what we had been teaching in the past was not at all close to what was happening in the real world. To educate future computer scientists in the skills that support the engineering and comprehension of large software systems, reengineering of existing systems, and application of innovative techniques (such as software reuse), our department deemed it necessary to begin introducing this material in the first course. Our software project chapters (Chapters 11 and 16) are vehicles for this introduction. These chapters provide several important experiences for the student. First, both projects use our EzWindows API. Using the API to do event-based programming and graphical input and output exposes students to the programming model typically used in real-world applications, and it permits students to develop more exciting and interesting programs. If desired, the software projects facilitate students' working together in groups of up to four. Again, this mirrors real-world practice, where it is rare for a lone programmer to develop an application. The software projects also illustrate software maintenance. Many of the exercises at the end of the software project chapters call for the student to make major modifications or non-trivial extensions to the project program.

CHAPTER SUMMARY

- *Chapter 1: Computing and the object-oriented design methodology —* basic computing terminology, machine organization, software, software development, software engineering, object-oriented design and programming.

- *Chapter 2: C++: the fundamentals* — program organization, function main(), include statement, comments, definitions, writing readable code, interactive input and output, fundamental types, literals, constants, declarations, expressions, conversions, precedence.

- *Chapter 3: Modifying objects* — assignment statement and conversions, extractions, const objects, increment and decrement, insertion and extractions, graphical objects and the EzWindows API.

- *Chapter 4: Control constructs* — logical values and operators, truth tables, bool, relational operators, general precedence, if statement, if-else statement, sorting, switch statement, enum, while statement, for statement, invariants, do statement.

- *Chapter 5: Function usage basics libraries* — functions, value parameters, formal parameters, actual parameters, invocation, flow of control, activation records, prototyping, preprocessor, inclusion directives, conditional compilation, macro definitions, software reuse, using libraries, standard streams, manipulators, and iostream, iomanip, math, ctype, string, assert libraries.

- *Chapter 6: Programmer-defined functions* — function definitions, parameters, invocation, flow of control, return statement, scope, local objects, global objects, initialization, name reuse, top-down design, recursion.

- *Chapter 7: Parameter passing* — reference parameters, file input and output, constant parameters, default parameters, parameter casting, function overloading, factory automation simulator/trainer.

- *Chapter 8: The class construct*: programmer-defined data types, class construct, information hiding, encapsulation, object-oriented analysis and design, access specification, data members, member functions, constructors, kaleidoscope program, object-oriented factory automation simulator/trainer.

- *Chapter 9: Abstract data types* — data abstraction, object-oriented design, default and copy constructors, inspectors, mutators, facilitators, auxiliary functions, memberwise assignment, const member functions, arithmetic operator overloading, reference return, insertion and extraction overloading, pseudorandom number generation, ADTs for rational and pseudorandom numbers, and the red-yellow-green guessing game.

- *Chapter 10: Arrays* — one-dimensional arrays, subscripting, parameter passing, initialization, strings, multi-dimensional arrays, tables, matrices, sorting, InsertionSort, QuickSort, binary search, list representation, ADTs for playing cards, decks, and poker hands.

- *Chapter 11: The EzWindows API* — Application programmer interfaces, graphical user interface, event-based programming, window coordinate system, call backs, mouse and timer events, EzWindows API mechanics, ADTs for simple windows, bitmaps, text labels, and a Simon Says game.

- *Chapter 12: Pointer types* — lvalues, rvalues, pointer types, addressing, indirection, pointer assignment, indirect assignment, pointers as parameters, simulating reference parameters, pointers to pointers, constant pointers, pointers to constants, equivalence of array and pointer notation, character string processing, command-line parameters, pointers to functions.

- *Chapter 13: Dynamic data types* — dynamic objects, free store, operators new and delete operators, new library function set_new_handler(), dangling pointers, memory leak, destructors, copy constructors, member assignment, this pointer, friend to a class, ADTs for string tables and large numbers.

- *Chapter 14: Inheritance* — object-oriented design, reuse, base class, derived class, single inheritance, is-a relationship, has-a relationship, uses-a relationship, shape hierarchy, controlling inheritance, protected members, multiple inheritance, ADTs for rectangles, circles, ellipses, and triangles, an object-oriented kaleidoscope program.

- *Chapter 15: Templates and polymorphism* — generic actions and types, function template, class template, container class, sequential lists, linked list, iterator class, polymorphism, virtual function, pure virtual function, abstract base class, virtually derived class, virtual multiple inheritance, ADTs for list elements, sequential lists, and list iterators.

- *Chapter 16: Software project: bug hunt!* — encapsulation, inheritance, virtual functions, object-oriented design, Bug Hunt game, ADTs for various kinds of bugs and a game controller.

- *Appendices* — ASCII character set, general precedence table, iostream, stdlib, time and string libraries, vector class, string class, namespaces, using statements, EzWindows API.

USING THIS BOOK

This text has more material than can be covered in a single course. The extra coverage was deliberate—it allows instructors to select their choice of topics on programming and software development. The book was also designed for flexibility in teaching. For example, if an instructor desires to move the introduction of classes earlier in the course, he or she can cover iteration after classes and our development of the rational number ADT. If an instructor desires to introduce classes after arrays, then sections 10.1 – 10.7 of Chapter 10 can precede Chapters 8 and 9. Also, the discussion of inheritance in Chapter 14 can precede the coverage of pointers and dynamic objects in Chapters 12 and 13. Instructors who do a breadth-first coverage of computer science may choose to omit the software project chapters and instead substitute material from other sources that cover topics such as the social and ethical aspects of computing or elementary formal logic.

The version of the course we teach has the following layout.

Week	Topic	Readings
1	Computing and object-oriented design	Chapter 1
2	Programming fundamentals	Chapter 2
3	Object manipulation	Chapter 3
4	Conditional statements	Chapter 4 (sections 4.1 – 4.3)
5	Iteration statements	Chapter 4 (sections 4.7 – 4.11)
6	Functions and reuse	Chapter 5, Chapter 6
7	Parameter passing	Chapter 7
8	Classes and object-oriented analysis and design (OOA/OOD)	Chapter 8, Chapter 9 (sections 9.1 – 9.3)
9	ADTs	Chapter 9 (sections 9.3 – 9.7)
10	Lists	Chapter 10 (sections 10.1 – 10.5)
11	List manipulation	Chapter 10 (sections 10.5 – 10.9)
12	Project—Simon Says, OOA/OOD	Chapter 11
13	Pointers	Chapter 12
14	Dynamic data types	Chapter 13
15	Inheritance, OOA/OOD	Chapter 14

Depending upon faculty interests, the material covered in week 12 can vary. In the introductory course at our university, we spend one week every semester on a problem in detail. Generally this examination leads to a final project. If the project involves dynamic data types, then the problem study is delayed until after dynamic objects are introduced.

SUPPLEMENTARY MATERIALS

In addition to the included floppy disk, which contains source code for much of our programs and listings, we have developed other materials. For example, there is a complete set of slide transparencies (approximately 300 slides). The course we teach also has a closed-laboratory component that meets once a week for reinforcing current course topics. For these laboratories, we have developed a student laboratory manual. These materials are available from the publisher. For more detailed information, visit their World Wide Web (WWW) site at location http://www.irwin.com.

SYMBOLS

The following icons are used in the margins throughout the text.

The floppy disk icon is associated with some code listings and programs. The icon indicates that the code is available on the disk supplied with the book. When the icon is associated with the label Program, the program consists of a single file. If the icon is associated with the label Listing, a library file or one file in a multi-file program is being made available.

The flag icon indicates a warning about programming. Often these are tips on how to avoid common programming errors.

The book icon indicates that the associated material is concerned with the C++ programming language itself. The two typical uses of this icon are for advanced C++ topics or for describing a proposed language extension that can have an impact on future software development.

The column icon indicates that the associated material is related to programming style. At the current time, there are a number of conventions being used. The manner that code is presented in this text generally reflects the dominant convention. (Of course, our variation is the best!)

The checked book icon is used to signify programming tips or to highlight material that presents a more detailed discussion or a side bar to the current topic.

The abacus icon is used to indicate discussion on the history of computing. Many people often mistakenly think that computing is simply writing programs. While designing and writing programs is certainly an important part of computing, it is by no means the only thing encompassed by computing. Each chapter contains at least one anecdote regarding triumphs and failures of the pioneers in computing.

THE AUTHORS

James P. Cohoon is a professor in the Computer Science department at the University of Virginia and is a former member of the technical staff at AT&T Bell Laboratories. He joined the faculty after receiving his Ph.D. from the University of Minnesota. He has been nominated twice by the department for the university's best teaching award. In 1994, Professor Cohoon was awarded a

Fulbright Fellowship to Germany, where he lectured on C++ and software engineering. Professor Cohoon's research interests include algorithms, computer-aided design of electronic systems, optimization strategies, and computer science education. He is the author of over fifty papers in these fields. He is a member of the Association of Computing Machinery (ACM), the ACM Special Interest Group on Design Automation (SIGDA), the ACM Special Interest Group on Computer Science Education (SIGCSE), the Institute of Electrical and Electronics Engineers (IEEE), and the IEEE Circuits and Systems Society. He is currently chairperson of SIGDA. He can be reached at cohoon@virginia.edu. His WWW home page is http://www.cs.virginia.edu/~cohoon

Jack W. Davidson is also a professor in the Computer Science department at the University of Virginia. He joined the faculty after receiving his Ph.D. from the University of Arizona. In 1990, Professor Davidson received an NCR Faculty Innovation Award for innovation in teaching. Professor Davidson's research interests include compilers, computer architecture, systems software, and computer science education. He is the author of over fifty papers in these fields. He is a member of the ACM, the ACM Special Interest Group on Programming Languages (SIGPLAN), the ACM Special Interest Group on Computer Architecture (SIGARCH), SIGCSE, the IEEE, and the IEEE Computer Society. He serves as an associate editor of *Transactions on Programming Languages and Systems*, ACM's flagship journal on programming languages and systems. He can be reached at jwd@virginia.edu. His WWW home page is http://www.cs.virginia.edu/~jwd.

DELVING FURTHER

The following are primary references on the C++ language.

- M. A. Ellis and B. Stroustrup, *The Annotated C++ Reference Manual*, Reading, MA: Addison-Wesley, 1990.
- Working Paper for the Draft Proposed International Standard for Information Systems—Programming Language C++, X3J16/96-0018 WG21/N0836, Washington: American National Standards Institute, 1996.

The following are good sources on libraries and more-advanced object-oriented design and program development.

- M. D. Carroll and M. A. Ellis, *Designing and Coding Reusable C++*, Reading, MA: Addison-Wesley, 1995.
- J. Bergin, *Data Abstraction: The Object-Oriented Approach Using C++*, New York: McGraw-Hill, 1994.
- M. P. Cline, G. A. Lomow, *C++ FAQs*, Reading, MA: Addison-Wesley, 1995.
- S. B. Lippman, *C++ Primer*, Reading, MA: Addison-Wesley, 1993.
- S. Meyers, *Effective C++*, Reading, MA: Addison-Wesley, 1992.

- S. Meyers, *More Effective C++*, Reading, MA: Addison-Wesley, 1996.
- S. Maguire, *Writing Solid Code*, Redmond, WA: Microsoft Press, 1993.
- D. R. Musser and A. Saini, *STL Tutorial and Reference Guide*, Reading, MA: Addison-Wesley, 1995.
- P. J. Plauger, *The Standard C Library*, Englewood Cliffs, NJ: Prentice-Hall, 1992.
- P. J. Plauger, A. Stepanov, M. Lee, and D. R. Musser, *The Standard Template Library*, Englewood Cliffs, NJ: Prentice-Hall, 1996.
- B. Stroustrup, *The Design and Evolution of C++*, Reading, MA: Addison-Wesley, 1994.
- S. Teale, *C++ IOStreams*, Reading, MA: Addison-Wesley, 1993.

The following are good sources for learning more about the history of computing.

- S. Augarten, *Bit by Bit: An Illustrated History of Computers*, New York: Ticknor & Fields, 1984.
- J. Palfreman and D. Swade, *The Dream Machine: Exploring the Computer Age*, London: BBC Books, 1991.
- M. R. Williams, *A History of Computing Technology*, Englewood Cliffs, NJ: Prentice-Hall, 1985.
- H. G. Stine, *The Untold Story of the Computer Revolution*, New York: Arbor House, 1985.

ACKNOWLEDGMENTS

We thank the University of Virginia and its department of Computer Science for providing an environment that made this book possible. In particular, we thank Mark Bailey, Alan Batson, Clark Coleman, James Ortega, and Jane Prey for their many comments. We also thank Bruce Childers who helped design and implement the EzWindows API. We are grateful to the Technical University of Munich and Princeton University for providing environments that allowed us to do much of the early development.

We thank all of the people at Irwin for their efforts in making this project a reality. In particular, we thank: Tom Casson, for his support and encouragement; Laurie Sander for her product management skills; Brian Kibby and Denise Mariani, for their creative marketing ideas; Michael Warrell, for his cover design; and June Waldman, for her copy-editing ability. Special thanks go to Elizabeth (Betsy) Jones, our sponsoring editor, for support, direction, and focus throughout this project, Kelley Butcher, our developmental editor, for managing and synthesizing the reviewing process, and Beth Cigler for her timely project management and last minute copy-editing.

We thank Elizabeth Lee Falta of Louisiana Tech University for class testing, reviewing, and providing very helpful feedback.

We also thank the following reviewers for their valuable comments and suggestions:

Rhoda Baggs Koss, Florida Institute of Technology
Kenneth Bayse, Clark University
Leslie Blackford, Wheaton College
Joanne Cohoon, University of Virginia
Gerald Dueck, Brandon University
H. E. Dunsmore, Purdue University
Ann Ford, University of Michigan
Robert Holloway, University of Wisconsin
Van Howbert, Colorado State University
Leon Jololian, New Jersey Institute of Technology
Michael Jones, Encyclopedia Brittanica, Inc.
Edward Keefe, Des Moines Area Community College
R. Raymond Lang, Xavier University
John Lowther, Michigan Technological University
Lewis Lum, University of Portland
Bruce Maxim, University of Michigan at Dearborn
Jin Mazumdar, State University of New York at Fredonia
Michael McCarthy, University of Pittsburgh
Suzanne Miller Dorney, Grand Valley State University
Howard Pyron, University of Missouri at Rolla
Donna Reese, Mississippi State University
Charles Riedesel, University of Nebraska
Carol Roberts, University of Maine
W. Brent Seales, University of Kentucky
Shashi Shekhar, University of Minnesota
Neelam Soundarajan, Ohio State University
M. A. Sridhar, University of South Carolina
Phil Sweany, Michigan Technological University
Ralph Tomlinson, Iowa State University
Jane Turk, LaSalle University

We thank our spouses Audrey and Joanne and our children for their efforts, cooperation, and sacrifices in making this book happen.

Finally, we thank the users of this book. We welcome your comments, suggestions, and ideas for improving this material. Please write in care of the publisher, Richard D. Irwin, Inc., or send E-mail to cohoon@virginia.edu or jwd@virginia.edu.

J. P. C
J. W. D

Contents

CHAPTER 1

Computing and the object-oriented design methodology

Introduction

Computers are an integral part of life in the 90s. For example, most of us have used a word processing program. Computers are also being used in ways that are not as obvious. For example, every time you use your telephone, it likely connects to a computer system. Similarly, on your next plane trip, it may be that the aircraft was landed by a computer system and not the pilot! The term, *computer system*, is used to emphasize that there are two distinct components: hardware and software. The hardware is the computer itself. The software is the programs that tell the computer what to do. In the telephone system, it is the software that provides special features such as call waiting. Designing and building software is especially challenging today where a piece of software may consist of millions of lines of code. In recent years, the object-oriented programming design methodology has emerged and shown much promise for managing and coping with such complexity. In this chapter, we introduce basic computing terminology and the concepts behind object-oriented design. In successive chapters, we show how to design and write software using the object-oriented programming language C++.

Key Concepts

- CPU
- binary number system
- machine language
- system software
- application software
- operating system
- translation system
- compiler
- abstraction
- information hiding
- encapsulation
- modularization
- hierarchy
- reuse
- object-oriented design
- object-oriented language
- inheritance
- polymorphism

1.1

BASIC COMPUTING TERMINOLOGY

One of the most daunting aspects of learning a new discipline is mastering the terminology. This is particularly true for computer science because computer scientists are fond of using acronyms and abbreviations for almost everything having to do with computers. Sometimes a conversation between two computer scientists can sound like a totally different language if you don't understand the jargon. Indeed, much of the terminology involving computers has become so ubiquitous that it is difficult to discuss computers without using the terminology.

1.1.1

Computing units of measure

Much of the computer terminology computer scientists use involves measures that are used to compare various aspects of the computer. These measures usually involve the size or capacity of some aspect of the machine or the speed of the machine. In measuring speed, computer scientists sometimes discuss how long it takes to do some operation. In these cases, the units of measures are thousandths, millionths, billionths, and trillionths of a second. Table 1.1 shows the most frequently used measures. As we shall see, current computers do most arithmetic operations in nanoseconds, but computer scientists expect computers to do operations in picoseconds in the near future.

Table 1.1
Common units of measure of computer speed

Fraction of a Second	Value	Abbreviation
10^{-3}	$\dfrac{1}{1,000}$	millisecond or ms
10^{-6}	$\dfrac{1}{1,000,000}$	microsecond or μs
10^{-9}	$\dfrac{1}{1,000,000,000}$	nanosecond or ns
10^{-12}	$\dfrac{1}{1,000,000,000,000}$	picosecond or ps

Rather than use the duration of an operation as a measure of speed, computer scientists sometimes use what is known as the clock rate. The *clock rate* is how many operations the computer can perform in a second and is typically expressed as *cycles per second* or hertz. For example, a computer with a clock rate of 50,000,000 hertz, does something every 20ns (i.e., $1 \div 50,000,000$). Scientists use the prefixes in Table 1.2, which are from the metric system. For our previous example, we would write 50 MHz (spoken as 50 megahertz). Clearly, the higher the clock rate the faster the computer.

Value	Abbreviation
1,000	kilo or K
1,000,000	mega or M
1,000,000,000	giga or G
1,000,000,000,000	tera or T

In terms of measures of capacity or size, computer scientists prefer to count things using powers of two. This system is convenient because digital computers use the binary number system. Table 1.3 shows the powers of two that are most often used. As the table shows, 2^{10} is known as a K, where the K comes from the stem "kilo." The prefix kilo is used because 1024 is closest to 1000. Similarly, the prefix mega is used for 2^{20} because its value is closest to a million. When these units are used to specify storage capacity of a machine, we really do mean the exact power of two. For example, a machine that has 8 megabytes of memory has 8×2^{20} bytes, or 8,388,608 bytes of memory. The use of these prefixes to mean different things can sometimes be confusing. However, the meaning is usually clear from the context. If someone says that he or she got a job offer with a salary of $30K, the person most likely means $30,000, not $30,720 (i.e., 30×1024).

Power of Two	Value	Abbreviation
2^{10}	1,024	kilo or K
2^{20}	1,048,576	mega or M
2^{30}	1,073,741,824	giga or G
2^{40}	1,099,511,627,776	tera or T

1.1.2

Computer organization

Every computer has four parts (see Figure 1.1). The brains of the computer is the *central processing unit*, or CPU. This is where computations are performed and decisions are made. *Memory* is where the data and programs are stored while being processed by the CPU. The bidirectional arrow in Figure 1.1 indicates that the CPU can both fetch information from and store information in the memory. Two very important components of a computer are the *input devices* and *output devices* because they are used to communicate information between humans and the computer. The following sections discuss the four components of a computer in more detail.

Figure 1.1

Computer organization

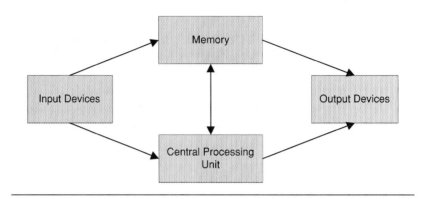

The CPU is where arithmetic calculations are performed. The arithmetic/logical unit (ALU) of the CPU performs the typical arithmetic operations such as addition, subtraction, multiplication and division. Interestingly, computers use the binary number system not the decimal number system to represent numbers. The binary number system has only two digits, 0 and 1. The binary number system is used because the fundamental building block of a computer is a switch, much like the familiar on/off switch for an electric lamp. The state of the switch indicates the value of the digit. In early computers, these switches were built from mechanical relays. The resulting machines were huge. They occupied an entire room, and they required special power and cooling. In today's machines, the switches are made from ultrasmall transistors. Consequently, an entire computer can fit on a single *chip* made of silicon. Because the entire computer fits on a chip, these chips are sometimes referred to as *microprocessors*. Intel's Pentium® processor contains about 3,000,000 transistors in an area a little larger than a square inch (see Figure 1.2). The follow-on to the Pentium, the Pentium Pro®, has about 5,500,000 transistors.

Figure 1.2

A Pentium chip

The principles behind the binary number system are the same as those used in our decimal number system. Both the decimal and binary number systems are *positional number systems*, that is, the position of the digit indicates its relative value. For example, in the decimal number 4,506, the five is in the hundred's place and thus indicates a value of 500. Reading the number from the right, each digit represents an increasing power of 10. Thus, the value of the 4,506 can be expressed as

$$4 \times 10^3 + 5 \times 10^2 + 0 \times 10^1 + 6 \times 10^0$$

The binary number system works exactly the same way except that we use increasing powers of two. For example, the binary number 1101 represents the value

$$1 \times 2^3 + 1 \times 2^2 + 0 \times 2^1 + 1 \times 2^0$$

which is the decimal value 13 (8 + 4 + 0 + 1). To indicate a number is in a base other than decimal, the base is written as a subscript at the end of the number. So 100100_2 is the binary representation of the decimal value 36, while 1001 represents the decimal value 1,001.

The individual digits of a binary number are referred to as *bits* (from *binary digit*). Writing out binary numbers for even moderately large numbers can be tedious, so the bits of a binary number are often grouped together to correspond to a bigger radix (which will be a power of two, of course). Grouping bits together in threes starting from the right gives a base eight or octal representation ($2^3 = 8$). Thus, the number

01011101_2

can be converted to its octal representation by first grouping the bits in threes. This yields

$(01)(011)(101)_2$

and the individual groupings can be converted to octal digits. Converting each digit yields

01_2 $= 1$
011_2 $= 3$
101_2 $= 5$

which is the number 135_8. This value can be converted to its decimal value in the same way that a binary number is converted. The difference is that powers of eight are used. The number 135_8 is

$$1 \times 8^2 + 3 \times 8^1 + 5 \times 2^0$$

which is the decimal value 93.

It's not too hard to convert a decimal representation of a value into its binary or octal representation. To convert a number in the decimal system to its octal equivalent (which is much less work than converting the same value into binary), we can think of the number in octal as ...*wxyz*, denoting

$...w \times 8^3 + x \times 8^2 + y + 8^1 + z \times 8^0$ or $...w \times 512 + x \times 64 + y \times 8 + z \times 1$

So the first step is to determine the number of 8s in the number. This is computed by dividing by 8. The remainder is the value of z. The value of y is computed by dividing the quotient of the previous operation (i.e., the original number divided by 8), which gives the number of 64s in the value. The remainder is the value of y. The process continues until the number we are dividing is less than 8.

To give an example, let's determine the octal and binary representation for the decimal value 458. The computation would proceed as follows:

$$\frac{458}{8} = 57 \text{ with remainder 2}$$

$$\frac{57}{8} = 7 \text{ with remainder 1}$$

$$\frac{7}{8} = 0 \text{ with remainder 7}$$

So the octal representation of 458_{10} is 712. The binary representation is easily obtained by expanding each octal digit to its binary equivalent. The process is

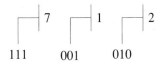

which gives the binary number 111001010.

The standard unit of computer storage on most machines is 8 bits. An 8-bit quantity is known as a *byte*. Because the octal system groups bits in threes and three does not evenly divide eight, base 16 is more commonly used. The base 16 number system is called the *hexadecimal* number system. In the hexadecimal number system, the bits are grouped together in sets of four. Thus, there are two hexadecimal digits per byte. Taking the binary representation of 89_{10} and dividing the bits into groups of four starting from the right yields (101) (1001), which is 59_{16}. As a check to see if we converted the number correctly, we can convert it back to decimal. We use the same process as we did for converting an octal or binary number to decimal except, of course, the base is 16. The number 59_{16} is

$$5 \times 16^1 + 9 \times 16^0 = 80 + 9 = 89$$

which is correct.

Since a hexadecimal digit can take on 16 possible values, extra symbols are required to represent the digits greater than nine. The convention is to use the letters A through F to represent the digits 10 through 15. So the hexadecimal representation of the octal value 712 is $1CA_{16}$, which was obtained by writing the binary equivalent of each octal digit, dividing the bits into groups of four—starting from the right as shown in the following diagram.

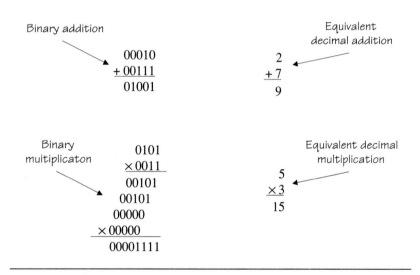

$$1 \qquad 12 = C \qquad 10 = A$$

$$1 \qquad 1100 \qquad 1010$$

Performing arithmetic on positive binary numbers is the same as performing arithmetic on decimal numbers. Both addition and multiplication are illustrated in Figure 1.3. For addition, the binary digits are added starting from the right. When the sum of the two digits is greater than one, a carry is propagated to the next column. For multiplication, the multiplicand (the top number) is multiplied by the digits of the multiplier starting from the right. For the binary number system, multiplication is particularly simple because we are always multiplying by either a zero or a one. The last step is to sum all the partial products to produce the final product.

Figure 1.3
Binary addition and multiplication

Binary addition

$$
\begin{array}{r}
00010 \\
+\,00111 \\
\hline
01001
\end{array}
$$

Equivalent decimal addition

$$
\begin{array}{r}
2 \\
+\,7 \\
\hline
9
\end{array}
$$

Binary multiplicaton

$$
\begin{array}{r}
0101 \\
\times\,0011 \\
\hline
00101 \\
00101 \\
00000 \\
\times\,00000 \\
\hline
00001111
\end{array}
$$

Equivalent decimal multiplication

$$
\begin{array}{r}
5 \\
\times\,3 \\
\hline
15
\end{array}
$$

A world consisting of ones and zeros leaves no room for the plus or minus sign, and so we need to adopt some convention for the representation of negative integer values. All computers use a fixed number of binary digits to represent a value. This basic unit of storage is usually called a *word*. To keep things simple, we assume that we are dealing with a computer with an 8-bit word, which is usually called a *byte*.

Based on what we already know, it is clear that the nonnegative integers 0 through 255 ($2^8 - 1$) can be represented in this amount of storage. However, if we want to represent negative values and be able to perform subtraction, then we have to sacrifice the largest positive value.

Most computers represent negative integers by their *two's complement.* Mathematically, the two's complement of an integer N in n bits is $2^n - N$. Practically, the easy way to find the two's complement of a value is to follow these steps:

Step 1.   Write the number in binary.

Step 2.   Complement each bit (replace each 1 by a 0, and each 0 by a 1).

Step 3.   Add 1 to the complemented number.

To give an example, let's choose the value 127_{10}. The steps are

Step 1.   01111111   (127_{10} in eight binary digits)

Step 2.   10000000   (its bit-wise complement)

Step 3.   10000001   (add one to the bit-wise complement)

So, the two's complement representation of -127_{10} is 10000001.

The acid test is to verify that the addition of the binary representations of 127 and -127 yields zero. The addition is

$$01111111$$
$$+\underline{10000001}$$
$$100000000$$

Notice the carry out of the most significant bit position. When performing binary arithmetic in which negative numbers are represented using two's complement, the carry out of the most significant bit is discarded. Thus the sum is zero.

Another check is to find the two's complement of -127_{10}, which should be the value 127_{10}. Perform the steps outlined above.

Step 1.   10000001   (-127)

Step 2.   01111110   (its bit-wise complement)

Step 3.   01111111   (127, the correct result)

So, $-(-127)$ does indeed equal 127 using the two's complement representation.

From the above examples, we can see that the most significant bit of the word serves as the sign bit. A one in the most significant bit position indicates a negative value, and a zero indicates a positive value. The range of values that can be represented in an 8-bit word is -128 to 127. In general, the range of values that can be represented in two's complement notation in a word of n bits is -2^{n-1} through $2^{n-1}-1$.

Two's complement is also important because it gives the computer a way to perform subtraction without having to use a specialized unit. To compute the difference between two binary numbers, x and y, the two's complement of y is produced and then added to x. The result is the difference $x - y$.

An important characteristic of a CPU is the size of the numbers it handles and how fast it can perform an arithmetic operation. The size of the numbers it can handle is usually given as the number of bits in the largest integer that the CPU can manipulate. On a typical machine today, the largest integer is 32 bits, but CPUs that can handle 64-bit integers are beginning to appear. An n-bit integer can represent the decimal values 0 through 2^n-1. For example, on a machine with 8-bit integers, the largest number is 2^8-1 or 255. The speed at which a CPU can perform an arithmetic operation is often specified by the time it takes to add two integers. Computers built in the 1940s could add two 31-bit numbers in 150 to 200 microseconds. A typical computer today can add two 32-bit numbers in 20 to 50 nanoseconds.

In addition to the ALU, a CPU contains a control unit. The control unit is responsible for fetching instructions from memory and causing the action specified by the instruction to be carried out (e.g., an add or subtract). Performing the action specified by the instruction is referred to as *executing the instruction*, and the instructions in memory are known as the *program*. The control unit performs these steps of fetching and executing instructions repeatedly. This process, called the *fetch/execute cycle*, is illustrated in Figure 1.4.

Figure 1.4

Fetch/execute cycle of a computer

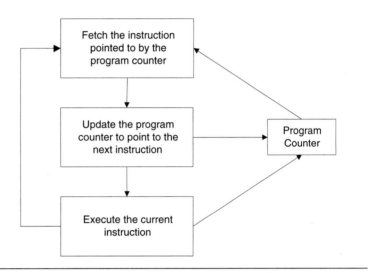

To keep track of which instruction to fetch and execute next, the control unit contains a program counter. The *program counter* holds the memory address of the next instruction to fetch and execute. In most cases, the program counter steps through the program sequentially. That is, instructions are fetched and executed in the order in which they are stored in memory. However, if we could only execute instructions sequentially, the computer would be of limited use. The control unit can test data fetched from memory and can change the program counter based on the outcome of the test. This ability enables the CPU to decide which actions to take based on the data that is being processed. This decision ability is fundamental to all computing devices.

Closely connected to the CPU is *main memory* where data and the instructions that control the operation of the CPU are stored. As we mentioned earlier, for most computers being built today, main memory is organized as a series of locations each of which can hold 8 bits, or 1 byte, of information. An important property of main memory is that any location or byte can be accessed in a fixed amount of time. For this reason, main memory is sometimes referred to as *random access memory* or RAM. This is in contrast to storing information on a tape, where to read information in the middle of the tape requires advancing the tape to the proper location. Thus the time to access information depends on where the information is located. This type of memory is called *sequential access memory.*

Two important characteristics of main memory are its size and its speed. The size of main memory is measured in terms of the number of bytes it contains. In a personal computer, main memory may range from a few hundred kilobytes up to 32 or 64 or more megabytes. Usually, megabytes is abbreviated to MB. So one will often see advertisements for machines saying the machine has 8MB of memory. The speed of main memory is measured in terms of how long it takes to read information from a particular location. Typical speeds on a personal computer range from 80 to 120 nanoseconds.

For most types of random-access memory, the contents are lost when the computer is turned off. This type of memory is called volatile memory. We need some memory that does not lose its contents when the power is turned off. Consequently, in addition to RAM, most computers have *read-only memory* or ROM. This type of memory is nonvolatile, that is, the information stored in it remains there when the computer is turned off. The contents of ROM are set at the time the computer is assembled. After assembly, it cannot be written; but only read. Hence, the name read-only memory. This memory, sometimes called ROM BIOS (Basic Input/Output Subroutines), contains information that identifies the type of computer and instructions that start the computer when it is first turned on. When the computer is turned on and the ROM BIOS program executes, the process is called *booting the machine.*

While a CPU performs computations and main memory is used to store programs and results, we need the ability to get information into the computer for processing and we need to be able to get the results back out. We also need to be able to store information so that when the computer is turned off we do not lose any results that have been produced. Input devices and output devices handle these two functions. There are hundreds of different types of input devices for transmitting data and instructions to the computer. Some common and familiar devices are a keyboard, a mouse, and a CD-ROM reader. Some not so familiar devices are image scanners, voice input units, joysticks, and light pens. Similarly, there are hundreds of different output devices, each tailored to outputting different kinds of information. Common output devices include laser and inkjet printers (for printed information), display screens and plotters (for graphical type information), and loudspeakers (for sound). Figure 1.5 shows some common input and output devices.

Some devices are capable of both input and output, and they are typically referred to as *input/output devices.* Most input/output devices are based on some type of magnetic recording technology. Typical input/output devices are floppy drives, hard or fixed disk drives, and magnetic tape units. Floppy drives write and read small removable disks. Early floppy drives could read and write disks that would hold 360K bytes of information. Current floppy drives have capacities of 1.2 megabytes and 1.44 megabytes. The 1.2 megabyte drives accept disks that have a diameter of 5.25 inches. These are often referred to as

Figure 1.5

*Common input and
output devices*

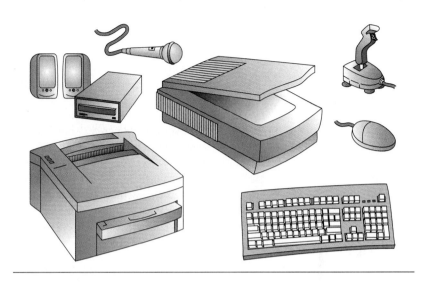

5¼-inch drives. These drives are slowly being replaced by the smaller but higher capacity drives that accept 3.5 inch floppies. Naturally, these drives are referred to as 3½-inch drives. Fixed or hard disks have a much greater capacity than floppy disks. Typical hard disks can hold 400 to 500 megabytes of information, and disks that hold more than 1 gigabyte of information are readily available. The disk cannot be removed from a hard disk drive as the disk is held in an airtight container to keep dust and any other foreign particles from interfering with reading and writing information.

A disk must be formatted before we can use it. The formatting operation writes information on the disk so that data can be written and retrieved efficiently. The process of formatting a disk is analogous to the process of drawing lines in a parking lot and numbering the slots. It allows the information to be placed (parked) and retrieved (find your car without wandering through the parking lot) efficiently. This explains why a disk has less space on it after it has been formatted. The lines and numbering take up space.

A very important output device on personal computers is the video display or monitor (see Figure 1.6). The monitor is sometimes referred to as a *CRT (cathode ray tube)* and it operates much like a television. The monitor is controlled by an output device called a *graphics card*. The graphics card sends the data to be displayed to the monitor in a form that the monitor can handle. Important characteristics of the monitor and graphics card are the refresh rate, resolution, and number of colors supported. The refresh rate is how fast the graphics card updates the image on the screen. This process must be done periodically because the phosphors used in the picture tube must be reenergized or they fade. A low refresh rate, such as 60 KHz, can cause eye fatigue because the image flickers imperceptibly. You can often detect the flicker by looking at the screen out of the corner of your eye. Many graphics cards can refresh the screen at rates of 70 to 100 KHz. This rate eliminates the flicker and the accompanying eye fatigue.

The other characteristics of the graphics card are the resolution and number of colors displayed. These two characteristics are related. The *resolution* is how many dots per inch can be displayed across and down the screen. A dot in this context is often referred to as a *pixel,* which stands for "picture element." A standard resolution supported by graphics cards that are video graphics array (VGA) compatible is 640 by 480. This means that there are 640 pixels across the screen and 480 pixels down the screen. The graphics card stores the information to display at each pixel in its own memory. This way it can constantly refresh the screen without interrupting the operation of the CPU. Only when the information changes do the CPU and graphics card need to communicate. Graphics cards that can display at higher resolutions require more memory. For example, many graphics cards support resolutions running from 800 by 600 to 1280 by 1024. Such a card requires from 1MB to 2MB of memory.

Figure 1.6

Video display or monitor on a desktop computer

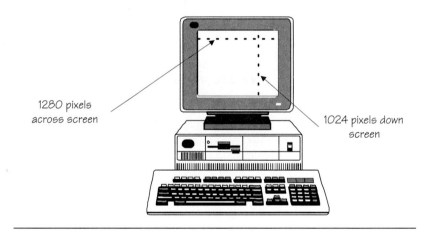

1280 pixels across screen

1024 pixels down screen

Related to the amount of memory and resolution is the number of colors that can be displayed. The graphics card must store the color information to display for each pixel on the screen. To display 256 (i.e, 2^8) colors, we need 1 byte for each pixel. To display "true color," which is defined to be 16.7 million colors, requires 24 bits per pixel. Thus we can see that the number of colors that can be displayed and the resolution are both related to the amount of memory on the graphics card. More memory means a higher resolution or more colors. In most graphics cards, it is possible to trade off more colors and higher resolution. For example, at a resolution of 800 by 600 you can display true color, but at a higher resolution, say 1024 by 768, you can display only 65,536 colors.

Two very common input devices are the keyboard and mouse. As keys are typed on the keyboard, the software reads the keystrokes and interprets them appropriately. The mouse is also a very useful input device. The typical mouse has one or two buttons and a little ball on the bottom that permits the mouse to be rolled around. As the mouse is rolled, the pointer on the screen moves accordingly. The pointer on the screen is usually referred to as the *sprite*. By moving the mouse so the sprite is pointing to a particular region of the screen (say a menu that has been displayed by an application) and clicking a mouse button, we can signal the computer to perform the command indicated by the menu item. Using menus and buttons to give commands to the computer is much simpler than having to type complicated commands that must be memorized.

1.1.3

Programming

By itself, a computer will not do anything useful. There must be a *program* that directs the computer to perform some specific task. Indeed, the ability to program a computer to do different tasks is what makes the computer so powerful. A program is a sequence of instructions that tells the computer what to do. The instructions are written in a language that is specifically designed for giving commands to a computer. We call these languages *programming languages*. One type of programming language is called *machine language*. A machine-language program is one that a particular computer can understand directly. A machine language consists of instructions that represent the fundamental operations the computer can perform. Consequently, different types of computers use different machine languages. For example, the machine language understood by Intel's Pentium processor is quite different from the machine language understood by IBM's PowerPC processor.

Part of the design of a computer is determining the fundamental operations the computer can perform and the binary encoding of these instructions. The *binary encoding* is the bit pattern that represents a particular instruction. The operations and their binary encodings are called the machine's *instruction set*. Most machines include instructions for performing arithmetic operations such as add, subtract, multiply, and divide. Another class of instructions is the jump instructions, which can change the program counter.

Even for today's modern computers, machine languages are quite primitive and writing a program directly in machine language is quite tedious. To make matters worse, without some type of assistance, we must directly use the binary encoding of the instructions. To get a first hand idea of the difficulties of writing machine-language programs, let's write a small program for the hypothetical Pop Machine 100, or PM100 for short.

The PM100 has been designed for use in soda machines. It has a very simple instruction set. A machine instruction on the PM consists of seven bits. The first three bits indicate the operation to perform. This is referred to as the *operation code,* or *opcode* for short. The remaining four bits are used only by the jump instruction. These four bits specify the address of the memory location to fetch the next instruction. Notice that because we have four bits for the address, the PM100 can contain up to 16 memory locations. Table 1.4 contains the machine's instruction set.

Let's consider the encoding of the jump instruction. Its encoding is

```
110 AAAA
```

The space between the two parts of the binary instruction separates the opcode from the address. This is purely for our convenience. The bit pattern `110` will be interpreted by the machine to mean that it should perform a jump operation. We use the notation `AAAA` for the next four bits to indicate that these bits are an address. When the PM100 executes a jump instruction, the four bits that specify the address are moved into the program counter (see Figure 1.4). Consequently, the next instruction fetched is from that memory location.

Table 1.4

PM100 instruction set

Instruction Description	Binary Encoding
Reset machine	000 0000
Wait for coin	001 0000
Skip next instruction if coin is not counterfeit	010 0000
Add coin amount to total	011 0000
Skip next instruction if total is less than the cost of a can of soda	100 0000
Take picture and call police	101 0000
Jump to specified location	110 AAAA
Dispense a can of soda and give change if any	111 0000

We want to write a program in the machine language of the PM100 that delivers a can of soda and appropriate change when enough money has been deposited. Because there has been a lot of trouble with people putting counterfeit coins in the machine, if a counterfeit coin is detected, the program should direct the PM100 to take a picture of the offender and call the police. It should then reset itself. We hope that the offender will hang around and pound on the machine and the police will have enough time to make an arrest on the spot. If not, the police have a picture of the offender. The PM100 has a special instruction for detecting bogus coins. It also has an instruction that telephones the police and activates a camera that takes a photograph of whoever is standing in front of the machine.

The machine language program for carrying out the desired actions follows. The instructions are stored sequentially in memory beginning at location zero. The first thing you should do is cover up the comments on the right and examine the program. It is very difficult to determine what the program does. For each instruction, you have to refer to the table that contains the PM100 instruction set and decode the binary instruction. Because we have to use the primitive instructions of the PM100, just getting the logic of the program correct is hard. We have to be concerned with every detail.

Memory Location	Instruction	Comments
0000	0000000	Reset the machine
0001	0010000	Wait for a coin
0010	0100000	Skip if coin is not counterfeit
0011	1101000	Jump to location 1000
0100	0110000	Add coin amount to total
0101	1000000	Skip if not enough money received
0110	1101010	Jump to location 1010
0111	1100001	Jump to location 0001
1000	1010000	Take picture and call police
1001	1100000	Jump to location 0000
1010	1110000	Dispense soda and return change
1011	1100000	Jump to location 0000

How can we tell if the program does what it is supposed to do? One activity a programmer often does when writing or trying to understand a program is to "hand execute" the code. In this procedure the programmer acts like the computer and fetches and executes the instructions in the program to see if the program will perform properly when executed by the real machine. This is sometimes called *tracing the execution of the program*. To see how this technique works, let's trace the execution of our simple, machine-language program.

We assume that we will begin executing instructions at location zero, and that the cost of a soda is 55 cents. The trace of the execution of the program is shown in Table 1.5.

The first step resets the state of the machine. This action sets the total amount of money received thus far to zero. Next, the instruction at location 0001 is executed. This instruction waits for a coin to be deposited. For the sake of the simulation, we assume that a quarter was deposited. When the coin is deposited, execution continues at location 0010 (Step 3). This instruction tests to see if the coin is counterfeit. It is not, so the instruction at location 0011 is skipped and execution continues at location 0100. This instruction adds the value of the coin to the total. Notice that the total is now 0.25. Next the program tests to see if enough money has been deposited to purchase a soda. The amount in total is less than 55 cents, so the next instruction is skipped and the instruction at location 0111 is executed. This instruction jumps the program

Table 1.5

Hand execution of the soda machine program

Step	Program Counter	Action	Value of Total
1	0000	Reset the machine	0.00
2	0001	Wait for coin	0.00
		Receive a quarter	
3	0010	Skip if coin not counterfeit	0.00
4	0100	Add coin amount to total	0.25
5	0101	Skip if not enough money	0.25
6	0111	Jump to location 0001	0.25
7	0001	Wait for coin	0.25
		Receive a quarter	0.25
8	0010	Skip if coin not counterfeit	0.25
9	0100	Add coin amount to total	0.50
10	0101	Skip if not enough money	0.50
11	0111	Jump to location 0001	0.50
12	0001	Wait for coin	0.50
		Receive a dime	
13	0010	Skip if coin not counterfeit	0.50
14	0100	Add coin amount to total	0.60
15	0101	Skip if not enough money	0.60
16	0110	Jump to location 1010	0.60
17	1010	Dispense soda; return a nickel	0.60
18	1011	Jump to location 0000	0.60
19	0000	Reset machine	0.00

back to location 0001, which waits for the next coin to be deposited. The program continues and another quarter and then a dime are deposited (steps 7 through 13).

After the dime is deposited and added to the total, execution continues at step 14. This time there is enough money, and the instruction following the skip instruction is executed. This instruction jumps to location 1010. At step 17, a soda is dispensed and a nickel is returned as change. At step 18, the instruction at location 1011 is executed so the program jumps back to location 0000 and the machine is reset to await another customer.

Based on our hand execution, it appears the program works correctly when no counterfeit coins are encountered. To ensure that the piece of the program that handles counterfeit coins works, we should also "walk through" that portion of the code.

Such hand executions are extremely valuable in determining what a program is doing. In hindsight, what we did might seem quite tedious. We went into quite a lot of detail to illustrate exactly what was happening. As you develop your programming skills, you will find that you can perform such hand executions on small sections of code with ease. You might need a piece of scratch paper to record values as they change, but generally it is not necessary to write down the steps taken.

Obviously, writing and checking even a medium-size program (500 to 1,000 instructions) in machine language would be quite tedious and error prone. Over the years, programmers have put much effort into developing languages that permit people to write programs in a way that is more natural. At a level slightly above binary machine language is assembly language. Although we still write programs by writing sequences of machine instructions, we no longer write them in binary. Rather we write instructions in a symbolic language called *assembly language*. Then a program called an *assembler* translates the assembly-language instructions into the binary form. Assembly-language programming is a great improvement because it allows the programmer to focus attention on solving the problem at hand rather than on the tedious job of encoding instructions in binary.

One of the characteristics of machine- and assembly-language programming is that you need to know the details of the machine being programmed. As we mentioned, each type of machine has its own, unique machine language. The next level of computer languages are referred to as high-level programming languages. A distinguishing characteristic of a high-level programming language is that detailed knowledge of the machine being programmed is not required. Another characteristic is that a high-level programming language usually uses a vocabulary and structure that is close to the type of problem being solved. For example, the programming language FORTRAN, which is used to solve scientific and engineering programs, uses a notation that is mathematical. Indeed, the name FORTRAN is derived from the phrase *formula translation*. Because of the close coupling of a programming language to a problem domain, there are literally hundreds of high-level programming languages.

1.2

SOFTWARE

Comparing the use of computers today and as recently as 15 years ago, we have seen an explosion in their use. Certainly part of the reason for this growth is the dramatic decline in the cost of a computer. However, another reason for this explosive growth in the usage of computers has been the development of useful, high-quality software that has made using the computer easy, even for novices. Software can be broadly classified as either application software or system software. The distinction between the two can sometimes be fuzzy, but generally application software involves solving a problem or providing a service in a particular problem domain or application area. Obviously, the range of applications is quite large and continues to grow rapidly. This growth is largely because of the increases in computing power at ever lower prices. Indeed, the personal computer revolution fostered the development of several new application areas: spreadsheets, desktop publishing (DTP), personal information managers (PIMs), personal financial managers (PFMs), and presentation managers (PMs).

System software, on the other hand, is the software that supports the development and execution of other programs. In some sense, system software bridges the gap between application software and the underlying hardware. The goal is to isolate the programmer from the low-level details of the machine and thus increase productivity. This organization view of a computer system is illustrated in Figure 1.7.

Figure 1.7

Organizational view of a computing system

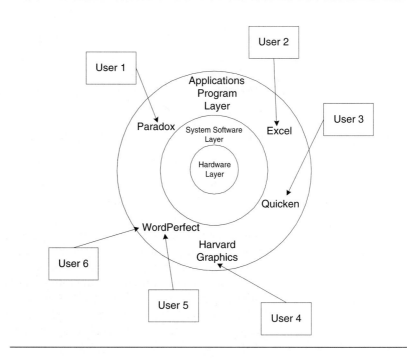

1.2.1

System software

One very important piece of system software is the operating system. An *operating system* is the software that controls and manages the computing resources. These resources include memory, input and output (I/O) devices, and the CPU. The operating system provides services such as allocating memory to a program, handling the control of I/O devices such as the display, the keyboard, and the disk drives. Currently popular operating systems for personal computers are MS-DOS, OS/2, and Unix.

An important service provided by the operating system is the file system. The file system controls how information is organized on a disk so that it can be found and retrieved quickly. The disk has areas where related information is stored together. These areas are analogous to drawers in a file cabinet. One drawer might contain all the files that pertain to first-year students. In the case of a file system, such an area is called a directory. Unlike a file cabinet, a directory can contain other directories. Such an organization is called a *hierarchical file system*. Computer scientists like to visualize a file system organized this way as an upside-down tree-like structure.

Figure 1.8 contains such a tree diagram of the organization of the files on a disk called C:. This is called the *root* of the tree. Below the root are files and

Figure 1.8

Hierarchical file system

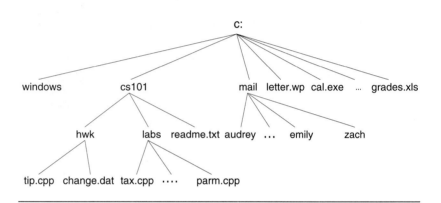

directories. For example, `cs101` is a directory that contains files that have to do with a course called cs101. The directory `cs101` contains files and directories. In Figure 1.8, `cs101` contains two subdirectories, `hwk` and `labs`, and one file `readme.txt`. The names you choose should indicate the contents of the directory. In this example, the name `hwk` indicates that the files it contains have to do with homework for the course cs101. Similarly, the name `labs` indicates the directory contains information about the course laboratories.

Similarly, the filename should indicate the type of information contained in a file. A filename has two parts. The part before the period is called the *basename*, and the part after the period is called the *extension*. The extension indicates the format of the file. There are some common extensions. For example, in the `cs101` directory, the file `readme.txt` has an extension of `txt`. This indicates the file contains text that can be read by printing the file to the display or using an editor to read its contents. Another common extension is `exe`. This extension is used for files that contain an executable program. This type of file cannot be processed by a word processor or text editor.

The basename tells what information the file holds. For example, the `readme` basename indicates that anyone wishing to understand what the `cs101` directory contains should read the contents of this file. As another example, consider the file `grades.xls`. The `xls` extension indicates that this file was produced by Excel, a popular spreadsheet application. The `grades` basename indicates that this file contains a spreadsheet of grades. If you carefully organize files into subdirectories and choose appropriate names, a hierarchical file system provides an effective way to organize information so that it can be found quickly.

Another important part of an operating system is its file management commands. The command names and how to invoke them vary for different operating systems, but their functionality is identical. Most systems have commands for deleting files, renaming files, copying files, and creating directories.

The operating system also provides basic services for performing input and output on a variety of devices. This means that a program need not know exactly how to interact with a particular input/output device because the low-level details are handled by the operating system. For example, if a program wants to read a particular file on a disk, rather than access the disk directly, it sends a request to the operating system. The operating system finds the file on the disk and reads the appropriate portions, and then returns the desired information to the program that made the request.

Another operating system service is the management of running programs. Most modern operating systems let multiple programs share the CPU. For example, with the OS/2 operating system you can download a file from a bulletin board to your computer, run a backup program, and run a word processor all at the same time. The operating system's job is to manage these running programs and make sure that each is provided with the necessary memory and is allowed to execute on the CPU when necessary.

Another class of system software is called *translation systems*. A translation system is a set of programs that we use to develop software. A key component of a translation system is a *translator*, or program that reads a program written in one programming language and outputs a new program, possibly in a different programming language. The input to a translator is called the *source program*, and the output is called the *target program*. The language used for the source program is called the *source language*, and correspondingly, the language used for the target program is called the *target language*. Figure 1.9 illustrates the translation process.

Figure 1.9

The translation process

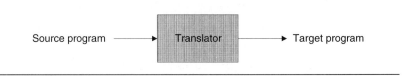

Source program ⟶ Translator ⟶ Target program

There are several types of translators, and they are typically categorized by source and target languages. In Section 1.1.3 on page 13, we said that an assembler translates a symbolic machine-language program to a binary machine-language program. A binary machine-language program is sometimes called *object code* or *object file*. A *compiler* is another type of translator. A compiler processes a program written in a high-level programming language and produces an object file. The process of using a compiler to translate a high-level language program is called *compilation*.

Another type of translator is called a *linker*. A linker combines object files and library files so that they can be executed as a unit. A library contains files of object code for routines that have been developed to perform some particular function or task. Libraries are often supplied by the developer of the compiler or by a company that specializes in providing libraries for a particular purpose. For example, it is common to provide a library that supports doing input and output. Another typical library is one that provides routines that support developing programs that use graphical user interfaces (GUIs). Such a library would contain routines for opening and displaying windows, creating menus, and handling input and output from the mouse.

The output of the linker is a file that can be executed by the computer. This file is sometimes called an *executable*. Using an operating system tool called a *loader*, the executable file can be loaded into the computer's memory and executed.

When doing software development, programmers repeatedly perform the actions of editing a program, compiling it, linking it with already compiled object files and library modules, and then loading and executing it. After viewing how the program behaves, programmers usually must make changes to the program, possibly because the program did not work correctly or because it did work correctly and they must continue developing the program. This process, known as the edit/compile/execute cycle, is illustrated in Figure 1.10.

Because this cycle is repeated many times as software is being developed, translation systems have been constructed that assist us with this process. These systems are sometimes referred to as *integrated development environments* (IDEs). The idea is that the editor, compiler, linker, and loader are integrated together and one set of controls is used to invoke them.

Several IDEs are available for supporting software development using C++. While they differ in how they look, they essentially offer the same features. The various menu selections allow the programmer to type in code, compile it, link the resulting object file with other object files and libraries to create an executable, and to execute the resulting code. Figure 1.11 contains the screen image of the Borland C++ IDE. An IDE can be a great time saver because it automates much of the drudgery of developing software.

1.2.2

Application software

While we certainly use the services provided by system software, it is applications programs that make the computer an indispensible tool for most people. Application software can be classified according to the type of application. For

Figure 1.10

*Edit/compile/execute
software development
cycle*

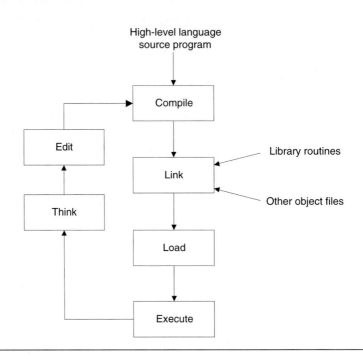

example, one category is word processors. These are programs that help produce documents. Some popular word processors are WordPerfect, Microsoft Word, and AmiPro. These programs simplify editing, and they are capable of printing documents on high-resolution printers. Over the years, the power of these word processors has grown tremendously. Early word processors included spelling checkers but that was about it. Today's versions include grammar checkers, a thesaurus, drawing tools, table creation tools, and hundreds of other features to facilitate document creation.

Closely related to the word processors, and indeed today there is some overlap, are the desktop publishing (DTP) programs. These programs support the design of documents. For example, they have tools for creating layouts for newsletters and company reports. These application programs support importing text and pictures from other sources. In comparison to word processors, these programs have more sophisticated facilities for handling color, graphics, and large documents such as books.

Another class of application program that has become very popular is the spreadsheet. Indeed, some believe that it was the invention of the electronic spreadsheet that helped initiate the personal computer revolution. Spreadsheets provide a simple and natural way to deal with a wide variety of problems. Accounting operations use spreadsheets extensively because they provide an easy way to do forecasting. For example, simply by changing a few numbers, business people can get an idea of the effect of reduced sales on overall profitability. Most of today's spreadsheets include facilities for presenting data

Figure 1.11
C++ IDE

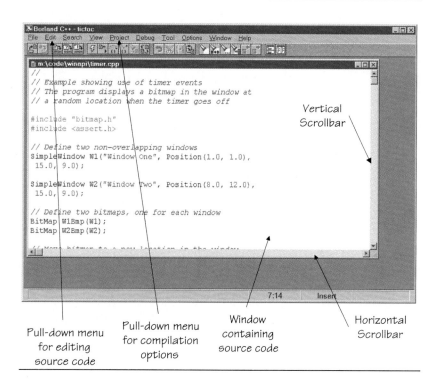

Pull-down menu
for editing
source code

Pull-down menu
for compilation
options

Window
containing
source code

Horizontal
Scrollbar

graphically using several types of line graphs, bar charts, or pie charts. The user selects the data to be graphed and the type of chart to graph it on, and the spreadsheet produces the chart using appropriate colors, keys, and legends.

Another type of application programs, personal information managers (PIMs), allow people to organize important personal information. These programs typically include modules for maintaining to-do lists, appointments, and phone directories. On the other hand, personal financial managers (PFMs), allow people to manage personal financial information. Typical packages include modules for maintaining checking account information, monthly budgets, tax estimates, personal net worth, and stock and bond portfolios. One new feature of these programs is the ability to connect to an online service and download a record of charges that have been made on a credit card. This eliminates the task of having to manually enter transactions into the program. As the power of the computer continues to grow, we can expect to see additional types of application programs offered, and the features offered by existing programs grow more sophisticated.

We now have enough computing terminology under our belts to take a brief look at software development and the object-oriented programming paradigm.

History of Computing

The beginnings

One way to discuss the history of computing is to discuss the devices that man developed to assist with computing. Most of the early devices were for doing counting and simple arithmetic. One of the earliest devices for computing is still used by small children—fingers. Indeed, early man developed various systems for counting and doing simple arithmetic such as addition, subtraction, and multiplication using fingers. These systems were quite complicated and permitted large numbers to be manipulated. Some of these systems are still in use in parts of Asia.

As an aid to counting and calculation, the ancient Chinese used a system of rows of grooves in the sand. Pebbles were placed in the grooves to denote a value. One pebble in the first groove would represent the value one; two pebbles would represent the value two. Each successive groove represented a power of 10. Thus, two pebbles in the second groove and three pebbles in the first represented the value 23.

Later, the system of grooves and pebbles was refined into the form we know as the abacus. An abacus consists of beads (the pebbles) strung on parallel wires (the grooves in the sand) (see Figure 1.12). Addition, subtraction, multiplication, and division are performed by moving beads appropriately. In the late 1940s, contests between someone experienced with the abacus and an electromechanical calculator were popular. The contest consisted of performing a set of arithmetic computations. The first to complete the computation won. Interestingly, the person using the abacus almost always won. The abacus, or soroban as it is called in Japan, is still in use in isolated parts of Asia and the Middle East.

Figure 1.12

An abacus

1.3

ENGINEERING SOFTWARE

As computers have become faster, cheaper, and more powerful, they have become indispensable tools for scientists and engineers. Perhaps more importantly though, they have become part of our everyday life. Computers are in common appliances such as televisions, video cassette recorders, and microwave ovens. Furthermore, every time we use the telephone or an automated teller at a bank, we are accessing a network of computers. However, faster, cheaper computers are only one-half of the equation. Recall that previously we used the term *computer system* to indicate that there are two components—hardware and software. While there have been tremendous advances in hardware technology, there have not been commensurate advances in software design. Part of the problem is that the expectations for software have grown considerably. Figure 1.13 illustrates what is known as the *complexity paradox*: the complexity of the system grows as we attempt to make a system easier to use.

Figure 1.13

Graph showing that as software is made simpler to use, the internal complexity increases

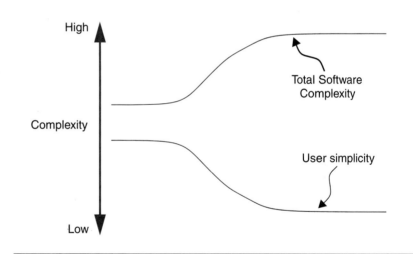

For example, early systems for graphing data required users to specify in detail how the graph should look such as supplying the end points of the graph, the scale, and how and where the graph should be labeled. Essentially, the user had to do most of the work. However, new spreadsheet tools contain 'experts' which analyze the data and produce a graph automatically. Such automatic graphing systems are much easier to use, but this ease of use comes at a price—increased software complexity.

Several factors account for the increased complexity. First, to do more, the software is larger. It is not unusual for application programs, such as spreadsheets, word processors, and drawing programs to consist of millions of lines of code. Another factor that increases complexity is the interaction between components. For example, a word processor may contain a component that does spell checking and correction, while another component provides the services of a thesaurus.

Let's consider the spell-checking component. When a possible spelling error is detected, the spelling checker must report the possible error to the user. To do this, the spelling checker must interact with the component of the application that creates a window or a dialog box so that the possible error can be displayed and the user queried about what action, if any, to take. If the user acknowledges it is a spelling error, the checker can correct the misspelling. To make the correction, the checker must interact with the component of the word processor responsible for replacing text in the document. As the number of components grows, the number of interactions between components grows rapidly.

Software engineering is the area of computer science that is concerned with how to build large software systems. The goal of a software engineer is to produce a software system that is

- Reliable
- Understandable
- Cost effective
- Adaptable
- Reusable.

Let's examine each of these properties.

A software system should be reliable. That is, it should work correctly and not fail. Imagine that you have spent several hours writing a paper for a course with a word processor and when you are nearly finished, the word processor quits unexpectedly. You lose all your work. Undoubtedly, you would be very upset and rightfully so.

While the failure of a word processor is annoying, the loss is insignificant when compared to the potential loss when a life-critical system fails. A *life-critical system* is one in which a failure could mean the loss of human life. Examples of life-critical systems where software is a major component include commercial and military aircraft, radiation therapy machines, and heart pacemakers. Obviously, a software failure in one of these systems could have disastrous consequences.

A way to make a software system reliable is to make it understandable; that is, the operation and design of the system should be readily determinable by other software professionals. Being understandable is extremely important because large software systems are constructed by many people working in teams. The construction of the software will go smoother with fewer errors if everyone working on it understands the overall operation of the system and its components.

Understandability is also important because of the long lifetime of software. A software product usually evolves over time, and often software engineers that had nothing to do with the original development of the software make enhancements and fix bugs. This process is sometimes called *software maintenance*. If the next generation of software engineers can understand the operation of the software, modifications to a complex system, while difficult, are doable. On the other hand, it is extremely difficult to make modifications or corrections to a poorly designed system. Indeed, it is often more cost effective to rebuild the system from scratch. As a measure of the difficulty of maintaining software, it is estimated that 67 percent of the cost of developing software is devoted to maintenance. This cost can be reduced when the design and operation of a system are comprehensible.

From the previous discussion, we can also see that a software system should be cost effective. That is, the cost to develop and maintain a software system should not exceed the expected profit from selling the system. Many software companies have gone bankrupt because they underestimated the cost of developing a system. A closely related component of cost is the time to design and build the software. Being the first to bring a product to market gives a company a decided advantage over its competitors. Reducing the time to build a software system can reduce costs, and it also can increase profits.

Because of the long lifetime of software, software should be adaptable. It is often difficult to predict what features and capabilities a client will eventually want in a software product. Adaptive maintenance involves changes and additions to the software that improve the effectiveness or competitiveness of the product. By designing software to which additional features and capabilities can be added easily in the future, the software engineer can again reduce overall maintenance costs. Clearly, in terms of adaptive maintenance, understandability is also a desirable property.

Because of the high development costs, software should be reusable. If many millions of dollars are to be spent to develop a software system, it makes sense to make its components flexible so they can be reused when developing a new system. This strategy is certainly common practice in other businesses. Consider the design and creation of a new model of car. The automotive engineer does not design a new car from scratch. Rather, the engineer borrows from the design of existing cars. For example, the engine design from an existing car may be used in a new model. Reuse can improve reliability, reduce development costs, and improve maintainability. Continuing with our car analogy, if the engine design has been used in a previous model, design problems have likely been resolved. Thus, development costs are reduced because a new engine does not need to be designed and tested. Finally, consumer maintenance costs are reduced because mechanics and others who must maintain the car are already familiar with the operation of the engine.

1.3.1

Software engineering principles

Software engineers have developed a number of design principles that help realize the goals in the previous section by managing the inevitable complexity of a large software system.

Abstraction is the process of extracting the relevant properties of an object while ignoring inessential details. The extracted properties define a view of the object. A car dealer might view a car from the standpoint of the selling features of the car. Relevant properties include price, color, optional equipment, and length of warranty. On the other hand, a mechanic views the car from the standpoint of the systems that require maintenance. Here relevant properties include the type of oil, the size of the oil filter, and the number and type of spark plug. The relevant properties are defined by how we use or manipulate the object. Clearly the properties of a car relevant to a car dealer are different from the properties relevant to a mechanic (see Figure 1.14). By focusing on the relevant properties and ignoring irrelevant details, the complexity of dealing with an object is reduced.

Figure 1.14

Two different views or abstractions of an automobile

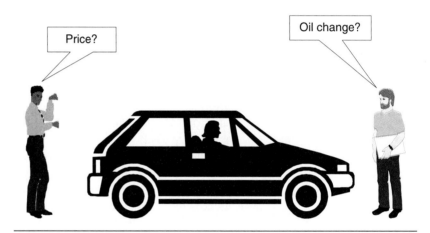

Abstraction is essential for managing the complexity of designing and writing software. As an example, let's consider the task of finding a file on a disk and reading its contents. If we had to handle the low-level details of exactly how a particular file is found on a disk and how to read its contents, accomplishing this task would be quite difficult. We would have to understand how data is stored on the disk as well as the low-level commands that control the operation of the disk drive. Fortunately, a file system provides an abstract view of the information on a disk that allows us to ignore such low-level details. We can access a file by simply supplying the name of the file. The file system handles the low-level details of reading the data on the disk drive and returning it to the program.

Encapsulation or *information hiding* is the process of separating the aspects of an object into external and internal aspects. The external aspects of an object are those that need to be visible or known to other objects in the system. The internal aspects are those details that should not affect other parts of the system. Hiding the internal aspects of an object means that they can be changed without affecting other parts of the system. Continuing with our automobile analogy, consider the radio in a car. The external aspects of the radio are the controls and the types of connectors needed to hook the radio to the electrical system, the speakers, and the antenna. The internal aspects of the radio are the details of how the radio works (see Figure 1.15). To install and use a radio in a car, we do not need to know anything about electrical engineering. Essentially, the radio can be viewed as a black box with buttons and cables.

Figure 1.15

Encapsulation of a car radio

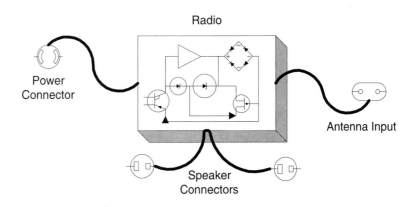

A big benefit of information hiding is that it is easier to make changes to complex systems. We can replace the radio in a car with one that includes a CD player without affecting other components of the car. Because the operation of the radio has been encapsulated and the external view of the radio is defined by the controls and connectors, we can simply remove the old radio and plug in the new one and connect it.

When applied to the design of a software system, encapsulation permits the internal operation of a software component to be changed without affecting other aspects of the system. For example, in an automated voice-mail system, if the principle of encapsulation has been applied correctly, it should be possible to change the component that handles storing the messages without affecting other parts of the system. For example, we might want to increase the number of messages that a user can store. If the message-storing system has been properly hidden and isolated, this change should not affect how users access the system and leave or retrieve messages.

Modularity refers to the process of dividing an object into smaller pieces or modules so that some goal is easier to attain. For example, we might structure a complex object into components so that each component can be tested individually. When an automobile is assembled, the various components, such as the engine, transmission, and radio have been individually tested already. Modularity reduces the time to test the completed car and it reduces the probability that a car will be assembled with a flaw. Similarly, we might structure an object so that we can easily reuse its components.

Most complex systems are modular. They are constructed by combining simpler working components or packages. Proper modularization of a complex system also helps manage complexity. Breaking things down into smaller, easier to understand pieces makes the larger system easier to understand. For example, an automobile can be decomposed into subsystems (see Figure 1.16). Automobile subsystems include the cooling system (radiator, water pump, thermostat, etc.), the ignition system (battery, starter, spark plugs, etc.), and the exhaust system (catalytic converter, muffler, etc.). By thinking about an automobile in terms of these groups of related abstractions, we can more readily grasp the car's overall structure and operation.

Figure 1.16

Subsystems of an automobile

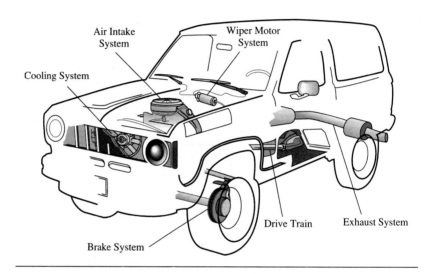

A ranking or ordering of objects based on some relationship between them is a *hierarchy*. Hierarchies help us understand complex organizations and systems. Figure 1.17 contains an organizational chart of a typical company. The chart shows the hierarchy of the employees based on the relationship of who reports to whom. The company hierarchy helps employees understand the structure of their company and their position in it.

For complex systems composed of abstractions, a very useful way of ordering similar abstractions is from most general to least general. Scientists have long used this technique to identify and classify species of the plant and animal kingdoms. A hierarchical ordering based on natural relationships is called a *taxonomy*. Such a hierarchy makes all the abstractions easier to understand because it exposes the relationship of the characteristics and behaviors they have in common. Figure 1.18 shows the taxonomy of the dinosaurs. We can see that the dinosaurs are divided into two groups depending on their hip structure. The Saurischia (lizard-hipped dinosaurs) contain the flesh-eating dinosaurs such as the Tyranosaurus and Velociraptor, while the Ornithischia (bird-hipped dinosaurs) contain the familiar Stegosaur and Triceratops.

Figure 1.17

*An organization chart
of a company*

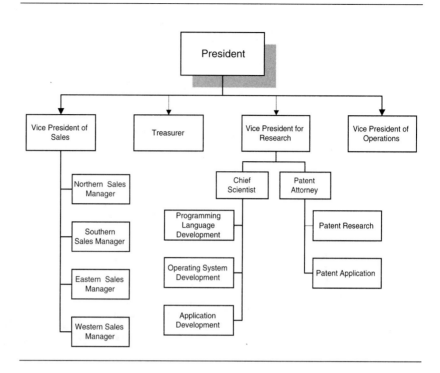

1.4

OBJECT-ORIENTED DESIGN

To support the previously described principles, several design and programming methodologies have been developed. Recently, one approach, object-oriented design and programming, has shown particular promise for helping software developers achieve the goals of reliability, cost effectiveness, adaptability, understandability, and reusability.

Object-oriented software design promotes thinking about software in a way that more closely models the way we think about and interact with the real world. At an early age, we learn about objects and how to manipulate them. Babies, for example, learn that if they shake a rattle, it will make noise. Later as we develop our cognitive skills, we realize that objects have properties, and we begin to be able to think about them abstractly. For example, a growing baby soon realizes that noise making is a property of all rattles.

To illustrate how viewing the world as objects with properties helps us manage complexity, let's consider an activity that many of us do. You are sitting at home watching television, and you remember that your favorite show will soon be starting on a different channel (see Figure 1.19). You take the remote control, push a button, and the television switches to the proper channel. You settle back and enjoy the show.

Figure 1.18

A taxonomy of dinosaurs

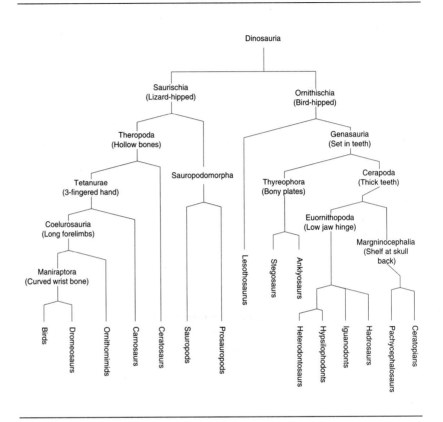

Let's analyze this activity. First, you picked up the remote control, which is a physical object. This object has properties like weight and size, and it also can do something. It can send messages to the television. It's not entirely clear how it does this or how the messages are encoded, but you don't need to know that. You only need to know which buttons to push. The buttons are the interface to the remote control. If you understand the interface to an object, you can use it to perform some task without understanding how the object works. Pushing the appropriate buttons caused the remote to send a message to the television. The television is also a physical object with various properties. Upon receipt of the message from the remote, the television changed to the desired channel.

Such interactions are so routine for us that it is easy to overlook how amazing this activity is. You were able to make two objects interact and perform a complex activity without understanding the internal operation of either object. You were able to do this because you had appropriate abstractions of both objects. Indeed your mental abstractions of the remote control and television mean that you could go to a friend's house and be able to use their remote control and television even though they have a different brand of television. Similar objects display similar behavior.

Figure 1.19

Objects interacting via messages

This way of dealing with the complex world around us can also be applied to software design and programming. A key step in developing a complex system using object-oriented design is to determine the objects that comprise the system. By carefully creating appropriate abstractions of these objects and separating their internal implementation from their external behavior, we can manage the complexity of a large software system.

So what exactly do we mean by an object? Certainly, physical things are objects. A ball, a file cabinet, an address book, a tree, a computer are all objects. What about things like a number, a word, a bank account, or a musical note? These aren't physical objects, but they are objects because they have properties or attributes and we can perform actions on them. A number has a value and we can add two numbers together. A word has a length and if we are talking about a word processor, a word can be inserted or deleted from a document. A musical note has pitch, duration, and loudness. For the most part, something is an object if it has

- a name,
- properties associated with it, and
- Messages that it can understand.

Typically, when an object receives a message, the message either causes the object to take some action or to change one of its properties. In our remote control example, when the television received the "change channel" message from the remote control, it switched channels.

If we are going to take an object-oriented approach to developing software, it makes sense to use a programming language that supports thinking and implementing solutions in terms of objects. A language that has features for supporting thinking about and implementing solutions in terms of objects is an *object-oriented programming language*. Using an object-oriented programming language to implement an object-oriented design is called *object-oriented programming*. Notice we were very careful to include the phrase "implement an object-oriented design." As you will see later, you can certainly use an object-oriented language, but not think in terms of objects.

Some of the currently popular object-oriented languages are Smalltalk, C++, Objective-C, and CLOS. The features they have for supporting object-oriented programming are, for the most part, identical. They differ mainly in the terminology they use to talk about objects and the syntax of the language. In the following section, we describe the key features of object-oriented languages for creating and using objects.

1.4.1

Object-oriented programming

To illustrate some of the features of an object-oriented language, let's sketch out the design of a simple computer game called Bug Hunt. The purpose of Bug Hunt, more than anything else, is to help people develop their coordination when using a mouse. The game works like this. A moving bug is displayed in a window on the screen. The bug changes directions randomly (see Figure 1.20). The object of the game is to eliminate the bug (just like programming). A bug is eliminated by "swatting" it, that is, by clicking the mouse when the pointer is positioned over the bug. These are tough bugs, and it takes several swats to kill one. When the first bug is eliminated, another faster bug takes its place. If a bug is missed (i.e., the mouse button is clicked, but the pointer is not over a shape), the player loses the game. A player wins when he or she eliminates both the slow bugs and the fast bugs without any misses.

Before beginning to design Bug Hunt, we need a more precise statement of what the program should do. A more precise problem statement is:

> The game Bug Hunt consists of a window containing an image of a bug. A bug moves in random directions within the window. There are two types of bugs—a slow bug and a fast bug. Obviously, a slow bug moves slower than a fast bug. However, the two types of bugs move differently. When a slow bug hits the border of the window, it reverses directions as if it hit a wall. When a fast bug hits a window border, it goes right on through and comes out the opposite window border.

> When the user positions the mouse pointer over a bug and clicks a mouse button, the bug is swatted. If the mouse button is clicked when the pointer is not positioned over a bug (i.e., the player misses), a pop-up window tells the player that he or she missed and the game starts at the beginning. It takes several swats to kill a bug. The game ends when the fast bug is eliminated.

The first step in the object-oriented design process is to determine the objects we will be working with. From the problem statement we can extract the objects by identifying the nouns that are objects according to our definition of object on page 33. The objects named in the problem statement are window, mouse, and bug. To illustrate the facilities available in an object-oriented lan-

Figure 1.20
The BugHunt game

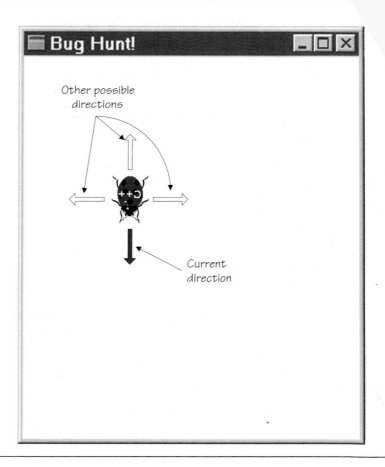

guage, we will focus on the design of the two bug objects. The design of the window and mouse objects are similar and are left as an exercise.

For each bug, we need to determine the properties associated with the bug and the actions it can perform. To implement Bug Hunt, a bug needs the following properties or attributes:

- Position in the window
- A display image or picture
- Current speed
- Current direction
- Strength (i.e., the number of swats it takes to eliminate the bug).

A bug needs to be able to handle the following messages or commands

- Draw
- Move the bug (i.e., update its current position)
- Change the direction the bug is moving

- Hit (i.e, tell the bug it was swatted)
- Kill (i.e., make the bug die)
- Is-pointed-at, which asks the bug to determine if the mouse cursor is pointing inside it.

These properties and messages form our abstraction of Bug Hunt's bugs.

Object-oriented languages provide a way of forming an abstraction by encapsulating properties and messages into a single concept. Such a concept is sometimes called a *class*. When a set of properties and messages are encapsulated in a class, we often say they are members of the class. The member properties of a class are sometimes called *data members* because they hold information. The messages a class of objects can handle are sometimes called *methods* or *member functions*.

The difference between a class and an object is subtle but important. Whereas a class is an abstract concept, an object is a concrete entity. For example, the concept of a car is a class, but a blue Ford Taurus with leather interior and a V-6 engine is an object. In practical terms, a class can be thought of as a stencil or mold for an object. From the class, objects with specific properties can be created, or instantiated.

The notion of instantiating a concrete object from a class abstraction is illustrated in Figure 1.21. Here, three different bugs, each with its own position, image, direction, and strength, are instantiated from the Bug class. The dotted enclosure for the class distinguishes it from a concrete object. In essence, a class defines what properties and messages an object has. Instantiation creates an object with specific values for each of the properties.

At this point, we could create one class for each type of bug (slow and fast) and instantiate different kinds of bugs as required. However, an important feature of object-oriented languages is that it lets the programmer exploit the similarity of objects. If we think about it, a fast bug and a slow bug have many common characteristics. Whether a bug is slow or fast, it has a position, a velocity, an image, a direction, and a strength. In fact, the distinguishing feature of a slow and a fast bug is how they move. A slow bug just reverses directions when it hits the edge of the window, while a fast bug tunnels through and reappears at the opposite side of the window. Thus we can think of creating a basic Bug that captures the attributes and behaviors that all bugs have in common, and using it to create two special types of bugs, SlowBug and FastBug, that behave differently when they hit the edge of the window. Thus, both Slow-Bug and FastBug are special types of Bug. These relationships, sometimes known as the *is-a* relationship, define a hierarchy. This hierarchy is shown in Figure 1.22.

At the top of the diagram is the Bug class. This, our most general class, is sometimes referred to as the *base class* or *super class*. Below the base class are the *subclasses* or *derived classes*. Derived classes inherit the properties and messages of their ancestors. Thus, both SlowBug and FastBug have the properties position, image, velocity, direction, and strength. Similarly, a FastBug and SlowBug understand the following messages or commands: draw, set the

Figure 1.21

*Instantiation of three
bug objects from class
Bug*

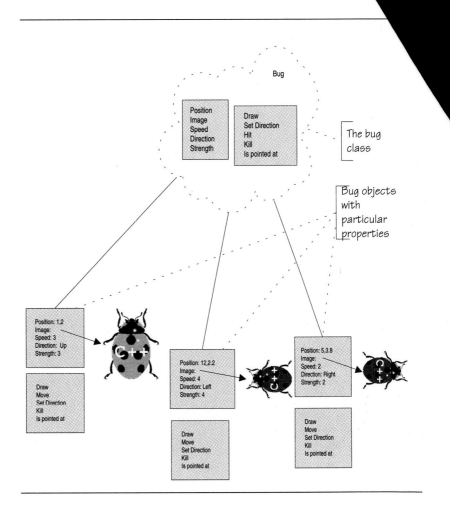

direction, hit, kill, and determine if the mouse is pointing at it. The notion of inheritance is a defining characteristic of object-oriented languages.

The ability of a class to inherit properties and member functions from an ancestor class supports the principle of reuse. Both bug types share the member functions of Draw, SetDirection, Hit, Kill, and IsPointedAt. These need to be implemented only once.

Our class hierarchy for bugs illustrates another feature of object-oriented languages—polymorphism. *Polymorphism* is the capability of something to assume different forms. In an object-oriented language, polymorphism is the property that a message can mean different things depending on the object receiving it. The message Move means one thing if it is sent to a SlowBug and something different if it is sent to an FastBug object. A SlowBug reverses directions when it hits the border of the window, while a FastBug tunnels through to the other side. This is illustrated in Figure 1.22 by including Move as a message for both the FastBug class and the SlowBug class.

viors

Polymorphism is a natural concept to apply to objects. Similar objects often accept the same message but do different things. For example, consider the graphical user interface of a computer. Here, the objects consist of icons that represent files. We use the mouse to send messages to these objects. A typical message is a double-click, which is sent to the object by moving the mouse cursor over the object and double-clicking a mouse button. For an executable file, the double-click message means execute the program, while for a text file, the double-click message means start up the text editor and open the file for editing.

The development of the Bug hierarchy illustrates many of the features available in an object-oriented language. However, to fully demonstrate the power of object-oriented design and programming we need to discuss how we can create a complete system from a group of objects. We can do this by sketching the high-level design of Bug Hunt.

Recall from the earlier description of Bug Hunt that the other objects explicitly mentioned were mouse and window. We will certainly need realizations of these objects. However, another very important object is mentioned in the description: the game itself! It's easy to overlook because the problem statement is a description of this object. If you think about it a moment, it makes sense to think of the game as an object. From an abstract point of view, the game object is the thing that coordinates the activities of the other objects, and it makes sure that the rules of the game are obeyed. We will call the object that is the game, the Game Controller.

We are now ready to complete the high-level design of Bug Hunt. As we mentioned, we certainly need mouse and window objects. For now, we can ignore the window object. While necessary for the implementation of the game, creation and control of a window does not play a major role in the operation of the game. The mouse, on the other hand, is a key component of the game. Indeed, most of the game's action centers around the activities of the mouse. Our abstract view of the mouse object, Mouse, is that it can send messages to the Game Controller. The Mouse sends a message to the Game Controller whenever a button is clicked. The message contains the screen location of the mouse pointer or sprite.

With the abstraction of the Mouse and Bug in hand, the design and operation of Bug Hunt is quite simple. The overall operation is illustrated in Figure 1.23. When a mouse button is clicked, the Mouse sends a MouseClick message to the Game Controller. The Game Controller extracts the mouse location from the message and sends an IsPointedAt message containing the location of the Mouse to the Bug on the screen. The Bug determines if the location in the message is within it. If the Mouse is pointing at it, the Bug responds yes to the IsPointedAt message; otherwise, it responds no. If the Game Controller receives a yes response, then the Game Controller sends a Hit message to the Bug. If the Bug's strength has been sapped, the bug responds to the hit message saying it has no strength. If this response is received, the Game Controller kills the Bug. If this was the SlowBug, the Game Controller creates a FastBug and the game continues. The interaction between the Game Controller and the Bug is illustrated in Figure 1.23.

If the Bug responds no, the mouse is not pointing at it; then the Game Controller creates a new window and displays a message telling the player that it missed the bug. If all the bugs are removed without a miss, the Game Controller displays a nice message in the window congratulating the player on her or his skill with a mouse. Of course, there are many details that still need to be worked out to complete the implementation of Bug Hunt. However, the high-level design is set, and in Chapter 15, we will complete the design and implementation of Bug Hunt. So don't go away!

1.5

POINTS TO REMEMBER

- The speed of a computer is usually expressed in cycles per second. Typical machines operate at 100 to 200 megahertz or 100 to 200 million cycles per second.

- Computers use the binary number system. A binary digit is called a bit.

- The basic unit of storage in a computer is a byte or eight bits.

Figure 1.23

Interaction of the game controller, mouse, and bug

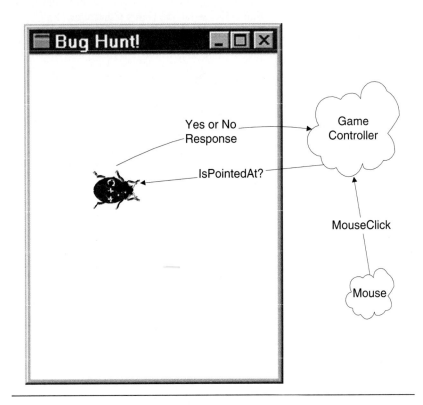

- Negative numbers are usually stored in two's complement representation. In this representation, an n-bit number can represent the values in the range -2^{n-1} through $2^{n-1}-1$.

- The central processing unit, or CPU, is the brains of a computer. It is where arithmetic and logical functions are performed.

- The size of a computer's random access memory, or RAM, is measured in megabytes (MB). Current desktop machines have memories that range from 8 to 128MB.

- The capacity of the hard disks found on current desktop machines ranges from .5 to 2.0 gigabytes (GB).

- A programming language is a language that gives commands or instructions to a computer.

- A compiler translates a programming language to machine language. A machine language consists of primitive operations that a computer can perform directly.

- Application software is software that solves a particular problem or provides a particular service.

History of Computing

Algorithms

Any system of counting or calculation whether mentally or by means of a device involves following a set of steps or directions. Computer scientists use the word *algorithm* to describe such as set of directions. The derivation of this word is of some interest. At the beginning of the ninth century, Caliph Al-Mamum established a great academic center in Baghdad. The center was known as the House of Wisdom. One of the scholars wrote a very influential textbook called *Kitab al jabr w' al-muqabala (Rules of Restoration and Reduction)*. The word *algebra* comes from the title of this book. The textbook introduced the use of Hindu numerals and included a systematic discussion of fundamental operations on integers. The book was influential because it fostered the use of Hindu numerals throughout the entire Arab empire and beyond. The word *algorithm* comes from the name of the scholar, Abu Ja'far Mohammed ibn Mûsâ al-Khowârizmî (literally, Father of Ja'far, Mohammed, son of Moses, native of Khowârizm).

A well-known example of an algorithm is Euclid's Algorithm which is a process for calculating the greatest common divisor (GCD) of two integers m and n. The algorithm is

Step 1. Let r be the remainder of m divided by n.

Step 2. If r is 0, the algorithm terminates and n is the GCD. Otherwise, set $m \leftarrow n$ and $n \leftarrow r$, and go back to Step 1.

To illustrate the use of the algorithm, let's calculate the GCD of 12 and 8. We perform each step in sequence.

Step 1. Step 1: $r \leftarrow 4$ (remainder of 12 divided by 8 is 4).

Step 2. Step 2: r is not 0, so $m \leftarrow 8$ and $n \leftarrow 4$, and we go back to Step 1.

Step 3. Step 1: $r \leftarrow 0$ (remainder of 8 divided by 4 is 0).

Step 4. Step 2: $r = 0$, so the algorithm terminates, and the GCD of 12 and 8 is 4.

Notice that the algorithm is expressed as a set of steps. Each step describes some action to take. In this algorithm, we have used English to describe the actions to perform at each step. In many algorithms, the steps are described using a combination of a natural language and mathematical notation. The notation we use to describe the steps is largely irrelevant; the important thing is to describe the actions to be performed clearly and unambiguously. In later chapters of this text, as we construct a program to perform a particular task, we will often begin with algorithms that describe how to do the task. We will use a notation similar to that shown above.

- Systems software is software that supports the development and execution of other programs.
- An operating system is system software that controls and manages the computing resources such as the memory, the input and output devices, and the CPU.

- Information is stored on a disk in a hierarchy of files so it can be found and retrieved quickly.
- An algorithm is a detailed, step-by-step description of how to perform some task.
- The goal of a software engineer is to produce software that is reliable, understandable, cost effective, adaptable, and reusable.
- Abstraction is the process of isolating the essential, inherent aspects of an object while ignoring inessential or irrelevant details.
- Encapsulation or information hiding is the process of separating the external aspects of an object, which can be viewed or accessed by other objects, from the internal implementation details which should be hidden from other objects.
- Modularity is the process of dividing an object into smaller pieces so each smaller object or module can be dealt with individually.
- An inheritance hierarchy is a way of organizing a set of abstractions from most general to least general.
- Object-oriented design and programming is a paradigm of programming in which a software system is modeled as a set of objects that interact with each other.
- In C++, an abstraction is formed by creating a class. A class encapsulates the properties and behaviors of an object.
- The data members of a class are the properties or attributes of a class.
- The member functions of a class are the behaviors of a class.
- A base class is one from which other, more specialized classes can be derived.
- A derived class is one that inherits properties from a base class.
- Polymorphism is the capability of something to assume different forms. In an object-oriented language, polymorphism is provided by allowing a message or member function to mean different things depending on the type of object that receives the message.
- Instantiation is the process of creating a concrete object from the class abstraction.

1.6

TO DELVE FURTHER

The following are excellent sources for learning more about the history of computing.

- Stan Augarten, *Bit by Bit: An Illustrated History of Computers*, New York: Ticknor & Fields, 1984.
- Jon Palfreman and Doron Swade, *The Dream Machine: Exploring the Computer Age*, London: BBC Books, 1991.

- Michael R. Williams, *A History of Computing Technology*, Englewood Cliffs, NJ: Prentice-Hall, Inc.,
- Harry G. Stine, *The Untold Story of the Computer Revolution*, New York: Arbor House, 1985.

1.7

EXERCISES

1.1   Suppose a microprocessor's clock rate is 120 MHz. If an addition operation can be done in one clock tick, how long, in nanoseconds, does it take to perform an addition?

1.2   Explain the difference between RAM and ROM.

1.3   Suppose a computer has a memory capacity of 16 megabytes. How many bits do we need to represent an address?

1.4   A computer has 640K bytes of memory. Exactly how many bytes of memory does it have?

1.5   How many bytes of information does a typical CD-ROM hold?

1.6   In a computer laboratory at your school. Find out all you can about one of the machines. At a minimum, you should find out

- the name of the company that manufactured the microprocessor in the machine,
- the clock speed of the processor,
- the amount of RAM in the machine,
- the size of the hard disk,
- the resolution of the graphics display, and
- the name and version of the operating system.

1.7   Find an advertisement for one of the mail-order companies that sell computers. Find out what the acronyms and terms in the advertisement mean. Some of the terms and acronyms you might see are cache, plug-and-play, SCSI, EIDE, burst mode, EDO, EPP, and 28.8.

1.8   The capacity of hard disk drives doubles every three years with cost remaining constant. Current 3.5-inch hard drives have a capacity of approximately 1 gigabyte and cost about $450. In six years, what can we expect a 2 gigabyte drive to cost?

1.9   For the operating system you are using, name the commands that manipulate files. In particular, give the name of the command that performs each of the following actions:

- delete a file
- rename a file
- copy a file
- create a directory
- delete a directory

1.10 Give the decimal value of the following numbers:

a) 01001_2

b) 0374_8

c) 0110100_2

d) 4033_5

e) $A32E_{16}$

f) 2345_8

g) 1211_4

h) 0111111_2

i) $02F3D_{16}$

j) 01010010011_2

k) 1776_8

l) $ABBA_{16}$

m) $ACDC_{16}$

1.11 Convert the numbers to the specified base.

a) 777_8 to hexadecimal

b) $AD11_{16}$ to binary

c) 01001011_2 to octal

d) 1111_{16} to octal

e) 01001111_2 to hexadecimal

f) 01001111_2 to octal

g) 3771_8 to binary

h) 4356_{16} to octal

1.12 Give the decimal value of the following 8-bit, two's complement numbers.

a) 10101100_2

b) 10000001_2

c) 11000000_2

d) 10100101_2

e) 11111111_2

f) 10000000_2

1.13 Compute the following sums and products. Your answers should be in binary.

a) $01000110 + 0001010$

b) $00111011 + 0101100$

c) $00000111 + 0000001$

d) $00100111 + 0001111$

e) $00010101 * 0001000$

f) $00001000 * 0000011$

g) 00001001 * 0000101

h) 00001011 * 0000100

1.14 Interview a computer scientist at your institution. Write a two-page summary of the interview. Here are some questions you might ask the interviewee:

- Why did you choose to become computer scientists?

- What are your areas of research expertise?

- What do you see as the most important research problems in your research area?

- What do you see as the most important research problems in the field of computer science?

- Do you work with industry in your research? What companies are your industrial partners? What are the advantages/disadvantages of working on research with industrial partners?

1.15 Consider an automated teller machine (ATM) at a bank. What are the relevant properties of an ATM for the following people?

a) ATM user

b) ATM repair person

c) Bank teller

d) Bank president

1.16 Give an example of encapsulation at work in a telephone-answering machine.

1.17 Most systems are modular. Name some of the components/modules of the following systems.

a) Boom box

b) Television

c) Washing machine

d) Television

e) Bicycle

1.18 Most organizations have a hierarchical structure. Pick an organization that you belong to and produce a diagram that illustrates its hierarchy.

1.19 Are the following things objects? Justify your answer.

a) Beauty

b) Time

c) Jealousy

d) Tree

e) Forest

1.20 Most electronic devices are designed using the principle of modularity, which makes the devices easier to manufacture and repair. Name the major components or modules of the following devices:

   a) Television

   b) VCR

   c) Microwave oven

   d) Boom box

   e) Radio

   f) Telephone

1.21 In an object-oriented inheritance hierarchy, the objects at each level are more specialized than the objects at the higher levels. Give three real-world examples of a hierarchy with this property.

1.22 Sketch the design of the Window class for the Bug Hunt game. Be sure to give the attributes (i.e., data members) and the actions (i.e., the member functions) that the class will have.

1.23 Sketch the design of the Mouse class for the Bug Hunt game. Be sure to give the attributes (i.e., data members) and the actions (i.e., the member functions) that the class will have.

1.24 Sketch the design of the Game Controller class for the Bug Hunt game. Be sure to give the attributes (i.e., data members) and the actions (i.e., the member functions) that the class will have.

1.25 Using the designs from questions 2.8 through 2.10, draw a diagram that shows how a game controller object, a bug, a mouse, and a window might interact.

1.26 Sketch the object-oriented design of the card game BlackJack. What are the key objects? What are the attributes and behaviors of these objects? How do the objects interact?

1.27 Sketch the object-oriented design of a system to control a pop machine. What are the key objects? What are the attributes and behaviors of these objects? How do the objects interact?

1.28 The inheritance example in Figure 1.22 ignored some details. Consider the following issues:

   a) Position is a property of all bugs. How might the position of a bug be specified?

   b) Outline the actions that a bug takes when it receives a kill message.

1.29 Extend the class hierarchy of Figure 1.22 to include a WarpBug class. A WarpBug occasionally disappears and reappears in a new position. Do you need to make any changes to the properties of Bug?

CHAPTER 2

C++: the fundamentals

Introduction

In this chapter, we examine and write several small C++ programs and introduce the fundamental objects supported by C++. The intent is to give an overall feel for the general structure of a C++ program and to help you become familiar with fundamental objects provided by C++. Indeed, a characteristic that often distinguishes one programming language from another is the primitive objects provided by the language. C++ has a rich set of fundamental objects, which allow integers, reals, and characters to be created and operated on.

Key Concepts

- function main()
- include
- comments
- definitions
- simple interactive input and output
- integer, floating-point, and character types
- integer, floating-point, and character literals
- C++ names
- declarations
- expressions
- usual unary conversions
- usual binary conversions
- operator precedence
- operator associativity
- iostream insertion and extraction

2.1

PROGRAM ORGANIZATION

Most programming languages have the concept of an executable unit. An executable unit is a named set of program statements. A program consists of a collection of these executable units. In some languages such as Fortran and Basic, the units are called subroutines or subprograms. In other languages, they are called procedures. In C++, the executable unit is called a function. These C++ executable units may be in one file or in several. A file containing C++ code is called a *translation unit*.

The ability to group program statements and functions into a named units has many advantages. First, it allows the programmer to structure the code as small, understandable units each of which performs a specific, well-defined task. This structure can reduce the complexity of the program significantly. Reduced complexity means the program is easier to understand, easier to modify, and more likely to run correctly. Organizing a program into translation units and functions is analogous to a writer structuring a book into a series of chapters (analogous to translation units) where each chapter consists of several sections (executable units). A well thought out organization helps the reader (programmer) understand the book (program).

The judicious use of functions can reduce the size of a program. In most programs a particular task must be performed at several points in the execution of a program. For example, an interactive program frequently queries users whether to proceed and perform some action. The user typically responds with a yes or no. If such queries occur often in a program, the size of the program can be reduced by placing the statements that prompt users and accept their responses in a separate function. Whenever user input is required, the programmer simply calls the function. In this chapter, we examine several simple C++ programs that consist of a single function.

2.2

A FIRST PROGRAM

Following a long-standing tradition, the first program we examine consists of a single function that outputs the following message:

```
Hello world!
```

Program 2.1 contains the source code for this program. Let's inspect this program in detail. The first three lines of the program are comments. Comments are program text that begin with two slashes. Comments are not translated by the compiler into executable code; they are inserted to describe and explain the operation of the program. The above program is so simple, we need not explain its operation. However, it is always useful to include comments that name the authors of the program. Later, if other programmers have a questions about the program, they know who to ask. In section 2.4 we will say much more about including comments in your programs

Program 2.1

Hello world program

```
// Program 2.1: Display greetings
// Authors: James P. Cohoon and Jack W. Davidson
// Date: 1/25/1996
#include <iostream.h>
int main() {
    cout << "Hello world!" << endl;
    return 0;
}
```

The fourth line of the program

```
#include <iostream.h>
```

is a preprocessor directive. The *preprocessor* is a program that runs before the compiler. Its job is to handle directives that control what source code the compiler sees as input. The `include` directive instructs the preprocessor to copy the contents of the specified file into the program. Essentially, the preprocessor replaces the directive with the contents of the specified file. In our example, the specified file is `iostream.h`. The left and right angle brackets surrounding the file name indicate that this is a system file and can be found in a special system directory. Any program that wishes to use the iostream library to perform input or output must contain this directive. It must appear before any code that uses the iostream library.

The fifth line of the program names the function and specifies the type of result the function will return. In a standard C++ program, the function named `main` is the first function called when the program is compiled and executed. The parentheses after the function name are used to delimit any arguments to the function. In this program, function `main()` requires no arguments, and hence nothing appears between the parentheses. The word **int** that appears before `main` indicates the type of result `main()` should return. The word **int** is C++'s name for an integer. By definition, `main()` always returns an integer result.

Following the parentheses is '{ ', a left brace character. Much like parentheses, braces are used to group things. In this case, the left brace and the right brace at the end of the function group the program statements that make up the function. This function consists of two statements:

```
cout << "Hello world!" << endl;
return 0;
```

The first statement is actually an expression like `a + b + c`. The operand `cout` is an object. Its definition along with the descriptions of the operations on it are found in the file `iostream.h`. The objects described in `iostream.h` are part of the iostream library, and they are used for doing input and output. `cout` is an output stream, and it typically corresponds to the display.

The second operand is a string literal. String literals are enclosed in double quotes. In C++ terminology, we say that the << operator inserts the string into the named stream. The result is that the string Hello World! is sent to the display. The third operand, endl, is also part of the iostream library. It is called a *manipulator*. A *manipulator* is a value that can be inserted into a stream to cause some special action to take place. The manipulator endl inserts a new-line character in the output stream (so that the next output will begin on a new line), and it forces all output that has been sent to the display to be printed immediately on the screen.

The second and final statement of the program is

```
return 0;
```

This statement ends execution of the function main, and control is returned to the code that called main. This code does some cleanup (e.g., files are closed), and then control is returned to the operating system. The zero in the return statement is the value returned by main. The convention is that a zero result from main indicates that the program ran successfully and no errors occurred. A nonzero result indicates that some type of error occurred, and the calling program or operating system can take appropriate action.

2.3

A SECOND PROGRAM

The previous program introduced several C++ components. However, it did not accept input and it performed no calculations. Program 2.2 reads the value of a purchase and computes the sales tax on it.

Program 2.2

Compute sales tax on a purchase

```
// Program 2.2: Compute sales tax on purchase
// Authors: James P. Cohoon and Jack W. Davidson
// Date: 1/25/1994
#include <iostream.h>
int main() {
    // Input price
    cout << "Purchase price ? " << flush;
    float Price;
    cin >> Price;

    // Compute and output sales tax
    cout << "Sales tax on $" << Price << " is ";
    cout << "$" << Price * 0.04 << endl;
    return 0;
}
```

The following lines illustrate the execution of the program.

```
Purchase price ? 55.50
Sales tax on $55.0 is $2.22
```

The underlined text was typed by the user in response to the request to input the amount of the purchase. We will use this convention for indicating user input throughout the textbook.

The first executable statement

```
cout << "Purchase price ? " << flush;
```

prompts the user to enter the purchase price. Such prompts are common in programs that interact with users. `flush` is a manipulator similar to `endl` except it does not output a carriage return so the cursor remains on the same line as the prompt.

In order to read the value of the purchase, we need a place to store the value. The seventh line of the program

```
float Price;
```

is a definition that instructs the C++ compiler to create an object named `Price` that can hold a floating-point value (i.e., a real). A floating-point object is used because we wish to enter the price as a decimal number.

The statement

```
cin >> Price;
```

waits for a number to be typed on the keyboard. When a value is typed, the value is converted to the internal format for floating-point numbers and stored in the object `Price`. The first operand, `cin`, is an object. Like `cout`, its definition along with the operations on it are found in the file `iostream.h`. `cin` is an input stream object, and it typically corresponds to the keyboard. The operator `>>` is called the *extraction operator*, and we say that it extracts a value from the named stream. The value extracted is stored in the right operand. The net effect is that the number typed on the keyboard is read and stored in `Price`.

The last two statements

```
cout << "Sales tax on $" << Price << " is ";
cout << "$" << Price * 0.04 << endl;
```

write the results to the display. The first statement writes a string, and the value stored in `Price`. The second statement outputs the result of the computation `Price * 0.04`, which is the sales tax. So, we see that the insertion operator can output the value of a object as well as the value of a computation. These two statements could have been written as a single statement, but they were split so they fit nicely on a line.

2.4

COMMENTS

A concept that is often difficult for beginning programmers to appreciate is that although a program is meant to be executed on a computer, it will be read by other human beings. Therefore, we want the program to be legal C++ (i.e., understandable by the computer), we also want other programmers to understand the program. Hundreds of programmers often work on large commercial software systems. Some might be adding additional features while others are fixing bugs. In order to accomplish their tasks, they must be able to understand how the program works. Thus it is important to write our programs so that other people can understand them.

It is our experience that even when we write programs for our personal use, there often comes a time when modification is necessary. While we might have understood how the program worked when we wrote it, after a few months or more have passed, important details about how the program worked are forgotten. *Comments* are a mechanism that allow us to include prose or commentary in the program that is not processed by the compiler. This commentary should explain how the program works.

In C++, there are two types or styles of comments. In the first type, the character '/' is immediately followed by another '/'. The compiler ignores the // and everything that follows it on the line. The following

```
// Comment
```

is a legal C++ comment, while

```
/ / Not a comment due to the space between the /'s
```

In the programs of section 2.1 and section 2.2, we used comments at the beginning of the program to identify the program, tell who wrote the program, and record when it was written. Including this information at the beginning of the program should be standard practice. Later, if other programmers have questions about the program, they know who to ask. Another common practice is that as a program is modified, each programmer who changes the program adds a comment after the comment naming the original authors, giving his or her name and a description of the changes. Program 2.3 gives an example.

Program 2.3

Modified hello world program

```
// Program 2.3: Display greetings updated
// Authors: James P. Cohoon and Jack W. Davidson
// Date: 1/25/1994
// Modified by:
//    Jane Student: added a good bye message
/     Date: 6/1/1994
#include <iostream.h>
int main() {
   cout << "Hello world!" << endl;
   cout << "Goodbye world!" << endl;
   return 0;
}
```

The second form of C++ comment begins with the characters /* and ends with a */. Such comments can span one or more lines. The compiler ignores everything between the beginning /* and the closing */. For example, the code

```
/* This is a multiline comment. It
   can span several lines.        */
```

Program 2.4 illustrates the use of this style of comment.

Program 2.4
Program with /...*/
style comments*

```
/****************************************************/
/* Program 2.4: Greetings variant                  */
/* Authors: James P. Cohoon and Jack W. Davidson   */
/* Date: 1/25/1994                                  */
/****************************************************/
#include <iostream.h>
int main() {
    cout << "Hello world!" << endl;
    cout << endl; /* output blank line */
    cout << "Bye world!" << endl;
    return 0;
}
```

Generally, C++ programmers use the // style of comment exclusively. The second form is used when blocks of code need to be temporarily removed, perhaps for debugging purposes. The block of code to be removed is surrounded by a /* */ pair. One must use this convention carefully because this style of comment does not nest. Thus if the block of code in question includes a /* */ style comment, the results will not be what's expected. Again, let's consider Program 2.4.

If we attempt to temporarily remove the last two statements by commenting them out, we get Program 2.5.

Program 2.5
Program with /...*/
style comments*

```
/****************************************************/
/* Program 2.5: Greetings variant                  */
/* Authors: James P. Cohoon and Jack W. Davidson   */
/* Date: 1/25/1994                                  */
/****************************************************/
#include <iostream.h>
int main() {
    cout << "Hello world!" << endl;
/*
    cout << endl; /* output blank line */
    cout << "Bye world!" << endl;
*/
    return 0;
}
```

The third insertion statement is not removed because the `*/` at the end of the previous line terminates the comment. In addition, the line following the third insertion statement (i.e., the `*/`) is treated as source code, but it is not a valid C++ expression. When the program is compiled, the compiler will report a syntax error.

2.5

ASSIGNING A VALUE

The third program we examine computes the y coordinate of a point on a line. The inputs to the program are the characteristics of the line (i.e., the slope and x intercept) and the x coordinate of the point of interest. The problem is illustrated in Figure 2.1.

Figure 2.1

Equation for a line

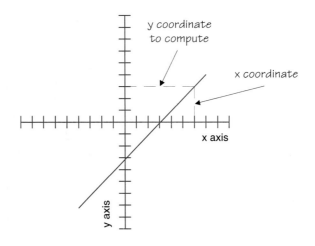

Program 2.6 contains the code. While this program is obviously larger than the previous two, it uses only one new C++ construct: the assignment expression. The first few lines of the program prompt the user for and read the slope of the line, the x intercept, and the x coordinate of interest. The statement

```
y = m * x + b;
```

computes the value of the y coordinate. This statement does not say that y is equal to m `*` x + b, but rather it says store the result of the computation m `*` x + b in the object y. The ability to compute and store values is fundamental to all computing.

Program 2.6

*Compute y coordinate
of a point on a line*

```
// Program 2.6: Compute the y coordinate of a
// point on a line given the line and an x coordinate
// Authors: James P. Cohoon and Jack W. Davidson
// Date: 1/25/1996
#include <iostream.h>
int main() {
    // Input line's parameters
    cout << "Slope of line? " << flush;
    int m; // Line slope
    cin >> m;
    cout << "Intercept of x axis? " << flush;
    int b;  // x intercept
    cin >> b;

    // Input x coordinate of interest
    cout << "X coordinate of interest? " << flush;
    int x;  // x coordinate of interest
    cin >> x;

    // Compute and display y coordinate
    int y;
    y = m * x + b;
    cout << "y = " << y << " when m = " << m << ";";
    cout << " b = " << b << "; x = " << x << endl;

    return 0;
}
```

**Programmer
Alert**

Using good style

Program 2.6 is an example of good programming style. The program begins with a brief statement of what the program does, lists the authors of the program, and gives the date the program was written. The program includes comments, and blank lines to delineate sections of the program. In the programs that follow, the authors and the date are omitted to keep the programs as short as possible. We encourage and recommend, however, that in practice you follow a programming style that is exemplified by Program 2.6.

2.6

FUNDAMENTAL C++ OBJECTS

C++ is notable because it has a large number of fundamental or built-in object types. The motivation was to give the programmer access to all the object types supported by typical hardware. The fundamental object types fall into one of three groups: the integer objects, the floating-point objects, and the character objects. Within each of these groups there are several variants. In the following sections, we discuss each group and the most commonly used variants. Other specialized variants of the fundamental types will be introduced throughout the text as they are needed.

2.6.1

Integer object types

Most programming languages have an object type for storing and manipulating integer values. The basic integer object type in C++ is called `int`. The definition of C++ does not specify the size of an `int`. The size of an `int` depends on both the underlying hardware and the compiler. Computer scientists say that the size of an `int` is *implementation dependent* or that the implementer of the compiler is free to choose the size of an `int`. Usually an `int` is chosen to be the most efficient integer data type on the underlying hardware. For most PC-based systems this size is 16 bits. A twos-complement 16-bit `int` can represent integers from -32,768 to 32,767. For Unix workstations, an `int` is usually 32 bits, although newer machines are now beginning to appear that support 64-bit integers. For these machines, the compiler designer could choose to use 64 bits to represent an `int`.

C++ provides several other integer object types. There are also **short** and **long**. Again, the specification of C++ does not dictate the size in bits of the **short** and **long** data types; however, it does specify that **long** be no shorter than **int** and that **int** be no shorter than **short**. That is,

$$NumberOfBits_{short} \leq NumberOfBits_{int} \leq NumberOfBits_{long}$$

The intent, however, is that **short** be smaller than **int** and **long** be greater than **int**. On PC-based systems, a **short** is usually 8 bits and a **long** is 32 bits. On Unix-based systems, a **short** is typically 16 bits, while a **long** is usually either 32 or 64 bits.

The question arises as to why C++ supports three different integer object types (actually, it provides support for others as well, but we defer discussion of those until later). Today many everyday objects are controlled by a computer. Examples include microwave ovens, automobiles, VCRs, and stereos. Systems in which a computer plays a central role in the operation of the system are called *embedded systems*. In most embedded systems, the memory used to hold the program that controls the system is a valuable resource that should not be wasted.

For example, many microwave ovens include a simple CPU that accepts input from a touch pad on the front and controls the operation of the oven. One of the costs associated with producing the oven is the number of memory chips required to hold the program that controls the operation of the oven. By providing support for integer objects of various sizes, C++ permits the programmer to optimize the usage of memory in the program. By picking the appropriate size object type, the programmer can reduce the memory requirements of the program. If this design results in fewer memory chips, the cost of the oven is lower.

As we mentioned earlier, an object is a set of attributes or values and behaviors or operations on the object. For the integer object types **short**, **int**, and **long**, C++ provides the usual arithmetic operations such as addition, subtraction, multiplication, and division. There are also C++ operators for comparing two integer objects. The six comparison operations are equal, not equal, less than, less than or equal, greater than, and greater than or equal.

2.6.2

Character object types

Closely related to the integer object type is the character object type **char**. Characters are encoded using some scheme where an integer represents a particular character. For example, the integer 98 might represent the letter *a*. The encoding scheme used is known as the *character set*. The two character sets in use today are ASCII and EBCDIC. Most computers use the ASCII character set, while the EBCDIC character set is used on IBM mainframe computers. The ASCII character set encodes the characters using seven bits, and the EBCDIC character set uses eight bits. For this reason, **char** is usually eight bits in length regardless of the character set in use. But again, we must point out that the definition of C++ leaves this decision to the implementer of the compiler.

Because the underlying representation of **char** is an integer, the operators defined on the integer types are defined on the character types as well. Regardless of the character set being used, we can always assume that the following relationships hold.

```
'a' < 'b' < 'c' < ... < 'z'

'A' < 'B' < 'C' < ... < 'Z'
```

and

```
'0' < '1' < '2' < ... < '9'
```

These relationships are useful, since they allow values that are made up of sequences of characters to be sorted into alphabetic order.

Additionally, with the ASCII character set we can assume that

```
'a' + 1
```

yields an integer that is the encoding for the character 'b' and that

```
'A' + 1
```

produces an integer that is the encoding for the character 'B'. That is, for any upper- or lowercase letter *c* except for 'z' and 'Z', the expression

```
'c' + 1
```

yields the next letter in the alphabet. Similarly, the expression

```
'2' + 1
```

yields an integer that is the encoding for the character '3'. That is, for any digit *d* except for '9', the expression

```
'd' + 1
```

yields the next sequential digit. These relationships are useful as they permit a character to be classified efficiently as to whether it represents a lowercase character, an uppercase character, or a digit.

For the EBCDIC character set, the above relationships do not hold for all characters. For example, with the EBCDIC character set, the expression

```
'i'+ 1
```

yields an integer that is the encoding of the character ':', not the letter 'j'. For this reason, when dealing with the object type **char**, from this point forward we will assume that the encodings are defined by the ASCII character set.

The integer and character object types, along with the enumeration types that are discussed in Chapter 4, form the set of types known as the integral types. They are called the *integral* types because they are represented by a binary encoding of the integers.

2.6.3

Floating-point object types

The floating-point object types are used to represent real numbers, that is, numbers that have both an integer part and a fractional part. For example,

```
3.1412
```

has an integer part of 3 and a fractional part of .1412. C++ provides three floating-point object types: **float**, **double**, and **long double**. Analogous to the situation with **int**, **short**, and **long**, the specification of C++ does not dictate the sizes of **float**, **double**, and **long double**. It depends on the underlying hardware. However, we can assume that values represented by the **float** type are a subset of the values represented by the **double** type and that values represented by the **double** type are a subset of the values represented by the **long double** type.

For a processor that supports only a single floating-point format, the **float**, **double**, and **long double** types would be equivalent. On a processor that supports two distinct formats, it is likely that the type **float** would be mapped to the smaller of the two formats and that **double** and **long double** would be mapped to the larger format.

As a concrete example, consider personal computers based on Intel's 80486 family of architectures. This family supports two floating-point representations. One is called *single real*. It is stored in 32 bits, and it can represent numbers in the range

$$1.18 \times 10^{-38} \le X \le 3.40 \times 10^{38}$$

with a precision of about seven decimal digits.

The second is called *double real,* and it can represent numbers in the range

$$2.23 \times 10^{-308} \le X \le 1.80 \times 10^{308}$$

with a precision of about 15 decimal digits. Double real requires 64 bits of storage. On this architecture, the type **float** would be mapped to single real. The types **double** and **long double** would be mapped to double real.

C++ provides the usual arithmetic operations on the floating-point data types as well as comparison operations.

From the above, one can guess that the rationale for different floating-point object types is somewhat analogous to that justifying the need for integer object types of different sizes. The larger floating-point formats are capable of representing numbers with a greater range and precision. It is up to the programmer to pick the format that best suits the application.

2.7
CONSTANTS

In the previous section, we discussed C++'s fundamental object types. We now examine how to write *constants* of each of these types. Again, in comparison with many other programming languages, C++ has a variety of ways that constants of each type can be written. We begin by examining string constants.

2.7.1
String and character constants

In Program 2.1, the string constant

```
"Hello World!"
```

was used. A *string constant* is a sequence of zero or more characters enclosed in double quotes.

This simple mechanism works well for characters that have a symbolic representation, but we also need to be able to specify special characters that do not have an obvious printable representation such as the bell, carriage return, or linefeed. To include a special character in a string constant, C++ defines an *escape mechanism*. The idea is that a special character, called the escape character, is used to change the meaning of the character following it. In C++, the escape character is the backslash '\', so, for example, to write a string constant that has the special newline character at the end, we would write

```
"Hello World!\n"
```

The backslash indicates that the character n is not to be interpreted as a constant n, but rather as a newline character.

Suppose we wish to write a string constant that includes the double quote. Again, we can use the escape mechanism and write

```
"\"Hello World!\""
```

The statement

```
cout << "\"Hello World!\"" << endl;
```

writes the string (including the double quotes)

```
"Hello World!"
```

to the display. Table 2.1 contains a list of the C++ character escape codes.

Table 2.1

Character escape codes

Character Name	ASCII Name	C++ Escape Sequence
newline	NL	\n
horizontal tab	HT	\t
backspace	BS	\b
form feed	FF	\f
alert or bell	BEL	\a
carriage return	CR	\r
vertical tab	VT	\v
backslash	\	\\
single quote	'	\'
double quote	"	\"
question mark	?	\?

C++ provides one additional escape mechanism for specifying characters in a string constant in which the numeric value of the character (from the ASCII character set definition) is given. Interestingly, the base of the number used must be either octal or hexadecimal. Decimal notation is not allowed. Thus a character can be included using one of the forms

```
\ooo
```

or

```
\xhh
```

where *ooo* and *hhh* are, respectively, octal or hexadecimal numbers. For example, the string constant

```
"Hello World!\012"
```

is exactly the same string as

```
"Hello World!\n"
```

because 12_8 is the ASCII encoding of the newline character. Generally, it is better to use the C++ character escape sequence for special characters because if the program is moved to a machine with a different character set, the C++ compiler will figure out the correct encoding for any special characters.

When a string constant is stored in memory, the individual characters are stored in consecutive memory locations. After the last character of the string, a null character ('\0') is added. This convention of terminating strings with the null character allows for easy checking for the end of the string. It also means that the length of the string need not be stored as part of the representation of the string. Figure 2.2 shows the memory allocation of the string constant

```
"Hello World!"
```

Figure 2.2

*Memory allocation for
a string literal*

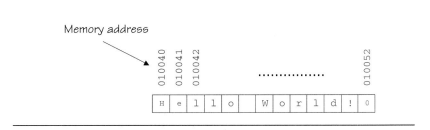

Each character takes up one byte of storage. The null character at the end of the string literal is not included when counting the number of characters in a string. Thus, the string literal above has 12 characters. This count is sometimes referred to as the *size of the string*.

The string constant with zero characters

```
" "
```

is often called the *null string,* or *empty string*. It contains zero characters, or has size zero. Remember, however, that it too has the null character at the end, so it takes up one byte of memory.

Sometimes we will need the representation of a single character. In C++, a character constant is created by enclosing the character desired with the ' character. For example,

```
'a' '1' '+' ';'
```

are valid C++ character constants.

We can use the character escape mechanism described for string constants to create character constants for any special characters that do not have an obvious printable representation. So, for example, to write a character literal that is the special newline character we write

```
'\n'
```

Again, the backslash indicates that the character n is not to be interpreted as a constant n, but rather as a newline. Suppose we wish to write a character constant that has the value of the single quote? Again, we can use the escape mechanism and write

```
'\''
```

This makes it clear that the middle single quote is the character being defined.

We can also use the numeric escapes to write a character constant. A character constant can be written using one of the forms

```
'\ooo'
```

or

```
'\xhhh'
```

where *ooo* and *hhh* are octal or hexadecimal numbers. The following are legal C++ character constants using the octal form

```
'\033' '\06' '\177'
```

They denote the ASCII characters ESC (escape), ACK (acknowledge), and DEL (delete), respectively. The literals

```
'\x1b' '\x6' '\x7f'
```

use the hexadecimal format, and they denote the same characters.

2.7.2

Integer constants

The simplest way to write an integer constant in C++ is to just write the number. For example,

```
23 45 101 55
```

are four valid C++ integer literals. When we write an integer constant, the compiler assigns it a C++ object type. Generally, it will usually be the type **int**, but the type assigned depends on the size of the constant and if it has a suffix. For example, to write an integer constant that will be treated as type **long**, the C++ programmer can append either an 1 or an L at the end of the number. Thus, the constants

```
23L 451 101L 55L
```

all have type **long**. We do not recommend using a lowercase 1 as it is easily confused with the digit 1. There is no way to specify an integer constant that is type **short**.

If the integer constant does not have a suffix, then the compiler chooses the type based on the size of the value. If the value can be stored as an **int**, then its type is **int**. However, if the value is too large to be stored as an **int**, but it can be stored as a **long**, then the compiler will treat the constant as type **long**. If the value is too large to be stored as a **long**, the compiler should report this as an error.

It is sometimes convenient to specify integer constants using a different base. C++ supports writing integer constants using both the base 8 and base 16. An integer constant that begins with a leading zero is assumed to be a base 8 number. The C++ constants

```
023 077L 045 010
```

C++
Language

Specifying C++ syntax

There are a variety of ways to form an integer constant. Looking at some examples is a good way to get a general idea of what constitutes a valid C++ constant, but it would be nice if we had a notation for describing how to construct valid constants as well as other C++ constructs we will discuss. In this textbook, C++ syntax is described using annotated syntax diagrams. For example, the syntax diagram that describes decimal constants is

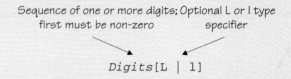

Sequence of one or more digits; Optional L or l type
first must be non-zero   specifier

Digits[L | l]

To specify one of several alternatives, the vertical bar ('l') is used. Square brackets around an item indicate that it is optional. Thus a type specifier can either be an L or an l, and it may be omitted. In a syntax diagram, italic symbols are known as *nonterminals*. That is, they represent a set of possibilities. In the diagram above, the symbol *Digits* represent the digits 0, 1, 2, ..., 9. The annotation notes that the first digit may not be a zero.

are all base 8 numbers and represent the decimal values 19, 63, 37, and 8. All but the second are type **int**. The second is type **long**. If the constant is base 8, then the characters 8 or 9 cannot appear in the constant. Thus the constants

    038 093 0779

are not valid C++ constants.

To use base 16, the prefix `0x` or `0X` is used. In a hexadecimal constant, the characters `f` through `f` or `A` through `F` represent the digits 10 through 15. The literals

    0x2a 0x45 0XffL 0xA1e

represent the decimal values 42, 69, 255, and 2590. The third value has type **long**, the others have type **int**. The general syntax for octal and hexadecimal integer constants is

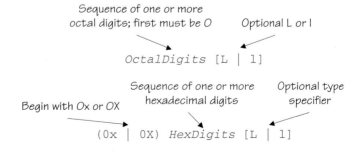

Sequence of one or more
octal digits; first must be 0   Optional L or l

OctalDigits [L | l]

Begin with 0x or 0X   Sequence of one or more   Optional type
                       hexadecimal digits   specifier

(0x | 0X) *HexDigits* [L | l]

Program 2.7 outputs the decimal values for octal, decimal, and hexadecimal constants.

Program 2.7

Output different base constants

```
// Program 2.7: Output different base constants
#include <iostream.h>
int main() {
    cout << "Display integer constants\n" << endl;

    cout << "Octal constant 023 is " << 023 << " decimal"
      << endl;    // outputs decimal value 19
    cout << "Decimal constant 23 is" << 23 << " decimal"
      << endl;    // outputs decimal value 23
    cout << "Hexadecimal constant 0x23 is " << 0x23
      << " decimal" << endl; // outputs decimal value 35

    return 0;
}
```

When executed, the program produces the following output:

```
Display integer constants
Octal constant 023 is 19 decimal
Decimal constant 23 is 23 decimal
Hexadecimal constant 0x23 is 35 decimal
```

Using different bases to represent numbers is the basis for the following really bad computer science riddle. Question: Why did the programmer get Halloween and Christmas confused? Answer: Because Oct 31 = Dec 25.

The observant reader might note that we have made no mention of negative numbers. The reason is that integer constants are always nonnegative. To form a negative value, a minus sign can be applied to a constant, but the formal interpretation is that a unary minus operator is applied to the constant. The minus sign is not part of the constant. A plus sign can also be applied to an integer constant. It does not change the value of the constant. The plus sign is included in C++ for symmetry with the unary minus operator.

2.7.3

Floating-point constants

C++ also provides a variety of ways to write floating-point constants. The syntax for one form of floating-point constant is

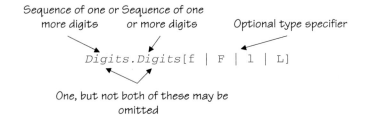

For example,

```
2.34 3.1416 29.00 .23 0.32
```

are all valid C++ floating-point constants. For floating-point constants, the type is always **double** unless otherwise specified. In a manner similar to that used for integer constants, the type can be specified using the letters f, F, l, and L as a suffix. The letters f or F specify that the constant is to be type **float**, while the letters l or L specify that the constant is to be of type **long double**. The types of the floating-point constants

```
23.4f 0.21L 45.3F 7456.1
```

are **float**, **long double**, **float**, and **long double**.

C++ also provides the ability to express floating-point constants using scientific notation. Recall that in standard scientific notation, a number is expressed as a power of 10. The number

$$1.23 \times 10^3$$

is in scientific notation. This is read as "one point two three times ten to the third power." The above number is equal to

$$1230.0$$

The general form for a number in scientific notation is

$$mantissa \times 10^{exponent}$$

The syntax for C++ scientific notation is

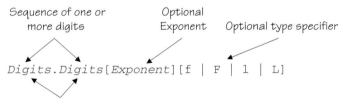

where *Exponent* is

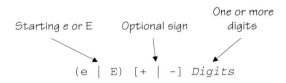

The mantissa can be an integer or a decimal number. The exponent is a signed integer. Examples of valid C++ floating-point constants using the scientific notation are

```
1.23E10        0.23E-4        45.e+23        23.68E12
```

These constants represent, respectively, the values

$$1.23 \times 10^{10} \qquad 0.23 \times 10^{-4} \qquad 45.0 \times 10^{23} \qquad 23.68 \times 10^{12}$$

in standard scientific notation. The type of a floating-point constant can be specified using the previously mentioned suffixes. In the previous example, since there is no type suffix, all of the above numbers are type **double**. The constants

```
1.23E10F       0.23E-4f       45.e+23L       23.68E12L
```

have the same values as above, but the first two are type **float** and the second two are type **long double**.

Program 2.8 illustrates the use of the various forms of floating-point constants.

Program 2.8

Output different forms of floating-point constant that represent the same value

```cpp
// Program 2.8: Illustrate different forms of
// floating-point constants that have the same value
#include <iostream.h>
int main() {
    cout << 230.E+3 << endl;
    cout << 230E3 << endl;
    cout << 230000.0 << endl;
    cout << 2.3e5 << endl;
    cout << 0.23E6 << endl;
    cout << .23e+6 << endl;
    return 0;
}
```

When the program is executed, it outputs the following values:

```
230000
230000
230000
230000
230000
230000
```

As the output shows, each of the constants represents the same value.

Analogous to the situation with integer literal constants described in section 2.7.2, floating-point constants are not signed. A constant can be negated by applying a minus sign to it.

2.8

NAMES

A fundamental requirement of computing is the ability to store and retrieve information. In the early days of computing, before assemblers and high-level programming languages, programmers wrote programs in machine language and they were required to keep track of where in the computer's memory values were stored. These values were accessed by specifying the address of the memory location that contains the value. To see first-hand how tedious and error-prone this process can be, let's write a simple machine-language program that computes a 6 percent sales tax on five items.

The prices of the five items are stored in memory. Figure 2.3 shows the layout of memory. The item prices are stored in memory locations 2000 through 2016. We also need memory locations to store the sum of the prices of the items and the computed tax. We must ensure that the locations we choose do not overlap with the memory locations where the cost of the items is stored. We arbitrarily pick memory location 2028 for the sum and memory location 2024 to hold the sales tax.

Figure 2.3

Memory layout for machine-language programming example

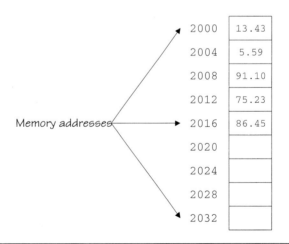

A memory location is accessed by writing M[n] where n is the address to access. The operation M[n] ← expr stores the value of expr in the memory location M[n]. A machine-language program to compute the sales tax is

```
M[2028] ← 0
M[2028] ← M[2028] + M[2000]
M[2028] ← M[2028] + M[2004]
M[2028] ← M[2028] + M[2008]
M[2028] ← M[2028] + M[2012]
M[2028] ← M[2028] + M[2016]
M[2024] ← M[2028] * .06
```

The first thing to notice about this program is that if you looked at it without knowing beforehand what it is supposed to do, it would be difficult to tell what it is computing. If we rewrite the instructions using symbolic names instead of machine addresses, we get the program

```
TotalCost  ←  0
TotalCost  ←  TotalCost + Price1
TotalCost  ←  TotalCost + Price2
TotalCost  ←  TotalCost + Price3
TotalCost  ←  TotalCost + Price4
TotalCost  ←  TotalCost + Price5
SalesTax   ←  TotalCost * .06
```

which is much easier to understand and less prone to errors.

Because of the overwhelming advantages of using symbolic names, all modern programming languages support the use of names to denote program values or objects. All high-level programming languages allow a programmer to use symbolic names to represent values as well as other program entities.

An important component of a programming language is the rule for forming valid names. In C++, a valid name is a sequence of letters (upper- and lowercase), digits, and underscores with the additional restriction that the name cannot begin with a digit. Examples of valid C++ names are

```
x _digit x1 Score do AverageScore for Nbr_Trials
```

Examples of strings that are not valid C++ names are

```
2BORNOT2B ToHot? $a1 A#
```

Names are case sensitive. This means that for two names to be the same, they must have exactly the same spelling including the case of the characters. For example, the names

```
NbrOfTrials      NbrofTrials
```

are different because *of* is capitalized in the first, but not in the second.

A question of interest is, How long can a name be? The definition of C++ sets no limit on the length of name. However, some C++ implementations are deficient in this area, and they may use only the first N characters of a name to determine uniqueness. For example, the Turbo C++ compiler uses the first 32 characters of the name. Other compilers may use more or less. Thus it is important to make sure that two long names for different objects are unique in the first part of the name rather than at the end. Otherwise, two names that appear different to the programmer may be treated as the same name by the compiler.

Like many other programming languages, C++ has two classes of names: keywords and identifiers. These names are discussed in the following sections.

2.8.1

Keywords

Some words are reserved as part of the language, and they cannot be used by the programmer to name things. These special names are called reserved words or in C++ terminology they are called *keywords*. Table 2.2 lists the C++ keywords.

Table 2.2
C++ keywords

asm	else	operator	throw
auto	enum	private	true
bool	explicit	protected	try
break	extern	public	typedef
case	false	register	typeid
catch	float	reinterpret_cast	typename
char	for	return	union
class	friend	short	unsigned
const	goto	signed	using
const_cast	if	sizeof	virtual
continue	inline	static	void
default	int	static_cast	volatile
delete	long	struct	wchar_t
do	mutable	switch	while
double	namespace	template	
dynamic_cast	new	this	

Keywords have special meaning to the compiler, and they cannot be changed by the programmer. We have already discussed a few of these keywords. The keywords **short**, **int**, **long**, **float**, **double**, and **char** are C++ fundamental types. As we delve deeper into C++, we will discuss the meaning of the other keywords.

Recall that names are case sensitive, and by definition keywords consist of lowercase letters only. Thus the strings

```
Continue DO Char
```

are not keywords. However, as we discuss below, they are valid C++ identifiers.

2.8.2

Identifiers

An *identifier* is a name defined by and given meaning to by the programmer. For example, in Program 2.1 on page 49, main, cout, and endl are symbolic names. main is the name of the function, cout is the name of an object that is used to do output to the display, and endl is the name of a manipulator.

The rule for forming a valid identifier is that it must be a valid C++ name and cannot clash with the keywords. Examples of valid C++ identifiers are

```
TaxRate    n    price    flow    first_value    tmp
```

Choosing identifiers that connote the purpose of the object being named is good programming practice. For example, suppose we are writing a program where we need to compute and store the number of students in a class. We could choose the identifier

```
s
```

to name the object that will hold the number of students in the class, but this identifier is not very descriptive. At the other end of the spectrum, we could use

```
Number_of_Students_in_Class
```

but this identifier would be tedious to write all the time. Usually, there is a reasonable middle ground. The identifier

```
NbrStudents
```

is much shorter and almost as clear. In this text, we will adopt several conventions for picking and constructing identifiers to name objects. First, we will strive to use single word identifiers. However, when we use identifiers constructed of two or more words so that the purpose of the object is clear, we will follow the convention of capitalizing the first letter of each word. So, for instance, we might use the identifiers

```
WordCount    Time    BitsPerSecond    LapTime
```

Second, we will often use abbreviations for obvious words. For example, abbreviations such as Nbr for *Number*, Obj for *Object*, and Cnt for *Count*, decrease the length of the identifier without loss of clarity. Identifiers illustrating this style of abbreviation are

```
WindowObj    EmployeeNbr    WordCnt
```

As we develop programs and the need for additional naming conventions becomes apparent, we will introduce them.

C++
Language

Use of underscores
While underscores are permitted at the beginning of C++ names, their use should be avoided. Identifiers beginning with a double underscore are reserved for use by the C++ compiler. Similarly, names that begin with a single underscore should be avoided as they are reserved by some C implementations for naming operating system routines. Some C++ implementations use C libraries.

2.9

DEFINITIONS

In C++, before we can use an object, we must define the object. A definition introduces the name of the object into the program, and it specifies the type of the object.

A common form of a C++ definition is

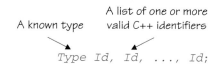

A known type

A list of one or more valid C++ identifiers

```
Type Id, Id, ..., Id;
```

where *Type* is a fundamental type or a type that has been previously defined by the programmer and *Id* is a C++ identifier. The definition

```
int Sum;
```

defines an object called Sum that has type **int** with no initial value. That is, the object is named, memory is allocated, but the object is given no initial value. Additional examples of this form of definition are

```
int x;
int WordCnt, Radius, Height;
float FlightTime, Mileage, Speed;
```

None of these objects is given an initial value. In general, it is not a good idea to define an object without initializing it. For example, if we attempt to use Mileage's value before we have explicitly given it one, the value we get is unknown or undefined.

Programming Tip

What is an object?

Some texts make a distinction between objects and the fundamental data types. In their view, an object is an instance of a programmer-defined data type where the data and the functions that operate on that data are combined into a single unit. Also in their view, a declaration of a fundamental data type is not an object, but a variable. Such a distinction is artificial. In our view, an object is a region of memory that contains values. How these values are interpreted depends on the type of the object and how it is accessed. It makes no difference whether the type was created by the programmer or provided by the programming language.

Program 2.9 illustrates the danger of using uninitialized objects. The program defines four uninitialized objects and then outputs their values. When the program is run, the output is unpredictable.

Program 2.9

Output the values of uninitialized objects

```
// Program 2.9: Output the values of uninitialized
// objects
#include <iostream.h>
int main() {
   float f;
   int i;
   char c;
   double d;
   cout << "f's value is " << f << endl;
   cout << "i's value is " << i << endl;
   cout << "c's value is " << c << endl;
   cout << "d's value is " << d << endl;

   return 0;
}
```

For instance, on one run of the program, the output was

```
f's value is 1.81825e+11
i's value is 8653
c's value is
d's value is 1.12975e-231
```

and on another run, the output was

```
f's value is 1.81825e+11
i's value is -1
c's value is b
d's value is 7.50781e-146
```

Thus it is always a good idea to initialize an object when it is defined.

Programmer Alert

Always give objects an initial value

A common error is to forget to give an object an initial value. To avoid this, it is a good idea to give an object an initial value when it is defined. The only exception is when the object will be initialized immediately after the definition by extracting a value from an input stream and storing it in the object. For example, the code

```
float Price;
cin >> Price;
```

is acceptable. However, it certainly would not hurt to write

```
float Price = 0.0;
cin >> Price;
```

However, some would argue that the above fragment could confuse the reader because the object Price is given a value that is immediately overwritten.

   In our code, we will follow the convention of always giving an object an initial value unless the object is immediately given a value through an extraction operation.

Another form of definition allows objects to be initialized when they are defined. The C++ syntax for this type of definition is

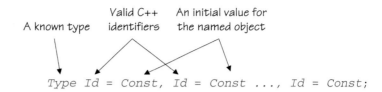

The definition

```
int Sum = 0;
```

is equivalent to the first definition, but it initializes Sum to zero. Other examples of this form of definition are

```
float TaxRate = 0.06;
char letter = 'a';
```

The first definition creates a float object called TaxRate with an initial value of 0.06, while the second creates an object named letter that has type **char** with an initial value of 'a'.

We will often use comments in conjunction with definitions to explain what the object represents. Some examples are

```
int Temp = 32;      // current Temperature (Fahrenheit)
char c;             // current input character
float PayRate;      // Hourly rate of pay (Dollars)
```

Notice, that when the object is a measure, it is helpful to state the units of measure in the comment.

Several objects can be defined and initialized in a single statement. For example, the C++ declaration

```
int Count = 0, Bits = 16, Small = -1;
```

declares three objects, all of type **int**. Count is initialized to 0, Bits is initialized to 16, and Small is initialized to -1.

Besides allowing us to use symbolic names for program objects, the use of definitions passes the burden of deciding where to place objects in memory to the compiler. In our machine-language sales tax program, we had to ensure that the memory locations for the various objects did not conflict or overlap. This process of assigning memory locations to objects is called *memory allocation*. To allocate memory manually, we had to know the amount of memory required to store each item. In our example, we assumed that a price was represented as a floating-point value and required four bytes of storage.

For a program with just a few objects, a programmer could probably keep track of where to store the objects. However, this task would be difficult for large programs with many objects, and perhaps more importantly, it would detract from the important job of writing a correct program.

Thus, a definition directs the compiler to do several things. Using the type information to determine the number of memory locations to hold the object, the compiler allocates memory locations to store the object. These memory locations are then reserved and cannot be used to hold subsequently defined objects. The compiler records that information along with the name so that when the name is used subsequently, the location of the object in memory can be found. And finally, it gives the object an initial value.

The two forms of definitions introduced above can be used together. The following C++ definition

```
int i, j = 4, k, l = 10;
```

creates four **int** objects: i, j, k, and l. The objects i and k have no initial value, while j and l are initialized to 4 and 10, respectively.

In this text, our rule of thumb will be to use a definition that initializes the object. Furthermore, we will typically define only one object per line. This convention allows us to include a comment with each definition that explains the purpose of the object.

2.10

EXPRESSIONS

In Chapter 1, we introduced the notion of an object. Recall that an object is a set of attributes or values and the operations that can be performed on them. An *expression* is C++'s mechanism for applying operations to objects. Conceptually, an expression is the means by which we calculate new objects from old ones. The objects or values being operated on are called the *operands*. The process of applying the operation to the operands is referred to as *evaluating the expression*. The evaluation of an expression yields a result that has a type as well as a value. The notion that the evaluation of an expression yields a result that has value and a C++ type is very important. To make this notion very clear, in the following sections that discuss expressions, we will present the result of evaluating an expression as a 2-tuple of the form

<value, type>

where *value* is the value of the expression and *type* is the C++ type associated with the value. Do not be put off by the term *2-tuple*. This is just a formal way of saying that a result consists of two components. As a reminder that this is the convention we have adopted for clarity, results expressed as 2-tuples will be italicized. In later sections, we will drop the notation and give only the value with the assumption that the type is implicitly part of the result.

2.10.1

Simple expressions

The simplest form of a C++ expression is a constant with no operation applied. For example, the evaluation of the expression

```
23;
```

yields the result *<23, int>*. Notice the semicolon after the expression. This is the C++ delimiter that separates or terminates an expression.

Similarly, the expression

```
18.53;
```

evaluates to *<18.53, double>*. The expression

```
'a';
```

evaluates to *<97, int>*.

An expression can also be an object with no operation applied. The result of evaluating this type of expression is the value of the object. For example, consider the following declaration and expression:

```
int XCoord = 23;      // x coordinate of point
XCoord;
```

The result of evaluating the expression is *<23, int>*. In some sense, an operation is being applied to the operand XCoord. The operation being applied is one that fetches the value stored in XCoord. Consider the following longer example:

```
double BattingAvg = .253;// current batting average
int AtBats = 301;         // at bats this season
short StolenBases = 34;   // stolen bases this season
float EarnedRunAvg = 1.7;    // Earned run average
                             // (pitchers)
char c = 'x';

// Begin expressions
AtBats;
BattingAvg;
EarnedRunAvg;
c;
StolenBases;
```

The results of the expressions are *<301, int>*, *<0.253, double>*, *<1.7, float>*, *<120, int>*, and *<34, short>*, respectively.

2.10.2

Binary arithmetic operations

C++ has several *binary* operators for performing arithmetic on the integer and floating-point types. The term binary indicates that the operator is applied to two operands. Because the C++ rules for performing binary operations are rather complicated, we first consider the binary operators applied to integer values. We will then consider expressions involving binary operators applied to floating-point values. The section will conclude with a discussion of how C++ handles expressions involving values of both integer and floating-point types.

The binary integer arithmetic operators are listed in Table 2.3. All the examples are done using the type **int**. As the table shows, the binary integer arithmetic operators, for the most part, do just what you think they should do. The simple expression

```
2 + 3;
```

produces the value *<5, int>*. Similarly, the expression

```
4 - 7;
```

produces the value *<−3, int>*. The division and modulus operators, however, deserve special attention. Notice that the expression

```
6 / 4;
```

produces the value 1, not 1.5. When applied to two positive integer values, the C++ division operator produces an integer result. If the divisor does not evenly divide the dividend, the fractional part of the quotient is discarded and the whole part of the quotient is the value component of the result. The process of discarding the fractional part is called *truncation*. In the second division example, the expression

```
11 / 4;
```

evaluates to the result *<2, int>*. That is, the result of the division 2.75 is truncated to produce the value 2. Note that truncation is not the same as *rounding*. In the previous example, rounding would have produced the value 3.

Table 2.3

Binary integer arithmetic operators

Operation	Operator	Example	Result
Addition	+	2 + 3; 5 + 10;	*<5, int>* *<15, int>*
Subtraction	−	13 - 4; 4 - 7;	*<9, int>* *<-3, int>*
Multiplication	*	3 * 4; 5 * 11;	*<12, int>* *<55, int>*
Division	/	8 / 2; 6 / 4; 11 / 4; 4 / 5; 6 / 0;	*<4, int>* *<1, int>* *<2, int>* *<0, int>* *<undef, int>*
Remainder	%	10 % 3; 23 % 4; 5 % 0;	*<1, int>* *<3, int>* *<undef, int>*

What happens if one of the operands is negative and the result is inexact? In this case, the definition of C++ allows one of two choices. The two choices are the integers that are closest to the mathematical quotient. The implementer of the compiler is free to choose the result that is most convenient for the target machine. For example, the choices for the value component of the expression

```
-11 / 2;
```

are −5 and −6. Thus, depending on the compiler and the machine, either of the results *<−5, int>* or *<−6 ,int>* may be produced.

Finally, there is a case that deserves special attention. If the divisor is zero, the result of the division operation is undefined. Indeed, for most machines, dividing by zero will cause the program to halt with an error. In many of the examples in this book, we take special care to ensure that we do not inadvertently perform a division by zero.

Closely related to division is the remainder operator %, which produces as a result the remainder of the division. It is also sometimes referred to as the *modulus* operator. The result of the expression

```
19 % 5
```

is *<4, int>* because 19 divided by 5 yields a quotient of 3 and a remainder of 4.

Because the remainder operator is typically implemented using the target machine's division instruction, it shares many characteristics of the division operator. First, if the right operand is zero, the result of the operation is undefined. Second, if either operand is negative and the result is not zero (i.e., there is a remainder), the value component of the result depends on how the target machine performs division. It is always the case that the expression

```
(a / b) * b + a % b
```

is equal to a if b is not 0. So for example, if

```
7 / -2
```

produces the result *<-4,int>*, it must be the case that the expression

```
7 % -2
```

produces *<-1,int>*. On the other hand, if the expression

```
7 / -2
```

produces the result *<-3, int>*, the remainder operator must produce the result *<1, int>*.

All the binary integer arithmetic operators have the potential to produce a value that is larger than the host machine can handle. This situation is called *overflow*. If an integer arithmetic operation produces an overflow, the value produced by the operation is undefined and the behavior of the program is unpredictable.

If you recall from section 2.6.1, C++ has three integer types—**short**, **int**, and **long**, as well as the **char** type. Up to this point, we have assumed that the operands are all of type **int**. How is arithmetic performed on the other integer types? For example, is the addition of two values of type **long** different from the addition of two values of type **int**? What if one value is of type **int** and the other of type **long**? With four types, there are 10 different possibilities for addition.

To reduce the number of cases that must be handled, C++ defines a set of conversions that is applied to operands before any operations are performed. These conversions are called the *usual unary conversions*. The usual unary conversions specify that values of type **char** and **short** should be converted to type **int** before any operations are performed. At this point, the operands of an integer binary operation can be either of type **int** or of type **long**. In addition, a set of conversions are applied to operands before binary operations are applied. These conversions are called the *usual binary conversions*. If the operands are the same type, no conversion is done, and the type of the result is the type of the operands. If the types of the operands are not the same, then the one that is type **int** is converted to type **long**, a **long** operation is performed, and the type of the result is **long**.

The above may seem a bit complicated, but it really is not that difficult. Just remember, the result is always **int** unless one of the operands is type **long**, then the result is type **long**. This rule is summarized in Table 2.4.

Table 2.4

Result types for integer binary operations

		Type of right operand			
		char	short	int	long
Type of left operand	char	int	int	int	long
	short	int	int	int	long
	int	int	int	int	long
	long	long	long	long	long

All the arithmetic operators, except for the remainder operator (%), can be applied to floating-point operands (i.e., **float**, **double**, and **long double**). The binary floating-point arithmetic operators are listed in Table 2.5. Again, for illustrative purposes, all operands are type **double**.

The remainder operator makes no sense when applied to floating-point operands. The C++ compiler will flag as illegal an expression where a floating-point value is an operand to the remainder operation.

The other binary floating-point arithmetic operators act as you would expect. Just as with the binary integer arithmetic operators, overflow is a possibility, and a floating-point division by zero will cause the program to halt.

Similar to the situation with the binary integer arithmetic operations, the usual binary conversions are applied when operands are of different floating-point types. The rule is similar in spirit to the rule for the integer types. That is, the less precise operand is converted so that it is at least as precise as the other

Table 2.5

Binary floating-point arithmetic operators

Operation	Operator	Example	Result
Addition	+	`2.0 + .33;` `5.1 + 10.0;`	*<2.33, double>* *<15.1, double>*
Subtraction	-	`13.6 - 4.2;` `4.0 - 7.0;`	*<9.4, double>* *<-3.0, double>*
Multiplication	*	`3.0 * 4.4;` `7.5 * 11.0;`	*<13.2, double>* *<82.5, double>*

Division	/	`8.6 / 2.0;`
		`5.0 / 4.0;`
		`-11.0 / 4.0;`
		`6.0 / 0.0;`
			<4.3, double>
			<0.125, double>
			<-2.75, double>
			<undef, double>

operand. To do otherwise would mean that we would unnecessarily loose precision in the result. For example, if one operand is type **float** and the other is type **double**, the operand that is type **float** is converted to type **double**. The operation performed is a double-precision addition, and the type of the result is **double**. The possibilities for the results of binary floating-point operators with operands of different precisions are summarized in Table 2.6.

Table 2.6

Result types for binary floating-point operations

		Type of right operand		
		float	double	long double
Type of left operand	float	float	double	long double
	double	double	double	long double
	long double	long double	long double	long double

To help understand the usual binary conversions when the operands are different floating-point types, let's study a code fragment that requires conversions.

```
float Temp = 23.3;
double Volume = 3.2;
long double AvogadroConstant = 6.023E23;
cout << Volume * AvogadroConstant;
cout << Temp / Volume;
```

In the arithmetic expression in the first insertion to `cout`, `Volume` is promoted from **double** to **long double** because `AvogadroConstant` is **long double**. In the following statement, `Temp` is promoted from **float** to **double** because Volume is **double**. Again, the key idea is that the operands are promoted so that the operation can be done using arithmetic that is as precise as the most precise operand.

2.10.3

Unary arithmetic operations

`C++` has several unary operators. The term *unary* means that the operator is applied to a single operand. As we mentioned in section 2.7.2 and section 2.7.3, `C++` has a *unary minus operator* for negating a value. The expression

```
-23;
```

is interpreted as

```
0-23
```

and obviously the result is *<−23, int>*. The unary minus operator can be applied to named objects that hold numeric values. For example, in the code fragment

```
int i = 10;
float x = 12.3;
long Time = 33;
// begin expressions
-i;
-x;
-Time;
```

the last three lines of code are expressions where the unary minus operator has been applied to the objects `i`, `x`, and `Time`. In each case, the value of the object is subtracted from zero to yield the result. The results are *<−10, int>*, *<−12.3, float>*, and *<−33, long>*.

`C++` also has a *unary plus operator*. This is included for symmetry with the unary minus operator. The expression

```
+244
```

is interpreted as

```
0+244
```

and the result is *<244,int>*.

2.10.4

Area of a circle

To illustrate the concepts covered thus far, let's write a program to solve a simple problem. The problem statement is

Compute the area and circumference of a circle given the radius. The input/output behavior of the program should be

```
Circle radius (real number)? 5.1
Area of circle with radius 5.1 is 81.710412
Circumference is 32.042299
```

Before we can write the program, we must consider a number of issues. Recall that the area of a circle is $Area = \pi r^2$. C++ does not have a exponentiation operator, but this operation is easily handled by multiplying the radius by itself. Thus if the name of the object that holds the radius is Radius, the area of the circle can be computed by the expression

```
3.1415 * Radius * Radius
```

Because we wish to allow the user to input a floating-point value as the radius, Radius should be a C++ floating-point type. Since the problem statement did not specify the possible size of the radius, or the accuracy of the result, we will arbitrarily choose type **float** for Radius. Program 2.10 contains the code that solves the problem.

Program 2.10

Compute area and circumference of a circle

```
// Program 2.10: Compute area and circumference
// of circle given radius
#include <iostream.h>
int main() {
    cout << "Circle radius (real number)? " << flush;
    float Radius;      // Radius of circle
    cin >> Radius;
    cout << "Area of circle with radius " << Radius
      << " is " << (3.1415 * Radius * Radius) << endl;
    cout << "Circumference is " << 3.1415 * 2
      * Radius << endl;

    return 0;
}
```

2.10.5

Mixed-mode expressions

Up to this point we have discussed the conversions that are done when an expression involves values that are either integer values or floating-point values. Mixed-mode expressions involve values with both integer and floating-point types. For example, in the expression

```
23 - 13.2;
```

the left operand is type **int**, and the right operand is type **double**. We need rules that tell us how to evaluate the expression so that the result makes sense. The only thing that makes sense is to convert the left operand to type **double** and perform a double-precision subtraction which produces the result *<9.8, double>*. In general, in a binary expression where either operand is a floating-point value, the operation will be performed using floating-point arithmetic and the result will be one of C++'s floating-point types.

Because the usual unary conversions always convert an integer operand to either **int** or **long**, we need add only two additional rows and columns to our table of usual binary conversions to cover mixed-mode arithmetic. Table 2.7 summarizes the possibilities.

Table 2.7

Result types for mixed-mode arithmetic operations

Type of left operand	Type of right operand				
	int	long	float	double	long double
int	int	long	float	double	long double
long	long	long	float	double	long double
float	float	float	float	double	long double
double	double	double	double	double	long double
long double	long double	long double	long double	long double	long double

Consider the following code fragment:

```
int MyDebt = 150;
double NationalDebt = 3.5E9;
float InterestRate = 0.06;
long USPopulation = 200000000;

MyDebt * InterestRate;
NationalDebt / USPopulation;
```

The first expression, which computes the interest due on MyDebt, yields the result *<9, float>*. The second expression, which computes the per capita national debt for each person in the United States, yields the result *<17.5, double>*.

2.10.6

Precedence

Like many programming languages, C++ allows the programmer to write expressions of arbitrary complexity using the binary and unary operators. As an example, consider the code fragment

```
int i = 4;
int j = 5;
i + 2 * j;
```

Depending on the order of operations, there are several possible results. Applying the operators in order from left to right, the result is *<30, int>*. Applying operators in order from right to left, the result is *<14, int>*. Clearly, we need a set of rules that tells us the order in which to apply the operators. These rules are called the *associativity* and *precedence* rules of the language.

Let us begin by discussing precedence. Each operator is assigned a precedence level. Table 2.8 contains the precedence level of the integer arithmetic operators we have discussed thus far. Informally, operators with higher precedence are applied before operators with lower precedence. Essentially, arithmetic expressions are evaluated just as we learned in high-school algebra. The two unary operators have highest precedence, and multiplication, division, and remainder have higher precedence than addition and subtraction. In the expression

```
i + 2 * j;
```

multiplication has higher precedence than addition, so the multiplication is done first and the result of that operation is added to the value of i to yield the value 14.

Table 2.8

Operator precedence and associativity

Operator	Operation	Precedence	Associativity
+ -	Unary plus and minus	15	Right
* / %	Multiplication, division, and remainder	13	Left
+ -	Addition and subtraction	12	Left

As other examples, consider the following expressions:

```
2 / 3 + 5;
-8 * 4;
8 + 7 % 2;
```

In the first expression, division has higher precedence then addition, so it is performed first. The result is 0, which is then added to 5 to yield a final value of 5. In the second example, the unary minus operator is applied to 8, and the resulting value -8 is multiplied by 4 to yield the final value of -32. In the third expression, the remainder operation is performed and yields the value 1. The final value of the expression is 9.

We will often want to override C++'s precedence rules. For example, consider writing an expression to compute the sales tax on five items. The expression

```
Price1 + Price2 + Price3 + Price4 + Price5 * 0.06
```

is obviously incorrect. The multiplication operator will be applied to Price5, and the product is added to the other four prices. C++ permits expressions to be parenthesized. Expressions enclosed in parentheses are evaluated first. Using parentheses, we can rewrite the expression as

```
(Price1 + Price2 + Price3 + Price4 + Price5) * 0.06
```

In this expression, the five prices are summed first, and then 6 percent of the total is computed.

Parenthesized expressions can be nested. In other words, a parenthesized expression can contain other parenthesized expressions. In these cases, the innermost parenthesized expressions are evaluated first. Consider the following expression:

```
(2 + (3 + 2) * 5) / (4 - 2);
```

The parenthesized subexpression (3+2) is nested within another parenthesized expression and is evaluated first. Now the expressions contained in the outer sets of parentheses can be evaluated. The final value is 13.

2.10.7

Associativity

Let's now consider the expression

```
3 * 5 / 2;
```

In this expression, the operators have the same precedence level. Depending on whether the multiplication is performed first or last, the value of the expression is either 7 or 6. In the case where an operand is surrounded by operators of the same precedence level, we need a rule that tells us which operator to apply to the operand. This is called the *associativity* of the operator. As shown in Table 2.8, multiplication and division are *left associative*. This means that in the previous example, the operand 5 "associates" with the operator on its left, and the correct value of the expression is 7. (Remember, integer division truncates!)

As a final check on the concepts covered thus far, consider the following code fragment:

```
int t1 = 17;
int t2 = 3;
int t3 = 7;
t1 % t2 * 5 / t3;
t3 * (5 / 2) + t2;
t3 + t1 * 4 + t1;
```

The values of these expressions are:

```
1
17
92
```

Style Tip

Use of parentheses

While it is important to know the rules of precedence, we recommend the use of parentheses to make the order of evaluation explicit even in cases where they are not needed. This technique helps the reader of the code, and it means that if the code gets changed later, other programmers are less likely to introduce an error.

Consider the unparenthesized expression

```
a * b + c / d - 3.0;
```

and the equivalent parenthesized expression

```
(a * b) + (c / d) - 3.0;
```

Both expressions perform exactly the same computation, but the meaning of the second one is much clearer.

In the code we present, we will always use parentheses to make the order of evaluation explicit in complicated expressions.

2.11

OUTPUT STATEMENTS

At this point we have discussed how to declare and initialize simple integral and floating-point objects and perform computations on these objects. These activities are not very useful unless we can display the results of the computation. We need a mechanism to output information computed by the program to the user.

Interestingly, unlike some other languages such as Fortran, Pascal, and Basic, C++ does not have special language constructs for doing output. Rather, output capability is provided by libraries that are implemented using ordinary C++.

Recall that in Program 2.1, we said that the C++ statement

```
cout << "Hello World!" << endl;
```

displays the message

```
Hello World!
```

on the user's screen. A complete description of how this statement achieves the desired effect requires understanding some of the more advanced features of C++, so we will not discuss all the details at this point. However, the statement does illustrate one of the nice features of C++: we can use objects developed by others without completely understanding exactly how they work. We do, however, need to know how to access these objects.

We will come back to our first program shortly, but for now let's discuss a simpler example. Consider the statement

```
cout << "C++";
```

In the above statement, the object we are accessing is cout (pronounced "C out"). It is an output stream object. The term *stream* refers to a flow of data to or from a device. Because cout is an output stream object, the flow of data is to the device rather than from it. Normally, the device that cout is associated with is the display. cout is part of the iostream library. Thus, to make data appear on the display, we must insert data into the stream. This is done via the insertion operator <<. In the example above, the characters 'C', '+', and '+' are inserted into the output stream. This is illustrated in Figure 2.4.

Figure 2.4
Output with cout

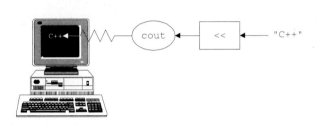

The characters inserted may or may not appear on the screen immediately. Many output devices are buffered. *Buffered* means that data are held internally, and when enough data have been collected, they are is written to the device. As an analogy, think of picking apples in an orchard. The basket you are carrying is the buffer. It does not make sense to pick a single apple, put it in your basket, and take the basket with the single apple and dump it in the collection bin. Rather, it is much more efficient to pick apples until your basket is full and then dump it. This is what buffering is all about. Rather than display each message as it is written, it is more efficient to buffer the output. When the buffer is full, the contents of the buffer are transferred to the output device.

However, for many programs we will want the output to appear immediately, and thus not be buffered. This is particularly true for *interactive* programs. In these programs, messages are sent to the display telling the user what action to take. This type of message is sometime called a *prompt*. Clearly, it would be very confusing if these messages were buffered, and then written to the display all at once. The process of writing the contents of the buffer to the output device is called *flushing* the buffer. The iostream library provides a mechanism for forcing the flushing of the buffer. In our first program, we used the special object endl. When endl is inserted into the output stream, it causes two things to happen. First, a newline character ('\n') is inserted into the stream, and second the current contents of the buffer are flushed to the display device. endl is a special class of object called a manipulator. A *manipulator* is an object that can be inserted into a stream to have some effect.

We could rewrite our previous example as

```
cout << "C++";
cout << endl;
```

and the second statement would ensure that a carriage return is inserted after the string `"C++"` and that the output is written to the display immediately.

The above insertion statements can be simplified into a single one. Like the arithmetic operators, the insertion operator can be composed or cascaded to output multiple values in a single statement. The two lines above can be written as the following single statement:

```
cout << "C++" << endl;
```

There is no limit on the number of insertion operations that can be cascaded in a single statement. The contrived statement

```
cout << "C++" << " is a " << "breeze" << endl;
```

illustrates this. It outputs the message

```
C++ is a breeze
```

to the display.

Cascading really becomes useful when we wish to output different types of values in the same statement. The insertion operator allows us to output any of C++'s fundamental types. For example, the statement

```
cout << "18 % 4 = " << 18 % 4 << endl;
```

outputs the following:

```
18 % 4 = 2
```

The statement outputs a string literal and the result of an arithmetic expression that produced a value of type **int**. The above statement also brings back up the concept of precedence. Notice that depending on the relative precedence levels of the << and % operators, the operand 18 could bind with either the << operator or the % operator. Fortunately, % has higher precedence than <<, so the statement does what we wanted it to do. However, as we have pointed out before, it's a good idea to add parentheses around the expression 18 % 4 so that the meaning of the statement is crystal clear.

We can also use the << operator to output the values of objects. When the code fragment

```
int Hours = 11;
cout << Hours << " hours is " << (Hours * 60)
  << " minutes " << endl;
```

is executed

```
11 hours is 660 minutes
```

is output. In the above code, the << operator handles inserting an **int** object operand, several string literal operands, and the result of an arithmetic expression into the stream cout.

The insertion operator can also output floating-point values. The expression

```
cout << (5.0 / 2.0) << " " (1.0 / 3.0) << endl;
```

writes

```
2.5 0.33333
```

to the display.

When a floating-point value is inserted into the output stream, the insertion operator attempts to output the value in a minimum amount of space. Thus, the code fragment

```
float x = 6.0;
cout << (x / 2.0) << endl;
```

writes

```
3
```

to the display. Later we will discuss some techniques for controlling how floating-point values are displayed.

As we do more programming, we will introduce other aspects of doing output using the iostream library. For now, it is sufficient to remember the following points:

- you must include the system header file `iostream.h` at the beginning of your program,

- The << operator can output any of C++'s fundamental types, and

- the << operator can be cascaded to output several values in a single statement.

2.12

COMPUTING AVERAGE VELOCITY

As a final case study, let's write a program that computes the average velocity of a car traveling on a road periodically marked with mileposts. The inputs to the program are the starting milepost and an ending milepost and time. Times are entered in hours, minutes, and seconds. The program should compute and output the average velocity in miles per hour. The problem statement is

> Compute the average velocity in miles per hour of a car. The input/output behavior of the program should be

```
All inputs are integers!
Start milepost? 321
Elapsed time (hours minutes seconds)? 2 15 36
End milepost? 458
Car traveled 137 miles in 2 hrs 15 min 36 sec
Average velocity was 60.619469 mph
```

The steps to solving this problem follow.

Step 1.   Issue the prompts and read the input.

Step 2.   Compute the elapsed time in hours.

Step 3.   Compute the distance traveled.

Step 4.   Compute the average velocity.

Each step seems relatively straightforward but converting each step to C++ code involves making some subtle, but important, decisions.

To implement step 1, we must select the types of the objects to store the input. The input/output behavior of the program shows that all values will be entered as integers. Thus it seems natural to use the type **int** to store the value of the starting point and ending point and the starting and ending time. However, if we use this method, we introduce a subtle problem that occurs in step 4. Recall that the formula for computing the average velocity of an object is

$$Velocity = \frac{Distance}{ElapsedTime}$$

Remember that in C++ division truncates. In most cases, truncation will not be a problem, but in the rare case where the elapsed time is greater than the distance traveled, the division will produce a zero result. This scenario points out one of the most difficult parts of programming. It's usually easy to write code that handles the common cases, but anticipating and handling the rare case is hard. Failure to anticipate a rare situation that could occur is the source of bugs in many programs. This type of error is particularly prevalent in interactive programs where the input is coming from a human.

Programming Tip

Interactive input and output

When writing an interactive program, it is important to tell the user what they are expected to do. For example, in Program 2.10, the user is told to input the radius and that a real number is expected. This may seem unnecessary as we know to enter a real number because we wrote the program and the source code is right in front of us. However, remember that someone else may run the program without seeing the source, so it is important that the program inform the user what is expected. Program 2.11 also tells the user what is expected.

In addition to telling the user what form the input should take, another general principle of good interactive I/O is to echo back the input typed by the user. This gives some assurance to the user that the input was received and interpreted correctly. In Program 2.10, the radius along with the computed area is printed. Thus, the user can see whether the program received the correct input. Similarly, in Program 2.11, when the output is produced, both the distance and the elapsed time are echoed along with the computed velocity.

There are a couple of solutions to this problem. We could make all the objects floating point and thus would ensure that floating-point arithmetic would be used for all computations. This approach is certainly the easiest, but it seems like overkill. A better solution is to accept the input as integers as was intended, but when a floating-point result is needed, make sure a floating-point result is computed. For example, we must convert the time that is entered as hours, minutes, and seconds into a single value that represents the elapsed time. The conversion can be done with the definition

```
float ElapsedTime = EndHour + (EndMinute / 60.0)
   + (EndSecond / 3600.00);
```

Because we used floating-point constants as the divisors, both divisions will be floating-point and the additions will also produce floating-point results.

Notice that the above definition is slightly different from the form we presented in Section 2.9 on page 71. There we said that the initial value could be a literal. Actually, C++ allows the initial value to be an arbitrary expression. Thus, the general form is

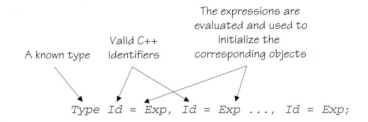

The expressions are evaluated and used to initialize the corresponding objects

Valid C++ identifiers

A known type

```
Type Id = Exp, Id = Exp ..., Id = Exp;
```

where *Exp* is an arbitrary expression.

Style Tip

Placement of declarations

In older style programs, the convention was to place all declarations at the beginning of the function. C++ permits declarations to appear almost anywhere in a function. As with any stylistic issue, there are pros and cons to each method.

Placing a declaration at the point of the first use of an object has the advantage that you don't have to look back at the beginning of the function to determine the type of the object. In addition, if you change the code, so that the object is no longer needed, you are much more likely to delete the now unnecessary declaration. We have encountered older style code that, after several years of maintenance, contains many useless declarations.

On the other hand, having all the declarations in a central location has some advantages. You know right where to look for the declaration. With the advent of integrated development environments and browsing tools, this advantage seems less significant. In our code, we will always place the declaration at or near the point of first use.

We can now compute the velocity with the following definition

```
float Velocity = Distance / ElapsedTime;
```

where `Distance` was computed earlier by the definition

```
int Distance = EndMilePost - StartMilePost;
```

The complete program is contained in Program 2.11.

Program 2.11

Compute average velocity of a car

```
// Program 2.11: Compute velocity of car
#include <iostream.h>
int main() {
    cout << "All inputs are integers!\n";
    cout << "Start milepost? " << flush;
    int StartMilePost;
    cin >> StartMilePost;

    cout << "End time (hours minutes seconds)? "
     << flush;
    int EndHour, EndMinute, EndSecond;
    cin >> EndHour >> EndMinute >> EndSecond;

    cout << "End milepost? " << flush;
    int EndMilePost;
    cin >> EndMilePost;

    float ElapsedTime = EndHour + (EndMinute / 60.0)
     + (EndSecond / 3600.0);
    int Distance = EndMilePost - StartMilePost;
    float Velocity = Distance / ElapsedTime;

    cout << "\nCar traveled " << Distance
    .<< " miles in ";
    cout << EndHour << " hrs " << EndMinute << " min "
     << EndSecond << " sec\n";
    cout << "Average velocity was " << Velocity << " mph"
     << endl;
    return 0;
}
```

2.13

POINTS TO REMEMBER

- The statement #include <iostream.h> is a preprocessor directive that includes the necessary definitions so that a program can do input and output using the iostream library.
- The C++ operator << is called the insertion operator. It is used to insert text into an output stream.
- The output stream cout normally corresponds to the display.
- The C++ operator >> is called the extraction operator. It is used to extract characters from an input stream.
- The input stream cin normally corresponds to the keyboard.
- The manipulator endl inserts a newline in the output stream. In addition, it forces all the output that has been sent to the stream to be written to the corresponding device.
- Standard C++ programs begin executing in function main. Function main returns an integer value that indicates whether the program executed successfully or not. A value of 0 indicates successful execution, while the

History of Computing

Napier's Bones

One of the early, influential contributions to computing was by John Napier, Baron of Merchison (1550–1617). Up until the 1600s, most computing was done by hand. Multiplication and division, in particular, were tedious to perform, requiring many individual calculations. Napier invented the principle of logarithms which allow multiplication and division to be reduced to the simpler operations of addition and subtraction. This principle, that numerical powers can be added and subtracted (e.g., $x^4 \times x^3 = x^7$ and $x^7 \div x^4 = x^3$), had far reaching effects.

To aid in computing logarithms, Napier also developed a device that came to be known as "Napier's bones." The device was essentially a multiplication table cut up into moveable columns. The term *bones* was coined because the columns were from bone or ivory. While primitive by our standards, Napier's bones were considered an indispensable computing device in the early 1600s.

The development of logarithms and Napier's bones spawned several "next generation" computing devices. One device that was developed in the 1600s that was still in use as late as the 1970s was the slide rule. A *slide rule* is essentially a physical analog of logarithms. A slide rule consists of three pieces of wood or metal with one piece sliding between two fixed pieces (see the photograph below). The pieces have scales etched on them that correspond to the logarithms. Numbers can be multiplied and divided by adding and subtracting distances. A cursor was used to help read the result. Later versions of slide rules had many different scales and could perform very complicated calculations. One problem with the slide rule was that the accuracy was limited to four or five decimal places.

Figure 2.5
A slide rule

value 1 indicates that a problem or error occurred during the execution of the program.

■ A value is returned from a function using the **return** statement. The statement

```
return 0;
```

returns the value 0.

■ A C++ style comment begins with // and continues to the end of the line.

■ Including descriptive and useful comments in a program is an important part of good programming. Remember, other programmers will read your program.

■ The assignment operator '=' is used to assign or give a new value to an object.

■ The C++ object types **short**, **int**, and **long** are used to represent integer values. On the PC, a **short** is stored in 8 bits, an **int** in 16 bits, and a **long** in 32 bits.

■ The C++ object type **char** is used to represent a character. For most machines, characters are encoded using the ASCII character set. Appendix A contains the ASCII character set.

■ The C++ object types, **float**, **double**, and **long double** are used to represent real values. On the PC, a **long** is stored in 32 bits, and a **double** is stored in 64 bits. On most PCs, a **long double** is the same size as a **double**, but on other machines it can be larger. For example, on some machines **long double** is 128 bits.

■ A C++ string constant is a sequence of characters enclosed in double quotes. Special characters such as the newline, tab, and bell can be included in a string constant using special character escapes. These are listed in Table 2.1 on page 60.

■ A C++ integer constant can be written in one of three bases: octal, decimal, or hexadecimal. An octal integer constant begins with a zero digit. Thus, the constant 040 is octal and represents the decimal value 32. Decimal constants begin with a digit other than zero, and hexadecimal constants begin with the prefix 0x or 0X. The constant 0x40 represents the decimal value 64.

■ C++ provides several ways to write a floating-point constant. The simplest way is to use standard decimal notation: 3.1416, 2.53, 0.3512. Floating-point constants can also be written using scientific notation. The C++ floating-point constant, 2.3E5, represents the value 2.3×10^5 or 230,000.

■ A C++ name consists of a sequence of letters (upper- and lower case), digits, and underscores. A valid name cannot begin with a digit character.

■ C++ names are case sensitive. For example, the names Temp and temp refer to two different objects.

- It is very important to pick meaningful and descriptive names for the objects in a program. Descriptive names help other programmers understand what your program is doing.

- An object must be defined before it can be used. Smart programmers give an object an initial value when it is defined.

- Integer division always produces a truncated result. The expression 5 / 2 produces the result 2, not 2.5.

- The usual unary conversions specify that operands of type **char** or **short** are converted to type **int** before proceeding with the operation.

- For an arithmetic operation involving two integral operands, the usual binary conversions specify that when the operands have different types, the one that is type **int** is converted to **long** and a **long** operation is performed to produce a **long** result.

- For an arithmetic operation involving two floating-point operands, the usual binary conversions specify that when the operands have different types, the operand with lesser precision is converted to the type of the operand with greater precision. The arithmetic operation is performed using the operation that produces a result with the same type as the operand with the greater precision. Thus for an addition operation involving a **float** operand and a **double** operand, the **float** operand is converted to **double**, and a double precision addition is performed.

- A mixed-mode arithmetic expression involves integral and floating-point operands. The integral operand is converted to the type of the floating-point operand, and the appropriate floating-point operation is performed.

- The precedence rules of C++ define the order in which operators are applied to operands. For the arithmetic operators, the precedence from highest to lowest is unary plus and minus; multiplication, division, and remainder; and addition and subtraction.

2.14

EXERCISES

2.1   What is the range of a 32-bit integer?

2.2   How many null bytes are at the end of the following string literal?

```
"What's going on here?\0"
```

2.3   Describe how integer division of two **int**s can produce a result that overflows.

2.4   Remove the statement

```
return 0;
```

from Program 2.1. Compile the modified program. Does the compiler report an error or warning? If so, what is the message?

2.5 Remove the `include` statement from Program 2.1 and compile the modified program. For which line of the modified program does the compiler first report an error?

2.6 Write a program that accepts the weight of an object in pounds and outputs the weight of the object in kilograms.

2.7 Write a program that computes the volume of an object. The program should ask the user to input the object's mass and density. The mass will be given in grams; the density will be in grams per cubic centimeter. The relationship of mass, density, and volume of an object is given by

$$Density = \frac{Mass}{Volume}$$

Your program should output the volume in cubic centimeters.

2.8 Write a program to compute the mass of a block of aluminum. The program should input the dimensions of the block (i.e., length, width, and height) in centimeters. The density of aluminum is 2.7 g/cm^3.

2.9 Modify Program 2.2 so that `Price` is of type **int**. Run the program. Explain why the output of the program is different.

2.10 In C++, the result of applying a backslash to a character that is not a character escape code is undefined. Many compilers do not catch this error. Try it with a compiler available to you and report the result.

2.11 Modify Program 2.11 so that it uses type **float** for all objects. Does the input/output behavior of the program remain the same?

2.12 Which of the following are invalid C++ identifiers?

a) GPA	i) T2	q) A
b) Grade.pnt	j) 3CPO	r) _dog
c) GradePtAvg	k) Avg__cost	s) Not!
d) Int	l) $Cost	t) _123
e) 1stNum	m) Era	u) Cat's
f) Num1	n) int	v) main
g) X-ray	o) PDQBach	w) Cost$
h) R2D2	p) ReturnV	

2.13 What is the result of the following expressions? Express your answer as *<value, type>*.

a) 25 / 7	h) 7 - 21
b) 21 / 3	i) 28 + 3 * 5
c) 26 / 2L	j) (27 / 3) + 15
d) 14 % 3	k) 2
e) 31 % 3	l) -23 + 7 * 2
f) 22.1 + 1.0	
g) 30L % 5	

2.14 Assume the following declarations:

```
float f1 = 23.3;
float f2 = 1.0;
double d1 = 3.1;
int i1 = 5;
int i2 = 10;
int i3 = 7;
```

What is the result of the following expressions? Express your answer as *<value, type>*.

a) `f1 + d1`

b) `i1 + d1`

c) `i1 + i2 * i3`

d) `i2 % i3`

e) `i3 / i2 + i1 * i5`

f) `f1 - f2`

g) `f1 - i3`

h) `f1 / i2 + d1`

i) `i2 + i3 + 3.0`

j) `i2 * f2 + 4`

2.15 Write `C++` expressions that are equivalent to the following mathematical formulas.

a) $b^2 + 4ac$

e) $-(a^2 - b^3)$

b) $a + \dfrac{b}{c} + d$

f) $a\left(\dfrac{b}{c}\right)$

c) $\dfrac{1}{1 + x^2}$

g) $(a + b)(c + d)(e + f)$

d) $\dfrac{4}{3}\pi r^2$

2.16 Write a program that accepts a Fahrenheit temperature and outputs the equivalent centigrade temperature. The equation for converting a Fahrenheit temperature to Celsius is

$$Celsius = \frac{5}{9}(Fahrenheit - 32)$$

2.17 Write a program that accepts a centigrade temperature and outputs the equivalent Fahrenheit temperature. The equation for converting a Celsius temperature to Fahrenheit is

$$Fahrenheit = \frac{9}{5}Celsius + 32$$

2.18 Write a program that accepts a distance in kilometers and outputs the distance as miles.

2.19 Write a program that accepts an integer between 10 and 12 digits long, and writes the integer with commas after every third digit starting from the right.

2.20 Write a program that prompts for and reads a floating-point number and evaluates the polynomial

$$3x^4 - 10x^3 + 13$$

The program should display both the number read and the result of evaluating the polynomial.

2.21 Write a program that prompts for and reads your age in years and outputs your age in days.

2.22 Suppose every person in China drank two beers a week. To brew a case of beer (24 bottles) requires a half bushel of barley. There are approximately 1 billion people in China. Write a program to determine the number of bushels of wheat that must be grown to satisfy the demand for beer.

2.23 Write a program that prompts for and reads five integers and computes the average.

2.24 Interest on credit card accounts can be quite high. Most credit card companies compute interest on an average daily balance. Here is an algorithm for computing the average daily balance and the monthly interest charge on a credit card.

Step 1. Multiply the net balance shown on the statement by the number of days in the billing cycle.

Step 2. Multiply the net payment received by the number of days the payment was received before the statement date.

Step 3. Subtract the result of the calculation from step 2 from the result of the calculation in step 1.

Step 4. Divide the result of step 3 by the number of days in the billing cycle. This is the average daily balance.

Step 5. Compute the interest charge for the billing period by multiplying the average daily balance by the monthly interest rate.

Here is an example to illustrate the algorithm. Suppose your credit card statement showed a previous balance of $850. Eleven days before the end of the billing cycle you made a payment of $400. The billing cycle for this month is 31 days, and the monthly interest rate is 1.32%. The calculation of the interest charge is as follows.

Step 1. $850 × 3 = $26,350
Step 2. $400 × 11 = $4,400
Step 3. $26,350 − $4,400 = $21,950

Step 4. $21,950 ÷ 31 = \$708.06$
Step 5. $\$708.06 × .0132 = \$9.34$

Write a program that computes the monthly interest charge on a credit card account. Your program should prompt for and accept the previous balance, the number of days in the billing cycle, the day of the billing cycle the payment was made, and the monthly interest rate.

2.25 We all like to exercise because it's good for us. Experts tell us to get the maximum aerobic effect from exercise that we should try and keep our pulse rate in a training zone. The training zone is computed as follows. Subtract your age from 220; 72% of that value is the low end of the range and 87% of that value is the high end of the range. Write a program that accepts an age and computes the training range.

CHAPTER 3

Modifying objects

Introduction

In this chapter we introduce operators that can modify objects and the use of programmer-defined object types. The operators are the assignment operators and the extraction operator. Of particular importance is =, the assignment operator. The assignment operation is common to most programming languages, and understanding the concept of assignment and its implementation in a language is a key concept that all programmers must master. The extraction operator >> modifies an object by extracting a value from a stream and storing that value in an object. The chapter concludes by introducing two programmer-defined object types: `SimpleWindow` and `RectangleShape`. We show how to define and manipulate instances of these programmer-defined object types by writing programs that produce graphical displays.

Key Concepts

- assignment operation
- assignment conversions
- assignment precedence and associativity
- extraction operations
- **const** declarations
- compound assignment operations
- input with `cin`
- increment and decrement operations

3.1

ASSIGNMENT

The C++ assignment operator is the =. This operator stores a value into an object. The code fragment

```
int x = 0;
x = 10;
```

stores the value 10 into the memory location assigned to x. The expression is read as "x gets 10" or "x is assigned 10."

To see better what the assignment operator does, let's examine the following code fragment:

```
float GrossSalary = 0.0;
float WithHolding = 0.0;
float TakeHomePay = 0.0;
GrossSalary = 50000.0;
WithHolding = GrossSalary * .05;
TakeHomePay = GrossSalary - WithHolding;
```

This fragment contains three objects, each of type **float**. Each object has memory allocated for it. As we discussed in Chapter 2, the C++ compiler handles assigning the objects to memory locations. Some people find it convenient to think of these memory locations as "mailboxes." The assignment operator places information in the mailbox. The object name acts like the address.

In Figure 3.1, the left diagram represents the state of memory before execution of the three assignment statements in the preceding code fragment. Notice that all three objects have zeros in their mailboxes. These were the initial values given when these objects were defined. The right diagram of Figure 3.1 represents the state of memory after the assignment expressions execute. Notice that the value of TakeHomePay was computed using the value of WithHolding that was computed and assigned in the previous statement.

A common programming job is to swap or interchange the values of two objects. For example, let's suppose that the following objects are defined and initialized and we want to swap their values.

```
int Score1 = 90;
int Score2 = 75;
```

We want to copy the value of Score1 into Score2 and the value of Score2 into Score1. It is tempting to write the assignment statements as follows:

```
Score2 = Score1;    // Copy Score1 into Score2
Score1 = Score2;    // Copy Score2 into Score1
```

Unfortunately, this code would result in both Score1 and Score2 having the original value of Score1, which is 90. The problem was that the first assignment statement overwrote the value of Score2.

In order to do the job correctly, we need a temporary object where we can store the value of one of the objects before we change its value. Assuming a

Figure 3.1
Illustration of assignment statement changing the value of objects

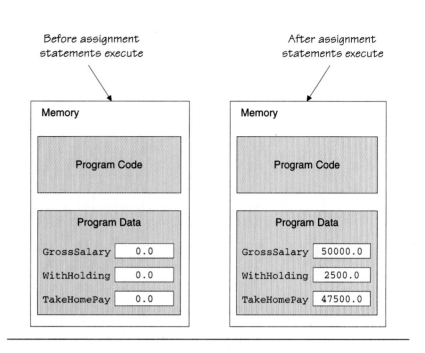

Before assignment statements execute

After assignment statements execute

temporary **int** object named Temp has been defined, a correct sequence for swapping the values of Score1 and Score2 is

```
int Temp = Score2;  // Copy original value of Score2
Score2 = Score1;    // Copy Score1 into Score2
Score1 = Temp;      // Copy original value of Score2
                    // into Score1
```

The step-by-step process is illustrated in the following diagram:

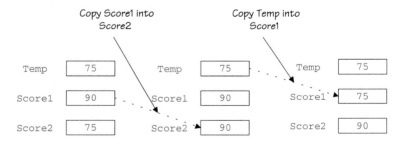

3.1.1

Assignment conversions

In the previous section, we used the simplest form of assignment statement.

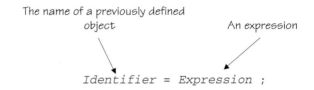

The rules of C++ state that the types of the left and right operands should be the same. In the following code fragment

```
int x;
float y;
double z;
x = 1;
y = 2.3F;
z = 0.81;
```

the left and right operands of each assignment expression match. If the left and right operands do not have the same type, it is necessary to convert the operands appropriately. In the case of the assignment operator, the generated code converts the right operand so that its type matches that of the left operand. This type of conversion is called the *assignment conversion*.

For example, in the fragment

```
int x = 0;
x = 2.3;
```

the type of the left operand is **int**, while the type of the constant right operand is **double**. Before performing the assignment, the assignment conversion conventions convert the right operand *<2.3, double>* to *<2, int>*. Recall that a conversion from a floating-point type to an integral type causes a truncation to occur.

For the most part, the assignment conversions behave exactly as you would expect. The only situation where unexpected results occur is when the type of the left operand is less precise than the type of the right operand and the value of the right operand is larger than what can be stored in the memory that corresponds to the left operand. The following code fragment shows this problem.

```
short s1 = 0;
long i2 = 65536;
s1 = i2;
cout << "i2 is " << i2 << endl;
cout << "s1 is " << s1 << endl;
```

When this fragment is executed on a machine where a **short** is 16 bits and a **long** is 32 bits (like most PCs), the following output is produced.

```
i2 is 65536
s1 is 0
```

In this case, assignment conversion maps i2's value from a **long** to a **short** by discarding the most significant 16 bits and storing the least significant 16 bits, which are all zero.

In the previous discussions of the assignment operator, we used the term *assignment expression* to emphasize that the assignment operator, besides storing a value in memory, also produces a result just like the arithmetic operators. Assuming x has been declared to be an **int**, the statement

```
x = 1;
```

stores a one in the object x, but it also produces the result *<1, int>*. The type of the result of the assignment operator is the type of the left operand, and the value of the result is the value stored into the left operand.

3.1.2

Assignment precedence and associativity

Because assignment is an operator, we can write expressions like

```
x = y = z + 2;
```

The question is, Exactly what does this mean? The answer lies in knowing the precedence and associativity of the assignment operator. First, let's consider precedence. Because z is surrounded by two different operators, the relative precedences of the operators determine whether z binds with + or =. The natural interpretation is that z and 2 are added together. Thus, the precedence of = must be lower than that of +. Indeed, assignment has a very low precedence. Thus, the interpretation of the previous expression is

```
x = y = (z + 2);
```

A complete precedence table for all C++ operators is included in Appendix A.

Continuing with this example, we notice that y is surrounded by the = operator. In this situation, the associativity of = determines whether y binds with the = on the right or the = on the left. Unlike the arithmetic operators, assignment is right associative. Consequently, the interpretation of the previous expression is

```
x = (y = (z + 2));
```

which says that the result of the assignment of the sum of z + 2 to y is assigned to x. Again this interpretation is natural because if assignment was left associative, the interpretation would be

```
(x = y) = (z + 2);
```

which makes no sense.

3.2

CONST DEFINITIONS

In addition to the definitions that we have seen thus far, C++ has another form of definition that is very handy. It is called a **const** definition. For a fundamental type object, a **const** definition has the form

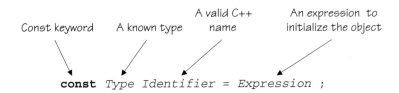

Const keyword   A known type   A valid C++ name   An expression to initialize the object

const *Type Identifier = Expression* ;

For example, the declarations

```
const double AvogadroNmber = 6.02E23;
const float SpeedOfLight = 186000;
```

are valid **const** definitions.

A **const** definition is similar to a normal definition in that the object named *Identifier* is defined and given the value of the expression *Expression*. However, the keyword **const** tells the compiler that this object can no longer be modified once it has been assigned its initial value. This seems strange, but it is very useful. In most programs, we use literals to represent an unchanging value. For example, many scientific and engineering programs use physical constants (e.g., Avogadro's number, the speed of light, π. Rather than use the literal value, it is better to define a **const** object that holds the value and use the object name throughout the program rather than the literal value.

For example, Program 3.1 is a rewrite of Program 2.10 using a **const** definition. The object Pi holds the constant 3.1415, and the **const** definition signals the compiler that this value is a constant and should not be changed.

Program 3.1

Compute area and circumference of a circle

```
// Program 3.1: Compute area and circumference
// of circle given radius
// Program modified to use const declaration
#include <iostream.h>
int main() {
    cout << "Circle radius (real number)? " << flush;
    float Radius;
    cin >> Radius;

    const float Pi = 3.1415;
    cout << "Area of circle with radius " << Radius
      << " is " << (Pi * Radius * Radius) << endl;
    cout << "Circumference is " << Pi * 2 * Radius
      << endl;
    return 0;
}
```

One of the advantages of using **const** definitions to declare program constants is that if we decide to change the constant, we need to make a change at only one place in the program. For example, in Program 3.1, if we decide to use more precision for π, we would need to change only the **const** declaration and recompile. On the other hand, Program 2.10 requires making two changes. For a large program, where a constant may be used in many places, changing all occurrences is tedious and error prone. In addition, if we choose a name that connotes the value of the constant, the program will be easier to understand.

Programming Tip

Using const

A good programming practice is to use a **const** object for any value that will not change during the execution of the program. The **const** definition tells the reader of the program that the value of this object will not change. Furthermore, if someone modifies the program and accidentally inserts a statement that would change the value of the object, the compiler will report the error. Additionally, if the compiler knows that an object will not change during the execution of a program, it can often generate more efficient code than it could if the object can be modified.

3.3

INPUT STATEMENTS

In Chapter 2, we discussed how to do output using the cout object and the insertion operator <<. The iostream library also provides an object for doing input. This object, cin (pronounced "C in"), is an input stream object. It is normally associated with the keyboard. That is, as we type characters on the keyboard the sequence of characters typed forms the input stream. For input, we must extract data from the stream. This is done via the extraction operator >>. The code fragment

```
int Value;
cin >> Value;
```

reads a single integer from the cin input stream and places the value in the **int** object Value. At this point it would be counterproductive to try and cover all the details of input. However, we do need to understand the basic behavior of the extraction operator when applied to the fundamental types.

When extracting integers or floating-point numbers, by default the extraction operator skips white space characters while looking for a character that can begin a number. The white space characters are the blank, the vertical and horizontal tabs, the form feed, and the newline. The characters that can begin an integer are the digits and the sign characters (+ and -). For a floating-point type, the possible initial values also include the period (i.e., the decimal point). When extracting a **char** value, the extraction operator also by default skips white space and stores the next character into the **char** object.

What happens if we are trying to extract an integer, but the next non-white space character encountered is not one that can begin an integer? In this case, the input stream object `cin` is put into an error state. When a stream object is in an error state, no additional characters can be extracted from the stream. Subsequent extractions do not change the value of the object being modified. In later chapters we will discuss how to test for errors in processing input and how to recover from them.

To illustrate `cin`'s behavior, let's consider the operation of the following code fragment when the user has typed the input shown in Figure 3.2.

```
int Ivalue;
cin >> Ivalue;
float Fvalue;
cin >> Fvalue;
char Cvalue;
cin >> Cvalue;
```

For the first extraction operator, the leading blanks are skipped. On encountering the character two, the characters that comprise the integer are read and converted to the internal machine representation of an **int** and this value is stored in the object. No further input is consumed, and subsequent extraction operations will begin processing the input stream at this point (i.e., the next character of the input stream is the blank following the three). Thus, the object `Ivalue` now has the value 23 stored in it.

The next operation is to extract a floating-point value from the input stream. In our example, the next non-white space character is a comma. At this point, `cin` is placed into an error state and the remaining extraction operations have no effect. Both `Fvalue` and `Cvalue` remain uninitialized.

Figure 3.2
Input from stream cin

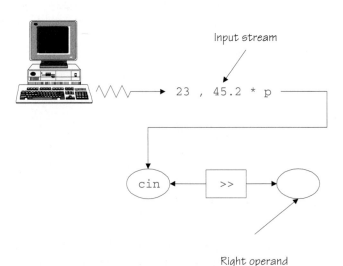

Recall that integer literals can take several forms. For example, `0x40` is a hexadecimal literal that has the decimal value 64. Similarly, 0100 is an octal literal with that same value. The extraction operator knows how to interpret these numbers correctly when they are encountered in a stream. When the input

```
0x52 034
```

is processed by the code fragment

```
int Ivalue1;
int Ivalue2;
cin >> Ivalue1 >> Ivalue2;
```

the objects `Ivalue1` and `Ivalue2` are given the decimal values 82 and 28, respectively. Notice that the extraction operator can be cascaded just like the insertion operator.

The iostream library provides a variety of mechanisms for extracting data. For example, at times we will want to process every character in an input file and not skip any. Similarly, we may wish the extraction operator to interpret the numbers being extracted as being in a different base. Chapter 5 provides a thorough introduction to the various stream libraries.

3.4

COMPUTING THE NUMBER OF MOLECULES IN A HYDROCARBON

A common problem in elementary chemistry is to compute the number of atoms or molecules contained in a particular amount of a substance. The substances we are interested in are the hydrocarbons. These are substances that contain only two elements: carbon and hydrogen. Examples of familiar hydrocarbons are the fuels methane, propane, and butane.

The computation of the number of molecules in a hydrocarbon is best illustrated with an example. Recall that a mole of any substance contains 6.02×10^{23} molecules. This number is known as Avogadro's constant. It is the case that one mole of a substance is always equal to the formula weight in grams. The formula weight is the sum of the atomic weights of the constituent elements. The computation of formula weight of methane, CH_4, is

1 carbon atom	=	1×12.0 amu	=	12.0
4 hydrogen atoms	=	4×1.0 amu	=	4.0
1 mole of CH_4			=	16.0 g.

Therefore, 16 grams of methane contain 6.02×10^{23} molecules. The following equation expresses the relationship between the mass of a substance and the number of molecules.

$$Molecules = Mass \times \frac{1\,mole}{FormulaWeight} \times \frac{6.02 \times 10^{23}\,molecules}{1\,mole}$$

We can now write the problem statement

Compute the number of molecules in an amount of hydrocarbon. The amount of hydrocarbon will be given in grams. Carbon's atomic weight is 12 amu, and hydrogen's is 1 amu. An example of the input/output behavior of the program is:

```
Enter mass of hydrocarbon (in grams)
followed by the number of carbon atoms
followed by the number of hydrogen atoms
(e.g. 10.5 2 6): 16 1 4
16 grams of a hydrocarbon
with 1 carbon atom(s) and 4 hydrogen atom(s)
contains 6.02e+23 molecules
```

An algorithm for computing the number of molecules in any hydrocarbon substance follows.

Step 1. Prompt for and read the mass of hydrocarbon, the number of carbon atoms, and the number of hydrogen atoms

Step 2. Compute the formula weight of one mole

Step 3. Compute the number of molecules in given mass of hydrocarbon (using above formula)

Step 4. Output the input and the computed result

Program 3.2 implements this algorithm. The definitions and insertion and extraction statements

```
float Mass;
cout << "Enter hydrocarbon mass (in grams)\n"
  "followed by the number of carbon atoms\n"
  "followed by the number of hydrogen atoms\n"
  "(e.g. 10.5 2 6):" << flush;

int CarbonAtoms;
int HydrogenAtoms;
cin >> Mass >> CarbonAtoms >> HydrogenAtoms;
```

implement step 1 of the algorithm. Because the mass need not be an integral value, we have defined it to be type **float**. Notice that we cascaded the extraction operation. This technique is more efficient than three separate statements, and it is shorter.

The next three lines compute the formula weight of one mole of hydrogen. They are

```
const int CarbonAMU = 12;
const int HydrogenAMU = 1;
long FormulaWght = (CarbonAtoms * CarbonAMU)
 + (HydrogenAtoms * HydrogenAMU);
```

Program 3.2

Compute number of molecules in a hydrocarbon

```
// Program 3.2: Compute number of molecules in
// a hydrocarbon
#include <iostream.h>
int main() {
  cout << "Enter mass of hydrocarbon (in grams)\n"
    "followed by the number of carbon atoms\n"
    "followed by the number of hydrogen atoms\n"
    "(e.g. 10.5 2 6): " << flush;

  float Mass;
  long CarbonAtoms;
  long HydrogenAtoms;
  cin >> Mass >> CarbonAtoms >> HydrogenAtoms;

  const int CarbonAMU = 12;
  const int HydrogenAMU = 1;
  long FormulaWght = (CarbonAtoms * CarbonAMU)
   + (HydrogenAtoms * HydrogenAMU);

  const double AvogadroNmbr = 6.02e23;
  double Molecules = (Mass / FormulaWght) *
   AvogadroNmbr;
  cout << Mass << " grams of a hydrocarbon\nwith "
   << CarbonAtoms << " carbon atom(s) and "
   << HydrogenAtoms << " hydrogen atom(s)\ncontains "
   << Molecules << " molecules" << endl;

  return 0;
}
```

The atomic weights of carbon and hydrogen are defined to be **const int**. The **const** tells the compiler and other readers of the program that these values are constant values that will not change during the execution of the program. We chose type **long** for the formula weight because for very complex hydrocarbons, the computation might have overflowed an object of type **int**.

In the computation of the formula weight, the subexpression

```
(HydrogenAtoms * HydrogenAMU)
```

appears. Because HydrogenAMU's value is 1, it can be argued that this is a useless expression and the entire statement can be written as

```
long FormulaWght = (CarbonAtoms * CarbonAMU)
 + HydrogenAtoms;
```

However, recall that an important part of programming is to write your program so others can easily understand it and possibly modify it. Thus, we argue that the first way of writing the expression is clearer. Furthermore, compilers routinely do code optimizations like the one above. Thus, there is no need for us to worry about such minor details.

The remaining statements in Program 3.2 compute and display the number of molecules. Because we are dealing with the number of molecules in a substance, the values involved can become quite large. Because we wish to be as precise as possible, we have used type **double** for the objects that hold

Programming Tip

Don't sacrifice clarity for speed

Even the most experienced programmers are tempted to "optimize" their programs so they run faster. While efficiency is important, clarity and correctness are always more important. Who wants to use a program that runs fast but produces incorrect results? Thus we should never sacrifice clarity and correctness for efficiency. Furthermore, it is very hard for a programmer to "tweak" a program so that it runs measurably faster. One rule of thumb in programming is that 90 percent of a program's running time is spent in 10 percent of the code. Consequently, without some idea of where a program spends most of its time, most changes to a program to speed it up will have little or no effect on the overall running time. If efficiency becomes an issue, a more effective approach is to wait until the program is complete and then use a special tool called a *profiler* to identify the program's hot spots. *Hot spots* are where the programs spends most of its time running. These areas of the program can be tuned to reduce the running time of the program.

Avogadro's number and the number of molecules. Of course, the **const** modifier is used to define Avogadro's number.

3.5

COMPOUND ASSIGNMENT

C++ has several special operators for performing commonly occurring operations. One can think of these as idioms or the shorthand of the language. For example, a common operation is to apply an operator to an object and then store the result back into the object. As an example, consider adding five to an object called i. In many programming languages, this might be written as

```
i = i + 5;
```

C++, on the other hand, has a compound assignment operator that accomplishes the same thing. In C++, the above expression is more properly written as

```
i += 5;
```

C++ has compound assignment operators for all of the binary arithmetic operators. Program 3.3 demonstrates the use of this type of operator.
The output from this program is

```
i is 2
j is 40
m is 3
```

What happens when the operands of a compound assignment operator are not the same type? For example, consider the following code fragment

Style Tip

Multiline expressions

As Program 3.2 illustrates, we often need to write long expressions that will not conveniently fit on the screen or a printed page. This is particularly true of output statements where we wish to label and output a number of values. For example, the expression

```
cout << "X-coordinate: " << Xcoord <<
"Y-coordinate: " << Ycoord << "Z-coordinate: " <<
Zcoord << endl;
```

is quite long and will most likely not fit in the window. A good convention to follow for breaking a long expression into a multi-line expression is that the continuation line should always begin with an operator and that it should be indented one space. Both of these serve to signal the reader that the line is a continuation of the previous line.

For example, we write the previous expression as

```
cout << "X-coordinate: " << XCoord
  << "Y-coordinate: " << YCoord
  << "Z-coordinate: " << ZCoord << endl;
```

As another example, we can write a long arithmetic expression as

```
((XCoord1 - YCoord1) / 2) * Distance1 + ((XCoord2
- YCoord2) / 2) * Distance2;
```

Taking some care as to where you break an expression can also improve the readability of the code. The above arithmetic expression can be written more clearly as

```
((XCoord1 - YCoord1) / 2) * Distance1
+ ((XCoord2 - YCoord2) / 2) * Distance2;
```

For insertion statements where the value being inserted is a long string, we can split the line wherever we choose and just continue the string on the next line. The compiler will automatically handle concatenating the strings together into one large string and inserting it into the stream in a single operation. The first insertion statement of Program 3.2 illustrates this technique.

```
int i = 10;
float y = 3.2;
i += y;
```

What conversions/operations are performed, and what is the type and value of the result? To answer these questions, it is convenient to think of the preceding assignment operation as

```
i = i + y;
```

We can then use the conversion rules for applying binary operators and doing assignment. First, the usual unary and binary conversions of the operands are

Program 3.3

Illustrate use of the compound assignment operators

```
// Program 3.3: Illustrate compound assignments
#include <iostream.h>
int main() {
    int i = 5;
    int k = 2;
    i /= k;
    cout << "i is " << i << endl;

    int j = 20;
    j *= k;
    cout << "j is " << j << endl;

    int m = 15;
    m %= 4;
    cout << "m is " << m << endl;
    return 0;
}
```

performed and then the operation is done. In our example, i is converted to **float**, and a floating-point addition is done yielding a result of *<13.2, float>*. Next, assignment conversion is done. Thus the value 13 is stored in i. Just as with simple assignment, the result of the expression is *<13, int>*.

3.6

INCREMENT AND DECREMENT

C++ also has special operators for incrementing or decrementing an object. The operator ++ is the increment operator, while the operator -- is the decrement operator. Now the reason for the name C++ is clear. It is really "C incremented!"

When applied to the arithmetic objects, these operators add or subtract one from the value of the object. For example, the following code fragment:

```
int i = 4;
++i;
cout << "i is " << i << endl;
```

results in the output

```
i is 5
```

For all intents and purposes, the expression

```
++i
```

is equivalent to

```
i += 1;
```

but it is shorter still. Interestingly, there are two forms of the increment and decrement operators—prefix and postfix. The term *prefix* means the operator appears before the operand. The expression ++i is an example. There is also a postfix form. The previous code fragment could have been

```
int i = 4;
i++;
cout << "i is " << i << endl;
```

which would produce exactly the same output. So what is the difference between the postfix and prefix versions of the increment operator? The difference becomes apparent when the operation is used as part of a larger expression. Consider the code fragment

```
int i = 4;
int j = 5;
int k = j * ++i;
cout << "k is " << k ", i is " << i << endl;
```

Is the multiplication operation performed before or after i is incremented? In the case of the ++ prefix operator, i is incremented first and then the multiplication is performed. The output is therefore

```
k is 25, i is 5
```

If the fragment is modified to be

```
int i = 4;
int j = 5;
int k = j * i++;
cout << "k is " << k ", i is " << i << endl;
```

the output would be

```
k is 20, i is 5
```

Thus, the *postfix* increment returns the value of the object before it is incremented, while the *prefix* increment returns the value of the object after it has been incremented. The decrement operator is similar to the increment operator except that it subtracts one. An important point to note is that the increment and decrement operators can be applied only to objects. For example, it is tempting to interpret the expression

```
(x - 2)++;
```

to mean

```
x - 2 + 1;
```

However, the previous expression is illegal and will not compile. The increment operator is being applied to an expression. See Appendix D for the precedence and associativity of the increment and decrement operators.

Increment and decrement

As was noted in the text, the increment and decrement operators are C++ shorthand for adding one or subtracting one from an arithmetic object. A good C++ programmer would never write

```
i = i + 1;
```

Whether to use the prefix or postfix incrementing in the above situation is a question of style. Our experience is that most good C++ programmers seem to favor the prefix version. Believing that imitation is the sincerest form of flattery, we also use the prefix version. Whichever you choose, the really important thing is be consistent!

3.7
ESTIMATING YEARLY SAVINGS OF CHANGE

If you are like most people, you collect a fair amount of change in your pocket. A painless savings plan is to dump all the loose change into a jar at the end of the week. However, we'd like some idea of the amount of money we'll have saved in a year so we can start thinking about what we want to buy. The final case study of this chapter is the construction of a program to estimate the yearly savings based on four weeks of data. The problem statement is

Compute the estimated yearly savings based on the amount of change saved at the end of each of four weeks. The amount of change saved at the end of each week is recorded as four numbers: the number of pennies, the number of nickels, the number of dimes, and the number of quarters. An example of the input/output behavior of the program is

```
For each week enter 4 numbers:
 pennies nickels dimes quarters (e.g.: 3 2 4 1)

Week 1 change: 8 2 5 3
Week 2 change: 4 3 3 5
Week 3 change: 8 5 6 3
Week 4 change: 5 2 7 6
Over four weeks you collected
 25 pennies
 12 nickels
 21 dimes
 17 quarters
which is $7.20 and a weekly average of $1.80.
Estimated savings in one year is $93.60.
```

The algorithm for solving this problem is straightforward

Step 1. Prompt for and read each week's data and keep a running total of the number of pennies, nickels, dimes, and quarters saved.

Step 2. Print the total number of pennies, nickels, dimes, and quarters saved.

Step 3. Compute and print the total amount saved and the weekly average.

Step 4. Compute and print the estimated year end saving.

Listing 3.1 contains the code that implements the first two steps of the algorithm. The program begins by displaying directions telling the user how to input the data. The next four sections of code read each week's data and update the total number of pennies, nickels, dimes, and quarters. Notice the use of the += operator to update the totals. The fifth section prints the totals.

Listing 3.1

Estimate yearly savings by saving pocket change (part 1)

```cpp
// Program 3.3: Compute estimated yearly savings
// by saving pocket change
#include <iostream.h>
int main() {
    cout << "For each week enter 4 numbers:\n"
        " pennies nickels dimes quarters (e.g.: 3 2 4 1)\n"
        << endl;

    // Prompt for and read the amount of change for
    // 4 weeks
    cout << "Week 1 change: " << flush;
    int Pennies, Nickels, Dimes, Quarters;
    cin >> Pennies >> Nickels >> Dimes >> Quarters;
    int TotalPennies = Pennies;
    int TotalNickels = Nickels;
    int TotalDimes = Dimes;

    int TotalQuarters = Quarters;

    cout << "Week 2 change: " << flush;
    cin >> Pennies >> Nickels >> Dimes >> Quarters;
    TotalPennies += Pennies;
    TotalNickels += Nickels;
    TotalDimes += Dimes;
    TotalQuarters += Quarters;

    cout << "Week 3 change: " << flush;
    cin >> Pennies >> Nickels >> Dimes >> Quarters;
    TotalPennies += Pennies;
    TotalNickels += Nickels;
    TotalDimes += Dimes;
    TotalQuarters += Quarters;

    cout << "Week 4 change: " << flush;
    cin >> Pennies >> Nickels >> Dimes >> Quarters;
    TotalPennies += Pennies;
    TotalNickels += Nickels;
    TotalDimes += Dimes;
    TotalQuarters += Quarters;

    cout << "Over four weeks you collected\n " <<
        TotalPennies << " Pennies\n " << TotalNickels
        << " Nickels\n " << TotalDimes << " Dimes\n "
        << TotalQuarters << " Quarters" << endl;
```

The second part of the program computes the total amount saved and the weekly average (see Listing 3.2). Displaying the dollar amounts in the proper format is the only complicated part of the program. This step is done by separately computing the number of dollars and the number of cents separately, using the division and remainder operators. The statement

```
int TotalDollars = Total / 100;
```

computes the number of dollars, while the statement

```
int TotalCents = Total % 100;
```

computes the cents. This sequence of operations is done whenever we need to print out a dollar and cents amount. An amount is output by inserting a dollar sign, followed by the dollar amount, followed by a period, followed by the cents. This technique is also used to output the average savings and the estimated year end savings computed in step 4.

Listing 3.2

Estimate yearly savings by saving pocket change (part 2)

```
// Compute and print total savings and the
// weekly average
int Total = TotalPennies + TotalNickels * 5
 + TotalDimes * 10 + TotalQuarters * 25;
int Average = Total / 4;
int TotalDollars = Total / 100;
int TotalCents = Total % 100;
int AverageDollars = Average / 100;
int AverageCents = Average % 100;
cout << "which is $" << TotalDollars << "."
 << TotalCents << " and a weekly average of $"
 << AverageDollars << "." << AverageCents
 << "." << endl;
// Compute and print estimated yearly savings
int YearSavings = Average * 52;
int YearDollars = YearSavings / 100;
int YearCents = YearSavings % 100;
cout << "Estimated savings in one year is $"
 << YearDollars << "." << YearCents << "." << endl;
return 0;
}
```

3.8

USING PROGRAMMER-DEFINED OBJECTS

Up to now, we have worked with the fundamental objects in C++: char, int, long, float, double. The real power of C++ comes from the ability to use object types that are specially developed for the task at hand. For example, in Chapter 1 we discussed creating a new type or class called Bug in order to implement the Bug Hunt game.

While we are not quite ready to discuss how to create classes, we can begin to write programs that use programmer-defined classes of objects that have already been designed and implemented. To begin, we will use two classes that will enable us to write programs that use the graphical display capabilities available on most computers. The two programmer-defined classes are `SimpleWindow` and `RectangleShape`.

3.8.1

Class SimpleWindow

`SimpleWindow` is a class that lets us create window objects that we can use to display graphical objects. Objects of type `Label` and `Rectangle` can be displayed in a `SimpleWindow` window. A programmer-defined type of object is created just like a fundamental type object is created—it is defined. For example, the code fragment

```
SimpleWindow W;
```

defines a `SimpleWindow` object named `W`. One thing to notice about this definition of `W` is that it was done using the same syntax we used to define a fundamental or built-in object.

As we mentioned in Chapter 1, a class has a set of attributes and messages that it understands. `SimpleWindow` has the following attributes:

- the text to display in the title bar at the top of the window, and
- the length and width of the window.

The behaviors or messages that a `SimpleWindow` object understands are open and close. The open message causes the window to appear on the screen, and it enables the window so that objects can be displayed in it. The close message causes the window to shut down and remove its image from the screen.

The `C++` syntax for sending an object a message is

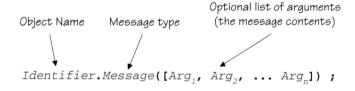

$$Identifier.Message([Arg_1, \ Arg_2, \ ... \ Arg_n]) \ ;$$

So, for example, the `C++` statement to send `SimpleWindow` object `W` an open message is

```
W.Open();
```

In this instance, the `Open` message does not require any arguments.

For example, the code fragment

```
SimpleWindow W;
W.Open()
```

creates and displays the window shown in Figure 3.3.

Since we made such a big deal about initializing objects, you might wonder why `W` was not initialized. Actually, `W` was initialized. For most programmer-

Figure 3.3

A SimpleWindow with default attributes

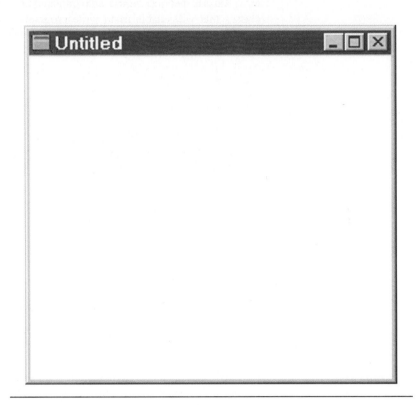

defined classes, when a class is designed, the designer can specify default initial values for the attributes of an object when it is defined without initializing it explicitly. We can, however, define an object and give its attributes different initial values by using a slightly different syntax than we used for initializing fundamental objects when we defined them. The reason is that we need a way to specify several initial values, one for each attribute. The syntax for defining an object and explicitly giving initial values for its attributes is:

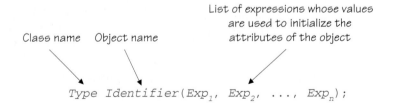

For the `SimpleWindow` class, for example, the definition

```
SimpleWindow N("Narrow Window", 8, 2);
N.Open();
```

creates the following window:

The window title is Narrow Window, and the window is 10 centimeters in length and 2 centimeters high. Thus, when defining a `SimpleWindow` object, the first argument is the title of the window and the second and third arguments are the length and the width of the window, respectively.

This new syntax for initializing objects can also be used to initialize fundamental objects. For example, the definition

```
int x(2);
```

is equivalent to the definition

```
int x = 2;
```

While the first definition can be used to initialize a complex object with several attributes, the second definition can be used to initialize a simple object only.

Style Tip

C++ definition styles

Since the new definition style works with both programmer-defined objects and fundamental objects, we could use this style of definition for all our objects. This convention would have the advantage of uniformity, which is definitely a plus. However, the new style of definition can be confusing for a fundamental object, especially when the object is being initialized with the value of an expression. Consider the following definition from Program 3.2 rewritten in the using the new style of definition:

```
double Molecules((Mass / FormulaWght) *
    AvogadroNmbr);
```

We think this is much harder to read and understand.

Our convention will be to continue to use the = style of definition for fundamental objects and to use the new style of definition only for complex objects that have more than one attribute that needs to be initialized.

Definitions of complex objects can be long, so we need a convention for splitting this type of definition into multiple lines. Our convention will be to split the definition between arguments. The following definition illustrates this style:

```
SimpleWindow Display("A Window for Display",
    DisplayLength, DisplayWidth);
```

3.8.2

Class RectangleShape

Now that we have a window, we need something that we can draw in a window. A simple but useful type of object is a rectangle. The class `Rectangle` has the following properties or attributes:

- a `SimpleWindow` object in which the rectangle is displayed,
- a position in the window,
- a color, and
- a length and width.

A `Rectangle` object understands the following messages:

- `Draw`—display the rectangle in the window.
- `GetColor`—return the color of the rectangle.
- `GetLength`—return the length of the rectangle.
- `GetWidth`—return the width of the rectangle.

The following code

```
SimpleWindow W("A Blue Rectangle", 8, 4);
W.Open();
RectangleShape R(W, 4.0, 2.0, Blue, 3, 2);
R.Draw();
```

creates and displays the following window and the object inside it.

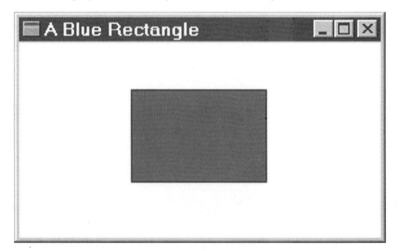

The definition of R instantiated a blue `RectangleShape` named R whose center is 4 centimeters from the left edge of the window and 2 centimeters from the top edge of the window. R is 3 centimeters in length and 2 centimeters high. Thus, R is centered within `SimpleWindow` W.

We can use the messages to obtain information about an object. For the object R above, the statement

```
int Length = R.GetLength();
```

sends a message to `RectangleShape R` requesting that it return its length. The value is stored in the `int` object `Length`. As another example, let's write code that displays the default length and width of a RectangleShape. The code fragment

```
SimpleWindow W("Default Rectangle", 8, 5);
W.Open();
RectangleShape D(W, 4.0, 2.5);
D.Draw();
cout << "D's length is " << D.GetLength() << endl;
cout << "D's width is " << D.GetWidth() << endl;
```

creates the following display window

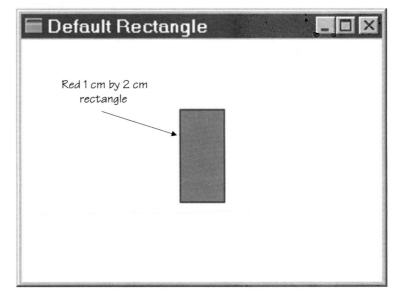

and writes the following output to the text output window:

```
D's length is 1
D's width is 2
```

We see that when the color and size of a `RectangleShape` are not specified in the definition, the default color of a `RectangleShape` is red and the default length and width are, respectively, 1 centimeter and 2 centimeters.

3.9

MOWING LAWNS

Your kid brother plans to start a lawn-mowing service this summer, and he wants to earn $5 an hour. He wants you to write a program that computes how much he should charge to mow a lawn. The problem statement is

> The input to the program is (1) the length and width of a rectangular lawn and (2) the length and width of a house situated on the lawn. All inputs

Programmer Alert

will be in meters. The average speed of mowing is 1 square meter a second. This average takes into account water breaks and periodically refueling the lawn mower. The amount to charge should be printed in dollars and cents. The input and output should look like the following:

```
Please use meters for all input
Please enter the length of the yard: 150
Please enter the width of the yard: 100
Please enter the length of the house: 25
Please enter the width of the house: 20

Yard size: 150 by 100 meters
House size: 25 by 20 meters
Time to cut: 4 hour(s) and 1 minute(s)
Cost to cut: 20 dollar(s) and 13 cent(s)
```

In addition, the program should create a window that graphically displays a plot of the house and the lawn. The scale of the display should be 10 meters equals 1 centimeter. The lawn should be green and the house should be yellow.

The steps necessary to solve the problem are straightforward.

Step 1.   Prompt for and read the inputs.

Step 2.   Print the input so the user can verify that it was correctly entered.

Step 3.   Compute the mowable area. The mowable area is the total size of the lawn minus the area the house takes up.

Step 4.   Compute and print the time required to mow the lawn.

Step 5.   Compute and print the amount to charge for mowing the lawn.

Step 6.   Create a display showing the lawn and the house.

Before implementing the first step of the program, we should define any constants we will use. We will group these at the beginning of the program so that they are easy to find and modify if necessary.

The constants we need are:

```
// Mowing rate in square meters per second
const float MowRate = 1.0;
// Pay rate desired
const float PayRate = 5.0;
// Seconds in an hour
const int SecondsPerMinute = 60;
// Minutes in an hour
const int SecondsPerHour = SecondsPerMinute * 60;
// Length and width of display window
const int DisplayLength = 20;
const int DisplayHeight = 20;
// Scale factor for display: 100 meters equals
// 1 centimeter
const float ScaleFactor = 0.01;
```

To prompt for and read the input is straightforward. The code is

```
cout << "Please use meters for all input\n" << endl;

long LawnLength; // Length of the lawn in meters
cout << "Please enter the length of the lawn: ";
cin >> LawnLength;

long LawnWidth; // Width of the lawn in meters
cout << "Please enter the width of the lawn: ";
cin >> LawnWidth;
```

In both code fragments, notice the use of descriptive names for the objects.

The code to echo the input is equally straightforward:

```
cout << endl;
cout << "Yard size: " << LawnLength << " by "
 << LawnWidth << " meters" << endl;
cout << "House size: " << HouseLength << " by "
 << HouseWidth << " meters" << endl;
```

The next step is to compute the mowable area. The statement accomplishes this task.

```
int MowableArea = (LawnLength * LawnWidth)
 - (HouseLength * HouseWidth);
```

Using MowableArea and MowRate, we can compute the time needed to mow the lawn. We initially compute the time to mow in seconds and then use that value to calculate the number of hours and minutes. The code to calculate and display the time is:

```
long MowTimeInSeconds = MowableArea / MowRate;
long Hours = MowTimeInSeconds / SecondsPerHour;
long Minutes = (MowTimeInSeconds - (Hours
 * SecondsPerHour)) / SecondsPerMinute;
cout << "Time to cut: " << Hours << " hour(s) "
 << Minutes << " minute(s)" << endl;
```

Step 5 is to compute and display the amount to charge for the job. To compute the cost requires simply converting the pay rate, which is in dollars per hour, to dollars per second and multiplying this amount by the time in seconds to mow the lawn. The cost calculation is

```
float DollarCost = MowTimeInSeconds
* (PayRate / SecondsPerHour);
```

and the output calculation is

```
int Dollars = DollarCost;
int Cents = (DollarCost - Dollars) * 100;
cout << "Cost to cut: " << Dollars << " dollar(s)"
    << " and " << Cents << " cent(s)" << endl;
```

Notice that the number of dollars was obtained by assigning DollarCost, which is a **float**, to Dollars, which is an **int**. Recall that assignment from a floating-point type to an integral type results in a truncated value being stored. Using DollarCost and Dollars, the number of cents in the amount is computed.

The final step of the program is to produce the graphical display. Like our previous examples, the first step is to instantiate and open a window. The code

```
SimpleWindow Display("Lawn and House Plot",
  DisplayLength, DisplayHeight);
Display.Open();
```

instantiates a window named Display with the title Lawn and House Plot. The window is DisplayLength centimeters long and DisplayHeight centimeters high.

To create the display we want, we will first draw the lawn and then we will draw the house. If we did it the other way, the larger rectangle would overwrite the smaller rectangle, and it would not be visible. The code to display a scaled image of the lawn is

```
RectangleShape Lawn(Display, DisplayLength / 2.0,
  DisplayHeight / 2.0, Green, LawnLength
  * ScaleFactor, LawnWidth * ScaleFactor);
Lawn.Draw();
```

The position attributes of Lawn are set to the values

```
DisplayLength / 2.0
```

and

```
DisplayHeight / 2.0
```

so it is positioned in the center of the window.

The final step is to draw the rectangle representing the house in the proper position. This code is similar to the previous code

```
RectangleShape House(Display, DisplayLength / 2.0,
DisplayHeight / 2.0, Yellow,
  HouseLength * ScaleFactor,
  HouseWidth * ScaleFactor);
House.Draw();
```

The final action of the program is to close the display window. The statements

```
cout << "Type a character followed by a\n"
  << "return to remove the display and exit" << endl;
char AnyChar;
cin >> AnyChar;
Display.Close();
```

displays a message in the console window and waits for the user to type a character followed by a return. This pauses the program so that the display window does not disappear. When the user types a character and a return, the program continues and sends the close message to the window.

Program 3.4 contains the complete code for the program and Figure 3.4 shows the display window that the program creates. There are several important things to notice about this program. First, the include statement

```
#include "rect.h"
```

incorporates the file `rect.h` into the program. This file contains the definitions necessary to access and use the programmer-defined types `SimpleWindow` and `RectangleShape`. Including a `.h` file is the standard way to gain access to new types and classes of objects.

Program 3.4

Compute time and cost to mow a lawn

```
// Program 3.4: Compute the time and cost required to mow
// a lawn
#include <iostream.h>
#include "rect.h"
int ApiMain() {
    // Mowing rate in square meters per second
    const float MowRate = 1.0;
    // Pay rate desired
    const float PayRate = 5.0;

    // Seconds in an hour
    const int SecondsPerMinute = 60;
    // Minutes in an hour
    const int SecondsPerHour =
     SecondsPerMinute * 60;

    // Length and width of display window
    const int DisplayLength = 20;
    const int DisplayHeight = 20;

    // Scale factor for display. 100 meters equals
    // 1 centimeter
    const float ScaleFactor = 0.01;

    cout << "Please use meters for all input\n" << endl;

    long LawnLength; // Length of the lawn in meters
    cout << "Please enter the length of the lawn: ";
    cin >> LawnLength;

    long LawnWidth; // Width of the lawn in meters
    cout << "Please enter the width of the lawn: ";
    cin >> LawnWidth;

    long HouseLength; // Length of the house in meters
    cout << "Please enter the length of the house: ";
```

```
cin >> HouseLength;

long HouseWidth; // Width of the house in meters
cout << "Please enter the width of the house: ";
cin >> HouseWidth;

// Echo the input so they can be verified
cout << endl;
cout << "Yard size: " << LawnLength << " by "
 << LawnWidth << " meters" << endl;
cout << "House size: " << HouseLength << " by "
 << HouseWidth << " meters" << endl;

// Compute the mowable area
long MowableArea = (LawnLength * LawnWidth)
 - (HouseLength * HouseWidth);

// Compute the time to cut and display it
long MowTimeInSeconds = MowableArea / MowRate;
long Hours = MowTimeInSeconds / SecondsPerHour;
long Minutes = (MowTimeInSeconds - (Hours
 * SecondsPerHour)) / SecondsPerMinute;

cout << "Time to cut: " << Hours << " hour(s) "
 << Minutes << " minute(s)" << endl;
// Compute the cost and display it
float DollarCost = MowTimeInSeconds * PayRate
 / SecondsPerHour;
int Dollars = DollarCost;
int Cents = (DollarCost - Dollars) * 100;
cout << "Cost to cut: " << Dollars << " dollar(s)"
 << " and " << Cents << " cent(s)" << endl;

// Open the window and display the lawn
SimpleWindow Display("Lawn and House Plot",
 DisplayLength, DisplayHeight);
Display.Open();

RectangleShape Lawn(Display, DisplayLength / 2.0,
 DisplayHeight / 2.0, Green,
 LawnLength * ScaleFactor,
 LawnWidth * ScaleFactor);
 Lawn.Draw();
// Display the house
RectangleShape House(Display, DisplayLength / 2.0,
 DisplayHeight / 2.0, Yellow,
 HouseLength * ScaleFactor,
 HouseWidth * ScaleFactor);
House.Draw();

cout << "Type a character followed by a\n"
 << "return to remove the display and exit" << endl;
char AnyChar;
cin >> AnyChar;
Display.Close();

return 0;
}
```

The second thing to notice is that this program does not contain a function
main(), but rather the code is contained in a function called ApiMain().
Because we are creating our own windows and managing the display of objects

Figure 3.4
*A graphical depiction of
the house and lawn*

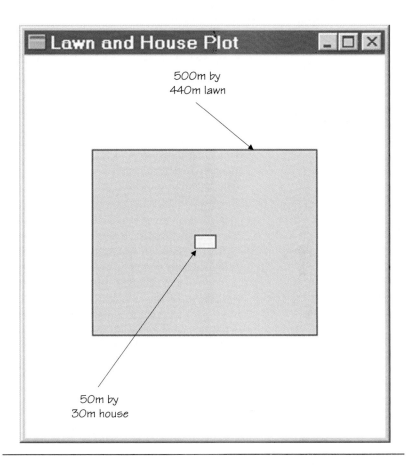

within these windows, we must bypass the normal window creation mechanism provided by the C++ compiler. The reason we need this special function is described more completely in Chapter 11 where we discuss the mechanics of graphical programming. So for now, just remember than when we write a program that creates a separate window for the display of graphical objects, the starting point for the execution of the program is in a function called Api-Main(), not main().

Careful examination of the code reveals a couple of potential problems. What would happen if the size of the lawn was so large that when it was scaled, it was larger than the display window? Similarly, what if the house size is larger than the size of the lawn? You could try running the program and see what happens, but clearly these are situations that we should avoid. In an interactive program, it is important to validate the input and make sure it is reasonable. We do not yet have a mechanism for doing this type of checking, but the next chapter introduces several C++ constructs that will allow us to check user input to make sure it is acceptable.

History of Computing

Mechanical devices

The seventeenth century saw the development of the first primitive mechanical calculators. The person now credited with constructing the first mechanical calculator is Wilhelm Schickard (1592–1635). The principal innovation of Schickard's device, which he called the "calculating clock" (see Figure 3.5), was the use of gears to propagate a carry from one digit place to the next highest digit place. This mechanism was used in one form or another in many of the later mechanical calculating devices. Unfortunately, the details of Schickard's invention were lost until the 1960s when references to his work were discovered in letters to the great mathematician and astronomer, Johannes Kepler. Because of this accident of history, much more attention has been paid to another inventor of a mechanical calculator—Blaise Pascal.

Blaise Pascal (1623–1662) was certainly a child prodigy. At an early age, he discovered several mathematical theorems and wrote several highly regarded essays. In his thirties, not long before he died, he invented the syringe and the hydraulic press. Pascal is best known for his design and construction of a mechanical calculator known as the Pascaline (see Figure 3.6). The *Pascaline* was a small box that had a series of toothed wheels. Each wheel corresponded to a digit, and the digit was displayed above the wheel in a small window. Addition was performed by dialing the numbers to be added on the wheels and reading the result in the windows above the wheels. The machine could also be used to do subtraction, but it was a bit more complicated. This may seem like a simple device, but in Pascal's day, it was a great accomplishment. To produce the machine, Pascal had to overcome several difficult problems. One of the most serious, and one that has plagued inventors throughout history, was that his ideas outstripped the technology of the time. Pascal designed several machines only to find that the craftsmen of the day could not build the components required.

Pascal addressed one of the problems with Schickard's calculating clock. The problem of using simple gears to propagate a carry to the next digit is that if the carry must be propagated several places, the force required to turn all the gears is quite large and the gears could break. Pascal devised a device that used a gravity-assisted mechanism to help propagate carries. Essentially, when a carry was needed, a weight would fall to activate a spring mechanism that would advance the next wheel. This mechanism eliminated any strain on the gears.

Gottfried Wilhelm Leibnitz (1646–1716) was a man of many talents. He worked in the areas of logic, mathematics, philosophy, law, and theology. He is best known for his independent invention of differential calculus, which he invented 20 years after Sir Isaac Newton but in a more usable form.

Figure 3.5
*Wilhelm Schickard
(1592–1635) and his
Calculating Clock*

Leibnitz also invented a calculator, called the "stepped reckoner" (see Figure 3.7), that had a special drum that acted as mechanical multiplier. The wheel had nine teeth that ran horizontally across the drum. The first tooth went one-tenth the distance of the drum, the second two-tenths, etc. By adjusting a sliding gear the appropriate distance, a multiplier was shifted one decimal place to the left. Leibnitz, like Pascal, could not find craftsmen able to do the exacting work required to construct his calculator. The only surviving device was found to not work properly, in large part, because of construction flaws. Indeed, some scholars feel that it is unlikely that the stepped reckoner ever worked properly. Nonetheless, the use of the "Leibnitz wheel" in later working calculators was common.

Figure 3.6
Blaise Pascal (1623–1662) and his Pascaline

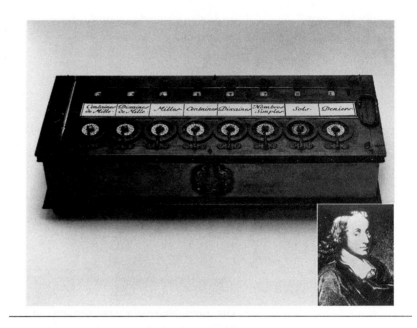

Figure 3.7
Gottfried Wilhelm Leibnitz (1646–1716) and his Stepped Reckoner

3.10

POINTS TO REMEMBER

- Always initialize an object when it is declared.

- When a floating-point value is stored in an integer object, the floating-point value is converted to an integer value by truncating its value. For example, after the code

```
int x = 0;
x = 23.6;
```

is executed, the value of x is 23.

- The assignment operator is right associative and has lower precedence than the arithmetic operators.

- The C++ keyword **const** is used to define objects that should not be modified. This technique is useful for defining objects that hold values that represent physical constants, values that are conversion factors, and other values that should not be changed during the execution of the program.

- The iostream object cin is an input stream. It is normally associated with input from the keyboard.

- Input is extracted from an input stream using the extraction operator >>. The extraction operator can extract integer, floating-point, and character values from an input stream.

- When writing a program that accepts input from a human user, it is important that the program issues prompts that clearly indicate what input is requested and the form of the input.

- The most important characteristic of a program is correctness and comprehensibility. When faced with the choice between clarity and a possible gain in performance, the correct choice is almost always clarity.

- The C++ compound assignment operators +=, -=, *=, /=, %= perform an arithmetic operation on an object and store the resulting value back into the object. For example, the statement

```
x += 5;
```

is equivalent to

```
x = x + 5;
```

- C++ has special operators, ++ and --, for incrementing and decrementing integral and floating-point objects. There are pre– and post– versions of these operators. With the *post*increment and *post*decrement operators, the value of the expression is the value of the object before it is modified. For example, when the code fragment

```
int x = 10;
int i = x++;
```

is executed, the value of i is set to 10 and the value of x becomes 11. With the *pre*increment and *pre*decrement, the value of the expression is the incremented value of the object. For example, when the code fragment

```
int x = 9;
int i = --x;
```

is executed, the value of i is set to 8 and the value of x becomes 8.

- Objects with more than one attribute or value are defined and initialized using a special syntax. The syntax is

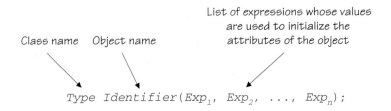

Class name   Object name

List of expressions whose values
are used to initialize the
attributes of the object

$$Type\ Identifier(Exp_1,\ Exp_2,\ \ldots,\ Exp_n);$$

3.11

EXERCISES

3.1   What is the name of the C++ >> operator?

3.2   Explain why the following code fragment is illegal.

```
int x = 5;
int y;
int z;
(z = y) = x;
```

3.3   Explain why the following code fragment is illegal.

```
const float PayRate = 6.50;
OldSalary = PayRate * 40;
PayRate = 7.25;
NewSalary = Payrate * 40;
```

3.4   What is the collective name of the C++ operators *=, +=, -=, /=, and %=?

3.5   What file must be included before the stream cin can be used?

3.6   For the following expressions, give the final values of the objects Cost and Price. The objects of interest are

```
int Cost = 5;
int Price = 10;
```

a) ++Cost;

b) Cost++;

c) Cost = Price++;

d) Cost = ++Price;

e) Cost = Price++
   + ++ Price;

f) Cost += Price;

g) Cost *= 5;

h) Cost += Price * 5;

i) Cost--;

j) Cost = Price++;

k) Price /= Cost++

3.7 Give the values of the defined objects after the execution of the following objects. If the value of an object is unknown, report its value as undefined.

a)
```
int i = 15;
int k = 10;
int j = 0;
j = k;
k = j;
j = i;
```

b)
```
int i = 5;
int j = 6;
int k= 7;
j = i;
i = 3;
k = j;
```

c)
```
int i = 21;
int j = 0;
int k = 11;
j = k;
k = i;
j = k;
```

d)
```
double x = 5.2;
double y = 0.0;
double z = 0.0;
y = x;
z = y;
x = z;
```

e)
```
double x = 32.1;
double y = 45.0;
double z = 0.0;
x = z;
y = z;
x = y;
y = x;
```

f)
```
char a = 'a';
char b = 'b';
char c = 'c';
a = b;
b = c;
c = a;
```

3.8 For each of the assignment statements below, give the value that is stored into the object on the left-hand side of the assignment operator. For this exercise, assume that a **char** is 8 bits, a **short** is 16 bits, and an **int** is 32 bits. The objects of interest are declared as

```
char c;
short s;
int i;
```

Give your answer as a decimal value.

a) c = 101.3;

b) i = 101.8;

c) s = 0x3a1;

d) i = 25;

e) i = 3e2;

f) c = 'a';

g) i = 31 + 0.7;

h) s = 12.2 + 13;

i) c = 55L;

j) c = 0xff1;

k) s = 0773451;

l) i = 0.23;

m) i = 143F;

n) c = '0';

o) i = '9';

p) s = 31000;

3.9 Give a single assignment statement that is equivalent to

```
j += 1;
i = j;
```

3.10 Give a single assignment statement that is equivalent to

```
i = j;
j += 1;
```

3.11 For each assignment expression below, give the result (using the *<value, type>* notation). If the assignment is invalid, give the result *<undef, undef>*. The objects of interest are declared as

```
char c = 'A';
int i = 23;
float x = 3.1;
double z = 5.0;
```

The value portion of your answer should be expressed as a decimal value.

a) i = c;   g) x = i = z;
b) i = x;   h) i = x = z;
c) c = i;   i) z = x = i;
d) x = i;   j) x = i = c;
e) z = x;   k) i = c = z;
f) x = i = c;

3.12 For each of the following **const** definitions, indicate whether or not they are valid C++ definitions.

a) **const** x = 23;
b) **const** float z = 5;
c) **const** int i = 5;
d) **const** double int = 5;
e) **const** double x = 33;
f) **const** char Blank(040);
g) **const** float f = +3;
h) **const** double x = 3.0;
i) **const** float z(2e3);

3.13 Consider the following code fragment.

```
int NumberOfDays = 30;
float PayRate = 5.0;
float AverageHours = 5;
cin >> PayRate >> NumberofDays >> AverageHours;
cout << "Salary is " << PayRate * NumberofDays
    * AverageHours << endl;
```

Give the output when the input stream contains the following characters.

a)   4.50 023 4

b)   6.00 23 010

c) 7.00,5,12

d) 7.00*5*12

3.14 Add a statement to Program 3.1 directly before the computation of the circumference that attempts to change the value of π to 3.1415926. Compile the modified program. Does the compiler report an error? If so, what is the error message?

3.15 Modify Program 3.2 so that it computes the number of molecules in a sugar. Sugars are composed of hydrogen, oxygen, and carbon. You will need to look up the atomic weight of oxygen. Use your program to compute the number of molecules in 10 grams of glucose ($C_6H_{12}O_6$).

3.16 Find a machine with a C++ compiler where a **double** is more precise than a float (this is true for most implementations of C++ on PCs). On this machine, write a C++ program that demonstrates that a **double** is more precise than a **float**.

3.17 Modify Program 3.1 to accept the diameter of the circle instead of the radius.

3.18 Increase the precision of the value of π in Program 3.1. Do you see a difference in the output? Explain your observation.

3.19 Modify Program 3.3 so that the average computed is a daily one, rather than weekly. Does this change make a difference in the estimated year-end savings? If so, explain why.

3.20 Modify Program 3.3 so that it handles half-dollar coins.

3.21 Modify Program 3.4 so that it handles lawns that have two buildings. Assume the second building is an attached garage.

3.22 Write a program that creates a checkerboard pattern of red and blue squares in a window that is 8 centimeters wide and 8 centimeters high. The squares should be 2 centimeters on a side.

3.23 Write a program that draws a tower consisting of five rectangles. The rectangles should be displayed in a window that is 8 centimeters wide and 10 centimeters high. The base rectangle should be 6 centimeters long and 1 centimeter high. Each succeeding rectangle is 75 percent of the length of the one underneath. The height of all the rectangles is the same. The rectangles should be blue.

3.24 Write a program that draws an empty square. An empty square can be constructed by drawing two vertical rectangles that are tall and very narrow and two horizontal rectangles that are short and wide. The rectangles are positioned so their ends meet to form a square. The rectangles should be yellow.

3.25 Write a program to compute a water and sewer bill. The input is the number of gallons consumed. A water and sewer bill is computed as follows:

■ water costs .021 cents per 100 gallons

■ sewer service is .001 cents per 100 gallons consumed

- a service charge of 2 percent is applied to the total of the water and sewer service charges.

3.26 Write a program that prompts for and accepts a telephone number in the form *ddd–ddd–ddd* where *d* is a digit and prints it out in the following format: (*ddd*) *ddd–dddd*.

3.27 Write a program that prompts for and reads a floating-point value. The program prints the whole part on one line and the decimal part on a second line. For example, if the program was given the input 23.45, it would output

```
23
0.45
```

3.28 Write a program that prompts for and reads a distance in inches. The program prints the distance as miles, feet, and inches.

3.29 A safe investment is to buy a Treasury bill. Typically, Treasury bills are sold in denominations that are multiples of $1,000. For example, you might pay $960 for a $1,000 Treasury bill maturing in 91 days. At the end of 91 days, you receive $1000. To compare this investment to other investments, it is useful to compute the annual interest rate. The steps to compute the annual interest rate are:

1. Compute the interest factor per period. For our example, this is $1000 \div 960 = 1.0416$. The interest rate is .0416.

2. Compute the annual interest rate by multiplying the interest rate by the number of periods in a year. In our example, there are 4 periods in a year, so the annual interest rates is $4 \times .0416 = 16.64\%$.

Write a program that prompts for and reads the denomination of a Treasury bill, the cost of the Treasury bill, and the number of days until the bill matures. The program uses this information to compute the annual interest rate.

CHAPTER 4

Control constructs

Introduction

U p to this point, our programs—whether defined in a function `main()` or an `ApiMain()`—have had the property that each time they are run, the exact same sequence of statements is executed. Execution begins with the first statement in the function and proceeds in a straight-line manner to the last statement in the function with every statement along the way being executed once. This form of programming is adequate for solving simple problems. However, for general problem solving we need the ability to control which statements are executed and how often. In this chapter we consider two *conditional constructs*—the **if** and **switch**—that control whether a statement list is executed and three *iterative constructs*—the **while**, **for**, and **do**—that control how many times a statement list is executed. Except for the **switch** construct, which performs a matching process to determine which statements are executed, these control constructs use logical expressions to determine their course of action. To support these constructs, C++ has the logical type **bool**. Our examination of control constructs begins with a discussion of logical expressions.

Key Concepts

- logical values and operators
- truth tables
- **bool** type
- relational operators
- short-circuit evaluation
- **if-else** statement
- **switch** statement
- **break** statement

- **enum** statement
- **for** construct
- **while** construct
- **do** construct
- infinite loops
- invariants
- iterators

4.1

BOOLEAN ALGEBRA

A *logical expression* is an expression whose value is either the logical value *true* or the logical value *false*. For example, two logical expressions are

- Zero degrees Celsius is the same as 32 degrees Fahrenheit (true).

- A triangle has four sides (false).

The area of mathematics associated with the manipulation of logical values is called Boolean algebra. It is named after the 19th-century British mathematician George Boole who formalized its study.

Logical values and expressions are important mathematically because they are the fundamental building blocks of formal proofs. In the realm of computers, besides being used to control statement execution, logical expressions are important because they can be used to model hardware behavior.

We use three primary logical operators to combine logic values into logical expressions. These logical operators are *and*, *or*, and *not*. The three primary operators are used in the following examples:

- Angela is amazed *and* Michael is happy.

- Kyle is going skiing *or* Michelle is going skiing.

- It is *not* a sunny day.

In normal conversation there may be mild confusion over the meaning of a logical operator. For example, if Kyle is going skiing or Michelle is going skiing, can it be the case that they are both going skiing? However, there is no mathematical ambiguity—each operator has a well-defined specification for the value of the operation given the values of the operands.

4.1.1

Truth tables

A *truth table* is the principal way of defining under which conditions a logical operation is true and under which conditions it is false. A truth table lists all possible combinations of operand values and the result of the operation for each combination.

The truth table for the logical operator *and* is given in Table 4.1. In this and successive truth tables, we use P and Q as placeholders to represent the left and right operands of the binary logical operator being discussed. We also use P in the discussion of the unary logical operator *not*.

Binary logical operators have four possible logic value combinations and therefore four entries in their truth tables. Unary logic operators have only two table entries.

Table 4.1

Truth table for logical and

P	Q	P and Q
false	false	false
false	true	false
true	false	false
true	true	true

The logical *and* truth table shows that the operation is true only if both of its operands are true; otherwise, the operation is false. For example, the second entry of the truth table indicates that when *P* is true and *Q* is false, an *and* operation has the value false. In the fourth entry where both *P* and *Q* are true, an *and* operation has the value true.

Table 4.2 gives the truth table for the logical *or* operator. This truth table indicates that the *or* operation is true if at least one of its operands is true; otherwise, the operation is false.

Table 4.2

Truth table for logical or

P	Q	P or Q
false	false	false
false	true	true
true	false	true
true	true	true

Table 4.3 gives the logical *not* operator. The *not* operation is true if its operand is false, and the operation is false if its operand is true.

Table 4.3

Truth table for logical not

P	not P
false	true
true	false

4.1.2

Logical expressions

We can form *compound* expressions by combining logical operations. For example, the following expression is true when both *P* and *Q* are false; otherwise, the expression is false.

not (P or Q)

When *P* and *Q* are both false, subexpression (*P or Q*) is false and the negation of subexpression (*P or Q*) is true, making the overall expression *not (P or Q)* true. Any other combination of values for *P* and *Q* makes subexpression (*P or Q*) true, and the negation of that subexpression false, making the overall expression *not (P or Q)* false. The truth table in Table 4.4 verifies this analysis.

Note that the table has entries for both the subexpression (*P or Q*) and the overall expression *not (P or Q)*.

Table 4.4

*Truth table for
not (P or Q)*

P	Q	P or Q	not (P or Q)
false	false	false	true
false	true	true	false
true	false	true	false
true	true	true	false

As another example, the following expression is true only when *P* is false and *Q* is true.

$$(not\ P)\ and\ Q$$

Table 4.5 verifies this analysis.

Table 4.5

*Truth table for
(not P) and Q*

P	Q	not P	(not P) and Q
false	false	true	false
false	true	true	true
true	false	false	false
true	true	false	false

The exercises at the end of the chapter consider other operators and logical equivalences including DeMorgan's Law.

4.2

A BOOLEAN TYPE

The representation of logical values is one of the aspects of C++ that is still evolving. Older versions of C++ followed the same convention as the programming language C (C++ was derived from C, hence the ++ in C++), where a logical false is represented by the value 0 and all other numeric values are representations of logical true. Using these rules, the following expressions are true:

```
1
979 * 3
-45 + 83
```

And the following expressions are false.

```
0
5 - 5
0 * 46
17 % 17
```

With this convention, it is not necessary to explicitly have a logical type. Instead, objects of an integral type such as **int** or **char** can be used.

The proposed C++ standard includes a logical type. It is named **bool**, and associated with this type are two symbolic constants **true** and **false**. The presence of the **bool** type should contribute to program readability and programmer understanding.

4.2.1

Boolean operators

There are three logical C++ operators: &&, ||, and !. Operator && is used to perform a logical *and* operation, operator || is used to perform a logical *or* operation, and operator ! is used to perform a logical *not* operation. Suppose the following object definitions are in effect.

```
bool P = true;
bool Q = false;
bool R = true;
bool S = false;
```

The following expressions are then true.

```
P           // P has value true
P && R      // logical and is true when both operands
            // are true
P || Q      // logical or is true when at least one of
            // the operands is true
!S          // logical not is true when the operand is
            // false
```

And the following expressions are false.

```
Q           // Q has value false
P && S      // logical and is false when at least one
            // of the operands is false
Q || S      // logical or is false when both of the
            // operands are false
!R          // logical not is false when the operand
            // is true
```

The logical operators are also defined for the integral type objects such as **int** and **char**. When using the logical operators with integral type objects, the previously mentioned convention, where only zero represents a logical false, is used. We demonstrate this capability through some examples. Suppose the following definitions are in effect.

```
int i = 1;
int j = 0;
int k = -1;
int m = 0;
```

The following expressions are then true.

```
i           // i is nonzero
i && k      // logical and is true when both operands
            // are nonzero
```

```
i || m      // logical or is true when at least one
            // of the operands is nonzero
!j          // logical not is true when the operand
            // is zero
```

And the following expressions evaluate to false.

```
j           // j is zero
j && i      // logical and is false when at least one
            // of the operands is zero
j || m      // logical or is false when both operands
            // are false
!k          // logical not is false when the operand is
            // nonzero
```

C++
Language

> ### *What if your compiler does not yet have a bool type?*
>
> If your C++ compiler does not have the **bool** type, it is quite simple to create the type yourself. The following listing for a source file `boolean.h` defines this logical type.
>
> ```
> #ifndef BOOLEAN_H
> #define BOOLEAN_H
> typedef int bool;
> const bool false = 0;
> const bool true = 1;
> #endif
> ```
>
> The **typedef** statement in this context defines an alias **bool** for the type **int**. Programmers can now use the type **bool** to create objects whose type name is more suitable for their task. To allow your program to make use of this definition, add the following preprocessor statement at the beginning of your program file:
>
> ```
> #include "boolean.h"
> ```
>
> In the next chapter, we discuss the meaning behind the preprocessor directives that surround the three definitions.

4.2.2

Relational operators

In addition to the logical operators that manipulate logical values, there are also the relational operators that produce logical values. There are two kinds of relational operators: equality and ordering.

The *equality operators* are defined for the fundamental and pointer types (pointer types are discussed in Chapter 12). The two equality operators are == and !=. They can be used for determining whether two objects represent the same or different values.

An == operation is true if its two operands have the same value; otherwise, the operation is false. A != operation performs in the opposite manner. If its two operands represent different values, the operation is true; otherwise, the operation is false.

The *ordering operators* are also defined for the fundamental and pointer types. They are used to determine the relative size of two values. There are four ordering operators: <, >, <=, and >=.

The < operator corresponds to the mathematical concept of less than. A < operation is true if its left operand occurs before the right operand in an ordering of the two values; otherwise, the operation is false. The operator > corresponds to greater than. A > operation is true if its left operand occurs before the right operand in an ordering of the two values; otherwise, the operation is false. The operator <= corresponds to less than or equal to. A <= operation is true if its left operand can occur before the right operand in an ordering of the two values; otherwise, the operation is false. The operator >= corresponds to operator greater than or equal to. A >= operation is true if its left operand can occur after the right operand in an ordering of the two values; otherwise, the operation is false.

For the **bool** type, the value of the constant **false** is less than the value of the constant **true**. We are not guaranteed any particular integral values for **true** and **false**.

We now consider some examples. Suppose the following object definitions are in effect.

```
int i = 1;
int j = 2;
int k = 2;
char c = '2';
char d = '3';
char e = '2';
```

The following expressions are then true.

```
c == e        // == is true when the values of the two
              // operands are the same
i != k        // != is true when the two operands have
              // different values
i < j         // < is true when the value of the left
              // operand is smaller than the value
              // of the right operand
d > e         // > is true when the value of the left
              // operand is larger than the value of
              // the right operand
i <= k        // <= is true when the value of the left
              // operand is not larger than the value
              // of the right operand
j >= k        // >= is true when the value of the left
              // operand is not smaller than the value
              // of the right operand
```

And the following expressions are false.

```
i == j        // == is false when the values of the
              // two operands are different
c != e        // != is false when the values of the
              // two operands are the same
j < k         // < is false when the value of the left
```

```
                          // operand is not smaller than the value
                          // of the right operand
        c > e             // > is false when the value of the left
                          // operand is not larger than the value
                          // of the right operand
        d <= c            // <= is false when the value of left
                          // operand is larger than the value of
                          // the right operand
        i >= k            // >= is false when the value of the
                          // left operand is smaller than the
                          // value of the right operand
```

Programmer Alert

> ### *Confusing assignment and equality*
>
> A common programming error is misuse of the = operator. A programmer may intend to write the following expression:
>
> ```
>     i == 0
> ```
>
> But instead writes this expression:
>
> ```
>     i = 0
> ```
>
> The first expression is an equality expression and is true whenever i is zero. The second expression is an assignment expression and is never true, because the value of that expression is the value assigned to i, which is 0.

4.2.3

Operator precedence revisited

More complicated expressions can be built by using multiple operators in the same expression. To evaluate such expressions requires knowing the precedence of the relational and logical operators with respect to the other operators.

The not operator ! has the same high precedence as other unary operators. Among the binary operators, the relational and logical operators have lower precedence than the arithmetic operators and greater precedence than the assignment operators. Relational operators have greater precedence than the logical operators. Among the relational operators, the ordering operators have greater precedence that the equality operators. Among the logical operators, && has greater precedence than ||. Because of operator precedence, the following expressions are equivalent:

```
    i + 1 < j * 4 && ! P || Q
    (((i + 1) < (j * 4)) && (!P)) || Q
```

And the next expressions are also equivalent.

```
    P != i < j || Q && S
    (P != (i < j)) || (Q && S)
```

To ensure readability and understanding, we stress the use of parentheses.

The relative precedence of the arithmetic, relational, and logical operators is summarized in Table 4.6. A complete specification of the operator precedence is described in Appendix A.

Table 4.6

Precedence of selected operators arranged from highest to lowest

Operation
Unary operators
Multiplicative arithmetic
Additive arithmetic
Relational ordering
Relational equality
Logical and
Logical or
Assignment

Programmer Alert

Rounding errors

Beware of using the equality operators with the floating-point types. The finite precision of the floating-point types permits round-off errors to be introduced with repeated operations. For example, suppose the following definition is in effect:

```
float Sum = .1 + .1 + .1 + .1 + .1 + .1 + .1 + .1
    + .1 + .1;
```

The following expression, which should be mathematically true, is unlikely to be true within a program:

```
Sum == 1.0
```

Rather than directly testing for equality or inequality, we check whether the two values are sufficiently close to each other. The checking is done by specifying a maximal error tolerance and verifying that the absolute value of the difference is smaller than that tolerance. For example, suppose our maximum error tolerance is specified as the following constant:

```
const float Delta = 0.0001;
```

The following expression would detect whether the two values are sufficiently close. The expression makes use of the math library function `fabs()` that returns the absolute value of its floating-point parameter (the math library is discussed in the Chapter 5 examination of libraries).

```
fabs(Sum - 1.0) <= Delta
```

4.2.4

Short-circuit evaluation

In the evaluation of a logical expression it can be the case that the value of the expression is known before all the operands have been considered. For example, if one operand of an `&&` operation is known to be false, then we know that the result of `&&` operation is false, since the `&&` operation is only true when both operands are true. Similarly, if one operand of an `||` operation is known to be true, then we know that the result of the || operation is true, since the || operation is true when at least one of its operands is true.

The C++ proposed standard states that in evaluating a logical operation the left operand is evaluated before the right operand. It also states that if the value of an operation can be determined from the left operand, then the right operand is not evaluated. This kind of evaluation is known as *short-circuit evaluation*.

Short-circuit evaluation is typically used in a logical expression to ensure that the objects being considered have a particular property before they are manipulated. For example, consider

```
(i != 0) && ((j / i) > 5)
```

Since the left operand of the && is evaluated first, we know that if the right operand of the && is evaluated, i cannot be 0 and therefore dividing by i makes sense. Without short-circuit evaluation, the right operand of the && could be evaluated with i being 0, causing an illegal division to occur.

4.3

CONDITIONAL EXECUTION USING THE IF STATEMENT

The first control construct that we consider is the **if** statement. The **if** statement has two possible forms. The simpler of the two has the following syntax:

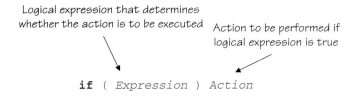

When an **if** statement is reached within a program, the parenthetic expression *Expression* following the keyword **if** is evaluated. If *Expression* is true, *Action* is executed, otherwise *Action* is not executed (in its simplest form, *Action* is a single statement). Either way, program execution continues with the next statement in the program. This description of the execution process of an **if** statement is its *semantic* definition. The semantics are demonstrated pictorially in Figure 4.1. The representation in that figure is called a *flowchart*—the chart indicates the flow of program execution.

Our first example using an **if** statement is Program 4.1 that echoes the absolute value of its input. The input is stored in the object Value. If the expression (Value < 0) is true, then Value is negative and reassigning it with the complementary value changes Value to the equivalent positive number. If instead the expression (Value < 0) is false, then Value must be non-negative and no action needs to be performed. In Program 4.1 and in the rest of the examples of this section, we are zealous in our commenting. We use the

Figure 4.1

Flowchart representation of a basic if statement

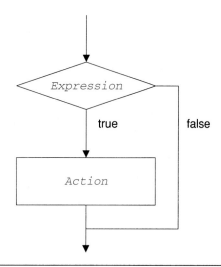

Program 4.1

Demonstration of an if statement

```
// Program 4.1: Display absolute value of input
#include <iostream.h>
int main() {
   cout << "Please enter a number: " << flush;
   int Value;
   cin >> Value;
   if (Value < 0)  // is Value less than zero?
     Value = -Value; // it is, so change its sign
   cout << Value << " is positive" << endl;
   return 0;
}
```

comments to reinforce new concepts. In practice, most of these comments should be eliminated. A flowchart of Program 4.1 is given in Figure 4.2.

We use an **if** statement in the following code segment to report whether an input is an even number. As in Program 4.1, the input is again stored in the object named `Value`. The term `(Value % 2)` is the remainder of `Value` divided by 2. If that value is not 0, then the input cannot be even.

```
cout << "Please enter a number: " << flush;
int Value;
cin >> Value;
cout << Value << " is ";
if ((Value % 2) != 0) // is Value odd?
   cout << "not ";     // Value is odd
cout << "even" << endl;
```

It is more often the case that several statements need to be executed based upon the value of an expression. To indicate that a group of statements is to be executed, the statements in the group are surrounded by left and right curly braces. The individual statements in the group are separated by semicolons. The semicolons are necessary so that the individual statements can be distinguished. An example of this kind of **if** statement is demonstrated in the fol-

Figure 4.2

*Flowchart
representation of
Program 4.1*

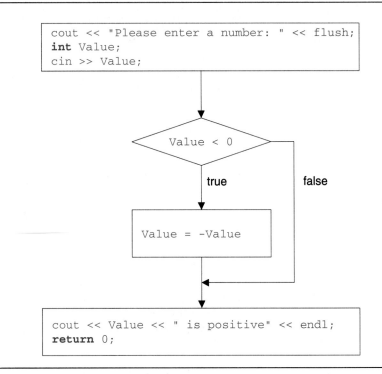

lowing code segment where two input values `Value1` and `Value2` are extracted and echoed back in sorted order.

```
cout << "Please enter two numbers: " << flush;
int Value1;
int Value2;
cin >> Value1 >> Value2;
if (Value1 > Value2) { // is Value1 larger?
    // as Value1 is larger, we need to do a swap
    int RememberValue1 = Value1;
    Value1 = Value2;
    Value2 = RememberValue1;
}
cout << "The input numbers in sorted order: "
  << Value1 << " " << Value2 << endl;
```

In the preceding segment, after the two numbers are extracted, they are compared. If `Value2` is smaller than `Value1`, the two values are swapped. The interchange is accomplished through the assistance of the object `RememberValue1`. Once the **if** statement has been completed, the objects `Value1` and `Value2` are displayed.

4.3.1

The if-else statement

A second form of the **if** statement deals with programming situations where different actions are to be taken based upon the value of a logical expression. This form of the **if** statement has the following syntax:

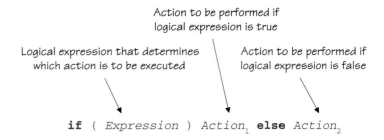

where $Action_1$ and $Action_2$ are individually either a single statement or a group of statements surrounded by curly braces. When this type of **if** statement is executed, *Expression* is evaluated. If *Expression* is true, $Action_1$ is executed; otherwise, $Action_2$ is executed. The flowchart in Figure 4.3 demonstrates the semantics of the **if-else** statement.

Figure 4.3

Flowchart representation of an if-else statement

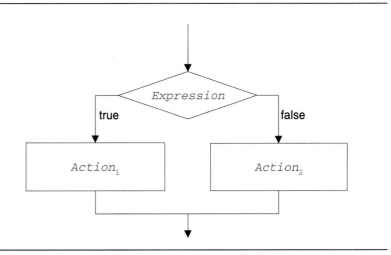

Suppose S and T are properly initialized objects of type Rectangle-Shape. The following code segment correctly reports whether these two objects have the same color.

```
if (S.GetColor() == T.GetColor()) // equal colors?
   cout << "Rectangles have the same color";
else // colors are not equal
   cout << "Rectangles have different colors";
cout << endl;
```

Consistent indentation and curly brace location

In examining the programs in this chapter you see that we have indented the *Action* statements associated with the **if** statements. The indentation is a clue to the reader that the execution of an *Action* statement depends upon the less indented **if** statement expression. A consistent indentation scheme is necessary for program readability. Most programmers typically use three or four characters per level of indentation. We will use a similar indentation scheme for actions associated with other control statements.

The placement of the curly braces that group the statement list is a matter of personal taste. The basis for our curly-brace placement is the following. We include the opening left brace on the initial line of the **if** statement to conserve line space. We place the closing brace on its own line at the same indentation level as the associated **if** as a visual clue that subsequent statements in the program are not associated with this **if** statement.

To get a sense of how hard it is to an understand a program, consider the following code segment, which is an nonindented version of our program that sorted two values.

```
#include <iostream.h>
int main() {
cout << "Please enter two numbers: " << flush;
int Value1;
int Value2;
cin >> Value1 >> Value2;
if (Value1 > Value2) {
int RememberValue1 = Value1;
Value1 = Value2;
Value2 = RememberValue1; }
cout << "The input numbers in sorted order: " <<
Value1 << " " << Value2 << endl;
return 0;
}
```

If the color of the rectangles is the same, then the equality operator returns true and the statement

```
cout << "Rectangles have the same color";
```

is executed, which displays the message denoting similarity. If the rectangles have different colors, then the equality operator returns false and the statement

```
cout << "Rectangles have different colors";
```

is executed, which displays the message denoting difference. Either way execution continues with the statement

```
cout << endl;
```

In the following code segment, two input values are extracted, and the larger of the values is displayed.

```
cout << "Please enter two numbers: " << flush;
int Value1;
int Value2;
cin >> Value1 >> Value2;
int Larger;
if (Value1 < Value2)   // is Value2 larger?
   Larger = Value2;    // yes, Value2 is larger
else // (Value1 >= Value2)
   Larger = Value1;    // no, Value1 is larger
cout << "The larger of " << Value1 << " and "
 << Value2 << " is " << Larger << endl;
```

After extracting input values Value1 and Value2, the code segment evaluates the expression (Value1 < Value2) in an **if-else** statement.

```
if (Value1 < Value2)   // is Value2 larger?
   Larger = Value2;    // yes, Value2 is larger
else // (Value1 >= Value2)
   Larger = Value1;    // no, Value1 is larger
```

If the expression is true, Value2 is the larger of the two inputs and it is used to set object Larger. Observe the semicolon following this assignment; it indicates that the action associated with a true test expression is completed.

If the expression (Value1 < Value2) is instead false, Value1 is at least as large as Value2. Therefore, in the **else** part, Value1 is used to set object Larger.

Thus our analysis shows that when this **if-else** statement is completed, Larger is appropriately set and can be used as needed.

Our next example, Program 4.2, extracts three values and determines the smallest of those values. This program uses **if-else** statements embedded within other **if-else** statements to accomplish its task.

After extracting the three input values Value1, Value2, and Value3, Program 4.2 compares Value1 with Value2. Suppose that Value1 is no larger than Value2; then in this case the program proceeds to evaluate whether Value1 is no larger than Value3. If Value1 is no larger than Value3, then Value1 is the smallest of the three values. If Value1 is larger than Value3, Value3 must be the smallest of the three inputs. This must be so because Value3 is smaller than Value1, which in turn is no bigger than Value2.

If in the initial comparison of Value1 and Value2, it is the case that Value1 is larger than Value2, then the smaller of Value2 and Value3 is the smallest of the three input values. Program 4.2 makes this determination within the **else** statement associated with the initial **if** statement.

As noted previously, a consistent indentation scheme makes the logic more understandable to a reader, but it does not affect the translation of the program. Language syntax and semantics rules precisely determine how a program is to be translated. They ensure that there is no ambiguity in determining which **else** is associated with which **if**. The rules in this regard are quite sim-

Program 4.2

*Demonstration of an
embedded if statement*

```
// Program 4.2: Determines smallest of three numbers
#include <iostream.h>
int main() {
    cout << "Please enter three numbers: " << flush;
    int Value1;
    int Value2;
    int Value3;
    cin >> Value1 >> Value2 >> Value3;
    int Smallest;
    if (Value1 <= Value2) {
        // Value1 is at most Value2
        if (Value1 <= Value3)
            // Value1 is also at most Value2
            Smallest = Value1;
        else // Value3 < Value1
            // Value3 is less than Value1 which is at most
            // Value2
            Smallest = Value3;
    }
    else { // Value2 < Value1
        // Value2 is less than Value1
        if (Value2 <= Value3)
            // Value2 is also at most Value3
            Smallest = Value2;
        else // Value3 < Value2
            // Value3 is less than Value2 which is at most
            // Value1
            Smallest = Value3;
    }
    cout << "The smallest of "
     << Value1 << ", " << Value2 << ", and " << Value3
     << " is " << Smallest << endl;

    return 0;
}
```

ple. Preceding the **else**, there must be either a single statement or a group of statements within curly braces. In front of this statement or statement list, there must be an **if** followed by a parenthetic expression. The **else** is associated with that **if**. For example, consider

```
if (P)
    if (Q)
        cout << "A" << endl; // P is true, Q is true
    else // not Q
        cout << "B" << endl; // P is true, Q is false
                            // true
```

In this segment, the **else** and its statement are associated with the **if** statement that evaluates Q. For the string "B" to be displayed, expression P must be true and expression Q must be false.

In the next code segment, curly braces surround the inner **if** statement.

```
if (P) {
    if (Q)
        cout << "A" << endl; // P is true, Q is true
}
else
    cout << "B" << endl;    // P is false, Q is
                            // unknown
```

Because of these braces, the **else** is matched to the first **if** statement. Therefore, string `"B"` is displayed whenever P is false, regardless of the value of Q.

4.3.2

Sorting three numbers

Sometimes we want to test which one of several expressions is true and then execute the appropriate action. For example, Program 4.3 extracts three input numbers and displays those numbers in sorted order; that is, nondecreasing order. We use the term nondecreasing rather than ascending because the input values may contain duplicates.

For three numbers, there are only six possible number orderings that need to be considered.

- Value1 ≤ Value2 ≤ Value3
- Value1 ≤ Value3 ≤ Value2
- Value2 ≤ Value1 ≤ Value3
- Value2 ≤ Value3 ≤ Value1
- Value3 ≤ Value1 ≤ Value2
- Value3 ≤ Value2 ≤ Value1

The program first tests whether the inputs Value1, Value2, and Value3 are already sorted. If the input values are sorted, then they are copied to Output1, Output2, and Output3. These three "output" objects record the correct sorted ordering. Observe that the test expression is

```
(Value1 <= Value2) && (Value2 <= Value3)
```

and not

```
(Value1 <= Value2 <= Value3)
```

This alternative expression has the right mathematical look but is wrong in terms of programming. Because of operator precedence, the alternative expression is equivalent to

```
(Value1 <= Value2) <= Value3
```

which compares a logical value (the result of comparing Value1 to Value2) to Value3. Thus the alternative expression does not accomplish what is needed and should not be used.

If the three input values are not in sorted order, then a test is made to determine whether Value1 is the smallest, Value3 is the middle value, and

Program 4.3

*Demonstration of an
if-else-if construct*

```cpp
// Program 4.3: Sorts three numbers
#include <iostream.h>

int main() {
  // extract inputs and define outputs
  cout << "Please enter three numbers:" << flush;
  int Value1;
  int Value2;
  int Value3;
  cin >> Value1 >> Value2 >> Value3;

  int Output1;
  int Output2;
  int Output3;

  // determine which of the six orderings is applicable
  if ((Value1 <= Value2) && (Value2 <= Value3)) {
    // Value1 <= Value2 <= Value3
    Output1 = Value1;
    Output2 = Value2;
    Output3 = Value3;
  }
  else if ((Value1 <= Value3) && (Value3 <= Value2)) {
    // Value1 <= Value3 <= Value2
    Output1 = Value1;
    Output2 = Value3;
    Output3 = Value2;
  }
  else if ((Value2 <= Value1) && (Value1 <= Value3)) {
    // Value2 <= Value1 <= Value3
    Output1 = Value2;
    Output2 = Value1;
    Output3 = Value3;
  }
  else if ((Value2 <= Value3) && (Value3 <= Value1)) {
    // Value2 <= Value3 <= Value1
    Output1 = Value2;
    Output2 = Value3;
    Output3 = Value1;
  }
  else if ((Value3 <= Value1) && (Value1 <= Value2)) {
    // Value3 <= Value1 <= Value2
    Output1 = Value3;
    Output2 = Value1;
    Output3 = Value2;
  }
  else { // (Value3 <= Value2) && (Value2 <= Value1)
    // Value3 <= Value2 <= Value1
    Output1 = Value3;
    Output2 = Value2;
    Output3 = Value1;
  }

  // display results
  cout << Value1 << " " << Value2 << " " << Value3
   << " in sorted order is " << Output1 << " "
   << Output2 << " " << Output3 << endl;
  return 0;
}
```

Value2 is the largest value. If this test evaluates true, then Value1 is copied to Output1, Value2 is copied to Output3, and Value3 is copied to Output2. If instead this test evaluates false, another ordering is considered. The testing process continues until five different orderings have been considered and rejected. At that point there is only one untried ordering, and it must represent the sorted ordering.

The multiple occurrences of **else if** in Program 4.3 are not applications of a new statement. Instead they are a repositioning of the **else** occurrences and the action statements associated with those occurrences. The indentation scheme and structuring of Program 4.3 reflects that the program is testing a series of expressions and executing the actions associated with the first expression that evaluates to true.

If in Program 4.3, we had instead consistently increased the indentation level as the **if** statements are embedded within the **else** statements, there would have been a considerable shifting of the code towards the right. That shifting would make it hard to present the statements in a coherent manner.

4.4
CONDITIONAL EXECUTION USING THE SWITCH STATEMENT

A software engineer is sometimes confronted with a programming task where the action to be executed depends upon the value of a specific integral expression. The **if-else-if** construct can be used to solve such tasks by separately comparing the desiring expression to a particular value and if the expression and value are equal, then executing the appropriate action. For example, suppose we need to report whether the current character ch is a vowel. Using **if** statements, the code would look like the following:

```
if ((ch == 'a') || (ch == 'A'))
   cout << ch << " is a vowel" << endl;
else if ((ch == 'e') || (ch == 'E'))
   cout << ch << " is a vowel" << endl;
else if ((ch == 'i') || (ch == 'I'))
   cout << ch << " is a vowel" << endl;
else if ((ch == 'o') || (ch == 'O'))
   cout << ch << " is a vowel" << endl;
else if ((ch == 'u') || (ch == 'U'))
   cout << ch << " is a vowel" << endl;
else
   cout << ch << " is not a vowel" << endl;
```

Because such programming tasks occur frequently, the C++ language includes a **switch** statement. Our vowel reporting task can be done in a more succinct and readable manner using that statement.

```
switch (ch) {
    case 'a': case 'A':
    case 'e': case 'E':
    case 'i': case 'I':
    case 'o': case 'O':
    case 'u': case 'U':
        cout << ch << " is a vowel" << endl;
        break;
    default:
        cout << ch << " is not a vowel" << endl;
}
```

As our example suggests, the **switch** statement has the following syntax:

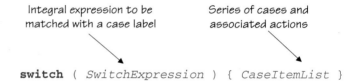

where *SwitchExpression* is an integral expression and *CaseItemList* has the following syntax:

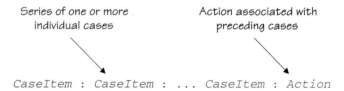

where an individual *CaseItem* consists of either the keyword **case** and a constant integral expression or the *CaseItem* is the keyword **default**.

Each *CaseExpression* must represent a different value.

The *Action* associated with a *CaseItemList* is either a single statement or a group of statements. Even if the *Action* is a group of statements, no enclosing curly braces are required.

When a **switch** statement is executed, its *SwitchExpression* is evaluated and if the value of that expression equals the value of a *CaseExpression* in that **switch** statement, then flow of control is transferred to the *Action* associated with the matching *CaseExpression*. As in our vowel code segment, an *Action* can be preceded by several cases. When this occurs, the *Action* is executed whenever one of the specified cases applies.

If no *CaseExpression* matches the value of the *SwitchExpression* and if a **default** case is supplied, then the *Action* associated with the **default** case is executed. In our preceding example, it is the **default** case that processes the nonvowel characters. In practice, most **switch** statements include a **default** *Action*—it checks that no unexpected condition has occurred.

What happens after the selected *Action* is executed depends upon the statements that make up the *Action*. Normally, the last statement in an *Action* is a **break** statement. The **break** statement indicates that the **switch** statement has completed its task and that the flow of control should continue with the statement after the **switch** statement. Thus, in the preceding vowel calculation example, the **break** statement ensures that after displaying a message indicating the character is a vowel, there is no second message indicating the character is not a vowel. Without a **break** statement, the remaining statements in the **switch** statement are *also* executed! This behavior may seem odd, but it is the way the **switch** statement works.

Because of the requirement that both the *SwitchExpression* and the individual *CaseExpressions* be integral, the **switch** statement cannot be used to determine actions based upon the value of a floating-point object. Such processing requires **if-else-if** statements.

In the next code segment, if the value of i lies between two and five, then one of the **case** expressions matches i and the string "Hello, world" is displayed i times.

```
switch (i) {
    case 5:
        cout << "Hello, world" << endl;
    case 4:
        cout << "Hello, world" << endl;
    case 3:
        cout << "Hello, world" << endl;
    case 2:
        cout << "Hello, world" << endl;
    default:
        cout << "Hello, world" << endl;
}
```

The multiple string insertions occur for these cases because the flow of control is allowed to continue through the various actions; that is, there are no **break** statements. If the value of i does not lie between two and five, then the **default** action is executed and the string is displayed just once. A flowchart of this segment is given in Figure 4.4.

Figure 4.4

Flowchart of switch statement without break statements

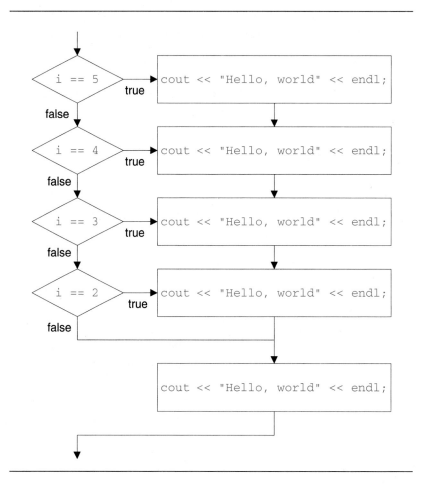

4.5

COMPUTING A REQUESTED EXPRESSION

We now consider developing a very simple calculator program that computes and displays the result of a single requested operation. Our problem has the following description:

> The input to the problem is a pair of operand numbers separated by an arithmetic operator. If the requested operation is defined for the values of its operands, then the operation is computed and displayed to the standard output stream. If either the requested operation is not defined or if its operands are inappropriate, then an error message is displayed to the standard output stream.

For example, if the input is

```
15 * 20
```

then the program displays

```
15 * 20 equals 300.
```

If the operator is not a legal one as in the following example

```
24 ~ 25
```

then the program displays

```
~ is unrecognized operation.
```

As a final example, if the denominator for a division operation is zero as in the following input

```
23 / 0
```

then the program displays the following

```
23 / 0 cannot be computed: denominator is 0.
```

An algorithm for the problem would have three simple steps.

Step 1.   Prompt and extract expression to be calculated. The expression operands are integers; the expression operator is a character.

Step 2.   Validate and compute expression.

Step 2.1   Determine type of operator

Step 2.2   Determine whether operands are appropriate

Step 2.3   Compute expression that corresponds to input operands and operator.

Step 3.   Display result.

Although an argument can be made that the validation and the computation of the expression should be made in separate steps, it is more easily done in a combined step. The translations of step 1 and step 3 into C++ are straightforward and can be found in Program 4.4.

The translation of step 2 in Program 4.4 is easily accomplished using a **switch** statement. The **switch** statement stores the result of the operation in object Result. The operands to be manipulated are objects LeftOperand and RightOperand. The operator is maintained in object Operator.

The **switch** statement treats each of the four arithmetic operators as a separate **case**. For addition, subtraction, and multiplication no validation of the operands is necessary, so the result can be immediately determined. If the input expression is a division operation, RightOperand must be checked to determine whether it is nonzero. If RightOperand is nonzero, the division is computed. If instead RightOperand is zero, an error is displayed and the program returns with a nonzero value. As noted previously, a program return value of zero indicates success, and a nonzero program return value indicates that the desired activity cannot be properly performed The flowchart for the switch statement is given in Figure 4.5.

Program 4.4

Calculate a simple input arithmetic expression

```cpp
// Program 4.4: Compute a simple arithmetic expression
#include <iostream.h>
int main() {
   // prompt and extract desired operation
   cout << "Please enter a simple expression "
    << "(number operator number): " << flush;
   int LeftOperand;
   int RightOperand;
   char Operator;
   cin >> LeftOperand >> Operator >> RightOperand;

   // validate and compute desired operation
   int Result;
   switch (Operator) {
      case '+':
         Result = LeftOperand + RightOperand;
         break;
      case '-':
         Result = LeftOperand - RightOperand;
         break;
      case '*':
         Result = LeftOperand * RightOperand;
         break;
      case '/':
         if (RightOperand != 0)
            Result = LeftOperand / RightOperand;
         else {
            cout << LeftOperand << " / "
             << RightOperand << "cannot be computed:"
             << " denominator is 0." << endl;
            return 1;
         }
         break;
      default:
         cout << Operator
          << " is unrecognized operation." << endl;
         return 1;
   }
   // display result
   cout << LeftOperand << " " << Operator << " "
    << RightOperand << " equals " << Result << endl;

   return 0;
}
```

4.6

VALIDATING A DATE

We next develop a program that prompts a user for a date and then determines whether that date is valid. The program is expanded in the exercises to compute the day of the year (e.g., February 12 is the 43rd day of the year). Our problem description is simple.

C++
Language

The ? : operator

The operator ? : can sometimes be used in place of a conditional statement. The operator has the following form:

TestExpression ? *Expression*$_1$: *Expression*$_2$

When executed, *TestExpression* is evaluated first. If *TestExpression* is true then the value of the operation is *Expression*$_1$; otherwise, the value of the operation is *Expression*$_2$. A colon separates the two expressions. The operator is used in the following code segment to assign the lesser of two input values to Min.

```
int Input1;
int Input2;
cin >> Input1 >> Input2;
int Min = Input1 <= Input2 ? Input1 : Input2;
```

Figure 4.5

Flowchart for switch statement using break statements

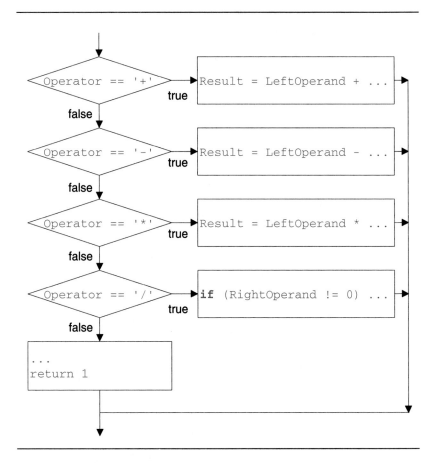

Extract a month, day, and year and determine whether the date is a valid one. If the program is given a valid date, an appropriate message is displayed. If instead the program is given an invalid date, an explanatory message is given. Note: To recognize whether the date is valid, we must be able to determine if the year is a leap year.

An example of the expected input/output behavior for a valid date follows.

```
Please enter a date (mm dd yyyy): 4 30 2000
4/30/2000 is a valid date.
```

An example of the expected input/output behavior for a date with an invalid month is

```
Please enter a date (mm dd yyyy): 13 1 2000
Invalid month: 13
```

Finally, an example of the expected input/output behavior for a date with an invalid day in a month is

```
Please enter a date (mm dd yyyy): 2 29 1899
Invalid day of month: 29
```

Before developing an algorithm for the problem, we first give the rules for determining whether a year is a leap year.

To be a leap year, the year must be evenly divisible by four. However, not all years evenly divisible by four are leap years. Years whose last two digits are zero are *century years*; for example, 1800, 1900, and 2000 are century years. Noncentury years that are evenly divisible by four are always leap years. However, century years are leap years only if they are evenly divisible by four hundred. The years 1600 and 2000 are leap years; 1700, 1800, and 1900 are not leap years. These rules are captured in the Venn diagram given in Figure 4.6.

Figure 4.6

Venn diagram capturing leap year specification

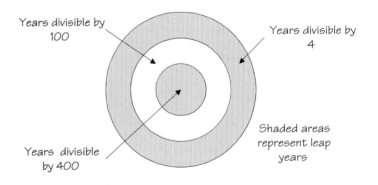

Using the problem description and the rules for determining whether a year is a leap year suggests the following algorithm:

Step 1. Prompt and read the month, day, and year.
Step 2. Determine whether year is a leap year.

Step 2.1	If the year is not evenly divisible by four, the year is not a leap year.
Step 2.2	If the year is evenly divisible by four hundred, the year is a leap year.
Step 2.3	If the year is a century year and not evenly divisible by four hundred, the year is not a leap year.
Step 2.4	If none of the previous situations apply, the year is a leap year.
Step 3.	Validate date.
Step 3.1	If the month is invalid, display an error message and quit.
Step 3.2	If the day is invalid for the month, display an error message and quit.
Step 3.3	If the month and day are valid, announce date is valid

Translating step 1 is straightforward and a code segment to accomplish it can be found at the end of this section in Program 4.5. Translating step 2 can be accomplished by examining the input year to determine which one of the four cases described in the step applies. The important piece of information to be derived in this step is knowing the number of days in February for the given year. This information is maintained in object `DaysInFebruary`. An **if-else-if** construct can be used to set that object.

```
int DaysInFebruary;
if ((Year % 4) != 0)
   DaysInFebruary = 28;
else if ((Year % 400) == 0)
   DaysInFebruary = 29;
else if ((Year % 100) == 0)
   DaysInFebruary = 28;
else
   DaysInFebruary = 29;
```

In the preceding code segment, if the test whether `((Year % 4) != 0)` is true, then the input year is not a leap year and February has 28 days for the input year. If instead `((Year % 4) != 0)` is false, then in the remainder of the **if-else-if** construct, it must be the case that the input year is evenly divisible by four.

If the test `((Year % 400) == 0)` is true, then the input year is automatically a leap year and therefore February has 29 days. If instead, the test `((Year % 400) == 0)` is false, then the input year can be a leap year only if it is not evenly divisible by 100. The last **else-if** test determines whether this is true.

The validation in step 3 can be accomplished by first determining how many days are in the input month and then making sure the input day lies in the interval defined by the first and last days of the month.

The number of days in the input month can be calculated by determining to which group the input month belongs: months with 31 days, months with 30 days, or February. Although an **if-else-if** construct would work, a **switch** statement provides a more readable code segment.

```
int DaysInMonth;
switch (Month) {
   case January: case March: case May: case July:
   case August: case October: case December:
       DaysInMonth = 31;
       break;
   case April: case June: case September:
   case November:
       DaysInMonth = 30;
       break;
   case February:
       DaysInMonth = DaysInFebruary;
       break;
   default:
       cout << "Invalid month: " << Month << endl;
       return 1;
}
```

The cases for the preceding **switch** statement use named constants for the various months that must be previously defined. The definition of these constants can be done in two ways. One method is to define each constant separately.

```
const int January = 1;
const int February = 2;
const int March = 3;
const int April = 4;
const int May = 5;
const int June = 6;
const int July = 7;
const int August = 8;
const int September = 9;
const int October = 10;
const int November = 11;
const int December = 12;
```

However, C++ provides the **enum** statement to define a collection of related symbolic constants. The collection of constants forms a type. In an **enum** definition, the constants are listed in ascending order of value. We can use the **enum** statement to define a type MonthsOfYear whose values are 1 through 12.

```
enum MonthsOfYear {January = 1, February = 2,
   March = 3, April = 4, May = 5, June = 6, July = 7,
   August = 8, September = 9, October = 10,
   November = 11, December = 12};
```

The preceding statement is our first definition of a nonfundamental type. Such types are called *programmer-defined* types. The use of **enum** method is usually preferred over the first method because it gives the programmer the ability to define objects of that derived type. Such a definition gives more information to a reader of code about the possible values for the object even if the name of the object itself does not.

```
MonthsOfYear M;
MonthsOfYear BirthdayMonth = April;
MonthsOfYear SpringBreak = March;
```

enum constants, while integral, are not **int** objects. This fact means we cannot use **int** arithmetic operators on **enum**-type objects. Also note that in referring to an **enum** constant, we do *not* use quotes. For example, to refer to our constant for the fourth month of the year, we use April and not "April". April is an identifier, while "April" is a string.

If the input month is a valid month, the **switch** statement correctly assigns the object DaysInMonth. An invalid month is processed by the **default** case of the **switch** statement. An invalid value causes an appropriate error message to be displayed and the program to terminate by returning a nonzero (unsuccessful) value.

Once object DaysInMonth is determined, an **if** statement can be used to test whether Day is valid. If Day is less than one or if it exceeds DaysIn-Month, an error message is displayed and the program terminated with a return value of one.

```
if ((Day < 1) || (Day > DaysInMonth)) {
    cout << "Invalid day of month: " << Day << endl;
    return 1;
}
```

C++
Language

Specifying "valueless" constants

Although **enum** type MonthsOfYear needs particular values for its constants, it is not a general requirement that the programmer supply actual values for **enum** constants. C++ will automatically generate values for the constants as is the case in this definition of musical genres.

```
enum Music {Classical, Country, Jazz, Popular,
    Soul, Rap, Rock};
```

Our type color used to describe the color of our various Rectangle-Shape objects is also defined automatically.

```
enum color {White, Red, Green, Blue, Yellow, Cyan,
    Magenta};
```

If the programmer does not supply a value, then the first constant in the list will have value 0, the second constant will have value 1, and so on. This feature is useful when concepts with no specific values need to be represented.

If the expression ((Day < 1) || (Day > DaysInMonth)) is false, then the input date is a valid date. It is not necessary to group the remaining actions in the program within an **else** statement because if the expression is true, the program terminates with the execution of the **return** statement. Therefore, if program execution reaches the insertion statement that follows this **if** statement, we know it is the case that Day has a proper value.

This completes our analysis and development of the date validation program. The entire implementation is given in Program 4.5.

4.7

ITERATION USING THE WHILE STATEMENT

Suppose we want to calculate the average of a list of five numbers that are to be extracted from the standard input stream. We might write something similar to the following code segment:

```
float Value1;
float Value2;
float Value3;
float Value4;
float Value5;
cin >> Value1 >> Value2 >> Value3 >> Value4
  >> Value5;
float Average = (Value1 + Value2 + Value3 + Value4
  + Value5)/5;
```

Now suppose that we needed to calculate the average of a list with 1,000 values. Simply modifying the previous code segment is too unwieldy. A better way is to write a code segment with an iterative component that repeatedly gets the next input value and then adds that value to a sum of values processed so far.

Step 1.   Set the running total to zero.

Step 2.   Set the number of values processed so far to zero.

Step 3.   If the number of values processed so far is equal to the list size proceed to step 6.

Step 4.   Process the next value.

Step 4.1   Extract the next value.

Step 4.2   Add the new value to the running total of values.

Step 4.3   Increment the number of values processed so far by one.

Step 5.   Repeat step 3.

Step 6.   Divide the running total by the list size to compute the average.

A simple way of having an action repeatedly executed in a program is through the **while** statement. The construct has the following form:

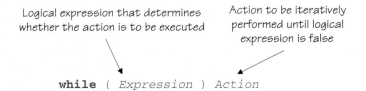

Logical expression that determines whether the action is to be executed

Action to be iteratively performed until logical expression is false

while (*Expression*) *Action*

Program 4.5

Determine whether an input date is valid

```cpp
// Program 4.5: Determine whether user date is valid
#include <iostream.h>
int main() {
  enum MonthsOfYear {January = 1, February = 2,
   March = 3, April = 4, May = 5, June = 6,
   July = 7, August = 8, September = 9,
   October = 10, November = 11, December = 12};

  // prompt and extract date
  cout << "Please supply a date (mm dd yyyy): "
   << flush;
  int Month;
  int Day;
  int Year;
  cin >> Month >> Day >> Year;

  // compute days in February
  int DaysInFebruary;
  if ((Year % 4) != 0)
    DaysInFebruary = 28;
  else if ((Year % 400) == 0)
    DaysInFebruary = 29;
  else if ((Year % 100) == 0)
    DaysInFebruary = 28;
  else
    DaysInFebruary = 29;

  // if month is valid, determine how many days it has
  int DaysInMonth;
  switch (Month) {
    case January: case March: case May: case July:
    case August: case October: case December:
      DaysInMonth = 31;
      break;
    case April: case June: case September:
    case November:
      DaysInMonth = 30;
      break;
    case February:
      DaysInMonth = DaysInFebruary;
      break;
    default:
      cout << "Invalid month: " << Month << endl;
      return 1;
  }

  // determine whether input day is valid
  if ((Day < 1) || (Day > DaysInMonth)) {
    cout << "Invalid day of month: " << Day << endl;
    return 1;
  }

  // display result
  cout << Month << "/" << Day << "/" << Year
   << " is a valid date" << endl;

  return 0;
}
```

where *Expression* is a logical expression and *Action* is either a statement or a list of statements nested within curly braces. The *Action* is often called the *body* of the **while** statement.

When a **while** statement is executed, its *Expression* is first evaluated. If the *Expression* is true, the *Action* is executed. The evaluation process is then repeated; if the *Expression* is again true, the *Action* is repeated. This process is called *looping* and it continues until the *Expression* is false. At that point, execution continues with the next statement in the program. This process is demonstrated pictorially in the flowchart of Figure 4.7.

Figure 4.7

Flowchart representation of a while construct

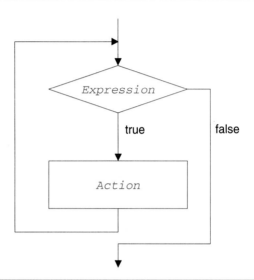

Program 4.6 uses a **while** statement to succinctly solve our problem of averaging five input values. The program first defines a constant ListSize to represent the number of values to be processed. Object ValuesProcessed is then defined. Its role is to reflect the number of values that have been processed. Since no values have been processed as of yet, ValuesProcessed is initialized to 0.

An *invariant* is a programmer-stated rule regarding program behavior. In discussing Program 4.6, we will show throughout its execution, the value of ValuesProcessed always reflects the number of values that have been processed. As a result, the behavior of ValuesProcessed is an invariant of the program. Ensuring that programmer claims regarding object behavior are invariants is an important part of programming with loops. The correct operation of loops can break down when an object's role is ambiguous.

A running total of the input values processed so far is maintained in ValueSum. Like ValuesProcessed, ValueSum is initialized to zero. That object ValueSum reflects the sum of the values processed is to be another invariant of our program.

Program 4.6

*Demonstration
program for the while
statement*

```cpp
// Program 4.6: Compute average of five numbers
#include <iostream.h>
int main() {
    const int ListSize = 5;

    int ValuesProcessed = 0;  // no values processed yet
    float ValueSum = 0;       // no running total

    cout << "Please enter " << ListSize
      << " numbers" << endl;

    while (ValuesProcessed < ListSize) {
        // there are more values to process
        float Value;
        cin >> Value;         // extract the next value
        ValueSum += Value;    // add value to running total
        ++ValuesProcessed;    // increment number of values
                              // that have been processed
    }

    float Average = ValueSum / ValuesProcessed;
    cout << "Average: " << Average << endl;

    return 0;
}
```

At this point in Program 4.6, we are ready to process the inputs, so a prompt is issued to the user.

As long as the number of values processed so far is less than the size of the list, there are more values to consider. This condition corresponds to the **while** loop's test expression (ValuesProcessed < ListSize). If the expression is true, there are still additional values to process; if the expression is false, there are no more values to extract. Since processing a value requires several statements, the **while** loop's body is surrounded by curly braces.

```cpp
while (ValuesProcessed < ListSize) {
    float Value;
    cin >> Value;
    ValueSum += Value;
    ++ValuesProcessed;
}
```

The first statement within the body defines an object local to the loop, named Value, to hold the extraction. The extraction then occurs, and the input value is added to the running total ValueSum. The processing of the current value is now finished. Therefore, the number of values that have been processed, ValuesProcessed, is incremented. Thus, our invariants regarding ValueSum and ValuesProcessed remain true.

The expression (ValuesProcessed < ListSize) is then reevaluated. If the expression evaluates to true, the **while** loop body is again executed. This process continues until ListSize values have been processed. At that point, expression (ValuesProcessed < ListSize) evaluates to false.

Execution then continues at the statement following the **while** statement, where the object Average is defined and initialized using the running total divided by the list size, which is the number of values processed. We know that the average is correctly computed because ValueSum and ValuesProcessed were correctly maintained.

```
float Average = ValueSum / ValuesProcessed;
```

By using this repetitive action approach, we gain flexibility. If the list size subsequently changes, updating the code segment is straightforward—just use the new list size value in the definition of constant ListSize.

Let's trace through Program 4.6 to better understand how it works. Suppose the input stream contains the values

```
3 9 4 7 17
```

After the first three definitions in our program, the objects defined so far have the following representation:

ListSize	10
ValuesProcessed	0
ValueSum	0.0

When the **while** test expression is evaluated, 0 is less than 5, so the body of the loop is executed. The extraction assigns a 3 to object Value because the 3 is the first value in our input stream. The two assignments then respectively increment ValueSum by 3 and ValuesProcessed by 1. After the first iteration, the objects have the following representation:

ListSize	5
ValuesProcessed	1
ValueSum	3.0
Value	3.0

The **while** test expression is then reevaluated. Because 1 is less than 5, the body of the loop is again executed. The extraction now assigns a 9 to Value (9 is the second value in the input stream). The assignment statements then respectively increment ValueSum by 9 and ValuesProcessed by 1. After the second iteration, the objects have the following representation.

ListSize	5
ValuesProcessed	2
ValueSum	12.0
Value	9.0

The **while** test expression is then evaluated for a third time. Because 2 is less than 5, the body of the loop is again executed. The extraction assigns a 4 to object Value (4 is the third value in the input stream). The two assignments then respectively increment ValueSum by 4 and ValuesProcessed by 1. After this iteration, the objects have the following representation.

ListSize	5
ValuesProcessed	3
ValueSum	16.0
Value	4.0

The **while** test expression is then evaluated for a fourth time. Because 3 is less than 5, the body of the loop is again executed. The extraction assigns a 7 to object Value (7 is the fourth value in the input stream). The two assignments then respectively increment ValueSum by 7 and ValuesProcessed by 1. After this iteration, the objects have the following representation.

ListSize	5
ValuesProcessed	4
ValueSum	23.0
Value	7.0

The **while** test expression is then evaluated for a fifth time. Because 4 is less than 5, the body of the loop is again executed. The extraction assigns a 17 to object Value (17 is the fifth value in the input stream). The two assignments then respectively increment ValueSum by 17 and ValuesProcessed by 1. After this iteration, the objects have the following representation.

ListSize	5
ValuesProcessed	5
ValueSum	40.0
Value	17.0

The **while** test expression is then evaluated for a sixth time. Because 5 is not less than 5, the **while** statement is terminated and execution continues with the definition of Average which is set to 8.0.

The average calculation problem can be solved in an alternative manner that provides even greater list processing flexibility. This alternative method is given in Program 4.7. This new program differs from Program 4.6 in one significant way. In Program 4.6, it is necessary to know the size of the list at the beginning of the computation, while in Program 4.7, the list size so far is calcu-

Program 4.7

Computing the average of an arbitrary list of values

```
// Program 4.7: Computes average of a list of values
#include <iostream.h>

int main() {
   cout << "Please enter list of numbers" << endl;

   int ValuesProcessed = 0;
   float ValueSum = 0;
   float Value;

   while (cin >> Value) {
      ValueSum += Value;
      ++ValuesProcessed;
   }

   if (ValuesProcessed > 0) {
      float Average = ValueSum / ValuesProcessed;
      cout << "Average: " << Average << endl;
   }
   else
      cout << "No list to average" << endl;

   return 0;
}
```

lated during program execution through the object `ValuesProcessed`. Note that the invariants regarding `ValuesProcessed` and `ValueSum` do not change.

The test expression in Program 4.7 that determines whether the **while** loop body is to be executed is `(cin >> Value)`. The value of an extraction operation is normally a reference to the input source stream. However, if the source stream has been exhausted (i.e., there are no more values to extract), then the value of the extraction operation is zero. Thus, the expression `(cin >> Value)` is nonzero, if and only if a value has been extracted. This fact means that the extraction expression can be used as the basis for determining whether another value needs to be processed. To indicate that there are to be no more input values, the user types an operating-system-specific escape sequence. For Unix systems, the sequence is normally Ctl-d; for DOS and Windows-based systems, the sequence is Ctl-z.

The processing of the current extracted value, `Value`, again requires that the value be added to the running total `ValueSum`. Similarly, the program must also increment `ValuesProcessed`, as its value represents the size of the list so far.

If a nonempty list was processed, the average can be calculated. To determine whether any values were extracted, a test is made using an **if** statement. If some input values were extracted, then `ListSize` is greater than zero. If instead no values were provided, then no extractions were made and object `ValuesProcessed` keeps its initial value of zero.

**Programmer
Alert**

Faulty while assumptions

It is important to realize that if a **while** expression initially evaluates to false, then its **while** body is never executed. Beginning programmers often make the mistake of assuming that the body is executed at least once. Your programs should never depend on an object getting its initial value within the body of a **while** statement. For example, if there is no more data in the standard input stream before the following code segment begins, then its insertion displays an object that has never been explicitly set.

```
int Number;
while (cin >> Number) {
    cout << "Extracted another value" << endl;
}
cout << "Last input: " << Number;
```

The **break** statement is sometimes used for the early termination of loops. The following code segment extracts and displays input values from the standard input stream `cin` until a specified value is found.

```
int KeyValue;
cin >> KeyValue;
int Input;
while (cin >> Input) {
    if (Input != KeyValue)
        cout << Input << endl;
    else
        break;
}
```

Use of the **break** statement in loops is sometimes discouraged because it can make the program's behavior harder to understand. In particular, it makes invariant claims more difficult to verify. Often, such loops can be easily rewritten to eliminate the **break** statements.

```
int KeyValue;
cin >> KeyValue;
int Input;
while ((cin >> Input) && (Input != KeyValue)) {
    cout << Input << endl;
}
```

4.7.1

Simple text processing

When a stream of text is to be processed, the **while** construct often comes into use. A text stream in general has an unknown number of lines with each line having an unknown number of characters.

In Listing 4.1, a model code segment is given for processing a stream of characters. The segment begins with a section that does whatever preparatory work is necessary for processing the text. A **bool** object MoreLinesToProcess is defined and initialized to keep track of whether additional processing is necessary. A **while** loop then occurs to process the individual lines. Iteration of the **while** loop is controlled by MoreLinesToProcess. The **while** body begins with a preparatory section for processing the characters on the current line. A **bool** object MoreCharactersOnCurrentLine is defined and initialized in this section. The purpose of the object is to indicate whether to process additional characters on the current line.

The values of the two **bool** objects MoreLinesToProcess and More-CharactersOnCurrentLine are to be invariants with respect to the text processing: as long as they are true, there are more lines to process and more characters to process on the current line.

Listing 4.1
Model for text processing

```
// prepare for processing text
bool MoreLinesToProcess = true;
...
while (MoreLinesToProcess) {
   // process next line
   bool MoreCharactersOnCurrentLine = true;
   ...
   while (MoreCharactersOnCurrentLine) {
      // prepare to process next character
      ...
      char CurrentCharacter;
      if (cin.get(CurrentCharacter)) {
         // process CurrentCharacter on current line
         ...
         if (CurrentCharacter == '\n') {
            // current line has no more characters
            MoreCharactersOnCurrentLine = false;
         }
         ...
      }
      else { // no more characters
         MoreCharactersOnCurrentLine = false;
         MoreLinesToProcess = false;
      }
   }
   // finish up processing of current line
   ...
}
// finish up overall processing
...
```

Once preprocessing of a line is finished, the actual processing begins. A **while** loop is used to process the individual characters. This inner **while** loop iterates for each character that needs to be processed. Embedding loops within loops is a powerful programming mechanism; it allows a significant amount of work to be accomplished as the inner loop is run for each iteration of the outer loop.

The body of the inner **while** begins with a preparatory section for an individual character. Part of this preparation is defining a **char** object Current-Character for representing the character that will be extracted.

The extraction into CurrentCharacter occurs in the test expression of an **if** statement. The extraction is not done via the extraction operator <<, but rather through a member function of `cin`. Like `RectangleShape` objects, object `cin` has member functions. This member function `get()` of `cin` attempts to extract the next character from the standard input stream and store it in `CurrentCharacter`. If the attempt is successful, the expression `(cin.get(CurrentCharacter)` evaluates to true; if the extraction is not possible, the expression will evaluate to false. The reason we use `get()` rather than `<<` is that `get()` does not ignore white space—function `get()` extracts all characters. We will discuss other member functions of `cin` in the next chapter.

If function `get()` does extract a character, then that character is processed. The actual processing depends upon the specific character and the specific task intended for the code segment. Since the inner loop needs some way of terminating, the processing of the `CurrentCharacter` generally includes a test of whether the `CurrentCharacter` is the newline character.

Once the characters on the current line have been individually processed and the inner **while** loop is terminated, the next section of code does any post-processing of the line that might be necessary. The outer **while** loop expression is then tested to see if an additional iteration of the inner **while** loop is necessary.

If function `get()` is unable to extract a character, then the code segment sets the two **bool** objects to indicate that the inner and outer **while** loops are to be terminated. Once the outer **while** loop is terminated, a final postprocessing section may occur.

This model segment is used in Program 4.8, which echoes each line of the input stream to the output stream. The echoing is done in a manner that displays uppercase input letters in the lowercase equivalent.

The processing of `CurrentCharacter` uses an **if**-**else**-**if** statement to decide to which one of three cases the `CurrentCharacter` corresponds: the `CurrentCharacter` is a newline; the `CurrentCharacter` is an uppercase alphabetic character; the `CurrentCharacter` is neither a newline nor an uppercase alphabetic character.

```
// process CurrentCharacter on current line
if (CurrentCharacter == '\n') {
    // found the newline that ends the line
    MoreCharactersOnCurrentLine = false;
}
else if ((CurrentCharacter >= 'A')
  && (CurrentCharacter <= 'Z')) {
    // CurrentCharacter is uppercase
    CurrentCharacter = CurrentCharacter - 'A' + 'a';
    cout << CurrentCharacter;
}
else { // nonuppercase character
    cout << CurrentCharacter;
}
```

If the `CurrentCharacter` lies in the ASCII interval `'A'` through `'Z'`, it is uppercase alphabetic. An uppercase alphabetic character can be converted to its lowercase equivalent by subtracting the representation of `'A'` from the rep-

Program 4.8

*Echoing input in its
lowercase equivalent*

```
// Program 4.8: Echo input to standard output
// converting uppercase to lowercase along the way
#include <iostream.h>
int main() {
    // prepare for processing text
    bool MoreLinesToProcess = true;
    while (MoreLinesToProcess) {
        // process next line
        bool MoreCharactersOnCurrentLine = true;
        cout << "Please type a line of text: " << flush;
        while (MoreCharactersOnCurrentLine) {
            // process next character on current line
            char CurrentCharacter;
            if (cin.get(CurrentCharacter)) {
                // process current character on current line
                if (CurrentCharacter == '\n') {
                    // found the newline that ends the line
                    MoreCharactersOnCurrentLine = false;
                }
                else if ((CurrentCharacter >= 'A')
                  && (CurrentCharacter <= 'Z')) {
                    // CurrentCharacter is uppercase
                    CurrentCharacter = CurrentCharacter - 'A'
                      + 'a';
                    cout << CurrentCharacter;
                }
                else { // nonuppercase character
                    cout << CurrentCharacter;
                }
            }
            else { // no more characters
                MoreCharactersOnCurrentLine = false;
                MoreLinesToProcess = false;
            }
        }
        // finish up processing of current line
        cout << endl;
    }
    // finish up overall processing
    return 0;
}
```

resentation of that uppercase alphabetic character and then adding to this difference the representation of `'a'` (the difference represents an offset of how far the `CurrentCharacter` is from the beginning of the alphabet).

```
CurrentCharacter = CurrentCharacter - 'A' + 'a';
```

The only postprocessing needed for a line is the issuing of the newline character (by using `endl` rather than `'\n'`, the insertion is immediately displayed).

4.8

ITERATION USING THE FOR CONSTRUCT

Although the **while** construct has sufficient flexibility to handle all iteration needs, many programming situations require similar forms of action. To make these situations more easily understood, C++ provides two other iteration constructs—the **for** and **do** constructs. We first consider the **for** construct, as it occurs more often; we then briefly consider the **do** construct.

The **for** construct has form

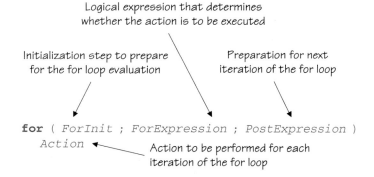

where *ForInit* is either an object definition(s) or an expression; *ForExpression* is a logical expression; *PostExpression* is an expression, and *Action* is either a single statement or a group of statements nested within curly braces. Any of *ForInit*, *ForExpression*, and *PostExpression* may be omitted. The semantics are demonstrated pictorially in Figure 4.8 which gives a flowchart for the **for** construct.

When a **for** statement is reached within a program, *ForInit* is first executed and then *ForExpression* is evaluated (note if *ForExpression* is not supplied, the value true is used instead). If *ForExpression* is true, then *Action* is executed and then *PostExpression* is executed. *ForExpression* is then reevaluated, and if it is again true, the execution of *Action* and *PostExpression* are repeated. This testing of *ForExpression* and execution of *Action* and *PostExpression* continues until *ForExpression* evaluates to false. Evaluation then continues with the next statement in the program.

If *ForExpression* is initially false, then neither *Action* nor *PostExpression* are ever executed—the program immediately continues with the next statement in the program. Most programmers use *ForInit* to do the necessary initialization for the **for** statement and *PostExpression* to do the necessary work to prepare for the next iteration of the **for** statement body.

Figure 4.8

Flowchart representation of a for construct

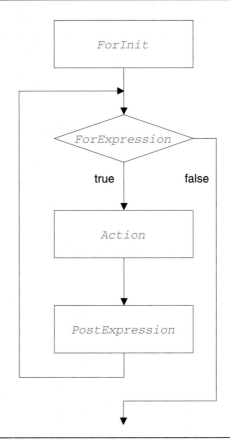

Our next example computes the product of the integers 1 through n. Mathematically this value is called *n*! (pronounced "en-factorial") and its definition is

$$
n! = \begin{cases} 1 & \text{if } n = 0 \\ n \times (n-1) \times \ldots \times 1 & \text{if } n \geq 1 \end{cases}
$$

The following code segment first prompts and extracts an integer value n. It then uses a **for** statement to compute the desired factorial. For simplicity in this and successive examples, we do not validate that the input has the correct form—such testing is left as exercises.

```
cout << "Please enter a postive integer: " << flush;
int n;
cin >> n;
int nfactorial = 1;
for (int i = 2; i <= n; ++i) {
   nfactorial *= i;
}
cout << n << "! = " << nfactorial << endl;
```

Suppose the extraction from the input stream supplies the value 4 for n. The code segment next defines `nfactorial` and initializes it to 1. These objects have representation

n	4
nfactorial	1

The **for** statement begins with a *ForInit* that defines and initializes an object i with the value 2 (the first factor with which we must be concerned). In traditional programming terminology i would be known as the *index variable*. In C++ terminology, i is known as an *iterator*—its value changes with each iteration. The value of i reflects the current factor used in our factorial computation. Since the factors are generated in ascending order, `nfactorial` always reflects the product of n's factors 1 through i-1. This behavior is our invariant. By appropriately updating `nfactorial` with the current factor i and then updating i to the next largest factor, our computation will be successful. At this point our objects have representation

n	4
nfactorial	1
i	2

The **for** statement next compares i with n. Because 2 is less than 4, the **for** loop body is executed. The body scales `nfactorial` by i. The result is that object `nfactorial` has value 2. The expression ++i is then evaluated, causing iterator i to be incremented by 1 so that it has the value 3.

n	4
nfactorial	2
i	3

The loop then reevaluates the expression i <= n. Because 3 is less than 4, the **for** loop body is again executed. In the body, object `nfactorial` is again scaled by object i. The result is that object `nfactorial` has value 6. The expression ++i is then evaluated, causing iterator i to be incremented by 1 so that it has the value 4.

n	4
nfactorial	6
i	4

The loop then reevaluates the expression i <= n. Because 4 equals 4, the **for** loop body is again executed. The scaling of nfactorial by object i gives it the value 24. The expression ++i is then evaluated, causing iterator i to be incremented by 1 so that it has the value 5.

n	4
nfactorial	24
i	5

The loop then reevaluates the expression i <= n. Because 5 is not less than or equal to 4, the **for** statement is over. Execution continues with the insertion statement

```
cout << n << "! = " << nfactorial << endl;
```

which causes output

```
4! = 24
```

Observe that if object n had been either 0 or 1, the *ForExpression* i <= n would be initially false. As a result, the value of nfactorial would remain 1, which is the correct value for 0! and 1!.

Programming Tip

Representing a for statement using a while statement

Any **for** statement can be converted

```
for (ForInit; ForExpression; PostExpression)
    Action;
```

into a **while** statement. This observation is demonstrated by the following code segment whose actions are equivalent to the preceding **for** statement

```
{ForInit;
while (ForExpression) {
    Action;
    PostExpression;
}
}
```

In Program 4.9, we use a **for** statement as the iterative construct to solve our earlier problem of computing the average of a list of input values. The objects used in this program have the same role as they had in Program 4.7 and the same invariants apply regarding their values.

The initialization of ValuesProcessed is the initialization expression of the **for** construct. The definition of ValuesProcessed preceded the **for** statement because the proposed C++ standard states that objects defined in the *ForInit* of a **for** loop can only be used in that **for** statement. If we had defined ValuesProcessed in the **for** statement, we would be unable to use it after the loop in the calculation of the average.

Program 4.9

Computing the average of a list of numbers using a for statement

```cpp
// Program 4.9: Compute the average of an arbitrary
// list of numbers
#include <iostream.h>
int main() {
   cout << "Please enter list of numbers" << endl;
   float ValueSum = 0;
   float Value;
   int ValuesProcessed;

   for (ValuesProcessed = 0; cin >> Value;
    ++ValuesProcessed) {
      ValueSum += Value;
   }

   if (ValuesProcessed > 0) {
      float Average = ValueSum / ValuesProcessed;
      cout << "Average: " << Average << endl;
   }
   else
      cout << "No list to average" << endl;

   return 0;
}
```

The incrementing of `ValuesProcessed` is the preparation statement for the next possible iteration. This organization is chosen because the processing of the current value can be viewed as an updating of the running total.

An important mathematical series is the Fibonacci sequence. We consider this sequence in more detail in Chapter 6. The sequence starts with the following numbers: 1, 1, 2, 3, 5, 8, 13, 21. After the initial two 1's, each number in the sequence is the sum of the two previous numbers. For example, $1 + 1 = 2$, $1 + 2 = 3$, $2 + 3 = 5$, $3 + 5 = 8$, and so on. The following code segment extracts a value n. A **for** loop is then used to display the first n numbers in the sequence. It is assumed that n is at least 2.

```cpp
cout << "Please enter an integer greater than 2: "
 << flush;
int n;
cin >> n;
cout << "The first " << n << " Fibonacci numbers:"
 << endl << 1 << endl << 1 << endl;
int PreviousNumber = 1;
int CurrentNumber = 1;
for (int i = 3; i <= n; ++i) {
   int Sum = PreviousNumber + CurrentNumber;
   cout << Sum << endl;
   PreviousNumber = CurrentNumber;
   CurrentNumber = Sum;
}
```

After the extraction of n, the code segment displays the first two numbers in the sequence. Next, objects `PreviousNumber` and `CurrentNumber` are defined. They represent the two previously processed numbers in the sequence. The **for** loop then iterates n-2 times. Object i is the loop iterator and it takes on the values 3 through n. Each loop iteration, an object Sum is defined to be the sum of two previously processed numbers. Next the value Sum is displayed. The **for** loop body then updates the values of PreviousNumber and CurrentNumber to reflect that another number has been processed.

In our next code segment, we use a **for** loop to display three square RectangleShape objects in a diagonal fashion. The output of the code segment is given in Figure 4.9.

```
SimpleWindow W("One diagonal", 5.5, 2.25);
W.Open();
int i = 0;
for (int j = 1; j <= 3; ++j) {
    RectangleShape S(W, i + j*0.75 + 0.25,
    j*0.75 -0.25, Blue, 0.4, 0.4);
    S.Draw();
}
```

Figure 4.9

Displaying squares along a diagonal

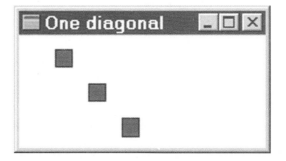

The diagonal producing segment begins by defining a SimpleWindow object W that has a suitable label and size for the task at hand. An object i is then defined and initialized to zero (our next example uses i in a generalization of this code segment to display three diagonals of rectangles). The **for** loop uses j as the iterator. Iterator j takes on in turn, the values 1, 2, and 3. The iterator takes on these values because it is initialized to 1, and it is incremented by 1 after iteration.

Window W, object i and iterator j are used in the definition of a RectangleShape S. Object S is redefined each time through the loop. Each definition assigns to Window W, a blue square RectangleShape whose sides have length 0.4 centimeters. In the first iteration, the center of the RectangleShape being defined is at coordinate (i + j*0.75 + 0.25, j*0.75 - 0.25) = (1, 0.5). In the second iteration, the center of the RectangleShape being defined is (1.75, 1.25). In the third and final iteration, the center of the RectangleShape being defined is (2.5, 2). Even though each time through the loop S is redefined and redrawn to occupy a different position in the window W, the previous versions of S also remain part of the display. This behavior is a characteristic of most windowing systems—an object is removed from a display only by actively invoking some kind of erasing command.

Our next code segment embeds the loop of the previous code segment within another **for** loop.

```
SimpleWindow W("Three diagonals", 5.5, 2.25);
W.Open();
for (int i = 0; i <= 2; ++i) {
    for (int j = 1; j <= 3; ++j) {
        RectangleShape S(W, i + j*0.75 + 0.25,
          j*0.75 -0.25, Blue, 0.4, 0.4);
        S.Draw();
    }
}
```

The outer **for** loop uses an iterator i, which takes on in turn, the values 0, 1, and 2. Because this loop iterates three times, the inner **for** loop is executed three times, and because each execution of the inner loop causes three squares to be drawn, a total of nine squares are drawn altogether. The output of a run of this segment is given in Figure 4.10.

Figure 4.10

Displaying nine squares along three diagonals

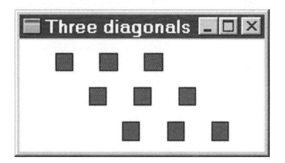

When the outer **for** loop is initiated, i has value 0, so the first three rectangles have centers (1, 0.5), (1.75, 1.25), and (2.5, 2) (as in our previous example). In the second iteration of the outer **for** loop, i now has value 1. This causes the inner **for** loop to generate rectangles with centers (2, 0.5), (2.75, 1.25), and (3.5, 2). The final iteration of the outer **for** loop, generates three more rectangles. They have centers (3, 0.5), (3.75, 4.25), and (2.5, 2).

Programming Tip

Infinite loops

All our **while** and **for** examples include some action that causes the iteration statement to eventually terminate. Without such an occurrence, the programs would have what is known as an *infinite loop*—they would continue to execute until some operating system command was eventually invoked to terminate them. When writing programs make sure that you understand what is going on in your iteration statements. In particular, make sure that they are designed to terminate.

4.9

SOLVING THE LAZY HOBO RIDDLE

The following riddle dates back to the late 19th century (its revival is credited to Will Shortz, crossword puzzle editor of the *New York Times*).

> There were once four hoboes traveling across the country. During their journey they ran short on funds, so they stopped at a farm to look for some work. The farmer said there were 200 hours of work that could be done over the next several weeks. The farmer went on to say that how they divided up the work was up to them. The hoboes agreed to start the next day. The following morning, one of the hoboes—who was markedly smarter and lazier than the other three—said there was no reason for them all to do the same amount of work. This hobo went on to suggest the following scheme. The hoboes would all draw straws. A straw would be marked with a number. The number would indicate both the number of days the drawer must work and the number of hours to be worked on each of those days. For example, if the straw was marked with a 3, the hobo who drew it would work 3 hours a day for 3 days. It goes without saying that the lazy hobo convinced the others to agree to this scheme and that through sleight of hand, the lazy hobo drew the best straw. The riddle is to determine the possible ways to divide up the work according to the preceding scheme.

A solution to the riddle consists of four numbers a, b, c, and d such that $a^2 + b^2 + c^2 + d^2 = 200$. So what we need to do is to systematically generate combinations of four numbers and check whether the current combination has the property that the squares of its numbers sum to 200.

Since the squares of numbers that are 15 or greater exceed 200, the only values that we need to consider for a, b, c, and d occur in the interval 1 to 14. As there is no advantage to evaluate the same combination more than once, we should generate the combinations in a manner that eliminates duplicate combinations. An easy way to ensure no duplications is to generate the combinations in ascending order. As a result, each generated combination will have the property that $a \leq b \leq c \leq d$.

To solve the riddle, we consider the various possibilities for a from the interval 1 to 14. For a given value of a, we consider all possibilities of b, c, and d subject to the constraints discussed above. In particular, the possibilities for b are a through 14. In a similar manner, given that a and b are fixed, we consider all possibilities for c and d. The possible values for c are b through 14. Once a, b, and c have been fixed, the possibilities for d are c through 14. This strategy is implemented in Program 4.10. The program consists essentially of four nested **for** statements where a, b, c, and d are iterators.

The output of a program run follows.

```
Lazy hobo possible solutions
2 4 6 12
6 6 8 8
```

Program 4.10

Solving the lazy hobo riddle

```
// Program 4.10: Display solutions for lazy hobo riddle
#include <iostream.h>
int main() {
   cout << "Lazy hobo possible solutions" << endl;
   for (int a = 1; a <= 14; a++) {
      for (int b = a; b <= 14; b++) {
         for (int c = b; c <= 14; c++) {
            for (int d = c; d <= 14; d++) {
               if (a*a + b*b + c*c + d*d == 200) {
                  cout << a << " " << b << " " << c
                     << " " << d << endl;
               }
            }
         }
      }
   }
   return 0;
}
```

It is interesting to determine how many possible solutions were considered during a run of the program. This task can be done by modifying the program to keep track of how many times the **if** expression is evaluated. It turns out that the **if** statement is executed 2,380 times. This number is large, but it still small compared to $14 \times 14 \times 14 \times 14 = 38,416$, which is number of sequences we would have considered if we had not generated unique combinations in ascending order. We can improve the efficiency of the program by causing the innermost **for** loop to terminate when a*a + b*b + c*c + d*d is greater than 200. Doing so will not cause any legal solutions to be missed (given that the a, b, and c is fixed, any unconsidered value for d will result in a sum of squares also bigger than 200). This modification turns out to lower the number of considered solutions to 1,214.

4.10

ITERATION USING THE DO CONSTRUCT

In some situations an action needs to be done at least once and possibly multiple times. To explicitly show this, a programmer can use the **do** construct. The **do** construct has the following form where *Expression* is a logical expression and *Action* is again either a single statement or a group of statements enclosed with curly braces.

Action to be performed at   Logical expression that determines
least once   whether action is repeated

do *Action* **while** (*Expression*)

The construct begins by executing *Action*. The *Expression* is then evaluated. If *Expression* is true, then the *Action* is repeated. This process continues until *Expression* is false. The semantics are demonstrated pictorially by the flowchart in Figure 4.11.

Figure 4.11

flowchart for do-while statement

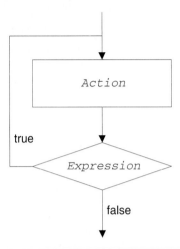

The **do** is sometimes used in the processing of a user reply to a prompt. For example, the following code segment repeatedly issues a prompt and then extracts a single character reply until the reply indicates yes or no. If no reply is given, no is assumed. To simplify the processing of this task, the reply is converted to its lowercase equivalent through the use of the ctype library function tolower() rather than mimicking the manual conversion of Program 4.8. The use of library functions is the focus of our next chapter.

```
char reply;
do {
    cout << "Decision (y, n): " << flush;
    if (cin >> reply)
        reply = tolower(reply);
    else
        reply = 'n';
} while ((reply != 'y') && (reply != 'n'));
```

4.11

POINTS TO REMEMBER

- A logical expression evaluates to true if the value of the expression is either a nonzero integer value or the **bool** value **true**.
- A logical expression evaluates to false if the value of the expression is integer zero or the **bool** value **false**.

History of Computing

The Difference Engine

A major milestone in the march toward the age of the computer occurred in the early 19th century. One of the great problems of that day was the accurate calculation and transcription of the various tables used by scientists and mathematicians. Accuracy was a very important problem because surveyors, bankers, navigators, and engineers relied on these tables. The problem was that the computation and printing of the tables was done largely by hand, and the process was extremely tedious. A young mathematician named Charles Babbage (1792–1871) had an idea for a solution. His idea was to use a machine to compute the tables. The proposed machine, called the "Difference Engine," would be powered by steam and would perform all computations mechanically, and the results would be recorded on metal plates. The metal plates would be used to print the tables, thereby eliminating the possibility of transcription and printing errors.

To understand the name *Difference Engine* and how it was to be used to automate the computation of mathematical tables, it is necessary to briefly discuss how tables were computed back in the 1800s. Most mathematical and physical functions can be approximated by evaluating a polynomial of the form $dx^n + \ldots + cx^2 + bx + a$. For a series of values, polynomials of this form can be evaluated by calculating a table of differences. To illustrate the concept, consider the 2nd-degree polynomial $n^2 + 2n + 22$ and Table 4.7

Table 4.7
Table of differences for a second order polynomial

n	$n^2 + 2n + 22$	Difference$_1$	Difference$_2$
0	22	—	—
1	25	3	—
2	30	5	2
3	37	7	2
4	46	9	2
5	57	11	2
6	70	13	2
7	85	15	2

From inspection of the table, it is easy to see that the last row can be easily computed without evaluating the formula. The value of Difference$_2$ is always 2. The value of Difference$_1$ for row n is the sum of Difference$_1$ and Difference$_2$ for row $n-1$. Thus, the entries for row 7 are 85, 15, and 2. In general, a polynomial of degree n can be evaluated by computing n differences. The Difference Engine was designed to handle polynomials of degree 6.

Babbage realized that construction of the Difference Engine would require considerable resources. He also realized that the construction of the Engine required manufacturing methods far superior to those available.

He addressed the first problem by petitioning the government for funds to support the construction of the equipment. With the support of the Royal Society of London, a preeminent scientific society, he was able to secure £1,500 (about $7,500 in 1823) from the British government. This support is one of the first examples of a government grant to carry out research. Babbage attacked the second problem by making a complete study of the manufacturing methods of the day. He found that better methods for building machine parts were necessary and he focused his efforts on that aspect of the project. Although this effort greatly advanced the state of the art in the milling of machine parts, it did little to advance the construction of the Engine. The project suffered a setback when Babbage lost two children and his wife in the space of a year. The project moved on slowly, and only a portion of the Difference Engine was ever completed (see Figure 4.12). It worked and could solve 2nd-degree equations to six digit accuracy. Unfortunately, Babbage never completed a full Difference Engine. He had conceived of a grander machine, the Analytical Engine, and he chose to devote his time to it.

The Analytical Engine was designed to be general purpose; that is, it could compute any mathematical function, not just one involving differences. Babbage attempted to convince the government to support the development of the Analytical Engine, but his request was refused. Babbage continued to work on the design of the Analytical Engine until his death. Despite the failure to build either the Difference Engine or the Analytical Engine, Babbage's influence should not be underestimated. The ideas embodied in his two engines had a profound influence on computing. For example, the Analytical Engine essentially had all the components that are a part of today's modern computers. It was programmed via punched cards. It had a memory, called the store, and a portion that performed computations that is similar in concept to the processing unit of today's computers.

- Logical expressions can be composed using the logical operators &&, ||, and !. These operators correspond respectively to *and*, *or*, and *not*.

- The relational operators also produce logical values. The relational operators fall into two categories: equality and ordering.

- The equality operators == and != and the ordering operators <, <=, >, and >= are defined for all fundamental and pointer types.

- A logical expression that is being evaluated is subject to the short circuit rule. This rule states that once the overall value of an expression is known, evaluation ceases; that is, if P is true, then the term Q is not evaluated in P || Q because the overall expression is true, and if P is false, then the term Q is not evaluated in P && Q because the overall expression is false.

- The **if** statement has two forms. In both forms, a logical expression is evaluated and if that expression is true, an action is executed. In one of the forms, an action is also specified for when the evaluated expression is false.

Figure 4.12
*Charles Babbage
(1792–1871) and a
portion of the
Difference Engine*

- The expression used to determine the course of action for a conditional or iterative construct is sometimes known as a test expression.

- The **switch** statement takes actions based upon the value of an integral expression. The programmer specifies the case values of interest for that expression, and for each case value the desired action is specified.

- Types defined by a programmer are known as programmer-defined or derived types.

- The **enum** statement is a method for organizing a collection of integral constants into a type.

- A loop is a group of statements whose actions are repeated using an iterative construct.

- The **while** statement permits actions to be repeated while a given logical expression evaluates to true. If the logical expression is initially false, then the action of the construct is never executed; otherwise, the action is repeatedly executed until the test expression evaluates to false.

- The **do** statement is similar in nature to the **while** statement; however, its action is always executed at least once. It has this property because its test expression is not evaluated until after its body is executed.

- The **for** statement is a generalization of the **while** construct that has a test expression and both a one-time loop initialization action and an action that is to be performed once for each execution of the loop body. All parts of a **for** statement are optional. In particular, if the test expression is omitted, then the value true is used instead.

- An iterator is an object that takes on a series of values. An iterator is sometimes known as an index variable. Iterators are generally assigned successive values in loops. The use of iterators is common in **for** loops.

- An object defined in the *ForInit* section of a **for** loop can be used only in that loop.

- As in other parts of programming, loops should be carefully constructed. Actions taken before and during the loop should ensure that the test expression for the loop always makes sense. These actions should also ensure that the loop eventually terminates.

- A invariant is a rule that should be always true. In developing a loop, the designer should be aware of the invariants that can be affected by the loop.

- A **typedef** statement creates a new name for an existing type. Both the new and old names can be used in subsequent definitions.

4.12

EXERCISES

4.1   Suppose the following object definitions are in effect.

```
bool P = false;

bool Q = true;

bool R = true;
```

Evaluate the following expressions:

a) `P && Q || !P && !Q`

b) `P || Q && !P || !Q`

c) `0 == 1 || 0 < 1`

d) `0 == 1 == true`

e) `P && (Q || R)`

f) `!!P`

g) `!i`

h) `!j`

i) `false < true`

j) `j = i`

4.2 Using the operator precedence rules, parenthesize the following expressions:

a) `1 + 2 == 3 * 4`

b) `1 + 2 == 3 * 4 && 5 / 6 == 7`

c) `P == Q <= R`

d) `P < Q == R`

e) `P == Q || R`

f) `P == Q && R`

g) `! 5 < 3 < 4`

h) `P || Q && R || S`

i) `P == Q = R || S`

j) `- 5 < 9 == P && 3 == 17`

4.3 Consider the following code segment:

```
if (i <= j)
    cout << "1" << endl;
else
    cout << "2" << endl;
cout << "3" << endl;
```

a) If `i` is 1 and `j` is 2, what is the output?

b) If `i` is 2 and `j` is 1, what is the output?

c) If `i` is 2 and `j` is 2, what is the output?

4.4 Consider the following code segment:

```
if (i == j)
    cout << "1" << endl;
else if ((i % j) < 3)
    cout <<"2" << endl;
else if (i < (j-1))
    cout <<"3" << endl;
else
    cout <<"4" << endl;
cout << "5" << endl;
```

a) If `i` is 9 and `j` is 4, what is the output?

b) If `i` is 4 and `j` is 9, what is the output?

c) If `i` is 5 and `j` is 6, what is the output?

d) If `i` is 5 and `j` is 9, what is the output?

4.5 Write code segments that implement the following actions:

a) If `i` divided by `j` is 4, then i is set to 100.

b) If `i` times `j` is 8, then i is set to 50, otherwise j is set to 60.

c) If `i` is less than `j`, then j is doubled; if instead i is even, then i is doubled; otherwise, both i and j are incremented by 1.

d) If both `i` and `j` are 0, then i is set 1 and j is set to 2; if instead only i is 0, then i is set to 5 and j is set to 10; if instead only j is 0, then i is set to 10 and j is set to 5; otherwise, both i and j are set to 4.

4.6   Assume the following object definitions are in effect:

```
bool P = false;
bool Q = true;
bool R = true;
```

Consider the following expressions. Determine if they have short-circuit evaluations, and if so, where.

a) `Q && P && R`

b) `Q && P || R`

c) `!Q || (i != j)`

d) `(P || Q && R) && (3 <= 4)`

e) `R || (P || !Q || !R && (4 > 3))`

4.7   Consider the following code segment using **bool** objects A, B, C, and D.

```
if (A && B)
    if (!C || !D)
        cout << "1" << endl;
    else if (D)
        cout << "2" << endl;
    else
        cout << "3" << endl;
else if (C != D)
    cout << "4" << endl;
else if (C)
    cout << "5" << endl;
else
    cout << "6" << endl;
```

a) Give values for A, B, C, and D that cause the preceding code segment to display 1 to the standard output stream.

b) Give values for A, B, C, and D that cause the preceding code segment to display 2 to the standard output stream.

c) Give values for A, B, C, and D that cause the preceding code segment to display 3 to the standard output stream.

d) Give values for A, B, C, and D that cause the preceding code segment to display 4 to the standard output stream.

e) Give values for A, B, C, and D that cause the preceding code segment to display 5 to the standard output stream.

f) Give values for A, B, C, and D that cause the preceding code segment to display 6 to the standard output stream.

4.8   Write the truth table that the following code segment computes.

```
if (P)
    Operation = true;
else if (Q)
    Operation = false;
else
    Operation = true;
```

4.9 Write the truth table that the following code segment computes.

```
if (P)
    if (Q)
        Operation = true;
    else
        Operation = false;
else if (Q)
    Operation = false;
else
    Operation = true;
```

4.10 Write the truth table for the logical binary operation of isomorphism (*iso*). The operation evaluates to true if the operands evaluate to the same value; otherwise, iso evaluates to false. Is there a C++ operator that computes *iso*? Explain.

4.11 Write the truth table for the logical binary operation of exclusive-or (*xor*). The operation evaluates to true if exactly one of its operands evaluates to true; otherwise, *xor* evaluates to false. Then write a code segment that tests whether P *xor* Q is true, where P and Q are **bool** objects.

4.12 Write the truth table for the logical binary operation for the complement of and (*nand*). The operation evaluates to false if both of its operands evaluate to true; otherwise, *nand* evaluates to true. Then write a code segment that tests whether P *nand* Q is true, where P and Q are **bool** objects.

4.13 Provide the truth table for the following logical expressions:

a) (*not P*) *and Q*

b) *not* (*not P*)

c) *P and* ((*not P*) *or Q*)

4.14 DeMorgan's law states that for logical variables *P* and *Q*

- *not* (*P and Q*) is equivalent to (*not P*) or (*not Q*).
- *not* (*P or Q*) is equivalent to (*not P*) and (*not Q*).

Prove these two equivalences through the use of truth tables. Hint: For the first equivalence, your truth table should have entries *P, Q, P and Q, not* (*P and Q*), *not P, not Q,* (*not P*) *or* (*not Q*).

4.15 Develop a boolean expression using an integer object year that is true if and only if the value of year corresponds to a leap year.

4.16 Develop flowchart representations of the following programs:

a) Program 4.2

b) Program 4.3

c) Program 4.6

d) Program 4.7

e) Program 4.10

4.17 Implement a program that extracts a single integer value as input. The program should display whether the input value is positive, negative, or zero.

4.18 Implement a program that extracts two integer values as input. The program should display whether the inputs are both positive, both negative, or one positive and one negative.

4.19 Implement a program that extracts two floating-point values as input. The program should determine whether the difference in the two values is at most Epsilon, where Epsilon is a program-defined constant equal to 0.00001.

4.20 Rewrite Program 4.2 so that it uses an **if-else-if** statement to determine the smallest value.

4.21 Suppose we want to sort four numbers. How many different orderings can there be?

4.22 Design and implement a program that sorts four input values.

4.23 Consider the following **switch** statement:

```
switch (i*j) {
    case 1: case 2: case 3: case 6:
        cout << "1" << endl;
    case 5:
        cout << "2" << endl;
        break;
    case 10:
        cout << "3" << endl;
        break;
    default:
        cout << "4" << endl;
}
```

a) If i is 11 and j is 2, what is the output?

b) If i is 1 and j is 5, what is the output?

c) If i is 3 and j is 2, what is the output?

d) If i is 5 and j is 2, what is the output?

4.24 Implement a program that extracts a single integer value. The input value should be in the range 1 through 10. The program should display whether the input value is a prime number. The program should categorize the input value using a **switch** statement.

4.25 Modify Program 4.4 so that it also computes remainder expressions of the form *LeftOperand % RightOperand* where % is the modulus operator.

4.26 Modify Program 4.4 so that it also computes simple relational expressions of the form *LeftOperand Operator RightOperand* where *Operator* is either less than (<) or greater than (>).

4.27 Define an **enum** type Days for days in the week.

4.28 Define an **enum** type for your local currency.

4.29 Show how a **do** statement can be converted into a **while** statement.

4.30 Suppose c is an object of **enum** type color. Write a **switch** statement to insert the name of its value to the standard output stream cout. For example, if c has the value red, then the string "red" is inserted.

4.31 Add input validation to Program 4.6.

4.32 Rearrange the following code segment so that it is properly indented.

```
if ((n > 0) && (m > 0)) { for (int i = 0; i < n;
++i) { for (int j = 0; j < m; ++j) { if (i ! =
j) { cout << "0" << endl; } else { cout << "1";
} } } } else { cout << "2" << endl; }
```

4.33 Correct the following code segment so that it displays the number of inputs that are bigger than the first input.

```
int FirstValue;
int CurrentValue;
int Sum = 1;
cin >> FirstValue;
while (cin >> FirstValue) {
    if (FirstValue == CurrentValue) {
        ++Sum;
    }
}
cout << Sum << endl;
```

4.34 Correct the following code segment so that it displays the sum of odd integers from 1 to n.

```
int i = 0;
for (int Sum = 1; Sum < n; ++i) {
    if (i % 2) {
        Sum += n;
    }
    cout << Sum << endl;
}
```

4.35 Correct the following code segment so that it displays the product of the integers in the inclusive interval 5 through 15.

```
int Factor = 5;
int Product = 1;
do {
    ++Factor;
    Product *= Factor;
} until (Factor == 15)
cout << Product << endl;
```

4.36 Consider the following code segment:

```
int i = 1;
while (i <= n) {
    if ((i % n) == 0) {
        ++i;
    }
}
cout << i << endl;
```

   a) What is the output if n is 0?

   b) What is the output if n is 1?

   c) What is the output if n is 3?

4.37   Consider the following code segment:

```
for (int i = 0; i < n; ++i) {
    --n;
}
cout << i << endl;
```

a)   What is the output if n is 0?

b)   What is the output if n is 1?

c)   What is the output if n is 3?

d)   What is the output if n is 4?

4.38   Design and implement a program that displays the absolute value of its inputs.

4.39   Design and implement a program that counts the number of its inputs that are positive, negative, and zero.

4.40   Design and implement a program that extracts values from the standard input stream and then displays the smallest and largest of those values to the standard output stream. The program should display appropriate messages for special cases where there are no inputs and only one input.

4.41   Design and implement a program that prompts the user for a nonnegative value n. The program then displays the value of powers of 2 from 2^0 to 2^n.

4.42   Design and implement a program that prompts the user for a nonnegative value n. The program then displays the value of n in reverse binary notation. For example, if n is 19, then 11001 is displayed.

4.43   Design and implement a program that prompts the user for a nonnegative value n that is less than 2^{16}. The program then displays the value of n in standard binary notation. For example, if n is 21, then 10101 is displayed.

4.44   Modify Program 4.4 so that it extracts a series of expressions and displays the output of each expression.

4.45   Design and implement a program that accepts a date as input. The program should display the date's position in the year. For example, if the date is 12 29 2002, then the displayed number is 363.

4.46   Design and implement a program that accepts as input starting and ending dates in the form expected by Program 4.5. The program then computes the number of days between the dates.

4.47   Design and implement a program that prompts its user for a non-negative value n. The program then displays as its output

```
1 2 3 ... n-1 n
1 2 3 ... n-1
...
1 2 3
1 2
1
```

(Note the ...'s are to be filled in with the appropriate numbers).

CHAPTER 5

Function usage basics and libraries

Introduction

Functions improve clarity and enable software reuse. A function is like an assistant that goes off to perform a particular task and then returns with its solution. In the next three chapters, the design and use of functions is considered in detail. We begin this exploration by examining fundamental concepts such as invocation and parameter passing. We do so by developing programs that use functions from standard software libraries including the iostream library. The iostream library is important because it permits an extensible method of displaying and extracting objects. The use of libraries is facilitated through preprocessor commands. The preprocessor commands support file inclusion, macro definitions, and conditional compilation.

Key Concepts

- functions
- value parameters
- invocation and flow of control
- function prototyping
- activation records
- preprocessor include directive
- preprocessor define directive
- preprocessor ifdef and ifndef directive
- iostream functionality
- iomanip manipulators
- fstream classes `ifstream` and `ofstream`
- string class
- math library
- ctype library
- assert macros

5.1

FUNCTION BASICS

The programs presented in previous chapters are interesting, but they are not typical software. Aside from their use of the iostream library and our EzWindows graphical library, the actions in those programs were completely specified within their individual function `main()`'s and `ApiMain()`'s. This was possible because the tasks they performed were simple and easy to code. However, significant software applications require hundreds of thousands, if not millions, of lines of code. It would be practically impossible to correctly produce a single piece of code for such large applications—a huge monolithic program of such magnitude would be far too complex to understand and validate. Even if the application could be built in this fashion, it would be a waste of resources—there are already many software modules that perform common computing tasks in readily available software libraries. For these reasons, all major application developments and even most simple programs use programming schemes that organize their information and its manipulation in a modular fashion. A principal part of all such schemes is the use of *functions*. Not surprisingly, functions are a crucial component of object-oriented programming.

Functions are used by programs as assistants to solve particular tasks. In C++, a program waits until an assisting function completes its task before continuing to the next statement. To solve its task, the assisting function can use other functions. In fact, as strange it may seem, a function can even use another instance of itself (this process is known as *recursion*, and it is considered in the next chapter).

Program 5.1 is a small program that uses a function `sqrt()` to assist its function `main()` to compute the roots of a quadratic expression whose coefficients are user-supplied input values. A quadratic expression is normally written with coefficients *a*, *b*, *c* in the form

$$ax^2 + bx + c = 0.$$

The roots of the expression are given by the formula

$$\frac{-b \pm \sqrt{b^2 - 4ac}}{2a}.$$

For pedagogical purposes, Program 5.1 limits its computation to a quadratic expression with two real roots (the general quadratic problem is left to the exercises).

The act of using a function is referred to as an *invocation* or *call* of the function. In Program 5.1, function `sqrt()` is invoked in the definition of **double** object `radical`.

```
double radical = sqrt(b*b - 4*a*c);
```

Program 5.1

*Computing roots of a
quadratic equation
$ax^2 + bx + c$*

```
// Program 5.1: Determines the roots of a quadratic
// equation
#include <iostream.h>
#include <math.h>
int main() {
   cout << "Coefficients for quadratic equation: "
   << flush;
   double a;
   double b;
   double c;
   cin >> a >> b >> c;
   if ((a != 0) && ((b*b - 4*a*c) > 0)) {
      double radical = sqrt(b*b - 4*a*c);
      double root1 = (-b + radical) / (2*a);
      double root2 = (-b - radical) / (2*a);
      cout << "The roots of " << a << "x**2 + " << b
      << "x + " << c << " are " << root1 << " and "
      << root2 << endl;
   }
   else {
      cout <<  a << "x**2 + " << b << "x + " << c
      << " does not have two real roots" << endl;
   }
   return 0;
}
```

During invocation, a function can be passed information to perform its task. The information is referred to as the function's *parameters* or *arguments*. For example, function sqrt() expects a **double** floating-point value to be passed as its parameter. It then computes the square root of that parameter.

When a function is invoked, the *flow of control* is temporarily transferred to that function. By this transfer, we mean that the next statement to be executed is the first one in the function that was invoked. To prepare for the execution of the function definition, a correspondence is established between the actual values used in the invocation with the parameters in the definition. After the invoked function completes its task, the flow of control returns to the statement in the function that did the invocation.

5.1.1

Interface specification

During program translation, three things must have been specified about a function before it can appear in an invocation: the type of value (if any) that the function will return, the function's name, and a description of its parameters. These three items form the function's *interface*. Note that the actual function definition is not required (although the definition must be eventually supplied so that the compilation process can be completed).

We have seen examples of a function interface in the various definitions of main() in our example programs. The interface is that portion of the definition of main() occurring before the left curly brace. Thus the interface for function main() in our programs has been

```
int main()
```

For Program 5.1 the interface for function `sqrt()` is specified in the math library header file `math.h`. The interface statement for function `sqrt()` in `math.h` resembles

```
double sqrt(double number);
```

The first part of an interface specification indicates what type of value (if any) the function produces as its result. We call that type the *function type* or *return type*. A function type can be any of the standard types or even a programmer-defined type. For `sqrt()`, the function type is **double**.

If the function does produce a value, we call the produced value in a particular invocation the *return value*. If a function's type is not **void**, then the function must *always* return a single value of the specified type. The return value that is produced by a function can vary with each invocation of the function. For example, if `sqrt()` is given the value 6.25 as its parameter, its return value is 2.5. If `sqrt()` is instead given the value 1.44 as its parameter, its return value is 1.2.

If a function's type is **void**, then the function *never* returns a value. It may seem strange to have a function that does not produce a return value, but **void** functions can be quite useful. For example, they are often used to display messages to the user.

The next part of the interface specification is the name of the function. The name must be an identifier. Programmers normally follow the same naming convention with function names as they follow with object names, which means using good names with a consistent capitalization scheme. Our naming convention, unless special conditions dictate otherwise, capitalizes the first letter in each word that makes up the name. Such a scheme makes it easier for readers of the code to recognize which functions are programmer-defined and which are part of the standard libraries (most standard library functions have lowercase names, e.g., `sqrt()`).

The last part of the interface specification describes the form of the parameters to be given to the function. The parameters are enclosed between a pair of parentheses. In our program examples so far, neither `main()` nor `ApiMain()` have required any information other than what was available through the standard input stream. Therefore, their parameter lists are empty. This is not the case for `sqrt()`. It requires a single piece of information to perform its computation—the value whose square root is to be determined. The description of that piece of information is called a *parameter declaration*. Functions that require multiple pieces of information have corresponding multiple parameter declarations; the individual declarations are separated by commas.

The interface specification for a function has the form

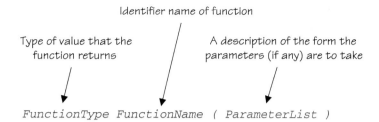

FunctionType FunctionName (ParameterList)

where *ParameterList* has the form

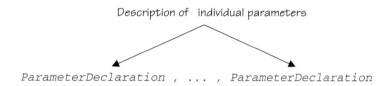

ParameterDeclaration , ... , ParameterDeclaration

C++ provides programmers with an extensive set of options for specifying a parameter. For now, we limit ourselves to the *value* parameter declaration form. The other possibilities are considered in later chapters. In its basic form, a value parameter declaration resembles a object declaration, since it consists of an identifier preceded by its type.

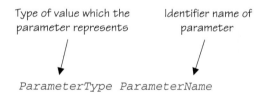

ParameterType ParameterName

Function `sqrt()` uses the basic form for its parameter declaration, so the declaration of its parameter resembles the following:

double number

5.1.2

Function prototyping

A *function prototype* statement indicates that a function of a particular form may be used to perform a program subtask. A function prototype statement resembles an interface specification followed by a semicolon. As mentioned earlier, at least the interface must be specified before a function can be used within a program. Function prototypes statement are typically placed near the beginning of the program file after the `#include` statements.

Some simple prototype declarations follow.

```
int PromptAndRead();
float CircleArea(float radius);
bool IsVowel(char CurrentCharacter);
```

The `PromptAndRead()` prototype indicates that the function does not expect a parameter but does return a value of type **int**. The prototype of `CircleArea()` indicates that the function computes and returns a value of type **float**. In addition, `CircleArea()` requires a single **float** value be given to it, or in programmer terminology *passed* to it. The prototype for function `IsVowel()` indicates that it returns a **bool** value. The function expects to be passed a single **char** value.

If a complete function definition is being given, the interface specification is followed by the list of statements directing the function's actions. The statement list is surrounded by left and right curly braces. This is the case for function `main()` in Program 5.1.

We say that a function prototype resembles an interface specification because the names of the parameters are not necessary in a prototype. However, it is our practice to include good names so as to contribute to program understandability.

5.1.3

Invocation and flow of control

The interesting statement in Program 5.1 is the definition of `radical`, which in its initialization invokes function `sqrt()`.

```
double radical = sqrt(b*b - 4*a*c);
```

The invocation supplies the value whose square root is desired, which in this case is the value of the expression `b*b - 4*a*c`. We call the expression `b*b - 4*a*c` the *actual parameter*. The object used in the definition of `sqrt()` to represent the actual parameter is called the *formal parameter*. At this point in the execution of the program, the flow of control is temporarily transferred from `main()` to `sqrt()`. This process is demonstrated in Figure 5.1, in which we depict the flow of control for Program 5.1.

Transfer of control to function `sqrt()` requires establishing a correspondence between the actual parameter given in the invocation and the object used by `sqrt()` to represent that parameter. In general, the relative positions of the parameters determines the correspondence between the actual parameters and the formal parameters. The first actual parameter is associated with the first formal parameter, the second actual parameter is associated with the second formal parameter, and so on. If a function's interface uses the basic value parameter declaration form, all invocations of the function must have that number of parameters.

For each invocation of a function, memory is set aside for its formal parameters. For functions such as `sqrt()` that have a value formal parameter, the formal parameter memory is initialized to the value of the actual parameter.

Figure 5.1

Depiction of the flow of control in Program 5.1 as it proceeds from main () to sqrt () back to main ()

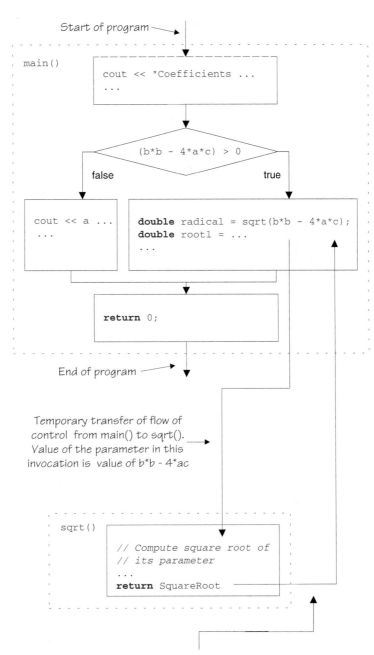

Start of program

main()

cout << "Coefficients ...
...

(b*b - 4*a*c) > 0

false   true

cout << a ...
...

double radical = sqrt(b*b - 4*a*c);
double root1 = ...
...

return 0;

End of program

Temporary transfer of flow of control from main() to sqrt(). Value of the parameter in this invocation is value of b*b - 4*ac

sqrt()

// Compute square root of
// its parameter
...
return SquareRoot

Transfer of flow of control from sqrt() back to main() to first complete the definition of radical using the double return value of sqrt() and to then complete the rest of main()

C++
Language

C++

> ### *The right type*
> The type of the actual parameter used in a function invocation should agree with the type of the corresponding formal parameter as specified in the function interface. If there is a mismatch between the type of the actual parameter and the type of the formal parameter, the usual conversions are tried automatically.

The memory that is set aside for the formal parameters of a function is part of the function's *activation record*. A fresh activation record is created for each invocation of a function. Even function `main()`, which is invoked by the operating system, has an activation record.

The activation record for a function is large enough to store the values associated with each object that is defined within the function. Depending upon the compiler, other information may be maintained in the activation record (e.g., a pointer to the current statement in the function being executed; a pointer to the statement in the function that invoked the function being executed; and if there is a return value, memory to temporarily hold that value).

The activation record for function `main()` in Program 5.1 includes the objects a, b, c, `radical`, `root1`, and `root2`. Suppose that the values supplied by the user for a, b, and c are respectively 6, 5, and 1 and that we are about to execute the initialization statement of `radical` in `main()`. A snapshot of `main()`'s activation record follows, where a question mark indicates that the value of the object has not yet been set by the program.

main()	
a	6
b	5
c	1
radical	?
root1	?
root2	?

When function `sqrt()` is invoked to initialize `radical`, an activation record is also created for `sqrt()`. In its activation record, its value formal parameter is initialized to the value of the actual parameter, the expression `b*b - 4*a*c`, which in this case has the value 1.

Once the expression `b*b - 4*a*c` has been used to initialize the value formal parameter, the actual parameter and formal parameter are then independent of each other. Whenever the formal parameter is used in `sqrt()`, the value used for the formal parameter is the one stored in the current activation record for `sqrt()`. Even if the invocation of `sqrt()` makes a change to the formal parameter, the change occurs within the memory of that invocation's activation record and the expression b*b - 4*a*c would be unaffected. This type of formal parameter–actual parameter relationship is referred to as *pass by value*. Essentially the formal parameter is an object that can be used only within function sqrt(). The formal parameter is created with the invocation of sqrt() and the formal parameter is destroyed when function sqrt() completes and releases its activation record memory.

The following code segment demonstrates some other legal invocations of sqrt().

```
double ScaledRoot = 25 * sqrt(1000);
sqrt(15.0);
```

The first of the two invocations initializes ScaledRoot. The invocation demonstrates that a function invocation can be used in combination with operators. The function invocation is permissible because it produces a return value and that return value can be used like any other value. In particular, the return value can be used in composing an expression. The second of the two invocations seems peculiar because nothing is done with the return value of the invocation. However, the statement is legal—an expression is a valid statement in C++, and a valid function invocation is a valid expression.

Next consider the statement

```
cout << sqrt(14) - sqrt(12);
```

This insertion statement twice invokes function sqrt(). Therefore, the flow of control is twice passed to function sqrt(), and two sqrt() activation records are created during the execution of the insertion statement. The two activation records are distinct and occur one after the other (i.e., they do not exist simultaneously). In each of the invocations, memory storage for the activation record—possibly different storage locations per invocation—is set aside to hold the value for the sqrt() formal parameter. In one invocation, that storage is initialized to the value 14, and in the other invocation that storage is initialized to the value 12.

The return value of the invocation with actual parameter 14 is used as the left operand for the subtraction, and the return value of the invocation with actual parameter 12 is used as the right operand of the subtraction. Conceptually, the following code segment *could* represent the insertion of sqrt(14) - sqrt(12).

```
double LeftOperand = sqrt(14);
double RightOperand = sqrt(12);
cout << LeftOperand - RightOperand;
```

Although these statements first evaluate the left operand and then the right operand of the subtraction, the original insertion statement did not require this evaluation ordering. C++ precedence rules specify the exact order of operator evaluation, but except for short circuit evaluation of logical expressions, the precedence rules do not specify which operand of an operator is evaluated first—the order of evaluation is left to the compiler. Thus the invocation of sqrt(12) can occur before the invocation sqrt(14). Therefore, the following code segment could also represent the insertion of sqrt(14) - sqrt(12).

```
double RightOperand = sqrt(12);
double LeftOperand = sqrt(14);
cout << LeftOperand - RightOperand;
```

Programmer Alert

Function side effects

For the evaluation of the expression sqrt(14) - sqrt(12), it makes no difference which operand is evaluated first. However, as we shall see in later chapters, it is possible to write functions where the value of an expression depends upon the order of evaluation. In such cases, the programmer should explicitly decompose the statement into multiple statements to ensure the correct evaluation. Functions that necessitate this process contain *side effects*. A side effect occurs when an internal action of a function modifies an object that is external to the function.

The ability to perform multiple invocations in a single statement is not limited to using return values as operands. A return value can also be used as the actual parameter in another function invocation. An example of such an invocation follows.

```
double QuarticRoot = sqrt(sqrt(5));
```

In this example, there are again two invocations and consequently two distinct activation records are created for sqrt(). However, this time the order of the invocations is specified. The expression sqrt(5) is computed first, and then its return value is used by the second invocation. This invocation sequence means that a sqrt() activation record is first created with memory storage for the formal parameter that is initialized to the value 5. The function then performs its computation using that activation record and produces a return value. The activation record is then discarded, and a new one is created that initializes the formal parameter to the return value of the previous sqrt() invocation. Using this value, the function again performs its computation and produces the return value that is used to initialize QuarticRoot. Thus the following actions occur (conceptually).

```
double Temporary = sqrt(5);
double QuarticRoot = sqrt(Temporary);
```

Not all function invocations are valid. For example, the following two invocations are invalid. The first has too few actual parameters and the second has too many.

```
double x = sqrt();      // illegal
double y = sqrt(5,3);  // illegal
```

5.2

THE PREPROCESSOR

It is important to remember that an invocation cannot appear until the function being invoked has been either prototyped or defined. In Program 5.1, a prototype of function `sqrt()` occurs in the file `math.h`. The prototypes and definitions in that file are in effect throughout function `main()` owing to the work of the C++ preprocessor.

The preprocessor examines the input program file for *file inclusion directives*, *macro definitions and invocations* and *conditional compilation* directives. Since the preprocessor carries out these directives on the input program file to produce the actual file to be compiled, the processing of these directives is the first step in program translation. The file produced by the preprocessor is called a *translation unit*.

5.2.1

File inclusion directives

A file inclusion directive specifies the name of a file that is to be part of the translation unit. The file named in the directive replaces the directive itself. If the file to be included cannot be found in the standard directories, the translation process is typically aborted and an error message is produced.

There are two file inclusion directive forms. One of the forms is given below.

```
#include <filename>
```

The octothorp symbol # indicates a preprocessor directive is to follow. The # must be the first non-white space character on the line. The angle brackets < and > both delimit the filename and indicate that the file is to be found in one of the standard directories of the system. The location of these standard directories is implementation dependent; that is, different systems can place the standard directories in different locations. For PC-based systems, the standard directories are typically within subdirectories of the directory that contains the compiler. These libraries are normally created when the compiler is installed on the PC.

The size of the translation unit is typically much bigger than the input program file. For example, using one popular PC-based compiler, the following five-line program file has an 884-line translation unit. This size increase indicates that the iostream library provides many capabilities other than just standard stream insertion and extraction.

```
#include <iostream.h>
int main() {
    cout << "Hello, World." << endl;
    return 0;
}
```

The second file inclusion directive has the following form:

```
#include "filename"
```

The quotes surrounding the filename indicate that an alternative set of directories should be searched to find the file in question. The process of considering alternative directories is implementation dependent. In practice, almost all compilers behave in the following manner:

- If the filename is given in terms of absolute file system pathname, then the file is taken from that absolute location. For example, the following directive states that the included file is `sample.h` and it can be found in the directory `\example\source` on the `C:` drive of the PC system.

  ```
  #include "C:\example\source\sample.h"
  ```

- If an absolute pathname is not specified, then the filename is taken to be a relative name with respect to the user's current directory on the computer system. For example, the following directive would look in the current directory for the file `hold.txt`. If the file was not found in that directory, the standard directories would then be searched.

  ```
  #include "hold.txt"
  ```

It is legal for included files to contain preprocessor directives. If they do contain directives, those directives are also processed. The processing of the directives in an included file is done before the processing of any remaining directives in the current file. For example, suppose the following line represents the contents of the input file to the preprocessor.

```
#include "a.txt"
```

where file `a.txt` contains the following line:

```
#include "b.txt"
```

where file `b.txt` contains for purposes of exposition, the following lines:

```
#include "c.txt"
#include "c.txt"
```

where the file `c.txt` contains the following line:

```
hello world
```

The output of the preprocessor would be a file with the following two lines:

```
hello world
hello world
```

Note that the preprocessor does not consider whether the lines it is creating are legal C++ statements. The preprocessor just executes its directives.

5.2.2

Macro definitions

A macro definition in its simplest form resembles the following:

```
#define MacroName MacroValue
```

where *MacroName* can be a string of letters, digits, and punctuation and *MacroValue* can be any string, character, number, or a line of text. The effect of the command is to associate the value with the name. After that point in the program file, whenever *MacroName* occurs, it is replaced by the associated *MacroValue*.

It was through the #define statements that constants were originally specified in the original C language, as that language did not have the modifier **const**. By tradition preprocessor constants are capitalized as in the following definitions:

```
#define PI 3.14159
#define BOILING_POINT 212
#define MESSAGE "Hello, World."
```

Note that semicolons are not used—if a semicolon was included, it too would be added to the program file everywhere the macro is invoked. With the preceding macro definitions in effect, the code segment

```
cout << PI << endl;
cout << BOILING_POINT << endl;
cout << MESSAGE << endl;
```

is translated into

```
cout << 3.14159 << endl;
cout << 212 << endl;
cout << "Hello, World." << endl;
```

Like functions, macros can also take parameters. For example, the following preprocessor directive defines a macro ADD that sums its two parameters.

```
#define ADD(a, b) a + b
```

The following code segment uses macro ADD to initialize the **int** object Sum to 7.

```
int Sum = ADD(5, 2);
```

When the preprocessor translates this statement, the result is

```
int Sum = 5 + 2;
```

The same macro is used in the following code segment to initialize the **float** object Total to the value 3.5.

```
float Total = ADD(1.25, 2.25);
```

When the preprocessor translates this statement, the result is

```
float Total = 1.25 + 2.25;
```

We next use the macro ADD to demonstrate that with macros the result is not necessarily what is expected.

```
int Result = ADD(2, 2) * 3; // Result is 8!
```

Because the preprocessor translates the statement into

```
int Result = 2 + 2 * 3;
```

Object `Result` is set to 8, not 12 as you might have expected. If `ADD` had been a function rather than a macro, it would be `ADD`'s return value that is multiplied by 3, thus producing the expected value of 12.

5.2.3

Conditional compilation

Because C++ has a **const** facility, and as we shall see in subsequent chapters, it allows for the safe *overloading* of function names, the *inlining* of function code, and generic parameters through template functions, the only real use for macros in C++ program files is to enable conditional compilation.

In our programs so far, it has been the case that each statement in the program file is always to be compiled. This feature can be overridden with the `#ifndef` and `#ifdef` conditional compilation directives.

The preprocessor directive `#ifndef` serves as the opening delimiter for a section of the file. An occurrence of the preprocessor statement `#endif` serves as the closing delimiter for the section. The delimited section is only compiled if the macro name following the `#ifndef` has not been previously defined. The ability to determine which statements should be compiled is useful because it enables us to prevent the illegal redefining of an object due to multiple inclusions. For example, many programs start off with

```
#include <iostream.h>
#include <iomanip.h>
```

even though the iomanip library includes the iostream library. Without the use of `#ifndef` statements by the iostream library, such programs would be illegal because there would be repeated definitions of standard streams `cin` and `cout`.

In the following example, **int** objects a and b can be defined at most once, no matter how many times this code segment is included into a program file.

```
#ifndef NO_MORE_A_AND_B
int a;
int b;
#define NO_MORE_A_AND_B
#endif
```

This behavior is the case, as one of the lines within these conditional compilation directives defines the macro `NO_MORE_A_AND_B`. Once this macro is defined, subsequent inclusions of the code segment will not redefine a and b.

It is possible to have a conditional compilation directive embedded within another conditional compilation directive (the embedding process is known as *nesting*). For example, in the following code segment, objects a and c are defined if the macro `NO_INTS` is undefined. Object b is defined only if macros `NO_INTS` and `NO_B` are both undefined. When conditional compilation directives are nested, a #endif statement is matched to the most recently occurring #if statement.

```
#ifndef NO_INTS
int a;
#ifndef NO_B
int b;
#endif
int c;
#endif
```

The #ifdef directive works in analogous manner. However, it requires that the macro name be defined for the associated statements to be part of the compilation process.

5.3

USING SOFTWARE LIBRARIES

Often the file to be included into a program file is a *header file* for a library. By programming convention, the file extension suffix *h* is used to indicate that a file is a header file. Thus, math.h is a header file. A library header file normally contains a related collection of function and operator prototypes, global constant and variable object definitions, and **class** descriptions. (A *global object* is one that can be used throughout the program). The collection is essentially an interface description for using the associated software library.

There are generally no function definitions in a library header file. Instead, the actual function definitions are placed in another file or files. Those definitions are combined with a program's other definitions during the linking stage of the translation process. The translation process was discussed in Chapter 1 and is reviewed in Figure 5.2.

If the library is a standard one, then the linking is automatically done by the compiler. If a library is a personal one, then compiling commands are given to specify where the definitions can be found. The linking of personal libraries can normally be automated through the use of *make* or *project* tools associated with the compiler. By only linking the library object modules to the program, the compilation process is greatly speeded up—no translation of the library is needed because it has been done previously.

In the next several sections we consider several libraries: iostream, fstream, math, ctype, and assert. We will also briefly consider the cstring library. The functions and objects defined by these libraries will be used in examples elsewhere in the text. Many other standard and nonstandard libraries are provided by a C++ compiler, for example, standard libraries for creating various kinds of lists, handling exceptions (improper program manipulations), and accessing time and date information. These other libraries are also useful, and the reader is directed to a language reference manual for complete definitions.

Figure 5.2

Translation process

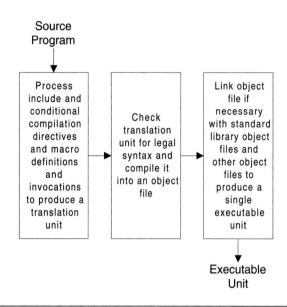

Source
Program

| Process include and conditional compilation directives and macro definitions and invocations to produce a translation unit | Check translation unit for legal syntax and compile it into an object file | Link object file if necessary with standard library object files and other object files to produce a single executable unit |

Executable
Unit

5.4

THE IOSTREAM LIBRARY

As in many programing languages, Input/Output (I/O) operations are not officially part of the C++ language. The I/O operations are instead defined in libraries that are associated with the language. While this separation from the language definition may seem quirky, it gives software developers the ability to choose the right library for the task at hand.

C++ I/O libraries provide an interface between the program and the hardware devices that make up the computer system. The interface spans two levels of abstraction. At the lower level is a file. In this context, a *file* is a logical concept that represents a particular hardware device like a monitor, modem, or keyboard, or instead represents a particular portion of a hardware device like a disk file on a floppy or on a CDROM. At the higher level of abstraction is a stream. The *stream* is a hardware-independent view of the actual device. The data coming from or going to the hardware device is just a sequence of bytes.

The stream and file views are both important. The stream view allows a program to issue generic I/O requests on flows of data while being unconcerned about how the requests are to be carried out. The file view captures the important physical characteristics of the actual device. The I/O requests of the stream view are translated automatically into file-level specific actions that accomplish the desired requests.

An important characteristic of the iostream library is its extensibility. This characteristic is not true of the other major alternative I/O library, the *stdio library*. The stdio library is the library C programmers use to do I/O. While there are stdio functions to input and output the standard types and strings, there is no method for extending or redefining these functions to operate on programmer-defined data types. And since pointers (discussed in Chapter 12) are extensively required in the processing of stdio-based input, most programmers are apt to make mistakes when using the stdio library. For these reasons, we recommend the use of the iostream library and confine our discussion to it.

Although the iostream library provides a hierarchy of basic I/O functionality, we are concerned now with only the top level of the hierarchy that allows for stream manipulation.

5.4.1

Standard streams

Header file iostream.h in part defines a collection of stream classes that are used to define streams capable of input, output, or both input and output. Header file iostream.h also defines four *standard* stream objects that are automatically created when program execution begins.

We have been using two of these stream objects, cin and cout, in most of our programs. The actual type of stream cin is istream_withassign, and the actual type of stream cout is ostream_withassign. The two other standard streams are cerr and clog. These other standard stream objects, like cout, are both of type ostream_withassign.

Figure 5.3 depicts the relationships among some of the classes defined in iostream.h. The class ios is the basis for all of the other depicted classes. In the figure, the arrows from istream and ostream indicate that they are directly *derived* from the base class ios. A derived class *inherits* attributes from its base class (i.e. the derived class takes its definition in part from the base class). We consider inheritance issues in detail in Chapter 14.

Figure 5.3
A portion of the ios hierarchy

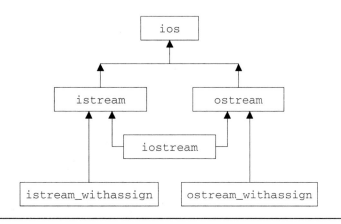

Class iostream is derived directly from classes istream and ostream and indirectly from the class ios. Classes istream and istream_withassign are for input streams. Classes ostream and `ostream_withassign` are for output streams. Class `iostream` is for defining streams that can serve as both input and output streams.

5.4.2

Standard error stream objects

Streams `cerr` and `clog` are used to insert output to the default error log. This log is normally the console monitor. These two streams, like `cin` and `cout`, have values as well as member functions and operators. The member functions and operators are the mechanisms to accomplish the desired input and output results on the streams.

If a program detects an abnormal situation, it is good practice to display a message indicating the nature of the problem to the user. Such a message should typically go to the monitor so that it will be immediately viewable. Since the output associated with stream `cout` is sometimes redirected to a file using operating system commands, `cout` is inappropriate for error or system status messages—you do not want the viewing of such messages to wait until the user gets around to looking at the output file. The preferred stream for error messages is `cerr`. Like `cout`, its insertion requests are directed by default to the monitor. However, unlike `cout`, `cerr` is normally always directed to the monitor.

The streams `cout` and `cerr` are also different with respect to buffering. Buffering is generally inappropriate for error messages because they tend to be time critical. So each insertion request to stream `cerr` is sent immediately for display. Several example error messages are given below.

```
cerr << "System being rebooted in 2 minutes\n";
cerr << "Zero balance: withdrawal ignored\n";
cerr << "Modem is not online, no call possible\n";
```

If for reasons of program efficiency, it is necessary to have buffered error and system status messages, the buffered error stream `clog` can be used. Like `cout` and `cerr`, `clog` is directed by default to the monitor. Some more example messages are given below.

```
clog << UserName << " has logged onto system\n";
clog << "Backup was successfully performed\n";
clog << "Mail has arrived\n";
```

5.4.3

The iostream manipulators

The iostream library also defines several input and output stream manipulators. These manipulators are listed in Table 5.1. Depending upon the individual I/O manipulator, a manipulator can occur as the right operand of an insertion operator << or of an extraction operator >> or even both.

We have already used the iostream manipulator `endl`. Manipulator `endl` when inserted to a output stream appends a newline character to the stream and causes the stream to be flushed. Manipulator `ends` operates in a similar man-

Table 5.1

Iostream manipulators

Manipulator	Purpose
dec	Display numeric values in decimal notation
endl	Output a newline character and flush the stream
ends	Output a null character
flush	Flush the stream buffer
hex	Display numeric values in hexadecimal notation
oct	Display numeric values in octal notation
ws	Skip over leading white space

ner except that it inserts a null character (the literal `'\0'`) to the target stream. This manipulator is sometimes useful in string processing.

Manipulators dec, hex, and oct are used to specify the base in which numbers are displayed to the associated output stream. Manipulator dec is used to specify decimal (the default base); manipulator hex is used to specify hexadecimal (base 16), and manipulator oct is used to specify octal (base 8). The three manipulators are all *persistent* (i.e., all numbers are expressed in the requested base for the affected stream until another base change is specified).

Manipulator ws is also persistent. Its use on an input stream indicates that the extraction operator for this stream should ignore leading white space before doing an extraction. Because this behavior is the default condition, it is normally never applied. To turn off this behavior, one can invoke the istream member function unsetf(), using as its parameter the constant ios::skipws. All input streams have such a member function, as all input streams are of a type that is indirectly derived from the class istream.

```
// turn off the skipping of white space during
// extractions from cin using its istream member
// function unsetf()
cin.unsetf(ios::skipws);
```

Manipulator flush has also been seen before. When it is applied to an output stream, the output buffer is immediately flushed. A flush operation is similar to endl except that it does not insert the newline character before flushing.

The following small example demonstrates some of these manipulators.

```
int i = 10;
int j = 20;
int k = 30;
cout << i << endl;
cout << i << "\n" << flush;
cout << oct;
cout << i << endl;
cout << j << endl;
cout << k << endl;
cout << hex << i << endl;
cout << j << endl;
```

```
cout << k << endl;
```

The first two insertion statements are effectively the same and cause i to be displayed on two separate lines in the default decimal base. The use of the oct manipulator in the third insertion statement of main() causes the insertion statements for i, j, and k that follow to be displayed in octal format. The use of the hex manipulator causes the insertions of i, j, and k to be displayed in hexadecimal. The output of the code segment follows.

```
10
10
12
24
36
a
14
1e
```

5.5

THE IOMANIP LIBRARY

Another collection of I/O stream manipulators is also available to modify the behavior of insertions and extractions. These additional manipulators are not strictly necessary because other functions associated with the stream objects can also accomplish these tasks. However, invoking those functions is generally cumbersome. The additional manipulators are defined in the standard header file iomanip.h. It is common practice for C++ programs to include the iomanip header file along with the iostream header file. A list of the manipulators provided by iomanip.h is given in Table 5.2. Except for manipulator setw(), all the manipulators are persistent.

Table 5.2

Iomanip manipulators

Output Manipulators	Purpose
setbase(**int** b)	Set the numeric base to b
setprecision(**int** d)	Set number of places of accuracy to d
setw(**int** w)	Set field width to w
setfill(**int** c)	Set the fill character to c
resetiosflags(**long** f)	Set flags indicated in f to 0
setiosflags(**long** f)	Set flags indicated in f to 1

Manipulator setbase() is strictly for output streams and requires a single parameter. The parameter specifies the base to be used in the display of numeric data (decimal, octal, or hexadecimal). The manipulator is not generally used because iostream manipulators dec, oct, and hex are also available. One could use setbase() when the desired base for inserting a value is the result of an earlier computation or input request. Such an example follows.

```
int number;
```

```
int base;
cout << "Provide a number and a base: " << flush;
cin  >> number >> base;
cout << number << " in decimal is "
 << setbase(base) << number << " in base " << base
 << endl;
```

If the input values for number and base are 9 and 8, then the output would be

```
9 in decimal is 11 in base 10
```

This result is not what we intended; the 10 in the preceding output is the representation of 8 in octal. This output happens because the effect of a setbase() invocation is persistent, so the cout insertions for number and base that occurred after the setbase() invocation are displayed in octal. To achieve the intended output, the insertion statement in the preceding code segment should be modified in the following manner:

```
cout << number << " in decimal is "
 << setbase(base) << number << " in base " << dec
 << base << endl;
```

This modification produces the desired output.

```
9 in decimal is 11 in base 8
```

If the input values for number and base are 19 and 16, then the output would be the following:

```
19 in decimal is 13 in base 16
```

Manipulator setprecision() is used to set the number of digits of precision (i.e., accuracy) when displaying a floating-point value. However, by default, output stream insertions do not display trailing zeroes. The following examples exhibit this behavior.

```
cout << setprecision(6)
 << 12.01234 << endl
 << 12.0123 << endl
 << 12.012 << endl
 << 12.01 << endl
 << 12.0 << endl;
```

The output of the fragment is given below.

```
12.0123
12.0123
12.012
12.01
12
```

The first two lines of the output are identical because six-place accuracy is the maximal display given the setprecision(6) invocation. The output serves as a warning that the display of floating-point values should always be considered approximate. In fact, given that there is finite precision to represent values, one must be cautious no matter how many places after the decimal are displayed. The next three output lines reflect that by default, only nonzero trailing digits are displayed. The last output line also shows that if all the places are zero, even the decimal point is dropped.

Now consider the following example:

```
cout << setprecision(0) << 12.01234 << endl;
```

The output of the insertion statement is

```
12.01234
```

This output occurred because a parameter of 0 in a `setprecision()` invocation indicates that the default precision is desired. For most C++ implementations, the default precision is six-place accuracy.

Manipulator `setw()` is used to set the desired width of an insertion. To the annoyance of many programmers, the `setw()` manipulator is *not* persistent. The width specified to the manipulator affects *only* the next insertion. After that next insertion, default behavior is again used. If the requested width to `setw()` is too small for the display of the next value, then the width of the next insertion is minimally increased to display the value correctly.

Determining the minimal width necessary to display a value depends upon the type of the value. In particular for character strings, if the width specified to `setw()` is less than the string length, then the string length is used. For integers, the entire number is always displayed along with a sign if one is necessary. For floating-point values, the necessary width varies according to whether scientific or decimal notation is being used. For either form, the minimal width that is used is large enough to include both the whole number and decimal portion, and if scientific notation is being used, the exponent.

If the specified width to `setw()` is larger then needed, then the value is displayed by default in a right-adjusted manner with the extra width portion being filled with the default fill character. By default, the fill character is a space.

Consider the following insertions of the character string `"Hello world"`.

```
cout << setw(1)  << "Hello world" << endl
     << setw(15) << "Hello world" << endl
     << "Hello world" << endl;
```

The insertions produces as their output

```
Hello world
    Hello world
Hello world
```

The middle output line differs from the first line because of the differing `setw()` invocations that precede the display of the string. The first invocation with `setw(1)` does not allow sufficient display width for the string, so the display width is temporarily increased to the length of the string. The second invocation with `setw(15)` provides more than sufficient display width for the string; therefore, the string is displayed in a right-adjust manner (i.e., four copies of the space fill character are displayed prior to the display of the string). The final display of the string again starts an output line. This behavior happens because the `setw()` manipulator is not persistent—the default width behavior, which uses minimal width, is again in effect.

Now consider the following insertion statement that displays representations of the floating-point value `10.12345`.

```
cout << setprecision(5)
  << setw(5) << 10.12345 << endl
  << setprecision(4)
  << setw(9) << 10.12345 << endl
  << setw(5) << 10.12345 << endl;
```

For the first of these insertions of `10.12345`, the requested decimal-place accuracy is five and the total display width is also 5. These widths are due respectively to the `setprecision(5)` and `setw(5)` invocations. The request for a five-decimal accuracy takes precedence, so the total display width is increased to six to allow for the display of five digits and a decimal point.

```
10.123
```

The next insertion which invokes `setprecision(4)`, causes four-place accuracy in the future.

```
10.12
```

This insertion of `10.12345` differs from the first one because the requested total display is now nine due to the `setw(9)` invocation. Since this width is more than necessary (given that four-place accuracy is in effect), the value is right adjusted by first displaying four fill characters. Since `setw()` is not persistent and `setprecision()` is persistent, the next insertion of `10.12345` starts off the output line and again uses four-place accuracy.

```
10.12
```

For large floating-point values, such as `123456789.123456789`, scientific notation is used by default. Consider the insertion statement

```
cout << setw(6) << 123456789.123456789 << endl
  << setprecision(3)
  << setw(15) << 123456789.123456789 << endl;
```

This statement produces the following lines of output:

```
1.23457e+08
      1.23e08;
```

The lines differ because of the `setw()` and `setprecision()` invocations in the insertion statement. Observe that the first insertion rounded the value to be displayed (rounding is standard practice).

Manipulator `setfill()` sets the fill character that is used when the width of an insertion request is larger than necessary. The following code segment demonstrates the use of this manipulator.

```
cout << setfill('#') << setw(15) << "Hello" << endl;
cout << setfill('$') << setw(5) << 100 << endl;
```

In the first insertion statement, the string `"Hello"` is right adjusted through the display of the octothorp character `'#'`. In the second statement, the integer `100` is right adjusted through the display of the dollar-sign character `'$'`.

```
##########Hello
$$100
```

Manipulators `setiosflags()` and `resetiosflags()` are general purpose manipulators. Through the use of formatting flags that are defined as `ios` constants, these manipulators can both duplicate the actions of the other manipulators and also achieve additional functionality. For example, there are formatting flags to ensure whether floating-point values are expressed in scientific or fixed point notation and whether uppercase or lowercase letters should be used in the display of hexadecimal values. To refer to these constants, as we did previously for constant `ios::skipws`, we use the scope operator `::`. Several of the particularly useful constants are `ios::left`, and `ios::right`, and `ios::showpoint`. Flags `ios::left` and `ios::right` are used to indicate whether a value should be left- or right-justified (as noted previously, values are right-justified by default). Flag `ios::showpoint` is used to indicate whether a decimal point should always be displayed for floating-point values. This flag needs to be set to have trailing zeros displayed after the decimal point.

Manipulator `setiosflags()` is used to indicate that a formatting option is in use; `resetiosflags()` is used to indicate that the formatting option is not in use.

The following code segment demonstrates how the `setiosflags()` manipulator can be used to obtain left-adjusted displays.

```
cout << setiosflags(ios::left)
  << setw(8) << "Tree" << "Type" << endl
  << "-----------------" << endl
  << setw(8) << "Maple" << "Deciduous" << endl
  << setw(8) << "Oak" << "Deciduous" << endl
  << setw(8) << "Cherry" << "Fruit" << endl
  << setw(8) << "Pine" << "Evergreen" << endl;
```

The output of the statement is the following.

```
Tree     Type
-----------------
Maple    Deciduous
Oak      Deciduous
Cherry   Fruit
Pine     Evergreen
```

5.6

THE FSTREAM LIBRARY

In the previous chapter we developed a program that extracts values from the standard input stream `cin` and then displays the average of those values to the standard output stream `cout`. The program is reproduced below.

```
#include <iostream.h>
int main() {
    cout << "Please provide list of numbers" << endl;
    int ValuesProcessed = 0;
    float ValueSum = 0;
    float Value;
    while (cin >> Value) {
        ValueSum += Value;
        ++ValuesProcessed;
    }
    if (ValuesProcessed > 0) {
        float Average = ValueSum / ValuesProcessed;
        cout << "Average: " << Average << endl;
    }
    else
        cout << "No list to average" << endl;
    return 0;
}
```

For a list with 10 or so values, running the program would be reasonable. But if we had a substantially larger list to process, we would like a program that gets its values from a file. By having the values in a file, their accuracy can be checked and, if necessary, errant values can be corrected. Similarly, if a program generates a significant amount of output, we would probably prefer to capture that output to a file so that we can review the information. Through the use of the standard library `fstream`, we can perform such file extractions and insertions. The interface for the library is specified in the standard file `fstream.h`.

The fstream library in part defines stream class types `ifstream`, `ofstream`, and `fstream`. The class `ifstream` is directly derived from the classes `istream` and `fstreambase`. Class `ifstream` is used to create instances of input streams whose values are extracted from files. The class `ofstream` is directly derived from the classes `ostream` and `fstreambase`. Class `ofstream` is used to create instances of output streams whose values go to files. The class `fstream` is for defining file-oriented streams capable of both input and output. Class `fstream` is directly derived from the classes `iostream` and `fstreambase`. A depiction of the `ios` hierarchy as it relates to these classes appears in Figure 5.4.

Suppose we need an input stream `fin` whose values are extracted from the file `mydata.nbr`. The desired stream can be created by defining an `ifstream` object `fin` while using the string `"mydata.nbr"` in its initialization.

```
ifstream fin("mydata.nbr");
```

Figure 5.4

*A portion of the ios
hierarchy associated
with ifstream, ofstream
and fstream*

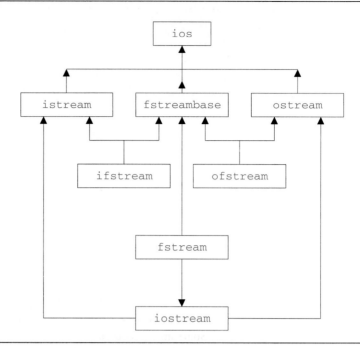

As seen in the definition, the name of the file that we want to process is passed as a string in defining the `ifstream` object. The definition sets up a correspondence between the stream `fin` and the file `mydata.nbr`.

Because class `ifstream` is derived from `istream`, the `istream` extraction operator `>>` is defined for `ifstream` objects. However, when the extraction operator is applied in conjunction with an `ifstream` object, the data comes from the associated file rather than from the standard input stream `cin`.

We can use both the iostream input manipulators and member functions, as well as the iomanip input manipulators, on `ifstream` objects. Likewise, we can use iostream output manipulators and member functions, as well as iomanip output manipulators, on `ofstream` objects.

For example, given the previous initialization of `fin`, the following statement extracts the next value from file `mydata.nbr`.

```
fin >> Value;
```

If we define an `ofstream` object, we can use it to capture insertions to a file. In the following example, we associate `ofstream` object `fout` with the file `average.nbr` and then insert the average of the inputs to that file. By default, the file associated with the `ofstream` object is made empty during the initialization of the object.

```
ofstream fout("average.nbr");
fout << Average << endl;
```

Using the above definitions, we can modify our average calculation program to extract values from file `mydata.nbr` and create a file `average.nbr` that holds the average of the values extracted from the input file. The result is Program 5.2.

Program 5.2

Calculates average of a file of numbers

```
// Program 5.2: Calculates average from program-
// specified file
#include <fstream.h>
int main() {
   ifstream fin("mydata.nbr");
   int ValuesProcessed = 0;
   float ValueSum = 0;
   float Value;
   while (fin >> Value) {
      ValueSum += Value;
      ++ValuesProcessed;
   }
   if (ValuesProcessed > 0) {
      ofstream fout("average.nbr");
      float Average = ValueSum / ValuesProcessed;
      fout << "Average: " << Average << endl;
   }
   else
      cerr << "No list to average" << endl;
   return 0;
}
```

Sometimes a requested input or output file is wrongly supplied or unavailable for some reason. There is a method of checking whether this is the case. If the stream of interest can be used, a nonzero value will be associated with it; otherwise, its value will be zero. The following code segment uses an **if** statement to test whether the input file is available before attempting an extraction.

```
ifstream fin("mydata.txt");
int Number;
if (fin) {
   fin >> Number;
   cout << Number << endl;
}
else {
   cout << "mydata.txt is unavailable, zero used "
      << " as value" << endl;
   Number = 0;
}
```

The value zero is also associated with an input stream for which there are no more values to extract. We say that a stream with this property has reached *end of file* or *eof* for short.

Backslash backlash

Consider the following object definition:

```
ifstream InStream("num\nbr.txt");
```

If you are familiar with MSDOS, you would expect that the file being associated with object `InStream` is `nbr.txt`, which can be found in the directory `num`. However, this is not what happens. As literal backslash character sequences are interpreted by the preprocessor, the `\n` in the filename is interpreted as the newline character. So the file in question is supposed to contain a newline as its fourth character. Because the newline is an illegal character in an MSDOS filename, `InStream` is improperly initialized. To achieve the correct initialization, we must use the `\\` literal sequence as in the following statement:

```
ifstream InStream("num\\nbr.txt");
```

5.7

A FIRST LOOK AT THE STRING LIBRARY

One way to achieve greater flexibility in file processing is to prompt the user for a filename and then process the file that the user specifies. The extraction of the filename can be done easily through the use of the proposed C++ standard library `string`. This library defines in part a class type `string` for representing character strings. Approximately 100 member functions and operators support the manipulation of `string` objects. The library also provides some important nonmember string processing functions and operators. For example, the library supplies insertion and extractions operators for `string` objects. These two operators are demonstrated in Program 5.3. This program prompts a user for some text and then iteratively displays the non-white space character sequences from that text.

Program 5.3
Extracting and inserting string objects

```
// Program 5.3: Extract words and insert one per line
#include <string>
#include <iostream.h>
int main() {
    string s;
    cout << "Please enter text: " << flush;
    while (cin >> s) {
        cout << s << endl;
    }
    return 0;
}
```

The following demonstrates a sample run of Program 5.3.

```
Please enter text: Good    day    to    you    all!
Good
day
```

```
to
you
all!
```

The `string` library also provides other operators such as `<`, `==`, and `!=` for making string comparisons. Observe that there is no use of a header suffix when including the `string` library (in previous versions of the proposed standard, the header file for this library was named `cstring.h`).

To help achieve our goal of flexible file processing, we use `string` member function `c_str()`. This member function returns a representation of its `string` object that can be used wherever a conventional character string is expected; for example, `ifstream` requires a conventional character string representation for the filename. Suppose we use `string` object `FileName` to store the name of the file to be processed; then `FileName.c_str()` provides a representation of that name, which is suitable as an `ifstream` initialization parameter.

The following code segment performs the actions and checks to make sure that stream `fin` is associated with a valid user-specified file.

```
cout << "File of values to be averaged: " << flush;
string FileName;
cin >> FileName;
ifstream fin(FileName.c_str());
if (! fin) {
    cerr << "Cannot open " << FileName
      << " for averaging." << endl;
    exit(1);
}
// ready to process file stream represented by fin
```

If the initialization is not successful, an error message is generated and the program is exited. Function `exit()` is defined in the `stdlib` library. This library is a collection of miscellaneous functions. Function `exit()` terminates the program with its parameter used as the program return value. Therefore, if the comment at the end of the code segment is reached, it must be the case that the expression `(! fin)` is false and that input stream `fin` represents a file that is available for processing. By adapting Program 5.2 and using this code segment, we can create a general-purpose average-calculating program. The resulting program is given as Program 5.4.

5.8

THE MATH LIBRARY

A significant amount of software development is concerned with scientific programming. The term *scientific programming* is a catch-all phrase for programming that makes extensive use of mathematical formulations and models. The programs that arise here often make use of trigonometric, exponential, and logarithmic functions. For software portability purposes, a standard math library

Program 5.4

A general-purpose average calculator

```
// Program 5.4: Prompts user for a file and then
// calculates the average of the values in that file
#include <fstream.h>
#include <iostream.h>
#include <stdlib.h>
#include <string>
int main() {
   cout << "File of values to be averaged: " << flush;
   string FileName;
   cin >> FileName;
   ifstream fin(FileName.c_str());
   if (! fin) {
      cerr << "Cannot open " << FileName
        << " for averaging." << endl;
      exit(1);
   }
   int ValuesProcessed = 0;
   float ValueSum = 0;
   float Value;
   while (fin >> Value) {
      ValueSum += Value;
      ++ValuesProcessed;
   }
   if (ValuesProcessed > 0) {
      float Average = ValueSum / ValuesProcessed;
      cout << "Average of values from " << FileName
        << " is " << Average << endl;
   }
   else {
      cerr << "No values to average in "
        << FileName << endl;
      exit(1);
   }
   return 0;
}
```

has been developed with many common math functions. The `sqrt()` function that we use in Program 5.1 is a math library function.

The interface for the math library is specified in the standard file `math.h`. Table 5.3 provides a listing of selected functions declared in that library. Unlike the other standard libraries discussed in this chapter, the actual math function definitions are not necessarily automatically linked to the program being translated. For compilers that are invoked from a command line prompt, the linking is typically requested via a parameter to the compilation command. For compilers that are part of larger programming environments, the linking is typically requested by setting an appropriate library option. The math library is treated differently because depending upon the circumstances, programmers may prefer to link to different library implementations. Possible library trade-offs can be floating-point accuracy and efficiency. The implementations of the components for the other libraries that we have considered are more straightforward than the implementation of the math library and thus do not normally require considering such trade-offs.

Table 5.3

Selected math library functions

Function	Computes
acos(**double** x)	Angle whose cosine is x
asin(**double** x)	Angle whose sine is x
atan(**double** x)	Angle whose tangent is x
atan2(**double** x, **double** y)	Angle whose tangent is x/y
ceil(**double** x)	Smallest whole number greater than or equal to x
cos(**double** x)	Cosine of angle x
cosh(**double** x)	Hyperbolic cosine of angle x
exp(**double** x)	e^x
fabs(**double** x)	Absolute value of x
floor(**double** x)	Largest whole number less than or equal to x
log(**double** x)	Natural log of x
log10(**double** x)	Log base 10 of x
pow(**double** x, **double** y)	x^y
sin(**double** x)	Sine of angle x
sinh(**double** x)	Hyperbolic sin of angle x
sqrt(**double** x)	Square root of x
tan(**double** x)	Tangent of angle x
tanh(**double** x)	Hyperbolic tangent of angle x

As indicated in Table 5.3, the math functions all return **double** values and generally expect **double** values as parameters. The **double** type is used as it typically provides greater precision than the **float** type (at a minimum it provides equal precision). If you invoke one of these functions with a numerical value that is not **double**, then a standard conversion is applied to *promote* the parameter to **double**. Parameter promotions are standard practice and are performed automatically if they are necessary on a fundamental type parameter to match an invocation with an applicable function. It is also possible to define promotion processes for programmer-defined types. We consider the promotion process in detail in subsequent chapters.

5.8.1

Computing compound interest

The formula for computing interest compounded on an annual basis follows.

$$EndingAmount = StartingAmount \cdot (1 + InterestRate/100)^{Years}$$

Using math library function pow(), the compound interest formula can be readily converted into C++.

```
                    float EndingAmount =
                     StartingAmount*pow(1+InterestRate/100.0,Years);
```

We use this definition of `EndingAmount` in Program 5.5. The program requires three user input values: the amount of deposit, the interest rate, and the term of deposit. After extracting these values, the program then computes how the principal will change.

Program 5.5

Computing compound interest

```
// Program 5.5: Computes the effect of the annual
// compounding of interest on a user-specified amount,
//interest rate, and term of deposit
#include <iostream.h>
#include <math.h>
int main() {
   cout << "Principal amount: " << flush;
   float StartingAmount;
   cin >> StartingAmount;
   cout << "Interest rate (%): " << flush;
   float InterestRate;
   cin >> InterestRate;
   cout << "Years of deposit: " << flush;
   float Years;
   cin >> Years;
   float EndingAmount =
    StartingAmount*pow(1+InterestRate/100.0, Years);
   cout << "Principal " << StartingAmount
    << " when compounded annually for " << Years << endl
    << "years at " << InterestRate << "% produces "
    << EndingAmount << endl;
   return 0;
}
```

An example of the input/output behavior of Program 5.5 follows.

```
Principal amount: 1000
Interest rate (%): 9
Years of deposit: 12
Principal 1000 when compounded annually for 12
years at 9% produces 2812.66
```

5.9

LIBRARY CTYPE

The ctype library is useful in text processing. The library provides a number of functions that test whether a character has a particular property. If the tested character has the property, the function returns a nonzero value; otherwise, the function returns 0. The library also provides two functions that convert an uppercase letter to its lowercase equivalent and vice versa. Table 5.4 provides a listing of these functions. The actual function actions are defined to be locally dependent to account for differences in the native languages of program users.

Program 5.6 uses function `toupper()` to echo its input characters in their uppercase equivalent. An example of its input/output behavior follows.

Function	Purpose
int isalnum(**int** c)	Tests whether isalpha() or isdigit() is true for character c
int isalpha(**int** c)	Tests whether islower() or isupper() is true for character c
int iscntrl(**int** c)	Tests whether c is a control character
int isdigit(**int** c)	Tests whether c is a decimal digit
int isgraph(**int** c)	Tests whether c is printable, non-space character
int islower(**int** c)	Tests whether c is a lowercase letter
int isprint(**int** c)	Tests whether c is a printable character
int ispunct(**int** c)	Tests whether both isgraph() is true and isalnum() is false for character c
int isspace(**int** c)	Tests whether c is one of the following characters: space ' ', form feed '\f', newline '\n', carriage return '\r', horizontal tab '\t', or vertical tab '\v'
int isupper(**int** c)	Tests whether c is an uppercase letter
int isxdigit(**int** c)	Tests whether c is a hexadecimal digit
int tolower(**int** c)	If isupper() is true for c and there is a corresponding lowercase equivalent character d for which islower() is true, then d is returned; otherwise, c is returned
int toupper(**int** c)	If islower() is true for c and there is a corresponding uppercase equivalent character d for which isupper() is true, then d is returned, otherwise; c, is returned

Table 5.4

Selected ctype library functions

```
Please enter text: hello world!
HELLO WORLD!
```

The exclamation point in the greeting is unaffected because it is not a lower-case letter in our local implementation.

5.10

THE ASSERT MACROS

The assert library provides a preprocessor macro assert that is useful during program development. The assert macro expects an integral expression as its single parameter. When an assert macro is invoked, its parameter expression is tested to see whether it has the value zero. If the expression is nonzero, the program continues in the normal fashion. If the expression is zero, the program produces a message to the standard error stream displaying the expression that

Program 5.6

Echoing input characters in their uppercase equivalent

```
// Program 5.6: Echoes input in uppercase equivalent
#include <iostream.h>
#include <ctype.h>
int main() {
    cin.unsetf(ios::skipws); // don't skip white space
    cout << "Please enter text: " << flush;
    char c;
    while (cin >> c) {
        c = toupper(c);
        cout << c;
    }
    cout << endl;
    return 0;
}
```

sion that caused the program to terminate, the name of the source file, and the line in that file where the failed `assert` expression occurred. After displaying the information, the program terminates.

Program 5.7 uses an `assert` statement to make sure that the denominator is nonzero for the quotient and remainder that it computes from two input values.

Program 5.7

Asserting a denominator is zero

```
// Program 5.7: Computes quotient and remainder of two
// inputs
#include <assert.h>
#include <iostream.h>
int main() {
    int Numerator;
    cout << "Enter numerator: " << flush;
    cin >> Numerator;
    int Denominator;
    cout << "Enter denominator: " << flush;
    cin >> Denominator;
    assert(Denominator); // really should be if test
    int Ratio = Numerator / Denominator;
    int Remainder = Numerator % Denominator;
    cout << Numerator << "/" << Denominator << " = "
      << Ratio << " with remainder " << Remainder << endl;
    return 0;
}
```

Suppose Program 5.7 is contained in the file `my.cpp`. If a zero is extracted for its object `Denominator`, then the `assert` macro will test to zero and the program will terminate after displaying an error message similar to the following:

```
Assertion failed: Denominator, file my.cpp, line 12
```

The assertion failure information while useful to a programmer is usually meaningless to a user. Thus the use of `assert` macros should not replace input validation or user-friendly error messages. Programmers normally use `assert` macros during debugging to help verify that their program logic is correct.

Programming Tip

Controlling the evaluation of assert invocations

For the expression in an `assert` invocation to be evaluated, the macro `NDEBUG` must be undefined. Thus, the default behavior of an `assert` invocation is to evaluate assertions. Through the use of the following preprocessor statement, the evaluation of subsequent assertions can be turned off.

```
#define NDEBUG
```

In some implementations, evaluation of assertions can be turned on again through the use of the following preprocessor statement:

```
#undef NDEBUG
```

This process works as the actions performed by an assert invocation are nested within a conditional evaluation directive that checks whether `NDEBUG` is defined.

It is normal practice to include the defining of `NDEBUG` at the start of a program that is distributed to users.

History of Computing

Punch card computing

The U.S.'s Census Department must perform a census every 10 years. In 1880, the actual head count required only a few months, but tabulating and analyzing the data took nine years to complete. Recognizing a problem in need of a solution, Herman Hollerith developed a system that used punched cards and special machines that could tabulate the data recorded on the cards. The system was quite simple. Data about a person, such as age, sex, and marital status, were recorded on a card by punching holes in the proper positions. The data on the card were counted by a machine operated by a human. The card was placed in a reader station. The operator applied a press containing pins that corresponded to each possible position that a hole could be punched. In locations where a hole was punched, a pin would make contact with a connection on the other side of the card and a counter would be incremented.

Through various trials and tests, Hollerith's system proved to be a vast improvement over previous tabulation methods. Hollerith formed a company, called the Tabulating Machine Company, and rented machines to the Census Department to perform the 1890 census. The tally of the total number of people in the United States was available six weeks after the head count was started. All the final statistics were available in seven years. This may not seem like much of an improvement, but the 1890 census included a far more thorough and detailed analysis of the raw data.

Hollerith's system was featured on the cover of the August 1890 issue of *Scientific American*, and it was adopted by countries all over Europe. Eventually, companies began using the system to do accounting and inventory. Hollerith's company experienced phenomenal growth and eventually merged with several others; it ultimately became one of the giants in the computing industry, International Business Machines (IBM).

5.11

POINTS TO REMEMBER

- Software reuse is important if programs are to be developed quickly and efficiently. One of the major sources of software is the standard libraries.

- C++ provides a significant number of libraries for a variety of application areas. Some of the more important stream libraries are the iostream, iomanip, and fstream libraries. These libraries provide mechanisms for the insertion and extraction of information in a controlled manner.

- Information to a function is passed via parameters. The function's computation is normally brought back as the return value. The type of value brought back by a function is the return type. A function that does not return a value has the type **void**.

- The parameters in the invocation are called the actual parameters. The actual parameters are represented in the invoked function by its formal parameters.

- When a function is invoked, flow of control is transferred from the invoking function to the invoked function. When the invoked function completes, control is transferred back to the invoking function. If the invoked function returns a value, then that value is essentially substituted for the invocation.

- Every function invocation creates an activation record. The values of the formal parameters and other objects defined in the function are kept in the activation record.

- Before a function is invoked, it must be prototyped or defined. A prototype is a description of the function's interface. A function definition contains both a description of the function's interface and its statement body. A description of the interface specifies the return type, function name, and the form of the parameter list.

- One way of passing actual parameters is the pass-by-value parameter-passing style. When an actual parameter is passed in this style, the formal parameter is called a value parameter because it is initialized to the value of the actual parameter. Subsequent changes to the formal parameter do not affect the actual parameter.

- All the standard libraries have header files that prototype the functions defined in those libraries. Depending upon the library, the header file may also contain object, class, and function definitions.

- The preprocessor is responsible for processing three kinds of commands in a program file. The file inclusion directives specify files that are to be part of the translation unit that is to be compiled. Macro definitions and invocations enable parameterized textual substitution. This ability is not important, as C++ has equivalent mechanisms that are type safe. Conditional compilation directives allow a programmer to restrict which lines of code are compiled.

- A hierarchy of classes exists for representing input and output streams. The root of this hierarchy is the class `ios`. Two other important classes are `istream` and `ostream`. Class `istream` is a root of the subhierarchy for input streams; class `ostream` is a root of the subhierarchy for output streams. In addition, there are the classes `ifstream` and `ofstream` for defining streams that manipulate files. These two streams process extractions and insertions respectively. The classes `iostream` and `fstream` define streams capable of both extractions and insertions.

- The iostream library defines two streams for error messages. Stream `cerr` is for unbuffered error messages; stream `clog` is for buffered error messages.

- The iostream provides manipulators for specifying how to perform insertions and extractions. In particular, these manipulators enable such actions (among others) as flushing the stream, ignoring white space, and specifying the number base.

- The iomanip library also provides stream manipulators. Two of its important manipulators allow the width and precision of an insertion to be specified easily.

- The string library defines a class `string` that can be used to represent a character string. The library provides an extensive set of member functions and operators for manipulating `string` objects. For some compilers, this library is called cstring.

- The math library provides access to trigonometric, exponential, and logarithmic functions.

- The ctype library provides functions for testing whether character objects have specific properties.

- The assert library defines an `assert` macro that enables an integral expression to be evaluated. If the expression is false, the program is terminated. If the expression is true, program execution continues in a normal manner.

5.12

TO DELVE FURTHER

The description of the functions and components of the various libraries in this chapter is adapted from the following sources:

- Working Paper for the Draft Proposed International Standard for Information Systems—Programming Language C++, X3J16/96-0018 WG21/N0836, American National Standards Institute, Washington, DC, 1996.

- P. J. Plauger, *The Standard C Library*, Englewood Cliffs, NJ: Prentice-Hall, 1992.

- S. Teale, *C++ IOStreams*, Reading, MA: Addison-Wesley, 1993.

5.13

EXERCISES

5.1 Search the directories on your system to find where the header files are stored.

5.2 Discuss flow of control.

5.3 Speculate on possible parameter-passing styles other than pass by value. Discuss how they could be effective.

5.4 Most operating systems designate one character as the end-of-file character. This character is different from the iostream **int** constant EOF. When this character is reached in standard input, the user is indicating that there are no more input values to follow. On most PC-based systems, the end of file character is Ctl-z. On many other systems, it is Ctl-d. Determine what the end-of-file character is on your system. Indicate how you determined it.

5.5 Suppose a cout output request was unsuccessful; that is, it returned zero. What could cause such an event? How could you inform the user of the program?

5.6 Prototype the following functions:

a) A function QuarticRoot() that takes a double-precision floating-point value x as its parameter and returns a value of that same type.

b) A function Area() that takes two integer values length and width and returns an integer result.

c) A function IsMathSymbol() that takes a character value c and returns a Boolean value.

d) A function GetNumber() that does not take any parameters and returns an integer.

5.7 Prototype the following functions:

a) A function that returns the volume of a specified sphere.

b) A function that returns the speed of an object starting at rest that accelerates at a specified rate for a specified number of seconds.

c) A function that converts a Celsius temperature to a Fahrenheit temperature.

d) A function that displays five spaces to the standard output stream cout.

e) A function that displays a specified number of spaces to the standard output stream cout.

5.8 Determine whether your implementation of the iostream library displays a **float** number by default in decimal or scientific notation. Does the default behavior have anything to do with how big or how small the number is? Does the default behavior have anything to do with where the most significant digit is found?

5.9 Modify Program 5.1 so that it correctly processes quadratic equations whose roots are imaginary or whose coefficient *a* is zero.

5.10 Is Program 5.1 a candidate for having its input coming from a file stream? Why?

5.11 Modify Program 5.3 so that the input comes from a user-specified file.

5.12 Should a program prompt a user for an input value using stream `cout` or `cerr`? Give reasons for the possible use of either stream.

5.13 What is the output of the following program? Why?

```
int main () {
    cout << "12345678901234567890" << endl;
    cout << setw(5) << 100 << endl;
    cout << 100 << endl;
    cout << setprecision(4) << 71.498000000001
      << endl;
    cout << setfill('0');
    cout << setw(10) << 88 << endl;
    cout << setw(20) << "Hello World" << endl;
    return 0;
}
```

5.14 Write C++ expressions for the following formulas.

a) $(\sin x)^2 \times (\cos x)^2$

b) $e^{\frac{1}{2}\sqrt{\tan \cos x}}$

c) $\dfrac{\left\lfloor \log\left(\dfrac{x^2}{1-x}\right)\right\rfloor}{\left\lceil x^{5+x}\right\rceil}$

5.15 Write a program that displays the following strings to standard output. The strings should be displayed one per line with each line centered within a field length that is extracted from standard input.

```
Greetings earth inhabitants
Take me to your leaders
Is that all there is
It is not our fault
```

5.16 Implement a program that extracts a character from standard input and then inserts a nicely displayed and labeled table to standard output. The information in the table is the values produced by the various functions in the ctype library when invoked with the extracted character as the parameter.

5.17 Rewrite your solution to Exercise 5.16 so that its output is inserted to the file `ctype.tbl`.

5.18 Implement a program without any loops that extracts five input values. The program displays these value in histogram form using astericks. For example, if the input is

```
5 9 4 12 7
```

then the output should be

```
 5:  *****
 9:  ********
 4:  ****
12:  ***********
 7:  *******
```

Hint: Use the iostream to modify the fill character.

5.19 Rewrite your solution to Exercise 5.18 so that `setw()` is the only stream manipulator used; that is, use loops.

5.20 Correct macro ADD (page 209) so that it ensures that the addition it performs takes precedence over other surrounding operators.

5.21 Design and implement a program that prompts a user for a filename and string. The program then counts the numbers of occurrences of that string in the specified file.

5.22 Design and implement a program that prompts a user for the sides, *a*, *b*, and *c* of a triangle, and if these sides do represent a triangle, the program displays the area of that triangle. The sides represent a valid triangle if the sum of the lengths for any two sides is greater than the length of the remaining side. The area of a triangle can be computed from its sides using the formula

$$\sqrt{s \cdot (s - a) \cdot (s - b) \cdot (s - c)}$$

where *s* is half of the sum of the sides (i.e., it is half the perimeter).

5.23 Design and implement a program that prompts a user for a starting amount and a number of years. The program determines the percentage rate that allows the amount to double in the required number of years.

5.24 Design and implement a program that prompts a user for a starting amount and a percentage rate. The program determines how many years are necessary for the amount to double given the percentage rate.

5.25 Is the starting amount a necessary input for Exercise 5.23 and Exercise 5.24? Explain.

5.26 Write a program that copies the characters in standard input stream `cin` to standard output stream `cout` except for the alphanumeric characters, which are to be ignored.

5.27 Write a program that copies the characters in standard input stream `cin` to standard output stream `cout` except for the digit characters. For a digit character, the program instead displays the digit's name; that is, zero for 0, one for 1, and so on.

5.28 Write a program that copies the characters in standard input stream `cin` to standard output stream `cout` while replacing all white space characters with the corresponding escape code. For example, if the input contains a tab, then the character `\t` is inserted.

CHAPTER 6

Programmer-defined functions

Introduction

The previous chapter explored the use of library functions to accomplish tasks. However, any significant software project also requires that new functions be designed and implemented. In this chapter, we consider the basics of programmer-defined functions with value parameters. Our examination includes a discussion of invocation, parameters, and the local and global scopes.

Key Concepts

- programmer-defined functions
- invocation and flow of control
- parameters
- prototypes
- activation records
- return statement
- local objects
- scope
- global objects
- name reuse
- implementation file
- header file
- standard class `strstream`
- class `Label`
- **extern** modifier

6.1

BASICS

Using existing software libraries to accomplish programming tasks is the preferred problem-solving strategy. This preference reflects the expectation that library use will be cost effective with respect to both time and money. However, for most software tasks using only library functions is not possible—it is also necessary to create programmer-defined functions.

Besides being concerned with correctness and efficiency when you design your own functions, you must also be concerned with software reuse. Reuse helps to minimize the expenses of maintenance and future projects.

With the exception of one program that demonstrates the use of global objects, the functions that we design in this chapter have two properties:

- External information to be used by a function comes from its value parameter list or by extractions from an input stream.

- Information to be communicated from a function is sent through its return value or by insertions to a output stream.

Such control over the information flow makes it easier for a function to be implemented and understood. This information flow is depicted in Figure 6.1.

Figure 6.1

Model for flow of information to and from a function using value parameters

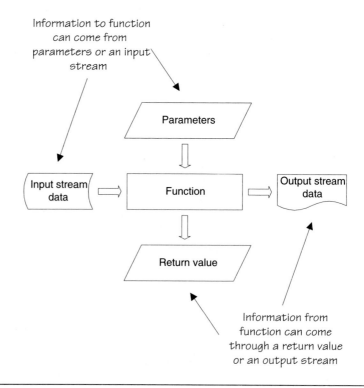

6.1.1

Function definition syntax

A *function definition* includes both a description of the interface and the statement list that comprises its actions. Since C++ allows different functions to have the same name, giving the function name alone is insufficient for a complete and unambiguous definition. Instead, the entire interface including the names and types of the formal parameters is used by C++ to indicate which function is being defined.

Program 6.1 contains the definition of a function CircleArea(). This function computes the area of a circle, and it is invoked by function main() in that same program. Function CircleArea() has a single **float** parameter r and has a **float** return type.

Program 6.1

Calling a user-defined function from main()

```
// Program 6.1: Compute area of a user-specified circle
#include <iostream.h>

// CircleArea(): compute area of circle of radius r
float CircleArea(float r) {
   const float Pi = 3.1415;
   return Pi * r * r;
}

// main(): manage computation and display of the area of
// a user-specified circle
int main() {
   // prompt and read the radius
   float DesiredRadius;
   cout << "Circle radius (real number)? " << flush;
   cin >> DesiredRadius;

   // compute the area
   float Area = CircleArea(DesiredRadius);
   cout << "Area of circle with radius "
   << DesiredRadius << " is " << Area << endl;

   // all done
   return 0;
}
```

As in previous examples using a function main(), the actions to be performed by a function are given in the *function body*. The function body is a statement list that is nested within left and right curly braces. The body of function CircleArea() from the definition in Program 6.1 is

```
   const float Pi = 3.1415;
   return Pi * r * r;
```

There are no restrictions on what kind of statements can be used in a function body. Any statement that would be permissible in function main() is permissible in any other function. The first statement defines an approximation Pi to the mathematical constant π. The next statement is the **return** statement for the function. It makes use of constant Pi and the circle area formula πr^2 to compute a **float** expression that corresponds to the area of a circle with a radius specified by parameter r.

A function uses a **return** statement to indicate that its task is completed. If the function return type is non-**void**, the statement also supplies the function's return value to the invoker of the function. A **return** statement has the form

For non-void functions, this value is returned to the
invoking function; for void functions, it is empty

return *ReturnExpression* ;

where *ReturnExpression* evaluates to a value whose type should be the same as the return type that is specified in the interface for the function. If the type of *ReturnExpression* is not the same as the return type, conversions are automatically attempted to transform the value of *ReturnExpression* to the return type. For function CircleArea(), the return value is the value of the expression Pi * r * r. Once a *ReturnExpression* is computed, execution continues at the invocation using the value of *ReturnExpression*.

Although it is not necessary, functions of type **void** can use **return** statements. In a **void** function, a **return** statement is an explicit indication that the function is finished and that flow of control should return to the function that did the call. The **return** statement for a **void** function is not permitted to include an expression.

6.1.2

Invocation and flow of control

As with library function invocations, the correspondence between the actual parameters in an invocation and the formal parameters of a programmer-defined function is determined by the relative positions of the parameters. The first actual parameter is associated with the first formal parameter, the second actual parameter is associated with the second formal parameter, and so on.

For function main() in Program 6.1, its activation record includes the objects DesiredRadius and Area. Suppose that the value extracted for DesiredRadius is 10 and that in terms of the execution of main() we are about to execute the definition of Area. A depiction of a snapshot of the activation record of main() follows (a question mark indicates that the object's value has not yet been set by the program).

main()	
DesiredRadius	10.000
Area	?

When function `CircleArea()` is invoked to initialize `Area`, an activation record is also created for it. In that activation record, formal parameter `r` is initialized to the value of the actual parameter, which in this case is the value of `DesiredRadius`. The activation record for this invocation has the following depiction:

CircleArea()	
r	10.0000
Pi	3.1415

Since the formal parameter `r` is a value parameter, once `DesiredRadius` has been used to initialize `r`, `DesiredRadius` and `r` are independent of each other. Whenever `r` is used in `CircleArea()`, the value used for `r` is the one stored in the current activation record for the function. If `CircleArea()` were to make a change to `r`, the change would occur within the memory of `CircleArea()`'s current activation record and object `DesiredRadius` would be unaffected. Essentially formal parameter `r` is an object that is *local* to function `CircleArea()`. The parameter is created with an invocation of `CircleArea()`, and it is destroyed when function `CircleArea()` completes and releases its activation record memory.

For our invocation of `CircleArea()`, the return value is 314.15, and this value is used to initialize `Area`. At that point, `main()`'s activation record has the following depiction:

main()	
DesiredRadius	10.000
Area	314.150

As noted in the previous chapter, it is important to remember that an invocation cannot appear until the function being invoked has been prototyped or defined. In Program 6.1, the definition of function `CircleArea()` occurs before the definition of function `main()`. This ordering allows `main()` to invoke `CircleArea()`. Although `CircleArea()` is defined before `main()`, program execution begins in `main()`.

6.2

A TASTY PROBLEM

Suppose we are interested in computing the size of a donut. For our purposes, a donut is a cylinder with a cylindrical core removed. This shape is demonstrated in Figure 6.2.

The size of a cylinder with radius r and height h is given by the formula $\pi r^2 h$. Based on our experience of computing the size of a circle, computing

Programming Tip

Constant value parameters

With one exception, the functions that we define in this chapter effectively use their formal parameters as constants that are initialized using the actual parameters. Because the formal parameters are used in this manner, we could have declared them to be **const** value parameters. For example, the following code segment defines function `CircleArea()` using a **const** parameter declaration.

```
float CircleArea(const float r) {
    const float Pi = 3.1415;
    return Pi * r * r;
}
```

In previous situations, when an object was not to be changed, we have applied the **const** modifier to provide extra information to the compiler and to the client programmer. However, in this context, we are giving information to the client regarding the implementation of the function that is not needed—the client cares only that the function does its job and that the actual parameter not be modified. Making the formal parameter a value parameter is sufficient to accomplish this. And by not making it a **const** formal parameter, we are free to change the implementation, and if necessary in this change, use the value formal parameter in a manner that allows it to be modified. This freedom, which does not affect the client, outweighs providing the **const** information.

Figure 6.2
A donut can be approximated as a cylinder with a cylindrical core removed

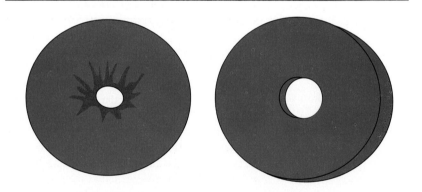

the size of a cylinder is straightforward. A function `CylinderVolume()` to do this computation is given below.

```
// CylinderVolume(): compute the size of a cylinder
// with radius r and height h
float CylinderVolume(float r, float h) {
    const float Pi = 3.1415;
    return Pi * r * r * h;
}
```

The size of a donut can be calculated by taking the difference in the sizes of two cylinders. Function `DonutSize()` does this job for us. It expects the radii of two corresponding cylinders as its parameters along with the thickness of the donut. It returns the difference in the cylinder volumes defined by those parameters.

```
// DonutSize(): compute the size of a donut with
// outer edge radius Outer from the donut center,
// inner edge radius Inner from the donut center,
// and thickness Width
float DonutSize(float Outer, float Inner, float
 Width) {
    float OuterSize = CylinderVolume(Outer, Width);
    float HoleSize = CylinderVolume(Inner, Width);
    return OuterSize - HoleSize;
}
```

Note that just as the invocation of `CircleArea()` in Program 6.1 requires that memory be set aside for an activation record to store the value associated with its parameter `r`, so do invocations of `DonutSize()` and `Cylinder-Volume()` require that memory be set aside for activation records to store the values of the parameters and objects that they use.

Once the `DonutSize()` parameter initialization is completed, parameters `Outer` and `Inner` are independent of the objects or expressions used to initialize them. As discussed previously, this independence is a characteristic of the value parameter passing. Inside `DonutSize()`, we are free to use `Outer`, `Inner`, and `Width` as **float** objects. In particular, we can use them in function invocations. Thus, in the definition of `OuterSize` there is no problem using `Outer` and `Width` to initialize parameters `r` and `h` in the first invocation of `CylinderVolume()`. Likewise, in the definition of `HoleSize` there is no problem using `Inner` and `Width` to initialize the parameters of `Cylinder-Volume()` in its second invocation.

The two invocations of `CylinderVolume()` by `DonutSize()` do require that `CylinderVolume()` be previously defined or prototyped in the program file. In Program 6.2, our complete solution to the donut problem, `CylinderVolume()` is prototyped before `DonutSize()` is defined.

In Program 6.2, we follow convention and define function `main()` before defining other functions. We also follow the convention of placing prototypes of the other functions defined in the program file prior to the definition of the `main()`. Since C++ allows a function to be used once it has been prototyped, the placing of these prototypes at the beginning of the program file allows us to define `DonutSize()` and `CylinderVolume()` in any order.

The prototyping of `CylinderVolume()` calls the parameters `Radius` and `Width` even though the definition of `CylinderVolume()` uses `r` and `h`. This difference is perfectly fine—a prototype declaration describes only the form of a function's interface. As remarked in the previous chapter, supplying identifier names is optional in a prototype—specifying the types of the formal parameters is sufficient. However, supplying a meaningful name makes it easier for programmers to understand the code. Because the great majority of soft-

Program 6.2

Computing the area of a donut through user-defined functions

```cpp
// Program 6.2: Compute size of a user-specified donut
#include <iostream.h>

// prototyping
float DonutSize(float Outer, float Inner, float Width);
float CylinderVolume(float Radius, float Width);

// main(): manage computation and display of user-
// specified donut size
int main() {
    // prompt for donut dimensions
    cout << "Outer edge donut radius: " << flush;
    float OuterEdge;
    cin >> OuterEdge;
    cout << "Hole radius: " << flush;
    float InnerEdge;
    cin >> InnerEdge;
    cout << "Donut thickness: " << flush;
    float Thickness;
    cin >> Thickness;

    // compute and display the size of our donut
    cout << endl << "Size of donut with" << endl
     << "    radius " << OuterEdge << endl
     << "    hole radius " << InnerEdge << endl
     << "    thickness " << Thickness << endl
     << "is "
     << DonutSize(OuterEdge, InnerEdge, Thickness)
     << endl;

    return 0;
}

// DonutSize(): compute the size of a donut with outer
// edge radius Outer from the donut center, inner edge
// radius Inner from the donut center, and thickness
// Width
float DonutSize(float Outer, float Inner, float Width) {
    float OuterSize = CylinderVolume(Outer, Width);
    float HoleSize = CylinderVolume(Inner, Width);
    return OuterSize - HoleSize;
}

// CylinderVolume(): compute the size of a cylinder with
// radius r and height h
float CylinderVolume(float r, float h) {
    const float Pi = 3.1415;
    return Pi * r * r * h;
}
```

ware development effort is spent modifying existing code, making code easy to understand should pay off.

We next trace through a sample running of the program. Suppose the dimensions extracted for OuterEdge, InnerEdge, and Thickness are 2.5,

0.5, and 0.75, respectively. After the three extractions, the activation record for function `main()` has depiction

main()	
OuterEdge	2.5000
InnerEdge	0.5000
Thickness	0.7500

The invocation of `DonutSize()` in the insertion statement causes a temporary transfer of control to a copy of function `DonutSize()`. The parameters `Outer`, `Inner`, and `Width` are initialized using the values 2.5 from `OuterEdge`, 0.5 from `InnerEdge`, and 0.75 from `Thickness`. The activation record associated with this invocation of `DonutSize()` after parameter initialization has depiction

DonutSize()	
Outer	2.5000
Inner	0.5000
Width	0.7500
OuterSize	?
HoleSize	?

The initialization of `Outer` causes a temporary transfer of control from `DonutSize()` to a copy of `CylinderVolume()`. The parameters `r` and `h` of `CylinderVolume()` are initialized using the values 2.5 and 0.75 of `Outer` and `Width`.

CylinderVolume()	
r	2.500
h	0.750

After defining `Pi`, `CylinderVolume()` computes and returns the value of expression `Pi * r * r * h`, which is approximately 14.7258. The return causes control to be transferred back to `DonutSize()` and the memory for

`CylinderVolume()`'s activation record to be released. The activation record for `DonutSize()` now has depiction

DonutSize()	
Outer	2.5000
Inner	0.5000
Width	0.7500
OuterSize	14.7258
HoleSize	?

The initialization of `Inner` in `DonutSize()` causes another temporary transfer of control from `DonutSize()` to a copy of `CylinderVolume()`. The parameters `r` and `h` of `CylinderVolume()` are now initialized respectively using the values 0.5 and 0.75 of `Inner` and `Width`.

CylinderVolume()	
r	0.500
h	0.750

After defining `Pi`, `CylinderVolume()` computes and returns the value of expression `Pi * r * r * h`, which for this invocation is approximately 0.5890. The return causes control to be transferred back to `DonutSize()` and the memory for `CylinderVolume()`'s activation record to be released. The activation record for `DonutSize()` now has depiction

DonutSize()	
Outer	2.500
Inner	0.500
Width	0.750
OuterSize	14.7258
HoleSize	0.5890

The return statement of `DonutSize()` is then executed. The return expression has value 14.1368. The return causes the activation record memory of `DonutSize()` to be released and control transferred back to `main()`, which uses the value 14.1368 in its insertion statement.

The input/output behavior of this tracing through Program 6.2 follows.

```
Outer edge donut radius: 2.5
Hole radius: 0.5
Donut thickness: 0.75

Size of donut with
    radius 2.5
    hole radius 0.5
    thickness 0.75
is 14.1368
```

6.3

SOME USEFUL FUNCTIONS

Two useful functions for many programs are `max()` and `min()`. For current purposes, both functions return an **int** value and require two **int** parameters. Function `max()` returns the larger value of its two parameters, and `min()` returns the smaller value of its two parameters.

Function `max()` can be implemented in the following manner:

```
// max(): determine larger of its two parameters
int max(int a, int b) {
    if (a < b)
        return b;
    else
        return a;
}
```

The function begins by comparing the values of its two parameters. If the expression a < b, which tests whether parameter a is less than parameter b, is true, then b is the larger of the values and the value of b is returned. If the test a < b is instead false, then a is no smaller than b, so the value of a is returned. The preceding function demonstrates that a function can have more than one **return** statement.

Function `min()` can be implemented in a similar manner to function `max()`. The only change is using the > operator rather than the < operator to compare the values of the two parameters.

```
// min(): determine smaller of its two parameters
int min(int a, int b) {
    if (a > b)
        return b;
    else
        return a;
}
```

Suppose we are required to prompt and extract two input values and then indicate the larger of the two values and the smaller of the two values. The following code segment using max() and min() accomplishes this task.

```
cout << "Please enter a number (integer): " << flush;
int Value1;
cin >> Value1;
cout << "Please enter a number (integer): " << flush;
int Value2;
cin >> Value2;
cout << "Max: " << max(Value1, Value2) << endl;
cout << "Min: " << min(Value1, Value2) << endl;
```

As noted previously, the actual parameters in an invocation of a function do not need to have the same name as the formal parameters. The correspondence between actual and formal parameters is always established using their positions in the parameter list. In the invocation of max() in the preceding code segment, the first formal parameter a is associated with the first actual parameter Value1 and the second formal parameter b is associated with the second actual parameter Value2. Once the correspondence is set, function max() performs its computation and returns the appropriate value. A similar correspondence is established between the actual parameters in the invocation of min() in the preceding code segment and the formal parameters contained in min()'s definition.

Another useful function is **int** function PromptAndRead() that first issues a prompt for a number to output stream cout. The function then extracts the response from the input stream cin. The response is used as the return value for PromptAndRead(). The function does not require any parameters because the invoking function provides no information to PromptAndRead() for its computation.

```
// PromptAndRead(): prompt and extract next integer
int PromptAndRead() {
    cout << "Please enter a number (integer): "
      << flush;
    int Response;
    cin >> Response;
    return Response;
}
```

Our code segment for determining the larger and smaller of two input values can be rewritten to use PromptAndRead() for acquiring the input.

```
int Value1 = PromptAndRead();
int Value2 = PromptAndRead();
cout << "Max: " << max(Value1, Value2) << endl;
cout << "Min: " << min(Value1, Value2) << endl;
```

In the previous chapter, we developed a code segment for determining whether a character is a vowel. For purposes of software reuse, it makes sense to encapsulate that code segment into a function so that it is not necessary to reproduce the statements every time such a computation is necessary. An appropriate name for this function would be IsVowel. The function would require a single **char** value as its parameter and return a **bool** value indicating whether that value is a vowel.

```
// IsVowel(): determine whether parameter is a vowel
bool IsVowel(char ch) {
    switch (ch) {
        case 'a': case 'A':
        case 'e': case 'E':
        case 'i': case 'I':
        case 'o': case 'O':
        case 'u': case 'U':
            return true;
        default:
            return false;
    }
}
```

In our next example, we define a function to compute the factorial of a number. As discussed in Chapter 4, this expression is denoted mathematically as *n*! where

$$
n! = \begin{cases} 1 & \text{if } n = 0 \\ n \times (n-1) \times \ldots \times 1 & \text{if } n \geq 1 \end{cases}
$$

Our function is named Factorial(). It expects a single **int** parameter n, and it returns an **int**.

```
// Factorial(): determine n! for parameter n
int Factorial(int n) {
    int nfactorial = 1;
    while (n > 1) {
        nfactorial *= n;
        --n;
    }
    return nfactorial;
}
```

Function Factorial() uses its parameter n to represent the current factor for updating the running product nfactorial. Once n has the value 1, all factors have been considered. Because n is a value parameter, the change made to it by the function does not affect the actual parameter. This independence is illustrated in the following code segment:

```
int i = 5;
int Result = Factorial(i);
cout << i << "! equals " << Result << endl;
```

which displays

```
5! equals 120
```

Our implementation of function Factorial() does not perform any checking to make sure that the value of n is sensible. Adding such a check is left as an exercise.

6.4

THE LOCAL SCOPE

Consider Program 6.3. What is its output?

Program 6.3

Program with a scope problem

```
// Program 6.3: Has a scope problem
#include <iostream.h>

void Mystery(int a, int b); // prototype

int main() {
    int i = 10;             // local object definition
    int j = 20;             // local object definition
    Mystery(i, j);          // invocation of mystery with
                            // local objects i and j
    cout << a << endl;   // insert?
    cout << b << endl;   // insert?
    return 0;
}

void Mystery(int a, int b) {
    cout << a << endl;
    cout << b << endl;
    a = 1;
    b = 2;
    cout << a << endl;
    cout << b << endl;
    return;
}
```

The question is a trick. Function `main()` would not execute because it could not compile. The references to a and b in function `main()` are illegal. Objects a and b do not exist in the *scope* of function `main()`. According to the C++ language specification, a function's parameters and the objects declared within the function can be used only within the function itself. Such objects are said to be *local* to the function. Depending upon where the definition occurs and what other definitions occur in the function, scope rules can also limit a local object or parameter to particular sections of code within the function.

6.4.1

Local scope rules

A *block* is a list of statements nested within curly braces. By this definition a function body is a block. It is legal in C++ to put a statement block anywhere a statement would be legal, and there is no restriction on what type of statements the block can include. This flexibility allows us to have a block within a block within a block and so on. A block contained within another block is called a *nested* block.

The statement list that comprises a block is naturally delimited, or *terminated* in C++ terminology, from the statement that follows it by the right curly brace. Thus no semicolon is needed after the right curly brace, as shown in the following example:

```
{
    int a = 1; // semicolon is necessary
}              // semicolon is not necessary
```

C++'s scope rules state that a local object can be used only in the block and the nested blocks of the block in which it has been defined. In particular, a local object can be used only in a statement or nested block that occurs after its definition. A formal parameter is considered to be defined at the beginning of its associated function body. This convention means that a formal parameter can normally be used throughout the function body.

6.4.2

Name reuse with objects

There is an additional scope rule that can limit the statements where an object can be used. This limitation has to do with the reuse of an object's name. While it often seems disconcerting to beginning programmers to reuse names, imagine how difficult it would be to write programs if name reuse was not permitted. Programmers would then need to know the name of every object used in every function in the software project, regardless of whether they were the author of a particular function. Not only would this task tend to be unmanageable; it would encourage poor names for the sake of uniqueness.

C++ allows identifier names to be reused as long as the declarations naming the same identifier occur in different blocks. This policy means that the following definition of main() is legal.

```
int main() {
    int a = 10;
    int b = 20;
    Mystery(a, b);
    cout << a << endl;
    cout << b << endl;
    return 0;
}
```

Function main()'s local objects a and b are different from the formal parameters a and b in the earlier definition of function Mystery(). The local objects a and b of main() exist only within main()'s statement block, and the formal parameters a and b of Mystery() exist only within Mystery()'s statement block.

This name reuse is reflected in the activation records for the two functions. They both contain entries for an a and b, but the a and b in one are independent of the a and b in the other.

main()	
a	10
b	20

Mystery()	
a	1
b	2

The output of the program is

```
10
20
1
2
10
20
```

Name reuse in two different blocks is permitted even if one of the blocks is nested within the other block. Once the nested block that reused the name is completed, the declaration of the encompassing block is back in effect. The following example demonstrates this rule.

```
{
    int i;
    // statement here using i references int object i
    {
        // statement here using i references int
        // object i
        char i;
        // statement here using i references char
        // object i
        {
            // statement here using i references char
            // object i
            float i;
            // statement here using i references float
            // object i
        }
        // statement here using i references char
        // char object i
    }
    // statement here using i references int object
    // i
}
// none of the preceding i's can be used here in a
// statement
```

The name reuse in the preceding code segment did not depend upon the use of different types for the various object i's. For example, the following code segment defines two objects with the same name and type.

```
{ // outer block
   int i;
   // statement here using i references outer
   // block i
   { // inner block
      int i;
      // statement here using i references inner
      // block i
   }
   // statement here using i references outer
   // block i
}
```

Although a name can be reused in a nested block, a name cannot be redefined in the same block in which it is initially defined. This restriction means the following program fragment is illegal.

```
int i;
float i; // illegal reuse: cannot reuse i within
         // the same block
```

Redefining a name within the same block is illegal even when a nested block occurs between the two definitions.

```
int i;
{
   char i; // legal: reuse occurs in a different
           // (nested) block
}
float i;   // illegal: cannot reuse i within the
           // same block
```

6.5

THE GLOBAL SCOPE

While an object can be defined within a statement block, a function definition is not allowed to occur within another function's statement block. This restriction does not contradict our use of function prototypes. A prototype is a declaration that describes a function's interface—it is not a definition. C++ requires that functions be defined at the *global* scope. The global scope occurs in the parts of your program that are not contained within any statement block. Object definitions and declarations, type definitions and declarations, as well as function prototypes are allowed to occur in the global scope.

6.5.1

Scope rules and name reuse with global objects

An object defined in the global scope is called a *global object*. The scope rules for global objects are similar to, but not the same as, the rules for local objects. As with local objects, a global object may be referenced by simply using its name in any desired block that occurs after its definition as long as no reuse for the object's name is in effect in the given block. Similarly, just as it is illegal to redefine a local object in the same block as it is initially defined, it is also illegal to reuse a global object's name for another object while the global scope is in effect.

C++ provides the unary scope operator :: as a way to use global objects even though name reuse has occurred. If a :: is placed in front of an object, it indicates that the definition being used is the global one. This fact means that it is illegal to use the scope operator on a local object.

To help understand these scope rules, let's consider the following example.

```
int i;
int main() {
    // statement here using i references global
    // int object i
    // statement here using ::i references global
    // int object i. the :: is unnecessary
    return 0;
}
void f() {
    // statement here using i references global
    // int object i
    // statement here using ::i references global
    // int object i. the :: is unnecessary
    char i;
    // statement here using i references local
    // char object i
    // statement here using ::i references global
    // global int object i
    {
        // statement here using i references local
        // char object i
        // statement here using ::i references global
        // int object i
        int i;
        // statement here using i references local
        // int object i
        // statement here using ::i references global
        // int object i
    }
    // statement here using i references local
    // char object i
    // statement here using ::i references global
    // int object i
    return;
}
void g() {
    // statement here using i references global
    // int object i
```

```
// statement here using ::i references global
// int object i. the :: is unnecessary
return 0;
}
```

In our example, functions main() and g() can both make use of global **int** object i throughout their entire function bodies. The scope resolution operator :: can be used there, but it is not necessary. Without using the scope resolution operator, function f() can make use of the global **int** object i in its outermost block until the definition of the local **char** object occurs. From that point on in that block and in its nested blocks, access to global **int** object i is possible only through the use of the scope operator. In the innermost nested block of function f(), a local **int** object i is in use. This object and the global object i are distinct. Changes to the local object will not affect the global object. The scope operator can also be applied to functions and programmer-defined types. This application is normally useful only in class definitions; we will examine its use in a later chapter.

6.5.2

Initialization of global objects

Unlike local objects, global objects are always initialized. If no explicit initialization is given for a fundamental type global object, then the value 0 is used. For example, the following program displays the value 0.

```
#include <iostream.h>
int a;
int main() {
    cout << a << endl;
    return 0;
}
```

Programmer Alert

Beware of global objects

There is strong potential for a programmer to lose track of just what a global object is supposed to represent. Consider the following scenario. A function f() written by a programmer does not itself change or even use a global object. However, f() invokes a function that invokes a function that invokes a function that does change a global object. Sounds pretty confusing, doesn't it? Because of situations like this, the use of global objects is strongly limited by most programming methodologies. Note: Our implementation of the stock-charting problem in section 6.6 requires a SimpleWindow object with global scope because we have not yet introduced reference parameters.

6.6

DISPLAYING A PRICE-INTERVAL CHART

Serious investors spend a lot of time trying to figure how the stock market is going to behave. Many of the software tools they use present information in a graphical manner to make any patterns in the market's behavior more apparent. The problem we now consider is how to graphically display a series of weekly high–low price intervals for a given stock. The problem description is

> The input to the price-interval problem comes from a file that contains a collection of weekly prices for the stock of interest. The name of the file is supplied by the user in response to a prompt (the filename and prices within the file should be tested for validity). Conceptually, the prices in the file come in pairs. A pair represents the low and high price of the stock for a week. All of the pairs are to be extracted, and a line interval is plotted on a labeled graph for each pair. For example, given the following sample input/output behavior for extracting the stock filename

>   Please enter file to be processed: <u>stock.dat</u>

> where file `stock.dat` contains the following values

>   2 4
>   1 5
>   4 6
>   4 8
>   5 9
>   3 8

> then Figure 6.3 shows the expected display. The graph includes labels for the axes, the file being processed, origins for both axes, the number of weeks of stock data, and the maximum occurring stock price.

Properly representing the weekly data is crucial to solving this problem. In a pure object-oriented design, we would probably create an object whose representation captures both the weekly low and high along with member functions that can test validity and chart the associated interval. Starting in Chapter 8 we introduce the class mechanism that allows us to define such objects. One of the exercises in that chapter is to rethink this problem. However, for now we need two independent objects to represent the weekly low and high. Given these two weekly values and the window for the display, it is straightforward to display a price interval using an object of type `RectangleShape`.

The display of the x-axis requires that we have a record of the maximum stock price seen over all weeks, and the display of the y-axis requires that we have a record of the number of weeks of stock data. Computing these two values is simple. For the maximum price, we iteratively compare the current weekly high with the maximum price seen so far, and if necessary update the

Figure 6.3

*Price-interval chart for
file stock.dat*

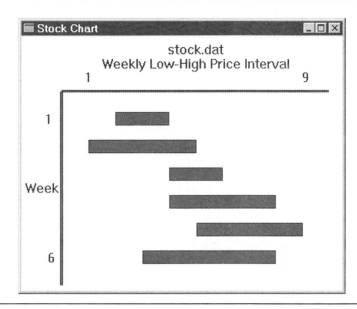

maximum price seen so far. For the number of weeks, we maintain a counter
that is incremented once per weekly extraction.

An algorithm for the problem quickly follows from the above analysis.

Step 1.   Prompt and extract filename.

Step 2.   Define an input stream associated with extracted filename.

Step 3.   Setup weekly counter and overall stock high.

Step 4.   While we can extract another weekly low and high do

Step 4.1   Validate stock data.

Step 4.2   Increment week counter.

Step 4.3   Compare weekly high with overall stock high so far and
update the overall stock high so far if necessary.

Step 4.4   Chart weekly interval.

Step 4.5   Repeat step 4.

Step 5.   Display x-axis.

Step 6.   Display y-axis.

The steps of the algorithm provide a framework for our program. The steps
are captured in the following code segment.

```
// Steps 1 and 2: extract filename and setup stream
string StockFile = GetFileName();
ifstream fin(StockFile.c_str());
if (! fin) {
    cerr << "Cannot open: " << StockFile << endl;
    exit(1);
}

// step 3: setup
float StockHigh = 0;
int WeekNbr = 0;

// step 4: iteratively process stock-price intervals
```

```
int WeeklyHigh;
int WeeklyLow;
while (fin >> WeeklyLow >> WeeklyHigh) {
    // step 4.1: check for valid data
    if (! Valid(WeeklyLow, WeeklyHigh)) {
        cerr << StockFile << ": Bad data for week "
          << ++WeekNbr << endl;
        exit (1);
    }

    // step 4.2: have another week of valid data
    ++WeekNbr;

    // step 4.3: update the overall high if necessary
    StockHigh = max(StockHigh, WeeklyHigh);

    // step 4.4: chart it
    ChartWeek(WeekNbr, WeeklyLow, WeeklyHigh);
}
// Steps 5 and 6: display axes
DrawXAxis(StockFile, StockHigh);
DrawYAxis(WeekNbr);
```

In the code segment, the portions of the algorithm steps that require further refinement are assigned to functions in what is essentially a *top-down design*. In this design method, you determine the basic tasks that must be performed to solve the problem. You also determine how these tasks must interface and interact. If necessary, the basic tasks are decomposed until all actions are well understood and (relatively) easy to implement. For our problem, we decompose six of the tasks into functions.

- GetFilename(): get the name of the file that contains the stock intervals to be charted.

- Valid(): verify that the current stock prices are sensible.

- max(): assist in the updating of the highest stock price seen so far.

- ChartWeek(): display the current weekly interval.

- DrawXAxis(): draw the x-axis and its associated labels.

- DrawYaxis(): draw the y-axis and its associated labels.

When developing functions to solve a problem, the functions are typically placed in files that group them by purpose. Essentially the function files are private libraries. At the same time, a software engineer will also create header files for these function files. If a private library is needed, the associated header file is then typically included at the start of the program file that requires the functions. It is the header file that is included rather than the implementation file. The implementation file is separately compiled just once and then linked as needed during the translation of applications that use the private library. The result is a faster application compilation.

Our stock charting program consists of two implementation files, stock.cpp and utility.cpp, and one header file, utility.h.

Implementation file stock.cpp principally contains ApiMain(). In fact except for some additions regarding windowing features, the previous code segment is the function body of ApiMain(). As discussed in Chapter 3, when using our graphical classes, `ApiMain()` is where your program logically starts. The complete contents of `stock.cpp` are shown in Listing 6.1.

Listing 6.1

Stock.cpp defines ApiMain() and global window object W

```
#include <iostream.h>
#include <fstream.h>
#include <string>
#include <stdlib.h>
#include "ezwin.h"
#include "utility.h"

// global window
SimpleWindow W("Stock Chart", 12, 9);

// ApiMain(): manage display of a stock chart
int ApiMain() {
   // extract filename and setup stream
   string StockFile = GetFileName();
   ifstream fin(StockFile.c_str());
   if (! fin) {
      cerr << "Cannot open: " << StockFile << endl;
      exit(1);
   }

   // setup
   W.Open();
   float StockHigh = 0;
   int WeekNbr = 0;

   // iteratively process stock-price intervals
   int WeeklyHigh;
   int WeeklyLow;
   while (fin >> WeeklyLow >> WeeklyHigh) {
      // check for valid data
      if (! Valid(WeeklyLow,WeeklyHigh)) {
         cerr << StockFile << ": Bad data for week "
          << ++WeekNbr << endl;
         exit(1);
      }

      // have another week of valid data
      ++WeekNbr;

      // chart it
      ChartWeek(WeekNbr, WeeklyLow, WeeklyHigh);

      // update the overall high if necessary
      StockHigh = max(StockHigh, WeeklyHigh);
   }
   // display axes
   DrawXAxis(StockFile, StockHigh);
   DrawYAxis(WeekNbr);

   // all done
   return 0;
}
```

Besides defining `ApiMain()`, implementation file `stock.cpp` includes the necessary standard library header files and our local library header files `ezwin.h` and `utility.h`. Library header file `ezwin.h` prototypes our basic graphical functionality. Header file `utility.h` prototypes the six functions from `utility.cpp` used by `ApiMain()`.

Listing 6.2 gives the contents of `utility.h`. The function prototypes are nested within preprocessor directives. The directives ensure that the prototypes are declared once per translation unit. The header file for a programmer-defined library is normally included at the beginning of an implementation file right after the inclusions of the header files for the standard libraries.

Listing 6.2

Utility.h prototypes the functions of utility.cpp

```
#ifndef UTILITY_H
#define UTILITY_H
#include <string>

// prototypes
string GetFileName();
bool Valid(float low, float high);
void ChartWeek(int week, float low, float high);
void DrawXAxis(string StockFile, float StockHigh);
void DrawYAxis(float WeekNbr);
int max(int a, int b);

#endif
```

Implementation file `stock.cpp` also defines a global `SimpleWindow` object W. Object W has a role that is analogous to `cout` in simple text-based programs—W is the target of all our graphical displays.

By making W global, `ChartWeek()`, `DrawXAxis()`, and `Draw-YAxis()` have access to it. The only other way at this point to give these functions access to W would be to add it as a value parameter to their definitions. However, this addition does not work because each function invocation would then display to a separate window. The separate window displays would occur because the invocations would be accessing their own `SimpleWindow` parameter objects. These value parameters would have characteristics identical to W but would be associated with different windows. We consider reference parameters in the next chapter, and we will then be able to define functions that manipulate their actual parameters. In the exercises of that chapter, we modify `ChartWeek()`, `DrawXAxis()`, and `DrawYAxis()` to have them display to accept W as a reference parameter.

The contents of `utility.cpp` is given in Listings 6.3 to 6.6. Listing 6.3 shows the initial portion of `utility.cpp`. Observe that the file includes header file `utility.h`. This inclusion ensures that the function definitions actually have the proper interface—if they did not, an error message would be generated by the compiler regarding an improper overloading of the function in question. After the file inclusions, several constants are defined. The constants describe axis and interval bar characteristics and how far the graph should be offset from the origin of the window. An **extern** declaration is made next. The modifier **extern** indicates that `SimpleWindow` object W has been defined in another program file. The declaration here enables the object to be used in this program file also. It is important to remember that when a global object is used in multiple files, it is defined in only one of those files. In the other files, the object is declared using an **extern** statement.

Listing 6.3

Contents of initial portion of utility.cpp

```cpp
#include <iomanip.h>
#include <strstream.h>
#include <string>
#include "rect.h"
#include "label.h"
#include "utility.h"

// utility constants
const float AxisThickness = 0.1;
const color AxisColor = Blue;
const float BarThickness = 0.5;
const color BarColor = Blue;
const float ChartXOffset = 1.5;
const float ChartYOffset = 2.0;

extern SimpleWindow W;

// GetFileName(): Prompt and extract filename
string  GetFileName() {
   cout << "Please enter file to be processed: "
    << flush;
   string s;
   cin >> s;
   return s;
}

// Valid(): are weekly stock prices sensible
bool Valid(float low, float high) {
   return (0 <= low) && (low <= high);
}

// max: determine larger of its two parameters
int max(int a, int b) {
   if (a < b)
      return b;
   else
      return a;
}
```

Functions `GetFileName()`, `Valid()`, and `max()` follow next in Listing 6.3. These functions are presented without comment, as they either are simple or have been previously discussed.

Listing 6.4 contains the **void** function `ChartWeek()` from utility.cpp. Function `ChartWeek()` has three **float** value parameters, `Week`, `Low`, and `High`, representing the week number and endpoints of the interval. The function displays a bar representing a weekly stock-price interval in the chart graph.

The x-coordinate of the center of the stock-price interval bar is the sum of the chart's x-axis constant offset `ChartXOffset` and the average of the values `Low` and `High`. The y-coordinate of the center of the bar is the value `Week` shifted by the chart's y-axis constant offset `ChartYOffset`. The length of the bar is given by the difference `High – Low`. The height of the bar is given by the constant `BarThickness`. The color of the bar is given by the constant `BarColor`. Once a `RectangleShape` object `Bar` has been defined with these characteristics, its `Draw()` member function displays the stock-price interval.

ChartWeek() from
utility.cpp

Listing 6.4

```
// ChartWeek(): Display current week's interval
void ChartWeek(int Week, float Low, float High) {
   float x = ChartXOffset + (Low + High)/2.0;
   float y = ChartYOffset + Week;
   float Length = High - Low;
   RectangleShape Bar(W, x, y, BarColor,Length,
    BarThickness);
   Bar.Draw();
   return;
}
```

Listing 6.5. of `utility.cpp` defines the **void** function `DrawXAxis()`, which displays the x-axis and its various labels. To accomplish the display, the function makes uses of two classes that we have not used before: `Label` and `ostrstream`.

DrawXAxis() from
Utility.cpp

Listing 6.5

```
// Display x-axis with labels
void DrawXAxis(string StockFile, float MaxX) {
   // draw axis
   float AxisLength = MaxX + 1;
   float CenterX = ChartXOffset + MaxX/2.0 + 0.5;
   float CenterY = ChartYOffset;
   RectangleShape Axis(W, CenterX, CenterY, AxisColor,
    AxisLength, AxisThickness);
   Axis.Draw();

   // display filename
   float FilenameX = CenterX;
   float FilenameY = ChartYOffset/4.0;
   Label Filename(W, FilenameX, FilenameY,
    StockFile.c_str());
   Filename.Draw();

   // display axis legend
   float LegendX = CenterX;
   float LegendY = ChartYOffset/2.0;
   Label Legend(W, LegendX, LegendY,
    "Weekly Low-High Price Interval");
   Legend.Draw();

   // display low label over axis
   float LowX = ChartXOffset + 1;
   float LowY = ChartYOffset/2.0 + 0.5;
   Label Low(W, LowX, LowY, "1");
   Low.Draw();

   // display high label over axis
   float HighX = ChartXOffset + MaxX;
   float HighY = ChartYOffset/2.0 + 0.5;
   ostrstream HighValue;
   HighValue << setw(3) << MaxX << ends;
   Label High(W, HighX, HighY, HighValue.str());
   High.Draw();

   // all done
   return;
}
```

Class `Label` is another of our graphical classes. `Label` objects are used to display messages in a `SimpleWindow`. In initializing a `Label` object, we need only to specify the `SimpleWindow` to which the object is to be displayed, its position in that window, and the desired character string message.

Class `ostrstream` is part of the `ios` hierarchy. An object of class `ostrstream` is known as an *in-memory* or *in-core* stream because insertions to it are stored in a character string memory buffer rather than being sent to the monitor or to a file. Once the insertions to `ostrstream` object have been completed, the constructed character string can be accessed via the `ostrstream` member function `str()`. The `ostrstream` class is declared in the standard header file `strstream.h`. This header file also declares an in-memory input stream class `istrstream` and an in-memory class `strstream` capable of both insertions and deletions.

Function `DrawXAxis()` begins by defining the length of the axis. For aesthetic purposes, the axis is one unit greater than parameter `MaxX`, which represents the maximum x-coordinate used in displaying the price-interval bars. The x- and y-coordinates `CenterX` and `CenterY` of the center of the x-axis are then defined. Like the display of price-interval bars, the center coordinates of the axis are shifted over from the origin of the window. Having defined these values, the axis is represented as a `RectangleShape` object and then drawn.

The name of the file being processed through `string` parameter `FileName` and a character string legend for the axis are displayed next, using `Label` objects. The positions of these two `Label` objects are relative to the center of the x-axis.

Function `DrawXAxis()` next constructs and displays the labels for low and high values on the x-axis. Because the low value is known to be 1, which can be represented as the string "1", it is easy to define a `Label` object `Low` for labeling the left end of the axis. However, labeling the right end of the axis is not as straightforward because there is no automatic conversion of a numeric value to a string. We can construct a string representation by inserting the value of `MaxX` to `ostrstream` object `HighValue`. The `setw(3)` manipulator ensures that the field width is (at least) three. The manipulator `ends` appends the character string termination character to our in-memory stream. Together, the three insertions produce a suitable character string representation of the value `MaxX`, which can then be accessed by invoking `HighValue.str()`.

Listing 6.6 of `utility.cpp` defines the **void** function DrawYAxis(). Its operation is analogous to `DrawXAxis()`, and therefore the function is not discussed.

This completes the discussion of our stock-charting program.

Listing 6.6

*DrawYAxis() from
Utility.cpp*

```
// DrawYAxis(): display y-axis with labels
void DrawYAxis(float MaxY) {
    // draw axis
    float CenterX = ChartXOffset;
    float CenterY = ChartYOffset + MaxY/2.0 + 0.5;
    float AxisLength = MaxY + 1;
    RectangleShape Axis(W, CenterX, CenterY, AxisColor,
     AxisThickness, AxisLength);
    Axis.Draw();

    // display legend
    float LegendX = ChartXOffset/2.0;
    float LegendY = CenterY;
    Label Legend(W, LegendX, LegendY, "Week");
    Legend.Draw();

    // display low label over axis
    float LowX = ChartXOffset/2.0 + 0.25;
    float LowY = ChartYOffset + 1;
    Label Low(W, LowX, LowY, "1");
    Low.Draw();

    // display high label over axis
    float HighX = ChartXOffset/2.0 + 0.25;
    float HighY = ChartYOffset + MaxY;
    ostrstream HighValue;
    HighValue << setw(3) << MaxY << ends;
    Label High(W, HighX, HighY, HighValue.str());
    High.Draw();

    // all done
    return;
}
```

6.7

RECURSIVE FUNCTIONS

Many programming languages, C++ included, support the use of recursion to solve problems. *Recursion* is the ability for a function to call itself. To illustrate what we mean by recursion and its use, let's reconsider the implementation of the factorial function. Our earlier definition of factorial

$$n! = \begin{cases} 1 & \text{if } n = 0 \\ n \times (n-1) \times \ldots \times 1 & \text{if } n \geq 1 \end{cases}$$

is not mathematically precise because we use an ellipsis (…). The ellipsis tells a reader to use her or his intuition to recognize the pattern. A formal definition of factorial removes any ambiguity.

$$n! = \begin{cases} 1 & \text{if } n = 0 \\ n \times (n-1)! & \text{if } n > 0 \end{cases}$$

In the preceding formal definition, we see that factorial is defined in terms of itself. That is, if $n > 0$, then $n!$ is $n \times (n\text{-}1)!$.

Using recursion, we can write a short and simple C++ function that computes factorial. The function is

```
int Factorial(int n) {
if (n == 0)
    return 1;
else
    return n * Factorial(n-1);
}
```

This function exactly mirrors the mathematical definition of factorial. If the value of n is 0, the value 1 is returned. If the value of n is not equal to 0, the product of n and Factorial(n-1) is returned.

To understand how recursion works, it is useful to visualize what is happening when a function calls itself. One way to do this is to picture the activation records that are created for each recursive call. Let's assume that we have the following main program:

```
#include <iostream.h>
int main() {
    cout << "Please enter a postive integer: "
     << flush;
    int n;
    cin >> n;
    cout << n << "! = " << Factorial(n) << endl;
    return 0;
}
```

The activation records after main() calls Factorial() are

Activation records

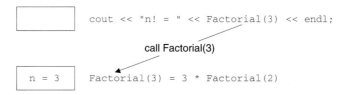

In Factorial() since n is 3, the **else** part

```
return n * Factorial(n-1);
```

of the **if** statement is executed. The **else** part calls Factorial() again, this time with an actual parameter with value 2. In this invocation of function Factorial() n is 2, so the **else** part

```
return n * Factorial(n-1);
```

of the **if** statement is executed again with an actual parameter with value 1. As shown in Figure 6.4, the process continues until n equals to 0. At this point, the **if** test expression evaluates to true, and

```
return 1;
```

is executed. This statement causes the recursion to start to *unwind* (i.e., no more recursive calls).

Figure 6.4

Activation records for recursive calls to Factorial()

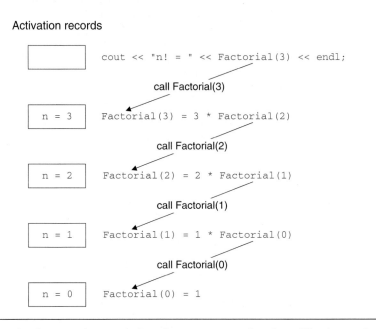

Activation records

```
                          cout << "n! = " << Factorial(3) << endl;

                                    call Factorial(3)

  n = 3          Factorial(3) = 3 * Factorial(2)

                                    call Factorial(2)

  n = 2          Factorial(2) = 2 * Factorial(1)

                                    call Factorial(1)

  n = 1          Factorial(1) = 1 * Factorial(0)

                                    call Factorial(0)

  n = 0          Factorial(0) = 1
```

As the recursion unwinds, values are returned to the calling invocation of the function. In effect, the return value is substituted for the call. The process of the recursion unwinding is illustrated in Figure 6.5. Using the returned value, the factorial of the n (for this invocation) is computed, and returned to the next level. This process continues until the call to Factorial() from function main() returns to main() with the value of 3!.

When the first call to Factorial() returns to main(), the insertion statement produces the following output:

```
3! = 6
```

One of the nice things about recursion is that it is a succinct way of expressing certain mathematical formulas, and the corresponding C++ implementation is equally short. A recursive function has generally two parts:

- a recursive call with simpler parameters, and
- a termination part that stops the recursion.

Figure 6.5

Unwinding the recursive calls to Factorial()

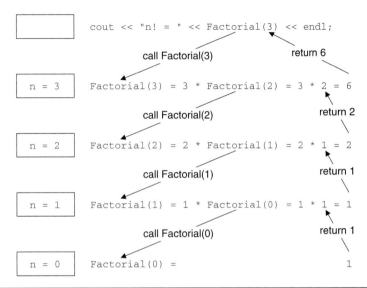

In the factorial code, the recursive call and the termination part were the two action parts of the **if-else** statement.

```
if (n == 0)                    ⎫ Termination part
       return 1;               ⎭
Recursive part ⎧ else
              ⎩       return n * Factorial(n - 1);
```

Let's consider the development of a recursive function to compute x^n. The C++ prototype of our power function is

```
int Power(int x, int n);
```

We know that x^0 is 1 for all x. This fact will be the termination part of our recursive function. We also know that $x^n = x \times x^{n-1}$ when n > 0. This will be the recursive part. Observe that because n is getting smaller, the recursion is sure to terminate. Writing the recursive version of the power function is simple.

```
int Power(int x, int n) {
   if (n == 0)
      return 1;
   else
      return x * Power(x, n-1);
}
```

As a final example of simple recursion, let's write a function that computes the *n*-th Fibonacci number. We considered briefly this number sequence in

Chapter 4. The Fibonacci sequence is denoted $F_1, F_2, F_3, ..., F_n$ where $F_1 = F_2$ = 1 and every further term is the sum of the preceding two. The first eight numbers in the sequence are 1, 1, 2, 3, 5, 8, 13, 21. The Fibonacci sequence was developed in 1202 by the Italian mathematician, Leonardo Pisano. The problem that he was investigating was how fast rabbits could breed in ideal circumstances. He assumed that a pair of rabbits (male and female) breed and always produce another pair of rabbits (male and female too). Furthermore, a rabbit becomes sexually mature after one month, and the gestation period is also one month. Thus a pair produces one new pair every month from the second month on. Assuming a rabbit never dies how many rabbits would there be after one year?

We can work out a solution by hand. At the end of the first month, there is still only one pair. At the end of the second month, another pair is born so there are now two pairs. At the end of the third month, the original pair produces another pair, but the second pair is just getting started, so there are only three pairs. At the end of the fourth month, the original pair has produced another pair and so has the second pair, so now there are five pairs. At the end of the fifth month, there will be eight pairs. In the sixth month, there will be thirteen pairs. The sequence being generated is

1, 1, 2, 3, 5, 8, 13, 21, 34, ...

That is, the number of pairs for a month is the sum of the number of pairs in the two previous months. At the end of 12 months, there will be 144 pairs of rabbits.

The mathematical definition of the n-th Fibonacci number is

$$F_n = \begin{cases} F_n = 1 & \text{if } n = 1 \\ F_n = 1 & \text{if } n = 2 \\ F_n = F_{n-1} + F_{n-2} & \text{if } n > 2 \end{cases}$$

The definition is a bit more complicated than the previous ones we coded, but we can use the same strategy. The pattern for our previous recursive functions has been

```
if (termination code statisfied)
    return value;
else
    make simpler recursive call;
```

and this will work for the Fibonacci numbers too. The code for the function is

```
int Fibonacci(int n) {
    if (n <= 2)
        return 1;
    else
        return Fibonacci(n-1) + Fibonacci(n-2);
}
```

The main difference between the current code and the code for the previous recursive functions is that the current code makes two "simpler" recursive calls. We know that these recursive calls eventually unwind because each recursive call is passing an n that is getting smaller. Figure 6.6 illustrates the recursive calls made by this code when computing F_5.

Figure 6.6

Computation of F_5

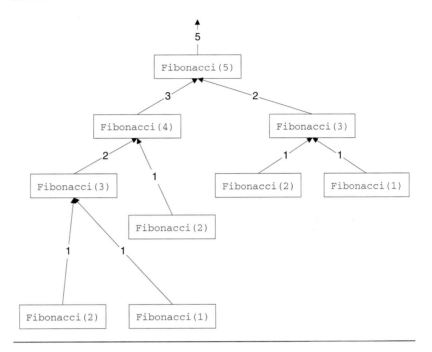

The Fibonacci numbers are interesting because they model many things in nature. For example, they model the reproductive behavior of bees, the number of branches in a tree, and the number of petals on a flower (e.g., buttercups have 5 petals, some asters have 21 petals, and there are daisies with 34, 55, and 89 petals). In the exercises, we explore some other interesting aspects of the Fibonacci numbers.

6.8

POINTS TO REMEMBER

- A function is a mechanism that permits modular programming and software reuse.

- The simplest functions take parameters in a manner similar to mathematical functions and then compute and return a value to be used in an expression.

- A statement block is a list of statements within curly braces.

- A nested block is a statement block occurring within another statement block.

History of Computing

A universal calculator

The period from 1900 to 1930 saw the refinement of mechanical calculators—they became faster and more sophisticated. Similarly, the punched card equipment developed by Hollerith was steadily improved and put to new uses. As of 1930, Babbage's dream of a general-purpose computer had not been advanced; however, from 1930 onward, advances occurred at a breakneck pace. Indeed, new developments happened so fast that historians have had a hard time determining who should be given credit for various inventions and ideas.

Two noteworthy ideas are credited to Konrad Zuse. Zuse was a German engineer, who like many before him, hated doing tedious engineering calculations. To make such calculations easier, Zuse decided to develop a universal calculator. Previous machines had used the decimal number system. Zuse recognized that a calculation machine could be made much simpler if it used the binary number system. Indeed, all of today's modern high-speed computers use the binary number system. Zuse's second contribution was that instead of using mechanical wheels, the calculator would use mechanical switches to manipulate the data. Again, all of today's modern machines use switches, although they are in the form of very small transistors.

Zuse's first machine was called the Z1. The Z1, besides being an innovative machine, is also notable because it may have been the first "home-brew" computer. Zuse constructed the Z1 in the living room of his parents' apartment in Berlin. Using the knowledge and experience gained from building the Z1, he built a larger machine called the Z2. The distinguishing feature of the Z2 was that it was an electromechanical calculator. In this machine, electrical relays replaced the mechanical switches. This replacement greatly increased the speed of the calculator. During World War II, Zuse continued to refine his designs producing the Z3 and Z4. After the war, the Z4 (see Figure 6.7) was installed at the Federal Polytechnical Institute (ETH) in Switzerland and used until 1955. Zuse, himself, went on to found a small computer company.

- To define a function, a programmer must completely specify its interface and actions. The actions occur within the function body. The function body is a statement block.
- A **return** statement supplies a value from the invoked function to the invoking function.
- A local object is an object defined within a statement block.
- A global object is an object defined outside of any function interface or function body.
- To complete their tasks, functions can use local and global objects and even other functions.
- To invoke a function, a programmer supplies actual parameters of the correct form. If the actual parameters are not of the correct form, the compiler

Figure 6.7
Konrad Zuse and the Z4

will attempt to perform conversions to put the actual parameters in the correct form.

- During a function invocation, an activation record is created in the computer memory. It is this memory that the function uses to store its parameters and local objects.

- Names can be reused as long as the declarations associated with the names occur in different blocks.

- The unary scope operator :: can be used to reference a global object whose name has been reused in the local scope.

- Global fundamental objects are initialized to zero by default.

- Typical programming efforts span multiple files. The files are individually compiled and linked together to produce an executable version of the program.

- A header file is often used to prototype functions that are defined in implementation files.

- Through the use of header files, functions defined in one implementation file can be invoked within another implementation file.

- A reference to a global object in an implementation file requires that the global object be either defined or declared using an **extern** statement within the translation unit of that implementation file.

- A global object can be defined only once in the global scope of the program.

- In top-down design you determine the basic tasks that must be performed and how these tasks must interface and interact. If necessary, the basic tasks are decomposed until all actions are well understood and can be easily implemented.

- The strstream library provides in-memory streams. Through a series of insertions, an `ostrstream` object can create a character string representation of other values.

- Recursion is where a function calls itself.

- A recursive function must have two parts. It has a termination part that ends the recursion, and a recursive call with simpler parameters.

6.9

EXERCISES

6.1   What is the purpose of name reuse?

6.2   Describe what happens during a function call.

6.3   How does a function prototype differ from a function definition?

6.4   What is an activation record?

6.5   What are the differences between an actual parameter and a formal parameter?

6.6   Can the name of a formal parameter be the same name as an actual parameter?

6.7   What is a local object?

6.8   What is a global object?

6.9   Does a **void** function necessarily contain a **return** statement? Explain.

6.10 Does a non-**void** function necessarily contain a **return** statement? Explain.

6.11 Define an **int** function `Cube()` that returns the cube of its single **int** formal parameter n.

6.12 Define a **float** function `Triangle()` that computes the area of a triangle using its two **float** formal parameters h and w, where h is the height and w is the length of the base of the triangle.

6.13 Define a **float** function `Rectangle()` that computes and returns the area of a rectangle using its two **float** formal parameters h and w, where h is the height and w is the width of the rectangle.

6.14 Define a **void** function `DoubleSpace()` that inserts two newline characters (`'\n'`) to standard output stream `cout`.

6.15 Define a **void** function `EndLine()` with a single **int** formal parameter n that indicates the number of newline characters to be displayed by the function.

6.16 Write a **float** function `GetRadius()` that prompts the user for a radius, extracts the user's response, and then returns the response as its value.

6.17 Rewrite Program 6.1 so that it uses the function GetRadius() from the previous exercise.

6.18 Write functions for the following formulas. Discuss your choice of which values are parameters, which values are constants, and what their types should be.

a) Speed(): Compute the speed of an object after t seconds of acceleration given that the object was initially traveling at v_0 meters per second and then accelerated at a meters per second per second.

$$v_0 + at;$$

b) Distance(): Compute the distance traveled in t seconds by an object that started at rest and then accelerated at a meters per second per second.

$$at^2/2;$$

c) BarVolume(): Compute the volume of a rectangular bar with width w, length l, and height h.

$$wlh;$$

d) SphereVolume(): Compute the volume of a sphere with radius r.

$$4\pi r^3/3;$$

6.19 What is the output of the following program? Explain.

```
#include <iostream.h>
int i = 0;
int I = 1;
int main() {
    int i = 2;
    int I = 3;
    ::i = i + 10;
    I = ::I + I + 20;
    ::I = ::i + 30;
    i = I + 40;
    cout << i << endl;
    cout << ::i << endl;
    cout << I << endl;
    cout << ::I << endl;
    return 0;
}
```

6.20 What is the output of the following program? Explain.

```
#include <iostream.h>
int counter = 0;
void f() {
    ++counter;
}
void g() {
    f();
    f();
}
```

```
void h() {
    f();
    g();
    f();
}
int main() {
    f();
    cout << counter << endl;
    g();
    cout << counter << endl;
    h();
    cout << counter << endl;
    return 0;
}
```

6.21 What is the output of the following program? Explain.

```
#include <iostream.h>
void f(int i, int j) {
    cout << "f: i = " << i << endl;
    cout << "f: j = " << j << endl;
    return;
}
int main() {
    int i = 10;
    int j = 20;
    f(i, j);
    cout << "main: i = " << i << endl;
    cout << "main: j = " << j << endl;
    return 0;
}
```

6.22 What is the output of the following program? Explain.

```
#include <iostream.h>
void f() {
    int i = 1;
    int j = 2;
    cout << "f: i = " << i << endl;
    cout << "f: j = " << j << endl;
    return;
}
int main() {
    int i = 10;
    int j = 20;
    f();
    cout << "main: i = " << i << endl;
    cout << "main: j = " << j << endl;
    return 0;
}
```

6.23 What is the output of the following program? Explain.

```
#include <iostream.h>
void f(int i, int j) {
    i = i + j;
    j = j + i;
    cout << "f: i = " << i << endl;
    cout << "f: j = " << j << endl;
    return;
```

```
    }
int main() {
    int i = 10;
    int j = 20;
    f(50, j);
    f(i, 50);
    cout << "main: i = " << i << endl;
    cout << "main: j = " << j << endl;
    return 0;
}
```

6.24 What is the output of the following program? Explain.

```
#include <iostream.h>
void f(int i, int j) {
    int temp;
    temp = i;
    i = j;
    j = temp;
    cout << "f: i = " << i << endl;
    cout << "f: j = " << j << endl;
    return;
}
int main() {
    int a = 10;
    int b = 20;
    f(a, b);
    f(b, a);
    cout << "main: a = " << a << endl;
    cout << "main: b = " << b << endl;
    return 0;
}
```

6.25 Write a function SwissCheese() with eight parameters w, l, h, m, b, n, r, and d that computes the volume of a rectangular hunk of Swiss cheese, where the hunk has width *w*, length *l*, height *h*, *m* internal spherical air bubbles of radius *b*, and *n* surface cylindrical holes of radius *r* and height *d*. The function should use function CylinderVolume() defined in this chapter and functions BarVolume() and SphereVolume() developed in Exercise 6.8. Then write a complete program that prompts a user for the characteristics of a Swiss cheese hunk and then appropriately displays the volume of the hunk.

6.26 In the U.S. coin system, the penny is the basic coin, and it is equal to one cent, a nickel is equivalent to 5 cents, a dime is equivalent to 10 cents, a quarter is equivalent to 25 cents, and a half-dollar is equivalent to 50 cents. Write the following **int** functions. Each function has a single **int** formal parameter Amount.

a) HalfDollars(): Compute the maximum number of half-dollars that could be used in making change for Amount.

b) Quarters(): Compute the maximum number of quarters that could be used in making change for Amount.

c) Dimes(): Compute the maximum number of dimes that could be used in making change for Amount.

d) `Nickels()`: compute the maximum number of nickels that could be used in making change for `Amount`.

6.27 Write a **void** function `MakeChange()` that expects a single **int** parameter `Amount` that displays to the standard output stream `cout` how to make change for `Amount` using a minimal number of U.S. coins. The function should use the functions developed in the previous exercise. Also write a complete program that prompts a user for an amount, and if the amount is sensible, the program then invokes `MakeChange()`, using that amount as its actual parameter.

6.28 Modify function `PromptAndRead()` to take a single parameter s of type `string` from the library `string`. Parameter s is to be the prompt message.

6.29 Modify the stock program to extract a third data value per week. The additional value is the weekly closing price. Modify `ChartWeek()` to use this value as parameter and to display a marker for the value in the appropriate spot on the price-interval bar.

6.30 The declaration of window `W` in Listing 6.1 is a potential problem in that its size is set before analyzing the data. Because the data comes from a file, it is possible to process the information more than once. Write functions `NumberOfWeeks()` and `HighStockPrice()` that respectively determine the number of weeks of stock data and the highest stock price in the file. Replace the definition of `W` in `stock.cpp` to use these functions in the initialization of `W` as the following code segment shows.

```
extern const float ChartXOffset;
extern const float ChartYOffset;
string StockFile = GetFileName();
SimpleWindow W("Stock Chart", 2.0, 2.0,
  HighStockPrice(StockFile)+ ChartXOffset+1,
  NumberOfWeeks(StockFile) + ChartYOffset+1);
```

6.31 Write a **bool** function `IsEndOfSentence()` that has a single value **char** parameter c. The function returns **true** if c is either a period, a question mark, or an exclamation point; otherwise, the function returns **false**.

6.32 Write an **int** function `Sum()` that expects a single integer number as its parameter. The function should return the sum of the integers from one to that number.

6.33 Modify the recursive version of function `Factorial()` so that it terminates if the value of its parameter is negative. Note: that 0! is defined mathematically to be 1, so your modification should not affect this computation.

6.34 Write a program that prompts a user for a number *n* and then computes and displays for integer values *i* in the interval one through *n* the nearest integer to the expression

$$\frac{1}{\sqrt{5}} \cdot \left(\left(\frac{1 + \sqrt{5}}{2} \right)^{i+1} - \left(\frac{1 - \sqrt{5}}{2} \right)^{i+1} \right)$$

Compare the output of the program with the output of function Fibonacci() for the same values. Speculate on their similarity.

6.35 Write a **void** function PrintChar() that expects two parameters: a character object c and an integer amount n. The function should make n copies of the character c to the standard output stream cout.

6.36 Write a **float** function EvaluateQuadraticPolynomial() that expects four **float** parameters a, b, c, and x. The function should return the value

$$ax^2 + bx + c$$

6.37 An angle is normally measured in either degrees or in radians where 360 degrees equal 2π radians. Write **float** functions DegreesToRadians() and RadiansToDegrees() that each expect a single **float** parameter. Function DegreesToRadians() treats its parameter as a value in degrees and returns the equivalent number of radians. Function RadiansToDegrees() treats its parameter as a value in radians and returns the equivalent number of degrees.

6.38 A light year is how far you could travel if you travel at the speed of light for one year. Write a **double** function LightYears() that expects a **double** value t as its parameter. The value t represents an amount of time in days. The function returns how far in light years you would travel if you went at the speed of light for t days.

6.39 Design a program that takes as its input two integer numbers that represent a range of integers. The program should display the sum of the integers in that range. Which functions from the chapters and exercises should be used? Explain.

6.40 Write a recursive function to compute the greatest common divisor (gcd) of two integers. The gcd of two integers is the largest integer that divides them both. A working definition of gcd is

$$gcd(m, n) = \begin{cases} n & \text{if } n \text{ divides } m \\ gcd(n, \text{remainder of } m \text{ divided by } n) & \text{otherwise} \end{cases}$$

6.41 If we take the ratio of successive numbers in the Fibonacci sequence, we see that the ratio is approaching a particular value. For example, 5/3 is 1.66666.... and 8/5 is 1.6, and 13/8 is 1.625. This ratio is called the *golden ratio* or *golden mean*. Write a program to compute the golden mean. To get an accurate estimation of its value, compute the golden mean of successive pairs of Fibonacci numbers until the difference between the computed golden means is less than 0.0005.

6.42 Below is a picture that illustrates the relationship between successive Fibonacci numbers.

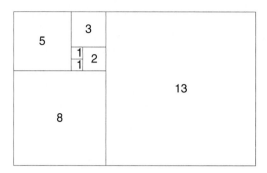

This picture was drawn by starting with two squares of size 1 drawn on top of each other. To the right, a square whose size is the sum of the previous two squares is drawn (i.e, a square of size 2). Each succeeding square's size is the sum of the size of the last two squares drawn. Let's call a diagram drawn in this fashion the Fibonacci squares picture. Write an EzWindows program using `RectangleShape` that draws a Fibonacci squares picture. Your program should prompt for and accept the number of squares to draw.

Interestingly, if you draw quarter circles in each square you get a spiral like the one shown in the figure below. This spiral is very similar to the ones that occur in nature in sea shells and snail shells.

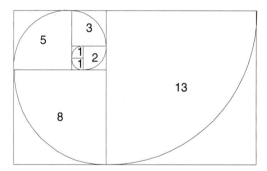

CHAPTER 7

Advanced parameter passing

Introduction

In addition to value parameters, C++ supports reference parameters. *Reference parameters* are a way to pass objects to functions so that they can be modified by the called function and the modified value passed back to the calling function. This type of parameter transmission is useful when the function computes several values and needs to return all of them to the calling function. Reference parameters are also useful when the function needs to modify one of its parameters in order to work properly. The chapter also describes some additional parameter passing features of C++ that support the development of flexible, robust functions.

Key Concepts

- reference parameters
- constant parameters
- default parameters
- function overloading
- function overload resolution
- side effects
- casting

7.1

REFERENCE PARAMETERS

One of the advantages of the call-by-value parameter transmission method is that it simplifies the understanding of a program. If the parameters are passed using the call-by-value method, we know that the called function cannot change the values of the actual parameters. For example, when reading a program encountering a call to a function with all call-by-value parameters, we know, without looking at the body of the function, that when the function returns, the actual parameters will have the same value as they did before the call. Consider the following code fragment:

```
// Prototype section
// Compute water flow (gallons per second) through
// a channel.
// Depth - depth of water
// Width - width of channel
float Flow(float Depth, float Width);
....
// more prototypes
....
int main() {
    ...
    f = Flow(CurrentDepth, ChannelWidth);
    ...
}
```

Without examining the body of function `Flow`, we can tell based on just the prototype for `Flow` that the objects `CurrentDepth` and `ChannelWidth` will not be changed by `Flow`. A function that does not modify the parameters passed to it and changes only values in the calling function via the function return value is said to have no *side effects*.

Because programs that use functions with no side effects are, in general, easier to understand, we should use call by value whenever possible. However, allowing a function to change the values of the actual parameters that are passed to it is sometime useful—for example, when the natural design of a function calls for it to return more than one value. For these and other situations, C++ provides *reference parameters*. In contrast to a value parameter where a copy of the actual parameter is passed, a reference parameter passes a reference or pointer to the actual parameter. Thus, when a formal reference parameter is changed in a function, the actual parameter is changed also.

Recall that the C++ syntax for specifying the interface of a function with value parameters is

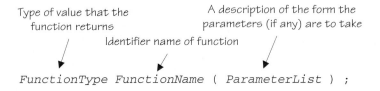

Type of value that the
function returns

A description of the form the
parameters (if any) are to take

Identifier name of function

FunctionType FunctionName (ParameterList) ;

where the *ParameterList* is a list of declarations of the form

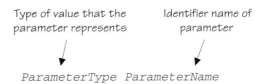

Type of value that the parameter represents

Identifier name of parameter

ParameterType ParameterName

To indicate that a parameter is a reference parameter, the syntax of a parameter declaration is extended slightly as follows

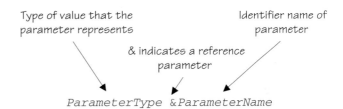

Type of value that the parameter represents

Identifier name of parameter

& indicates a reference parameter

ParameterType &ParameterName

The ampersand indicates that a reference to *ParameterName* is to be passed to the called function rather than a copy of *ParameterName*'s value.

To illustrate how reference parameters work, let's revisit the Mystery program from the previous chapter. In the original program, the interface to Mystery() was

```
void Mystery(int a, int b);
```

That is, Mystery() requires two **int** parameters that are passed by value. In addition, Mystery() does not return a value. It is a **void** function. We shall change the interface of Mystery() to use a reference parameter. The new interface is

```
void Mystery(int a, int &b);
```

The first parameter, a, is still a value parameter, while b is now a reference parameter. Program 7.1 is a complete program that uses Mystery(). Examination of the operation of this program helps illustrate the difference between call by value and call by reference. The output of Program 7.1 follows.

```
Output at beginning of main
i is 10
j is 20
Output at beginning of Mystery
a is 10
b is 20
Output after Mystery assignments
a is 5
b is 6
Output after Mystery returns
i is 10
j is 6
```

Thus, when Mystery() changed b, main()'s j was changed!

Program 7.1

Demonstrate call by reference

```
// Program 7.1: Demonstrate call by reference
#include <iostream.h>
void Mystery(int a, int &b) {
   cout << "Output at beginning of Mystery" << endl;
   cout << "a is " << a << endl;
   cout << "b is " << b << endl;
   a = 5;
   b = 6;
   cout << "Output after Mystery assignments" << endl;
   cout << "a is " << a << endl;
   cout << "b is " << b << endl;
   return;
}

int main() {
   int i = 10;              // local object definition
   int j = 20;              // local object definition
   cout << "Output at beginning of main" << endl;
   cout << "i is " << i << endl;
   cout << "j is " << j << endl;
   Mystery(i, j);           // invocation of Mystery with
                            // local objects i and j
   cout << "Output after Mystery returns" << endl;
   cout << "i is " << i << endl;
   cout << "j is " << j << endl;
   return 0;
}
```

To understand exactly what is happening, we need to look at the activation records of main() and Mystery(). The left-hand side of Figure 7.1 contains a depiction of the two activation records before the assignment statements in Mystery() are executed. Notice that in Mystery()'s activation record, the value of parameter object b is an arrow that points to the object j in main()'s activation record. The arrow signifies that when Mystery() accesses b, it really accesses j in main(). We can say it this way: When we *refer* to b in Mystery(), we are really *referencing* j in main(). Hence, b is a reference parameter, and objects that are passed via a reference parameter are *passed by reference*.

Figure 7.1

Activation records of main() and Mystery()

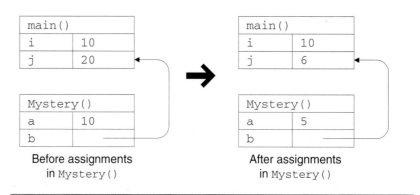

Before assignments
in Mystery()

After assignments
in Mystery()

The activation records of main() and Mystery() after the assignment statements in Mystery() are executed are shown on the right-hand side of Figure 7.1. Notice that j in main() has changed, while i has not. This is because a is a value parameter, so i was passed by value. Instead of a reference to i, a copy of i's value was passed.

To illustrate the usefulness of reference parameters, let's revisit a program we wrote in Chapter 4. This program read three values and output the values in sorted order. To obtain the proper ordering, the program checked for each of the possible six orderings of three values and executed the appropriate assignment statements to produce the correct order of the values. Using a function that employs reference parameters, we can achieve the same effect with much less code. Our approach will be to write a function that sorts three integer values. The function accepts three integer reference parameters and arranges the values such that when the function returns, the first parameter contains the smallest of the three values, the second parameter contains the next smallest, and the third parameter is the largest.

The strategy we use is to compare pairs of values and swap them if they are out of order. First, we compare the values contained in the first and second parameters, and if they are not in the correct order, we swap the values they contain. We repeat this operation on the first and third parameters. After these two steps, we know that the first parameter contains the smallest value. The last step is to compare the second and third parameters and swap their values if they are not in the correct order. In the case where the values are the same, we do not swap values. Thus to sort the three values we do three comparisons and, based on the results of the comparisons, potentially perform three swap operations.

The following code implements the operations described above.

```
void Sort3(int &a, int &b, int &c) {
    if (a > b) {
        int t = a;      // swap a and b
        a = b;
        b = t;
    }
    if (a > c) {
        int t = a;      // swap a and c
        a = c;
        c = t;
    }
    if (b > c) {
        int t = b;      // swap b and c
        b = c;
        c = t;
    }
    return;
}
```

In order for the function to work correctly, all three parameters must be reference parameters. Otherwise, any changes the function makes to the values of the parameters would not change the values of the actual parameters.

Using this function, we can now rewrite Program 4.3. Program 7.2 contains the revised program, which is shorter and easier to understand than the original.

Program 7.2

Sorting three numbers

```
// Program 7.2: Input three numbers and output
// them in sorted order
#include <iostream.h>
// sort three numbers into non-descending order
void Sort3(int &a, int &b, int &c) {
    if (a > b) {
        int tmp = a;    // b is smaller, swap a and b
        a = b;
        b = tmp;
    }
    if (a > c) {
        int tmp = a;    // c is smaller, swap a and c
        a = c;
        c = tmp;
    }
    if (b > c) {
        int tmp = b;    // c is smaller, swap b and c
        b = c;
        c = tmp;
    }
    return;
}

int main() {
    // Input the three numbers
    cout << "Please provide three integers: " << flush;
    int Input1;
    int Input2;
    int Input3;
    cin >> Input1 >> Input2 >> Input3;
    int Output1 = Input1;
    int Output2 = Input2;
    int Output3 = Input3;

    // Sort the three numbers
    Sort3(Output1, Output2, Output3);

    // Output the sorted numbers
    cout << Input1 << " " << Input2 << " " << Input3
      << " in sorted order is "
      << Output1 << " " << Output2 << " " << Output3
      << endl;

    return 0;
}
```

To make sure we understand the operation of the program, let's look at the activation records of main() and Sort3() at several key points. We will assume that the inputs to the program are the integers 20, 5, and 9. On entry to Sort3(), the activation records appear as shown in the left diagram of Figure 7.2. Notice that the parameters of Sort3(), a, b, and c, refer to Output1, Output2, and Output3 of function main(). At this point Sort3() compares the values of a and b, and because a is greater than b, it swaps them. Of course, it really swaps the values of Output1 and Output2. The activation records after this step are shown in the middle part of Figure 7.2. Notice that the values of Output1 and Output2 have been exchanged.

Figure 7.2

Activation records during execution of Program 7.2

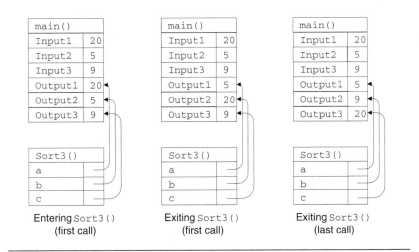

Entering Sort3()
(first call)

Exiting Sort3()
(first call)

Exiting Sort3()
(last call)

Next, the values of a and c are compared. Because they are already in sorted order, nothing happens. Next, the values of b and c are compared. Because they are out of order, they are swapped. The activation records just before Sort3() returns to function main() are shown in the right-most diagram of Figure 7.2. The values in the output variables are now in sorted order. The output of the program follows.

```
20 5 9 in sorted order is 5 9 20
```

Our program is fairly simple, but we can make it simpler still. Notice that Sort3() performs the same operation, a swap, on three different pairs of values. If we can write a function to do this, we can replace the three instances of the swap code with calls to a swap function. This function will shorten and simplify the code. Using reference parameters to write a function that swaps two values is easy. The code for swapping two integer values follows.

```
void Swap(int &x, int &y) {
    int tmp = x;
    x = y;
    y = tmp;
    return;
}
```

Program 7.3 contains the final code for our sorting program. This program is interesting because it contains a call to a routine that uses reference parameters (i.e., main() calls Sort3()) and that routine calls another routine that uses reference parameters (i.e., Sort3() calls Swap()). What do the activation records look like?

Program 7.3

Sort three numbers using a swap function

```cpp
// Program 7.3: Input three numbers and output them
// in sorted order
#include <iostream.h>
// swap two values
void Swap(int &x, int &y) {
   int tmp = x;
   x = y;
   y = tmp;
   return;
}

// sort three numbers into non-descending order
void Sort3(int &a, int &b, int &c) {
   if (a > b)
      Swap(a, b);
   if (a > c)
      Swap(a, c);
   if (b > c)
      Swap(b, c);
   return;
}

// read three numbers and output them in sorted order
int main() {
   cout << "Please enter three integers: " << flush;
   int Input1;
   int Input2;
   int Input3;
   cin >> Input1 >> Input2 >> Input3;
   int Output1 = Input1;
   int Output2 = Input2;
   int Output3 = Input3;

   // Sort the three numbers
   Sort3(Output1, Output2, Output3);

   // Output the sorted numbers
   cout << Input1 << " " << Input2 << " " << Input3
    << " in sorted order is "
    << Output1 << " " << Output2 << " " << Output3
    << endl;

   return 0;
}
```

Using the input from the previous example (20, 5, and 9), we can step through the program as we did in the previous example. Sort3() compares parameters a and b and determines that they are out of order. In this program, rather than swapping them directly, Sort3() calls Swap() passing it a and b. Since Swap()'s formal parameters, x and y, are both reference parameters, rather than pass the values of a and b, references to a and b are passed. However, since a and b are themselves reference parameters, the values that they reference are passed instead!

The left-most diagram of Figure 7.3 depicts the activation records just before the first statement of Swap() is executed. Notice that the parameters x and y refer to main()'s local variables Output1 and Output2 and the action

Swap() takes switches their values. The middle diagram of the figure depicts the activation records after Swap() has completed its operation, but before it returns to Sort3().

Figure 7.3

Activation records for sorting program with swap

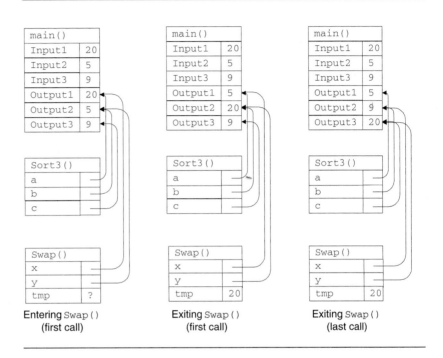

Function Swap() is called again to swap the values of b and c. The rightmost diagram in Figure 7.3 shows the activation records after Swap() completes the exchange. Notice that in this diagram, x and y refer to Output2 and Output3, respectively.

While the pictures of the activation records accurately depict what is happening with value and reference parameters, it is awkward to draw arrows all the time. A simple way to think about a reference parameter is that the formal parameter name is an *alias* for the actual parameter. In Sort3(), a is an alias for Output1 in main(). When we get or change a's value, we get or change the value of Output1. If we adopt this more convenient view, we can simplify our pictures by putting the actual name in the box that corresponds to the formal parameter's value instead of drawing a line that connects a formal reference parameter to the actual parameter. However, we need a way to show that the parameter is not a value, but really a reference to a named object. By putting an ampersand (&) in front of the name, we can indicate that a actual parameter is a reference to an object. Figure 7.4 reflects this simpler notation. It shows that when we access a in function Sort3(), we are really referencing Output1 in function main(). Similarly in Swap(), the formal parameter x references Output2 in Sort3().

Figure 7.4

Activation records for sorting program with swap

main()	
Input1	20
Input2	5
Input3	9
Output1	5
Output2	9
Output3	20

Sort3()	
a	&Output1
b	&Output2
c	&Output3

Swap()	
x	&Output2
y	&Output3
tmp	20

Exiting Swap()
(last call)

7.2

PASSING OBJECTS BY REFERENCE

One situation where it is absolutely mandatory that we use a reference parameter is when we pass a stream object to a function. The reason, of course, is that when we extract data from a stream or insert data into a stream, we are changing the stream. This change must be reflected in the stream object. As we know, if we passed the stream object by value, any changes that we made to the stream object would be made to a copy of the stream object, not the actual object. Thus whenever we need to pass a stream to a function, it must be passed by reference. In fact, most compilers make sure that when a stream object is passed to a function, it is passed by reference. If it is not, a compilation error occurs and no object file is produced.

The following function writes an integer value to a stream that is passed as the first parameter to the function.

```
void OutputValue(ostream &out, int Value) {
    out << "Value is " << Value << endl;
    return;
}
```

The next line of code uses the OutputValue() to write the value k to the stream cout.

```
OutputValue(cout, k);
```

Similarly, the code

```
OutputValue(cerr, k);
```

invokes OutputValue() that writes the value of k to the stream cerr.

Functions that output values to a stream are useful when we need to output several values along with labeling information from several places in a program. We might use such a function to write data to the display as well as to a log file for later examination. Another use would be to help debug the program. We can also use the function to output values of interest at strategic points in the program. Let's examine this latter use.

Suppose, for example, that we wish to "watch" our Sort3() function from Program 7.3 as it sorts the values. We want to show the values of a, b, and c after each step of the function. Rather than add three insertion statements after each **if** statement, we can call a function that outputs the three values. We want this function to be as general as possible, so one of its parameters is the stream to write the output to. The code for the function, called ShowValues(), is

```
void ShowValues(ostream &out, int a, int b, int c) {
    out << "a: " << a << endl;
    out << "b: " << b << endl;
    out << "c: " << c << endl;
    return;
}
```

and the revised code for Sort3() that uses ShowValues() to write the values to stream clog is

```
// sort three numbers into ascending order include
// iostream.h so that the function has access to clog
#include <iostream.h>
void Sort3(int &a, int &b, int &c) {
    if (a > b)
        Swap(a, b);
    ShowValues(clog, a, b, c);
    if (a > c)
        Swap(a, c);
    ShowValues(clog, a, b, c);
    if (b > c)
        Swap(b, c);
    ShowValues(clog, a, b, c);
    return;
}
```

We can also put the ability to pass an input stream as an parameter to a function to good use. For example, suppose we are writing a program to process data from a file. When we are creating the program, development and testing will go faster if the program takes input from the keyboard. We can quickly test the program by typing in data rather than having to create a test file each time we want to test the program on different data. However, eventually the program will be reading data from a file. We do not want to write the program so that it accepts input from the keyboard, and then when the program is complete, have to make extensive changes to the program so that it operates on a different stream. We can handle this situation by writing any functions that extract input to accept as a parameter the stream to read data from. This way, if we decide to take the data from a different source, the function need not be changed.

The function `ReadValues()` reads three values from the stream that is passed as its first parameter.

```
bool ReadValues(istream &in, int &v1, int &v2,
  int &v3) {
    if (in == cin)
        cout << "Please enter three numbers" << flush;
    if (in >> v1 >> v2 >> v3)
        return true;
    else
        return false;
}
```

The function is, for the most part, straightforward, However, the two **if** statements in the function deserve further discussion. When `ReadValues()` is used for interactive input (for example, during testing), we want it to prompt us for data. However, when it is used in the system that will read data from a file, we do not want it to output a prompt. The first **if** statement handles this requirement. If the stream being read from is `cin` (i.e., the keyboard), then a prompt is output.

Because `ReadValues()` is intended to be used as part of a larger system, it must tell the calling function whether it was able to read three values successfully. As was discussed in Chapter 5, an extraction expression returns true if the extraction operation succeeded; otherwise, it returns false. The second **if** statement checks to make sure that three values were read. If three values were read successfully, `ReadValues()` returns true; otherwise, it returns false.

Using `ReadValues()`, we can modify the main function of Program 7.3 so that it reads values from a file called `test.dat`. Program 7.4 contains the revised function. Notice the function checks to make sure that the file was successfully opened and that `ReadValues()` reports successfully reading three values. If either of these actions failed, the program writes an error message to `cerr` and returns a 1 to the operating system indicating that some type of failure occurred. This type of "defensive programming" is key when we are writing code that other programmers will use.

7.3

VALIDATING TELEPHONE ACCESS CODES

Many organizations require that users of their telephone system first provide a valid access code. It is a security measure to help prevent unauthorized long distance calls. The validation of the access code is made by a computer that connects the internal phone system with the outside world.

Program 7.4

*Sorting numbers read
from a file*

```
// Program 7.4: Sorting numbers read from a file
#include <iostream.h>
#include <fstream.h>
int main() {
   // Open the input file
   ifstream fin("test.dat");
   if (!fin) {
      cerr << "Could not open test.dat" << endl;
      return 1;
   }
   int Input1;
   int Input2;
   int Input3;
   if (!ReadValues(fin, Input1, Input2, Input3)) {
      cerr << "Could not read three values" << endl;
      return 1;
   }
   int Output1 = Input1;
   int Output2 = Input2;
   int Output3 = Input3;
   // Sort the three numbers
   Sort3(Output1, Output2, Output3);
   // Output the sorted numbers
   cout << Input1 << " " << Input2 << " " << Input3
    << " in sorted order is "
    << Output1 << " " << Output2 << " " << Output3
    << endl;
   return 0;
}
```

An example of a simple access and validation method is to have a user type a five-digit number. The first three digits are added together. The remainder of this sum when divided by the fourth digit should be equal to the fifth digit. If this is the case, the user is allowed to make the phone call; otherwise, the user is not allowed to make the phone call. As long as the algorithm that determines whether a number sequence is a valid access code is kept secret, the probability that a randomly typed number is valid is reasonably low.

Program 7.5 demonstrates the basics of access validation. After the include directives for the `iostream` and `ctype` libraries, the program prototypes **bool** functions `Get()` and `Valid()`.

The purpose of function `Get()` is to set its five reference parameters with the next five inputs supplied by the user. The purpose of the function `Valid()` is to examine the digit inputs and determine whether they represent a valid access code.

Function `main()` begins by defining five **int** objects to store the input values. The function then invokes `Get()`, and if it is successful, then invokes function `Valid()`. Finally, function `main()` uses its return value to signal whether the access code is valid. As noted previously, if a program returns zero, the program is indicating a successful computation. If the computation was not successful, the program should return a nonzero value. Different non-

Program 7.5

*Validate a telephone
access code*

```cpp
// Program 7.5: Validate a telephone access code
#include <iostream.h>
#include <ctype.h>

// Prototypes for utility functions that main will use
bool Get(istream &in, int &d1, int &d2, int &d3,
  int &d4, int &d5);
bool Valid(int d1, int d2, int d3, int d4, int d5);

int main() {
    int d1;
    int d2;
    int d3;
    int d4;
    int d5;

    if (Get(cin, d1, d2, d3, d4, d5)
      && Valid(d1, d2, d3, d4, d5))
        return 0;
    else
        return 1;
}

bool Get(istream &sin, int &d1, int &d2, int &d3,
  int &d4, int &d5) {
    char c1;
    char c2;
    char c3;
    char c4;
    char c5;

    if (sin >> c1 >> c2 >> c3 >> c4 >> c5) {
        if (isdigit(c1) && isdigit(c2) && isdigit(c3)
            && isdigit(c4) && isdigit(c5)) {
            d1 = c1 - '0';
            d2 = c2 - '0';
            d3 = c3 - '0';
            d4 = c4 - '0';
            d5 = c5 - '0';
            return true;
        }
        else
            return false;
    }
    else
        return false;
}

bool Valid(int d1, int d2, int d3, int d4, int d5) {
    if (d4 == 0)
        return false;
    else
        return ((d1 + d2 + d3) % d4) == d5;
}
```

zero values can be used to indicate how the program failed. Function `main()` follows this convention. It returns zero only if both `Get()` and `Valid()` return true. Otherwise it returns a one—this indicates that either an incomplete or invalid access code was supplied.

In our version of function Get(), the inputs are extracted from the stream sin, which is passed as the first parameter. The inputs are extracted as **char** objects in case the user supplies illegal values. The function uses the fact that an extraction operation returns a nonzero value only if the extraction was successful. Therefore, if the user did not supply five inputs, execution would flow to the **else** statement of the construct and the function would indicate that it was unsuccessful by returning **false**. If the user did supply five inputs, function Get() verifies that they are digits by calling the library function isdigit() whose definition is obtained from the include file ctype.h. This function returns true if its parameter is a decimal digit; otherwise, it returns false. If all the input characters are digits, then the reference parameters are appropriately set with the numeric equivalent of the digits. In this case the function was successful, and it returns **true**. If the inputs are not all digits, the function instead executes the **else** statement, where it signals that it was unsuccessful by returning **false**.

The conversion of the character representation of a digit to a numeric representation by Get() assumes that characters are encoded in ASCII format. As discussed in Chapter 2, the ASCII characters digits are arranged in a contiguous ascending order (i.e., '1' equals 0' + 1, '2' equals '1' + 1, and so on). By subtracting the character 0 from the character digit, Get() computes the numeric version of the digit. For example, '3' - '0' yields the integer value 3.

Program 7.5 next defines the function Valid() that examines its parameters and returns **true** if they correspond to a valid access code and returns **false** if they do not. The first step of the validation process is to examine the fourth digit—it must be nonzero, since its role is to be a divisor in the access algorithm. If the fourth digit is zero, Valid() returns **false**. If the fourth digit is not zero, then the first three digits are summed, and if this sum modulus the fourth digit is equal to the fifth digit, Valid() returns **true,** indicating a valid access code; otherwise, it returns **false** indicating an invalid access code.

7.4

CONSTANT PARAMETERS

For all of the programs that we have written thus far, we have used the **const** modifier to define program objects that represent constant values. These objects could be accessed but not modified. There are two justifications for using **const** objects. First, they make our programs easier to modify. For example, if we need to change the value of a literal constant that appears in many different places throughout a large program, we would have to find each instance of the literal constant and change it. Clearly, for a large program this task would be tedious and time consuming, and we would probably miss changing some of the literals. Any oversight could introduce a bug into the program.

The other justification for using a **const** modifier was that it gives anyone reading the program additional, useful information about the object. When we encounter a definition of an object that has the **const** modifier, we know that the program cannot change that object. That is, the object is "read only." This information is useful if we are trying to understand the program or make modifications to the program.

The **const** modifier can also be used with parameter declarations. The meaning is exactly the same as when it is applied to a local declaration—the function cannot change the object. Consider the following function that accepts three integer value parameters where the first is **const** value parameter.

```
void Example(const int a, int b, int c) {
    b = a + 3;      // legal assignment
    a = c + 5;      // illegal assignment
    return;
}
```

The first assignment statement is legal because it reads but does not modify a. The second statement is illegal because it attempts to modify a. The C++ compiler will report the violation and not produce an executable.

Here is another example illustrating the use of **const** parameters.

```
void AnotherExample(const RectangleShape &R1,
  RectangleShape &R2) {
    R2.SetColor(Blue);    // Legal
    R1.SetColor(Green);   // Illegal
}
```

The second statement in the function above is illegal because R1 is a **const** parameter. Function AnotherExample() cannot change its color even though it is passed by reference.

Programming Tip

Using const reference parameters for efficiency

When an object is passed by value, a copy of the object is made and the copy is passed to the called function. For large objects, copying can add considerable overhead to the program, and may in some instances adversely affect the performance of the program. For such objects, we can obtain efficiency, yet retain safety, by passing the object as a constant reference parameter. Thus a reference to the object is passed, which is usually more efficient than passing a copy, but the **const** modifier ensures that the actual object is not modified by the called function. Sometimes you can have your cake and eat it too!

Using the **const** modifier for parameters that a function will not change is a good software engineering practice. It provides additional information to readers of the code, and it allows the compiler to automatically check to make sure that the object is not intentionally or unintentionally changed.

**Programmer
Alert**

Compiler limitations on enforcing the const modifier

Most C++ compilers will issue an error message if they detect a **const** object on the left-hand side of an assignment. However, if a **const** object is passed by reference to another function, the compiler might issue a warning message only or no message at all.

Consider the following example:

```
void foo(int &p1, int p2) {
    p1 = p2 + p1 + 10;
    return;
}
void example(const int CValue) {
    foo(Cvalue, 3);
    return;
}
```

In function foo(), reference parameter p1 is changed. Of course, there is no problem with this. However, when function example() calls foo() and passes the **const** object CValue by reference, there is the possibility that the value of CValue could be changed. Most compilers will not issue an error message for the above situation. However, some compilers will issue a warning message letting you know that you passed a **const** object to a function that expects a reference parameter.

In general, when passing a **const** object to another function, we should take care that the function the object is passed to does not modify the object. We cannot rely on all compilers to catch this possibility.

7.5

DEFAULT PARAMETERS

Normally when we call a function, we must pass exactly the number of parameters to the function that the function expects. For example, suppose the prototype for a function called ThreeArgs is

```
int ThreeArgs(int a, int b, int c);
```

and it is invoked with the following code:

```
int x = ThreeArgs(1, 2);
```

The compiler will issue an error message because we did not pass a value for c.

Generally, we want the compiler to let us know if we have not supplied all the values necessary to invoke a function. However, it would be nice to not have to pass a value for each parameter a function expects, yet still have that parameter receive a value. This is useful when we want to write a function that has a default behavior, but occasionally we want to change or override that behavior. We can do this using *default parameters*.

The following function uses a default parameter for controlling whether the output should be double-spaced.

```
void OutputValues(ostream &out, int Value1,
  int Value2, bool DoubleSpace = false) {
    out << "Value 1 is " << Value1 << endl;
    if (DoubleSpace)
       out << endl;
    out << "Value 2 is " << Value2 << endl;
    if (DoubleSpace)
       out << endl;
    return;
}
```

The code

```
OutputValue(cout, 20, 30);
```

calls `OutputValues()` and passes values for the first three parameters. Since a fourth parameter value was not supplied, when the function executes, the fourth parameter `DoubleSpace` is given the value specified in the function header. Thus, when the above code executes, the output inserted into stream `cout` is

```
Value 1 is 20
Value 2 is 30
```

If we want the output to be double-spaced, we can invoke `OutputValues` and pass **true** as the fourth parameter. Since we supplied a fourth parameter, the default value for the fourth parameter is ignored and the value passed is used. Thus, the function call

```
OutputValues(cout, 20, 30, true);
```

inserts the output

```
Value 1 is 20

Value 2 is 30
```

When defining a function with default parameters, the default parameters must appear after any mandatory parameters. For example, the following function declaration is illegal.

```
void f(int x = 5, double z, int y); // illegal
```

This makes sense because here is no way for the compiler to know if a nontrailing parameter is missing.

We can use default parameters to simplify writing generalized input and output functions. In Program 7.5, we wrote an input function `Get()` that accepted an input stream as its first parameter. It read the access code from that stream. We can rewrite `Get()` so that unless specified otherwise, it reads from the stream `cin`, but it can also read from another stream if desired. The prototype for the new `Get()` is

```
bool Get(int &d1, int &d2, int &d3, int &d4,
  int &d5, istream &in = cin);
```

and when Get() is invoked as

```
if (Get(d1, d2, d3, d4, d5)
  && Valid(d1, d2, d3, d4, d5))
    return 0;
else
    return 1;
```

it will read from stream cin. When we want to use Get() to read from a file, we can do so by supplying the sixth parameter. Thus, the code

```
ifstream fin("telcodes.dat");
if (Get(d1, d2, d3, d4, d5, fin)
  && Valid(d1, d2, d3, d4, d5))
    return 0;
else
    return 1;
```

causes Get() to read from the stream fin, which is the file telcodes.dat.

> ### *Default parameters cannot be redefined*
> C++ does not allow the redefinition of a default parameter—not even to the same value—within a translation unit. The following code is illegal.
>
> ```
> void f(int x, int y = 3);     // prototype for f
> ...
> ...
> void f(int x, int y = 3) {    // illegal
> // body of f
> ...
> }
> ```
>
> In effect, either the prototype or the definition of the function, but not both, must specify the default values of the parameters. It will be our convention to specify the default value in the prototype of the function because we view the prototype as the interface to the function. However, you may encounter code that follows the opposite convention, or worse, sometimes specifies the default in the prototype and sometimes in the function definition.

7.6
CASTING OF FUNCTION PARAMETERS

One way to think about a function call is that it is just like an operator except that it can take many operands and it may or may not produce a value. For example, the statement

```
int Sum = Plus(a, b, c);
```

can be thought of as applying the Plus operator to the operands a, b, and c. Indeed, in many respects, C++ takes this view of functions, and many of the concepts which we discussed as applying to operators also apply to function calls.

For example, consider the following prototype and corresponding function invocation.

```
// ComputeInterest: compute simple compound interest
double ComputeInterest(double Principle,
 double InterestRate, int Days);
 . . .
 . . .
double Interest = ComputeInterest(4500, .075, 365);
```

Notice that in the call to function ComputeInterest() the type of the first parameter is **int**, while the prototype of the function specifies that ComputeInterest() expects a **double**. Similar to the way the C++ compiler converted operands of arithmetic operators to the appropriate type, it will convert parameter expressions to the appropriate type. In the above example, the compiler will convert the 4500 to a **double** and pass that as the first value.

Similarly, in the function invocation

```
double Interest = ComputeInterest(500.0, 0.8,
 155.8);
```

the third parameter 155.8 will be converted to an **int**. Thus, the parameter Days will receive the value 155.

7.7
FUNCTION OVERLOADING

Previously we discussed how C++, like many programming languages, has operators that are *overloaded*. That is, what an operator means or does depends on the type of its operands. For example, the + operator is overloaded. If its operands are integers, then it performs an integer addition. If its operands are floating point, then it performs a floating-point addition.

C++ also supports *function overloading*. That is, we can create several functions of the same name that behave differently. Function overloading is useful when we need to write functions that perform similar tasks, but need to operate on different data types. The following function min() from Chapter 6 illustrates the use of function overloading.

```
int min(int a, int b) {
    if (a > b)
        return b;
    else
        return a;
}
```

The function accepts two integer parameters and returns the minimum value. Suppose that we also needed a function that returned the minimum of two **double** values. Without function overloading, we would be forced to choose a different name for this function. We might call it `MinDouble()`. This could become awkward especially if we had many different versions of the minimum function.

With function overloading, we do not need to think up different names for functions that perform similar tasks on different data types. We can create two functions that have the same name but different parameter lists.

Suppose that we had defined the following two `min()` functions.

```
// integer version of min
int min(int a, int b) {
    if (a > b)
        return b;
    else
        return a;
}
// double version of min
double min(double a, double b) {
    if (a > b)
        return b;
    else
        return a;
}
```

When the compiler encounters a call to function `min()`, how does it decide which one to invoke? The answer is that the compiler uses a technique similar to the technique it uses to decide which type of operation to perform when it encounters an overloaded operator. With an overloaded operator, the types of the operands determined which operation to perform. With overloaded functions, the specifications of the actual parameters determine which function to invoke. The *signature* of a function is its parameter list. The compiler examines the parameter list of the function call, and it invokes the function whose signature best matches the actual parameter list.

For example, the function call

```
double z = min(1.2, 3.4);
```

would cause the double version of `min()` to be invoked because both actual parameters are type **double**. On the other hand, the statement

```
int x = min(2, 4);
```

invokes the integer version of `min()` because the parameters are integers. Determining which function to invoke when there is more than one function with the same name is called *function overload resolution*.

Function overload resolution is simple when there is a function definition where the types of the formal parameters exactly match the types of the actual parameters. The matching function is then called. When there is no exact match and the compiler must perform conversion of the actual parameters so that a function can be invoked, function overload resolution can become quite complicated. For example, the statement

```
int x = min(1.2, 4);
```

is illegal because there is no "best match" between the actual parameter list and the formal parameter lists of the two function definitions. There is no best match because there are two equally reasonable ways the compiler could cast the actual parameters to match the formal parameter lists. The compiler could convert the first actual parameter to an integer and call the integer version of `min()`, or it could cast the second actual parameter to a **double** and call the **double** version of `min()`.

As an indication of the complexity of overload resolution, the discussion of parameter matching requires fourteen pages of discussion and examples in *The Annotated C++ Reference Manual* by Ellis and Stroustrup. Because of the complexity of function overload resolution when parameter conversions must be done, we will not rely on its use. Rather, we will always ensure that a function definition exists with a parameter list where the types of the formal parameters exactly match the types of the actual parameters of any call. The interested or brave reader is referred to the annotated reference for the full details.

7.8

RANDOM NUMBERS

Random number sequences have an important role in many computer applications. For example, they are used in games to ensure that players do not experience the same situations each time they play the game. Random number sequences are also used in the design of complex systems such as a new highway. Before a highway is constructed, it is typically modeled and simulated on a computer. By using random number sequences that reflect the expected frequency and behavior of automobiles on the proposed highway, designers can estimate the impact of adding a lane or an interchange.

A particularly useful random number sequence is the *uniform random number sequence*. A uniform random number sequence has a specified set of numbers from which the sequence takes or *draws* its random numbers. In each position of the random number sequence, any number from the set is equally likely to occur.

Suppose you wanted to create a uniformly-distributed random number sequence drawn from the set {1, 2, 3, 4, 5, 6}. One way to do this is to get a normal six-sided die that has each of its sides labeled with a different element from that set. When the die is thrown, one of its sides will be facing up after the throw. For any given throw, each side is equally likely to be facing up. The sequence of values appearing on the face-up side will be a uniform random number sequence from the set {1, 2, 3, 4, 5, 6}.

Because a random number sequence is supposed to be random, there cannot be any computer algorithm that iteratively computes truly random numbers. The instructions that comprise an algorithm are deterministic rules—knowing them tells you the next number. However, some functions do produce sequences of numbers that appear to be random. These sequences are properly called *pseudorandom number sequences*, although most people are imprecise and drop the prefix *pseudo*.

The C++ stdlib library provides two functions that are useful in generating pseudorandom number sequences. They are rand() and srand(), and they are declared in stdlib.h. Function rand() takes no parameters. Each time it is invoked, it returns a uniform pseudorandom number from the *inclusive* interval 0 to RAND_MAX, where RAND_MAX is an implementation-dependent preprocessor macro constant defined in stdlib.h. In most implementations of rand(), the generation of the current pseudorandom number is a function of the previously generated pseudorandom number. The generation of the first pseudorandom number by a program is based on a similar manipulation of an initial value, called the *seed*, that is supplied to the pseudorandom number generator.

In Program 7.6 we give a simple program that displays five pseudorandom numbers through repeated invocations of function rand().

Program 7.6

Displays five random numbers without using srand()

```
// Program 7.6: Display of pseudorandom numbers
#include <stdlib.h>
#include <iostream.h>
int main() {
   for (int i = 1; i <= 5; ++i)
      cout << rand() << endl;
   return 0;
}
```

The program was run on a system where RAND_MAX equals 32,767. The output of the first run is as follows:

```
346
130
10982
1090
11656
```

The program was run a second time and produced the following output:

```
346
130
10982
1090
11656
```

That the two runs produce the same output is not a defect in the design of rand(). In fact, the repetition is part of the design of the function. By default, rand() always produces the same pseudorandom number sequence. That way, while a program is being tested or examined, it is possible to reproduce the same statement execution sequence.

To produce a different sequence of pseudorandom numbers, the function srand() is used. Function srand() expects an **unsigned int** as its parameter (the type modifier **unsigned** indicates that the value being represented does not use a sign bit in its representation, i.e., all values are nonnegative). The parameter is used to set the seed for generating the first pseudorandom number. Once the seed is set, `rand()` should produce a different sequence of pseudorandom numbers.

Program 7.7 is a modification of Program 7.6; in the new program, the user provides the seed value that is to be passed to `srand()`.

Program 7.7

Display five random numbers using prompted value for srand()

```
// Program 7.7: Display five pseudorandom numbers
#include <iostream.h>
#include <stdlib.h>
int main() {
   cout << "Random number seed (number): " << flush;
   unsigned int seed;
   cin >> seed;
   srand(seed);
   for (int i = 1; i <= 5; ++i)
      cout << rand() << endl;
   return 0;
}
```

The following is an example of the input/output behavior of Program 7.7.

```
Random number seed (number): 12
4155
30526
32049
23353
29576
```

Another run of Program 7.7 produced the following input/output behavior:

```
Random number seed (number): 13
4501
30310
10132
13461
7374
```

Program 7.8 is a modification of Program 7.7; the new program automatically generates the seed. Program 7.8 uses the current time as the basis for the seed value. By using the current time as the seed, the seed should be different for each run of the program that in turn should produce a different sequence of numbers for each run. The current time is determined using the function `time()`, which is defined in the time standard library. Function `time()` returns a value of type `time_t`, which is an integral type that is also defined in the time library. If the parameter to function `time()` is zero, function `time()` supplies the current time through its return value.

The following is an example of the input/output behavior of Program 7.8.

```
1372
20765
3967
26247
6928
```

Program 7.8

Automatic display of different pseudorandom number sequences

```
// Program 7.8: Display pseudorandom numbers
#include <iostream.h>
#include <stdlib.h>
#include <time.h>
int main() {
   srand((unsigned int) time(0));
   for (int i = 1; i <= 5; ++i)
      cout << rand() << endl;
   return 0;
}
```

The following is a display of another run of Program 7.8.

```
7084
8706
20276
6944
8322
```

The following statement in Program 7.8 is an example of a C++ cast expression.

```
srand((unsigned int) time(0));
```

A *cast expression* directs the compiler to convert the value of its operand to an explicit type. In this statement, the expression directs the compiler to convert the result of the call to time(), which is type time_t, to an **unsigned int**.

There are several common uses of casting expressions. You have just seen one. In this example, the cast expression is actually not required as casting of argument functions would have handled the conversion. However, it is good programming practice to use the cast expression so that it is clear to other programmers that a conversion is taking place and that this conversion is intended.

Another common use of casting expressions is to prevent the use of integer addition which produces a truncated result. Suppose that we wanted to compute a batting average. A batting average is defined to be the number of hits divided by the official number of times at bat. The following code fragment will not produce the correct results.

```
int AtBats = 3;
int NbrOfHits = 1;
float BattingAverage = NbrOfHits / AtBats;
```

The problem is that integer division truncates and BattingAverage is set to 0.0. One solution would be to define one of the objects, AtBats or NmbrOf-Hits, to be a floating-point type. This is artificial because you cannot have a fractional number of at bats or number of hits. The best solution is to use a casting expression. By casting either of the operands of the division to type **float**, we can force the compiler to perform floating-point division.

```
float BattingAverage = ((float) NmbrOfHits) / AtBats;
```

The above statement correctly computes the average .333. There are a few other situations where casting expressions can help make the code clearer. We will point these out as we encounter them.

There are two functions that are very useful in applications that use random numbers to pick something randomly from a selection of choices. One is a function that sets the random number seed so that a new random number sequence is generated each time the application is run. The other useful function is one that generates a random number in a specified interval. We shall make use of these functions in several of our programming examples. Later, we will generalize and encapsulate the capability of generating random numbers in a user-defined class. Listing 7.1 contains the prototypes for these utility functions.

Listing 7.1

Header file uniform.h

```
// Interface to random number utility functions
#ifndef UNIFORM_H
#define UNIFORM_H
void InitializeSeed();
int Uniform(int Low, int High);
#endif
```

Function `InitializeSeed()` sets the random number seed. It uses the same statement as Program 7.8 to set the pseudorandom number generator seed. The purpose of function `Uniform()` is to produce a pseudorandom number from a specified interval. The interval is specified to the function via its two parameters `Low` and `High`. The name `Uniform` indicates that the numbers generated will be uniformly chosen from the specified interval. That is, each number in the interval is equally likely to be generated. Listing 7.2 contains the implementations of the two functions.

The definition of `InitializeSeed()` is straightforward. It uses the same statement as function `main()` did in Program 7.8 to set the pseudorandom number generator seed. Function `Uniform()` is a bit more complicated. It first ensures that a valid interval has been specified, i.e., that `Low` is no bigger than `High`. If `Low` is bigger than `High`, an error message is issued and the function exits signalling an error.

If the interval is proper, the number of integers in the specified interval is then computed and assigned to `IntervalSize`.

```
int IntervalSize = High - Low + 1;
```

Next, a pseudorandom number produced by rand() is taken modulus `IntervalSize` and assigned to `RandomOffset`.

```
int RandomOffset = rand() % IntervalSize;
```

The expression `rand() % IntervalSize` produces pseudorandom numbers in the interval 0 to `IntervalSize - 1` in an equally likely manner. Since the value of `RandomOffset` is a pseudorandom number from the interval 0 to `IntervalSize - 1`, the value of the expression `Low + RandomOffset` is a pseudorandom number from the interval `Low` to `Low + IntervalSize - 1`.

Listing 7.2

Implementation of InitializeSeed and Uniform in file uniform.c

```
// Implementation of InitializeSeed and Uniform
#include <stdlib.h>
#include <iostream.h>
#include <time.h>
#include "uniform.h"

// InitializeSeed(): set the random number generator
// seed
void InitializeSeed() {
   srand(unsigned int time(0));
}

// Uniform(): generate a uniformly distributed random
// number between Low and High
int Uniform(int Low, int High) {
   if (Low > High) {
      cerr << "Illegal range passed to Uniform" << endl;
      exit(1);
   }
   else {
      int IntervalSize = High - Low + 1;
      int RandomOffset = rand() % IntervalSize;
      return Low + RandomOffset;
   }
}
```

Since `IntervalSize` equals `High - Low + 1`, the expression `Low + IntervalSize - 1` equals `High`. Therefore the value returned by `Uniform()` is a pseudorandom number from the interval `Low` to `High`.

7.9

A FACTORY AUTOMATION TRAINER

Most modern factories use automation wherever possible to reduce costs and to speed up the manufacturing process. Despite the advances in factory automation, many jobs are difficult to automate and require human input. For example, humans are still much better than machines at recognizing subtle differences in colors and recognizing complex patterns. In this section, we design and implement a program for training people to perform a particular task in a factory.

In this factory, groups of three parts proceed down a conveyor belt to an inspection station. At the inspection station a video image of the parts is sent to a display that is being watched by a human inspector. Figure 7.5 illustrates the operation of the inspection process. The inspector examines the video image of the three parts and determines if they should be accepted or rejected. To be accepted, two of the parts must be the same color. If two parts are the same color, the inspector punches the accept button and the parts proceed down the line and are assembled with other components. If no two parts are the same color, the inspector punches the reject button and the three parts are routed to a recycling station.

Figure 7.5

Factory automation system

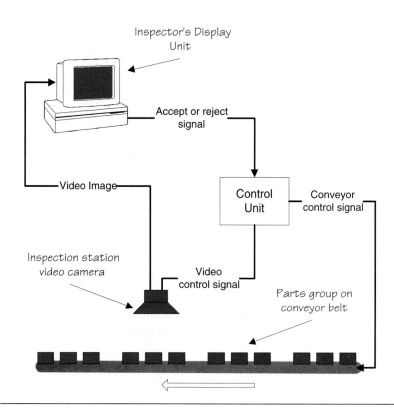

Inspector's Display Unit

Accept or reject signal

Video Image

Control Unit

Conveyor control signal

Inspection station video camera

Video control signal

Parts group on conveyor belt

Our job is to write a program that can be used to train and evaluate the performance of potential part inspectors. In addition, the program can be used to help determine at what rate inspectors can reliably inspect parts. This information is used to set the rate at which parts move through the system.

While we do not yet have all the C++ tools necessary to a complete object-oriented implementation, we can design the training system using object-oriented methods. From the above description, we see that the system consists of three components or objects—the inspection station on the conveyor belt, the display where the inspector views the parts, and the inspector. We will need to implement program components that simulate the behavior of the conveyor belt and the display. The actions of the inspector will, of course, be implemented by a real person. We must also have an object that controls and coordinates the operation of the system, much as we had in the Bug Hunt game discussed in Chapter 1. Before starting the detailed design and implementation of the trainer, we need a more precise description of exactly how the trainer should operate.

A more detailed description is:

> The parts inspection trainer will simulate the operation of the inspection component of the assembly line. To simulate parts moving

down the conveyor belt, we will create three rectangles with randomly chosen colors. The display system will consist of a display window where the three rectangles produced by the conveyor will be displayed. The input by the inspector will be accepted through the control window. The inspector can accept a group of parts by typing the letter "a" (for accept), or he/she can reject a group of parts by typing the letter "r" (for reject). A group of parts is acceptable if two of the parts are the same color. If no two parts are the same color, the parts should be rejected.

The trainer should maintain statistics about the performance of the inspector. The trainer should record the number of parts groups the inspector handles and the number of correct and incorrect decisions the inspector makes. After the training session is complete, the trainer should print the following statistics: the length of the training session, the number of part groups inspected during the session, the number of correct and incorrect decisions, and the percentage of correct decisions.

This description and the objects that make up the system drives the design of the program. Since we have not yet discussed how to create objects with C++, we will create functions that simulate the behavior of the objects we need. For now, we can think of these functions as the objects. One object corresponds to the video camera at the conveyor belt inspection station. The function is named `GetPartsImages()`. It generates images of the parts. We also need an object that corresponds to the display screen. This object displays the parts for the trainee to view. The display will be implemented by a function called `DisplayPartsImages()`. The other object is the object that controls and coordinates the simulation. A high-level description of the behavior of this object follows.

Step 1. Get part images.

Step 2. Display parts images in the display window.

Step 3. Read and record the response of the trainee.

Step 4. Score the response.

Step 5. Check to see if the training session should end. If time is not up, go back to step 1. If time is up, the final statistics of the training session are computed and printed.

Figure 7.6 shows the functional structure of the training system. In addition to the functions that correspond to the display and the video camera on the conveyor belt, two functions correspond to the two other main tasks of the training simulator. These functions, `CheckResponse()` and `PrintSessionResults()`, determine if the trainee correctly accepted or rejected a group of parts and print the results of the training session, respectively. The function `ApiMain()` implements the overall behavior of the system.

As the first step in the development of the trainer, let's write the first part of `ApiMain()`, which sets up the displays and creates the objects we will need for the training session. The first step of the ApiMain() is to set the ran-

Figure 7.6

Functional structure of the training simulator

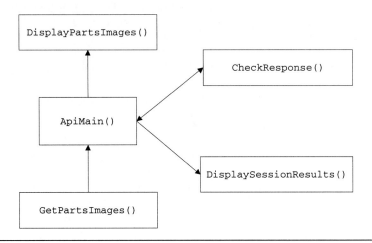

dom number seed so each simulation generates a different sequence of parts. Following that action, `ApiMain()` creates a display window and opens it. It then displays a message in the control window telling the trainee to arrange the windows so that they don't overlap. The next thing it does is define three `RectangleShape` objects, which will be used to represent the parts. We could try to declare them in the `GetPartsImages()` function, but when that function returns, the objects would be destroyed. Consequently, we must create these objects in `ApiMain()` because `ApiMain()` needs to pass these objects to the display function.

In addition to creating these display objects, `ApiMain()` also creates objects for keeping track of the responses of the trainee and the elapsed time of the session. The corresponding code follows.

```
InitializeSeed();
// Window for displaying the objects
SimpleWindow DisplayWindow("Training Window",
 DisplayLength, DisplayHeight);
DisplayWindow.Open();
assert(DisplayWindow.GetStatus() == WindowOpen);

// Print message telling user to arrange windows
cout << "Please resize this window so that\n"
 << "both windows are visible,\n"
 << "and they do not overlap.\n"
 << "Type any character followed by a return\n"
 << "when you are ready to proceed" << endl;
char Response;
cin >> Response;
cout << "\n\n\n" << flush;

// Create three rectangles for the three parts
RectangleShape Part1(DisplayWindow,
 3.0, YPosition, Blue, 2.0, 2.0);
RectangleShape Part2(DisplayWindow,
 7.0, YPosition, Blue, 2.0, 2.0);
RectangleShape Part3(DisplayWindow,
```

```
   11.0, YPosition, Blue, 2.0, 2.0);
// Define objects for scoring the trainee
int Attempts = 0;     // Number of tests done
int CorrectResponses = 0;
int IncorrectResponses = 0;

// Begin the training session
// Record starting time
const long StartTime = GetMilliseconds();
long ElapsedTime;
```

`Part1`, `Part2`, and `Part3`, are squares 2 centimeters on a side. Each part is initially colored blue, but function `GetPartsImages()` will randomly set the color of each part to simulate a variety of parts groups moving down the conveyor belt. The parts are centered within the display window and equidistant from each other. The constant `YPosition` is defined at the beginning of the program. The integer objects, `Attempts`, `CorrectResponses`, and `InCorrectResponses`, will be used to keep track of the trainee's performance.

To time the training session, we need access to a timer. The function `Get-Milliseconds()` provides this capability. Function `GetMilliseconds()` is part of the EzWindows library described in detail in Chapter 11. This function returns the value of a timer that is ticking continuously. The unit of time handled by the timer is milliseconds. Thus before we start the training session, we get the current value of the timer. During the training session, we will check the timer to determine the amount of time that has elapsed. Once one minute has elapsed, we will stop the session and print the statistics in the control window.

We are now ready to implement the main part of the training session, which consists of implementing the five steps outlined previously. The following code almost exactly parallels the five steps.

```
do {
    GetPartsImages(Part1, Part2, Part3);
    DisplayPartsImages(Part1, Part2, Part3);

    cout << "Accept or reject (a or r)? "
     << flush;
    char Response;
    cin >> Response;

    ++Attempts;
    if (CheckResponse(Response, Part1, Part2,
     Part3))
        ++CorrectResponses;
    else
        ++IncorrectResponses;

    ElapsedTime = GetMilliseconds();
} while ((ElapsedTime - StartTime) < TestTime);
PrintSessionResults(TestTime, Attempts,
 CorrectResponses, IncorrectResponses);
```

The function `GetPartsImages()` simulates the action of the video camera. It changes the color of the three objects, `Part1`, `Part2`, and `Part3` to simulate the image of the next three parts under the video camera. The function

`DisplayPartsImages()` takes the three objects and displays them on the inspector's display screen. The trainee then decides whether to reject or accept the parts. The trainee's response is checked for correctness by `CheckResponse()`. If the response was correct, the counter `CorrectResponses` is incremented; otherwise, the counter `IncorrectResponses` is incremented. The final part of the loop gets the current value of the timer and tests to see whether the elapsed time exceeds the time allocated for the test. If the time for the test has not elapsed, the code in the loop is repeated. Figure 7.7 shows the control and display windows created by the trainer.

Figure 7.7

Control and display windows for the training simulator

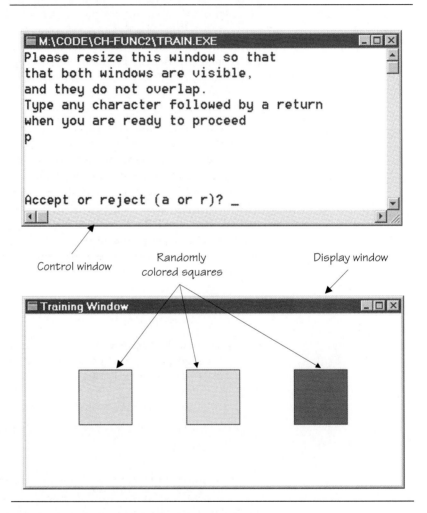

Control window

Randomly colored squares

Display window

To complete the implementation of the training simulator, we need to implement the functions `GetPartsImages()`, `DisplayPartsImages()`, `CheckResponse()`, and `DisplaySessionResults()`. Let's start with `GetPartsImages()`. This function simulates the video camera taking a picture of the parts by setting the three parts to a randomly generated color. The implementation of this function follows.

```
void GetPartsImages(RectangleShape &P1,
  RectangleShape &P2, RectangleShape &P3) {
    P1.SetColor(GenerateRandomColor());
    P2.SetColor(GenerateRandomColor());
    P3.SetColor(GenerateRandomColor());

    return;
}
```

Notice that the parameters to this function are passed by reference. This method is necessary because we are going to modify the objects by setting their colors. If the parts had been passed by value, then our changes would be made to copies of the objects, not to the actual objects. GenerateRandomColor() picks one of the five colors at random and returns it. The implementation of this function is:

```
color GenerateRandomColor() {
    switch (Uniform(0, 5)) {
        case 0: return Red;
        case 1: return Blue;
        case 2: return Green;
        case 3: return Yellow;
        case 4: return Cyan;
        case 5: return Magenta;
    }
}
```

We use our function Uniform() to generate a random integer in the range 0 through 5. Using this value, a part color is chosen.

The function DisplayPartsImages() displays the parts in the inspector's window simply by drawing each of the parts. When they were created by ApiMain(), they were positioned correctly and given the proper size. The code for this function is:

```
void DisplayPartsImages(const RectangleShape &P1,
  const RectangleShape &P2,
  const RectangleShape &P3) {
    P1.Draw();
    P2.Draw();
    P3.Draw();

    return;
}
```

Notice that the parameters P1, P2, and P3 are constant reference parameters, which ensures that the function will not modify the parts.

The job of CheckResponse() is to determine if the operator gave the correct response. If the operator's response was correct CheckResponse() returns true; otherwise, it returns false. If two of the three parts are the same color, the correct response is to accept the part; otherwise, the correct response is to reject the part. The implementation of `CheckResponse()` follows.

```
bool CheckResponse(char Response,
  const RectangleShape &P1, const RectangleShape &P2,
  const RectangleShape &P3) {
    if (P1.GetColor() == P2.GetColor()
       || P1.GetColor() == P3.GetColor()
       || P2.GetColor() == P3.GetColor())
      return Response == 'a';
    else
      return Response == 'r';
}
```

The final function for the training simulator is the function `DisplaySessionResults()`. This function computes and displays the statistics on how the trainee performed. It displays the length of the training session, the number of groups of parts inspected, the number of correct responses, the number of incorrect responses, and the percentage of correct responses. The implementation of `DisplaySessionResults()` follows.

```
void DisplaySessionResults(long Time, int Attempts,
  int Correct, int Wrong) {
    cout << "\n\nFor a training period of "
     << Time / 1000L << " seconds" << endl;
    cout << "Groups viewed: " << Attempts << endl;
    cout << "Correct responses: " << Correct << endl;
    cout << "Incorrect responses: " << Wrong << endl;
    cout << "Percent correct: "
     << Correct / ((float) Attempts * 100) << endl;

    return;
}
```

Figure 7.8 shows the control window after a training session has been completed, and Program 7.9 contains the complete code for the training simulator. Notice that the code includes the file `rect.h`. This file is included because it contains the declaration of the class `RectangleShape`.

7.10

TO DELVE FURTHER

The Annotated C++ Reference Manual by Margaret Ellis and Bjarne Stroustrup contains a complete discussion of function overload resolution. Another source of information about function overload resolution is the *Working Paper for Draft Proposed International Standard for Information Systems—Programming Language C++*. This document can be obtained from AT&T Bell Laboratories ftp repository.

Figure 7.8

Control window with statistics after a training session is over

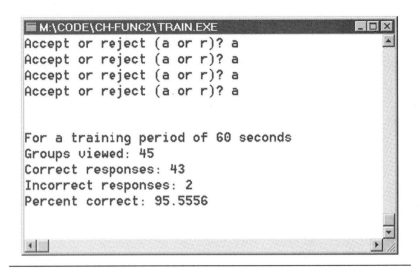

```
M:\CODE\CH-FUNC2\TRAIN.EXE
Accept or reject (a or r)? a
Accept or reject (a or r)? a
Accept or reject (a or r)? a
Accept or reject (a or r)? a


For a training period of 60 seconds
Groups viewed: 45
Correct responses: 43
Incorrect responses: 2
Percent correct: 95.5556
```

Program 7.9

A training simulator

```cpp
// Program 7.9: Program to train a parts inspector
#include <iostream.h>
#include <assert.h>
#include "uniform.h"
#include "rect.h"

// Length of Display window
const float DisplayLength = 14.0;
const float DisplayHeight = 6.0;

// Vertical position of the parts in the display
const float YPosition = DisplayHeight / 2.0;

// Length of the session (60 seconds)
const long TestTime = 60 * 1000L;

// Randomly pick one of the six colors
color GenerateRandomColor() {
    switch (Uniform(0, 5)) {
       case 0: return Red;
       case 1: return Blue;
       case 2: return Green;
       case 3: return Yellow;
       case 4: return Cyan;
       case 5: return Magenta;
    }
}

// Generate the test parts by randomly
// setting the color of the three parts
void GetPartsImages(RectangleShape &P1,
 RectangleShape &P2, RectangleShape &P3) {

    P1.SetColor(GenerateRandomColor());
    P2.SetColor(GenerateRandomColor());
    P3.SetColor(GenerateRandomColor());

    return;
```

```
   }
   // Display the shapes
   void DisplayPartsImages(const RectangleShape &P1,
    const RectangleShape &P2, const RectangleShape &P3) {
      P1.Draw();
      P2.Draw();
      P3.Draw();

      return;
   }

   // Print the results from the training session
   void DisplaySessionResults(long Time, int Attempts,
    int Correct, int Wrong) {

      cout << "\n\nFor a training period of "
       << Time / 1000L << " seconds" << endl;
      cout << "Groups viewed: " << Attempts << endl;
      cout << "Correct responses: " << Correct << endl;
      cout << "Incorrect responses: " << Wrong << endl;
      cout << "Percent correct: "
       << Correct / (float) Attempts * 100 << endl;
      return;
   }

   // Determine if the appropriate response was given
   bool CheckResponse(char Response,
    const RectangleShape &P1, const RectangleShape &P2,
    const RectangleShape &P3) {
      if (P1.GetColor() == P2.GetColor()
       || P1.GetColor() == P3.GetColor()
       || P2.GetColor() == P3.GetColor())
        return Response == 'a';
      else
        return Response == 'r';
   }

   int ApiMain() {
      InitializeSeed();
      // Window for displaying the objects
      SimpleWindow DisplayWindow("Training Window",
       DisplayLength, DisplayHeight);
      DisplayWindow.Open();
      assert(DisplayWindow.GetStatus() == WindowOpen);

      // Print message telling user to arrange windows
      cout << "Please resize this window so that\n"
       << "both windows are visible,\n"
       << "and they do not overlap.\n"
       << "Type any character followed by a return\n"
       << "when you are ready to proceed" << endl;
      char Response;
      cin >> Response;

      cout << "\n\n\n" << flush;

      // Create three rectangles for the three parts
      RectangleShape Part1(DisplayWindow,
       3.0, YPosition, Blue, 2.0, 2.0);
      RectangleShape Part2(DisplayWindow,
```

```
   7.0, YPosition, Blue, 2.0, 2.0);
RectangleShape Part3(DisplayWindow,
   11.0, YPosition, Blue, 2.0, 2.0);
// Define objects for scoring the trainee
int Attempts = 0;    // Number of tests done
int CorrectResponses = 0;
int IncorrectResponses = 0;
// Begin the training session
// Record starting time
const long StartTime = GetMilliseconds();
long ElapsedTime;
do {
   GetPartsImages(Part1, Part2, Part3);
   DisplayPartsImages(Part1, Part2, Part3);

   cout << "Accept or reject (a or r)? " << flush;
   char Response;
   cin >> Response;

   ++Attempts;
   if (CheckResponse(Response, Part1, Part2, Part3))
      ++CorrectResponses;
   else
      ++IncorrectResponses;
   ElapsedTime = GetMilliseconds();
} while ((ElapsedTime - StartTime) < TestTime);

DisplaySessionResults(TestTime, Attempts,
 CorrectResponses, IncorrectResponses);

return 0;
}
```

7.11

POINTS TO REMEMBER

- C++ supports two types of parameters—value parameters and reference parameters.

- When a parameter is passed by value, a copy of the object is passed to the called function. Any modifications made to the parameter by the called function change the copy, not the original object.

- When a reference parameter is used, instead of passing a copy of the object, a reference to the original object is passed. Any modifications made to the parameter by the called function change the original object.

- One common reason for using a reference parameter is that the called function needs to modify the object being passed, for example, when the called function needs to return several values to the calling function. The parameters that are used to pass values back to the calling function should be reference parameters.

History of Computing

- When an iostream object is passed to a function, either an extraction or an insertion operation implicitly modifies the stream. Thus, stream objects should be passed as reference parameters.

- A reason to use a reference parameter is for efficiency. When an object is passed by value, a copy of the object is passed. If the object is large, making a copy of it can be expensive in terms of execution time and memory space. Thus objects that are large, or objects whose size is not known are often passed by reference. We can ensure that the objects are not modified by using the **const** modifier.

- A **const** modifier applied to an parameter declaration indicates that the function may not change the object. If the function attempts to modify the object, the compiler will report a compilation error.

Figure 7.10

*ENIAC at the University
of Pennsylvania*

- C++'s default parameter mechanism provides the ability to define a function so that an parameter gets a default value if a call to the function does not give a value for that parameter. Thus for most calls to the function, only the necessary parameters are listed in the call to the function; default values are provided for the other parameters. When necessary, the function can be called with values provided for all the parameters.

- To make a function maximally useful, especially a library function, try to make the function as general as possible. This means the function accepts more parameters than are needed in the common, most heavily used cases.

- Default parameters can be specified for trailing parameters only.

- A function's parameter list is the signature of the function.

- Function overloading is when two or more function have the same name.

- The compiler resolves overloaded function calls by calling the function whose signature best matches that of the call.

- Casting expressions provide a facility to explicitly convert one type to another.

- A cast expression is useful when the programmer wants to force the compiler to perform a particular type of operation such as floating-point division rather than integer division.

- A cast expression is useful for converting values that library functions return to the appropriate type. This makes it clear to other programmers that the conversion was intended. This also avoids unnecessary warnings from the compiler.

- The stdlib library provides a function rand() that returns a pseudorandom number from the interval 0 through RAND_MAX, where RAND_MAX is an stdlib constant.

- The stdlib library provides a function srand() to alter the sequence of pseudorandom numbers that can be obtained through the use of rand(). The function invocation srand((**unsigned int**) time(0)) should initiate a different pseudorandom number sequence for each invocation.

7.12

EXERCISES

7.1 Consider the following function scramble():

```
void scramble(int i, int &j, int k) {
    i = 10;
    j = 20;
    k = 30;
    return;
}
```

a) What is the output of the following program fragment?

```
#include <iostream.h>
int main() {
        int i = 1;
        int j = 2;
        int k = 3;
        scramble(i, j, k);
        cout << "i = " << i << " j = " << j
            << " k = " << k << endl;
    return 0;
}
```

b) What is the output of the following program fragment?

```
#include <iostream.h>
int main() {
    int i = 1;
    int j = 2;
    int k = 3;
    scramble(j, j, j);
    cout << "i = " << i << " j = " << j
        << " k = " << k << endl;
    return 0;
}
```

7.2 Consider the following function scramble():

```
void scramble(int i, int &j, int &k) {
    i = 10;
    j = 20;
    k = 30;
```

```
        return;
    }
```

a) What is the output of the following program fragment?

```
int main() {
    int i = 1;
    int j = 2;
    int k = 3;
    scramble(k, j, i);
    cout << "i = " << i << " j = " << j
        << "k = " << k << endl;
    return 0;
}
```

b) What is the output of the following program fragment?

```
int main() {
    int i = 1;
    int j = 2;
    int k = 3;
    scramble(j, j, j);
    cout << "i = " << i << " j = " << j
        << "k = " << k << endl
    return 0;
}
```

7.3   Consider the following C++ program:

```
#include <iostream.h>
int funny(int &a, int b) {
    int c = a + b;
    a = b;
    b = c;
    return c;
}
int main() {
    int x = 3;
    int y = 4;
    int z = 5;
    cout << funny (x, y) << endl;
    cout << "x is: " << x << " and y is: " << y
        << endl;
    z = funny (x, z);
    cout << "z is: " << z << " and x is: " << x
        << endl;
    return 0;
}
```

What does the program display when it is executed?

7.4   Consider the following valid program:

```
#include <iostream.h>
int main() {
    int x = 1;
    f(x);
    cout << "x is " << x << endl;
    return 0;
}
```

When this program runs, the output is

```
x is 2
```

Write the function prototype for **void** function f().

7.5   Consider the following valid function tricky():

```
void tricky(const int x, int &y, int z) {
    x = 3;
    y = 3;
    z = 3;
}
```

When the function is compiled which assignment statements generate a compilation error? Write Yes beside the assignment statement if a compilation error occurs, write No if a compilation error does not occur.

a) x = 3;   _____

b) y = 3;   _____

c) z = 3;   _____

7.6   What is the output of the following C++ program?

```
#include <iostream.h>
void f(int &a) {
    cout << "int " << a << "\n";
    return;
}
void f(char &a) {
    cout << "char " << a << "\n";
    return;
}
int main() {
    int  i = 1;
    char c = 'c';
    f(i);
    f(c);
    return 0;
}
```

7.7   Find the errors in the following program fragments:

a)

```
int Update(const int &x, int y, int z) {
    y = z % 3;
    x = y + z;
    return x;
}
```

b)

```
int sum(int x, int y = 3, int z) {
    return x + y + z;
}
```

c)

```
void Flow(double x, int y) {
    return x + y;
}
```

d)

```
double Mul(const double a, const double b) {
    return a * b;
}
double Mul(double x, double y) {
    return x * y;
}
```

e)

```
#include <iostream.h>
bool GetInput(istream in, int &Value) {
    if (in >> Value)
        return true;
    else
        return false;
}
```

f)

```
#include <iostream.h>
bool GetInput(const istream &in, int &Value) {
    if (in >> Value)
        return true;
    else
        return false;
}
```

7.8   Write a program that reads a telephone number from a file called num-
      ber.dat. The program should determine whether the input is a valid
      telephone number. A valid telephone number has the following syntax:

      D D D '-' *D D D* '-' *D D D D*

      where the first *D* cannot be a zero.

      If the telephone number is valid, the program should print the telephone
      number followed by a colon (:) followed by a space and the word
      "Valid." If the telephone number is invalid, the program should print the
      telephone number followed by a colon (:) followed by a space and the
      words "Not Valid."

7.9   Write a program that prompts for and accepts two characters as input.
      The program determines if the two characters are a valid state abbrevia-
      tion. If the characters are a valid state abbreviation, the program prints
      the characters (in uppercase) followed by a colon (:) followed by a space
      and the word "Valid." If the characters are not a valid state abbreviation,
      the program prints the characters (in uppercase) followed by a colon (:)
      followed by a space and the words "Not Valid." For example, for the
      input

```
Va
```

the program should display

```
VA: Valid
```

For the input,

```
tz
```

the program should display

```
TZ: Not Valid
```

7.10 Consider the following functions:

```
#include <iostream.h>
void f(int a, double b) {
    cout << "f(int, double) says a is "
     << a << endl;
    cout << "f(int, double) says b is "
     << b << endl;
    return;
}
void f(int a, int b) {
    cout << "f(int, int) says a is "
     << a << endl;
    cout << "f(int, int) says b is "
     << b << endl;
    return;
}
void f(double a, double b) {
    cout << "f(double, double) says a is "
     << a << endl;
    cout << "f(double, double) says b is "
     << b << endl;
    cout << endl;
    return;
}
```

a) What is output when the following program is executed using these
    functions?

```
int main() {
    int i = 1;
    int j = 2;
    double x = 3.5;
    double y = 10.2;
    f(i, j);
    f(i, y);
    f(y, x);
    return 0;
}
```

b) What is output when the following program is executed using these functions?

```
int main() {
    f(1, 2.3);
    f(2, 4);
    f(2.6, 10.5);
    return 0;
}
```

c) When the following program is compiled using these functions, a compilation error occurs. What is wrong with the program?

```
int main() {
    f(1, 2.3);
    f(2.3, 4);
    f(2.6, 10.5);
    return 0;
}
```

7.11 The function `Valid()` in Program 7.5 contains the following if statement:

```
if (d4 == 0)
    return false;
else
    return ((d1 + d2 + d3) % d4) == d5;
```

Rewrite the if statement so that it is a single return statement. Which version of the program do you think is clearer? Why?

7.12 What is the output of the following program?

```
#include <iostream.h>
#include <assert.h>
void DisplayString(ostream &sout, char c = '*',
    int count = 1) {
    assert(count >= 0);
    for (int i = 0; i < count; ++i)
        sout << c;
    sout << endl;
}
int main() {
    DisplayString(cout);
    DisplayString(cout, '-', 10);
    DisplayString(cout, '+');
    return 0;
}
```

7.13 Modify Program 7.5 to read a file of access codes. The access codes are contained in a file called `access.dat`, one access code per line. For each access code, the program determines whether the code is valid or not. The program creates a file called `tested.dat` that contains each access code followed by either the word "Valid" or the word "Invalid".

7.14 Program 7.9 contains some hard-coded constants. For example, the squares are hard coded to be 2 centimeters on a side. Similarly, the horizontal position of the squares in the training window are hard coded to be at x-coordinates 3, 7, and 11. Modify the program to remove these hard-code constants. Document the changes you make at the beginning of the program.

7.15 In Program 7.9, the parts were accepted if two squares had the same color; size was not a factor. Modify the program so that the parts displayed are different colors and sizes. The parts should be accepted if two squares are the same color and size; otherwise, they should be rejected.

7.16 Modify Program 7.9 so that it computes and displays the trainee's speed. The speed should be expressed as parts inspected per minute. To get an accurate gauge of the trainee's speed, the simulation will have to be run for five minutes.

7.17 Modify Program 7.9 so that the squares are displayed in the following configuration in the display window.

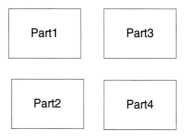

A group of parts should be accepted if the parts diagonally across from one another are the same color. That is, if `Part1` and `Part4` or `Part3` and `Part2` have the same color, the parts group should be accepted; otherwise, it should be rejected.

7.18 Modify Program 7.9 so that it displays three rectangles all of the same color. The rectangles, which represent parts, can have the following sizes: 3 by 2, 4 by 2, 6 by 2, 2 by 3, 2 by 4, and 2 by 6. The trainee should accept a parts group if two parts are the same size, regardless of the orientation of the parts.

7.19 Write a program that computes final averages for a set of grades. The program reads the grades from a file called `scores.dat`. The file `scores.dat` begins with a header line followed by a set of scores for each student. The format of the header line is

$$n \qquad weight_1 \; weight_2 \; ... \qquad weight_n$$

where n is the number of scores for each student and $weight_i$ is the weight of the ith score. The header line is followed by grades for each student. The format of a grade line is

$$name \qquad score_1 \; score_2 \; ... \qquad score_n$$

where *name* is the last name of the student and $score_i$ is the ith score. All scores must be between 0 and 100.

The program reads the file `score.dat` and writes a file called `average.dat` that has the following format:

name score₁ score₂ ... scoreₙ => nn.nn Average

<span></span>

The program reads the file `score.dat` and writes a file called `average.dat` that has the following format:

name score$_1$ score$_2$ ... score$_n$ => nn.nn Average

where *name* and *score$_i$* are as before and *nn.nn* is the weighted average of the student's scores. The weighted average is computed as

$$\frac{\sum_{i=1}^{n} score_i \times weight_i}{n}$$

Your program should validate its input. That is, it should make sure each score is between 0 and 100 and that each student has *n* scores. If a student's scores are invalid, the program should write an error message to `cerr` and that student's scores should not be written to the output file `average.dat`. Design hint: Your program should contain a routine that handles doing input and a routine that handles validating the input.

7.20 Extend Exercise 7.19 so that the program also determines a final letter grade. The letter grade ranges are:

Average	Letter Grade
0–59	F
60–69	D
70–79	C
80–89	B
90–100	A

The lines written to `average.dat` should have the following format:

name score$_1$ ... score$_n$ => nn.nn Average (Letter)

where *Letter* is the letter grade.

7.21 Extend Exercise 7.19 so that the program computes and displays an overall average for the class.

7.22 Modify the stock charting program of the previous chapter to make its `SimpleWindow` object `W` a local object of the program's `ApiMain()`. This change requires that you modify the invocations of functions `ChartWeek()`, `DrawXAxis()`, and `DrawYAxis()` to pass `W`. The definitions of these three functions must also include a `SimpleWindow` reference parameter.

7.23 An interesting baseball statistic is the slugging average. This statistic measures the ability of a batter to hit for power. The definition of slugging average is the total number of bases reached divided by the official number of times at bat. For example, in 12 official at bats (walks and sacrifices do not count as official at-bats), a player has 2 singles (2 bases), 2 doubles (4 bases), a home run (4 bases), and a strike out (0 bases), the player's slugging average is 10 ÷ 12 = .833. Incidentally, Babe Ruth holds the record for lifetime slugging average of .690.

Write a program to compute the slugging average of a set of players. The data for the players is contained in a file. The file has the following format:

name   AtBats   Singles   Doubles   Triples   HomeRuns   StrikeOuts

Name is the last name of the player. All other items are integer values. Your program should prompt the user for the name of the file that contains the data to be processed. Your program should create a new file called `slugging.dat` that contains the computed slugging average. The format of each line of this file should be:

```
name Total Bases: bb At-Bats: aa Slugging
Average: .nnn
```

all on one line. *Name* is the last name of the player, `bb` is the total bases for the player, `aa` is the number of at-bats, and `.nnn` is the slugging average.

CHAPTER 8

The class construct

Introduction

O bjects are the basic unit of programming in object-oriented languages like C++. Objects are models of information and are implemented as software packages that can encapsulate both attributes and behavior. The construct for defining new types of encapsulated objects in C++ is the **class**. A **class** is the "blueprint" from which an object can be created. In this chapter, we introduce how to create these blueprints or specifications of objects. We do so by showing the class declaration of a programmer-defined type we have used in previous chapters—RectangleShape.

Key Concepts

- **class** construct
- information hiding
- encapsulation
- data members
- member functions
- constructors
- inspectors
- mutators
- facilitators
- **const** functions
- access specification: **public** and **private**
- object-oriented analysis and design

8.1

INTRODUCING A PROGRAMMER-DEFINED DATA TYPE

The preceding chapters provided the basics of programming and software engineering practices. Knowing that material makes it possible for you to solve simple problems. However, to solve more complex problems, you must master additional language features, algorithmic skills, and engineering techniques. In this chapter, we introduce the C++ **class** construct for defining new types of objects. This construct is the basis of object-oriented programming using C++.

A fundamental-type object is an object that is provided by the programming language. For example in C++, the type **int** and the operations on it are part of the language definition of C++. That is, all C++ compilers must provide **int** objects. In addition to its fundamental types, C++ provides several mechanisms to define other types. These other types are called *programmer-* or *user-defined types*.

In the previous chapters we used the C++ **enum** construct to create new types. The type color, which we used in conjunction with the object RectangleShape, was created using the **enum** construct. In addition to the **enum** construct, C++ provides several other methods for creating new types. For example, C++ allows the programmer to define a type that is a list of objects. These are called arrays. A second example is the pointer mechanism that allows a programmer to define a type whose values are the memory addresses of other objects. Both of these mechanisms are considered in subsequent chapters.

The **class** construct that is introduced in this chapter is the most important mechanism for defining new types. With this construct, software engineers can define class-type objects that contain or *encapsulate* both an *attribute* component and a *behavior* component.

To illustrate the basics of creating a new object type using the **class** construct, we discuss the declaration of an programmer-defined type we have used in previous chapters—RectangleShape. Whenever one is designing something, it helps to know how the thing will be used. Our goal in designing RectangleShape is that we want a graphical object that is easy to create and simple to use. It can then be used, as we have seen in the previous chapters, whenever a rectangle shape can represent a real object.

The first thing to do when creating a class type is to determine the attributes of the object. For objects in our graphical display system, the necessary attributes of a rectangle are its size, its location within the viewport or display window, the window it will be displayed in, and its color. In C++, the attributes of a class-type object are referred to as the *data members* of the class. Later in this chapter when we consider how classes are defined, you will see that the data members are simply sub-objects of the class-type object.

The second step when creating a class-type object is to determine the messages the object can receive and the operations that can be performed on the object. This is its behavior component. The behavior component of a class-type object is a collection of *member functions* that provide the ability to send messages to an object requesting it perform some action. Continuing with the development of a class for a rectangle shape in a windowed graphical display system, a rectangle needs to handle two classes of messages. One set of messages returns the value of an attribute of a rectangle, and one set of messages changes the value of an attribute.

Messages that return the value of an attribute are called *inspectors*. For maximum flexibility, our definition of RectangleShape will include inspectors for all of the data members. Thus, RectangleShape's inspectors are GetColor(), GetSize(), GetPosition(), and GetWindow().

Messages that change or set an attribute are called *mutators*. They are called mutators because the messages change or mutate the object. Again, to make the RectangleShape as flexible as possible, we will have mutators for the attributes that control the appearance and location of a RectangleShape. Thus, RectangleShape's mutators are SetColor(), SetPosition(), and SetSize(). Each member function sets the attribute indicated by its name.

One additional message is neither an inspector or a mutator. The draw message tells the rectangle to display itself in the window. Draw() is an example of a facilitator. A *facilitator* causes an object to perform some action or service.

Notice RectangleShape has an inspector GetWindow(), but there is no corresponding mutator SetWindow(). Once a RectangleShape is created, it is bound to a display window, and once a shape is bound to a display window, it cannot be changed. Thus, we prevent a user from changing the window by not providing the necessary mutator. As we will see shortly, there are several good reasons for having this restriction.

Figure 8.1 illustrates our abstraction of a rectangle for our simple graphical display system. The dotted cloud shape indicates that this entity is a class definition of a rectangle, not an actual instance of a rectangle. Our convention is to label the class name with the letter C, the data members with the abbreviation DM, and the member functions with the abbreviation MF.

You might wonder why we say that class RectangleShape is an abstraction of a rectangle. After all, there are some concrete details about the rectangle such as size, color, and position within the window. Abstraction eliminates the irrelevant and focuses on the essential properties of an object. In our case, the essential properties are those that are required for making a RectangleShape useful for developing graphical programs. These properties are the size, color and position of a rectangle within a window. The irrelevant details are how a RectangleShape is drawn in a window. Our abstraction of a rectangle says nothing about that. By eliminating unessential details, we make RectangleShape easy to use. Furthermore, how we use RectangleShape is independent of the windowing system we use. Thus, our programs can run on a variety of operating systems without modification.

Figure 8.1

*Data members and
member functions for
class RectangleShape*

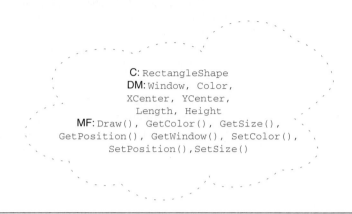

```
C: RectangleShape
DM: Window, Color,
    XCenter, YCenter,
    Length, Height
MF: Draw(), GetColor(), GetSize(),
GetPosition(), GetWindow(), SetColor(),
    SetPosition(),SetSize()
```

8.2

THE RECTANGLESHAPE CLASS

Now that we have determined an abstraction for a rectangle, we are ready to see how to declare a C++ **class** corresponding to an object abstraction. The syntax for declaring a class-type object is

Class keyword   A valid C++ name

```
        class ClassName {
Public  public:
keyword     // Prototypes for constructors
            // and public member functions
            // and declarations for public
            // data attributes go here
                 ...
                 ...
Private public:
keyword     // prototypes for private data
            // members and declarations for
            // private data attributes go here
                 ...
                 ...
        };
```

Public
keyword

Private
keyword

The declaration begins with the keyword **class** followed by the name of the class. Inside the class declaration are the prototypes for the functions that implement the inspectors, mutators, and facilitators. The class declaration also contains declarations for any member data that are part of the class.

For example, the **class** declaration for RectangleShape is

```
class RectangleShape {
    public:
        RectangleShape(SimpleWindow &Window,
          float XCoord, float YCoord, color Color,
          float Length, float Height);
        void Draw();
        color GetColor() const;
        void GetSize(float &Length,
          float &Height) const;
        void GetPosition(float &XCoord,
          float &YCoord) const;
        SimpleWindow& GetWindow() const;
        void SetColor(const color Color);
        void SetPosition(float XCoord, float YCoord);
        void SetSize(float Length, float Height);
    private:
        SimpleWindow &Window;
        float XCenter;
        float YCenter;
        color Color;
        float Length;
        float Height;
};
```

and the following program uses the class to create a 2-centimeter-by-3-centimeter blue rectangle named R in a window.

```
#include "rect.h"
SimpleWindow W("MAIN WINDOW", 8.0, 8.0);
int ApiMain() {
    W.Open();
    RectangleShape R(W, 4.0, 4.0, Blue, 2.0, 3.0);
    R.Draw();
    return 0;
}
```

Figure 8.2 shows the resulting window.

A C++ **class** declaration begins with the keyword **class** followed by the name of the **class**. As you would expect, the name of the **class** must be a valid C++ identifier. The data members and member functions of the **class** are enclosed in curly braces. Inside the curly braces, the data member and member function declarations are divided into two sections labeled **public** and **private**. For now, we will ignore the meaning of these labels.

Let's begin by examining the data attribute declarations that appear after the reserved word **private**. One declaration corresponds to each attribute of the object. For example, the declaration

```
SimpleWindow &Window;
```

declares a subobject called Window that will hold a reference to the SimpleWindow that will display the RectangleShape object. You are probably

Figure 8.2

*RectangleShape R in
MainWindow*

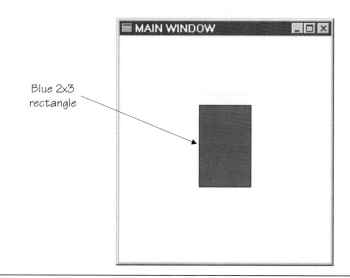

wondering why the declaration uses the reference operator &. If the declaration had been

```
SimpleWindow Window;
```

then a `RectangleShape` would contain a `SimpleWindow` object (not a reference to one). Just like the call-by-value parameter passing mechanism this declaration means that when a new `RectangleShape` object is instantiated a copy of a `SimpleWindow` object is made. This action is confusing because what should happen when you make a copy of a `SimpleWindow` object is unclear. Normally, when you copy an object, you get another identical object. Do we really want another window to appear each time we create a `RectangleShape`? Clearly, no. Therefore, rather than copy the `SimpleWindow` object, we just keep a reference to it. Just like the reference parameter passing mechanism, you can think of the reference attribute `Window` as an alias for the actual window that contains the object.

The declarations

```
float XCenter;
float YCenter;
```

are the declarations for the subobjects that will hold the coordinates of the center of the rectangle, and the declaration

```
color Color;
```

declares the data member that will hold the color of the rectangle. The attributes for the size of the rectangle are held in the following data members:

```
float Length;
float Height;
```

Now that we understand the attributes of a `RectangleShape`, let's examine the various public functions. The first prototype in `Rectangle-Shape`'s class declaration

```
RectangleShape(SimpleWindow &Window,
   float XCoord, float YCoord, color Color,
   float Length, float Height);
```

is a *constructor* for `RectangleShape`. A constructor function is automatically invoked when an object is defined. The constructor can initialize some or all of the object's data members to appropriate values. Constructor functions are easily recognized because they have the same name as the class.

The definition

```
RectangleShape R(W, 4.0, 4.0, Blue, 2.0, 3.0);
```

creates a `RectangleShape` called `R`, invokes the constructor, and passes it the values `W`, `4.0`, `4.0`, `Blue`, `2.0`, and `3.0` to initialize the data members of `R`. As you can guess, `Window` is initialized to the value `W`. `XCenter` and `YCenter` are given the values `4.0` and `4.0`, `Color` is set to `Blue`, and `Length` and `Height` are set to `2.0` and `3.0`, respectively. The process of creating an object and initializing its data members is called *instantiation*.

Similarly, the definitions

```
RectangleShape R1(W, 1.0, 4.0, Cyan, 3.0, 3.0);
RectangleShape R2(W, 6.0, 4.0, Red, 1.0, 2.0);
```

instantiate two objects of type `RectangleShape` named `R1` and `R2`. The process of instantiating a particular instance of an object from its abstraction is illustrated in Figure 8.3. The solid cloud shape indicates that the entity is an actual instance of the abstraction. Our convention is to label the name of the object with the letter O. The data members and member functions will be labeled with the same notation used with the illustration of a class.

The next part of `RectangleShape`'s definition lists the prototypes for the messages that a `RectangleShape` object can receive. The definitions of these functions and the constructors are contained in another module. While it is possible to include the definition of a member function or constructor in the class declaration, the principle of information hiding encourages us to put the implementation details in a separate module. The inclusion of the implementation of the constructor or member functions within the class would complicate the class declaration and make the interface to the class harder to see.

Figure 8.3

*Instantiation of two
RectangleShape objects
R1 and R2*

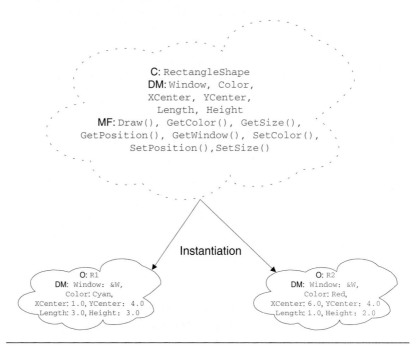

In C++, messages are sent to objects by invoking member functions. Recall the syntax for sending a message to an object by invoking a member function is

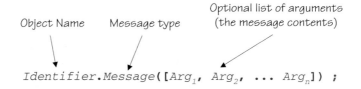

The '.' between the identifier and the message type is called the member access operator. The *member access operator* selects a member function or data member of an object.

Our class RectangleShape contains eight member functions. The first member function, Draw(), sends a message telling the object that it should make itself visible in the window. When a RectangleShape is instantiated, it does not appear in the window. Rather the programmer must explicitly tell a RectangleShape object to draw itself in the window by sending the object a draw message. For example, for RectangleShape object R, the code

```
R.Draw();
```

sends a message telling R to draw itself in the SimpleWindow that contains it.

You might wonder why we need a draw function at all. Why not just have the object appear in the window when it is instantiated? This is a reasonable question. As we shall see, having an explicit draw function makes `RectanglegleShape` more flexible. We will often want to create a shape before we know exactly what characteristics the shape should have. Similarly, we will often reuse an existing shape by giving it a new color, changing its position, and drawing it in its new location. By separating the actions of instantiation from the action of drawing, we can create a shape with default values, determine and set its attributes, and then when we are ready, cause the shape to appear by sending it a draw message.

Following the draw member function declaration, are declarations for the member functions `GetColor()`, `GetSize()`, `GetPosition()`, and `GetWindow()`. These are the declarations of the inspectors that return the attributes of a `RectangleShape`. Notice that the inspectors `GetSize()` and `GetPosition()` use reference parameters to return both values of their attributes. For example, `GetSize()` returns both the length and height of a `RectangleShape`. The declaration for `GetWindow()` specifies that it returns a reference to the `SimpleWindow` that contains the `RectangleShape`. Again, we use this method because we don't want to make a copy of the window that contains the shape.

You should also notice that each inspector has the reserved word **const** as part of its declaration. For example, the declaration of inspector `GetColor()` indicates that the member function is a constant function.

```
color GetColor() const;
```

That is, this function does not modify or change the object. Knowing that a function is specified to not change an object helps us read the code, and it allows the compiler to check to make sure that we do not mistakenly change the value of the object. If a constant function tries to change the value of the object or call a non-constant function, the compiler will report the error.

Following the declaration of the inspectors are the declarations of the mutators. The mutator member functions are `SetColor()`, `SetPosition()`, and `SetSize()`. Each attribute that can be changed has a mutator. For example, the code

```
R2.SetColor(Blue);
```

sends R2 a set color message with the argument `Blue`. When R2 receives this message, it will set its color attribute to `Blue`. The code

```
R2.SetPosition(2.5, 6.0);
R2.SetSize(1.0, 4.0);
```

sends messages to set R2's other attributes. The first message tells R2 that its center should be 2.5 centimeters from the left edge of the window and 6.0 centimeters from the top edge of the window. The final message tells R2 that its length should be 1.0 centimeters and its height 4.0. After setting the various attributes, we can display R2 in the window by sending it a draw message. The invocation

```
R2.Draw();
```

sends a message telling R2 to draw itself in its window at its x, y coordinates, with its color, and size. The process of instantiation, initialization of data members, and the drawing of R2 is illustrated in Figure 8.4.

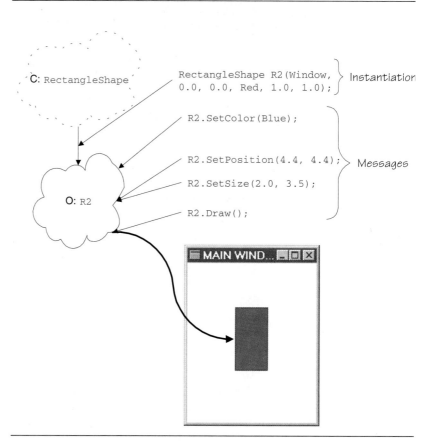

8.2.1

Public and private access

One of the principles of software engineering that we discussed in Chapter 1was information hiding or encapsulation. Recall that this process separates the aspects of an object into external and internal aspects. The external aspects of an object are those that need to be visible or known to other objects in the system. The internal aspects of an object are those that should not affect other parts of the system and therefore need not and should not be known to or available to other objects in the system. The labels **public** and **private** within a class declaration are one of the features that C++ provides to support information hiding or encapsulation.

Style Tip

Public before private

In a C++ class declaration, the public and private sections may appear in any order. Some programmers prefer to put the private section first since it contains the data attributes. We believe that the public section should be first because the public member functions and the constructors are the user's interface to the class. Indeed, the data attributes in the private section are somewhat secondary to the use of the class, and with a properly defined class, we really should never need to see how the data attributes are declared.

Data members and member functions declared following a **private** label are accessible only to other member functions of the class. Class members following a **public** label are accessible to functions that are not members of the class. This notion of controlling access to the members of a C++ **class** is illustrated in Figure 8.5.

Figure 8.5

Controlling access to class members with public and private

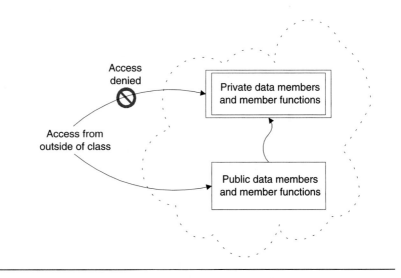

While public and private sections can be used to control access to data members and member functions, a more important use of access specifiers is to implement information hiding. *The information hiding principle states that all interaction with an object should be constrained to use a well-defined interface that allows underlying object implementation details to be safely ignored.* Thus, the member functions and data members in the **public** section form the external interface to the object, while the items in the **private** section are the internal aspects of the object that do not need to be accessible to use the object.

In the `RectangleShape` class, the member functions `Draw()`, `Get-Color()`, `GetSize()`, `GetPosition()`, `GetWindow()`, `SetColor()`, `SetPosition()`, and `SetSize()` are the public interface to `Rectangle-Shape`. Using `RectangleShape`'s public interface, we were able to write a code fragment that created a rectangle within a window by defining a `RectangleShape` object called `R` and by calling the appropriate member functions to set `R`'s attributes. The exact details of how a `RectangleShape` is represented and implemented are irrelevant.

For example, `RectangleShape`'s public interface says the size and position of a `RectangleShape` are specified using centimeter values that are stored floating-point objects. However, the underlying window system uses a system based on pixels, not centimeters. `RectangleShape`'s public interface lets us use a more familiar measurement system to position and size shapes. Furthermore, we do not know anything about the underlying coordinate system in which windows are represented. The beauty of encapsulation is that irrelevant and complicating details can be hidden, which simplifies the use of the object.

8.3

USING THE RECTANGLESHAPE CLASS

Now that we understand the basics of declaring a class, instantiating objects of that class, and interacting with the objects via the member functions, we can explore the use of class `RectangleShape` in more detail. Recall that the coordinate system used to position rectangles in a window assumes that the origin is the upper-left corner of the window. Figure 8.6 shows the `SimpleWindow` coordinate system.

Figure 8.6

The SimpleWindow coordinate system

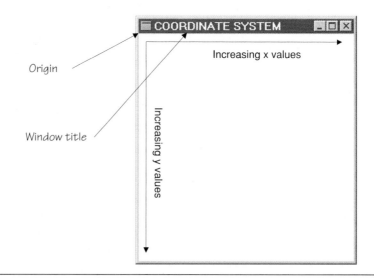

The units on the axes are centimeters. Thus, the definition

```
RectangleShape T(ExampleWindow, 2, 3, Red, 2, 2);
```

creates a `RectangleShape` named `T` with its center 2 centimeters from the left side of the window and 3 centimeters from the top of the window.

The unit of measure of all the arguments to `RectangleShape`'s member functions that have to do with position or size is centimeters. Having a consistent or uniform interface to a class of object is a key object-oriented design principle. For example, the program

```cpp
#include "rect.h"
SimpleWindow W("Double Square", 8, 8);
int ApiMain() {
    W.Open();
    RectangleShape B(W, 4, 4, Blue, 1, 1);
    B.Draw();
    // Create and draw another rectangle so that its
    // bottom-right corner touches the upper-left
    // corner of B
    RectangleShape M(W, 2.5, 2.5, Magenta, 2, 2);
    M.Draw();
    return 0;
}
```

creates and draws blue rectangle `B` 1 centimeter on a side and positioned 3 centimeters from the left and top of window `W`. Then the program creates rectangle `M`. `M`'s length and height is 2 centimeters, its color is set to magenta, and it is set to be displayed in window `W`. `M`'s position is set to coordinates (2.5, 2.5) so that its bottom-right corner touches `B`'s upper-left corner. Figure 8.7 shows the resulting window.

Figure 8.7

Display created by double square

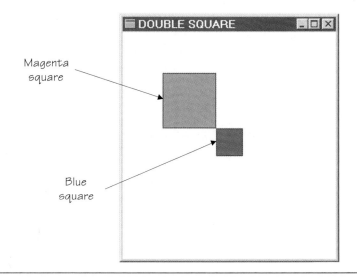

Another important characteristic of a window system is the color scheme that can be used. The color scheme is sometimes referred to as the palette. Let's write a program called `Colors` that displays all the colors that a `Rectangle-Shape` object can be.

Recall that the colors a `RectangleShape` object can be are specified by the enumeration

```
enum color {White, Red, Green, Blue, Yellow, Cyan,
            Magenta};
```

Thus, we need to display six squares—one for each color except `White`. Because white is the background color, we wouldn't be able to see it. We will display the six colors using 1-centimeter squares laid out side-by-side so that the screen resembles a color spectrum. Of course, we want to center the color spectrum within the window so it looks nice. Program 8.1 contains the code for this program.

Program 8.1

Create and display a color palette

```
// Program 8.1: Display color palette
#include "rect.h"
SimpleWindow ColorWindow("Color Palette", 8.0, 8.0);
int ApiMain() {
    const int SideSize = 1;
    float XPosition = 1.5;
    const float YPosition = 4;

    ColorWindow.Open();

    // Create a RectangleShape to use
    RectangleShape ColorPatch(ColorWindow,
     XPosition, YPosition, White, SideSize, SideSize);

    // Loop over colors drawing ColorSquare with
    // that color next to the previous square
    for (color c = Red; c <= Magenta;
     c = (color)(c + 1)) {
       ColorPatch.SetColor(c);
       ColorPatch.SetPosition(XPosition, YPosition);
       ColorPatch.Draw();
       XPosition += SideSize;
    }
    return 0;
}
```

With one minor exception, the code is quite straightforward. First, a few constants specify the size of the rectangle and the position of the first color patch. Following those definitions, the `RectangleShape` object `Color-Patch` is instantiated.

The for statement loops over the colors. The for loop contains another use of a cast expression. The increment expression of the for loop is

```
c = (color) (c + 1)
```

This statement sets `c` to the next color. You might ask why we did not write `++c` to advance to the next color. C++ does not allow enumeration objects to be incremented. The reason is that given a member of an enumeration the next member may not be represented by the next integer. However because the underlying implementation of an enumeration type is integer, we can perform arithmetic enumeration objects. The result is an integer. Since we know that the members of `color` are consecutive integers, we can safely cast the result of the expression `c + 1` to `color` to obtain the next color. This allows us to write the for loop in a natural way.

The body of the for statement sets the object `Colorpatch` to the appropriate color, draws the patch, and then repositions the patch so the next patch will appear adjacent to the previous one. Figure 8.8 shows the window created by the program.

Figure 8.8

Display created by the color palette program

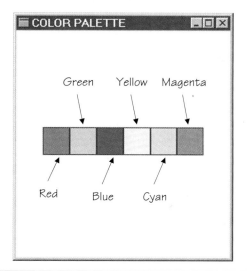

8.4

CONSTRUCTORS

In the previous examples, each time we defined a `RectangleShape`, we had to provide initial values for all the data members because the `Rectangle-Shape` constructor required them. We need a way to create a class-type object without having to specify all the data member values, especially if we are immediately going to change them or set them as we did in the color palette program. However, creating an object without specifying values for the attributes would be dangerous. For example, if we created a `Rectangle-Shape` and didn't give it a position and then sent it a message to draw itself, any number of strange things might happen—including our program crashing the system.

Fortunately, C++ provides a way to do exactly what we want. Remember the default parameters we discussed in Chapter 7? We can also use this mechanism in a constructor.

We can change the prototype of RectangleShape's constructor to be

```
RectangleShape(SimpleWindow &Window,
    float XCoord = 0, float YCoord = 0, color c = Red,
    float Length = 1, float Height = 2);
```

Using default parameter values in a constructor works just like using default parameter values in a function prototype. For example, the definition

```
RectangleShape C(ControlWindow);
```

creates a Rectangleshape named C and sets its SimpleWindow attribute to ControlWindow. The other attributes are given the default values as specified in the constructor's prototype. Thus, the position attributes XCenter and YCenter are given the value 0.0, the data member Color is set to Red, and the data members Length and Height are set to the values 1.0 and 2.0, respectively.

Similarly, the definition

```
RectangleShape D(ControlWindow, 3, 5);
```

instantiates a RectangleShape named D that is in the window Control-Window with its center 3 centimeters from the left edge of the window and 5 centimeters from the top edge of the window. Because the definition did not specify the values of the color and size attributes, they are given the default values of Red, 1.0, and 2.0.

Notice the argument Window does not have a default value. Thus the definition

```
RectangleShape E;
```

is illegal, and the C++ compiler will flag it as an error because reference data members must be initialized when the object is constructed. In addition, once a reference data member is initialized, it cannot be changed.

8.5

BUILDING A KALEIDOSCOPE

As a final demonstration of the use of class RectangleShape, we now design and implement a program that simulates a kaleidoscope display in a window. In this first implementation of a program to simulate a kaleidoscope, we will use objects, but the design of the program is not object-oriented. Chapter 14 contains an improved program that simulates a kaleidoscope. This version was designed using the object-oriented approach.

The kaleidoscope, invented in 1816 by Sir David Brewster, is a device, somewhat similar in size and shape to a small telescope, that creates symmetrical multi-colored patterns that can be viewed through an eyepiece. Many of us are familiar with the child's version of a kaleidoscope that is constructed from cardboard tubes. One tube contains bits of colored glass and mirrors; the other tube contains the eye piece for viewing the image. The image created is the result of combining reflections of the bits of colored glass. The pattern can be changed by rotating the tube with the colored glass and mirrors. As the bits of colored glass shift, they create new patterns.

A kaleidoscope image can be simulated by displaying images symmetrically positioned in a display window. In this first version of our kaleidoscope program, the images displayed will be squares of various sizes and colors. Rather than refer to the images as squares, which are their concrete representation, we will call them trinkets, which is more in keeping with the way a real kaleidoscope works

Thus, we need to write a routine, `Kaleidoscope()`, that displays trinkets of various sizes and colors symmetrically within the window to create a kaleidoscope effect. To simulate the changing patterns, `Kaleidoscope()` will be called repeatedly to add new trinkets to the display window.

Our strategy for creating the symmetrical patterns will be to partition the window into four quadrants (see Figure 8.9). To simulate the mirrorlike reflection, identical trinkets are displayed in diagonally opposite quadrants. All four trinkets are positioned symmetrically about the center of the window. The net effect is that the trinkets in opposite quadrants look like reflections. Four additional trinkets are positioned similarly with the color scheme reversed. Thus two trinkets are drawn in each quadrant for a total of eight trinkets.

Figure 8.9

Window layout to simulate a kaleidoscope

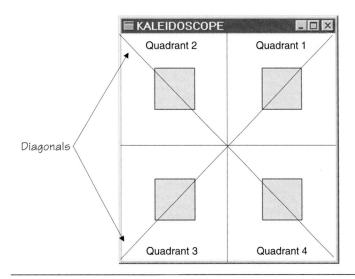

Three of the subtasks we need to do are to randomly pick a color, a trinket size, and an offset from the center of the window to position the trinkets. For all these tasks, we can use the function `Uniform()` that we developed in Chapter 7.

Generating a random color is easy using `Uniform()` and a casting expression. The following 3-line function generates a random color.

```
color RandomColor() {
    return (color) Uniform(1, MaxColors - 1);
}
```

Notice that in the return statement the random number returned by `Uniform()` is cast to be the type `color`. This works because `color` is an enumeration type and its underlying implementation is a sequence of integers starting at 0. Thus, the value 1 is mapped to red, 2 is mapped to green, 3 is mapped to blue, etc. Using the cast expression makes it explicit that we want to convert the integer returned by `Uniform()` to a color.

To generate a random trinket size, we can do something similar. We would like to generate a size that is between one and some maximum that we pick. We need to control the maximum size because we do not want the trinket to be larger than the window. To get some variability in the display, we want to use a range of trinket sizes and allow trinkets with fractional sizes. As a starting point, we decide that we will generate trinket sizes in the range one to some maximum size in 0.1 centimeter increments. The function

```
float RandomTrinketSize(int MaxSize) {
    return Uniform(10, MaxSize * 10) / 10.0;
}
```

generates a number in the range 1 to `MaxSize` in 0.1 increments. Using simple algebraic substitution, you can convince yourself that the function returns a number from the sequence of numbers 1, 1.1, 1.2,..., `MaxSize`.

We also need to generate a random offset to position the trinkets along the diagonals. Generating the offset is somewhat more difficult because we need to make sure that the offset is large enough so that when the trinket is drawn, it does not overlap the center of the window. Consequently, the offset depends on the size of the trinket. Additionally, if the offset is too large, part of the square will be displayed outside the window.

To take into account the size of the trinket, we need to make sure that the offset is at least as large as half the length of the trinket's side. Thus, if we make sure the offset is at least this length, we can be assured that the trinkets will not overlap at the center when drawn. The following function generates a random offset that meets our requirements.

```
float RandomOffset(int Range, float TrinketSize) {
    float offset = (Uniform(0, Range * 10)) / 10.0;
    if (offset < (TrinketSize / 2))
        offset = TrinketSize / 2;
    return offset;
}
```

We can now write `Kaleidoscope()`, the function that will draw the required eight trinkets. The following code creates the first four trinkets.

```
const float Center = WindowSize / 2.0;
float TrinketSize = RandomTrinketSize(MaxSize);
float Offset = RandomOffset(TrinketSize, MaxSize);
color FirstColor = RandomColor();
color SecondColor = RandomColor();

// Create four trinkets, one in each quadrant
RectangleShape TrinketQuad1(KaleidoWindow,
 Center + Offset, Center + Offset, FirstColor,
 TrinketSize, TrinketSize);
RectangleShape TrinketQuad2(KaleidoWindow,
 Center - Offset, Center + Offset, SecondColor,
 TrinketSize, TrinketSize);
RectangleShape TrinketQuad3(KaleidoWindow,
 Center - Offset, Center - Offset, FirstColor,
 TrinketSize, TrinketSize);
RectangleShape TrinketQuad4(KaleidoWindow,
 Center + Offset, Center - Offset, SecondColor,
 TrinketSize, TrinketSize);
```

The first part of the code computes various values needed to create the trinkets. The first line computes the center coordinate of the square window. Following that, the program computes the size of the trinkets and their offsets from the center of the window is computed by calling the appropriate functions. The last bit of set-up code gets two colors for the trinkets. Using this information, trinkets in each quadrant are instantiated. Once the trinkets are instantiated, the following code draws the trinkets.

```
TrinketQuad1.Draw();
TrinketQuad2.Draw();
TrinketQuad3.Draw();
TrinketQuad4.Draw();
```

The next job is to reposition the trinkets and draw them in their new positions. We call `RandomOffset()` to get a new offset. Using this offset, the trinkets are repositioned using `RectangleShape`'s `SetPosition()` mutator. The code for drawing the other four squares is identical to the code above. Program 8.2 contains the complete Kaleidoscope program.

The function `ApiMain()` contains calls to library functions that we have not seen before. In order to simulate the kaleidoscope turning slowly, we need to call function `Kaleidoscope()` periodically. The `SimpleWindow` class contains a timer object that is designed specifically for this purpose. The `SimpleWindow SetTimerCallback()` member function sets up the timer and tells the EzWindows system to call the `Kaleidoscope()` function when the timer goes off. The `SimpleWindow` member function `StartTimer()` starts the timer and tells it to go off every 1,000 milliseconds or once a second.

Despite its simplicity, function `Kaleidoscope()` creates a display that looks very much like an image created by a real kaleidoscope. Figure 8.10 shows the image created after the program has been running for about 30 seconds.

Program 8.2

*Simulate a
kaleidoscope*

```
// Program 8.2: Simulate a simple kaleidoscope
#include "uniform.h"
#include "rect.h"
// Size of the window
const float WindowSize = 10.0;

// Maximum size of a trinket
const float MaxSize = 4.0;

// Create a square window
SimpleWindow KaleidoWindow("Kaleidoscope",
 WindowSize, WindowSize);

color RandomColor() {
   return (color) Uniform(0, MaxColors - 1);
}

// RandomOffset - generate a random amount to offset
// a trinket from the center of the window. Generate
// a random offset in the interval 0..Range-1 in
// .1-centimeter increments. The size of the offset
// must take into account the size of the trinket so
// the shapes do not overlap at the center.
float RandomOffset(int Range, float TrinketSize) {
   float Offset = Uniform(0, Range * 10) / 10.0;
   if (Offset < TrinketSize / 2)
     Offset = TrinketSize / 2;
   return Offset;
}

// RandomSize - generate a random size in
// the interval 1 to MaxSize in .1-centimeter
// increments (i.e., 1, 1.1, 1.2, ..., MaxSize)
float RandomTrinketSize(int MaxSize) {
   return Uniform(10, MaxSize * 10) / 10.0;
}

int Kaleidoscope() {

   const float Center = WindowSize / 2.0;

   const float TrinketSize = RandomTrinketSize(MaxSize);
   float Offset = RandomOffset(MaxSize, TrinketSize);
   const color FirstColor = RandomColor();
   const color SecondColor = RandomColor();

   // Create four trinkets, one in each quadrant
   RectangleShape TrinketQuad1(KaleidoWindow,
    Center + Offset, Center + Offset, FirstColor,
    TrinketSize, TrinketSize);
   RectangleShape TrinketQuad2(KaleidoWindow,
    Center - Offset, Center + Offset, SecondColor,
    TrinketSize, TrinketSize);
   RectangleShape TrinketQuad3(KaleidoWindow,
    Center - Offset, Center - Offset, FirstColor,
    TrinketSize, TrinketSize);
   RectangleShape TrinketQuad4(KaleidoWindow,
    Center + Offset, Center - Offset, SecondColor,
    TrinketSize, TrinketSize);

   // Draw the trinkets
   TrinketQuad1.Draw();
```

```
   TrinketQuad2.Draw();
   TrinketQuad3.Draw();
   TrinketQuad4.Draw();

   // Reset their color
   TrinketQuad1.SetColor(SecondColor);
   TrinketQuad2.SetColor(FirstColor);
   TrinketQuad3.SetColor(SecondColor);
   TrinketQuad4.SetColor(FirstColor);

   // Relocate the trinkets to a new position for
   // a Kaleidoscope effect
   Offset = RandomOffset(MaxSize, TrinketSize);
   TrinketQuad1.SetPosition(Center + Offset,
    Center + Offset);
   TrinketQuad2.SetPosition(Center - Offset,
    Center + Offset);
   TrinketQuad3.SetPosition(Center - Offset,
    Center - Offset);
   TrinketQuad4.SetPosition(Center + Offset,
    Center - Offset);

   // Draw the trinkets at the new positions
   TrinketQuad1.Draw();
   TrinketQuad2.Draw();
   TrinketQuad3.Draw();
   TrinketQuad4.Draw();

   return 0;
}
int ApiMain() {
   InitializeSeed();
   KaleidoWindow.Open();
   KaleidoWindow.SetTimerCallback(Kaleidoscope);
   KaleidoWindow.StartTimer(1000);

   return 0;
}
```

8.6

OBJECT-ORIENTED ANALYSIS AND DESIGN

The class construct is the key C++ construct for realizing an object-oriented design. Object-oriented design, like most worthwhile disciplines, is difficult to master. However, once mastered it pays for itself by reducing the cost of maintaining and extending the software. Figure 8.11 illustrates the difference between object-oriented and traditional software development methods. With traditional software development methods, implementation and testing consume the largest portion of the development time. With the object-oriented approach, design consumes the largest portion of overall development time. In object-oriented design less time is spent on implementation and maintenance because a good design is easier to implement and has fewer errors, but a larger percentage of time is spent on the design itself because designing for reuse, maintenance, and extensibility is quite difficult. The overall time spent devel-

Figure 8.10

*Kaleidoscope display
after several calls to
Kaleidoscope*

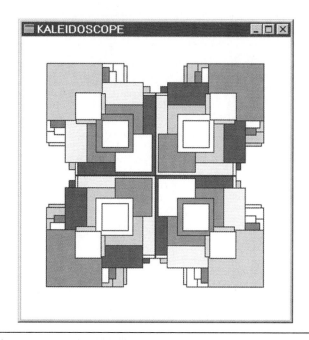

oping software using either method is likely the same. However, software designed using the object-oriented method costs less to maintain, is easier to extend, and parts of it can be reused in other applications. Thus, the cycle time for these efforts is greatly reduced.

To illustrate the basics of object-oriented analysis (OOA) and object-oriented design (OOD) and the realization of an object-oriented design using classes, let's revisit the factory automation trainer from Chapter 7. Figure 8.12 shows the overall operation of the factory system.

The first step of an object-oriented design is to discover or determine the objects that comprise the system. Generally, this is not too difficult, especially for concrete objects, such as a camera, an ATM machine, a sensor, or a telephone. Objects that represent some intangible entity in the system are more difficult to identify. Examples of such objects are a video image, a banking transaction, a sensor signal, or a telephone call.

From Figure 8.12, we can identify some of the classes we would need to realize in an object-oriented design. We do not necessarily need all the objects in Figure 8.12 because we are writing a training system—not a simulation of the entire factory automation system. Clearly, we need a video camera, a display device, an input device, and parts. For the training system, there's no need to simulate the conveyor belt. Because we are implementing a simulation, it will be useful to have a simulation controller that coordinates the operation of the simulation. Additionally, Figure 8.12 contains references to items like a video image, an accept or reject signal, and a video control signal. It's not so

Figure 8.11

Comparison the software life cycle of traditional and object-oriented software projects

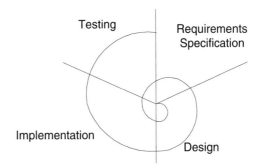

Traditional Software Life Cycle

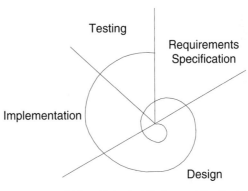

Object-Oriented Software Life Cycle

obvious as to whether we want objects to represent these entities. We will keep these objects in mind, but will not commit to creating classes for them just yet.

Once we have determined the objects we need, it is useful to draw a diagram showing how the objects interact. This step is important because how the objects interact affects what behaviors or responsibilities the objects have. Figure 8.13 contains a drawing showing the interaction of the objects. Not surprisingly, it corresponds closely to Figure 8.12. This is one of the strengths of object-oriented analysis and design: the design closely models the actual system. From Figure 8.13, we see that the video camera interacts with the control unit by sending it the video image, which the control unit forwards to the video display. Remember, we are building a training system for the factory automation system, so the control unit needs the video image to determine whether the trainee gave the correct response. In addition, the control unit interacts with the video camera, the conveyor belt, and the operator console.

After determining how the objects will interact, we can now think about the behaviors or responsibilities of an object. Let's determine the responsibilities and attributes of the video camera. The camera takes a picture of the parts

Figure 8.12

*Factory automation
system*

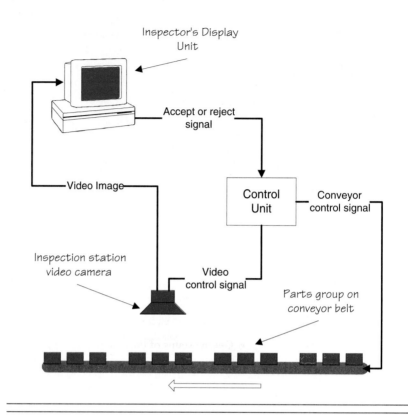

Figure 8.12

*Factory automation
system*

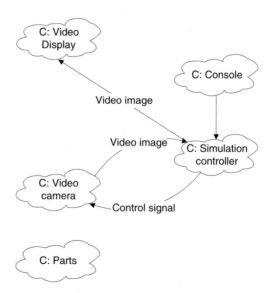

Figure 8.13

*Interaction of objects in
the factory automation
trainer*

as they pass under the camera, so one of its responsibilities is to capture an image of the parts when signaled by the control unit.

A common attribute of a physical device is its mode or *state*. For example, a photo copier has several states that it displays on an LCD panel: off, warming up, on, out of paper, and malfunction. A video camera also has state, and the various states depend on the type of camera. Typical states include on, off, or error. In determining the states of an object it is important to use abstraction, which means to eliminate the irrelevant and focus on the essential. For the factory automation trainer, the essential state is whether the camera is on or off. If it is on, then it can take a picture; if it's off, it cannot. Thus our abstraction of a video camera will have a state attribute that can have two values: on and off. We will want to manipulate the state of the camera so it accepts messages that turn it on and off. We will also want to determine the state of the camera. These will be additional behaviors of the camera.

Based on the following discussion, our abstraction of the video camera has a single attribute—its status—and the following behaviors:

- Capture an image.

- Turn on the camera.

- Turn off the camera.

- Get the status of the camera.

Using our picture notation, the class `VideoCamera` is

C:`VideoCamera`
DM: `Status`
MF: `CaptureImage(), TurnOn(),`
`TurnOff(), GetStatus()`

We can realize this abstraction through the C++ class declaration in Listing 8.1.

Listing 8.1

Declaration of class VideoCamera from vcam.h

```
#ifndef VIDEOCAMERA_H
#define VIDEOCAMERA_H
#include "image.h"
enum CameraStatus { CameraOn, CameraOff };
class VideoCamera {
    public:
        VideoCamera();
        CameraStatus GetStatus() const;
        VideoImage CaptureImage();
        void TurnOn();
        void TurnOff();
    private:
        CameraStatus Status;
};
#endif
```

Notice that our design process has 3 steps:

1. Determine the object or classes in the system.
2. Determine how the objects interact.
3. Determine the responsibilities (behaviors) and attributes of the objects.

These are the typical steps in any object-oriented design methodology. Like most design processes, the steps are repeated as the design is refined. For example, when determining the behaviors of an object, you might discover that you overlooked an interaction between that object and another. Similarly, when determining the attributes of an object it is common to discover that additional objects to represent the attributes are needed.

In the declaration of the class `VideoCamera`, the member function `CaptureImage()` returns an `VideoImage` object. This object is an abstraction of a video image. It is the object sent from the camera to the simulation controller. Let's apply the OOA/OOD process to realize this object. The video image is an interesting object because it is not at all clear how to represent it. From Figure 8.13, we see that the video image is sent to the simulation controller. The simulation controller forwards it to the display unit. Because the display unit will display the image of the parts group, clearly the video image needs enough information so the video display can synthesize an appropriate image (e.g., a `RectangleShape` of the appropriate size and color). Consequently, it is tempting to represent this object using our graphical object `RectangleShape`. However, we would be making a common design mistake.

Using `RectangleShape` to realize the object `VideoImage` would prematurely tie the abstraction of the video image object to how we plan to display it. To illustrate our erroneous logic, suppose we decided to move the simulation to a machine that did not have a windowing system like EzWindows. On this machine, we need to output a character string that indicates the parts group under the camera (e.g., output the string `Red Blue Red` for a parts group with a red part, a blue part, and another red part). To make this change when the video image is represented by a `RectangleShape` would be time consuming and would require changing more code than we would like. In general, it is a good idea to decouple the display of information from the operation of the rest of the system because we often want to change how information is displayed.

To solve this problem, we again apply abstraction—eliminate the irrelevant and focus on the essential. For the factory automation trainer, the essential aspects of the video image are the parts viewed. Thus, a video image can consist of three parts. Listing 8.2 contains the class declaration for `VideoImage`.

Since `VideoImage` contains a `Part`, let's design it next. `Part` has no uses outside of `VideoImage`. For our simulation, the essential properties or state of a part is its color. As usual, we will want an inspector for the color attribute. We will not need a corresponding mutator because once a part is created we will never need to change its color. Listing 8.3 contains the class declaration for `Part`.

The final two objects in the training simulator are the video display and the console. These objects are the user interface objects. The operator views

Listing 8.2

*Declaration of class
VideoImage from
image.h*

```
// class VideoImage
#ifndef VIDEOIMAGE_H
#define VIDEOIMAGE_H
#include "part.h"
class VideoImage {
   public:
      VideoImage(const color c1, const color c2,
       const color c3);
      Part GetPart1() const;
      Part GetPart2() const;
      Part GetPart3() const;
   private:
      Part Part1;
      Part Part2;
      Part Part3;
};
#endif
```

Listing 8.3

*Declaration of class
Part from part.h*

```
#ifndef PART_H
#define PART_H
#include "ezwin.h"
class Part {
   public:
      Part(const color c = Red);
      color GetColor() const;
   private:
      color Color;
};
#endif
```

the parts of the video display, and he or she records a response using the console. Let's begin with the video display unit. The responsibility of the video display is to project the image so the operator can view it and make a decision as to whether to accept or reject the parts group. Like the video camera, the video display maintains state information about whether it is on or off. To display the images of the parts, we will use the SimpleWindow class from the EzWindows library. The SimpleWindow used for the display will be another attribute of the display unit. This is appropriate because we want to encapsulate all aspects of how we display the parts in the video display unit class. The declaration of class VideoDisplayUnit is shown in Listing 8.4.

The constructor requires a string parameter, which is the string displayed in the title bar of the SimpleWindow that is created. The member function DisplayImage() is the message that causes the VideoDisplayUnit to display the images of the parts. The content of the message is the video image.

The final object in our design is the console. The console's responsibilities are to display any instructions to the trainee, to accept all input from the operator trainee, and to display the results of the training session. The only attribute of the console is its state: on or off. Listing 8.5 contains the declaration of class Console.

Listing 8.4

*Declaration of class
VideoDisplayUnit from
dunit.h*

```
#ifndef DISPLAYUNIT_H
#define DISPLAYUNIT_H
#include <cstring.h>
#include "ezwin.h"
#include "image.h"
enum DisplayStatus { DisplayOn, DisplayOff };
class VideoDisplayUnit {
   public:
      VideoDisplayUnit(string Title);
      void DisplayImage(const VideoImage &Image);
      void TurnOn();
      void TurnOff();
   private:
      SimpleWindow W;
      DisplayStatus Status;
};
#endif
```

Listing 8.5

*Declaration of class
Console from console.h*

```
#ifndef CONSOLE_H
#define CONSOLE_H
enum ConsoleStatus { ConsoleOn, ConsoleOff };
class Console {
   public:
      Console();
      void TurnOn();
      void TurnOff();
      char GetResponse();
      void PrintSessionResults(long Time, int Attempts,
        int Correct, int Wrong);
   private:
      ConsoleStatus Status;
};
#endif
```

Member function `TurnOn()` sets the state of the console to on and it prints the introductory message that directs the operator to resize the windows. `GetResponse()` reads the response and returns it to the simulation controller so it can be verified. Member function `PrintSessionResults()` displays the results of the training session on the console when the simulation is finished.

Using these class definitions, we can reimplement the training simulator. Listing 8.6 contains code that implements the training simulator. There are four points about the code worth noting. First, we have chosen to keep most of the logic of the program in the routine `ApiMain()`. We could have created a simulation control object and placed the code there, but this seemed like overkill and so we opted against it. Second, the heart of the program, the do-while loop, reads more naturally than it did in our first implementation. The program closely corresponds to a physical realization of the trainer. Third, this implementation will be easier to maintain and extend than our original implementation. For example, an exercise in a later chapter is to modify the program so that the operator can use the mouse to indicate whether a parts group should be accepted or rejected. Because of the object-oriented design, this change will be simple and easy to make. Fourth, the objects we developed can be reused in implementations of other simulations. Suppose we were asked to implement a

Listing 8.6

Implementation of the factory automation training simulator in trainer.cpp

```cpp
// ApiMain(): a factory automation training simulator
#include <iostream.h>
#include "uniform.h"
#include "dunit.h"
#include "ezwin.h"
#include "vcam.h"
#include "console.h"

// Length of the session (60 seconds)
const long TestTime = 60 * 1000L;

// Determine if the appropriate response was given
bool CheckResponse(char Response,
 const VideoImage &v) {
   Part Part1 = v.GetPart1();
   Part Part2 = v.GetPart2();
   Part Part3 = v.GetPart3();
   if (Part1.GetColor() == Part2.GetColor()
      || Part1.GetColor() == Part3.GetColor()
      || Part2.GetColor() == Part3.GetColor())
      return Response == 'a';
   else
      return Response == 'r';
}

int ApiMain() {
   VideoDisplayUnit TrainingMonitor("PARTS DISPLAY");
   VideoCamera InspectionCamera;
   Console TrainingConsole;
   TrainingMonitor.TurnOn();
   TrainingConsole.TurnOn();
   InspectionCamera.TurnOn();

   InitializeSeed();
   // Define objects for scoring the trainee
   int Attempts = 0;      // Number of tests done
   int CorrectResponses = 0;
   int IncorrectResponses = 0;

   // Record starting time
   const long StartTime = GetMilliseconds();
   long ElapsedTime;

   do {
      VideoImage Image =
       InspectionCamera.CaptureImage();
      TrainingMonitor.DisplayImage(Image);

      char Response;
      Response = TrainingConsole.GetResponse();

      ++Attempts;
      if (CheckResponse(Response, Image))
         ++CorrectResponses;
      else
         ++IncorrectResponses;
      ElapsedTime = GetMilliseconds();
```

```
    } while ((ElapsedTime - StartTime) < TestTime);

    TrainingConsole.PrintSessionResults(TestTime,
     Attempts, CorrectResponses, IncorrectResponses);
    TrainingMonitor.TurnOff();
    TrainingConsole.TurnOff();
    InspectionCamera.TurnOff();
    return 0;
}
```

simulator of a central highway traffic monitoring station. Much of the code we developed for the factory training simulator could be reused. In the highway traffic monitoring system, an operator sits in a control room and monitors video screens showing traffic moving down a highway. Video cameras are placed at key points on the highways. If there is some interruption in traffic, the operator notifies the highway patrol. To implement this system, we could reuse many of the objects we developed for the factory automation trainer. We could reuse the class `VideoImage`, but instead of parts, the video image would consist of cars. The classes `VideoDisplayUnit` and `VideoCamera` could be reused with little or no modification. Because of reuse, we could likely design, implement, and test the simulation of the highway monitoring system in half the time it would take to do it from scratch. The third and fourth points, extensibility and reuse, are two of the key benefits of object-oriented design and implementation.

8.7

POINTS TO REMEMBER

- New data types that represent real-world objects are created using C++'s class construct.
- A class-type object consists of two components—a set of attributes and a set of behaviors. The attributes are called the data members, and the behaviors are called the member functions.
- When creating a new class type, two important initial steps are determining the attributes and the behaviors of the objects.
- Member functions that return the value of an attribute of an object are called inspectors.
- Member functions that set or change the value of an attribute of an object are called mutators.
- Member functions that direct an object to perform some function or action are called facilitators.
- A constructor is a special member function that is invoked when an object is created. It is typically used to initialize the attributes of an object.
- A class declaration is divided into two sections: public and private. The public section contains declarations for the attributes and behaviors of the object that are meant to be accessible to users of the object. Constructors

3334433

3344

History of Computing

Stored programs

The next major advance in computing involved how computers were programmed. The ENIAC computer was programmed using plug boards. These boards consisted of an array of sockets into which wires could be plugged. By connecting the appropriate sockets, the machine circuitry could be changed and a different computation could be performed. The problem was that this task was a very time consuming. For complex problems, it could take several days to reprogram the machine.

This problem was solved with the development of the Electronic Discrete Variable Computer (EDVAC). While there is some controversy over the development of the ideas embodied in EDVAC, most historians agree that John von Neumann played a pivotal role in the design of the stored-program computer.

John von Neumann was a well-known and highly-respected brilliant mathematician. In addition to his contributions to computing, which we are about to discuss, von Neumann made significant contributions in areas such as game theory, physics, pure mathematics, and meteorology. Von Neumann, a consultant to BRL, became interested in computers after visiting the University of Pennsylvania to review the work on ENIAC. After meeting with Eckert and Mauchly, von Neumann produced a paper, "First Draft of a Report on EDVAC," that outlined the components and basic operation that would be part of all modern computers. One of the most important ideas was to store the program that controlled the computer in memory along with the data. This meant that the program could be manipulated like data, an ability that is fundamental to all computers.

At this point, it is worthwhile to step back and discuss some of the controversy involving the development of the ideas embodied in ENIAC and EDVAC. Many at the University of Pennsylvania felt that von Neumann slighted them by leaving their names off his paper and not mentioning their contributions to the project. Indeed, because of this and other conflicts involving intellectual property, Eckert and Mauchly left the University in 1946 and founded a company to design, build, and sell electronic computers. To protect their invention, they filed for a patent to cover the operation of their electronic computer.

In 1942, three years before the completion of ENIAC, John Atanasoff, a professor at Iowa State University, and Clifford Berry, a graduate student, constructed the Atanasoff-Berry Computer, or ABC for short. The ABC also used vacuum tubes, and it performed binary arithmetic. In fact, Mauchly visited Atanasoff in Iowa and reviewed a proposal written by Atanasoff to build an electronic calculator. Many of the ideas in the proposal found their way into the ENIAC. Unfortunately for Atanasoff, his attorney never filed for a patent to cover the innovations in the ABC, and the credit rightfully due him never materialized.

It was not until 1964, when the Mauchly–Eckert patent for the ideas in ENIAC was finally granted, that the full story of the development of the electronic computer was revealed. At that time, the patent was held by Sperry Rand. In 1968, Sperry decided to begin enforcing the patent and collecting royalties. One company, Honeywell, rather than pay royalties, decided to fight in court. Honeywell's strategy was to have the ENIAC patents declared invalid. A patent can be declared invalid if it can be shown that the idea in the patent was developed previously. As you can probably guess, Atanasoff was one of the star witnesses during the lawsuit. After a five-year court battle, the judge hearing the case invalidated the ENIAC patents, and the judgment stated, "Eckert and Mauchly did not themselves first invent the automatic electronic digital computer, but instead derived that subject matter from one Dr. John Vincent Atanasoff." After more than 25 years, Atanasoff's contributions to the development of the electronic digit computer were finally made public.

With the development of the concept of a stored-program computer, systems for storing information became a critical issue. In this area, Britain had the lead because of their work with radar. Consequently, it is not surprising that the first operational stored-program machine was constructed in England. A prototype machine employing the stored-program concept, called the Manchester Mark I, was completed in 1948 at the University of Manchester in Manchester, England. It had a memory of 32 words each containing 32 bits. One year later, in Cambridge England, another stored-program computer was unveiled, the Electronic Delay Storage Automatic Computer (EDSAC). Interestingly, the EDVAC, whose original design spawned all this development, was not completed until 1952.

must always be declared in the public section. The private section contains the member functions and data members that are hidden or inaccessible to users of the object. These member functions and data attributes are accessible only by the object's member function.

- The process of creating an object is called instantiation.

- Data members and member functions are accessed using . the member access operator.

- A constant member function is one that cannot change its objects' attributes.

- Default arguments make a constructor more flexible and useful.

- Reference data members must be initialized when an object is instantiated. Once initialized, a reference data member cannot be changed.

- Abstraction eliminates the irrelevant properties of an object and focuses on the essential.

- Object-oriented design consists of three basic steps: 1) determine the objects in the system, 2) determine how the objects collaborate or interact, and 3) determine the behaviors and attributes of the objects.

■ Good design is hard. Do not be afraid to spend time designing a system. In the long run, it will save time.

8.8
TO DELVE FURTHER

There are several excellent books that discuss object-oriented analysis and design.

■ R. Martin, *Designing Object-Oriented C++ Applications using the Booch Method*, Englewood Cliffs: NJ, Prentice-Hall, 1995.

■ G. Booch, *Object-Oriented Analysis and Design with Applications*, Redwood City, CA: Benjamin-Cummings, 1994.

■ J. Rumbaugh, M. Blaha, W. Premerlani, F. Eddy, and W. Lorensen, *Object-Oriented Modeling and Design*, Englewood Cliffs: NJ, Prentice-Hall, 1991.

■ R. Wirfs-Brock, B. Wilkerson, and L. Wiener, *Designing Object-Oriented Software*, Englewood Cliffs: NJ, Prentice-Hall, 1990.

8.9
EXERCISES

8.1 A _____ is a function that is called to create an instance of a class.

8.2 A _____ is a member function that gets the value of a data member of an object.

8.3 A _____ is a member function that changes or sets the value of a data member of an object.

8.4 A _____ is a member function that performs some action or service.

8.5 Structured design is traditional design method. Find out about structured design and compare it to object-oriented design.

8.6 Give a C++ **class** declaration to represent the following geometric objects.

　　a) Circle

　　b) Rectangle

　　c) Ellipse

　　d) Triangle

　　e) Quadrilateral

8.7 Give a C++ **class** declaration to represent the following objects:

　　a) A digital clock

　　b) A home thermostat

c) A digital timer

d) A cassette player

8.8 Do an object-oriented design like the one for the factory automation trainer for the following applications:

a) A calculator application

b) A calendar application

c) An bank ATM

d) A library check-out system

e) A computer version of a Las Vegas slot machine

f) A spelling checker application

In your design, be sure and show how the objects collaborate or interact.

8.9 Other messages can be useful with `RectangleShape`, for example, an erase message that directs a rectangle to remove its image from the display. Can you think of other useful messages? Extend class `RectangleShape` to include member functions for each message.

8.10 For questions (a) through (d), use the following declaration for a square object.

```
class Square {
   public:
      Square(SimpleWindow &W);
      void Draw();
      void SetColor(color Color);
      void SetPosition(float XCoord,
        float YCoord);
      void SetSize(float Length);
   private:
      color Color;
      int XCenter;
      int YCenter;
      float SideLength;
      SimpleWindow &Window;
};
```

a) Write a code fragment that defines and draws a square object with 1.5-centimeter sides called `GreenSquare` that is displayed in the window `Sample`. Position `GreenSquare`'s center 3.5 centimeters from the left edge of the window and 2.5 centimeters from the top edge of the window. `GreenSquare` should be green.

b) Write a code fragment that defines and draws a square object with 2-centimeter sides called `MagentaSquare`. `MagentaSquare` is displayed in the window `Sample`. Position `MagentaSquare`'s upper-left corner at the upper-left corner of the window. Color `MagentaSquare` magenta.

c) Write a code fragment that defines and draws two square objects both with 2.5-centimeter sides. Display both squares in the window `DoubleSquare`. One square should be called `TopSquare`, and the other square should be called `BottomSquare`. Position `Top-`

Square 3 centimeters from the left edge of the window and 1.5 centimeters from the top edge of the window. Position Bottom-Square below TopSquare so that BottomSquare's top side touches TopSquare's bottom side. Color TopSquare red and BottomSquare blue.

d) Write a code fragment that defines and draws three square objects. One square is 3 centimeters on a side, another square is 2 centimeters on a side, and the last square is 1 centimeter on a side. Display all three squares in the window OverlappedSquares. Position all three squares at the screen coordinates contained in the variables XCenterWindow and YCenterWindow. The 3-centimeter square is called BigSquare and is yellow. The 2-centimeter square is called MiddleSquare and is green. The 1-centimeter square is called SmallSquare and is red.

8.11 Design a Kaleidoscope class.

8.12 Design a class for the following objects. Give a C++ class declaration that corresponds to your design.

a) A screen position for use in the EzWindows graphical system.

b) A line object for use in the EzWindows graphical system.

c) A mouse object for use in the EzWindows graphical system.

8.13 Redesign the VideoImage class of the factory automation trainer so a parts group consists of 5 objects. What other classes must you modify?

8.14 Redesign the Part class of the factory automation trainer so that a part has a length and a width. What other classes must you modify?

8.15 Redo Exercise 8.10 assuming the following declaration for Square is available.

```
class Square {
    public:
        Square(SimpleWindow &W, float XCoord = 0,
          float YCoord = 0, color c = Red,
          float Length = 1);
        void Draw();
        void SetColor(const color Color);
        void SetPosition(float XCoord,
          float YCoord);
        void SetSize(float Length);
    private:
        color Color;
        int XCenter;
        int YCenter;
        float SideLength;
        SimpleWindow &Window;
};
```

8.16 Revise the Kaleidoscope program so that the color of each trinket is picked randomly.

8.17 Revise the Kaleidoscope program so that it also draws trinkets along axes that divide the screen into the four quadrants (see Figure 8.14). The

program should randomly decide whether to place the trinkets on the
diagonals or on the vertical axes.

Figure 8.14

*Trinkets positioned on
vertical and horizontal
axes*

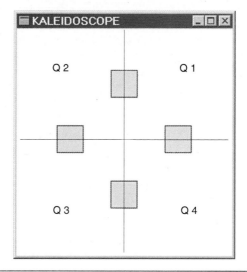

CHAPTER 9

Abstract data types

Introduction

A representation of information and the operations to be performed on it is a data abstraction. An abstract data type or ADT is a well-defined and complete data abstraction that uses the information-hiding principle. An ADT allows the creation and manipulation of objects in a natural manner. In this chapter, we introduce ADTs in the C++ framework of classes, functions, and operators. We do so by developing ADTs for rational numbers, uniform pseudorandom numbers, and a simple guessing game. Our development of ADTs includes discussion of their interfaces and implementations.

Key Concepts

- data abstraction
- abstract data type (ADT)
- rule of minimality
- class minimality principle
- default constructors
- copy constructors
- memberwise assignment
- inspectors
- mutators
- facilitators
- **const** member functions
- auxiliary functions and operators
- operator overloading
- overloading insertion and extraction operators
- reference return
- pseudorandom number sequence

9.1

INTRODUCING ABSTRACT DATA TYPES

All the problems that we previously considered were carefully chosen so that if an object was used in the solution, it was best represented using a fundamental type or a class type that was defined in an available library. More sophisticated problem solving requires that we develop our own representations for the information to be manipulated. In object-oriented programming terminology, the representation and the operations to be performed on the representation form a *data abstraction*. In this chapter, we develop abstractions for rational numbers, for random numbers, and for a simple guessing game. The abstractions are developed using classes, functions, and operators.

In developing an abstraction, the information-hiding principle is normally followed. By enforcing information hiding through encapsulation, it is easier to maintain the integrity of the data (e.g., preventing a rational number with a denominator of zero). In addition, by using public methods, client programs are generally immune to changes in the implementation of the abstraction.

A well-defined abstraction allows its objects to be created and used in an intuitive manner. Therefore the programming syntax for the definition and manipulation of objects of an abstraction should have a form analogous to fundamental-type and standard-class objects doing comparable activities. For example, suppose we have an abstraction `Rational` for rational numbers and we want to display the result of summing 1/2 and 1/3. A code segment such as the following should be possible.

```
Rational a(1,2);          // a = 1/2
Rational b(2,3);          // b = 2/3
cout << a << " + " << b << " = " << a + b << endl;
```

The insertion has the same form as the corresponding display of the sum of two **int** or **float** objects would have. This analogous form would not be the case in traditional, non-object-oriented languages like C. In traditional languages, a programmer can neither have objects with methods nor extend existing operators to work with new types of objects. The programmer is forced to define functions and additional temporary objects. The resulting code is generally unnatural and awkward looking.

We will call a well-defined class using the information-hiding principle coupled with the appropriate library functions an *abstract data type* or ADT.

9.2

RATIONAL ADT BASICS

Our exploration of ADTs begins with development of an ADT `Rational` for representing rational numbers. To remind you, a rational number is the ratio of two integers that is typically represented in the manner *a/b*. We call *a* the

Programming Tip

numerator and b the denominator. The denominator is required to be nonzero. The basic arithmetic operations have the following definitions:

- Addition: $\dfrac{a}{b} + \dfrac{c}{d} = \dfrac{ad + bc}{bd}$

- Subtraction: $\dfrac{a}{b} - \dfrac{c}{d} = \dfrac{ad - bc}{bd}$

- Multiplication: $\dfrac{a}{b} \times \dfrac{c}{d} = \dfrac{ac}{bd}$

- Division: $\dfrac{a/b}{c/d} = \dfrac{ad}{bc}$

Our goal in developing `Rational` is to create a type whose objects are as natural to use as objects defined using the fundamental types.

To represent a rational number, we need to represent a numerator and denominator. This necessity implies that a class representing rational numbers should define objects with two data members—one member to represent the particular numerator and the other member to represent the particular denominator of the object. Both data members will be **int** objects.

The member functions of our `Rational` ADT should provide methods to initialize and manipulate a rational number object in the following ways:

- Construct the rational number with default or particular attributes.

- Add, subtract, multiply, and divide the rational number to another rational number.

- Copy the value of the rational number to another rational number.

- Compare the rational number to another rational number.

- Display the value of the rational number.
- Extract the value of the rational number.

To support these client-programmer activities and information hiding, the following methods should also be present for a rational number object.

- Inspect the values of the numerator and denominator.
- Set the values of the numerator and denominator.

To supplement the `Rational` class, we also need to define some auxiliary operators in the class library. The *auxiliary operators* are not members of the class but are overloaded versions of the arithmetic, relational, and stream operators. They use the public members of the class to accomplish their tasks. These operators are vital because they enable `Rational` objects to be manipulated in a consistent natural manner. Together the class and the auxiliary operators compose the rational library.

The definitions of objects a and b in the earlier code segment are depicted in Figure 9.1. The figure shows that the memory associated with a rational number object has portions that are reserved for the numerator and denominator being represented. Other portions of memory are reserved for the code associated with the various member functions.

9.2.1

A client program using the rational library

Before presenting a C++ implementation of the rational number ADT, we first consider Program 9.1. This client program is a simple illustration of the look-and-feel that we want in the various components of the `Rational` ADT. If the rational library it uses truly represents an abstract data type, Program 9.1 should be easy to understand.

Suppose the two inputs to our client program are the rational numbers 1/2 and 1/3. The input/output behavior of the program is then

```
Enter rational number (a/b): 1/2
Enter rational number (a/b): 1/3
1/2 + 1/3 = 5/6
1/2 * 1/3 = 1/6
```

Program 9.1 begins by including the header files for both the standard iostream library and the nonstandard rational library. Header file `rational.h` is similar to `iostream.h` in that the file is really an interface specification for an ADT (the implementation of `Rational` and the auxiliary operators is in file `rational.cpp`).

Function `main()` of Program 9.1 first defines `Rational` objects r and s.

```
Rational r;
Rational s;
```

No initialization is specified for these objects, so their initial values are determined by the default constructor for the class `Rational`.

Figure 9.1

*Depiction of two
Rational objects being
instantiated from a
class definition*

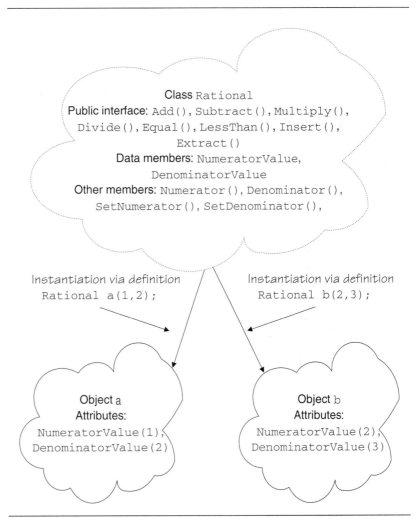

The default constructor takes no parameters and assigns default values to the various data members of the object. It is standard practice that constructors initialize all data members to appropriate values. The default rational representation is 0/1.

A class can often have several different constructors. The constructors will differ in their parameter list specifications. If no constructor has a parameter list that matches the actual initialization parameters given in the object definition, then an error message is generated.

One constructor that is always present is the copy constructor. The *copy constructor* has a single constant reference parameter that is of the same type as the new object. The new object becomes a copy of the actual parameter. The constructor is always present, because if the class designer does not specify a

Programming Tip

Program 9.1

Demonstration of some Rational ADT capabilities

```
// Program 9.1: Demonstrate some member functions and
// auxiliary operators of the Rational ADT
#include <iostream.h>
#include "rational.h"

int main() {
    Rational r;
    Rational s;
    cout << "Enter rational number (a/b): " << flush;
    cin >> r;
    cout << "Enter rational number (a/b): " << flush;
    cin >> s;

    Rational t(r);
    Rational Sum = r + s;
    Rational Product = r * s;

    cout << r << " + " << s << " = " << Sum << endl;
    cout << r << " * " << s << " = " << Product << endl;

    return 0;
}
```

copy constructor, one is automatically supplied by the compiler. In Program 9.1 the copy constructor makes t a duplicate of r.

```
    Rational t(r);          // t is a copy of r
```

Another member that is always present, regardless of whether the designer includes it, is the assignment operator that modifies an existing object.

The copy constructor and assignment operator provided by the compiler do what is known as a memberwise copying of the data members of the source object to the target object. In a *memberwise copy*, the various data members are copied member-by-member with each member being directly copied in a bit-by-bit manner from the source data member to the corresponding target data member. This bit-by-bit assignment is the same kind of assignment performed on an object defined from one of the fundamental types. Because memberwise copying of data members is appropriate for the classes that we consider in this chapter, we do not define a copy constructor or a member assignment operator.

In spite of the difference in form from the definition of object t, the copy constructor is also used by Program 9.1 in the definitions of objects Sum and Product.

```
Rational Sum = r + s;
Rational Product = r * s;
```

No — Not just copy assignment

In a definition where an initialization expression follows the <u>assignment operator</u> (=), the constructor that is invoked is the one whose definition allows a single parameter of the same type as the expression. The invoked constructor uses the initialization expression as its actual parameter. Thus, the definitions of Sum and Product both invoke the copy constructor because the type of values produced by Rational addition and multiplication is Rational.

In the following code segment, Rational object w is made a copy of Rational object v through the assignment operator.

```
Rational v;
cin >> v;
Rational w;
w = v;
```

The assignment operator rather than the copy constructor is used on w because w is being modified, not defined.

A class may also define other constructors depending upon what kind of information is reasonable for initializing a new object of the desired class. For a Rational ADT, another constructor should exist. This constructor would expect either one or two integer values as parameters. The first parameter is the initial value of the new object's numerator. The second parameter is an optional parameter that supplies the initial value of the new object's denominator with a default value of one. Examples of this constructor's application are given in the following code segment:

```
Rational x(3,4);      // x = 3/4
Rational y(5);        // y = 5/1
```

The modifier **const** can be used in conjunction with creating **class** objects. If the modifier is applied, then after the construction of the object, it is illegal to modify the values of its data members. In the following statement, a **const** Rational object representing 1/2 is defined.

```
const Rational OneHalf(1,2);
```

Program 9.1 performs two extractions from cin to assign values to objects r and s. The Rational number extraction operator >> is not a member operator of the Rational class, but is an auxiliary operator. Rational extraction is not a member method because we expect a particular form for an extraction. We expect that the left operand of the extraction operator is the source stream and the right operand is the target object. However, if operator >> is overloaded as a member operator of the Rational class, then the two operands need to be reversed (it is the left operand that invokes the method). This would result in extractions with form

```
r >> cin;
```

This extraction form would be confusing to a reader of the code and should be avoided. Thus, the extraction operator and, for similar reasons, the insertion operator are defined as auxiliary operators in the rational library.

As noted previously, Program 9.1 contains definitions of `Rational` objects `Sum` and `Product`. The expressions used in their definitions demonstrate that + and * have also been overloaded.

This completes our overview of the behavior that we expect with `Rational` class objects. We are now ready to proceed with the actual development of the rational library. The only rational arithmetic operations we consider are addition and multiplication. The other rational arithmetic operations, as well as the rational relational operations, are left to the exercises.

The rational library encompasses two files: a header file, `rational.h`, and an implementation file, `rational.cpp`. We begin with an examination of the header file.

9.3
RATIONAL CLASS INTERFACE DESCRIPTION

Header file `rational.h` is given in Listing 9.1. The header file is strictly an interface description. This property is not necessarily the case with all class header files. For example, header files like `iostream.h` define global objects (e.g., `cin` and `cout`).

The two major declaration sections in `rational.h` are surrounded collectively by preprocessor statements. The first section is the definition of the `Rational` class. Following that description is a prototyping of the auxiliary operators. Neither the definitions of the member functions nor the definitions of auxiliary operators are given in the header file. The definitions of these functions and operators are given in implementation file `rational.cpp`.

Preceding the two declaration sections in Listing 9.1 are several preprocessor statements of familiar form. The first two preprocessor statements coupled with the final line in the header file ensure that the file is included only once into a translation unit. The other preprocessor statement in the header file includes the iostream library. The iostream library is included because of the auxiliary overloading of the insertion and extraction operators.

9.3.1
Access restrictions

As demonstrated by our definition of `RectangleShape` for the kaleidoscope program of the previous chapter, a class declaration or definition begins with

Listing 9.1

Header file rational.h

```
// rational.h: declaration of Rational ADT
#ifndef RATIONAL_H
#define RATIONAL_H

#include <iostream.h>

// Rational ADT: class description
class Rational {
   public: // member functions
      // constructors
      Rational();
      Rational(int numer, int denom = 1);
      // some arithmetic and stream facilitators
      Rational Add(const Rational &r) const;
      Rational Multiply(const Rational &r) const;
      void Insert(ostream &sout) const;
      void Extract(istream &sin);
   protected:
      // inspectors
      int Numerator() const;
      int Denominator() const;
      // mutators
      void SetNumerator(int numer);
      void SetDenominator(int denom);
   private:
      // data members
      int NumeratorValue;
      int DenominatorValue;
};

// Rational ADT: auxiliary operator description
Rational operator+(const Rational &r,
 const Rational &s);
Rational operator*(const Rational &r,
 const Rational &s);

ostream& operator<<(ostream &sout, const Rational &s);
istream& operator>>(istream &sin, Rational &r);

#endif
```

the reserved word **class**. It is then followed by the name of the class. If only the class name is being introduced, then the declaration is immediately followed by a semicolon. If it is a definition (i.e., the data members and member functions and operators are also being declared), then the name is followed by a sequence of declarations and definitions. The sequence is delimited by a pair of left and right curly braces. Through the use of *access-specifier* labels, the sequence is divided into sections with different access permissions.

The Rational class definition in Listing 9.1 has three sections. They begin respectively with the access-specifier labels **public**, **protected**, and **private**. The members declared within a **public** section can be directly used by client programs. For that reason, Program 9.1 can make use of the various Rational constructors. Members declared within a **protected** section of a class definition can normally be used only by other member functions and operators of the class and by member functions and operators from a derived class (e.g., istream is derived from ios, so an istream object has access to its `ios` members). Members declared within a **private** section can normally be used only by other member functions and operators of that class.

9.3.2
Constructor member functions

The prototypes of the two `Rational` constructors in Listing 9.1 are different from typical function prototypes.

```
Rational();
Rational(int numer, int denom = 1);
```

As observed for the class `RectangleShape` in the previous chapter, a constructor prototype does not specify a return value. Because a constructor function for a class is required to have the same name as the class, no other special syntax is necessary to identify the function as a constructor.

The first constructor being declared is the default constructor because it uses no parameters.

The second constructor expects either one or two **int** objects as parameters. As the two parameter names suggest, they are used respectively to set the new `Rational` object's numerator and denominator data members. The default value for the denominator is one.

As neither a copy constructor nor a member assignment operator is declared in its class definition, the `Rational` class uses the ones provided by the compiler.

9.3.3
Facilitator member functions

To reference a data member or member function or operator of an object, a client programmer uses the access operator (.). The left operand of the access operator is an object; the right operand is the particular member of that object being referenced. For example, the following code segment uses the access operator to invoke several `Rational` member functions.

```
Rational r;
Rational s;
r.Extract(cin);
s.Extract(cin);
Rational t = r.Add(s);
t.Insert(cout);
```

Although the access operator provides the mechanism to access a member, it must also be the case that the operator is used in a valid context. In the preceding code segment, the `Rational` members that are accessed are all declared in the public section of the class declaration; therefore, they can be accessed in both client and member code.

Because of the information-hiding principle, data members are almost never public members. Consequently, data members cannot normally be referenced with the access operator in nonmember functions and operators. The nonpublic access rights act as a barrier that helps ensure the integrity of the data.

Without access restrictions, the improper use of an object can introduce inconsistencies or illegal values. Therefore, a well-constructed public interface supplies member functions and operators to safely manipulate the data members. Their presence supports information hiding. These member functions fall into three categories: inspectors, mutators, and facilitators. Inspector functions provide methods to access representations of the data members of an object. Mutator functions provide methods to modify the representations of the data members of an object. Facilitator functions provide methods for achieving the abstraction intended with the object being represented.

After the constructor declarations, Listing 9.1 prototypes a collection of four arithmetic and stream facilitator functions. (We consider the relational facilitators and the other arithmetic facilitators in the exercises.)

```
// arithmetic and stream facilitators
Rational Add(const Rational &r) const;
Rational Multiply(const Rational &r) const;
void Insert(ostream &sout) const;
void Extract(istream &sin);
```

The two arithmetic facilitators each have a single formal parameter r. The facilitators use the invoking object's value and the actual parameter's value to determine the result of the member function.

Stream facilitator `Insert()` expects a reference to an `ostream` as its parameter. The facilitator inserts a representation of its rational number to that stream. Stream facilitator `Extract()` expects a reference to an `istream` as its parameter. The facilitator extracts a representation of a rational number from that stream to be used for its object. In this regard, `Extract()` is also a mutator. The two stream facilitators have reference parameters because the act of inserting or extracting modifies the stream.

The `Rational` facilitators are public members, so they can be used by client programs. However, they are not used in practice. Instead the auxiliary operators with their natural interfaces are used. The facilitators are the underlying mechanisms that allow the auxiliary arithmetic and stream operators to do their jobs.

Facilitators `Add()`, `Multiply()`, and `Insert()` make use of the *qualifier* **const**. The **const** in this context indicates that the member's invocation does not change any of the data members. Member functions and operators with the qualifier **const** can be used by **const** and non-**const** objects. Member functions without the qualification cannot be used by **const** objects.

In the following example, the **const** object `OneHalf` can invoke the `Insert()` facilitator, but it cannot invoke the `Extract()` facilitator.

```
const Rational OneHalf(1,2);
OneHalf.Insert(cout); // legal
OneHalf.Extract(cin); // illegal
```

In the following code segment, we use these facilitators to accomplish the task of Program 9.1.

```
Rational r;
Rational s;
cout << "Enter rational number (a/b): " << flush;
r.Extract(cin);
cout << "Enter rational number (a/b): " << flush;
s.Extract(cin);
Rational t(r);
Rational Sum = r.Add(s);
Rational Product = r.Multiply(s);
r.Insert(cout);
cout<< " + ";
s.Insert(cout);
cout << " = ";
Sum.Insert(cout);
cout << endl;
r.Insert(cout);
cout<< " * ";
s.Insert(cout);
cout << " = ";
Product.Insert(cout);
cout << endl;
```

The code segment shows the importance of the auxiliary operators in making the code natural looking. Clearly, the statements in Program 9.1 are preferable.

9.3.4

Inspector member functions

The next declarations in the definition of the `Rational` class in Listing 9.1 are two prototypes of **protected** inspector member functions.

```
int Numerator() const;
int Denominator() const;
```

These inspectors give access to representations of the numerator and denominator. Their use of the qualifier **const** allows them to be invoked on **const** objects. Because they are in a **protected** section, a client program cannot use these two inspectors. However, they can be used by other `Rational` member functions. For example, the following code segment is legal in `Rational` member functions, but not in a client program.

```
// legal in member code, illegal in client code
Rational z;
cout << z.Numerator() << z.Denominator() << endl;
```

9.3.5

Mutator member functions

The `Rational` class definition in Listing 9.1 next declares two **protected** mutators.

```
void SetNumerator(int numer);
void SetDenominator(int denom);
```

The declarations indicate that the member functions are both of type **void** and both expect a single **int** object as a parameter. The mutators are used respectively to set the numerator and denominator of the rational number being represented. Like the two inspectors, because they are declared in a **protected** section, the two mutators cannot be used in a client program. However, the mutators can be used by other `Rational` member functions.

Because mutators modify data members, they cannot use the qualifier **const**. Therefore, mutator methods cannot be used by **const** objects.

9.3.6

Data members

Data members are normally declared in a **private** section. This convention requires that any access or modification to data members by client programs or by other classes derived from this class use the public member inspector and mutator functions. As noted previously, information hiding helps ensure the integrity of the data members and also normally makes it possible to update or correct the library without requiring changes to code developed by clients. When the library is updated, clients need only relink their code.

Non-**const** data members cannot be initialized in their class declaration. Constructors are instead used to perform the initialization of the data members. It is good software engineering practice to make sure that every data member of an object is initialized by its constructor to some appropriate value. If all constructors and mutators guarantee that only appropriate values are set for the data members, the other member functions and operators do not need to validate that the data members contain appropriate values.

The definition of the `Rational` class in Listing 9.1 indicates that all `Rational` objects have two **int** data members associated with them.

```
int NumeratorValue;
int DenominatorValue;
```

The intended use of these two data members is self-explanatory from their names—data member `NumeratorValue` holds a representation of the numerator of the rational number being represented, and data member `DenominatorValue` holds a representation of the denominator of the rational number being represented.

The two data members are declared within a **private** section, so it is illegal to directly reference them in a nonmember function or operator. Thus, an

error message would occur if the following statement is placed in function
`main()` of Program 9.1 to display the value of `r`'s numerator.

```
cout << "Numerator of rational number: "
  << r.NumeratorValue << endl; // illegal access
```

The error message would indicate that a nonpublic member is being illegally
referenced.

This completes our introduction of the `Rational` class definition in Listing 9.1. We next consider the prototypes of the `Rational` auxiliary operators.

9.3.7

Overloaded operators

The prototypes of the `Rational` auxiliary arithmetic operators are also in
Listing 9.1. These prototypes are our first examples of operator overloading
declarations.

```
Rational operator+(const Rational &r,
  const Rational &s);
Rational operator*(const Rational &r,
  const Rational &s);
```

Operator prototypes serve the same purpose as function prototypes—they
describe an interface that enables other functions and operators to invoke the
prototyped operator. The reserved word **operator** is used to indicate that an
operator overloading is being performed.

Whether an operator prototype declaration or definition is being given, the
interface to the operator is described first. The interface description begins
with the return type of the operator. Unless it is a member operator being
defined outside of the class definition, the operator return type is followed by
the reserved word **operator**. (If a member operator is being defined outside
of its class definition, then the class name and the scope operator (`::`) precede
the reserved word **operator**.) The reserved word **operator** is followed by
the actual operator to be overloaded. The interface is completed with the declaration of the operands. The declaration of the operands is given as a parameter
list.

Because the result of rational arithmetic is a rational value, the `Rational`
arithmetic operator declarations have `Rational` as their return types. Both
`Rational` arithmetic operator declarations specify two operands (parameters). The left operand is declared first and then the right operand. Since the
operands should not be modified as a result of an operation, the operands are
declared as **const** parameters. The operands are defined as **const** reference
parameters for efficiency reasons. (If they were value parameters, then copies
of the objects would be created and passed into the arithmetic operators.)

The ability to overload the insertion operator for `Rational` objects is an
example of why software engineers prefer the iostream library with its *extensibility* to the stdio library. The functionality designed into the iostream library
makes its possible to overload the insertion and extraction operators so that

there is a consistent interface for all input and output requests. This expressiveness is not possible with the stdio library, which constrains all input and output requests to involve only the fundamental types and character strings.

The prototypes of the insertion and extraction operators also specify two operands.

```
ostream& operator<<(ostream &sout,
 const Rational &r);
istream& operator>>(istream &sin, Rational &r);
```

The left operands of the insertion and extraction operators are declared as reference parameters. The left operands are reference parameters because inserting or extracting a Rational object modifies the stream and this change is permanent with respect to the client program. Type ostream is a base class for all output streams. Type istream is a base class for all input streams. By using these base classes, the operators can be invoked with standard streams, file streams, and in-memory streams.

The insertion and extraction operators perform *reference returns*. The modifier & in conjunction with a return type indicates this type of return. In a standard return, the return value of a function or operator is a temporary object that is created to hold the value being returned. The existence of the temporary object is bound to the invocation expression. In a reference return, no temporary object is created. The return value is instead supplied in an object with the property that its scope includes the scope of the function or operator that contained the invocation. For a member operator or function, the invoking object has this property. A reference parameter also has this property.

With a reference return, a Rational object insertion or extraction can be part of a larger insertion or extraction operation. For example, in the following code segment, first Rational r is displayed and then a newline character is displayed.

```
Rational r(1,2);
cout << r << endl;
```

Without a reference return, two separate insertion expressions would have been required.

```
Rational r(1,2);
cout << r;
cout << endl;
```

A reference return is more efficient than a standard return because no object needs to be created. This efficiency is particularly obvious when using classes more complex than Rational.

If a reference return uses a local object to supply a reference return value, the compiler should generate an error message. If it did not, then any use of that object in the invoking function would have undefined behavior. The behavior is undefined, because any use of the return value would be to activation record memory that has already been released.

Programming
Tip

9.4

IMPLEMENTING THE RATIONAL CLASS

Thus far the description of the rational library has not included the definitions of the member functions nor the definitions of the auxiliary operators. Listings 9.2 through 9.6 contain a possible implementation of the functions and operators described in `rational.h`. The source file for the listings is named `rational.cpp`.

As you examine the listings you will see that in the definitions of the Rational member functions, the name of the function being defined is always preceded by the class name and the scope operator. For example, the definition of the Rational mutator `SetNumerator()` has the following syntax:

```
void Rational::SetNumerator(int numer) {
    NumeratorValue = numer;
}
```

The scope identification is necessary because a source file can contain definitions of member functions and operators from different classes that use the same member name and interface. Without some scope resolution, it is not possible to match the definitions with the appropriate class.

Within a member definition, there is no similar difficulty in recognizing which member function or operator is being referenced by default. The lack of difficulty is because the default nonlocal scope in a member function is the class scope. Therefore, inside member definitions it is not necessary to use the scope resolution operator in conjunction with the class name to reference members of that class.

9.4.1

Constructor definitions

Both constructors in Listing 9.2 use the mutators `SetNumerator()` and `SetDenominator()` to do their actual work.

Listing 9.2

*Implementation of
Rational constructors
from rational.cpp*

```cpp
#include <iostream.h>
#include "rational.h"

// default constructor
Rational::Rational() {
   SetNumerator(0);
   SetDenominator(1);
}

// (numer, denom) constructor
Rational::Rational(int numer, int denom) {
   SetNumerator(numer);
   SetDenominator(denom);
}
```

The default constructor is defined first, and it invokes the mutators with parameters 0 and 1, respectively, to initialize the new object so that it represents the rational number 0/1.

```cpp
SetNumerator(0);
SetDenominator(1);
```

The use of mutators `SetNumerator()` and `SetDenominator()` isolates the underlying data member implementation. The information-hiding principle encourages localizing data member manipulations to as few functions and operators as possible. This localization generally makes it simpler to incorporate changes in the data representation.

The second constructor defined in Listing 9.2 uses the values of its parameters `numer` and `denom` in its invocations of mutators `SetNumerator()` and `SetDenominator()`, respectively, to initialize the new object so that it represents the rational number `numer/denom`.

```cpp
SetNumerator(numer);
SetDenominator(denom);
```

For this constructor, the second parameter is an optional parameter. The C++ language rules specify that the declaration of the default value should occur only once. Therefore, the declaration of the default value can occur either in the class definition or in the definition of the member function. It is our practice to specify the default value in the class definition—for it is this section of the ADT library that is normally examined by client programmers.

9.4.2

Inspector definitions

The `Rational` class supports information hiding, so it provides inspector and mutator member functions to control references to the data members.

The definitions of the inspectors `Numerator()` and `Denominator()` in Listing 9.3 are straightforward. The numerator of the rational number being represented is maintained in the data member `NumeratorValue` and the denominator is maintained in the data member `DenominatorValue`. The values of these data members are the ones returned by the inspectors. There is no need to use the scope operator or even the access operator in the listing to qualify which `NumeratorValue` and `DenominatorValue` are being referenced—by default, references are to the data members of the object whose inspector is invoked.

Listing 9.3

Implementation of Rational inspectors and mutators from rational.cpp

```
// get the numerator
int Rational::Numerator() const {
   return NumeratorValue;
}

// get the denominator
int Rational::Denominator() const {
   return DenominatorValue;
}

// set the numerator
void Rational::SetNumerator(int numer) {
   NumeratorValue = numer;
}

// set the denominator
void Rational::SetDenominator(int denom) {
   if (denom != 0)
      DenominatorValue = denom;
   else {
      cerr << "Illegal denominator: " << denom
        << "using 1" << endl;
      DenominatorValue = 1;
   }
}
```

9.4.3
Mutator definitions

The definitions of the mutators `SetNumerator()` and `SetDenominator()` in Listing 9.3 are also straightforward. These functions each have a single **const int** parameter that is used to be the new value of the object's data members `NumeratorValue` and `DenominatorValue`. It is the responsibility of ADT member functions to validate manipulation requests. For the `Rational` ADT checks must be made to ensure that the denominator is not zero.

9.4.4
Arithmetic facilitator definitions

The two arithmetic facilitators in Listing 9.4 are direct implementations of rational arithmetic. The parameter supplied to each of the facilitators is conceptually the right operand of the arithmetic operation being computed where the left operand is the object doing the invoking.

Listing 9.4

Implementation of arithmetic and stream facilitators

```
// adding Rationals
Rational Rational::Add(const Rational &r) const {
   int a = Numerator();
   int b = Denominator();
   int c = r.Numerator();
   int d = r.Denominator();
   return Rational(a*d + b*c, b*d);
}

// multiplying Rationals
Rational Rational::Multiply(const Rational &r) const {
   int a = Numerator();
   int b = Denominator();
   int c = r.Numerator();
   int d = r.Denominator();
   return Rational(a*c, b*d);
}

// inserting a Rational
void Rational::Insert(ostream &sout) const {
   sout << Numerator() << '/' << Denominator();
   return;
}

// extracting a Rational
void Rational::Extract(istream &sin) {
   int numer;
   int denom;
   char slash;
   sin >> numer >> slash >> denom;
   SetNumerator(numer);
   SetDenominator(denom);
   return;
}
```

For example, the following segment displays 5/6:

```
Rational a(1,2);
Rational b(1,3);
Rational c = a.Add(b); // 1/2 + 1/3 is 5/6
cout << c << endl;
```

9.4.5

Stream insertion and extraction facilitator definitions

The definition of facilitator `Insert()` is also given in Listing 9.4. The facilitator has an `ostream` reference parameter `sout` that is the target output stream for the insertion that it performs. The process to insert a `Rational` object is quite simple—display its numerator, display a slash character, and display its denominator.

The definition of the facilitator `Extract()` is also given in Listing 9.4. The parameter list specifies a single `istream` reference parameter `sin` that is the source stream of the rational number representation that is to be extracted into the invoking object.

The definition begins by extracting an **int** value `numer` that should correspond to the numerator of the rational number being extracted. A character is then extracted; in this case, it should be the slash that separates the numerator from the denominator. Proper code would verify that the extracted character is indeed a slash. This modification is left to the exercises.

The definition of facilitator `Extract()` next uses the two extracted values in its invocations of mutators `SetNumerator()` and `SetDenominator()` to reset the invoking object's data members.

Programming Tip

> ### *Think before overloading*
> When overloading an operator, try to imagine how it will be used. Look at the operator in its traditional setting with fundamental objects and make sure that the analogous behavior is present in your overloaded version.

9.4.6

Auxiliary arithmetic operator definitions

The two overloaded arithmetic operators in Listing 9.5 simply use the appropriate facilitator to perform the desired action.

Listing 9.5

Implementation of the arithmetic operators from rational.cpp

```
// adding Rationals
Rational operator+(const Rational &r,
  const Rational &s) {
    return r.Add(s);
}

// multiplying Rationals
Rational operator*(const Rational &r,
  const Rational &s) {
    return r.Multiply(s);
}
```

In Chapter 3, we discussed how promotions are automatically attempted during expression evaluation if operands of mixed fundamental types are present. The same is true if the mixed-type operands involve class-type objects. For example, in the following code segment the right operand of the addition and the left operand of the subtraction are promoted to `Rational` objects.

```
Rational u(3,4);
cout << u + 2 << endl;
cout << 2 - u << endl;
```

Promotions are attempted when there is no definition for the relevant combination of operator and operands. A promotion is achieved by invoking a constructor on an operand. In the preceding example, the `Rational` constructor with the default second parameter can construct a `Rational` from the **int** 2. Thus the preceding example is equivalent to the following code segment:

```
Rational u(3,4);
Rational Two(2,1);
cout << u + Two << endl;
cout << Two - u << endl;
```

The complete promotion rules are quite involved. For a formal definition of these rules examine a C++ reference manual (e.g., Ellis and Stroustrup).

9.4.7

Auxiliary stream operator definitions

The definition of the insertion operator in Listing 9.6 expects two operands. The left operand `sout` is the target output stream for the insertion. The right operand `r` is the `Rational` object to be displayed.

Listing 9.6

Implementation of the stream auxiliary operators from rational.cpp

```
// inserting a Rational
ostream& operator<<(ostream &sout, const Rational &r) {
    r.Insert(sout);
    return sout;
}
// extracting a Rational
istream& operator>>(istream &sin, Rational &r) {
    r.Extract(sin);
    return sin;
}
```

Like the overloading of the arithmetic operators, the overloading of the insertion operator is straightforward given the existence of the facilitators. After finishing the insertion using public member `Insert()`, a reference to `ostream sout` is returned. As discussed previously, the reference return enables `Rational` insertions to be cascaded with other insertions in a single expression.

The definition of **operator**>>() in Listing 9.6 for overloading extraction is similarly straightforward. After resetting the object through the use of a facilitator `Extract()`, a reference to `istream sin` is returned. The reference return enables a `Rational` extraction to be cascaded with other extractions in a single expression.

This completes our discussion of the rational library.

9.5

DEVELOPING A RANDOM ADT LIBRARY

In Chapter 7, functions `Uniform()` and `InitializeSeed()` were developed to assist in the generation of pseudorandom number sequences. We now take a more object-oriented view and develop an ADT for uniform pseudoran-

C++
Language

Struct

The **class** construct is a generalization of the **struct** construct of C. The **struct** construct in C permits public data members, but not member functions or operators. In addition, there cannot be any **protected** or **private** sections. This restriction prevents information hiding and makes C less suitable than C++ for significant software engineering applications.

C++ also has a **struct** construct. However, it is more like the **class** construct than its counterpart in C. The C++ **struct** permits both data members and member functions and operators. There can also be access specifiers. The **struct** construct differs from the **class** construct only in that the default access specification is **public**.

The **struct** construct is rarely used in C++ programs because the class construct with its default access specification of **private** better supports the information-hiding principle.

History of
Computing

Snow White and the seven dwarfs

One of the first companies to achieve prominence with its computer was Remington Rand. Mauchly and Eckert—the designers of ENIAC—produced Remington Rand's successful line of computers called UNIVAC (Universal Automatic Computer). The UNIVAC caught the public's eye when CBS used it to help predict the outcome of the 1952 presidential election. Because of this television exposure, the term UNIVAC became synonymous with computer.

Although much development of computer technology was done by new companies, some existing companies slowly entered the field. In 1952, after prodding by Thomas J. Watson Jr., IBM added computer manufacturing to its business. Their first successful machine was the IBM 701. In 1964, with the introduction of the IBM System 360, IBM established its leadership in the industry. During this time period, IBM's dominance of the business-computer market was so great that the computer industry was often referred to as "Snow White and the Seven Dwarfs," with IBM being Snow White. The seven dwarfs were Sperry Rand, Control Data, Honeywell, RCA, NCR, General Electric, and Burroughs, none of which manufactures mainframe computers anymore.

dom number sequences. We will use this ADT in developing a simple guessing game in section 9.6 of this chapter.

As a reminder, functions Uniform() and InitializeSeed() made use of stdlib library functions rand() and srand(). Each time function rand() is invoked it returns a uniform pseudorandom number from the inclusive interval 0 to RAND_MAX, where RAND_MAX is defined in stdlib.h. To produce a different sequence of pseudorandom numbers, function srand() can be used. Function srand() expects an **unsigned int** as its parameter, which is used to set the seed for generating the next pseudorandom number. Once the seed is set, rand() should produce a different sequence of pseudorandom numbers. By using the current time as the seed, the seed should be different for each run of the program. The different seeds should cause a different sequence of numbers to be generated in each run. The current time can be determined using the function `time()` from time standard library. Function `time()` with a parameter of 0 supplies the current time through its return value.

An abstraction for uniform random number sequences should allow different kinds of uniform pseudorandom number sequences to be generated (e.g., sequences from the interval 1 through 6 or from the interval 1 to 32). An object to represent a random number sequence would need to support public methods to

- Reproduce the same pseudorandom number sequence.

- Generate different pseudorandom number sequences.

- Restrict pseudorandom numbers in the sequence to a specified interval.

- Draw the next number in a sequence.

To support these public methods, several other methods would be useful.

- Set the interval from which the numbers are drawn.

- Set the seed for the random number sequence.

- Inspect the low value in the interval from which the numbers are drawn.

- Inspect the high value in the interval from which the numbers are drawn.

The only data our representation requires is knowledge of the endpoints for the interval from which the pseudorandom numbers are to be drawn. The data members to represent these values should be placed in a private section to support information hiding.

A possible library interface for this behavior is given in Listing 9.7.

The class `Random` defined in Listing 9.7 has two constructors. The first constructor is the default constructor. It constructs an object representing a default sequence. We specify that the default sequence is the same as you would get through repeated calls to stdlib function `rand()` without using `srand()`. To achieve this behavior, the default interval is 0 through `RAND_MAX` (`RAND_MAX` is an implementation-dependent preprocessor macro constant defined in `stdlib.h`).

The second constructor takes either two or three parameters. The first two parameters specify the inclusive interval from which the numbers in the sequence are drawn. The optional parameter specifies a seed for generating the initial pseudorandom number in the sequence. A default value of 1 causes it to mimic the behavior of `srand()`, which also has a default value of 1.

In the following code segment, we define `Random` objects R, S, and T. Object R uses the default constructor; objects S and T use the other constructor to specify the intervals from which the numbers in their sequences are drawn. For object S, it is the inclusive interval 1 through 6. For object T, it is the inclu-

Listing 9.7

Header file random.h
for random library

```
#ifndef RANDOM_H
#define RANDOM_H
class Random {
   public:
      // default constructor
      Random();
      // constructor for generating from interval (a,b)
      Random(int a, int b, unsigned int seed = 1);
      // mutators
      int Draw();
      unsigned int Randomize();
   protected:
      // mutators
      void SetInterval(int a, int b);
      void SetSeed(unsigned int s);
      // inspectors
      int GetLow();
      int GetHigh();
   private:
      // data members
      int Low;
      int High;
};
#endif
```

sive interval 1 through 32. For object T, an initial seed value of 88 is also specified.

```
// sequence with numbers from 0 ... RAND_MAX
Random R;
// sequence with numbers from 1 ... 6
Random S(1, 6);
// sequence with numbers from 1 ... 32 using seed 88
Random T(1, 32, 88);
```

The mutator member function Draw() returns as its value the next pseudorandom number in the sequence. For example, the following code segment defines a Random object U and then displays the first five numbers in its sequence.

```
Random U;
for (int i = 1; i <= 5; ++i) {
   cout << U.Draw() << endl;
}
```

Because our implementation mimics the behavior of repeated invocations of rand(), the output of the segment is the same as the output of Program 7.6 from Chapter 7.

```
346
130
10982
1090
11656
```

The purpose of mutator `Randomize()` is to set the current seed for the pseudorandom number sequence to an unspecified value that should be different for each invocation of the mutator.

There are also two protected mutators. Mutator `SetInterval()` expects as its two parameters the desired endpoints of the integer interval from which the pseudorandom numbers are drawn. Mutator `SetSeed()` expects as its single parameter the seed value for generating the next pseudorandom number.

The protected inspectors `GetLow()` and `GetHigh()` have analogous roles. They return representations of the low and high endpoints of the interval from which the pseudorandom numbers are drawn.

9.5.1

Random number implementation

The implementation file for the random library member functions is `random.cpp`. A copy is presented in Listing 9.8. An examination of the listing shows that stdlib functions `rand()` and `srand()` establish the `Random` class functionality.

The two constructors for the `Random` class are straightforward implementations that practice information hiding.

```
Random::Random() {
    SetInterval(0, RAND_MAX);
}
Random::Random(int a, int b, unsigned int s) {
    SetInterval(a, b);
    SetSeed(s);
}
```

Mutator `SetInterval()` is used by both constructors to specify the endpoints of the interval from which the numbers are to be drawn. The nondefault constructor also uses mutator `SetSeed()` to specify the seed for the pseudorandom number sequence.

In accomplishing its task, mutator `SetInterval()` first examines its parameters to make sure that the requested endpoints are sensible.

```
void Random::SetInterval(int a, int b) {
    if (a > b) {
        cerr << "Bad random number interval: " << a
        << " ... " << b << endl;
        exit(1);
    }
    Low = a;
    High = b;
}
```

If the endpoints are sensible, data members `Low` and `High` are set using the parameter values.

Listing 9.8

*Implementation file
random.cpp for
random library*

```cpp
#include <stdlib.h>
#include <iostream.h>
#include <time.h>
#include "random.h"

// Random default pseudorandom number sequence
// constructor
Random::Random() {
   SetInterval(0, RAND_MAX);
}

// Random constructor specifying interval and seed for
// pseudorandom number sequence
Random::Random(int a, int b, unsigned int s) {
   SetInterval(a, b);
   SetSeed(s);
}

// SetInterval(): sets low and high endpoint of interval
// for sequence
void Random::SetInterval(int a, int b) {
   if (a > b) {
      cerr << "Bad random number interval: " << a
      << " ... " << b << endl;
      exit(1);
   }
   Low = a;
   High = b;
}

// SetSeed(): set seed for sequence
void Random::SetSeed(unsigned int s) {
   srand(s);
}

// Randomize(): set and return an arbitrary seed value
// for sequence
unsigned int Random::Randomize() {
   unsigned int CurrentSeed = time(0);
   SetSeed(CurrentSeed);
   return CurrentSeed;
}

// Draw(): return next value in sequence
int Random::Draw() {
   int IntervalSize = GetHigh() - GetLow() + 1;
   int RandomOffset = rand() % IntervalSize;
   int Number = GetLow() + RandomOffset;
   return Number;
}

// GetLow(): return low endpoint of interval
int Random::GetLow() {
   return Low;
}

// GetHigh(): return high endpoint of interval
int Random::GetHigh() {
   return High;
}
```

The mutator member function `SetSeed()` uses its parameter in an invocation of function `srand()`.

```
void Random::SetSeed(unsigned int s) {
    srand(s);
}
```

Because member function `Draw()` uses `rand()` in its generation of pseudo-random numbers, an invocation of `SetSeed()` affects the sequence of numbers that are generated.

The definition of mutator `Randomize()` is similar to function `InitializeSeed()` of Chapter 7.

```
unsigned int Random::Randomize() {
    unsigned int CurrentSeed = time(0);
    SetSeed(CurrentSeed);
    return CurrentSeed;
}
```

Function `Randomize()` first invokes function `time()` to initialize object `CurrentSeed` with the current time. It then invokes `srand()` using `CurrentSeed` as the actual parameter. Finally, `Randomize()` returns the value of `CurrentSeed`. This value is returned so that the client program, if need be, can record the seed of the pseudorandom number sequence thus allowing the sequence to be replicated.

The `Draw()` function performs several small steps to produce a uniform pseudorandom number from the desired interval. The steps are similar to function `Uniform()` of Chapter 7.

```
int Random::Draw() {
    int IntervalSize = GetHigh() - GetLow() + 1;
    int RandomOffset = rand() % IntervalSize;
    int Number = GetLow() + RandomOffset;
    return Number;
}
```

Function `Draw()` first calculates the size of the interval in an object `IntervalSize`. To do so it uses inspectors `GetLow()` and `GetHigh()`. Next, a uniform pseudorandom number produced by `rand()` is taken modulus `IntervalSize` and assigned to `RandomOffset`.

```
int RandomOffset = rand() % IntervalSize;
```

Suppose `IntervalSize` is 2, then the value of the expression `rand() % IntervalSize` is either 0 or 1. If the value of RAND_MAX is odd then the values 0 and 1 are assigned to `RandomOffset` in an equally likely pseudorandom manner, because you would expect that half the time `rand()` produces an even number and the other half of the time it produces an odd number. If the value of RAND_MAX is instead even, then 0 has a slightly increased chance of being assigned to `RandomOffset` because there is one more even number than odd number in the interval 0 to RAND_MAX.

If the value of RAND_MAX is very large compared to IntervalSize, then the fact that some numbers have an extra $1/(\text{RAND\_MAX} + 1)$ chance of occurring can be ignored. Thus in general, the expression rand() % IntervalSize produces pseudorandom numbers in the interval 0 to IntervalSize - 1 in a near-equally likely manner; that is, in a uniform pseudorandom manner.

Since the value of RandomOffset is a uniform pseudorandom number from the interval 0 to IntervalSize - 1, the value of the expression GetLow() + RandomOffSet is a uniform pseudorandom number from the interval Low to Low + IntervalSize - 1. As IntervalSize equals the value High - Low + 1, the value assigned to Number and returned by Draw() is a uniform pseudorandom number from the interval Low to High.

```
int Number = GetLow() + RandomOffset;
```

Program 9.2 demonstrates the use of Randomize() and Draw() to generate five pseudorandom numbers from the interval 10 to 15.

Program 9.2

Demonstration of random library

```
// Program 9.2: Display pseudorandom numbers from
// the interval 10 to 15.
#include <iostream.h>
#include "random.h"
int main() {
   Random U(10,15);
   U.Randomize();
   for (int i = 1; i <= 5; i++) {
      cout << U.Draw()<< endl;
   }
   return 0;
}
```

The output of a run of a Program 9.2 follows.

```
15
11
10
14
14
```

The output of another run of the program follows.

```
12
14
10
13
11
```

We shall use our random library in the implementation of the ADT for the red-yellow-green game.

9.6

RED-YELLOW-GREEN GAME

A fun, relatively simple guessing game is the red-yellow-green game. It is normally a two-person game in which one person picks a number between 100 and 999, and the other person tries to guess it. Every time a guess is made, the picker responds by telling the guesser the number of red digits, yellow digits, and green digits in the guess.

A guess digit is a green digit if the guess digit and the corresponding answer digit are the same. A guess digit is a red digit if it does not correspond to any of the answer digits. A guess digit is a yellow digit if it is neither a red digit nor a green digit. Suppose the answer is 123 and the guess is 422. The initial guess digit 4 is a red digit because it is neither 1, 2, nor 3. The middle guess digit 2 is a green digit because it matches the corresponding answer digit. The final guess digit 2 is a yellow digit because it does not match the corresponding answer digit but does match another of the answer digits (the middle answer digit).

When supplying the red-yellow-green information in response to a guess, the reply gives the number of red digits first, the number of yellow digits next, and then the number of green digits. By giving totals only, the game is made harder. Suppose the answer is 653 and the guess is 616; the picker would reply one red, one yellow, and one green. Suppose instead the answer is 492 and the guess is 249; the picker would reply zero red, three yellow, and zero green.

9.6.1

Abstraction and interface

Our goal is to develop an electronic version of the game in which the program plays the role of the number picker.

The initial step in the object-oriented design is to determine the objects that will comprise the system. The system in this case is the red-yellow-green game. Overall, there must be a game controller that initiates and runs the game. Also, there must be objects for representing each kind of user input and output. So, objects associated with the controller will represent the current three-digit user guess and the three-color response to that guess. Another object associated with the controller will be the three-digit number picked by the program. Notice that all of the controller's objects have three numeric components. Thus, it will be advantageous to develop a class to represent an object with three numeric components. Objects of such a class can be used for representing the guess, the response, and the number to be picked.

The next step in object-oriented design is to determine how the objects will interact. For our system, the controller must be able to react to a user guess by producing the red-yellow-green count response. The response should then generate another user guess. This interaction continues until either the user correctly guesses the number or quits.

We now turn our attention to a more refined view of the behaviors of our various objects. The behaviors associated with a guess object are

- Getting a guess.
- Assigning a value to a component digit in a guess.
- Inspecting the value of a component digit in a guess.

The behaviors associated with a response object are

- Initializing a response in reaction to a guess.
- Assigning the number of reds, greens, and yellows in the response.
- Inspecting the number of reds, greens, or yellows in the response.

The behaviors associated with a game controller object are

- Randomly choosing a three-digit number from the interval 100 to 999 to start the game.
- Welcoming the user.
- Prompting the user to supply a guess.
- Acquiring the guess.
- Evaluating the guess to produce a response.
- Displaying a response.
- Detecting a winning guess.
- Congratulating a winning guess.
- Permitting the user to quit.
- Coordinating the play of the game.

Other behaviors associated with several of these controller behaviors are

- Inspecting the digits in the number to be picked.
- Assigning the digits in the number to be picked.
- Determining the number of reds, yellows, and greens for creating the response.

The necessary behaviors associated with the object composed of three numeric components are

- Inspecting the individual components.
- Setting the individual components.

The name of our class to represent an object with three numeric components (data members) is `Element`. A copy of the header file for `Element` is given in Listing 9.9. The class has a constructor that by default initializes its members to 0. To support the behaviors discussed previously, there are three public inspectors and three public mutators. These member functions support information hiding.

The three private data members of `Element` are named `X`, `Y`, and `Z`. These names were chosen because an `Element` object resembles a coordinate in three-dimensional space, where the axes are called the x-axis, y-axis, and the z-axis. Given these names for the data members, the names for the associated inspectors and mutators follow immediately.

Listing 9.9

Header file element.h for the class Element

```
#ifndef ELEMENT_H
#define ELEMENT_H

class Element {
  public:
    // default constructor
    Element(int x = 0, int y = 0, int z = 0);
    // inspectors
    int GetX() const;
    int GetY() const;
    int GetZ() const;
    // mutators
    void SetX(int x);
    void SetY(int y);
    void SetZ(int z);
  private:
    // data members
    int X;
    int Y;
    int Z;
};

#endif
```

Listing 9.10

Header file guess.h for the class Guess

```
#ifndef GUESS_H
#define GUESS_H
#include "element.h"

class Guess {
  public:
    // default constructor
    Guess();
    // inspector
    int GetDigit(int i) const;
    // mutator
    bool Update();
  protected:
    // mutator
    void SetDigit(int i, int v);
  private:
    Element Number;
};

// auxiliary operators
ostream& operator<<(ostream &sout, const Guess &G);

#endif
```

The name of our class to represent a user guess object is `Guess`. A copy of the header file for `Guess` is given in Listing 9.10.

The member functions given in the class definition for Guess follow from our earlier discussion of object behavior. Public inspector `GetDigit()` gives access to a particular digit in the user's guess. Mutator `Update()` acquires the next user guess. In the implementation given in a later section, `Update()` extracts the user's guess from the standard input stream. Other implementations are also possible by simply modifying `Update()`. Protected mutator `SetDigit()` is used to set an individual digit in the representation of the guess. Private data member `Number` stores the three digits in `Element` form.

The first digit in the guess will be associated with the X member of Number, the second digit in the guess will be associated with the Y member of Number, and the third digit in the guess will be associated with the Z member of Number. The header file also includes a prototype of an overloaded version of the extraction operator for Guess objects.

Response is the name of our class for representing a response to a user. The header file for Response is given in Listing 9.11. The member functions given in the class definition again follow from our earlier discussion of object behavior. The public inspectors give access to the number of reds, yellows, and greens. The protected mutators are used by the constructor to set the counts for the number of reds, yellows, and greens in a response. The mutators are in a protected section, because once the response is constructed, there is no reason for it to be modified. The color counts are represented using private data member Counts of type Element. In the implementation, the red count is associated with the X member of Counts, the yellow count is associated with the Y member of Counts, and the red count is associated with the Z member of Counts.

Listing 9.11

Header file response.h
for the class Response

```
#ifndef RESPONSE_H
#define RESPONSE_H
#include "element.h"
class Response {
   public:
      // constructor
      Response(int r = 0, int y = 0, int g = 0);
      // inspectors
      int GetRed() const;
      int GetYellow() const;
      int GetGreen() const;
   protected:
      // mutators
      void SetRed(int r);
      void SetYellow(int y);
      void SetGreen(int g);
   private:
      Element Counts;
};
#endif;
```

The name of our class to manage the game is RYG. The header file for RYG is given in Listing 9.12. Together with their auxiliary operators, the classes Element, Guess, Response, and RYG form our red-yellow-green game data abstraction.

The header files for Guess, Response, and Element are included in the header file for RYG because of data members UserInput, UserFeedback, and SecretNumber. In addition, there are two public members. One public member is the default constructor that principally initializes Element object SecretNumber, which represents the number picked by the program. The other public member is Play(), which manages the control of the game. To

Listing 9.12

Header file ryg.h for the class RYG

```
#ifndef RYG_H
#define RYG_H

#include "guess.h"
#include "response.h"
#include "element.h"

class RYG {
   public:
      // default constructor
      RYG();
      // facilitator
      void Play();
   protected:
      // facilitators
      void Welcome() const;
      void Prompt() const;
      Response Evaluate(const Guess &G) const;
      bool Winner(const Response &R) const;
      void Congratulations() const;
      void Display(const Guess &G, const Response &R)
       const;
      void GoodBye() const;
      int Red(const Guess &G) const;
      int Yellow(const Guess &G) const;
      int Green(const Guess &G) const;
   private:
      // data members
      Element SecretNumber;
      Guess UserInput;
      Response UserFeedback;
};
#endif
```

gain insight into the other members of RYG, the implementation of Play() is provided in Listing 9.13.

Listing 9.13

RYG member function Play() from ryg.cpp

```
void RYG::Play() {
   Welcome();
   Prompt();
   while (UserInput.Update()) {
      UserFeedback = Evaluate(UserInput);
      if (Winner(UserFeedback)) {
         Congratulations();
         return;
      }
      else {
         Display(UserInput, UserFeedback);
         Prompt();
      }
   }
   GoodBye();
}
```

Member function Play() begins by invoking member functions Welcome() and Prompt(). Member function Welcome() displays a welcoming message, and Prompt() asks the user for an initial guess. A **while** loop is then initiated. The **while** loop test expression (UserInput.Update())

updates the user's guess. The loop is iterated once for every guess. If the test expression is false, the user did not supply a value and instead gave up. Under this condition, the loop is exited and an appropriate message is displayed by member `GoodBye()`. (It will be the case that if the user wins the game, the program executes a return statement from within the loop body.) Member function `Evaluate()` examines the user's guess to determine the appropriate response. Member function `Winner()` examines the response and determines whether it indicates three greens. If it is the winning response, member function `Congratulations()` indicates this fact and function `Play()` returns. If the response is not the winning response, member function `Display()` displays the result of the guess and then `Prompt()` is executed to prepare for the next iteration of the loop. At that point, the **while** loop test expression attempts to update the guess, and if successful, the loop body is executed again. A sample run of function `Play()` follows.

```
Welcome to the red-yellow-green game.
A number between 0 and 999 has been chosen
for you to guess.

What is your guess? 456
Guess 456 corresponds to 1 red 1 yellow 1 green

What is your guess? 536
Guess 536 corresponds to 1 red 0 yellow 2 green

What is your guess? 526
Guess 526 corresponds to 1 red 0 yellow 2 green

What is your guess? 596
Guess 596 corresponds to 3 green

Congratulations on your win!
```

Member function `Play()` is invoked from a function `main()`. The function `main()` consists of two statements: a definition of an RYG object `Game` to create a game instance, and an invocation of `Play()` for the instance. Function `main()` is given in Listing 9.14.

Listing 9.14

Red-yellow-green game controller from rygmain.cpp

```
#include <stdlib.h>
#include <iostream.h>
#include "ryg.h"

int main() {
   RYG Game;
   Game.Play();
   return 0;
}
```

To assist member function `Evaluate()`, three other member functions are defined for analyzing a guess with respect to a particular color: `Red()`, `Yellow()`, and `Green()`.

9.6.2

Implementation of the class Element

We will now consider the implementation of the various class member functions and auxiliary operators. We begin with the class `Element`. Its implementation is given in Listing 9.15.

Listing 9.15

Implementation of class Element from element.cpp

```cpp
#include "element.h"

// Element(): constructor
Element::Element(int x, int y, int z) {
   SetX(x);
   SetY(y);
   SetZ(z);
}
// GetX(): return X attribute
int Element::GetX() const {
   return X;
}
// GetY(): return Y attribute
int Element::GetY() const {
   return Y;
}
// GetZ(): return Z attribute
int Element::GetZ() const {
   return Z;
}
// SetX(): set X attribute
void Element::SetX(int x) {
   X = x;
}
// SetY(): set Y attribute
void Element::SetY(int y) {
   Y = y;
}
// SetZ(): set Z attribute
void Element::SetZ(int z) {
   Z = z;
}
```

The three inspectors and three mutators given in Listing 9.15 are all straightforward in their implementation. These member functions exist to support information hiding.

9.6.3

Implementation of the class Guess

Listing 9.16 contains the implementation of the class `Guess`, and Listing 9.17 contains the implementation of the overloaded insertion operator for `Guess` objects.

Listing 9.16

*Implementation of
Guess member
functions from
guess.cpp*

```cpp
#include <iostream.h>
#include <stdlib.h>
#include "guess.h"

// Guess(): default constructor
Guess::Guess() {
    Number.SetX(0);
    Number.SetY(0);
    Number.SetZ(0);
}

// GetDigit(): get aspect of guess
int Guess::GetDigit(int i) const {
    switch (i) {
        case 1: return Number.GetX();
        case 2: return Number.GetY();
        case 3: return Number.GetZ();
        default:
            cerr << "Unexpected digit request: " << i
                << endl;
            exit(1);
    }
}

// SetDigit(): Set aspect of guess
void Guess::SetDigit(int i, int v) {
    switch (i) {
        case 1: Number.SetX(v); break;
        case 2: Number.SetY(v); break;
        case 3: Number.SetZ(v); break;
        default:
            cerr << "Unexpected digit request: " << i
                << endl;
            exit(1);
    }
}

// Update(): acquire new guess from player
bool Guess::Update() {
    int Value;
    if (cin >> Value) {
        if ((Value >= 100) && (Value <= 999)) {
            int d1 = Value / 100;
            int d2 = (Value - (d1 * 100)) / 10;
            int d3 = Value % 10;
            SetDigit(1, d1);
            SetDigit(2, d2);
            SetDigit(3, d3);
        }
        else
            cerr << "Illegal guess ignored." << endl;
        return true;
    }
    else
        return false;
}
```

Listing 9.17

Overloaded insertion operator from guess.cpp

```
// operator <<: insert a guess
ostream& operator<<(ostream &sout, const Guess &G) {
   sout << G.GetDigit(1) << G.GetDigit(2)
     << G.GetDigit(3);
   return sout;
}
```

The `Guess` class constructor initializes its data member `Number` to represent a guess of all zeros.

```
Number.SetX(0);
Number.SetY(0);
Number.SetZ(0);
```

Such a guess cannot generate any information about the number picked by the program because the number picked is always greater than 99.

The `Guess` inspector member function `GetDigit()` of Listing 9.16 uses its parameter `i` to determine which digit of the user's guess is to be returned. As discussed previously, the first digit is maintained in the `X` member of `Number`, the second digit is maintained in the `Y` member of `Number`, and the third digit is maintained in the `Z` member of `Number`. A **switch** statement is used by the inspector to invoke the proper member function of `Number`.

```
switch (i) {
    case 1: return Number.GetX();
    case 2: return Number.GetY();
    case 3: return Number.GetZ();
    default:
        cerr << "Unexpected digit request: " << i
          << endl;
        exit(1);
}
```

The **default** case in the **switch** statement detects when parameter `i` does not correspond to a valid digit position. In this case, an error message is generated and the program terminates.

The `Guess` mutator member function `SetDigit()` of Listing 9.16 uses its parameters `i` and `v` to set the ith digit in a guess to the value `v`. Like `Get-Digit()`, `SetDigit()` uses a **switch** statement to determine which mutator member function of `Number` should be invoked. As implemented, the `SetDigit()` does not check that `v` is valid for the specified digit. Such validation of `v` is left to the exercises at end of the chapter.

The task of `Guess` mutator member function `Update()` of Listing 9.16 is to get the next user input. In our implementation, the user input is extracted as an integer `Value` and then converted to `Element` form.

If there is a successful extraction, a test is made to verify that `Value` is valid (i.e., `Value` falls in the interval 100 to 999). If `Value` is invalid, no updating of the current guess is performed. If `Value` is valid, the following actions are then taken:

```
int d1 = Value / 100;
int d2 = (Value - (d1 * 100)) / 10;
int d3 = Value % 10;
```

Object `d1` is the leading digit of `Value`, and it is determined by dividing `Value` by 100. Object `d2` is the middle digit of `Value`, and it is determined by subtracting `Value` rounded down to the 100s place from `Value` and then by dividing that difference by 10. Object `d3` is the trailing digit of `Value`, and it is determined by computing the remainder of `Value` when it is divided by 10; that is, `Value` mod 10.

Once the component digits of the guess are determined, mutator `Set-Digit()` is invoked to set the first, second, and third digits of the guess to their new values.

```
SetDigit(1, d1);
SetDigit(2, d2);
SetDigit(3, d3);
```

After the extraction has been processed, the value **true** is returned. This value indicates that the user has supplied another guess. If no extraction into `Value` was possible (i.e., the expression `(cin >> Value)` evaluated to false), `Update()` returns **false**.

The implementation in Listing 9.17 of the insertion operator `<<` for a `Guess` object consists of two statements. The first statement performs the actual insertion:

```
sout << G.GetDigit(1) << G.GetDigit(2)
  << G.GetDigit(3);
```

The insertion uses `G`'s member function `GetDigit()` to individually display the three digits. The other statement is a reference return of the stream `sout`. As in the overloading of the insertion operator for `Rational` objects, the reference return enables a `Guess` insertion to be part of a larger insertion statement. For example, in the following code segment, `Guess` object `MyGuess` is displayed first, and then a newline character is displayed.

```
Guess MyGuess;
cout << MyGuess << "\n";
```

9.6.4

Implementation of the class Response

The implementation of the class `Response` is given in Listing 9.18.

The `Response` constructor uses its parameters `r`, `y`, and `g` to initialize the three counts associated with a response. (The parameters have default values of 0.) The counts are maintained in data member `Element` object `Counts`. The

Listing 9.18

Implementation of Response member functions from response.cpp

```cpp
#include "response.h"
// Response(): default constructor
Response::Response(int r, int y, int g) {
    SetRed(r);
    SetYellow(y);
    SetGreen(g);
}

// GetRed():  get number of reds
int Response::GetRed() const {
    return Counts.GetX();
}

// GetYellow(): get number of yellows
int Response::GetYellow() const {
    return Counts.GetY();
}

// GetGreen(): get number of greens
int Response::GetGreen() const {
    return Counts.GetZ();
}

// SetRed(): set number of reds
void Response::SetRed(int r) {
    Counts.SetX(r);
}

// SetYellow(): set number of yellows
void Response::SetYellow(int y) {
    Counts.SetY(y);
}

// SetGreen(): set number of greens
void Response::SetGreen(int g) {
    Counts.SetZ(g);
}
```

initialization is done using mutators `SetRed()`, `SetYellow()`, and `Set-Green()`.

```cpp
SetRed(r);
SetYellow(y);
SetGreen(g);
```

Verification that the values of the three parameters make sense is left to the exercises at end of the chapter.

As noted previously, the red count is associated with the X member of the `Element Counts`, the yellow count is associated with the Y member of `Counts`, and the green count is associated with the Z member of `Counts`. The `Response` inspectors and mutators support information hiding. Their implementation is straightforward.

9.6.5

Implementation of the class RYG

We will now consider the implementation of the RYG member functions. The implementation spans Listings 9.19 – 9.21, as well as the earlier Listing 9.13 of member function Play().

Listing 9.19

Initial portion of RYG implementation file from ryg.cpp

```
#include <iostream.h>
#include <stdlib.h>
#include "random.h"
#include "ryg.h"
// default RYG constructor
RYG::RYG() {
    Random x(1, 9);
    Random y(0, 9);
    Random z(0, 9);
    x.Randomize();
    y.Randomize();
    z.Randomize();
    SecretNumber.SetX(x.Draw());
    SecretNumber.SetY(y.Draw());
    SecretNumber.SetZ(z.Draw());
}

// Welcome(): display opening message
void RYG::Welcome() const {
    cout << "Welcome to the red-yellow-green game.\n"
    << "A number between 100 and 999 has been chosen\n"
    << "for you to guess.\n" << endl;
}

// Prompt(): request next guess
void RYG::Prompt() const {
    cout << "What is your guess? " << flush;
}

// Congratulations(): announce their success
void RYG::Congratulations() const {
    cout << "Congratulations on your win!";
}

// GoodBye(): tell player the answer and so long
void RYG::GoodBye() const {
    cout << "Better luck next time" << endl;
}
```

Listing 9.19 begins with the inclusion of several libraries, one of which is the random library that was discussed in this chapter. The default constructor is the first member defined in Listing 9.19. The constructor begins by defining three Random objects x, y, and z. These objects are used to generate the three digits that comprise the number picked by the program.

```
Random x(1, 9);
Random y(0, 9);
Random z(0, 9);
```

Object x is used to generate the first digit. Because the number must fall in the interval 100 to 999, the pseudorandom value drawn for the digit must come from the interval 1 to 9. Objects y and z are used to draw pseudorandom values for the second and third digits. These two digits have no restriction on their values, so y and z are associated with the interval 0 to 9.

After defining the three Random objects, the objects' member functions Randomize() are invoked to ensure that the same digits are not picked each time the game is played.

```
x.Randomize();
y.Randomize();
z.Randomize();
```

Next, the RYG constructor sets the three components of its Element data member SecretNumber. As noted previously, the X member of Secret-Number is associated with the first digit of the number picked by the program, the Y member of SecretNumber is associated with the second digit of the number picked by the program, and the Z member of SecretNumber is associated with the third digit of the number picked by the program. The appropriate mutators of SecretNumber are invoked using pseudorandom numbers drawn from the proper intervals as their parameters.

```
SecretNumber.SetX(x.Draw());
SecretNumber.SetY(y.Draw());
SecretNumber.SetZ(z.Draw());
```

The other member functions Welcome(), Prompt(), Congratulations(), and GoodBye() of Listing 9.19 perform only insertions and require no analysis.

RYG member function Winner() of Listing 9.20 determines whether its parameter R represents the winning response. Parameter R is the winning response if the number of greens associated with it is 3. The member function GetGreen() of R computes the actual number of greens.

Listing 9.20

Some RYG member functions from implementation file ryg.cpp

```
// Winner(): reports whether response is all greens
bool RYG::Winner(const Response &R) const {
    return R.GetGreen() == 3;
}
// Display(): announce reds, yellows, greens
void RYG::Display(const Guess &G, const Response &R)
 const {
    int red = R.GetRed();
    int yellow = R.GetYellow();
    int green = R.GetGreen();
    cout << "Guess " << G << " corresponds to "
     << red << " red "
     << yellow << " yellow "
     << green << " green "
     << "\n" << endl;
}
```

The other `RYG` member function given in Listing 9.20 is `Display()`. This function has two parameters: a `Guess` G and a `Response` R. Function `Display()` reports the result of the guess. In our implementation, function `Display()` inserts a text message. (In the exercises we consider a graphical display.) Our implementation begins by invoking the inspectors of R to initialize local objects `red`, `yellow`, and `green` with the counts associated with R.

```
int red = R.GetRed();
int yellow = R.GetYellow();
int green = R.GetGreen();
```

An insertion statement then displays parameter G along with these counts to the standard output stream `cout`.

```
cout << "Guess " << G << " corresponds to "
 << red << " red "
 << yellow << " yellow "
 << green << " green "
 << "\n" << endl;
```

Notice that the insertion statement uses the overloaded version of the << operator for a `Guess` object to display G.

Listing 9.21 contains the definitions of `RYG` facilitator functions `Green()`, `Red()`, `Yellow()`, and `Evaluate()`. All four facilitators have a formal parameter G of type `Guess`.

Facilitator `Green()` reports the number of greens associated with G. This is kept in the local **int** object `green`, which is initialized to 0. The inspector `Green()` then compares the first guess digit with the first digit of the number picked by the program. The value of the first guess digit is obtained through inspector `GetDigit()` of G. The value of the first digit of the number picked by the program is obtained through the inspector `GetX()` of `SecretNumber`.

```
if (G.GetDigit(1) == SecretNumber.GetX())
    ++green;
```

If the digits test the same, the count of green digits is incremented by one. If there is a mismatch, no special action is taken. Next, the function compares the second digit of the guess and the second digit of the number picked by the program, and, if they test the same, the count of green digits is incremented by one. Finally, the inspector compares the third guess digit with the third digit of the number picked by the program, and, if it is appropriate, the inspector increments the count of green digits. Once the comparisons and increments are completed, the count of green digits is returned.

The actions of the inspector `Red()` are similar to `Green()`: a count is initialized to 0, the guess digits are compared with the digits of the number picked by the program, the count is incremented for each match, and the count is returned after making the three comparisons. For ease of expression in accom-

Listing 9.21

*More RYG member
functions from
implementation file
ryg.cpp*

```
// Green(): return number of green responses to guess
int RYG::Green(const Guess &G) const {
    int green = 0;
    if (G.GetDigit(1) == SecretNumber.GetX())
        ++green;
    if (G.GetDigit(2) == SecretNumber.GetY())
        ++green;
    if (G.GetDigit(3) == SecretNumber.GetZ())
        ++green;
    return green;
}

// Red(): return number of red responses to guess
int RYG::Red(const Guess &G) const {
    int sx = SecretNumber.GetX();
    int sy = SecretNumber.GetY();
    int sz = SecretNumber.GetZ();
    int gx = G.GetDigit(1);
    int gy = G.GetDigit(2);
    int gz = G.GetDigit(3);

    int red = 0;
    if ((gx != sx) && (gx != sy) && (gx != sz))
        ++red;
    if ((gy != sx) && (gy != sy) && (gy != sz))
        ++red;
    if ((gz != sx) && (gz != sy) && (gz != sz))
        ++red;
    return red;
}

// Yellow(): return number of yellow responses to guess
int RYG::Yellow(const Guess &G) const {
    return 3 - Green(G) - Red(G);
}

// Evaluate(): determine reds, yellows, and greens
Response RYG::Evaluate(const Guess &G) const {
    return Response(Red(G), Yellow(G), Green(G));
}
```

plishing these tasks, function `Red()` makes copies of the guess digits and the digits of the number picked by the program.

```
int sx = SecretNumber.GetX();
int sy = SecretNumber.GetY();
int sz = SecretNumber.GetZ();
int gx = G.GetDigit(1);
int gy = G.GetDigit(2);
int gz = G.GetDigit(3);
```

For a guess digit to be red, it cannot match any of the digits in the number picked by the program. Because three mismatches are required, the comparison expression for determining whether a guess digit is a red digit has three terms that are conjuncted together (combined using the `&&` operator). An individual term is true if the guess digit differs from the currently considered digit of the number picked by the program. If all three terms are true, the guess digit is a red digit. For example, the first guess digit gx is a red digit if the expression in Figure 9.2 is true.

Figure 9.2

An expression testing whether a guess digit is a red digit

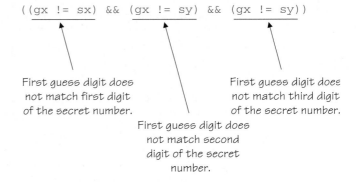

Given the existence of member functions Red() and Green(), member function Yellow() of Listing 9.21 is straightforward. Function Yellow() simply returns the number of reds and greens subtracted from 3.

```
return 3 - Green(G) - Red(G);
```

Function Evaluate() is also given in Listing 9.21. The function constructs and returns the Response object that corresponds with Guess G. The Response object is constructed by using the values of expressions Red(G), Yellow(G), and Green(G) as the actual parameters of the Response constructor.

```
return Response(Red(G), Yellow(G), Green(G));
```

This completes our discussion of the RYG ADT.

Programming Tip

Safe input extraction

Professional software normally extracts its input in a character representation. The input is then validated and translated into the desired representation. For example, in the red-yellow-green game, we can extract the guess as three **char** objects. This method provides a safe way of extracting the guess. For example, if an **int** representation is used, and a user provides a nondigit, the program terminates with an error message that is incomprehensible to most users. By using the **char** representation, a Guess object can do its own validation. In one of the exercises, this modification to the ADT is considered.

History of Computing

9.7

POINTS TO REMEMBER

- A representation of information and the operations to be performed on it is a data abstraction.

- An abstract data type or ADT is a well-defined and complete data abstraction that uses the information-hiding principle.

- An ADT allows the creation and manipulation of objects in a natural manner.

- The ADT rule of minimality states: Unless a behavior is generally needed, it should not be part of the ADT.

- The class minimality principle states: If a function or operator can be defined such that it is not a member of the class, then do not make it a

Figure 9.3

*A vacuum tube and an
early transistor*

member. This practice makes a nonmember function or operator generally independent of changes to the class's implementation.

■ By practicing information hiding in an ADT, client programs are generally immune from changes in the implementation of the ADT.

■ In C++, an ADT is implemented using classes, functions, and operators.

■ Constructors initialize objects of the ADT type. It is standard practice to ensure that every ADT object has all of its data members appropriately initialized.

■ A default constructor is a constructor that requires no parameters.

■ A copy constructor initializes a new object to be a duplicate of a previously defined source object. If a class does not define a copy constructor, the compiler automatically supplies a version.

■ A member assignment operator copies a source object to the invoking target object in an assignment statement. If a class does not define a member assignment operator, the compiler automatically supplies a version.

■ A memberwise copy is a copy where all data members of a source object are copied bit-by-bit to a target object.

■ The versions of the copy constructor and member assignment operator supplied by the compiler perform memberwise copying.

■ Some of the other member functions that commonly exist are called inspectors, mutators, and facilitators.

■ An inspector member function returns the value of an attribute of an object.

■ A mutator member function provides a method to modify an attribute of an object.

Figure 9.4

An integrated circuit

- A facilitator member function performs a task that depends in part upon the attributes of an object.
- The qualifier **const** appended to a function interface indicates that the function does not modify any of the data members. A **const** member function can be used by **const** objects of the class.
- The client interface to a class object occurs in the **public** section of the class definition.
- Any member defined in any section—whether **public**, **protected**, or **private**—is accessible to all of the other members of a class.
- Members of a **protected** section are intended to be used by other members of the class or by a class derived from the class.
- Data members are normally declared in a **private** section. By restricting direct client program access to the data members in an ADT, it is easier to ensure the integrity and consistency of their values.

- Members of a **private** section are intended to be used only by other members of the class.

- An & in the return type for a function or operator indicates that a reference return is being performed. In a reference return, a reference to the actual object in the return expression rather than a copy is returned. The scope of the returned object should not be local to the invoked function or operator.

- Iostream behavior is extensible. Objects of program-defined types can also have insertion and extraction operations defined for them.

- ADT libraries often contain auxiliary functions and operators that are not part of the ADT class, but do provide behavior that is expected with the objects.

- Two commonly provided auxiliary operators are insertion and extraction. They are not made members in part to give them the same form as insertions and extractions for fundamental type objects.

- A pseudorandom number sequence has the appearance and statistical properties of a random number sequence.

9.8

EXERCISES

9.1 Does every class definition define an ADT? What properties do you expect in an ADT?

9.2 Why is the information-hiding principle so important to the object-oriented programming paradigm?

9.3 What are the differences between a data member and a member function?

9.4 What are the differences between a mutator and an inspector member function?

9.5 What are the differences between member and auxiliary functions and operators?

9.6 What are the differences in using the various access-specifier labels?

9.7 What is the purpose of the qualifier **const**?

9.8 Why is it unnecessary for constructors to have return types?

9.9 How does a reference return type differ from the standard return type?

9.10 Why are class objects that are not modified in a function or operator typically passed as constant reference parameters rather than as value parameters?

9.11 Suppose the following definitions are in effect.

```
class Widget {
   public:
      bool Flag;
      Widget();
      Widget(int Value);
```

```
        int GetValue() const;
    protected:
        int DataItem;
        void SetValue(int Value);
};
```

a) How many member functions does class `Widget` have? Explain.

b) How many data members does class `Widget` have? Explain.

c) Is the function `SetValue()` defined in the `class Widget` a constructor? Explain.

d) Is the function `SetValue()` a public member function of the class `Widget`? Explain.

e) Can the `Widget public` member functions access the `Widget` data member `DataItem`? Explain.

f) Can a client function access the `Widget` data member `Flag`? Explain.

g) Does the class `Widget` support information hiding? Explain.

9.12 Develop a cloud representation for the class `Random`. Show an instantiation of the class for a `Random` object that is associated with the interval 1 through 10.

9.13 Develop a cloud representation for the class `RYG`. Also show an instantiation of the class.

9.14 Modify the rational library header file to include prototypes for the other arithmetic and relational operators.

9.15 Modify the rational library to include implementations of public arithmetic `Subtract()` and `Divide()` facilitators for subtraction and division.

9.16 Modify the rational library to include an implementation of auxiliary relational operators `-` and `/`. The implementation should use the facilitators developed in the previous exercise.

9.17 Modify the rational library to include an implementation of a public mutator `Reduce()` that ensures that the rational number representation has a relatively prime numerator and denominator. Hint: Divide the numerator and denominator by their greatest common divisor (use Euclid's algorithm to determine their greatest common divisor).

9.18 Modify the rational library to include implementations of public relational facilitators `Equal()` and `LessThan()` for testing equality and less-than relationships.

9.19 Modify the rational library to include an implementation of auxiliary relational operators `==` and `<`. The implementation should use the facilitators developed in the previous exercise.

9.20 Modify the rational library to include implementations of the relational operators `<=`, `>`, and `>=`. Your implementation should make use of the operators defined in the previous exercise.

9.21 Modify the definition of `Rational` member function `Extract()` so that it verifies that a slash was extracted between the numerator and denominator. Discuss whether the function should do its own validation, or should the validation by `SetDenominator()` suffice.

9.22 Place two insertion statements inside each of the member functions defined in `rational.cpp`. The first insertion should be placed at the beginning of the statement body, and it should display which member has been invoked. The second insertion should be placed at the end of the statement body, and it should indicate which member has finished executing. Run Program 9.1 and examine the output. Account for each occurrence in the output of these member-identifying statements.

9.23 The `Rational` constructors and the `Rational` member function `Extract()` invoke the mutators `SetNumerator()` and `SetDenominator()` in a similar manner. The two invocation statements in these members can be replaced by the single invocation of a new `Rational` member `SetRational()`, which in turn does the two invocations. This member function would have two **int** value parameters `numer` and `denom` that are used to set the numerator and denominator of the invoking object. Add a prototype of the new member to the `Rational` class definition and its implementation to source file `rational.cpp`. Discuss your choice of making the new member **public**, **protected**, or **private**.

9.24 Modify the rational library to include an explicitly defined copy constructor.

9.25 Modify the rational library to include a public member function `FloatingPoint()` that returns a floating-point representation of the object.

9.26 Modify `Rational` member function `Insert()` to have default parameter value of `cout`. Where should the default value be specified? Why?

9.27 Modify `Rational` member function `Extract()` to have default parameter value of `cin`. Where should the default value be specified? Why?

9.28 Design an auxiliary function `power()` with two parameters `r` and `n`. Parameter `r` is a `Rational` and n is an **int**. The function should return r^n. Discuss your choices for parameter declarations and return type.

9.29 Design an ADT library `complex` for complex numbers. Discuss your decisions for member functions and operators as well as for auxiliary functions and operators. Also discuss your access restrictions. Compare your decisions to those made in the standard complex library.

9.30 Implement your version of the complex library of Exercise 9.29. Also implement a program that demonstrates the features of your library.

9.31 Design an ADT library `Position` for graph coordinates. There should be two floating-point data members in each class object representing the x-value and y-value of a coordinate. Discuss your decisions for member functions and operators as well as auxiliary functions and operators. Also discuss your access restrictions.

9.32 Implement the `Position` library of Exercise 9.31. Also implement a program that demonstrates the features of your library.

9.33 Use the `Position` ADT of Exercise 9.31 to construct an ADT `Line` for representing lines. A line object will have two data members both of which are coordinates. This is an example of a *has-a* relationship—a line has a coordinate attribute.

9.34 Design and develop an ADT to represent the weekly stock information for the stock-interval problem of Chapter 6. Implement the ADT and a program that uses the ADT to solve the stock-interval problem. Because stock prices are normally kept as rational numbers, your ADT should represent stock information as `Rational` objects.

9.35 Create a simulation of die rolling. Define two `Random` objects `Dice1` and `Dice2` whose pseudorandom number sequences are from the interval one through six. Simulate 10,000 rolls of the die. For each role, compute the sum of the two numbers. Maintain the number of times each sum occurs. Compare your totals with the expected number of times each sum should occur.

9.36 Modify the `Random` class so that it has a single constructor with three optional parameters. This constructor should replace the existing constructors, so the default values for the optional parameters should be set in a manner that maintains the current behavior.

9.37 Modify the `RYG` class so that the response given by member function `Display()` is colored squares rather than text as in the following figure.

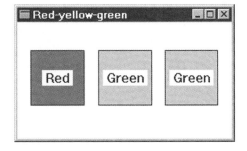

Use `RectangleShape` objects to create the squares. This change requires that the red-yellow-green-game `main()` of Listing 9.14 be replaced with an `ApiMain()`. You may also find it convenient to add a reference parameter `W` of type `SimpleWindow` to `Display()`. The actual `SimpleWindow` object used by `Display()` should be an object local to `Play()`.

9.38 Modify the `Guess` class so that a user guess is extracted as three **char** objects. If the extracted objects are of the correct form, then convert the character digit representation to numeric digit representations. If the extracted objects are not of the correct form, then generate an error message. What are the advantages of doing the extraction this way?

9.39 Design an ADT for the red-yellow-green game where the ADT object takes on the role of the guesser.

9.40 Modify `Guess` member function `SetDigit()` to validate that the new digit value is a proper value.

9.41 Modify the `Response` constructor to verify that its parameters correspond to valid color counts (i.e., the parameter sum is 3 and the individual parameters are part of the interval 1 ... 3).

9.42 Modify the `Response` mutators `SetRed()`, `SetYellow()`, and `SetGreen()` to verify that the new counts falls in the interval 1 to 3. If these member functions do this testing, is it necessary for the modified constructor of Exercise 9.42 to verify their individual values? Why?

9.43 Design and implement an ADT to represent an instance of the game of tic-tac-toe. Your implementation of the ADT should use the EzWindows library to display a graphical view of the game's progress as in the following figure.

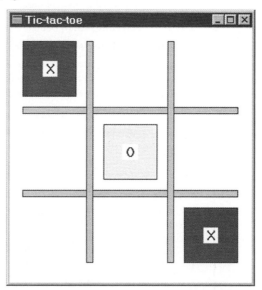

CHAPTER 10

Arrays

Introduction

In many problem situations, a programmer needs the ability to define a group of objects or, in programming parlance, an array. Arrays can be defined to represent both one-dimensional and multidimensional lists. Our examination of arrays considers how to define and manipulate them. We also consider how to efficiently sort and search an array of values.

Key Concepts

- one-dimensional arrays
- subscripting
- first-class type
- arrays as parameters
- array elements as parameters
- strings
- multidimensional arrays
- tables
- matrices
- sorting
- function `InsertionSort()`
- function `QuickSort()`
- searching
- function `BinarySearch()`
- member initialization list

10.1

NAMED COLLECTIONS

Suppose you need to find the minimum value from a group of five **int** objects Value1, Value2, through Value5. The following code segment computes that value.

```
int MinimumSoFar = Value1;
if (Value2 < MinimumSoFar)
    MinimumSoFar = Value2;
if (Value3 < MinimumSoFar)
    MinimumSoFar = Value3;
if (Value4 < MinimumSoFar)
    MinimumSoFar = Value4;
if (Value5 < MinimumSoFar)
    MinimumSoFar = Value5;
```

Notice that a separate **if** statement is needed for each object in the group because, although the object names are similar, each object is totally independent of the other objects.

Now suppose that you need the minimum value from a group of 1,000 objects Value1 through Value1000. Because of object independence, you cannot simply introduce iteration into the solution as was done for the averaging problem in Chapter 4. And if you proceed as above, with a separate **if** statement for each object in the group, the resulting very large code segment would be both clumsy and error prone. Instead, what you need is the C++ *array* type mechanism that allows a group of objects of the same type—an array—to be created in a single definition.

The objects in the array can be referenced collectively or individually. They can be any fundamental type, pointer type, or previously defined derived type (we delay our discussion of pointer object arrays until Chapter 12).

10.2

ONE-DIMENSIONAL ARRAYS

Like other objects, arrays can be defined either with or without initialization. If initialization is not used, then a one-dimensional array has the following form:

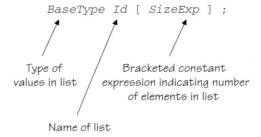

BaseType Id [*SizeExp*] ;

Type of
values in list

Bracketed constant
expression indicating number
of elements in list

Name of list

where *BaseType* is the type of the individual elements in the array; *Id* is an identifier that is the name of the array; and *SizeExp* is a constant, positive expression that uses literals or constants derived from literals to specify the number of objects in the array.

Suppose the following constant definitions are in effect.

```
const int N = 20;
const int M = 40;
const int MaxStringSize = 80;
const int MaxListSize = 1000;
```

Then the following are all correct C++ array definitions.

```
int A[10];                  // array of 10 ints
char B[MaxStringSize];      // array of 80 chars
float C[M*N];               // array of 800 floats
int Values[MaxListSize];    // array of 1000 ints
```

A, B, C, and Values are now one-dimensional arrays. Each of these objects is a collection of individual *array elements*. Each array element is itself an object that can be used like any other object.

The act of referring to an individual array element is called *subscripting* or *indexing*. Just as brackets are used in a definition to indicate that an array is being created, so too are brackets used to subscript a particular element of an array. Each element of an array has its own subscript value. The first element of an array has subscript value 0, the second element of an array has subscript value 1, and so on. For array A, the last element has subscript value 9. The following figure shows a representation of A. A dash indicates that the element is uninitialized.

In the following code segment, the references to individual array elements of A are all correct.

```
int i = 7;
int j = 2;
int k = 4;
A[0] = 1;              // element 0 of A given value 1
A[i] = 5;              // element i of A given value 5
A[j] = A[i] + 3;       // element j of A given value
                       // of element i of A plus 3
A[j+1] = A[i] + A[0];  // element j+1 of A given value
                       // of element i of A plus
                       // value of element 0 of A
A[A[j]] = 12;          // element A[j] of A given
                       // value 12
cout << A[2];          // element 2 of A is displayed
cin >> A[k];           // element k of A given next
                       // extracted value
```

If the value extracted from the standard input stream was the value 3, then the effect of executing the preceding code segment is

A	1		8	6	3			5	12	
	A[0]	A[1]	A[2]	A[3]	A[4]	A[5]	A[6]	A[7]	A[8]	A[9]

Programmer Alert

Bad subscripting

C++ does not provide an automatic way for ensuring that proper subscripts are used. For example, the following code segment does not generate an error message.

```cpp
int A[10];
int B[5];
B[-5] = 1;
```

Instead of an error message, the likely effect of the preceding assignment is to modify the memory location of object `A[5]` because most compilers would assign array `B` immediately after array `A` in their activation record. Therefore, `B[-5]` would be referring to the fifth element from the end of `A`, which is `A[5]`.

The most common subscript error is misreferencing the last element of an array. Both beginning and experienced programmers sometimes forget that the last element of the array has a subscript one less than the size of the array.

10.2.1

Array initialization

Individual array element objects are initialized in a manner similar to other objects. In particular, arrays defined in the global scope with fundamental base types have their array elements set to zero unless there is explicit initialization. In addition, arrays defined in a local scope with fundamental base types have their array elements uninitialized unless there is explicit initialization.

The following four array definitions initialize all five of their elements to zero.

```cpp
int Frequency[5] = {0, 0, 0, 0, 0};
int Total[5] = {0};
int Sum[5]({0, 0, 0, 0, 0});
int Count[5]({0});
```

The definition of `Frequency` explicitly sets all of its elements to zero. The definition of `Total` explicitly sets its first array element `Total[0]` to zero and uses the C++ rule that if only a partial initialization is given, the unspecified elements are set to zero. The definitions of `Sum` and `Count` are analogous using the alternative initialization form.

The following array definitions also do explicit initialization. Since no *SizeExp* is provided, the number of elements in each definition is determined by the number of initialization expressions.

```
int Digits[] = {0, 1, 2, 3, 4, 5, 6, 7, 8, 9};
int Zero[] = {0};
char Alphabet[] = {'a', 'b', 'c', 'd', 'e', 'f', 'g',
 'h', 'i', 'j', 'k', 'l', 'm', 'n', 'o', 'p', 'q',
 'r', 's', 't', 'u', 'v', 'w', 'x', 'y', 'z'};
```

The definition of array `Digits` results in a 10-element array with `Digits[0]` being initialized to zero, `Digits[1]` being initialized to 1, and so on. The definition of `Zero` results in a single-element array with `Zero[0]` being initialized to 0. A single element array is still an array and is treated by C++ consistently in that manner. The definition of `Alphabet` defines a 26-element array with `Alphabet[0]` being initialized to `'a'`, `Alphabet[1]` being initialized to `'b'`, and so on.

When an array is defined with a class base type, initialization is always performed regardless of the scope. The default constructor for the class is automatically applied to each individual array element. Since the default constructor is applied, no explicit initialization is given.

In the following example, an array R of 10 `Rational` objects is defined. Each of the array elements is initialized to represent the default `Rational` value of 0/1.

```
Rational R[10]; // ten rationals initialized to 0/1
```

10.2.2

Constant arrays

As in other object definitions, the modifier **const** can be applied in an array definition. The modifier has the usual effect—after applying the initialization, the object is treated as a constant. For an array this means that the values of the individual array elements cannot be changed. The following example defines and initializes a two-element array B. Afterwards, neither of the array element values can be changed.

```
const int B[2] = {10, 100};
```

With the preceding **const** definition in effect, the following statements are invalid.

```
B[0] = 20;       // illegal: a const object cannot be
                 // the target of an assignment
cin >> B[1];     // illegal: a const object cannot be
                 // the target of an extraction
```

A **const** array element is properly used in contexts where only a value is needed.

```
int i = B[1];    // legal: i is a copy of B[1]
cout << B[0];    // legal: B[0] is inserted to the
                 // standard output stream
```

10.2.3

Simple array processing

The following code segment extracts up to `MaxListSize` values from standard input and assigns them in turn to an array A.

```
const int MaxListSize = 10;
int A[MaxListSize];
int n = 0;
int CurrentInput;
while ((n < MaxListSize) && (cin >> CurrentInput)) {
    A[n] = CurrentInput;
    ++n;
}
```

The array A can represent up to `MaxListSize` list values. Because the user may not necessarily provide that many values, an object n is defined to represent the number of elements in the list that have been assigned values. It will be the case during the processing that the assigned elements (if any) are A[0] through A[n-1]. Thus, the place to store a newly extracted value is A[n]. At the beginning of the code segment none of the array elements has yet been assigned a value, so n is initialized to zero.

The preceding code segment also defines an object `CurrentInput` to store the current extracted value from the standard input stream.

A **while** construct is then used to process the extractions. The **while** loop body iterates if the two terms in the test expression are both true.

- The term (n < ListSize) when true indicates that there is an unassigned element in A to store a value. Because of the short-circuit evaluation of logical expressions, if this term is false, the second term is not evaluated.
- The term (cin >> CurrentInput) when true indicates that there is an extracted value.

If the **while** loop body is executed, the next available array element is used to store the current input value.

```
A[n] = CurrentInput;
```

After this assignment n is incremented to reflect that another value has been added to the list.

```
++n;
```

The **while**-test expression is then reevaluated, and if it is true, the process is repeated.

Suppose the input stream looks like the following:

```
4 9 5
```

The first time through the loop, n is zero, so A[0] is assigned the input value 4. The memory associated with array A would now look like the following:

A	4	–	–	–	–	–	–	–	–	–

In the next iteration, n will have been incremented to 1, and A[1] will be assigned the input value 9.

A	4	9	–	–	–	–	–	–	–	–

In the following iteration, n will have been incremented to 2, and A[2] and will be assigned 5.

A	4	9	5	–	–	–	–	–	–	–

Notice by incrementing n after each assignment of an input value to an array element, n does represent the number of elements in A that have been set.

If after n has been incremented it is equal to MaxListSize, the test expression is false, and the loop is terminated. The termination is necessary because there are no more unassigned elements in A for storing additional input values. If the loop is instead terminated because there are no more input values, then n also has the correct value for this case.

If the input stream is initially empty, the loop body is never executed and n remains 0, reflecting the correct value for this case.

Thus, no matter how many times the loop body is executed, when the loop is finished, n reflects the number of values assigned to the list.

In the next example, an array List with m elements is searched for a particular value that is commonly called the *key*.

```
cout << "Enter the search value (number): ";
int Key;
cin >> Key;
int i;
for (i = 0; (i < m) && (List[i] != Key); ++i) {
    continue;
}
if (i == m)
    cout << Key << " is not in the list" << endl;
else
    cout << Key << " is the " << i
        << "-th element in the list" << endl;
```

Suppose m is the number of array elements in List that have been set so far (it has the role of n for A). Therefore, only array elements List[0] through List[m-1] must be examined. Because the number m of array elements that have been set is known, a **for** statement easily expresses the subscripts of the array elements that need to be considered—0 through m-1 in increments of one. We use iterator i, to represent the current subscript value. The value of i must be available after the loop, so we cannot declare it in the **for** loop.

The **for**-loop test expression processes the current array element List[i]. As in the **while** loop that initialized A, there are two terms that must be true for the loop to be iterated. The terms for the **for** loop are

■ The term (i < m) when true indicates that there is a current element in List for testing whether it matches the key value. Because of short-circuit evaluation, if this term is false, the second term is not evaluated.

■ The term (List[i] != Key) when true indicates that the current element is not equal to the key value.

If the test expression is true, we must continue our search for the key value in the next element of List. Because the increment of i in the **for**-loop post expression sets up the next evaluation of the test expression, no actions need to be taken in the **for**-loop body itself.

There are several ways to indicate that the loop body requires no action. For example, an empty statement is a legal statement in C++, so the loop could be represented in the following manner:

```
for (i = 0; (i < m) && (List[i] != Key); ++i) {
    ;
}
```

We chose to use the keyword **continue** in a **continue** statement.

```
for (i = 0; (i < m) && (List[i] != Key); ++i) {
    continue;
}
```

A **continue** statement in a loop body indicates that the execution of the body is finished for this iteration. It is thus vaguely similar to the **break** statement.

By examining the value of i after the **for** loop has terminated, we can determine whether one of the array elements of List has the same value as Key.

If i has value m, then all of the array elements were examined and the loop was terminated because there were no more elements to consider (remember List[0] through List[m-1] were the elements to consider). In this case, the key value is not present, and an appropriate message is inserted to the output stream.

If i does not have the value of m, then it must be that the **for** loop terminated because (List[i] != Key) was false for some i with a value between 0 and m-1. In this case, List[i] is the key value, and the appropriate message is inserted to the standard output stream.

We now trace through the code segment using the following representation for List, m, Key, and i. In terms of execution, we are about to begin the **for** loop.

List | 4 | 9 | 5 | — | — | — | — | — | — | — |

m | 3 |

Key | 5 |

i | — |

The initialization step of the **for** loop is first executed, and iterator i is assigned the value 0.

List	4	9	5	–	–	–	–	–	–	–

m	3

Key	5

i	0

The test expression is then evaluated. Based upon the values of List, m, key, and i, both terms are true (0 is less than 3, and 4 is not equal to 5). Iterator i is then incremented to 1, to prepare for the next evaluation.

List	4	9	5	–	–	–	–	–	–	–

m	3

Key	5

i	1

The test expression is then reevaluated. Based upon the values of List, m, key, and i, both terms are again true (1 is less than 3, and 9 is not equal to 5). Iterator i is then incremented to 2 to prepare for the next evaluation.

List	4	9	5	–	–	–	–	–	–	–

m	3

Key	5

i	2

The test expression is again reevaluated. Based upon the values of List, m, key, and i, the first term remains true, but the second term is now false (2 is less than 3, but 5 is equal to 5). Because the terms must both be true for the loop to iterate, the **for** loop is terminated.

The **if** statement is then evaluated, and its test expression is found to be false (2 is not equal to 3). As a result, the following output occurs.

```
5 is the 2-th element in the list
```

The key value search code segment is typical of array processing. There is initialization to prepare for the processing of the array, a loop to process each array element in turn, and a check to see whether the processing of the list is completed. For example, the following code segment finds the minimum value of a list Values where the list size m is at least 1.

```
int MinimumSoFar = Values[0];
for (int i = 1; i < m; ++i) {
    if (Values[i] < MinimumSoFar)
        MinimumSoFar = Values[i];
}
```

To find the minimum value in an array requires examining each element in turn. If the code segment keeps track of the minimum array element value seen so far, the lesser of that value and the current element is the minimum value seen so far. If this processing is done for each array element, then after the last array element has been considered, the minimum value seen so far is in fact the minimum. Notice that the above code segment for finding the minimum of an arbitrarily sized list is even smaller than the code segment that was presented at the start of this chapter for finding the minimum of five values!

The following code segment is a commented version of the previous code segment. The numbered comments reflect the preceding discussion. The comments are essentially invariants regarding the value of `MinimumSoFar`.

```
int MinimumSoFar = Values[0];
// (1): MinimumSoFar is minimum in Values[0] ...
// Values[0]
for (int i = 1; i < m; ++i) {
    // (2): MinimumSoFar is minimum in Values[0]
    // ... Values[i-1]
    if (Values[i] < MinimumSoFar)
        MinimumSoFar = Values[i];
    // (3): MinimumSoFar is minimum in Values[0]
    // ... Values[i]
}
// (4): MinimumSoFar is minimum in Values[0] ...
// Values[m-1]
```

The first comment is true because `MinimumSoFar` is initially set to `Values[0]`. The second comment is true the first time the **for** body is executed because `i-1` at that point is zero and the first comment is known to be true. The third comment is true if the second comment was true because the **if** statement that precedes the third comment updates `MinimumSoFar` if in fact `List[i]` is the minimum value in `Values[0]` through `Values[i]`. If the **for** body is repeated, the second comment is again true because the comment at that point is simply a restatement of the third comment from the previous iteration using the incremented value of `i`. The fourth comment is true because it is simply either a restatement of the third comment (if m is greater than one) or a restatement of the first comment (if m is one). Since the fourth comment is true, we have correctly determined the minimum value in the list.

10.3

REPRESENTING STRINGS AS CHARACTER STRINGS

C++ provides another initialization style for **char** arrays to support the representation of character strings. For example, the following definition of `Letters` defines and initializes a *27*-element array.

```
char Letters[] = "abcdefghijklmnopqrstuvwxyz";
```

The first 26 elements of the array—Letters[0] through Letters[25]—get their initialization character from the corresponding position in the initialization string. That is, the array element Letters[0] gets the first character 'a' in the string, the second array element Letters[1] gets the second character in the string 'b', and so on through the 26th element Letters[25] that gets the 26th character in the string 'z'.

The last array element Letters[26] is initialized to the null character '\0'. Array element Letters[26] is created because the C++ representation for character strings includes a null character at the end of a string.

The following array definition creates a 13-element array with Greetings[0] being initialized to 'H', Greetings[1] being initialized to 'e', and so on through Greetings[11] being initialized to 'd' and Greetings[12] being initialized to '\0'.

```
char Greetings[] = "Hello, world";
```

The iostream library includes a definition of the insertion operator << for a right operand that is a **char** array. The operation displays all of the characters of the array that precede the first null character in the array. For example, the following insertion causes the phrase "Hello, world" to be displayed to the standard output stream.

```
cout << Greetings;
```

The extraction operator is also defined in the iostream library for a right operand that is a **char** array. The extraction by default first skips leading whitespace characters and then extracts the next sequence of non-white-space characters from the input stream. A null '\0' is automatically stored in the array element that occurs after the element that holds the last extracted character. If the standard input stream contains

```
how    are you    today?  i am fine
```

then the following code segment

```
const int MaxStringSize = 10;
char S[MaxStringSize];
while (cin >> S) {
   cout << S << endl;
}
```

will display the non-white-space strings one per line.

```
how
are
you
today?
i
am
fine
```

Upon completion of the code segment, the memory associated with array S would look like the following:

S	'f'	'i'	'n'	'e'	'\0'	'?'	'\0'	—	—	—

The question mark character and the second end-of-string character remain as array values in S because the final extraction involved only four characters.

Although the extraction operator is defined to work with **char** array objects, its use is generally avoided because we cannot be sure that the size of the array will be sufficiently large to hold the next input string. Instead the characters are either explicitly extracted character-by-character and assigned to an array or one of the overloaded versions of the istream member functions get() or getline() is used.

One version of member function get() has two required parameters and one optional parameter (see Appendix B for a description of other iostream member functions). The required parameters are an array of type **char** and a length. The optional parameter is a **char** whose default value is the newline '\n'. This character is called the *delimiter*. Characters are extracted from the input stream and assigned to the next available array element until one of the following conditions has occurred.

- There are no more characters to extract; that is, end of file is reached.
- The next character to be extracted would be the delimiter.
- The number of extracted characters is one less character than the value of the second parameter.

Regardless of which of the three conditions causes the string extraction process to terminate, a null '\0' is stored in the element following the array element that holds the last extracted value.

The istream member function getline() operates in a similar manner to the preceding member function get() except that if the delimiter is encountered, it is also extracted. However, the delimiter is not assigned to its array parameter.

If the standard input stream contains

```
A
multi-line
  example.
```

then code segment

```
const int MaxStringSize = 10;
char S[MaxStringSize];
while (cin.getline(S, MaxStringSize)) {
    cout << S << endl;
}
```

produces

```
A
multi-lin
e
  example.
```

Upon completion, the memory associated with array S would look like the following:

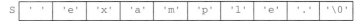

S | ' ' | 'e' | 'x' | 'a' | 'm' | 'p' | 'l' | 'e' | '.' | '\0' |

Programming Tip

Character strings or string class strings?

Prior to this chapter, when we had string processing needs, we used the class `string` from the string library. In subsequent chapters, we will continue to do so because the `string` class is a first-class type. We will use a character string representation when we want access to older style library functions that are based on character strings. Although we need not be concerned with how the `string` class is implemented, we can expect that it uses in part a character string.

So far our examples have used arrays as local objects. In the next section we develop several useful functions that have arrays as parameters. These functions perform list extraction, list insertion, and list searching.

10.4

ARRAYS AS PARAMETERS

The original developers of C, the predecessor language of C++, were concerned with efficiency. For this reason they did not make an array type a *first-class type*. By this we mean that array objects cannot be used in conjunction with certain language features that are applicable to objects of other types. This limitation has carried over into the C++ language in two major ways.

- A function return type cannot be an array.

- An array parameter can only be a reference parameter.

Relaxing these restrictions would require a copy to be made of each individual array element. This requirement could be quite costly with respect to both memory and processing time if an array is composed of many elements.

The syntax for an array parameter reflects that it can be passed only by reference. No `&` is required or expected in the definition of an array parameter.

The syntax for an array parameter definition allows the size of a one-dimensional array to be omitted from within the brackets. This flexibility means that the same function can process arrays of different sizes. This flexibility does not occur in other languages such as Pascal, which makes the size of the array an integral part of the parameter declaration. Although C++ functions do not need the size of the array as part of the parameter declaration, another parameter usually indicates how many elements of the array should be processed.

We now define a **void** function GetList() that has three formal parameters. This function will extract values from input stream cin and store them in an array.

```
void GetList(int A[], int MaxN, int &n) {
   for (n = 0; (n < MaxN) && (cin >> A[n]); ++n) {
      continue;
   }
}
```

The first parameter is the array A that holds the extracted values. The second parameter MaxN is the maximum number of values to be extracted. The third parameter n upon completion of the function indicates the number of extracted values. It will be the case that MaxN differs from n only if cin does not contain sufficient input values. Both A and n are reference parameters—A because arrays are always passed by reference and n because of the reference parameter syntax.

The body of function GetList() consists of a single **for** statement. As in the key searching code segment, no action is required in the **for** loop body.

The loop test expression has two terms that must be true for the loop to be iterated. The test expression was designed to use the short-circuit evaluation feature of C++. The first term ensures that the number of extracted values so far is less than the maximum number of values to be extracted. Only if this term is true, is the second term evaluated. The evaluation of the second term causes an extraction to be attempted from cin that assigns a value to the next available element of A, which is A[n]. If the extraction is unsuccessful, the value of the operation is 0, which corresponds to false and results in the loop being terminated. If the extraction is successful, the value of the operation is nonzero, which corresponds to true. Thus if a value is assigned to element A[n], the overall test expression is true.

If the test expression is true, n is incremented. The incrementing reflects that another value has been extracted and assigned to the array.

Suppose the standard input stream contained the following values:

```
6 9 82 11 29 85
11 28 91
```

Then code segment

```
const int MaxListSize = 10;
int Scores[MaxListSize];
int NbrScores;
GetList(Scores, MaxListSize, NbrScores);
```

would assign array Scores in the following manner:

Scores	6	9	82	11	29	85	11	28	91	—

Scores is modified because when an element of formal reference parameter array A is set, we in fact change the corresponding element of Scores. The preceding code segment also sets NbrScores to 9.

It is important to observe that the invocation of `GetList()` does not use brackets in passing the actual array parameter `Scores`. In the code segment, it is known that `Scores` is an array; therefore, no brackets are needed.

The next function that we consider is `PrintList()`.

```
void PrintList(const int A[], int n) {
   for (int i = 0; i < n; ++i) {
      cout << A[i] << endl;
   }
}
```

This **void** function has two formal parameters: A and n. The first parameter is the **int** array to be displayed. Because displaying a list does not require any modification to its elements, the modifier **const** is used. The second parameter is a value parameter that represents the number of elements in the array to be displayed. The function uses a **for** statement to iteratively display n array element values one per line to the standard output stream. For example, the following invocation displays our previously defined array `Scores`.

```
PrintList(Scores, NbrScores);
```

The following output results.

```
6
9
82
11
29
85
11
28
91
```

We next consider an **int** function `Search()`, which has three formal parameters. The first parameter is an **int** array `List`; the second parameter is the number of elements m to be considered, and the third parameter is the key value `Key`.

```
int Search(const int List[], int m, int Key) {
   for (int i = 0; i < m; ++i) {
      if (List[i] == Key) {
         return i;
      }
   }
   return m;
}
```

Function `Search()` is similar in purpose to the code segment that searched an array for a key value earlier in this chapter. However, function `Search()` does not display a message indicating whether it found the value. If `Search()` finds the key value in the list, it returns the subscript of the first matching element. If the key value is not among the array element values, `Search()` returns the number of elements m in the list. Because the list elements occupy subscript positions 0 through m-1 in the array, the value m indicates that the key value is not in the list.

In the following code segment, the previously defined array `Scores` is searched for two values.

```
int i1 = Search(Scores, NbrScores, 11);
int i2 = Search(Scores, NbrScores, 30);
```

The first invocation initializes `i1` to 3 because the first match of the value 11 in the array `Scores` is with `Scores[3]`. The second invocation initializes `i2` to 9 (the value of `NbrScores`) because none of array elements `Scores[0]` through `Scores[8]` matches the value 30.

Although when using an array as an actual parameter there is no use of subscripts, subscripts are used when an individual array element is passed as an actual parameter. The use of brackets is necessary here because it is the subscript that allows a particular element to be specified. For example, the function `main()` of Program 10.1 invokes the function `Swap()`—originally defined in Chapter 7—to interchange the values of a pair of elements from the **int** array `Number`.

```
Swap(Number[i], Number[n-1-i]);
```

The definition of function `Swap()` specifies that its two arguments are **int** reference parameters. Because the base type of `Number` is **int**, passing two `Number` array elements to `Swap()` is appropriate.

Program 10.1 initializes the array `Number` using function `GetList()`. After reversing the order of the values in the list, function `PrintList()` is used to display the list.

10.5

SORTING

In Chapter 4 we introduced the notion of sorting when we considered Program 4.3 that would display its three input values in nondecreasing order. We used the term nondecreasing rather than increasing because there can be duplicate values. In this chapter we consider the general sorting problem of arranging the values in an array of arbitrary size into nondecreasing order.

A sort is often an iterative process that rearranges some of the values in the array on each iteration. For example, on iteration i the method known as `SelectionSort()` finds the ith smallest element of A and exchanges the value of that element with the value of array element `A[i]`. In another example, on iteration i the method known as `InsertionSort()` correctly places the value of `A[i]` with respect to the values stored in array elements `A[0]` through `A[i-1]`.

Some sorts are recursive rather than iterative. The recursive methods typically decompose an array into sublists that are then separately sorted. If it is necessary to complete the task, the sorted sublists are merged into a single sorted list.

Program 10.1

Display input values in reverse order

```
// Program 10.1: Display inputs in reverse order
#include <iostream.h>

void GetList(int A[], int MaxN, int &n);
void Swap(int &Value1, int &Value2);
void PrintList(const int A[], int n);

// main(): manage extraction, reversal, and display of
// list
int main() {
   const int MaxListSize = 100;
   int Number[MaxListSize];
   int n;
   GetList(Number, MaxListSize, n);
   for (int i = 0; i < n/2; ++i) {
      // swap element from front of list with
      // corresponding element from the end of the list
      Swap(Number[i], Number[n-1-i]);
   }
   PrintList(Number, n);
   return 0;
}

// GetList(): extract up to MaxN value from input into A
void GetList(int A[], int MaxN, int &n) {
   for (n = 0; (n < MaxN) && (cin >> A[n]);++n) {
      continue;
   }
}

// Swap(): interchange values of parameters
void Swap(int &Value1, int &Value2) {
   int RememberValue1 = Value1;
   Value1 = Value2;
   Value2 = RememberValue1;
}

// PrintList(): display n elements of A
void PrintList(const int A[], int n) {
   for (int i = 0; i < n; ++i) {
      cout << A[i] << endl;
   }
}
```

We consider here the iterative sort `InsertionSort()` and the recursive sort `QuickSort()`. Function `SelectionSort()` and another sort are considered in the exercises.

In the discussion that follows, we assume the array to be sorted is a **char** array. The same sorts can be modified easily for other types of values.

10.5.1

The InsertionSort() method

On iteration `i`, the task of `InsertionSort()` is to place the value of array element `A[i]` correctly with respect to the previously arranged values of array elements `A[0]` through `A[i-1]`. For example, suppose the list to be sorted is

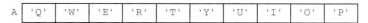

and that we have completed the iterations that placed the first seven values correctly among themselves. The array at that point would look like this:

On the next iteration with `i` being 7, we are to place the value in `A[7]` correctly with respect to the sorted values in `A[0]` through `A[6]`. In this case, the value `'I'` in `A[7]` should come between the value `'E'` in `A[0]` and the value `'R'` in `A[1]`. To do so, we first copy the value of `A[7]` to a temporary object `v` and then shift the values in `A[1]` through `A[6]`. At that point, the array would look like this:

```
A   'E'   'R'   'R'   'Q'   'T'   'U'   'W'   'Y'   'O'   'P'
```

We then copy the value `'I'` from object `v` to `A[1]` to complete the iteration.

```
A   'E'   'I'   'R'   'Q'   'T'   'U'   'W'   'Y'   'O'   'P'
```

Although there are several ways to accomplish the shifting process, the preferred method begins by comparing array elements `A[i]` and `A[i-1]`. If these two elements are in the proper order, then no shifting is necessary for iteration `i`, as the first `i` elements of the array are already in sorted order—the sublist composed of the first `i-1` elements was previously put in sorted order, and the value of `A[i]` is no smaller than the largest value in that sublist.

If `A[i]` is not less than `A[i-1]`, then to make room for the correct value to be placed into `A[i]`, a copy `v` of `A[i]` is made. Determining which array element values require shifting is straightforward. An iterator `j` is used to indicate which element in `A` should be the target of the next shifting. The initial value for `j` is `i`, and the first value to be shifted is `A[j-1]`. Once the shift has been performed, `j` is decremented. It is decremented because its new value is the index of the location in `A` now available as a target of shifting, or if appropriate, as the location of value `v`. A test is then made to determine which case applies. If `A[j-1]` exists and if `v` is less than `A[j-1]`, the shifting and comparison process is repeated. Otherwise, the right spot for value `v` has been found, and the shifting process is terminated.

For example, suppose i is now 8, and A[i], which is 'O', is less than A[i-1], which is 'Y'. A shifting process must be performed. A copy of 'O' is made and placed in v, and the iterator j is set to 8.

The shifting of A[j-1] and the decrementing of j results in the following situation:

Because 'O' is less than 'W', another shift is performed copying the 'W' to A[j]. In addition, j is decremented.

Because 'O' is also less than 'U', another shift is performed copying the 'U' to A[j]. Iterator j is again decremented.

Because 'O' is also less than 'T', another shift is performed copying the 'T' to A[j]. Iterator j is again decremented.

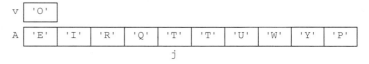

Because 'O' is also less than 'Q', another shift is performed copying the 'Q' to A[j]. Iterator j is again decremented.

Because 'O' is also less than 'R', another shift is performed copying the 'R' to A[j]. Iterator j is again decremented.

Because 'O' is not less than 'I', no shifting is necessary. Instead the 'O' is copied from v into A[j].

A **void** function InsertionSort() that implements the preceding discussion is given in Listing 10.1. An outer **for** loop is used to generate the various values for iterator i, and an inner **do** loop is used to control the shifting process. Two terms in the logical expression control whether the **do** loop is iterated again. The first term determines whether j is greater than 0. If this term is true, element A[j-1] is available for comparison; if instead j is 0, then the shifting has ended—element A[j], which is A[0], is the proper location for v. The second term determines whether A[j-1] is larger than v. If this term is true, additional shifting is necessary. If instead A[j-1] is not larger than v, no more shifting is necessary—element A[j] is the location for v. Observe that regardless of whether the first or second term becomes false, when the loop is completed, A[j] is the location for v.

Listing 10.1

InsertionSort()

```
// InsertionSort(): sort A using a shifting process
void InsertionSort(char A[], int n) {
   for (int i = 1; i < n; ++i) {
      // find proper spot for A[i]
      if (A[i] < A[i-1]) {
         // some shifting is necessary
         char v = A[i];     // copy A[i] so its spot can
                            // be used for shifting
         int j = i;         // set up iterator where
                            // available array element
                            // spot is located

         do {
            A[j] = A[j-1];  // do the value shift
            --j;            // prepare for next
                            // comparison
         } while ((j > 0) && (A[j-1] > v));
         A[j] = v;          // put v in its spot
      }
   }
}
```

10.5.2

Quality of InsertionSort()

In analyzing a sorting algorithm, we are normally concerned with the total number of array element comparisons and the total number of array element copies/assignments performed by the sort. For InsertionSort(), the number of array element comparisons and copies/assignments is maximized when, for each iteration i, the value of A[i] is the smallest of the first i element values (i.e., A is in reverse-sorted order). This means when i is 1, at most 1 element comparison and 3 element copies/assignments are made. When i is 2, at most 2 element comparisons and 4 element copies/assignments are made.

In general, on iteration i, at most i element comparisons and i+2 element copies/assignments are made by InsertionSort(). The total number of element comparisons is therefore at most 1 + 2 + ... + n-1, which is proportional to n^2. The total number of element copies/assignments is at most 3 + 4 + ... + n+2, which is also proportional to n^2. These totals reflect the worst-case performance of InsertionSort(). Because the performance is proportional to the square of the number of array elements, we say that the algorithm has *quadratic* worst-case performance.

Suppose InsertionSort() is given an array of values in arbitrary order. For an average iteration, with an arbitrary initial ordering of values, value v is shifted on average into the middle element of the current sublist. This means that both the expected number of element comparisons and the expected number of element copies/assignments for an arbitrary list of n elements are proportional to one-half the worst-case performance. Because $n^2/2$ is proportional to n^2, the *arbitrary-case* performance of InsertionSort() is also quadratic.

When InsertionSort() is given an array of elements with the values already in sorted order, only one element comparison is made per iteration and no element copies/assignments are made. This means for an already sorted array of n elements, that n-1 comparisons are made and no element copies/assignments are made. This behavior represents the *best-case performance* of InsertionSort(). Because the performance is proportional to the number of elements, we say that InsertionSort() has a *linear* best-case performance.

Many data processing experts believe that the typical list to be sorted has been systematically generated and is already nearly sorted. A nearly sorted list is hard to quantify precisely, but roughly speaking in a nearly sorted list, the starting position of each value is near its position in the sorted version of the list. Under this scenario, both the average number of element comparisons and the average number of element copies/assignments performed by InsertionSort() are proportional to n. Because of this performance quality, InsertionSort() is typically the sorting method of choice when we know that the data was systematically generated.

10.5.3

The QuickSort() method

Although `InsertionSort()` has excellent average-case and best-case per-formances, its worst-case and arbitrary-case performances are substandard. For time-critical client applications that need to sort a list of n elements, `InsertionSort()` can be unacceptable. Instead, such applications often use the `QuickSort()` method. The `QuickSort()` method when fully implemented has best-case, arbitrary-case, and average-case performances that are all pro-portional to the expression n log n. This performance is sometimes known as *linearithmic* performance. We note that the worst-case performance of `QuickSort()` is quadratic and arises when the values in the list are in reverse or nearly reverse sorted order. However, such pathological cases are generally deemed too infrequent to matter.

The `QuickSort()` method begins by choosing a pivot value. The list is then rearranged into three sublists or *partitions*. The middle sublist is com-posed of an element whose value is the *pivot value*; the values of the elements in the left sublist are no larger than the pivot value, and the values of the ele-ments in the right sublist are no smaller than the pivot value. Since the sublists are partitioned in this manner, the left and right sublists can be sorted indepen-dently to produce a totally sorted list. The sublists are sorted by making recur-sive calls to the `QuickSort()` method. For example, suppose we are to again sort the following list:

A	'Q'	'W'	'E'	'R'	'T'	'Y'	'U'	'I'	'O'	'P'

If `'P'` is the pivot value, partitioning could rearrange A in the following man-ner (the shaded portion is the middle sublist).

A	'I'	'O'	'E'	'P'	'T'	'Y'	'U'	'R'	'W'	'Q'

We can now separately sort the left sublist A[0] through A[2] and the right sublist A[4] through A[9]. Doing so makes the entire list sorted.

If the pivot element value is chosen well, then the left and right sublists both have approximately n/2 elements. It can be shown mathematically that this partitioning method leads to linearithmic performance.

Listing 10.2 provides the header file `qsort.h`. The header file is a collec-tion of prototypes for functions `QuickSort()`, `Pivot()`, `Partition()`, and `Swap()`. Listing 10.3 provides the implementation file `qsort.cpp` for the `QuickSort()` method.

Listing 10.2

Header file qsort.h for QuickSort()

```
#ifndef QSORT_H
#define QSORT_H

void QuickSort(char A[], int left, int right);
void Pivot(char A[], int left, int right);
int Partition(char A[], int left, int right);
void Swap(char &Value1, char &Value2);

#endif
```

Listing 10.3

Implementation file
qsort.cpp for
QuickSort()

```cpp
#include "qsort.h"

// QuickSort(): sort using variation of Hoare's method
void QuickSort(char A[], int left, int right) {
   if (left < right) {
      Pivot(A, left, right);
      int k = Partition(A, left, right);
      QuickSort(A, left, k-1);
      QuickSort(A, k+1, right);
   }
}

// Pivot(): prepare A for partitioning
void Pivot(char A[], int left, int right) {
   if (A[left] > A[right])
      Swap(A[left], A[right]);
}

// Partition(): rearrange A into 3 sublists, a sublist
// A[left] … A[j-1] of values less than A[j], a sublist
// A[j], and a sublist A[j+1] … A[right]
int Partition(char A[], int left, int right) {
   char pivot = A[left];
   int i = left;
   int j = right+1;
   do {
      do ++i; while (A[i] < pivot);
      do --j; while (A[j] > pivot);
      if (i < j) {
         Swap(A[i], A[j]);
      }
   } while (i < j);
   Swap(A[j], A[left]);
   return j;
}

// Swap(): interchange elements
void Swap(char &Value1, char &Value2) {
   char RememberValue1 = Value1;
   Value1 = Value2;
   Value2 = RememberValue1;
}
```

Function `QuickSort()` first makes sure that the list to be sorted requires some processing, that is, there are at least two elements to be ordered. Indexes `left` and `right` indicate the left-most and right-most elements of the portion of array `A` to be sorted in the current invocation of `QuickSort()`. If there are indeed multiple array elements, then function `Pivot()` is invoked first.

The task of `Pivot()` is to rearrange the array so that the pivot value is in `A[left]`. It also ensures that the value of `A[right]` is no smaller than the pivot value. In our basic implementation, `Pivot()` compares elements `A[left]` and `A[right]`. If `A[left]` is greater than `A[right]`, the element values are swapped (in the exercises, we consider a more intelligent function

`Pivot()`). Suppose the array `A` to be sorted had the following representation before the invocation of `Pivot()`.

A	'Q'	'W'	'E'	'R'	'T'	'Y'	'U'	'I'	'O'	'P'

After the invocation of `Pivot()`, `A` would have the following representation.

A	'P'	'W'	'E'	'R'	'T'	'Y'	'U'	'I'	'O'	'Q'

`QuickSort()` next partitions the elements of array `A` that have subscripts in the range `left` through `right`. This task is done by function `Partition()`. When it is done, `Partition()` returns the index of the array element that now contains the pivot value. `QuickSort()` then performs two recursive calls to sort the elements to the left and right of the pivot element.

The bulk of the sorting is done by the invocations of `Partition()`. This function begins by making a copy `pivot` of the pivot value `A[left]`. Two iterators `i` and `j` are then defined. These iterators are used to index array elements from the left and right sides of the array respectively.

The major loop in `Partition()` is a **do** loop that iterates until the iterators `i` and `j` *cross* (the value of the left-side iterator `i` is greater than the value of the right-side iterator `j`).

For each iteration of the **do** loop, `i` is incremented in an inner **do** loop until an array element is found whose value is at least `pivot`. Next `j` is decremented in another inner **do** loop until an array element is found whose value is at most `pivot`. Such array elements must exist because `Pivot()` made `A[left]` the smaller of `A[left]` and `A[right]` and it made `A[right]` the larger of `A[left]` and `A[right]`. We say that `A[left]` and `A[right]` are *sentinels* whose values guarantee that both inner loops of `Partition()` terminate.

If after indexes `i` and `j` have been updated, it is determined the indexes have not crossed each other, then the values of `A[i]` and `A[j]` are in the wrong partitions and need to be swapped. For our example problem, the situation immediately before the first partition swap is the following:

A	'P'	'W'	'E'	'R'	'T'	'Y'	'U'	'I'	'O'	'Q'
	i								j	

After swapping, the situation becomes

A	'P'	'O'	'E'	'R'	'T'	'Y'	'U'	'I'	'W'	'Q'
	i								j	

The process is then repeated. Continuing with our example, the situation immediately before the next swap is

A	'P'	'O'	'E'	'R'	'T'	'Y'	'U'	'I'	'W'	'Q'
				i			j			

and after swapping, the situation becomes

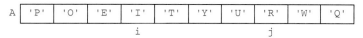

The process continues until the indexes cross each other. For our problem example, the next iteration of outer **do** loop results in the following situation with crossed indexes.

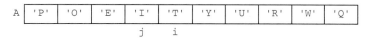

When the indexes cross, the partition has been constructed except for putting the pivot value in the proper spot. At this point in the function's execution, the value of index j represents the subscript of the right-most element belonging to the left partition. If A[j] and A[left] are swapped, then elements A[left] through A[j-1] form the left sublist to be sorted and elements A[j+1] through A[right] form the right sublist to be sorted.

The swapping of A[j] and A[left] results in the following situation:

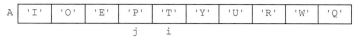

QuickSort() would then make the two recursive calls to sort separately the left sublist composed of the first four elements of A and the right sublist composed of the last five elements of the array A. Figure 10.1 illustrates all of the invocations of QuickSort() to arrange our list correctly. Each entry shows the values of parameters left and right at the start of an invocation.

The arrangement of the values in the array at start of each invocation follows.

```
0 ...  9:  QWERTYUIOP
0 ...  2:  IOEPTYURWQ
0 ... -1:  EOIPTYURWQ
1 ...  2:  EOIPTYURWQ
1 ...  0:  EIOPTYURWQ
2 ...  2:  EIOPTYURWQ
4 ...  9:  EIOPTYURWQ
4 ...  3:  EIOPQYURWT
5 ...  9:  EIOPQYURWT
5 ...  5:  EIOPQRTUWY
7 ...  9:  EIOPQRTUWY
7 ...  6:  EIOPQRTUWY
8 ...  9:  EIOPQRTUWY
8 ...  7:  EIOPQRTUWY
9 ...  9:  EIOPQRTUWY
```

Figure 10.1

Left and right indexes into list
Q W E R T Y U I O P
during QuickSort()
invocations

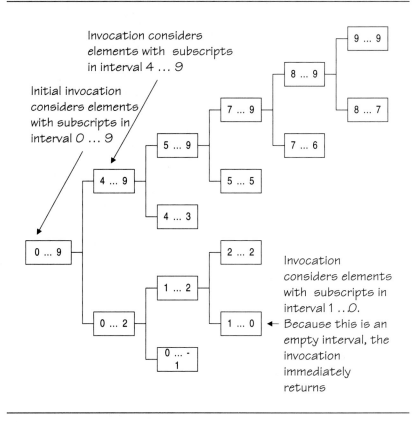

QuickSort() comments

The `QuickSort()` algorithm was developed in 1960 by C. A. R Hoare and is probably the most analyzed computer science algorithm. Our implementation is closest to the version developed by R. Sedgwick in his text *Algorithms in C++*, Reading, MA: Addison-Wesley, 1992. This text also presents, in part, a wide collection of other sorting and searching algorithms useful to programmers.

Because of the importance of `QuickSort()`, implementations of the algorithm are included in the stdlib and standard template libraries.

10.6

BINARY SEARCHING

When the values of a list are in sorted order, there are better searches than function `Search()` for determining whether a particular value is in the list. For example, when you look up a name in the phone book, you do not start in the beginning and scan through until you find the name—you use the fact that the

**Programming
Tip**

names are listed in sorted order and use some intelligence to jump quickly to the right page and then start scanning.

The function `BinarySearch()` given in Listing 10.4 conducts a series of tests that allows it to iteratively reduce the portion of the array `A` that can possibly contain the value `Key`.

Listing 10.4

BinarySearch()

```
// BinarySearch(): examine sorted list A for Key
int BinarySearch(int A[], int n, int Key) {
   int left = 0;
   int right = n-1;
   while (left <= right) {
      int mid = (left + right)/2;
      if (A[mid] == Key)
         return mid;
      else if (A[mid] < Key)
         left = mid + 1;
      else
         right = mid - 1;
   }
   return n;
}
```

The portion of the array that can contain the key value is represented by the indexes `left` and `right`. Prior to the first **if** test, any of the array elements can contain the `Key` value. For this reason, `left` is initialized to 0 and `right` is initialized to n-1, where n is the number of elements in the array. Suppose the array and key value have the following representation:

Function `BinarySearch()` follows the same convention as `Search()`. If the `Key` value is present, then `BinarySearch()` returns the index of a matching element; if the `Key` value is not present, then `BinarySearch()` returns n.

A **while** loop performs the tests that update indexes `left` and `right`. The loop iterates until either the `Key` value has been found or it has been determined that no portion of the list contains the `Key` value.

The body of the **while** loop starts by assigning the average of the current values of `left` and `right` to object `mid`. If element `A[mid]` is equal to the `Key` value, then `mid` is returned.

If element `A[mid]` is less than the `Key` value, then because the array is sorted, all elements to the left of `A[mid]` are also less than the `Key` value. If the `Key` value is to be in the array, it must occur to the right of `A[mid]`. Therefore, index `left` is reset to be to the immediate right of `mid`, that is, `left` becomes `right + 1`. For our example, the value of `Key`, which is `'R'`, is greater than the value of `A[mid]`, which is `'Q'`. This results in the following situation after `mid` is updated in the next iteration.

If element `A[mid]` is neither equal to nor less than the `Key` value, it must be greater than the `Key` value. As the array is sorted, all elements to the right of `A[mid]` are also greater than the `Key` value. If the `Key` value is in the array, it must occur to the left of `A[mid]`. Therefore, in this case index `right` is reset to be to the immediate left of `mid`, that is, `right` becomes `left - 1`. For the previously depicted situation, the value of `Key`, which is `'R'`, is less than the value of A[mid], which is 'U'. This results in the following situation after mid is updated in the next iteration.

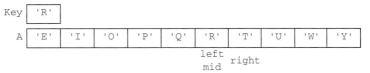

In this situation, the values of Key and A[mid] test equal, so the function returns the value of mid.

It can be shown that in the worst case BinarySearch() performs approximately 2·log n comparisons to process a list of n elements. Consequently, for a sorted list of a 1,000 elements, 20 comparisons are sufficient for BinarySearch() to determine whether the key value is present. It also means that for a sorted list of 1,000,000 elements, BinarySearch() can determine whether a particular value is present using no more than 40 comparisons!

It can also be shown using an information-theoretic argument that any comparison-based search algorithm requires on the order of log n comparisons in the worst case.

10.7

MULTIDIMENSIONAL ARRAYS

In addition to defining one-dimensional lists, it is also possible to define multidimensional lists of objects. For example, the object M defined below is a two-dimensional array.

```
char M[3][4];
```

Array M can be viewed as consisting of three one-dimensional subarrays M[0], M[1], and M[2] with each of these subarrays consisting of four elements. The subarrays are commonly referred to as *rows*. To refer to an individual element of a row, an additional subscript is used. For example, M[i][j] is the jth element of the ith row in M.

Arrays with more than two dimensions are also possible. However, in practice, arrays with three dimensions are seldom used, and arrays with more than three dimensions are almost never used.

When memory is reserved in an activation record for a two-dimensional array, the array's elements are assigned memory locations in *row-major* order, which means the 0th row occurs first, the 1th row occurs next, and so on. Within a row, the elements are assigned memory locations in increasing order of subscript. For M, this convention means that M[0][0] is assigned the first unit of the array memory, and `M[2][3]` is assigned the last unit of the array memory.

M	–	...	–	–	...	–	–	...	–

M[0][0]   M[0][3]M[1][0]   M[1][3]M[2][0]   M[2][3]

In general, element `M[i][j]` of M is assigned the `i*4+j` unit of array memory. (The 4 in the expression `i*4+j` comes from the size of a row in M.) For arrays with higher dimension, an analogous scheme is used to assign array elements to memory locations.

The definition of a multidimensional array can include initialization. For a two-dimensional array whose base type is a fundamental type, the array initialization can be a given as a list of values, a collection of initial row values, or a combination of the two. For example, the following definitions of A, B, and C all initialize the corresponding elements to the same value.

```
int A[3][3] = {1, 2, 3, 4, 5, 6, 7, 8, 9};
int B[3][3] ={{1, 2, 3}, {4, 5, 6}, {7, 8, 9}};
int C[3][3] = {1, 2, 3, {4, 5, 6}, 7, 8, 9};
```

As with one-dimensional arrays, if an insufficient number of values is specified, the trailing elements are initialized to zero.

For a multidimensional array whose base type is a class type, no explicit initialization can be given. Instead each array element is initialized using the default constructor for the class.

Functions with parameters that are multidimensional arrays are permitted. Like one-dimensional array parameters, a multidimensional array parameter must be a reference parameter. It is also possible to use a subarray of a multidimensional array as a parameter. For example, we can separately invoke `QuickSort()` on the three rows of the two-dimensional array M that was defined at the beginning of this section.

```
QuickSort(M[0], 0, 3);
QuickSort(M[1], 0, 3);
QuickSort(M[2], 0, 3);
```

We can make these invocations using rows of M because we are able to consider each row of a two-dimensional array as a one-dimensional array object.

When defining a function with a multidimensional array parameter, the size of each dimension other than the first dimension must be specified. For example, the following function `Zero()` has a two-dimensional array parameter A with a constant `MaxCols` that defines the number of elements per row. Parameters `rows` and `columns` are used to indicate how many rows and how many elements per row are to be set to 0 by the function.

```
void Zero(int A[][MaxCols], int rows, int columns) {
    for (int r = 0; r < rows; ++r)
        for (int c = 0; c < columns; ++c)
            A[r][c] = 0;
}
```

The following **void** function GetWords() extracts non-white-space strings from the standard input stream cin and stores them in a two-dimensional array. The function has three parameters: the two-dimensional **char** array List to store the strings, the maximum number of strings to be extracted MaxSize, and the count n, which is the number of extracted strings when the function has completed. The maximum length of a string is assumed to be MaxStringSize. This constant, which must be defined elsewhere, is the size of the second dimension in List.

```
void GetWords(char List[][MaxStringSize],
  int MaxSize, int &n) {
    for (n = 0; cin >> List[n]; ++n) {
      continue;
    }
}
```

Function GetWords() is similar to GetList() except it extracts character strings rather than **int** values. In the exercises, an alternative version of Get-Words() is developed that makes use of the cin member function get-line().

Suppose standard input contained the following:

```
a list of words
to be read.
```

Then

```
const int MaxStringSize = 10;
const int MaxListSize = 10;
char A[MaxListSize][MaxStringSize];
int n;
GetWords(A, MaxListSize, n);
```

would set A in the following manner:

A[0]	'a'	'\0'	—	—	—	—	—	—	—	—
A[1]	'l'	'i'	's'	't'	'\0'	—	—	—	—	—
A[2]	'o'	'f'	'\0'	—	—	—	—	—	—	—
A[3]	'w'	'o'	'r'	'd'	's'	—	—	—	—	—
A[4]	't'	'o'	'\0'	—	—	—	—	—	—	—
A[5]	'b'	'e'	'\0'	—	—	—	—	—	—	—
A[6]	'r'	'e'	'a'	'd'	'.'	'\0'	—	—	—	—
A[7]	—	—	—	—	—	—	—	—	—	—
A[8]	—	—	—	—	—	—	—	—	—	—
A[9]	—	—	—	—	—	—	—	—	—	—

As you see, the two-dimensional array representation for a list of strings is quite wasteful—most of the array elements are unused. In Chapter 13, we consider mechanisms that can represent character strings with a minimal amount of excess storage.

10.7.1

Matrices

A two-dimensional array is sometimes known as a *matrix* because it resembles that mathematical concept. A mathematical matrix A with m rows and n columns is represented in the following manner:

$$\begin{bmatrix} a_{1,1} & a_{1,2} & \cdots & a_{1,n} \\ a_{2,1} & a_{2,2} & \cdots & a_{2,n} \\ \cdots & & & \cdots \\ a_{m,1} & a_{m,2} & \cdots & a_{m,n} \end{bmatrix}$$

Addition is defined for two matrices with the same corresponding number of rows and columns. If A and B are both matrices with m rows and n columns, then their sum C has the following form:

$$\begin{bmatrix} a_{1,1}+b_{1,1} & a_{1,2}+b_{1,2} & \cdots & a_{1,n}+b_{1,n} \\ a_{2,1}+b_{2,1} & a_{2,2}+b_{2,2} & \cdots & a_{2,n}+b_{2,n} \\ \cdots & & & \cdots \\ a_{m,1}+b_{m,1} & a_{m,2}+b_{m,2} & \cdots & a_{m,n}+b_{m,n} \end{bmatrix}$$

Matrix addition is implemented in the following function `Add()` whose body is a double-nested **for** loop.

```
void Add(const int A[][MaxCols],
  const int B[][MaxCols], int C[][MaxCols],
  int rows, int columns) {
    for (int r = 0; r < rows; ++r) {
       for (int c = 0; c < columns; ++c) {
          C[r][c] = A[r][c] + B[r][c];
       }
    }
}
```

The outer **for** loop of `Add()` supplies the iterator `r` to process the current row. The inner **for** loop supplies the iterator `c` to process the current column in the current row. Together the two iterators enable the sum of a pair of array elements from `A` and `B` to be calculated and assigned to the corresponding array element of `C`.

10.7.2

Find that word

A popular word puzzle is to search a two-dimensional list for hidden words. For example, can you find the names Emily, Hannah, Jenna, James, and Zachary among the letters given in Figure 10.2. The names can occur horizontally, vertically, or diagonally in either forward or reverse order.

Programming Tip

Accessing multidimensional arrays

Because multidimensional arrays are stored in row-major order, it is generally more efficient to process array elements row-by-row rather than column-by-column. The efficiency comes about in how memory values are brought into the central processing unit. Often contiguous sections of memory called *pages* are brought in with the expectation that values near a desired value are more likely to be referenced than values defined elsewhere in memory. Since a page is contiguous memory, it is more likely to contain a complete row than a complete column.

Figure 10.2

Several names are hidden in this two-dimensional list of letters

```
A  N  N  E  J  Z  E

S  J  A  M  I  J  N

Y  L  Z  I  Q  W  N

E  R  A  L  U  V  A

R  S  C  Y  N  N  O

D  H  H  L  K  F  J

U  J  A  M  E  S  L

A  A  R  N  F  H  I

S  C  Y  D  N  D  O

U  K  T  Z  A  A  R

A  S  D  F  G  Q  H
```

In Listing 10.5 a function `PuzzleSearch()` supervises the search for a given word in a two-dimensional array of characters. To make the search for the hidden word easier, the rows and columns of alphabetic characters are surrounded by null characters. For example, if an array `T` with 12 rows and 8 columns was to represent the puzzle instance of Figure 10.2, the array would have the form depicted in Figure 10.3.

Function `PuzzleSearch()` considers, in turn, each interior array element in the table as a possible starting location for the word. There are eight directions in which the word can proceed. The eight directions differ in how the row and column indexes must be modified to proceed from element to element. For example, to proceed rightward from an element, the row index does not change and the column index increases by one. Similarly, to proceed diagonally upward and leftward, both the row and column indexes must decrease by one. For each possible starting array element, an **if-else-if** construct is executed with the **if** statements in the construct considering different directions. If the word is found, an appropriate message is displayed and the function returns. If none of the eight directions works out with the current starting element, the process continues with a new starting element. The process terminates either with the word being found or having exhausted all possible starting elements. If the latter occurs, an appropriate message is displayed. The func-

Listing 10.5

*Function
PuzzleSearch() of
puzzle.cpp*

```cpp
// PuzzleSearch(): look for Word in T
void PuzzleSearch(const char T[][MaxColumns],
 int r, int c, const char Word[]) {
   for (int i = 1; i <= r; ++i) {
      for (int j = 1; j <= c; ++j) {
         if (CheckWord(T, i, j, Word, 0, 1)) {
            cout << Word << " is at " << i << ", " << j
              << " going horizontally right" << endl;
            return;
         }
         else if (CheckWord(T, i, j, Word, 0, -1)) {
            cout << Word << " is at " << i << ", " << j
             << " going horizontally left" << endl;
            return;
         }
         else if (CheckWord(T, i, j, Word, 1, 0)) {
            cout << Word << " is at " << i << ", " << j
             << " going vertically down" << endl;
            return;
         }
         else if (CheckWord(T, i, j, Word, -1, 0)) {
            cout << Word << " is at " << i << ", " << j
             << " going vertically up" << endl;
            return;
         }
         else if (CheckWord(T, i, j, Word, 1, 1)) {
            cout << Word << " is at " << i << ", " << j
             << " going diagonally right and down"
             << endl;
            return;
         }
         else if (CheckWord(T, i, j, Word, 1, -1)) {
            cout << Word << " is at " << i << ", " << j
             << " going diagonally left and down"
             << endl;
            return;
         }
         else if (CheckWord(T, i, j, Word, -1, 1)) {
            cout << Word << " is at " << i << ", " << j
             << " going diagonally right and up"
             << endl;
            return;
         }
         else if (CheckWord(T, i, j, Word, -1, -1)) {
            cout << Word << " is at " << i << ", " << j
             << " going diagonally left and up"
             << endl;
            return;
         }
      }
   }
   cout << Word << " is not in the Puzzle" << endl;
   return;
}
```

Figure 10.3

Array representation of puzzle search list

T[0]	'\0'	'\0'	'\0'	'\0'	'\0'	'\0'	'\0'	'\0'	'\0'
T[1]	'\0'	'A'	'N'	'N'	'E'	'J'	'Z'	'E'	'\0'
T[2]	'\0'	'S'	'J'	'A'	'M'	'I'	'J'	'N'	'\0'
T[3]	'\0'	'Y'	'L'	'Z'	'I'	'Q'	'W'	'N'	'\0'
T[4]	'\0'	'E'	'R'	'A'	'L'	'U'	'V'	'A'	'\0'
T[5]	'\0'	'R'	'S'	'C'	'Y'	'N'	'N'	'O'	'\0'
T[6]	'\0'	'D'	'H'	'H'	'L'	'K'	'F'	'J'	'\0'
T[7]	'\0'	'U'	'J'	'A'	'M'	'E'	'S'	'L'	'\0'
T[8]	'\0'	'A'	'A'	'R'	'N'	'F'	'H'	'I'	'\0'
T[9]	'\0'	'S'	'C'	'Y'	'D'	'N'	'D'	'O'	'\0'
T[10]	'\0'	'U'	'K'	'T'	'Z'	'A'	'A'	'R'	'\0'
T[11]	'\0'	'A'	'S'	'D'	'F'	'G'	'Q'	'H'	'\0'
T[12]	'\0'	'\0'	'\0'	'\0'	'\0'	'\0'	'\0'	'\0'	'\0'

Listing 10.6

Function CheckWord() from puzzle.cpp

```cpp
// CheckWord(): look for Word in T starting at [i][j]
// changing row value by RowOffset and column value by
// ColOffset
bool CheckWord(const char T[][MaxColumns], int i,
 int j, const char Word[], int RowOffset,
 int ColOffset) {
  int Length = strlen(Word);
  int row = i;
  int col = j;
  for (int k = 0; k < Length; ++k) {
    if (Word[k] != T[row][col])
      return false;
    else {
      row += RowOffset;
      col += ColOffset;
    }
  }
  return true;
}
```

tion to check a particular starting location and direction is `CheckWord()`, and it is given in Listing 10.6.

Function `CheckWord()` has six parameters. The first parameter is the two-dimensional array of characters `T` to be searched. The second and third parameters are, respectively, the row `i` and column `j` that form the subscript of the array element in `T`, which is to be the start of the search. The fourth parameter `Word` is an array of characters that represents the hidden word. The fifth and sixth parameters `RowOffset` and `ColOffset` indicate, respectively, by what amount the current row and column indexes should be incremented to access the next array element in `T` in the search for the hidden word.

The actual check for a given direction is simple. First, the length of string represented by `Word` is computed using the C-based string library function `strlen()`. The current row index `row` and column index `col` for subscripting

T are then initialized using i and j. Each character in Word is considered in turn. If the current character Word[k] from Word and the current character T[row][col] from T mismatch, then our guess for the word's location is wrong and the function returns **false**. If the current characters in Word and T match, then the indexes row and column are incremented by the appropriate offsets so that together they form the subscript of the new current array element in T. If the **for** loop completes with all the letters matching, then the hidden word has been found and the function returns **true**.

A simple function main() that initializes the puzzle search table and then allows the user to specify a series of searches is given in Listing 10.7. The function does not perform any validation; an improved version is left as an exercise.

Listing 10.7

Function main() from
puzzle.cpp

```cpp
// main(): manage play of puzzle search game
int main() {
    char S[MaxColumns];

    cout << "Enter puzzle table file name: " << flush;
    cin >> S;

    ifstream fin(S);

    char Table[MaxRows][MaxColumns];

    int n;
    int m ;
    for (n = 0; fin >> S; ++n) {
        m = strlen(S);
        for (int i = 0; i < m; ++i) {
            Table[n+1][i+1] = S[i];
        }
        Table[n+1][0] = Table[n+1][m+1] = ' ';
        Table[n+1][m+2] = '\0';
    }

    for (int i = 0; i <= m+1; ++i) {
        Table[0][i] = Table[n+1][i] = ' ';
    }
    Table[0][m+2] = Table[n+1][m+2] = '\0';

    for (int j = 0; j <= n+1; ++j) {
        cout << Table[j]   << endl;
    }

    cout << "Enter your puzzle search word: " << flush;

    while (cin >> S) {
        cout << endl;

        PuzzleSearch(Table, n, m, S);

        cout << endl;
        cout << "Enter your next search word: " << flush;
    }

    return 0;
}
```

10.8

REPRESENTING A POKER HAND

One of the more popular games of chance is poker, which uses playing cards from a standard deck. In this section, we first develop two ADTs to support the basic modeling of playing cards. Using these ADTs we then develop another ADT to model a poker hand.

A standard deck consists of 52 playing cards. Each card has two characteristics—its *suit* and *face*. There are four different suit values. These values in increasing order of preference are club, diamond, heart, and spade. There are 13 different face values. These values in increasing order of preference are two, three, four, five, six, seven, eight, nine, ten, jack, queen, king, and ace. In a standard deck each card represents a different combination of suit and face value (e.g, ace of clubs, nine of diamonds).

Both the equal relationship and less than relationship are defined for cards. Two cards are equal if both their face values and suit values match.

A card *c* is less than a card *d* if either

■ The face value of *c* is less than the value of *d*.

■ The face value of *c* and *d* are the same and the suit value of *c* is less than the suit value of *d*.

By this definition, the following relationships are true:

Two of spades < eight of diamonds.

Four of hearts < four of spades.

And the following relationships are false:

Two of spades < two of hearts.

Four of hearts < three of hearts.

For our purposes, a new standard deck has its cards arranged in ascending order by suit, that is, two of clubs, three of clubs, …, ace of clubs, two of diamonds, …, two of hearts, …, two of spades, …, ace of spades. Before a standard deck is used in a game, the ordering of the cards is randomized through shuffling.

10.8.1

An ADT for playing cards

An abstraction for a playing card needs to represent two pieces of information—the suit and face of a card. This requirement suggests the use of a type `CardSuit` that represents the possible suits and a type `CardFace` that represents the possible faces. These types can be easily defined in C++ using **enum** statements.

In the following definitions we create two collections of **enum** constants. The first collection is of type `CardSuit`, and the second collection is of type `CardFace`.

```
enum CardSuit {club, diamond, heart, spade};
enum CardFace {two, three, four, five, six,
  seven, eight, nine, ten, jack, queen, king,
  ace};
```

For example, based upon the `CardSuit` and `CardFace` definitions, the following expressions are true (remember **enum** constants are specified in order of least value to greatest value).

```
club < diamond
diamond < spade
two < ten
king < ace
```

In manipulating a playing card representation, we need the following behaviors:

- Inspect the suit and face.
- Modify the suit and face.
- Insert a representation of the face and suit.
- Extract a representation of the face and suit.
- Compare two cards to determine whether they represent the same value.
- Compare two cards to determine whether one playing card is less than the other.

These requirements can be implemented using the class definition `Card` and the auxiliary operator prototypes of Listing 10.8. The listing corresponds to the header file for the card library.

The `Card` class definition of Listing 10.8 shows two constructors: a default constructor that initializes its `Card` object to represent the two of clubs and a constructor that initializes its `Card` object to represent a particular card. The class definition also shows that there are two member inspectors, `GetFace()` and `GetSuit()`. In addition, there are two member mutators, `SetFace()` and `SetSuit()`. The inspectors and mutators perform their tasks using the two data members `Face` and `Suit`. These two data members are defined in a **private** section to support information hiding.

The `Card` ADT does not require any facilitators. The public member inspectors and mutators enable auxiliary operators to accomplish their tasks directly.

Basic implementations of the member functions are provided in Listing 10.9, and auxiliary operators for the `Card` class are provided in Listing 10.10. Together these two listings constitute the implementation file `card.cpp`.

Mutators `SetFace()` and `SetSuit()` are defined first in Listing 10.9. It is their tasks to set the data members `Face` and `Suit`. For example, the following assignment is used by `SetFace()` to assign data member `Face`.

```
Face = f;
```

Representing a poker hand **453**

Listing 10.8

Header file card.h for card library

```
#ifndef CARD_H
#define CARD_H
#include <iostream.h>
enum CardSuit {club, diamond, heart, spade};
enum CardFace {two, three, four, five, six, seven,
 eight, nine, ten, jack, queen, king, ace};
class Card {
  public:
    // construct default card (two of clubs)
    Card();
    // construct specific card
    Card(const CardFace &f, const CardSuit &s);
    // face and suit inspectors
    CardFace GetFace() const;
    CardSuit GetSuit() const;
    // face and suit mutators
    void SetFace(const CardFace &f);
    void SetSuit(const CardSuit &s);
  private:
    // data members
    CardFace Face;
    CardSuit Suit;
};
// auxiliary operators
bool operator==(const Card &c1, const Card &c2);
bool operator<(const Card &c1, const Card &c2);
ostream& operator<<(ostream &sout, const Card &c);
istream& operator>>(istream &sin, Card &c);
#endif
```

The two constructor definitions in Listing 10.9 use mutators `SetFace()` and `SetSuit()` to initialize the data members. In particular, the default constructor uses the following code segment to initialize its playing representation.

```
SetFace(two);
SetSuit(club);
```

The other constructor uses the following code segment to initialize its playing representation.

```
SetFace(f);
SetSuit(s);
```

An alternative method of doing the construction is using a member initialization list. A *member initialization list* is a series of data members with a specification of their initial values. The data members are separated using commas. The initialization list for a constructor immediately precedes the constructor body. It is separated from the constructor parameter list by a colon.

Listing 10.9

*Card member functions
from card.cpp*

```
#include <iostream.h>
#include "card.h"
// SetFace(): face mutator
void Card::SetFace(const CardFace &f) {
   Face = f;
}
// SetSuit(): suit mutator
void Card::SetSuit(const CardSuit &s) {
   Suit = s;
}
// Card(): default constructor
Card::Card() {
   SetFace(two);
   SetSuit(club);
}
// Card(): specific constructor
Card::Card(const CardFace &f, const CardSuit &s) {
   SetFace(f);
   SetSuit(s);
}
// GetFace(): face inspector
CardFace Card::GetFace() const {
   return Face;
}
// GetSuit(): suit inspector
CardSuit Card::GetSuit() const {
   return Suit;
}
```

For example, the Card constructors can be implemented using initialization lists in the following manner.

```
Card::Card() : Face(two), Suit(club) {
   // no body needed. initialization list does it
   // all
}
Card::Card(const CardFace &f, const CardSuit &s)
 : Face(f), Suit(s) {
   // no body needed, initialization list does it
   // all
}
```

It is important to note that the elements of the initialization list are constructed in the order that they are defined in the class definition rather than then their position in the initialization list.

When using initialization lists be sure that the data member constructors take appropriate actions if the initial values are not sensible. For the **enum** types CardFace and CardSuit all of their **enum** constants are appropriate so using an initialization list for Face and Suit is fine.

Member inspectors GetFace() and GetSuit() both have straightforward implementations—they simply return the value of the associated data member. For example, the body of `GetSuit()` consists of the single statement

```
return Suit;
```

Listing 10.10

Auxiliary operators from card.cpp

```
// ==: auxiliary equality operator
bool operator==(const Card &c1, const Card &c2) {
  CardFace f1 = c1.GetFace();
  CardSuit s1 = c1.GetSuit();
  CardFace f2 = c2.GetFace();
  CardSuit s2 = c2.GetSuit();
  return (f1 == f2) && (s1 == s2);
}

// <: auxiliary less than operator
bool operator<(const Card &c1, const Card &c2) {
  CardFace f1 = c1.GetFace();
  CardSuit s1 = c1.GetSuit();
  CardFace f2 = c2.GetFace();
  CardSuit s2 = c2.GetSuit();
  return (f1 < f2) || ((f1 == f2) && (s1 < s2));
}

// <<: basic insertion operator
ostream& operator<<(ostream &sout, const Card &c) {
  switch (c.GetFace()) {
    case two:    sout << "2"; break;
    case three:  sout << "3"; break;
    case four:   sout << "4"; break;
    case five:   sout << "5"; break;
    case six:    sout << "6"; break;
    case seven:  sout << "7"; break;
    case eight:  sout << "8"; break;
    case nine:   sout << "9"; break;
    case ten:    sout << "10"; break;
    case jack:   sout << "J"; break;
    case queen:  sout << "Q"; break;
    case king:   sout << "K"; break;
    case ace:    sout << "A"; break;
  }
  switch (c.GetSuit()) {
    case club:    sout << "C"; break;
    case diamond: sout << "D"; break;
    case heart:   sout << "H"; break;
    case spade:   sout << "S"; break;
  }
  return sout;
}
```

The definitions of the equality operator and less than operator are given in Listing 10.10. These operators both call their formal `Card` parameters `c1` and `c2`. The operators set local objects with the suit and face values of those `Card` objects.

```
CardFace f1 = c1.GetFace();
CardSuit s1 = c1.GetSuit();
CardFace f2 = c2.GetFace();
CardSuit s2 = c2.GetSuit();
```

For the two cards are to be equal, the faces and suits must both match. This situation corresponds to the following logical expression:

```
(f1 == f2) && (s1 == s2)
```

As discussed previously, two cards have a less than relationship if either the face of the first is less than the face of the second, or the two faces are the same and the suit of the first is less than the suit of the second. This situation corresponds to the following logical expression:

```
(f1 < f2) || ((f1 == f2) && (s1 < s2))
```

Our overloading of the insertion operator in Listing 10.10 is rudimentary. For example, if the following code segment is executed

```
Card a(ace, club);
Card b(seven, heart);
Card c(queen, spade);
cout << a << " " << b << " " << c << endl;
```

then the following output is produced.

```
AC 7H QS
```

Each invocation of the insertion operator for a `Card` object translates that insertion into two character string insertions. The actual strings to be displayed are determined using **switch** statements. The first **switch** statement controls the display of the card face, and the second **switch** statement controls the display of the card suit.

Depending upon which system is being used (e.g., MSDOS), an extended character set may be available that includes iconic representations of the four suits. For such systems we can modify our insertion definition to use those iconic characters to produce output such as the following:

```
A♣ 7♥ Q♠
```

Another alternative is the graphical display of playing cards. This approach requires access to a graphical API. The EzWindows API supports such a representation. It requires that you have access to bitmap representations of each kind of playing card. Such representations are considered in Chapter 11.

The overloading of the extraction operator is left for an exercise.

10.8.2

An ADT for a deck of playing cards

A data abstraction of a deck should maintain the order and value of 52 playing cards. Activities commonly associated with a deck follow.

- Inspect individual cards.
- Swap pairs of cards.
- Shuffle the cards.
- Sort the cards.

For our purposes, it also convenient to display a deck. These methods can be implemented using the class definition `Deck` and auxiliary operator prototypes of Listing 10.11. This listing corresponds to the library header file `deck.h`.

Listing 10.11

Header file deck.h for deck library

```
#ifndef DECK_H
#define DECK_H
#include <iostream.h>
#include "card.h"

class Deck {
   public:
      // initialize a canonical deck
      Deck();
      // put deck in random order
      void Shuffle();
      // put deck in sorted order
      void Sort();
      // put deck in canonical order
      void Arrange();
      // inspect i-th card
      Card GetCard(int i) const;
      // assign a specific value to the i-th card
      void SetCard(int i, const Card &c);
      // swap i-th & j-th cards
      void SwapCards(int i, int j);
   private:
      Card Cards[52];
};

// auxiliary operator prototypes
ostream& operator<<(ostream &sout, const Deck &d);
istream& operator>>(istream &sin, Deck &d);
#endif
```

Figure 10.4

Cloud representation of the class Deck

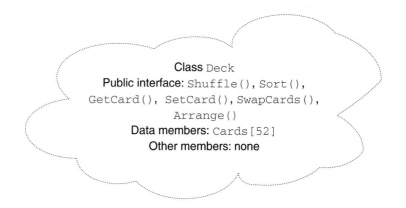

Class `Deck`
Public interface: `Shuffle()`, `Sort()`,
`GetCard()`, `SetCard()`, `SwapCards()`,
`Arrange()`
Data members: `Cards[52]`
Other members: none

The ADT `Deck` has a single constructor. The purpose of this default constructor is to construct a representation of a deck of cards in *canonical* order where canonical order is the clubs in increasing order, followed by the diamonds in increasing order, followed by the hearts in increasing order, followed by the spades in increasing order.

The individual cards in the deck are represented using the **private** data member Cards. This data member is an array of 52 Card objects. It is important to realize that although an object of type Deck *has* a data member that is an array, the Deck object itself is not an array. This property is demonstrated pictorially in Figure 10.4.

The class definition for Deck supplies several member mutators for reordering the cards in the deck. These mutators include Shuffle() for putting the cards in random order, Arrange() for putting the cards in canonical order, and Sort() for putting the cards in nondecreasing order.

The class definition provides an inspector GetCard() for getting the value of a particular card and a mutator SetCard() for setting the value of a particular card. There is also a mutator SwapCards() that interchanges the values of two cards in the deck. The interchange is specified by giving the positions of the two cards in question.

Member functions GetCard(), SetCard(), and SwapCards() expect that deck positions are numbered starting at one. This numbering scheme reflects that Deck is an ADT and that a user of an ADT does not need to be concerned how the ADT is implemented. It is natural for a user of the ADT to reference the first card in the deck using the value 1, to reference the second card in the deck using the value 2, and so on (the member functions can internally map a deck position to an index into the array cards by subtracting 1 from the position).

In the following code segment, a Deck d is initialized and displayed.

```
Deck d;
cout << "Canonical deck:" << endl;
for (int i = 1; i <= 52; ++i) {
   cout << d.GetCard(i) << " ";
   if ((i % 13) == 0)
      cout << endl;
};
```

The segment displays

```
Canonical deck:
1C  2C  3C  4C  5C  6C  7C  8C  9C  10C  JC  QC  KC
1D  2D  3D  4D  5D  6D  7D  8D  9D  10D  JD  QD  KD
1H  2H  3H  4H  5H  6H  7H  8H  9H  10H  JH  QH  KH
1S  2S  3S  4S  5S  6S  7S  8S  9S  10S  JS  QS  KS
```

because Deck d upon initialization has its cards in canonical order. The insertion of d.GetCard(i) in the preceding segment use the overloading of the insertion operator that was defined for a Card object. This definition is being invoked because d.GetCard() returns a value of type Card.

The implementation of several Deck member functions is given in Listing 10.12 and Listing 10.13. Other Deck member functions and the overloading of the insertion and extraction operators for Deck objects are left to the exercises.

The first member function defined in Listing 10.12 is SetCard(). This member function is given two parameters: a position i in the deck and the

Listing 10.12

*Member function
definitions from
deck.cpp*

```cpp
// SetCard(): assign a specific value to ith card
void Deck::SetCard(int i, const Card &c) {
   if ((i >= 1) && (i <= 52))
      Cards[i-1] = c;
   else {
      cerr << "Bad deck reference" << endl;
      exit(1);
   }
}

// Deck(): initialize a canonical deck
Deck::Deck() {
   int p = 1;
   for (int i = 1; i <= 4; ++i) {
      CardSuit s;
      switch (i) {
         case 1: s = club;    break;
         case 2: s = diamond; break;
         case 3: s = heart;   break;
         case 4: s = spade;   break;
      }
      for (int j = 1; j <= 13; ++j) {
         CardFace f;
         switch (j) {
            case  1: f = two;   break;
            case  2: f = three; break;
            case  3: f = four;  break;
            case  4: f = five;  break;
            case  5: f = six;   break;
            case  6: f = seven; break;
            case  7: f = eight; break;
            case  8: f = nine;  break;
            case  9: f = ten;   break;
            case 10: f = jack;  break;
            case 11: f = queen; break;
            case 12: f = king;  break;
            case 13: f = ace;   break;
         }
         Card c(f, s);
         SetCard(p, c);
         ++p;
      }
   }
}
```

value c for the card at that position. The function begins by testing whether i is valid.

```cpp
   if ((i >= 1) && (i <= 52))
      Cards[i-1] = c;
   else {
      cerr << "Bad deck reference" << endl;
      exit(1);
   }
```

If i is a valid position, then the array element in Cards representing position i is updated. As noted previously, element Cards[i-1] is used to represent the

i^{th} card in the deck. If i is invalid, then an error message is generated and the program terminates using the stdlib function exit().

The other function defined in Listing 10.12 is the Deck default constructor. The default constructor uses a **for** loop nested with another **for** loop to systematically generate the various card values for the deck. Each playing card in the deck is set by invoking SetCard() with the current deck position and card value.

The outer **for** loop is used to generate suit values. Object i ranges from 1 to 4 where 1 corresponds to clubs, 2 corresponds to diamonds, and so on. This correspondence is achieved through a **switch** statement.

The inner **for** loop is used to generate card values. The inner loop is executed four times—once for each value of i. For each execution of the inner loop, object j ranges from 1 to 13 where 1 corresponds to card value two, 2 corresponds to card value three, and so on. This correspondence is also established through a **switch** statement.

Using the current face f and suit value s, a Card object c is defined and initialized. Object c is then used to initialize the next available position p in the deck. Position p is initialized to 1 prior to the **for** loops, and p is incremented by 1 after each invocation of SetCard().

```
Card c(f,s);
SetCard(p, c);
++p;
```

The Deck member function GetCard() is defined in Listing 10.13.

Listing 10.13

More member function definitions from deck.cpp

```
// GetCard(): return value of ith card
Card Deck::GetCard(int i) const {
   if ((i >= 1) && (i <= 52))
      return Cards[i-1];
   else {
      cerr << "Bad deck reference" << endl;
      exit(1);
   }
}

// SwapCards(): swap ith and jth cards
void Deck::SwapCards(int i, int j) {
   Card ci = GetCard(i);
   Card cj = GetCard(j);
   SetCard(i, cj);
   SetCard(j, ci);
}

// Shuffle(): put deck in random order
void Deck::Shuffle() {
   for (int i = 1; i <= 52; ++i) {
      Random r(i,52);
      r.Randomize();
      int j = r.Draw();
      SwapCards(i, j);
   }
}
```

Function `GetCard()` is the inspector counterpart to mutator `Set-Card()`. The function supports information hiding. `GetCard()` is given a deck position i as its parameter, and it returns the value of the card at position i in the deck. Like `SetCard()`, `GetCard()` validates its parameter before using it to index into the array `Cards`.

```
if ((i >= 1) && (i <= 52))
    return Cards[i-1];
else {
    cerr << "Bad deck reference" << endl;
    exit(1);
}
```

If the position is valid, then the value of element `Cards[i-1]` is returned. If the position is invalid, then an error message is generated and the program terminates.

`Deck` member function `SwapCards()` is next to be defined in Listing 10.13. This mutator interchanges the cards at the positions specified by its parameters i and j. To accomplish its task, `SwapCards()` first defines two local `Card` objects ci and cj that are initialized to the current card values at deck positions i and j.

```
Card ci = GetCard(i);
Card cj = GetCard(j);
```

Objects ci and cj are then used to reset the values at those positions. There is no need for `SwapCards()` to validate whether its parameters have proper values because member functions `GetCard()` and `SetCard()` both do validation.

```
SetCard(i, cj);
SetCard(j, ci);
```

The final `Deck` member function defined in Listing 10.13 is `Shuffle()`. Function `Shuffle()` makes use of the Chapter 9 ADT `Random` whose objects can generate pseudorandom number sequences from specified intervals. For example, object r in the following definition generates pseudorandom number sequences from the interval i through 52.

```
Random r(i,52);
```

A **for** loop is used by function `Shuffle()` to rearrange the cards. In the ith iteration, the card for the ith deck position is determined. The possibilities for the ith position are the card values stored at the positions that are not yet fixed. These unfixed positions are i through 52. An invocation of `r.Draw()` selects one of these positions in a pseudorandom manner. (The invocation of `r.Randomize()` should cause a different sequence to be generated every time `Shuffle()` is executed).

```
r.Randomize();
int j = r.Draw();
```

The card value at the selected position j is then swapped with the value at position i.

```
SwapCards(i, j);
```

The following code segment demonstrates the effect of invoking member function `Shuffle()` on a deck.

```
Deck d;
d.Shuffle();
cout << "Shuffled deck:" << endl;
for (int i = 1; i <= 52; ++i) {
    cout << d.GetCard(i) << " ";
    if ((i % 13) == 0)
        cout << endl;
};
```

The segment produces the following output:

```
Shuffled deck:
5C 7C 7D 4S 1D JC 4H 6H 10D 1C 2C QS 10C
6D 1S 3D KD 5H 10S 2H 5D 3H 8H JS 4C 7H
8D 2D 6S 5S 10H KH 9D 9C 7S QH JH 3C 9S
1H QC KS 8S 6C 4D 2S JD KC QD 8C 3S 9H
```

10.8.3

An ADT for a poker hand

A poker hand consists of five playing cards. The rules of poker rank a poker hand according to its combination of cards. There are eight combinations of interest. If a hand does not represent one of these combinations, then the hand is said to have *nothing*. A nothing hand is the worst hand to have. The other kinds of hands are given below in increasing order of quality.

- *One pair:* Two cards of the five cards in the hand have matching faces (e.g., 2♣ 7♥ J♦ J♥ Q♠).

- *Two pair:* Two sets of two cards out of the five cards have matching faces (e.g., 2♣ 2♥ 9♥ Q♦ Q♠).

- *Three of a kind:* Three out of the five cards in the hand have matching faces (e.g., 2♣ 7♥ 9♦ 9♥ 9♠).

- *Straight:* The five cards in the hand have face values that represent a contiguous ascending sequence (e.g., 2♣ 3♥ 4♥ 5♦ 6♠).

- *Flush:* All five cards in the hand have matching suits (e.g., 2♦ 7♦ 9♦ J♦ Q♦).

- *Full house:* Two of the cards in the hand have matching faces and the other three cards also have matching faces (e.g., 3♣ 3♥ 3♠ 5♦ 5♠).

- *Four of a kind:* Four of the five cards in the hand have matching faces (e.g., 2♣ 2♦ 2♥ 2♠ Q♠).

- *Straight flush:* The five cards in the hand form both a straight and a flush (e.g., 2♣ 3♣ 4♣ 5♣ 6♣).

For example, the above ranking tells us that a hand with two pair is worth less than a hand with a straight. For our purposes, hands with the same rank are considered equivalent (e.g., we do not distinguish between a pair of jacks and a pair of tens).

A poker-hand ADT must provide the following methods:

- Inspect and modify the individual cards in the hand.
- Display the poker hands.
- Provide information on the kind of the hand (e.g., one pair, two pair, etc.).
- Compare two hands for the equality relationship.
- Compare two hands for the less than relationship.

These requirements can be implemented using the definitions `Rank` and `Hand`, and the auxiliary operator prototypes of Listing 10.14.

Listing 10.14

Header file poker.h for poker library

```
#ifndef POKER_H
#define POKER_H
#include <iostream.h>
#include "card.h"

enum Rank {Nothing, OnePair, TwoPair, ThreeOfAKind,
   Straight, Flush, FullHouse, FourOfAKind,
   StraightFlush};

class Hand {
   public:
      // create empty poker hand
      Hand();
      // return ith card in hand
      Card GetCard(int i) const;
      // set ith card in hand
      void SetCard(int i, const Card &c);
      // returns type of poker hand
      Rank Quality() const;
      // arrange hand in ascending card order
      void Sort();
      // test for hand properties
      bool HasOnePair() const;
      bool HasTwoPair() const;
      bool HasThreeOfAKind() const;
      bool HasStraight() const;
      bool HasFlush() const;
      bool HasFullHouse() const;
      bool HasFourOfAKind() const;
      bool HasStraightFlush() const;
   private:
      Card Cards[5];
};

// auxiliary operators
bool operator==(const Hand &a, const Hand &b);
bool operator<(const Hand &a, const Hand &b);
ostream& operator<<(ostream &sout, const Hand &h);
istream& operator>>(istream &sin, const Hand &h);
#endif
```

The **enum** collection Rank defines nine constants representing the various kinds of poker hands. The ordering of these constants correctly captures the ranking of poker hands.

The class Hand defines an object with a **private** data member Cards that is accessed and manipulated by both **public** member functions. The member functions include a default constructor, an inspector GetCard(), a mutator SetCard(), and some facilitator functions. The facilitator function Quality() returns the hand type. The other facilitator functions are **bool** functions that indicate whether the hand has a given combination.

You should notice that both Deck and Hand objects have member functions GetCard() and SetCard(). Similarly, they both have a **private** data member Cards. This name reuse is not a problem. By class scope context, a C++ compiler can tell whether a Deck member or a Card member is being used.

An implementation of the Hand constructor, inspector, and mutators is given in Listing 10.15.

Listing 10.15

Hand member function definitions from poker.cpp

```
// Hand(): create empty poker hand
Hand::Hand() {
   return;
}
// GetCard(): return ith card in hand
Card Hand::GetCard(int i) const {
   if ((i >= 1) && (i <= 5))
      return Cards[i-1];
   else {
      cerr << "Bad poker hand reference" << endl;
      exit(1);
   }
}
// SetCard(): set ith card in hand
void Hand::SetCard(int i, const Card &c) {
   if ((i >= 1) && (i <= 5)) {
      Cards[i-1] = c;
   }
   else {
      cerr << "Bad poker hand reference" << endl;
      exit(1);
   }
}
```

The Hand constructor has nothing to do, as each element of the array Cards is initialized using the default Card constructor. The default values will be replaced by the actual cards in the hand by copying cards from a shuffled deck. For example, function main() of Listing 10.16 deals and then displays three hands of cards. An invocation of the function produced the following output:

```
9C 9D JC AD AH
6S 4H 10D QC QD
2D 9H 10H 10S KC
```

Listing 10.16

Function main() of pokemain.cpp deals and displays three hands

```cpp
#include <iostream.h>
#include "deck.h"
#include "poker.h"
// main(): deal and display three hands
int main() {
    Deck d;
    d.Shuffle();
    Hand h[3];
    int k = 1;
    for (int i = 1; i <= 5; ++i) {
        for (int j = 0; j < 3; ++j) {
            // deal i-th card in j-th hand using the
            // k-th card in deck
            h[j].SetCard(i, d.GetCard(k));
            ++k;
        }
    }
    for (int j = 0; j < 3; ++j) {
        h[j].Sort();
        cout << h[j] << endl;
    }
    return 0;
}
```

The definitions of Hand member functions GetCard() and SetCard() in Listing 10.15 are similar to their Deck counterparts. The only change is that the size of the array is five in a poker-hand representation.

The 'Has' member functions are used by member function Quality() in determining the kind of poker hand. A Has member function returns **true** if the poker hand has the desired property; otherwise, it returns **false**. This means, for example, that a hand with four aces has the following properties: one pair, two pair, three of a kind, and four of a kind. Given that the Has functions operate this way, member function Quality() is straightforward to implement. As shown in Listing 10.17, Quality() uses an **if-else-if** construct to determine the highest rank property that its hand possesses.

The implementation of several other Hand inspector functions is provided in Listing 10.18. Most of the 'Has' functions would have an easier task if the cards could be put in sorted order. However, because they are **const**-qualified, the functions cannot modify the data members. Instead, a copy h is made of the Hand whose member function is being invoked. After making the copy, the copy is sorted. The sorted copy is then examined to see if it has the particular property. If the copy has the property, the original hand also does.

The copy h is defined using the copy constructor with the parameter *this. The expression *this is defined by C++ to be the current object. We will use the keyword **this** again in Chapter 13 when we consider dynamic memory.

Sorting the cards in the copy makes it straightforward to determine whether a hand has a particular property. For example, after sorting, function HasOnePair() needs to make only four comparisons of face values to determine whether a hand has a pair of matching face values: the first and second

Listing 10.17

Hand member function
Quality() from
poker.cpp

```
// Quality(): returns rank of poker hand
Rank Hand::Quality() const {
    if (HasStraightFlush())
        return StraightFlush;
    else if (HasFourOfAKind())
        return FourOfAKind;
    else if (HasFullHouse())
        return FullHouse;
    else if (HasFlush())
        return Flush;
    else if (HasStraight())
        return Straight;
    else if (HasThreeOfAKind())
        return ThreeOfAKind;
    else if (HasTwoPair())
        return TwoPair;
    else if (HasOnePair())
        return OnePair;
    else
        return Nothing;
}
```

cards, the second and third cards, the third and fourth cards, and the fourth and fifth cards.

```
CardFace f1 = h.GetCard(1).GetFace();
CardFace f2 = h.GetCard(2).GetFace();
CardFace f3 = h.GetCard(3).GetFace();
CardFace f4 = h.GetCard(4).GetFace();
CardFace f5 = h.GetCard(5).GetFace();
return (f1 == f2) || (f2 == f3) || (f3 == f4)
    || (f4 == f5);
```

The initialization of the five local `CardFace` objects by `HasOnePair()` is interesting in that the `Card` value returned by `GetCard()` invokes its member function `GetFace()` to get the actual face value.

Function `HasThreeOfAKind()` is also given in Listing 10.18. If the hand has three of a kind, then after sorting, the three cards with matching face values will be next to each other. Therefore, we need to compare only the face values of the first and third cards, the second and fourth cards, and the third and fifth cards. If any of these face values agree, then those two cards and the card between them form three of a kind.

```
CardFace f1 = h.GetCard(1).GetFace();
CardFace f2 = h.GetCard(2).GetFace();
CardFace f3 = h.GetCard(3).GetFace();
CardFace f4 = h.GetCard(4).GetFace();
CardFace f5 = h.GetCard(5).GetFace();
return (f1 == f3) || (f2 == f4) || (f3 == f5);
```

The next function defined in Listing 10.18 is function `HasFlush()`. This function determines whether the cards in the hand all have the same suit. It

Listing 10.18

*Hand member function
definitions from
poker.cpp*

```
// Has functions
bool Hand::HasOnePair() const {
  Hand h(*this);
  h.Sort();
  CardFace f1 = h.GetCard(1).GetFace();
  CardFace f2 = h.GetCard(2).GetFace();
  CardFace f3 = h.GetCard(3).GetFace();
  CardFace f4 = h.GetCard(4).GetFace();
  CardFace f5 = h.GetCard(5).GetFace();
  return (f1 == f2) || (f2 == f3) || (f3 == f4)
    || (f4 == f5);
}

bool Hand::HasThreeOfAKind() const {
  Hand h(*this);
  h.Sort();
  CardFace f1 = GetCard(1).GetFace();
  CardFace f2 = GetCard(2).GetFace();
  CardFace f3 = GetCard(3).GetFace();
  CardFace f4 = GetCard(4).GetFace();
  CardFace f5 = GetCard(5).GetFace();
  return (f1 == f3) || (f2 == f4) || (f3 == f5);
}

bool Hand::HasFlush() const {
  CardSuit s1 = GetCard(1).GetSuit();
  CardSuit s2 = GetCard(2).GetSuit();
  CardSuit s3 = GetCard(3).GetSuit();
  CardSuit s4 = GetCard(4).GetSuit();
  CardSuit s5 = GetCard(5).GetSuit();
  return (s1 == s2) && (s2 == s3) && (s3 == s4)
    && (s4 == s5);
}

bool Hand::HasStraightFlush() const {
  return HasStraight() && HasFlush();
}
```

does so by examining the suit values of each pair of adjacent cards. If each pair of adjacent cards has the same suit, the hand is a flush.

```
CardSuit s1 = GetCard(1).GetSuit();
CardSuit s2 = GetCard(2).GetSuit();
CardSuit s3 = GetCard(3).GetSuit();
CardSuit s4 = GetCard(4).GetSuit();
CardSuit s5 = GetCard(5).GetSuit();
return (s1 == s2) && (s2 == s3) && (s3 == s4)
  && (s4 == s5);
```

The last function defined in Listing 10.18 is `HasStraightFlush()`. This member function simply uses `HasStraight()` and `HasFlush()` to determine whether the hand has a straight flush.

```
return HasStraight() && HasFlush();
```

This completes our discussion of an ADT for poker hands. In the exercises, we continue its development and use it in some applications.

History of Computing

10.9

POINTS TO REMEMBER

- Arrays are the C++ type mechanism for defining an object that represents a list of objects.

- In defining an array, we must specify the size of the array, that is, the number of elements in the array. The size must be a bracketed expression whose terms represent literal constants.

- The typical array is a one-dimensional list. However, multidimensional arrays can also be defined.

- By using the subscript operator [], we can reference an individual element of the array.

- Each element has its own subscript value: The first element in the array has a subscript of 0, the second element has a subscript of 1, and so on until the last element of the list which has a subscript that is one less than the size of the list.

- Once subscripted, an individual array element can be used like any other object—it can be accessed, assigned, displayed, extracted to, passed as a value or reference parameter, and so on.

- Arrays are normally processed using iteration. Each time through a loop, a different element is processed.

- A **continue** statement indicates that the body of the innermost loop that contains the statement is finished for the current iteration.

- An array is not a first-class object. As such, we cannot use an array as the target of an assignment or as the return value for a function. In addition, when an array is passed as a parameter, it must be passed by reference. These limitations are a carry over from the C language.

- When defining a function with an array parameter, the formal parameter definition does not need to include the size of the first dimension. This property makes C++ functions more flexible than their counterparts in languages such as Pascal that require separate functions to process arrays of different sizes.

- The elements of an array are always stored in contiguous memory. For a one-dimensional array, at the beginning of its memory will be the first element, next will be the second element, and so on. For multidimensional arrays, the array elements are stored in row-major order.

- The traditional way to represent a string value is a character string. When an array is used to represent a character string, a null value '\0' is stored in the element that immediately follows the last character in the string.

- Elements of a global array whose base type is a fundamental type are initialized to 0 by default.

- Elements of a local array whose base type is a fundamental type are not initialized by default.

- Elements of an array whose base type is a class type are initialized using the default constructor of the base type.

- Elements of an array whose base type is a fundamental type can be set to specific values in their definition using initialization lists. If the initialization list does not specify sufficient values, the unspecified elements are set to 0.

- Two of the major activities performed in conjunction with arrays are sorting and searching.

- An array is sorted if the values in it are arranged in order by value. The standard ordering is nondecreasing.

- There are a number of sorting methods. The performance of these methods typically varies with the distribution of values in the array.

- Two of the more important sorting methods are InsertionSort() and QuickSort().

- The task of `InsertionSort()` on its ith iteration is to correctly place the value of the element with subscript i with respect to the values of array elements with subscripts 0 through i-1. `InsertionSort()` works well in practice.

- `QuickSort()` is typically implemented as a recursive sort. The method begins by choosing a pivot value. The list is then rearranged into three sublists. The middle sublist is composed of an element whose value is the pivot value; the values of the elements in the left sublist are no larger than the pivot value, and the values of the elements in the right sublist are no smaller than the pivot value. Since the sublists are partitioned in this manner, the left and right sublists can be sorted independently of each other to produce a totally sorted list. The sublists are sorted by making recursive calls to the `QuickSort()` method. `QuickSort()` can be implemented so that it has very good average-case and worst-case performance characteristics.

- If a list needs to be searched frequently for different key values, consideration should be given to sorting the list first. This preprocessing can be helpful because `BinarySearch()`, which is designed for examining a sorted list, is far more efficient than a standard sequential search through an unsorted list.

- A member initialization list is a means of specifying the initial values of the data members of a class object. The initialization list is part of the constructor definition and it immediately precedes the constructor body. The initialization list is separated from the constructor parameter list by a colon. The elements of the initialization list are evaluated in the order that they are defined in the class definition.

10.10

EXERCISES

10.1   What operator is used to refer to a particular element of an array?

10.2   Can an array represent more than one type of value? Explain.

10.3   Why do we tend to use named constants rather than literals when defining the size of an array?

10.4   Can an array be a value parameter? Explain.

10.5   Can an object that contains an array as a data member be a value parameter? Explain.

10.6   What is a first-class object?

10.7   Can an array element be a value parameter? Explain.

10.8   Can an array element be a reference parameter? Explain.

10.9   Does a global array with a base type that is a fundamental type have its elements automatically initialized? Explain.

10.10 Does a local array with a base type that is a fundamental type have its elements automatically initialized? Explain.

10.11 Does a local array with a base type that is a class type have its elements automatically initialized? Explain.

10.12 What is meant by row-major order?

10.13 How many objects are defined in the following statements? Explain.

```
int A[100];
float B[25][30];
char C[9][4][4];
Rational D[2];
```

10.14 Write a code segment that does the following:
   a) Defines a constant `MaxSize` equal to 20.
   b) Defines an array `List` whose base type is integer that can represent at most 20 values.
   c) Sets the first element of `List` to the value 19.
   d) Sets the last element of `List` to the value 54.
   e) Sets the other elements of `List` to 0.
   f) Displays `List`.

10.15 Write a code segment that does the following:
   a) Defines a constant `MaxN` equal to 40.
   b) Defines an array `Scores` whose base type is floating point that can represent at most 40 values.
   c) Sets the value of each element in `Scores` so that it matches its subscript value.
   d) Displays the values of last five element of `Scores`.
   Answer the following questions regarding `Scores`.
   e) Is the value 3.1415 a legal element value? Explain.
   f) Is the value 3.1415 a legal subscript value? Explain.

10.16 Write a code segment that does the following:
   a) Defines constants `MaxRows` equal to 25 and `MaxColumns` equal to 10.
   b) Defines an array `Data` whose base type is **bool** that can represent a table of values. There are at most 25 rows in the table with at most 10 entries per row.
   c) Initializes array `Data` so that the elements whose row subscript value is odd have the value **true**. Initialize the other elements to **false**.

10.17 Examine the following code segment:

```
cin >> A >> B;
cout << A << B << endl;
B = A;
C = A + B;
```

   a) Which of the statements are legal if A, B, and C are **int** arrays?

b) Which of the statements are legal if A, B, and C are **char** arrays?

c) Which of the statements are legal if A, B, and C are **float** arrays?

10.18 What would happen during execution if the **for** loop of function main() in Program 10.1 is as follows:

```
for (int i = 0; i < n; ++i)
    Swap(Number[i], Number[n-1-i]);
```

10.19 Design and implement a **void** function Initialize() that has three parameters: A, n, and val. Parameter A is an array of **int** objects; **int** parameter n is the size of array; and **int** parameter val is the value of interest. The function sets each of the n elements of A to val.

10.20 Design and implement a **bool** function Equal() with three parameters: A, B, and n. Parameters A and B are **int** arrays; **int** parameter n is the size of the arrays. The function iteratively compares the elements of the arrays. If each of the n pairs of elements is the same, the function returns **true**; otherwise, the function returns **false**.

10.21 Design and implement an **int** function LessThan() with three formal parameters: an **int** array A, the number of valid elements n, and an **int** value v. The value v is to be optional with a default value of 0. Function LessThan() returns the number of elements in list A[0], ..., A[n-1] that are less than v.

10.22 Design and implement the following statistical functions. Each of the functions returns a **float** value and has two parameters: A and n. Parameter A is an array of **float** objects; parameter n is the size of array.

a) Function Mean(): returns the average of the n values in the list.

b) Function Median(): if n is odd, it returns the middle value of the n values in the list; if n is even, it returns the average of the two middle values of the n values in the list.

10.23 Reimplement function GetWords() so that it uses the istream member function getline().

10.24 Reimplement function Pivot() so that if the sublist to be partitioned has at least three elements, then the pivot value is the median value of the left-most, right-most, and middle elements in the sublist.

10.25 Implement the iterative sorting function SelectionSort(). This function on its ith iteration finds the ith smallest element in the list and interchanges that value with the ith element in the array.

10.26 Modify function InsertionSort() so rather than specifying the number of elements to be sorted, a range of elements is specified.

10.27 Modify function QuickSort() so that it invokes the modified InsertionSort() of the previous exercise if the number of elements to be sorted is 20 or less.

10.28 Implement the recursive sorting function MergeSort(). This function conceptually divides the current list of n elements into two sublists of size n/2. If a sublist contains more than one element, the sublist is sorted by a recursive call to `MergeSort()`. After the two sublists of size n/2 are sorted, they are merged together to produce a single sorted list of size n.

10.29 Implement a recursive version of function `BinarySearch()`.

10.30 Design and implement a function `InitializeTable()` that prompts a user for a file name and then extracts a puzzle search table from that file. The extractions are stored in a reference parameter that is suitable for `PuzzleSearch()`. Function `InitializeTable()` also has two other reference parameters m and n, where m is the number of rows extracted and n is the number of columns per row. The function should perform all appropriate validation.

10.31 Given a matrix *A* with *m* rows and *n* columns and a matrix *B* with *n* rows and *p* columns, we can compute the product matrix *AB*. The product *C* has *m* rows and *p* columns where element C_{ij} has the following definition:

$$C_{ij} = \sum_{k=1}^{n} A_{ik} \cdot B_{kj}$$

Implement a function `Multiply()` that performs matrix multiplication. Function `Multiply()` has the following prototype:

```
void Multiply(const int A[][MaxCols],
  const int B[][MaxCols], int C[][MaxCols],
  const int m, const int n, const int p);
```

10.32 Complete the implementation of the card library by implementing a `Card` extraction operator `>>`.

10.33 Implement the `Deck` member function `Sort()`, which puts the current cards in the deck in sorted nondecreasing order.

10.34 Implement the `Deck` member function `Arrange()`, which puts the current cards in the deck in canonical order.

10.35 Implement the `Deck` auxiliary insertion operator `<<`, which displays the current cards in the deck from first card to last card. The cards should be displayed 13 cards per line, with a single space following each card representation.

10.36 Implement the `Deck` auxiliary extraction operator `>>`, which extracts the next 52 card values and assigns them to the individual cards in the deck.

10.37 Implement the `Hand` member function `HasTwoPair()`, which determines whether the hand has two different pairs of matching face values.

10.38 Implement the `Hand` member function `HasStraight()`, which determines whether the hand has face values that represent a contiguous ascending sequence.

10.39 Implement the `Hand` member function `HasFullHouse()`, which determines whether two of the cards in the hand have matching faces and the other three cards also have matching faces.

10.40 Implement the `Hand` member function `HasFourOfAKind()`, which determines whether four of the cards in the hand have matching faces.

10.41 Implement the `Hand` member function `Sort()`, which puts the five cards in the hand in sorted order.

10.42 Implement the `Hand` auxiliary operator `==`, which returns **true** if and only if the two `Hand` operands have the same rank.

10.43 Implement the `Hand` auxiliary operator `<=`, which returns **true** if and only if the left `Hand` operand has a rank that is less then the rank of the right `Hand` operand.

10.44 Implement the `Hand` auxiliary insertion operator, which displays the five cards in the hand. The cards should be displayed with a single space following each card representation.

10.45 Implement the `Hand` auxiliary extraction operator, which extracts the next five card values and assigns them to the individual cards in the hand.

10.46 Add a `Hand` constructor that initializes a `Hand` object using an array of five cards.

10.47 A variation on normal poker is stud poker. In stud poker you receive seven cards, and use five of those cards to determine a poker hand. You can form 21 different poker hands from seven cards. Display in sorted order, the possible poker hands associated with a random seven-card stud hand. This can be accomplished by implementing two functions:

a) Function `InitializeHand()` with two parameters: an array `C` of seven `Card` objects and an array `List` of 21 `Hand` objects. The function determines the various hands associated with `C` and assigns them to `List`.

b) Function `Display()` with two parameters: an array `List` of Hand objects and an **int** n. The function displays the first n elements of the array `List` to the standard output stream `cout`.

To test your functions, use them in conjunction with the following code segment:

```
Deck d;
d.Shuffle();
Card StudCard[7];
cout << " Stud hand: ";
for (int i = 1; i <= 7; ++i) {
    StudCard[i-1] = d.GetCard(i);
    cout << StudCard[i] << " ";
}
cout << " produces poker hands" << endl;
Hand List[21];
InitializeHand(StudCard, List);
Display(List, 21);
```

CHAPTER 11

The EzWindows API

Introduction

At this point, it should be clear that designing and writing good programs, while fun and interesting, is an intellectually demanding and time-consuming task. As we mentioned in Chapter 1, the time-consuming nature of programming is one factor that has led to the software crisis. In this chapter, we introduce the concept of an application programmer interface, or API. Using an API is one way that professional programmers reduce the time and cost of producing software. Essentially, an API provides a set of basic building blocks or infrastructure for constructing particular kinds of programs. Rather than building each program from scratch, the programmer uses facilities provided by the API when possible. Properly designed APIs can significantly reduce the effort to construct complicated programs. Indeed, most commercial software is constructed using a variety of APIs. To illustrate the use of an API, we introduce an API for displaying simple graphical objects in a window. The EzWindows API is an object-oriented API that provides facilities for building programs that use a windowing system for input and output. Using the EzWindows API, we will be able to build good programs that look good too!

Key Concepts

- application programmer interface
- graphical user interface
- event-based programming
- callbacks
- mouse events
- timer events
- bitmaps

11.1
APPLICATION PROGRAMMER INTERFACES

Designing, building, and testing a program is difficult and time-consuming work. To simplify and speed up the development of software, programmers have developed several approaches for shortening the time required to build a program. One of these techniques is to use an *application programmer interface* (API). The basic idea is similar to that of using standard libraries. If a library routine exists for doing a particular job or task, we should use it rather than writing code from scratch to do the job. Programmers call writing code to do a job when code already exists for doing the job reinventing the wheel. We want to avoid reinventing the wheel whenever possible.

An API is also a set of library routines. What distinguishes an API from a standard library is that an API supports building a specific kind of application or a component of an application with a specific capability. For example, there are numerous APIs for building the graphical user interface (GUI) component of an application. Some popular APIs for developing GUIs include Open Software Foundation's Motif®, Microsoft's Foundation Classes® (MFC), and Borland's ObjectWindows Library® (OWL).

APIs exist for almost every type of application imaginable. For example, there are APIs for building applications that

- Process and produce HTML, the language used to produce documents for distribution via the World-Wide Web.
- Use multimedia.
- Employ cryptography.
- Use virtual reality.
- Use the telephone to communicate.
- Access network facilities.
- Control and monitor scientific instruments.
- Produce graphs and plots of data.
- Perform statistical analysis.
- Perform database queries.

Obviously, using an API is a form of software reuse. However, a few ancillary advantages to using an API are worth mentioning. First, APIs usually handle application-specific details that the programmer should not have to worry about. For example, the designers of an API for a GUI have already dealt with issues, such as consistency of look and behavior, user friendliness, and flexibility, as well as low-level details about how to construct and draw elements on a variety of display devices. Thus the application programmer need not worry about these details. In turn, the programmer can concentrate on the application—not on the details having to do with the GUI. Second, use of an API ensures consistency across applications. All applications that use the API have the same look and feel. This consistency makes the applications easier to learn and use.

Because of the overwhelming benefits of using an API, most applications of any size are developed using one. In this chapter, we introduce and use a simple object-oriented API designed for building programs that use the graphical display capabilities and input devices that are available on most modern desktop machines. The name of the API is EzWindows, for easy windows. We have several goals in introducing and using EzWindows.

First, it illustrates a style and method of programming that is used in the real world. Most programs are not developed from scratch. They build on an existing infrastructure, such as an API. Second, it allows us to use the input/output paradigm that is common today. Most of today's popular applications use a graphical user interface to communicate with the user. It is rare these days to see an application where the human communicates with the application by typing commands and data on the keyboard. Similarly, the application communicates with the user via graphical displays rather than by printing only text on a screen. Third, EzWindows enables us to develop much more interesting and fun programs than we could otherwise create.

11.2

A SIMPLE WINDOW CLASS

EzWindows contains two major classes that are publicly available. In this section, we discuss `SimpleWindow`, a class that encapsulates the creation and control of windows for displaying graphical objects. The following section discusses `BitMap`, a class that encapsulates the creation and manipulation of bit-mapped screen images.

11.2.1

Event-based programming

Previously, our programs contained a function `main()` or a function `ApiMain()`. With the exception of the Kaleidoscope program of Chapter 8, a program began executing when the operating system called `main()` or `ApiMain()`, and it stopped executing when `main()` or `ApiMain()` returned or the program called `exit()`.

This method works well for conventional programs, but not for programs that use the mouse for input and a graphical display for output. This type of program must respond to events or messages from the operating system. These events include mouse clicks and timer events. For programs that use this paradigm of user interaction, the object-oriented programming model is more appropriate.

With the object-oriented model, we think of the operating system as one object and the program as another. The operating system communicates with the program by sending it messages. Using this approach, it is easy to see that we do not want a program that runs sequentially, starting with a call to function `main()` or `ApiMain()`. In fact, the program needs to be able to receive and send messages. Rather than have an application directly receive from and send messages to the operating system, we will use EzWindows to provide a consistent and simplified set of methods for communicating with the operating system. In effect, EzWindows will handle the interaction between the operating system and a user application. With EzWindows, the messages or events that a program can receive are start program, mouse click, timer click, refresh, and end program. The interaction between the EzWindows class `SimpleWindow` and a user program is shown in Figure 11.1.

Figure 11.1

Interaction between the EzWindows SimpleWindow class and a user program

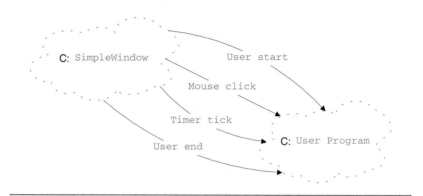

In addition to the messages that EzWindows forwards to the user program, the user program can send messages to the operating system through EzWindows. For example, a user program can tell EzWindows the user routine to call when a mouse click or a timer tick occurs. Telling EzWindows the user routine to invoke when a certain event occurs is called *registering a callback*. In addition to the event services, EzWindows provides facilities for creating windows and displaying various types of objects in a window. For example, a user program can send EzWindows's `SimpleWindow` class a message that directs it to display a text string at a specified location in a particular window. As we proceed through the chapter, we describe some of the capabilities of EzWindows and illustrate their use by writing some simple programs.

11.2.2

SimpleWindow coordinate system

Before exploring the EzWindows API further, we need to revisit the coordinate system for positioning objects as well as a system for specifying the size of objects. EzWindows uses the metric system for specifying both the position of an object and its size. For example, the EzWindows declaration

```
SimpleWindow TestWindow("Sample Window",
    10.0, 5.0, Position(4.0, 4.0));
```

creates a window labeled "Sample Window" that is 4 centimeters from the left edge of the screen and 4 centimeters from the top edge of the screen. The window is 10 centimeters in length and 5 centimeters in height. Figure 11.2 shows the window and its position on the screen.

Figure 11.2

*The EzWindows
coordinate system*

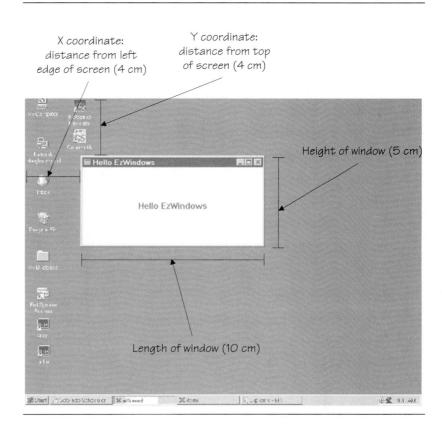

The prototype of the constructor for the SimpleWindow class is

```
SimpleWindow(string WindowTitle = "Untitled",
  float Width = 8.0, float Height = 8.0,
  const Position &WindowPosition
  = Position(0.0, 0.0));
```

Notice that the position of the window relative to the upper-left corner of the screen is specified using an object called Position. In earlier chapters, the position of a window object was specified by passing both an x and y coordinate to any function that dealt with the position of a window object. We did this to keep the number of objects we were dealing with to a minimum. Now that we have a better understanding of objects and object-oriented programming, it makes sense to begin to use objects whenever appropriate. It is convenient and natural to encapsulate a window location as a single entity. Consequently, we have created a new class, Position, that holds the logical window coordinates of a window object. The class declaration of Position is contained in Listing 11.1.

Listing 11.1

*Declaration of Position
from file position.h*

```
#ifndef POSITION_H
#define POSITION_H
class Position {
   public:
      Position(float x = 0.0, float y = 0.0);
      Position Add(const Position &p) const;
      int GetXDistance() const;
      int GetYDistance() const;
   protected:
      void SetXDistance(float x);
      void SetYDistance(float y);
   private:
      float XDistance;
      float YDistance;
};
// Auxilary function for computing new positions
Position operator+(const Position &x,
 const Position &y);
#endif
```

The declaration of `Position` follows our normal convention with a constructor that uses default values of zero for the x and y distances and inspectors and mutators for the private data. `GetXDistance()` and `GetYDistance()` are public because some of the low-level window manipulation routines need access to the values of the coordinates. The mutators are not public because we do not want clients of `Position` to be able to change the private data. However a derived class created from `Position` might need to change the values of the private data. Making the mutators protected gives the derived class access to the mutators. Listing 11.2 contains the implementation `Position`.

The existence of the class `Position` means that we can conveniently define a location. For example, the definition

```
Position p(2.0, 4.0);
```

instantiates a `Position` object named p whose value is the location that is 2 centimeters from the left edge of the screen and 4 centimeters from the top. Similarly, the definition

```
Position Origin;
```

defines a `Position` object called `Origin` whose value is the upper-left corner of the screen (i.e., location 0,0).

It will sometimes be convenient to compute a new position given a position and an offset from that position. For this purpose, the + operator has been overloaded so that it operates on two positions. For example, suppose we are given the position

```
Position p1(5.0, 5.0);
```

Listing 11.2

Implementation of class Position from position.cpp

```
#include "position.h"
Position::Position(float x, float y) :
 XDistance(x), YDistance(y) {
   // No code needed
}
Position Position::Add(const Position &p) {
   return Position(GetXDistance() + p.GetXDistance(),
    GetYDistance() + p.GetYDistance());
}
float Position::GetXDistance() const {
   return XDistance;
}
float Position::GetYDistance() const {
   return YDistance;
}
void Position::SetXDistance(float x) {
   XDistance = x;
   return;
}
void Position::SetYDistance(float y) {
   YDistance = y;
   return;
}
Position operator+(const Position &a,
 const Position &b) {
   return x.Add(y);
}
```

and we need to compute a new position named p2 that is 2 centimeters to the left and 3 centimeters down from p1. We can compute this new location by adding the proper distance to p1. The code

```
Position p2 = p1 + Position(-2.0, 3.0);
```

creates p2 with the value (3.0, 8.0). As we shall see, the use of the class Position simplifies the use of EzWindows objects.

11.2.3

Hello EzWindows

To demonstrate some of the basics of using EzWindows, let's rewrite the hello world program using EzWindows. We want the new program to open a window and display the greeting Hello EzWindows in the center of the window.

To create a window, we need only instantiate a SimpleWindow object. The API will handle all of the details. Generally, the definition of a SimpleWindow object will be done via a global declaration. While we normally avoid global declarations, we need to use one in this situation because we want the window to persist during the execution of our program. Recall that an object defined inside a function block is destroyed when the block containing the definition ends. With event-based programming, there is no function where we can safely define a window and have it persist throughout the execution of the program.

The global declaration for the window is

```
SimpleWindow HelloWindow("Hello EzWindows",
  10.0, 4.0, Position(5.0, 6.0));
```

which, when executed, will create a `SimpleWindow` object named `HelloWindow` with the label Hello EzWindows. The window will by 10 centimeters by 4 centimeters, and will be positioned 5 centimeters from the left edge of the screen and 6 centimeters from the top edge of the screen.

When a `SimpleWindow` object is created, it is not immediately displayed. It is up to the programmer to open the window. Our program will open the window and display the text when EzWindows sends the user start message. EzWindows sends this message by calling the function `ApiMain()`, where most of the work is done for our program. The first thing we need to do is to get `HelloWindow` to display itself, so we send an open message to the window. The following call

```
HelloWindow.Open();
```

sends the message. Similar to calls for opening files, we should check to make sure the window indeed opens. The class `SimpleWindow` includes the member function `GetStatus()` that returns the status of the window. The prototype for `GetStatus()` is

```
WindowStatus GetStatus();
```

where type `WindowStatus` is

```
enum WindowStatus { WindowClosed, WindowOpen,
  WindowFailure };
```

Thus, a better, safer way to open a window is

```
HelloWindow.Open();
assert(HelloWindow.GetStatus() == WindowOpen);
```

If the open fails, the assert macro will print a message for us.

To print our message, we will use two additional `SimpleWindow` public member functions. The first, `GetCenter()`, returns the position of the center of the window. The second, `RenderText()`, displays a text string at a specified location in the window. The following code displays the message in the center of the window.

```
Position Center = HelloWindow.GetCenter();
Position UpperLeft = Center + Position(-1.0, -1.0);
Position LowerRight = Center + Position(1.0,  1.0);
HelloWindow.RenderText(UpperLeft, LowerRight,
  "Hello EzWindows", White);
```

When the location of the center of `HelloWindow` is obtained, a bounding box is computed to position the text. A bounding box is specified by giving the coordinates of the upper-left corner and lower-right corner of an imaginary rectangle. The text is positioned so that its center is the center of the bounding box. The size of the bounding box for `RenderText()` is somewhat irrelevant because `RenderText()` allows the text to extend past the edges of the bounding box (see Figure 11.3). Consequently, we use a box that is 1 centimeter on a side.

Figure 11.3

*Text bounding box used
by RenderText( )*

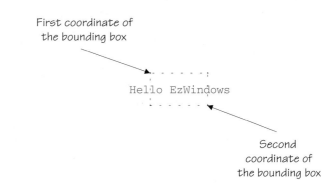

The third argument to `RenderText()` is the string to display, and the last argument is the background color to use for the text. Since, by default, a `SimpleWindow` window has a white background, the text is displayed with a white background. The colors supported by EzWindows are defined by the following enumeration:

```
enum color { White, Red, Green, Blue, Yellow,
    Cyan, Magenta };
```

The last piece of our program handles the user end message that the program receives when the operating systems sends a terminate message through EzWindows. Such messages are generated when the controlling window is closed. When EzWindows receives a terminate message, it sends a message to the user application by calling `ApiEnd()`. For the hello program, the only thing `ApiEnd()` needs to do is close the window. If the user does not supply an `ApiEnd()` function, a default `ApiEnd()`, which performs no actions, is loaded from the EzWindows library. Figure 11.4 shows the window created when our application runs and Listing 11.3 contains the complete code for the program.

Figure 11.4

*Window created by
hello program*

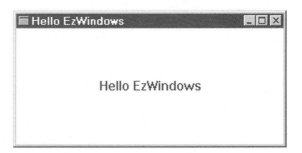

Listing 11.3

*Implementation of
EzWindows hello
program in hello.cpp*

```
// Hello EzWindows program
#include "ezwin.h"
#include <assert.h>
// Create a 10 x 4 window
SimpleWindow HelloWindow("Hello EzWindows", 10.0, 4.0,
  Position(5.0, 6.0));
// ApiMain(): create a window and display greeting
int ApiMain() {
   HelloWindow.Open();
   assert(HelloWindow.GetStatus() == WindowOpen);

   // Get Center of Window
   Position Center = HelloWindow.GetCenter();

   // Create bounding box for text
   Position UpperLeft = Center + Position(-1.0, -1.0);
   Position LowerRight = Center + Position(1.0,  1.0);

   // Display the text
   HelloWindow.RenderText(UpperLeft, LowerRight,
    "Hello EzWindows", White);

   return 0;
}
// ApiEnd(): shutdown the window
int ApiEnd() {
   HelloWindow.Close();

   return 0;
}
```

SimpleWindow has additional capabilities, such as handling events from the mouse and a timer and displaying pop-up messages. Before covering these topics, we review the other major class contained in EzWindows—Bitmap.

11.2.4

EzWindows API mechanics

The EzWindows API code and the examples discussed in this chapter are supplied on a floppy disk that is included with the textbook. Appendix E contains a reference summary of the EzWindows API. EzWindows is designed so that it can be used on PCs running Windows 3.1®, Windows 95®, and Windows NT®. It has been tested using both the Borland® C++ and the Microsoft Visual® C++ compilers.

Since the EzWindows API code is being supplied to you, to build and run an EzWindows program requires that your program be compiled and linked with the EzWindows code. Figure 11.5 illustrates this process for the hello program. The dotted box labeled EzWindows API library contains the EzWindows modules that will be linked with the program. The object code for these modules are contained in the library file ezwin.lib. The C++ linker is smart and it only pulls modules out of the library that the program being built requires. The dotted box labeled Application module contains the modules written by the programmer.

Figure 11.5

Building an EzWindows application

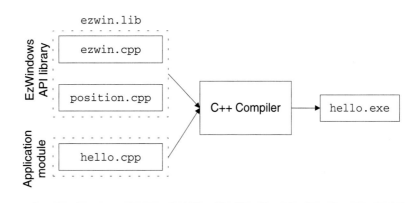

Because most software projects, even those of modest size, consist of more than one module, commercial C++ program development environments provide facilities for specifying the files that need to be compiled in order to produce an executable. Some compilers use what is known as a project file, others use a "Makefile." In both methods, the programmer specifies the files that need to be compiled, the libraries that should be used, and where to place the executable. Once this is done, building the executable usually requires simply clicking on the appropriate button. Indeed, these environments know which files have been modified since the last time the executable was built and they recompile only the files that have changed since the last build. For large software projects, this selective recompilation can save an enormous amount of time.

Throughout this chapter, most of the projects consist of several modules. To help get the big picture, we will provide a diagram like the one above that shows the program modules that go into the application.

One of the common difficulties of writing a program that uses the graphical interface is that it is sometimes hard to debug the program because there is no easy way to display debugging information. The EzWindows API solves this problem by always opening a window that text can be displayed in by inserting text into the cout stream. This window is also used for sending input to a program by extracting from the stream cin. We call this window the control window.

To illustrate the use of the EzWindows control window to do text input and output, we have modified the hello program so that it prompts for and reads the location to write the hello message. Listing 11.4 contains the code for this program. Its module structure is identical to the previous hello program. Because the program will be using cin and cout, the file iostream.h must be included. When this program is compiled and executed, two windows are created. One is the text window; the second is the window explicitly created by the program. The two windows are shown in Figure 11.6. As the figure illustrates, the text that is inserted into stream cout is displayed in the text window. Simi-

Listing 11.4

Program to illustrate stream I/O in an EzWindows program

```
// Program to illustrate mechanics of API program
#include "ezwin.h"
#include "iostream.h"
#include <assert.h>

// Create a 10 x 4 window
SimpleWindow HelloWindow("Hello EzWindows",
 10.0, 4.0, Position(5.0, 6.0)));

// ApiMain(): demonstrate using cin with EzWindows
int ApiMain() {
  HelloWindow.Open();
  assert(HelloWindow.GetStatus() == WindowOpen);

  cout << "Enter the location in the window\n"
   << "to write the text (e.g., 4 6): " << flush;
  int XCoordinate;
  int YCoordinate;
  cin >> XCoordinate >> YCoordinate;

  Position Location(XCoordinate, YCoordinate);
  Position UpperLeft = Location + Position(-1.0, -1.0);
  Position LowerRight = Location + Position(1.0, 1.0);

  // Display the text
  HelloWindow.RenderText(UpperLeft, LowerRight,
   "Hello EzWindows", White);
  cout << "Text was rendered at " << XCoordinate << ","
   << YCoordinate << endl;
  return 0;
}
// ApiEnd(): shutdown the window
int ApiEnd() {
  HelloWindow.Close();
  return 0;
}
```

larly, when the window is active, characters typed on the keyboard are placed in the stream `cin` where they can be extracted.

11.3

THE BITMAP CLASS

Most windowing systems have facilities for displaying graphical images. There are many different formats for storing images. One popular format is called a bitmap. For example, many painting programs save the drawing using the bitmap file format. On many systems, a file containing a bitmap has the extension bmp. EzWindows supports the display of bitmap images.

To illustrate some of the basic EzWindows facilities for displaying a bitmap file, we will write a program that loads and displays a bitmap photograph

Figure 11.6

Windows created by the program in Listing 11.4

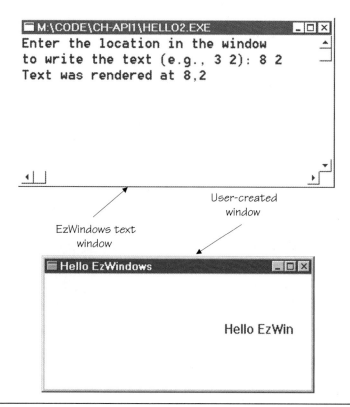

EzWindows text
window

User-created
window

of the authors of this book. The modules needed for this program are shown in the following diagram.

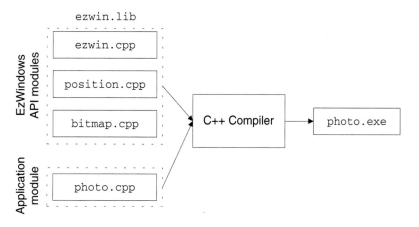

To display bitmaps, in addition to `ezwin.cpp` and `position.cpp`, the module `bitmap.cpp` is also required. This module contains the implementation of the bitmap class. The code we write is contained in the file `photo.cpp`. Figure 11.7 shows the window created and displayed by the program.

Figure 11.7

*Window created by
photo program*

Cohoon

Davidson

Photo centered in window

Like our hello program in Listing 11.3, we need to instantiate a window. We create a `SimpleWindow` object named `PhotoWindow`. Its global definition is

```
SimpleWindow PhotoWindow("The Authors", 10.0, 7.0,
    Position(5.0, 3.0));
```

Again, all the work is done in `ApiMain()`. `PhotoWindow` is opened, and the location of its center is obtained. We then instantiate a `BitMap` object named `PhotoBmp`. Its definition is

```
BitMap Photo(PhotoWindow);
```

That is, the `BitMap` constructor requires a single argument which is the `SimpleWindow` that the `BitMap` should be attached to or associated with. The declarations of `BitMap`'s constructor is

```
BitMap(SimpleWindow &DisplayWindow);
```

Thus, a `BitMap` object is constructed by giving a reference to a `SimpleWindow` object.

The next step is to load the image into the `BitMap` object. The code

```
Photo.Load("photo.bmp");
assert(Photo.GetStatus() == BitMapOkay);
```

loads the photo image from the disk into the `BitMap` object. The `BitMap` member function `GetStatus()`, like `GetStatus()` for `SimpleWindow`, returns a status indication. The declaration of `GetStatus()` is

```
BitMapStatus GetStatus();
```

and the definition of `BitMapStatus` is

```
enum BitMapStatus {NoBitMap, BitMapOkay, NoWindow};
```

Status `NoBitMap` indicates that the file specified either did not exist or was not a file containing a bitmap, and status `NoWindow` indicates that no window is associated with the `BitMap` object. This situation can happen if the `SimpleWindow` object that was bound to the `BitMap` when it was constructed was closed. In either of these cases, no image is loaded. Status `BitMapOkay` indicates the image was loaded successfully.

The last step is to compute the position within `PhotoWindow` to display the image. Unlike some of the other graphical objects we have used, `BitMap` objects are positioned by specifying the position of the upper-left corner of the image. The following code computes the proper position of the `Photo` bitmap so that it is centered in the window, sets its position, and displays the image in the window.

```
Position PhotoPosition = WindowCenter +
  Position(-.5 * Photo.GetWidth(),
  -.5 * Photo.GetHeight());
Photo.SetPosition(PhotoPosition);
Photo.Draw();
```

The code uses `BitMap` public member functions `GetWidth()` and `GetHeight()` to obtain the width and height in centimeters of the image. Listing 11.5 contains the complete code for the module `photo.cpp`.

Listing 11.5

Program that illustrates loading and displaying a bitmap

```
// Display a bit map image of the authors in the
// center of a window
#include "bitmap.h"
#include <assert.h>

// Open a window to display photograph of the authors
SimpleWindow PhotoWindow("The Authors", 10.0, 7.0,
  Position(5.0, 3.0));

// ApiMain(): display a bitmap photo
int ApiMain() {
  PhotoWindow.Open();
  assert(PhotoWindow.GetStatus() == WindowOpen);

  Position WindowCenter = PhotoWindow.GetCenter();

  // Create a bitmap
  BitMap Photo(PhotoWindow);

  // Load the image
```

```
    Photo.Load("photo.bmp");
    assert(Photo.GetStatus() == BitMapOkay);

    // Compute position of logo so it is centered
    // in the window
    Position PhotoPosition = WindowCenter +
     Position(-.5 * Photo.GetWidth(),
     -.5 * Photo.GetHeight());

    Photo.SetPosition(PhotoPosition);
    Photo.Draw();

    return 0;
}

// ApiEnd(): shutdown the window
int ApiEnd() {
    PhotoWindow.Close();

    return 0;
}
```

11.4

MOUSE EVENTS

One of the innovations that has made computers much easier to use is the mouse. A mouse lets a user interact with a program without having to type obscure or hard to remember commands. EzWindows provides a simple facility for using the mouse. The basic idea is that the application tells EzWindows what function to call when a mouse click occurs in an EzWindows `SimpleWindow`. As we mentioned earlier, this procedure is called registering a callback. The `SimpleWindow` declaration of the member function for registering a callback for a mouse event is

```
    void SetMouseClickCallback(MouseCallback f);
```

where `MouseCallback` is the **typedef**

```
    typedef int (*MouseCallback)(const Position &);
```

This declaration specifies that when an application registers a callback for a mouse-click event, we need to give the name of a function that returns an **int** and accepts a **const** Position as its argument. The value of the argument is the position of the mouse sprite when the mouse button was clicked. To illustrate how mouse-click events are handled, let's write an application that opens two windows and displays a different image in each window. When the mouse is positioned in a window and clicked, the bitmap image for that window is redisplayed at that location.

As usual, we define two global `SimpleWindow` objects. We also use global definitions for the two bitmaps because we do not want to keep instantiating them and destroying them when messages are sent to the application from EzWindows. The definitions are

```
    SimpleWindow W1("Window One", 15.0, 9.0,
     Position(1.0, 1.0));
```

```
SimpleWindow W2("Window Two", 15.0, 9.0,
  Position(8.0, 12.0));
// Define two bitmaps, one for each window
BitMap W1Bmp(W1);
BitMap W2Bmp(W2);
```

Function `ApiMain()` opens the two windows, loads the bitmaps, and displays the bitmaps in each window at a default location. This code is similar to the code we wrote for the previous program. See Listing 11.5 for the details. The last action of `ApiMain()` is to register the functions to call back on a mouse click. We need to register a callback function for each window. The code

```
W1.SetMouseClickCallback(W1MouseClick);
W2.SetMouseClickCallback(W2MouseClick);
```

sends a message to `W1` telling `W1` to call function `W1MouseClick` when it receives a mouse-click event. The code sends a similar message to `W2`.

The definition of `W1MouseClick` is

```
int W1MouseClick(const Position &p) {
    // Erase the bitmap
    W1Bmp.Erase();

    // Set its new position and display it
    W1Bmp.SetPosition(p);
    W1Bmp.Draw();

    return 1;
}
```

The mouse-event handler for `W1` erases its associated bitmap, resets its position using the position passed to it from EzWindows, and draws the bitmap at the new position. Our code is contained in the module `mevent.cpp`. The required module structure follows.

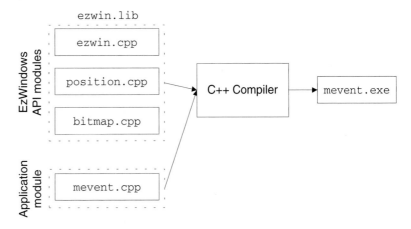

When the modules are compiled and linked, the executable will be placed in the file `mevent.exe`. Figure 11.8 illustrates what happens when the program runs.

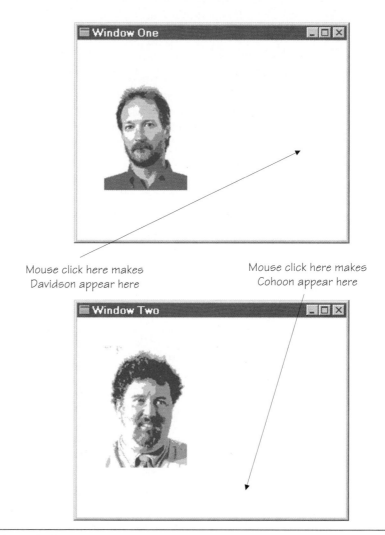

Figure 11.8

*Window created by
mouse-event program*

The code for `W2MouseClick` is similar and is contained in Listing 11.6, which contains the entire program.

Listing 11.6

Program to illustrate responding to mouse events

```
// Example showing use of the mouse
// The program displays a bitmap in the window at
// the place where the mouse is click
#include "bitmap.h"
#include <assert.h>

// Define two non-overlapping windows
SimpleWindow W1("Window One", 15.0, 9.0,
 Position(1.0, 1.0));

SimpleWindow W2("Window Two", 15.0, 9.0,
 Position(8.0, 12.0));

// Define two bitmaps, one for each window
BitMap W1Bmp(W1);
BitMap W2Bmp(W2);

// W1MouseClick(): call back function for Window one
int W1MouseClick(const Position &p) {

    // Erase the bitmap
    W1Bmp.Erase();

    // Set its new position and display it
    W1Bmp.SetPosition(p);
    W1Bmp.Draw();

    return 1;
}
// W2MouseClick(): call back function for Window two
int W2MouseClick(const Position &p) {

    // Erase the bitmap
    W2Bmp.Erase();

    // Set its new position and display it
    W2Bmp.SetPosition(p);
    W2Bmp.Draw();

    return 1;
}

int ApiMain() {

    // Open the windows
    W1.Open();
    assert(W1.GetStatus() == WindowOpen);
    W2.Open();
    assert(W2.GetStatus() == WindowOpen);

    // Load the images
    W1Bmp.Load("c1.bmp");
    assert(W1Bmp.GetStatus() == BitMapOkay);
    W2Bmp.Load("c2.bmp");
    assert(W2Bmp.GetStatus() == BitMapOkay);

    // Display the bit maps at a starting position
    W1Bmp.SetPosition(Position(1.0, 1.0));
    W2Bmp.SetPosition(Position(1.0, 1.0));
    W1Bmp.Draw();
    W2Bmp.Draw();

    // Register the call backs for each window
    W1.SetMouseClickCallback(W1MouseClick);
    W2.SetMouseClickCallback(W2MouseClick);
```

```
    return 0;
}
int ApiEnd() {
    // Close the windows
    W1.Close();
    W2.Close();

    return 0;
}
```

11.5

BITMAPS AND MOUSE EVENTS

A useful feature of a bitmap is the ability to determine if a location is inside a bitmap. EzWindows `BitMaps` have this capability built in. The declaration of this member function is

```
    int BitMap::IsInside(const Position &AtPosn);
```

which returns one if `AtPosn` is contained with the bitmap and zero otherwise. In conjunction with the mouse, this capability provides the facilities for designing simple controls. For example, we can display a `BitMap` that represents some action to take. We can cause this action to take place by positioning the mouse sprite inside the bitmap and clicking a button. To illustrate this capability, we will write a program that displays the bitmap images of a card. When the mouse is clicked inside the card, the card is flipped over. The application code is contained in the file `flip.cpp`, and the required modules for this program follow.

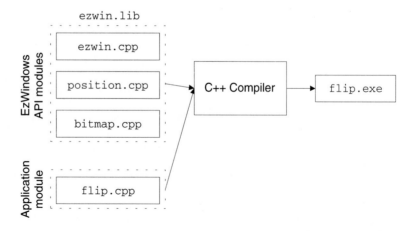

Just like the previous EzWindows sample programs, we define a window. We also need two bitmaps: One is the front of the card and the other is the back. In addition to these global objects, we need an object that remembers which side of the card is showing. Recall that this is known as a state variable. The following definitions do the job.

```
// Define a window
SimpleWindow FlipWindow("FlipCard", 15.0, 9.0,
  Position(1.0, 1.0));

// Define bitmaps for the front and back of a card
BitMap CardFront(FlipWindow);
BitMap CardBack(FlipWindow);

// Need a type and object for remembering which side
// of the card is showing
enum Side { Front, Back };
Side SideShowing;
```

The `ApiMain()` function is similar to some of the previous code we have written. What's new here is what happens in our mouse call-back function. When the program receives the message, it checks to see if the mouse is pointing inside the card. The implementation of the function is:

```
int MouseClickEvent(const Position &MousePosition) {
    if (CardFront.IsInside(MousePosition)) {
        // card is selected so flip it
        if (SideShowing == Back) {
            SideShowing = Front;
            CardFront.Draw();
        }
        else if (SideShowing == Front) {
            SideShowing = Back;
            CardBack.Draw();
        }
    }
    return 1;
}
```

If the mouse was clicked inside the card, the code checks the state variable to see which side is showing. If the back side is showing, the code draws the front of the card and changes `SideShowing` to `Front`; if the front side is showing, the code draws the back of the card and changes `SideShowing` to `Back`. The effect on the screen is that the card is "flipped" each time the mouse is clicked inside it. The complete code for this demonstration program is contained in Listing 11.7.

Listing 11.7

Program to illustrate checking to see if the mouse points at an object

```
// Demonstrate selecting an action
// by clicking in a bitmap
#include <assert.h>
#include "bitmap.h"

// Define a window
SimpleWindow FlipWindow("FlipCard", 15.0, 9.0,
  Position(1.0, 1.0));

// Define bitmaps for the front and back of a card
BitMap CardFront(FlipWindow);
BitMap CardBack(FlipWindow);

// Need a type and object for remembering which side
```

```
                        // of the card is showing
                        enum Side { Front, Back };
                        Side SideShowing;

                        // MouseClickEvent(): come here when user clicks mouse
                        int MouseClickEvent(const Position &MousePosition) {
                            if (CardFront.IsInside(MousePosition)) {
                                    // card is selected so flip it
                                if (SideShowing == Back) {
                                    SideShowing = Front;
                                    CardFront.Draw();
                                }
                                else if (SideShowing == Front) {
                                    SideShowing = Back;
                                    CardBack.Draw();
                                }
                            }

                            return 1;
                        }

                        int ApiMain() {
                            // Open the window
                            FlipWindow.Open();
                            assert(FlipWindow.GetStatus() == WindowOpen);

                            // Load the images
                            CardFront.Load("c1.bmp");
                            assert(CardFront.GetStatus() == BitMapOkay);

                            CardBack.Load("cardbk1.bmp");
                            assert(CardBack.GetStatus() == BitMapOkay);

                            // Compute position to display the card
                            Position CardPosition = FlipWindow.GetCenter() +
                             Position(-.5 * CardFront.GetWidth(),
                             -.5 * CardFront.GetHeight());

                            CardFront.SetPosition(CardPosition);
                            CardBack.SetPosition(CardPosition);

                            SideShowing = Front;
                            CardFront.Draw();

                            // Set up mouse call back
                            FlipWindow.SetMouseClickCallback(MouseClickEvent);

                            return 0;
                        }

                        int ApiEnd() {
                            FlipWindow.Close();

                            return 0;
                        }
```

11.6

TIMER EVENTS

Another feature of EzWindows is the ability to set up a timer. A timer is useful when we want our program to perform some action at a predetermined time or interval. You can think of a timer as an alarm clock managed by EzWindows.

When the alarm clock goes off, EzWindows informs the application program by sending it a message through a call-back function. The `SimpleWindow` member functions for setting up and managing a timer are `SetTimerCall-back()`, `StartTimer()`, and `StopTimer()`. `SetTimerCallback()` is similar to `SetMouseClickCallback()`. It registers the user's call-back function with EzWindows. The call-back function will be invoked when a timer event occurs.

The member function `StartTimer()` starts a timer. It takes a single argument, which is how often to generate a timer event. The argument is in milliseconds. For example, the statements

```
SWin.SetTimerCallback(TimerHandler);
SWin.StartTimer(1000);
```

set up a timer for the `SimpleWindow` `SWin`. The timer will go off every 1,000 milliseconds, or once a second. When it goes off, the user routine `TimerHandler()` is called.

When no further timer events are required, a timer is turned off by calling `StopTimer()`. The statement

```
SWin.StopTimer();
```

stops the timer started in the code above.

To illustrate the use of timer events, let's modify `mouse.cpp` from section 11.4 so that the bitmaps are displayed at a random location in the window every half second. The module structure for this example program follows.

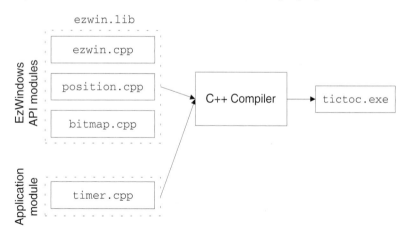

The new module is called `timer.cpp`, but most of the code is the same as the code in `mouse.cpp`. Instead of setting up two mouse call-back functions, we set up two timer-event call-back functions. The statements that set up the call-back for our two windows are

```
W1.SetTimerCallback(W1TimerEvent);
W2.SetTimerCallback(W2TimerEvent);
W1.StartTimer(500);
W2.StartTimer(500);
```

and the timer-event call-back functions are

```
int W1TimerEvent() {
    Redisplay(W1, W1Bmp);

    return 1;
}
int W2TimerEvent() {
    Redisplay(W2, W2Bmp);

    return 1;
}
```

Function ReDisplay() handles the details of generating a random location to display the bitmap. See Listing 11.8 for its implementation.

Listing 11.8

Program to demonstrate use of a timer

```
// Example showing use of timer events
// The program displays a bitmap in the window at
// a random location when the timer goes off
#include "bitmap.h"
#include <assert.h>

// Define two non-overlapping windows
SimpleWindow W1("Window One", 15.0, 9.0,
 Position(1.0, 1.0));

SimpleWindow W2("Window Two", 15.0, 9.0,
 Position(8.0, 12.0));

// Define two bitmaps, one for each window
BitMap W1Bmp(W1);
BitMap W2Bmp(W2);

// Redisplay(): move bitmap to a new location
void Redisplay(SimpleWindow &W, BitMap &B) {
    // Erase the bitmap
    B.Erase();

    // Compute a new position and display it
    // Make sure the bitmap is completely in the window
    int XCoord = Uniform(1, W.GetWidth());
    if (XCoord + B.GetWidth() > W.GetWidth())
      XCoord = XCoord - B.GetWidth();
    int YCoord = Uniform(1, W.GetHeight());
    if (YCoord + B.GetHeight() > W.GetHeight())
      YCoord = YCoord - B.GetHeight();
    B.SetPosition(Position(XCoord, YCoord));
    B.Draw();
}

// W1TimerEvent(): call-back function for Window one
int W1TimerEvent() {
    Redisplay(W1, W1Bmp);

    return 1;
}

// W2TimerEvent(): call back function for Window two
int W2TimerEvent() {
    Redisplay(W2, W2Bmp);

    return 1;
}
// ApiMain(): open the windows and start the timers
```

```
int ApiMain() {
   // Open the windows
   W1.Open();
   assert(W1.GetStatus() == WindowOpen);
   W2.Open();
   assert(W2.GetStatus() == WindowOpen);

   // Load the images
   W1Bmp.Load("c1.bmp");
   assert(W1Bmp.GetStatus() == BitMapOkay);
   W2Bmp.Load("c2.bmp");
   assert(W2Bmp.GetStatus() == BitMapOkay);

   // Display the bit maps at a starting position
   W1Bmp.SetPosition(Position(1.0, 1.0));
   W2Bmp.SetPosition(Position(1.0, 1.0));
   W1Bmp.Draw();
   W2Bmp.Draw();

   // Register the callbacks for each window
   // and start the timers to go off every 500 ms
   W1.SetTimerCallback(W1TimerEvent);
   W2.SetTimerCallback(W2TimerEvent);
   W1.StartTimer(500);
   W2.StartTimer(500);

   return 0;
}
int ApiEnd() {
   // Stop the timers and close the windows
   W1.StopTimer();
   W2.StopTimer();
   W1.Close();
   W2.Close();

   return 0;
}
```

11.7

ALERT MESSAGES

It is often handy to pop up a window and display a message that the user cannot ignore. One way to make sure the message is not ignored is to block the user from working in any of the windows that the application has open. Such windows are sometimes called alert windows or modal dialog boxes. The class SimpleWindow provides a facility for displaying alert windows. For example, if there is an open SimpleWindow called Jitterbug, the statement

```
Jitterbug.Message("Nice swatting!");
```

would cause an alert window to appear. Furthermore, the user cannot work in any of the windows belonging to the application until the message box is dismissed. (Program execution is suspended until the message box is dismissed.) To illustrate the behavior of message boxes, let's modify our hello program so that a message box pops up before the text is displayed. The module structure follows.

```
                    ezwin.lib
```

The revised `ApiMain()` is

```cpp
int ApiMain() {
    HelloWindow.Open();
    assert(HelloWindow.GetStatus() == WindowOpen);
    // Get Center of Window
    Position Center = HelloWindow.GetCenter();
    // Create bounding box for text
    Position UpperLeft = Center
     + Position(-1.0, -1.0);
    Position LowerRight = Center
     + Position(1.0,  1.0);
    HelloWindow.Message("Click Ok to continue");
    // Display the text
    HelloWindow.RenderText(UpperLeft, LowerRight,
     "Hello EzWindows", White);
    return 0;
}
```

This program creates the windows in Figure 11.9. Notice that the main window does not have any text displayed in it. Furthermore, if the mouse is clicked inside the main window, a beep warns the user that the program is suspended. When the user clicks on OK, the alert box disappears and the text Hello EzWindows is displayed in the window.

11.8

SIMON SAYS

We all remember the childhood game Simon Says. We conclude this chapter on the EzWindows API by developing a computer version of this game. In this game, which we call Simon, a set of cards are displayed in the window. The game starts when the computer flips the cards over momentarily in a random sequence. After the computer has flipped the cards, the player must select the

Figure 11.9

*Message box displayed
with window*

objects in the same order as they were flipped. If the player successfully recalls the order in which the cards were flipped, the computer displays another, longer sequence. The game continues until the player makes a mistake or the player successfully remembers the longest sequence.

Writing the game is actually not too hard when we use the EzWindows API, especially if we design the game using object-oriented principles. First we need to decide what objects we need, and how they will communicate or collaborate with one another. A more formal description of the game will help with the first tasks.

The game Simon consists of a window in which several types of images are displayed. One type of image is a card that can be flipped over. Four cards are displayed adjacent to one another across the window. In addition to the cards, there are control images. One image is a restart button. When the mouse is clicked on this button, the game starts over at the beginning level. Another image is a quit button. When it is selected, the game is terminated.

Simon is played as follows. Cards are flipped over momentarily in a random sequence. Initially, three cards are flipped. After a sequence is shown, the player must select the cards in the same order. If the player is successful, a new sequence, one longer than before, is shown. The player wins the game when a sequence of six cards is recalled successfully.

From the above statement, it is clear that we need an object to represent the cards. One behavior of the cards is that they should be able to be flipped. We also need to be able to determine if the mouse is pointing at a card. We will call this class SimonObject. It should be obvious that the EzWindows Bit-Map class provides much of functionality needed by SimonObject. Other, similar objects are the control objects. These are also represented by EzWindows `BitMap` objects.

Another object that is required is something that controls the play of the game. It will be responsible for generating the sequence, causing the cards to be flipped in the proper order, and then checking to see if the player recalls the correct sequence. It will also be responsible for setting up the game and determining when the game is over. We will call this class `SimonGame`.

One other important object is mentioned in our description—the player. Fortunately, we do not need to implement the player because this function is provided by one of us.

The objects in the game provide a natural partitioning of the program into modules, as shown in Figure 11.10. Module `simobj.cpp` contains the implementation of class `SimonObject`, and module `simon.cpp` contains the implementation of class `SimonGame`. Function `ApiMain()` and the mouse and timer call-back functions are in module `simmain.cpp`.

Figure 11.10

Module structure of Simon

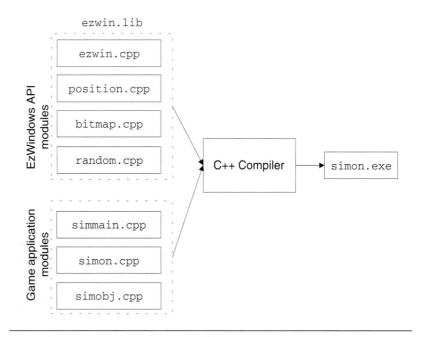

`SimonGame` controls the game, so let's get a rough cut at what it should do and what attributes and objects it should contain. The behaviors or actions provided by `SimonGame` include setting up the game board in the window, generating a sequence to flip the cards, flipping the cards, and dealing with mouse clicks in the window. A mouse click could be in one of the control bitmaps, which means the player is asking either to restart the game or to quit, or it could be inside the card, which means the player is selecting that card as the one that was next flashed in the sequence. The behaviors or responsibilities of `SimonGame` are:

- Initialize the game.
- Handle mouse-click events.
- Generate a sequence to flip the cards.
- Manage the play of the game.
- Flip the cards.

Obviously, SimonGame should contain all the attributes of the game. These include the length of the sequence, whose turn it is to go (computer or human), and the sequence to play. In addition to these attributes, SimonGame will contain the SimonObjects, a SimpleWindow to display the SimonObjects, and the bitmaps for controlling the game. The bitmaps for controlling the game will be called Restart and Quit. The attributes of SimonGame are:

- A SimpleWindow object for the game.
- An array of SimonObjects.
- The restart and quit bitmaps.
- The order to flash the cards.
- A state attribute that contains whose turn it is to go.
- The current sequence length.

Our first version of class SimonGame follows.

```
class SimonGame {
    enum Turn { Simon, Player };
    public:
        SimonGame(SimpleWindow &Window);
        void Initialize();
        void Play();
        int MouseClick(const Position &MousePosn);
        int Timer();
        void PickOrder();
    private:
        SimpleWindow &W;
        SimonObject Posn[MaxPositions];
        BitMap Restart;
        BitMap Quit;
        int Order[MaxSequenceLength];
        Turn WhoseTurn;
        int SequenceLength;
};
```

Let's examine the data members first. Like all the objects we have used before that involve a window, SimonGame includes a reference to the window that will display the game. Posn is an array of SimonObjects. These objects are displayed across the window and flipped in a random sequence. Restart and Quit are the bitmaps for controlling the game. The array Order contains the sequence to flip the SimonObjects. The state object WhoseTurn contains whose turn it is to go—the computer or the player. Finally, the data member SequenceLength contains the length of the sequence to generate. As the game progresses, SequenceLength gets larger.

The public member functions include a constructor, which takes as a single argument the window that will display the game. `Initialize()` sets up the game board. `Play()` puts the game is put into its initial state and starts it. `MouseClick()` and `Timer()` will be called on mouse-click and timer-tick events, respectively. These functions handle much of the logic of the game. `PickOrder()` generates the random sequence to flip the cards.

Now we turn to `SimonObject`. From the description of the game, it is clear that a `SimonObject` should have a flip behavior. We will also need to be able to determine if the mouse is clicked inside a `SimonObject`. Finally, we will need to be able to draw the `SimonObjects`. As we noted, many of these properties will be supplied by `BitMap`. We can think of a `SimonObject` as packaging a `BitMap` with some additional properties. At this point, the behaviors of a `SimonObject` are:

- Flip itself over.
- Determine if the mouse is clicked inside it.
- Draw itself.

A `SimonObject` contains two bitmaps—one for the front of the object and one for the back. It also has an attribute that indicates which side is currently showing.

The declaration of `SimonObject` follows.

```
enum Side { Front, Back };
class SimonObject {
   public:
       SimonObject();
       void Initialize(SimpleWindow &GameWindow,
        string FrontFile, string BackFile,
        const Position &Posn);
       void SetSide(const Side s);
       Side GetSide() const;
       void Draw();
       void Flip();
       bool IsInside(const Position &MousePosition);
   private:
       BitMap FrontSide;
       BitMap BackSide;
       Side SideShowing;
};
```

In addition to the behaviors previously listed, a `SimonObject` contains an inspector and mutator for the data member `SideShowing`.

Now that we have a good idea of what our two main objects look like, we can describe how the program will work. The board will consist of some `SimonObjects` and the control buttons. These will be EzWindows `Bitmaps`. We will be able to determine if the mouse is pointing at a `SimonObject` or control button using `BitMap`'s `IsInside` member function. The flow of the game is controlled by timer events and mouse-click events, which are handled by `SimonGame`. Figure 11.11 shows the classes and the messages that they send one another. As the diagram shows, the `BitMap` class is the key building block for the game.

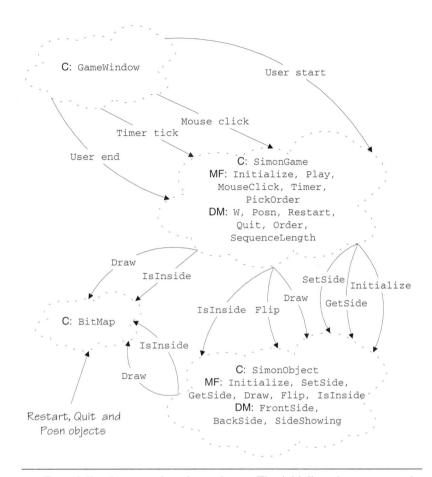

Figure 11.11

Simon classes and the messages they send

Essentially, the game has three phases. The initialize phase sets up the board and gets everything ready to play. The second phase is where the Simon-Objects are flashed, and the third phase is where the player selects the SimonObjects and the selection is checked to see if it was correct.

The first phase is straightforward. We can write it first and then check to see that the board looks like we want it to. The first thing is to write the constructor for SimonGame.

```
SimonGame::SimonGame(SimpleWindow &Window) :
W(Window) {
    // No code needed!
}
```

It simply initializes the W data member. All the real work is done in Simon-Game::Initialize(). The first part draws the SimonObjects and uses

SimonObject::Initialize() to load the BitMap for each position. The code follows.

```
assert(W.GetStatus() == WindowOpen);
SequenceLength = BeginningSequenceLength;
X = InitialPosition.GetXDistance();
Y = InitialPosition.GetYDistance();
string BitMapFile[MaxPositions] =
  { "c1.bmp","c2.bmp", "c3.bmp", "c4.bmp" };
for (p = 0; p < MaxPositions; ++p) {
    Posn[p].Initialize(W, BitMapFile[p],
    "cardbk1.bmp", Position(X, Y));
    Posn[p].Draw();
    X += Posn[p].GetWidth() + 0.5;
}
```

BitMapFile contains the filenames of the images to load for each position on the board. We will use bitmaps of cards. The for loop initializes each position by calling SimonObject::Initialize() and passing it the window, the bitmap for the front side of the SimonObject, the bitmap for the back side, and the position of the SimonObject. Based on the width of the bitmap, the position of the next SimonObject is computed.

The next part of SimonGame::Initialize() sets up the control buttons. This code simply loads the bitmaps that contain the images of the buttons and draws them at the proper location. Listing 11.9 shows the complete implementation of SimonGame::Initialize().

Listing 11.9

SimonGame's Initialize() member function from simon.cpp

```
// Initialize(): initialize the game, init'ing simon
// game objects
void SimonGame::Initialize() {
  int p;
  float X, Y;
  InitializeSeed();
  assert(W.GetStatus() == WindowOpen);
  SequenceLength = BeginningSequenceLength;

  X = InitialPosition.GetXDistance();
  Y = InitialPosition.GetYDistance();

  string BitMapFile[MaxPositions] =
    { "c1.bmp","c2.bmp", "c3.bmp", "c4.bmp" };
  for (p = 0; p < MaxPositions; ++p) {
    Posn[p].Initialize(W, BitMapFile[p],
    "cardbk1.bmp", Position(X, Y));
    Posn[p].Draw();
    X += Posn[p].GetWidth() + 0.5;
  }

  // Set up the control buttons
  Restart.SetWindow(W);
  Restart.Load("rbutton2.bmp");
  assert(Restart.GetStatus() == BitMapOkay);
  X = InitialPosition.GetXDistance();
  Y += Posn[0].GetHeight() + 2.0;
  Restart.SetPosition(Position(X, Y));

  Quit.SetWindow(W);
  Quit.Load("qbutton2.bmp");
```

```
    assert(Quit.GetStatus() == BitMapOkay);
    X = Restart.GetWidth() + 2.0;
    Quit.SetPosition(Position(X, Y));

    Restart.Draw();
    Quit.Draw();
}
```

`SimonObject`'s `Initialize()` member function uses `BitMap` member functions to initialize the `FrontSide` and `BackSide`. It also sets the data member `SideShowing` to `Back`. The code for this function is contained in Listing 11.10.

Listing 11.10

SimonObject's Initialize() member function from simobj.cpp

```
// Initialize(): load a card face and back for this
// simon object
void SimonObject::Initialize(SimpleWindow &GameWindow,
 string FrontFile, string BackFile,
 const Position &Posn) {
  FrontSide.SetWindow(GameWindow);
  FrontSide.SetPosition(Posn);
  FrontSide.Load(FrontFile);
  assert(FrontSide.GetStatus() == BitMapOkay);

  BackSide.SetWindow(GameWindow);
  BackSide.SetPosition(Posn);
  BackSide.Load(BackFile);
  assert(BackSide.GetStatus() == BitMapOkay);
  SetSide(Back);
}
```

With these functions implemented, we can write an `ApiMain()` that will display the game window. As usual, we declare a global `SimpleWindow` for the display. We also instantiate a `SimonGame`. The two definitions are

```
SimpleWindow GameWindow("Simon Game", 14.0, 7.0,
 Position(0.25, 0.25));
SimonGame Simon(GameWindow);
```

The preliminary version of `ApiMain()` that displays the game window only is

```
int ApiMain() {
   GameWindow.Open();
   Simon.Initialize();

   return 0;
}
```

Figure 11.12 shows the resulting window.

Before going further with the game, let's go ahead and complete the implementation of `SimonObject`. After all, we will need to use its capabilities to implement the game. The inspector `GetSide()` and mutator `SetSide()` are much like all the other inspectors and mutators we have implemented. See Listing 11.11 for their implementations.

Figure 11.12

*Window for Simon
before play starts*

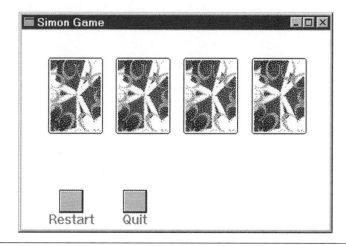

Member function `Draw()` is

```
void SimonObject::Draw() {
    if (SideShowing == Back)
        BackSide.Draw();
    else
        FrontSide.Draw();
}
```

which simply decides which `BitMap`, `BackSide` or `FrontSide`, to draw based on the value in `SideShowing`. `Flip()` simply sets `SideShowing` to the opposite of what it currently is and then invokes `Draw()`. Member function `Flip()`'s definition is

```
// Flip(): flip the object and redraw it
void SimonObject::Flip() {
    SetSide(GetSide() == Back ? Front : Back);
    Draw();
}
```

Finally, `SimonObject::IsInside()` simply invokes `BackSide.IsInside()`. It doesn't matter whether we use `BackSide` or `FrontSide`, as they are both at the same position. We note that because EzWindows provides much of the underlying capabilities, all the member functions of `SimonObject` were short and simple.

Listing 11.11

Module simobj.cpp

```
#include <iostream.h>
#include <string>
#include <stdio.h>
#include <stdlib.h>
#include <assert.h>
#include "simobj.h"

SimonObject::SimonObject() {
};
```

```
// Initialize(): load a card face and back for this
// simon object
void SimonObject::Initialize(SimpleWindow &GameWindow,
 string FrontFile, string BackFile,
 const Position &Posn) {
   FrontSide.SetWindow(GameWindow);
   FrontSide.SetPosition(Posn);
   FrontSide.Load(FrontFile);
   assert(FrontSide.GetStatus() == BitMapOkay);

   BackSide.SetWindow(GameWindow);
   BackSide.SetPosition(Posn);
   BackSide.Load(BackFile);
   assert(BackSide.GetStatus() == BitMapOkay);
   SetSide(Back);
}

// SetSide(): set the current object's side
void SimonObject::SetSide(const Side s) {
   SideShowing = s;
}

// GetSide(): get the current object's side
Side SimonObject::GetSide() const {
   return SideShowing;
}

// GetHeight(): get the height of the bitmap
float SimonObject::GetHeight() const {
   return FrontSide.GetHeight();
}

// GetWidth(): get the width of the bitmap
float SimonObject::GetWidth() const {
   return FrontSide.GetWidth();
}

// Flip(): flip the object and redraw it
void SimonObject::Flip() {
   SetSide(GetSide() == Back ? Front : Back);
   Draw();
}

// IsInside(): determine if a mouse click falls in
// this object
bool SimonObject::IsInside(const Position &p) const {
   return BackSide.IsInside(p);
}

// Draw(): draw the object to the window
void SimonObject::Draw() {
   if (SideShowing == Back)
     BackSide.Draw();
   else
     FrontSide.Draw();
}
```

With the game board set up and SimonObject implemented, we can now implement the play. The play of the game is controlled by member function Play(), which is called to play a round of the game. A round consists of two phases. In the first phase, the computer flashes the SimonObjects in random order. In the second phase, the player must select the objects in the same order. We can think of this as Simon and the player taking turns.

The first step of `Play()` is to mark that it is Simon's turn and to make sure all the objects are flipped over and ready to be flashed. We need to do this because some of the objects were undoubtedly flipped over in a previous round. The code for this step follows.

```
WhoseTurn = Simon;
for (int p = 0; p < MaxPositions; ++p) {
    Posn[p].SetSide(Back);
    Posn[p].Draw();
}
```

We can now generate the sequence to flash the objects, which is accomplished by the member function `PickOrder()`. The random sequence to flip the objects is held in the `SimonGame` data member `Order`. The elements of this array are integers that select a `Posn`. For example, in Figure 11.13 the array `Order` contains the values 1, 0, 2, 3, 3, and 1. This array indicates that the `SimonObject` in `Posn[1]` should be flashed first, then the one in `Posn[0]`, `Posn[2]`, and so on. The idea is to shuffle the values in `Order` to determine the order to flash the objects held in `Posn`. This process is similar to shuffling a deck of cards, which we implemented in Chapter 10.

Figure 11.13

Selecting an object to flip in a random sequence

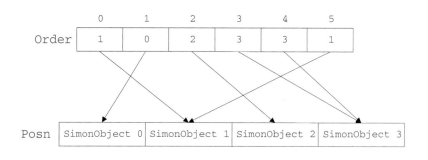

The shuffling of `Order` is done by member function `PickOrder()`. The first step is to initialize `Order`. We need to initialize only the elements of the array that will be used to generate the sequence. The length of the sequence is held in data member `SequenceLength`. The following code initializes the array.

```
for (i = 0; i < SequenceLength; ++i)
    Order[i] = i % MaxPositions;
```

Notice that because `Order` has more elements than `Posn`, we take the modulus of `i`. This ensures that the values stored in `Order` are in the range zero to three.

Once we have initialized the array, we can shuffle the values around. We use the technique we developed in Chapter 10 to shuffle a deck of cards. For the ith element of `Order`, we generate a random number `j`, in the range 0 to

MaxPositions-1. Then we swap the jth element of Order with the ith element. Listing 11.12 contains the definition of SimonGame::PickOrder().

Listing 11.12

SimonGame's PickOrder() member function from simon.cpp

```
// PickOrder(): generate a random sequence
void SimonGame::PickOrder() {
   for (int i = 0; i < SequenceLength; ++i)
      Order[i] = i % MaxPositions;
   Random R(0, MaxPositions - 1);
   R.Randomize();
   for (int i = 0; i < SequenceLength; ++i) {
      int j = R.Draw();
      int tmp = Order[j];
      Order[j] = Order[i];
      Order[i] = tmp;
   }
}
```

After Play() calls PickOrder() to produce the sequence, we are ready to flash the cards. Here is where event-based object-oriented programming really comes into its own. In fact, without events, this program would be difficult, if not impossible, to write. The basic idea is that we will use an EzWindows timer to flip the SimonObjects. To keep track of the next SimonObject to be flipped, we add the data member Selection to the private section of SimonGame. Its declaration is

```
int Selection;
```

Selection will also be used in the next phase of the game to keep track of the order that the player should pick the cards.

So the last step of SimonGame::Play() is to set Selection to zero and start the timer. Listing 11.13 contains the complete code for Play().

Listing 11.13

SimonGame's Play() member function from simon.cpp

```
// Play(): go play the simon game at the current level
void SimonGame::Play() {
   // it's simon's turn to flash the objects in order
   WhoseTurn = Simon;
   // turn all objects over ready for flashing
   for (int p = 0; p < MaxPositions; ++p) {
      Posn[p].SetSide(Back);
      Posn[p].Draw();
   }
   // pick a random order to flash the simon objects
   PickOrder();
   // Selection keeps track of the number of
   // objects flashed so far
   Selection = 0;

   // Start the timer for flashing the SimonObjects
   W.StartTimer(FlashInterval);
}
```

The timer for the GameWindow is set up in ApiMain(). The call is

```
GameWindow.SetTimerCallback(TimerEvent);
```

and function `TimerEvent` calls Simon's `Timer()` member function. The implementation of `TimerEvent()` is

```
// TimerEvent(): pass timer ticks to the game
// to flip the appropriate card
int TimerEvent() {
    return Simon.Timer();
}
```

The basic idea behind using the timer to flip the `SimonObjects` is that we set up the timer to generate a callback at twice the speed we want the objects to be flipped. When `SimonGame::Timer()` receives the first timer-tick message, it flips the first object in the sequence onto its front. When it receives the next tick message, it flips that same object onto its back. When the next timer tick occurs, the next object in the sequence is flipped onto its front, and so on. When the last object in the sequence has been flipped back onto its back, we turn off the timer and mark that it is now the player's turn. The data member `Selection` is used to select the values from the array `Order`. Listing 11.14 contains the implementation.

Listing 11.14

*Simon's Timer()
member function from
simon.cpp*

```
// Timer(): process timer tick events, flipping
// simon objects
int SimonGame::Timer() {
    // see if we are done flashing objects
    if (Selection == SequenceLength) {
        WhoseTurn = Player;
        W.StopTimer();
        Selection = 0;
        return 1;
    }
    // Get the current object
    int p = Order[Selection];
    // flip object to back side, if not on that side
    // if on that side, flip it to front and
    // go to next object
    if (Posn[p].GetSide() == Back)
        Posn[p].Flip();
    else {
        Posn[p].Flip();
        ++Selection;
    }
    return 1;
}
```

The final step in the development of Simon is to handle mouse-click events. The mouse is used by the player to select the cards in the order the player remembers them being flipped. The mouse can also be used to either quit the game or restart the game.

The setup for handling mouse-click events is similar to the setup for timer events. We send a message to `GameWindow` telling it to call the function `MouseClickEvent()` when a mouse click occurs inside it. The code is

```
GameWindow.SetMouseClickCallback(MouseClickEvent);
```

Function `MouseClickEvent()` forwards the message to Simon's `Mouse-Click()` member function. The code for `MouseClickEvent()` is

```
int MouseClickEvent(const Position &MousePosn) {
   return Simon.MouseClick(MousePosn);
}
```

The first thing `MouseClick()` should do is check to see if the control buttons `Restart` or `Quit` have been selected. If the `Restart` button was selected, the code should set `SequenceLength` back to the beginning sequence length and call `Play()` to start a new game. If the `Quit` button was selected, we should exit the program. The initial part of `MouseClick()` is

```
int SimonGame::MouseClick(const Position
 &MousePosn) {
   int p;
   // restart button clicked?
   if (Restart.IsInside(MousePosn)) {
       SequenceLength = BeginningSequenceLength;
       Play();
       return 1;
   }
   // quit button clicked?
   else if (Quit.IsInside(MousePosn))
       Terminate();
```

The function `Terminate()` is an EzWindows function that terminates an application. Before EzWindows terminates the application, it sends an `Api-End()` message to the application so any necessary clean up can be done.

If the mouse was not clicked inside one of the control buttons, the next step is to determine if it's the player's turn, and if so, whether the mouse was clicked inside a card. If the mouse was clicked inside a card, then we need to check if the card was selected in the correct order. The data member `Selection` is again used to step through the array `Order`. Notice that in `Simon::Timer()`, when all the objects were flipped, `Selection` was set back to zero.

To help determine whether the mouse was clicked while pointing inside a card, we add a member function `Find()` to class `Simon`. `Find()` determines if the mouse was clicked inside a `SimonObject`.The implementation of this member function follows.

```
// Find(): find the selected simon object
int SimonGame::Find(const Position &MousePosn) {
   for (int p = 0; p < MaxPositions; ++p)
       if (Posn[p].IsInside(MousePosn))
           return p;
   return -1;
};
```

The code for `Simon::Find()` simply loops over the array `Posn` invoking the member function `IsInside()` on each `SimonObject`. If `IsInside()` returns true, the index is returned. If the loop completes, the mouse was not pointing at a `SimonObject` and the value –1 is returned.

With the addition of `Find()`, the development of class `SimonGame` is complete. Listing 11.15 contains the final version of its declaration.

Listing 11.15

Declaration of SimonGame from simon.h

```
#ifndef SIMON_H
#define SIMON_H

#include "simobj.h"

const int MaxPositions = 4;
const int BeginningSequenceLength = 3;
const int MaxSequenceLength = 6;

// Lower this to make the game harder
const int FlashInterval = 800;

// Position of first SimonObject
const Position InitialPosition(1.0, 1.0);

class SimonGame {
    enum Turn { Simon, Player };
  public:
    SimonGame(SimpleWindow &Window);
    void Initialize();
    void Play();
    int Refresh();
    int MouseClick(const Position &MousePosn);
    int Timer();
    int Find(const Position &MousePosn);
    void PickOrder();
  private:
    SimpleWindow &W;
    SimonObject Posn[MaxPositions];
    BitMap Restart;
    BitMap Quit;
    int Order[MaxSequenceLength];
    int SequenceLength;
    Turn WhoseTurn;
    int Selection;
};
#endif
```

Using `Find()`, we can complete `MouseClick()`. The last part of the function follows.

```
else if (WhoseTurn == Player) {
    // see if object selected
    if ((p = Find(MousePosn)) >= 0) {
        // flip the object over to show it
        Posn[p].SetSide(Front);
        Posn[p].Draw();
        // check whether the object was selected in
        // the right order
        if (p != Order[Selection]) {
            WhoseTurn = Simon;
            W.Message("Wrong Order!");
        }
        // check for successful selection of the
        // entire sequence
        else if (Selection + 1 == SequenceLength) {
            // reached highest level -- game over
```

```
if (SequenceLength
  == MaxSequenceLength) {
    WhoseTurn = Simon;
    W.Message("You Win!!!");
}
// go to the next level
else {
    ++SequenceLength;
    Play();
}
}
// next user selection in the order
else
    ++Selection;
}
}
return 1;
}
```

If it's not the player's turn, we just ignore the mouse click. If it is the player's turn, `Find()` is invoked to see if the mouse was pointing at a `SimonObject`. If it's not, the mouse click is ignored. If the mouse is pointing at one of the `SimonObjects`, we flip it over and check to see if it is the next card in the sequence. If the player incorrectly selected the next `SimonObject`, we output a message telling the player he/she is wrong and reset the game so it is Simon's turn. The player can restart the game by dismissing the alert message and clicking on the restart control button.

If the next `SimonObject` is correctly selected, the code checks to see if the end of the sequence is reached. If the end of the sequence has not been reached, Selection is incremented to the next object in the order. If the last object in the sequence was picked, the code checks to see if this sequence is the last sequence required to win the game. If it is, a winning message is displayed (see Figure 11.14) and Simon gets another turn. If the longest sequence wasn't reached, the sequence length is increased by one and the next round is played.

Figure 11.14

Simon after player wins a game

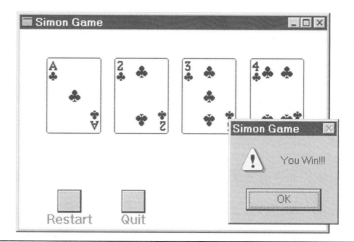

This completes the development of Simon. Listing 11.16 contains the complete code in `simmain.cpp`.

Listing 11.16

Module simmain.cpp

```
#include <iostream.h>
#include <assert.h>
#include <stdio.h>
#include "simon.h"

SimpleWindow GameWindow("Simon Game",
  11.5, 7.0, Position(0.25, 0.25));
SimonGame Simon(GameWindow);

// RefreshEvent(): pass window refresh to the game
int RefreshEvent() {
  return Simon.Refresh();
}

// MouseClickEvent(): pass mouse events to player
int MouseClickEvent(const Position &MousePosn) {
  return Simon.MouseClick(MousePosn);
}

// TimerEvent(): pass timer expirations to the game to
// check for card matches
int TimerEvent() {
  return Simon.Timer();
}

// ApiMain(): open the game window, set callbacks, and
// begin play
int ApiMain() {
  GameWindow.Open();
  GameWindow.SetMouseClickCallback(MouseClickEvent);
  GameWindow.SetRefreshCallback(RefreshEvent);
  GameWindow.SetTimerCallback(TimerEvent);
  Simon.Initialize();
  return 0;
}

// ApiEnd(): shut down the window
int ApiEnd() {
  GameWindow.Close();
  return 0;
}
```

11.9

POINTS TO REMEMBER

- Avoid reinventing the wheel. Use library code and APIs to develop applications.

- Applications that use graphical interfaces are simpler to use than a text-based interface, but they harder to develop.

- Event-based programming involves handling events that are generated outside the program. Typical events include mouse clicks, timer ticks, and messages from the operating system.

History of Computing

■ A bounding box is a way of specifying the location of an object on the screen. For most window systems, a bounding box is specified by giving the screen coordinates of the upper-left corner and lower-right corner of a rectangle that either enclose the object or that the object is centered within.

11.10

EXERCISES

11.1 Write an EzWindows program that displays a flashing message in a window. The message should be read from `cin`. The message should flash every two seconds.

11.2 Go to the library and create a list of the APIs that are available for building different types of applications. Your list should give the name of the API, the types of applications it was designed to help build, the name of the company that sells the API, and what computing platforms it works on.

Figure 11.15
*Steven Jobs and
Stephen Wozniak with
the Apple I*

11.3 Write an EzWindows program that displays a bitmap that is too large for the window. What happens?

11.4 Write an EzWindows program that opens a window. When the mouse is clicked in this window, the mouse coordinates are displayed in the text control window.

11.5 Write an EzWindows program for displaying bitmaps. The program should prompt the user for the name of the file that contains the bitmap. The program should center the bitmap within the window.

11.6 Write an EzWindows program that reminds someone to do something. The program should prompt for and accept a time specified in minutes. After this specified time has elapsed, the program should remind the user to do whatever they needed to do by displaying an appropriate pop-up window.

11.7 Write an EzWindows program that has two windows. The first window contains two buttons. One button is an on switch and the other is an off switch. The second window is the message window. When the on switch is clicked on, the message in the window flashes every two seconds. When the off switch is clicked on, the message does not flash. Be sure to use the object-oriented approach to your design. Determine the objects and develop classes for them.

11.8 The quit and restart buttons used in Simon are not very professional looking. Find two bitmaps that look better and modify the program to use the new bitmaps.

11.9 The supplied version of Simon provides no facility for pausing the game once it is started. Add a pause button to the game.

11.10 A problem with the current version of Simon is that if one of the cards is repeated, when the player is selecting the cards in sequence, the mechanism for giving the player feedback is that the card is flipped over. This method works fine when no card was repeated, but if a card is repeated, the player receives no feedback that they selected the card because it is already flipped over. Devise and implement a method for giving a player feedback that works even when a sequence contains a duplicate card.

11.11 Modify the Simon program so that the game has another level of difficulty. In this version of the game, after the player has completed one round of correctly guessing the sequences, the next round flips the cards faster. The new version of the game should have three levels: slow, medium, and fast.

11.12 Modify the Simon program so that it uses four different bitmaps. You might consider bitmaps that represent related objects like fruits (e.g., orange, apple, cherry, and lemon), shapes (e.g., square, triangle, circle, and ellipse), or musical instruments (e.g., drum, trumpet, violin, and tuba). The bitmaps should be arranged as shown in the following diagram:

11.13 Using the EzWindows API, create a digital timer. It should have three control buttons: start, stop, and reset. The display should consist of minutes and seconds (e.g., mm:ss). To create the display, use the bitmaps for the digits and colon supplied with the EzWindows API code. The timer display should be updated every second.

11.14 Redo the program in Exercise 12.13 so that the display includes a 10th of a second. The timer display should be updated every 10th of a second.

11.15 Write an EzWindows program that displays a poker hand of five cards. Your program should display the cards in a way that minimizes the space taken but still makes the hand visible.

11.16 Write an EzWindows program that simulates a screensaver. The program opens and closes random-size windows at random locations on the screen. It does this at a random time interval between 2 and 6 seconds.

11.17 Write an EzWindows program that simulates a screensaver. It opens a window that is as large as the screen and displays a bitmap of your choice at random locations within the window. It draws the bitmap at a new location at a random time interval between two and six seconds.

11.18 A card game kid's sometimes play is to deal the cards face down in a rectangular pattern. The following diagram shows how the screen should look at the beginning of the game.

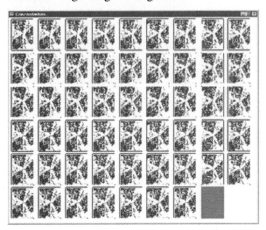

To start the game, a player turns over two cards with the goal of picking two cards of the same face (e.g., two queens or two aces). If the card faces match, the player gets a point; otherwise, the cards are flipped back over. If the player does turn over a matching pair, he or she gets another turn. If the player doesn't pick a match, it's the other player's turn. This game is sometimes called Concentration.

Write an EzWindows program for practicing Concentration. The program should display the cards as shown above. A player chooses two cards by clicking on the cards. If the cards match, they are removed from the display; if not they are flipped back over. The play continues until no cards remain.

11.19 Write an EzWindows program for playing Concentration (see Exercise 11.18). One player is the computer. The computer always remembers the cards it turns over, but for some reason, it does not remember the cards the player turns over. Be sure to include a display that shows the current score. A player's score is how many pairs he or she finds. In this implementation, the computer always goes first.

11.20 Implement the game as described in Exercise 11.19 but include buttons that allow the player to choose who should go first—the computer or the player.

11.21 Implement the game as described in Exercise 11.20 but modify the program so that the computer remembers the position of a card that is flipped over 60 percent of the time. Can you beat the computer? Modify the program so that the computer has an 80 percent recall of the cards flipped over.

CHAPTER 12

Pointer types

Introduction

A pointer is an object whose value is the location of another object. To support the use of pointers, C++ provides two complementary operators—the address operator `&` and the indirection operator `*`. The address operator allows the location of another object to be computed, and the indirection operator allows the value stored at another location to be computed. One important use of pointers is accessing the command-line parameters that users provide to programs.

Key Concepts

- lvalues
- rvalues
- pointer types
- null address
- indirection operator `*`
- indirect member selector operator `->`
- address operator `&`
- pointer assignment
- indirect assignment
- pointers as parameters
- pointers to pointers
- constant pointers versus pointers to constants
- arrays and pointers
- command-line parameters
- pointers to functions

12.1

LVALUES AND RVALUES

In C++ there are two kinds of expressions. There are expressions that represent objects that can be evaluated and modified, and there are expressions that can only be evaluated. Suppose the following definitions are in effect.

```
int a = 1;
int b;
int c[3];
```

Then the following code segment contains both kinds of expressions.

```
b = 5;
cout << b << endl;
c[0] = 2*a;
```

The expression b represents an object whose value can be both evaluated or modified depending upon the circumstances. In the first assignment statement, the object represented by expression b is being modified. In the insertion statement, it is the evaluation of the object represented by expression b that is important. In the second assignment, the expression c[0] represents an object whose value can be evaluated and modified.

Expressions that represent objects that can be both evaluated and modified are *lvalues* (pronounced "el-values"). Thus, object names—such as a and b in the preceding code segment—are lvalues, but not all lvalues are object names, as discussed below.

Although the typical assignment statement uses the name of an object as its left operand, the syntax of an assignment statement requires only that the left operand be an lvalue. This flexibility is important because not all objects have names. For example, while an array has a name, its individual elements do not—individual array elements are referenced using lvalue subscript expressions. Thus, the assignment to c[0] in the preceding code segment is an example of assignment to an lvalue that corresponds to an object without a name.

The two right operands of our assignment statements, 5 and 2*a, are not lvalues—it would not make sense to allow either 5 or 2*a to be the target of an assignment. These kinds of expressions are *rvalues* (pronounced "are-values"); they cannot be used as the left operand of an assignment. Lvalues do not have such restrictions. Lvalue expressions can be used as either left or right operands of an assignment.

12.2

POINTER BASICS

A pointer is an object whose value represents the location of another object. Pointer objects are defined in conjunction with the unary *indirection* operator *. The following code segment defines three pointer objects: iPtr, s, and rPtr.

```
int *iPtr;
char *s;
Rational *rPtr;
```

Object iPtr is of type pointer to **int**, object s is of type pointer to **char**, and object rPtr is of type pointer to Rational. These pointer types are all different just as **int**, **char**, and Rational are all different types. Because these definitions did not include initialization, the three objects are uninitialized. The following figure depicts the result of these definitions (a dash indicates an uninitialized value).

iPtr   [—   ]

s   [—   ]

rPtr   [—   ]

For explanatory purposes in referring to a pointer type, we use the associated type concatenated with the indirection operator, that is, **int*** should be read as "pointer to **int**," and **char*** should be read as "pointer to **char**."

There is one literal value that can be assigned to any pointer object. This literal is 0, which in this context is known as the null address. For example, the following statements all assign the null address.

```
int *iPtr = 0;
char s = 0;
Rational rPtr = 0;
```

A pointer object whose value is the null address is not pointing to an object that can be accessed. In depicting pointer objects whose values are null, we use a filled-in square.

In the next section we discuss operators that allow a pointer to be associated with specific objects. In doing so, we will be able to achieve representations like the one in Figure 12.1.

Figure 12.1

*Three pointer objects
and the values to which
they point*

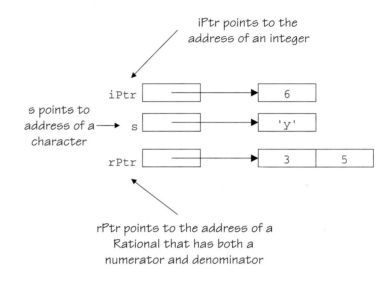

The assignment operator is defined for pointer objects. If Ptr1 and Ptr2 have the same pointer type, then the following assignment is legal.

```
Ptr1 = Ptr2;
```

The meaning of the preceding assignment is the same as it is for other objects—the value represented by Ptr1 is modified to hold the value represented by Ptr2. As a result of this assignment, objects Ptr1 and Ptr2 both point to the same object. The preceding example uses the name of a pointer object as the right operand. This did not need to be the case. The right operand can be any expression that evaluates to the same type as the left operand.

Suppose the following definitions are in effect.

```
int i = 1;
int *iPtr;
char *cPtr;
```

Then none of the following three assignment statements is legal—their right operands do not produce values of the proper type.

```
iPtr = i;     // illegal: i is not an int*
i = iPtr;     // illegal: iPtr is not an int
iPtr = cPtr;  // illegal: cPtr is not an int*
```

In the first of these illegal assignment statements, iPtr is the target of the assignment. Therefore, the right operand must evaluate to an **int*** value, but i is an **int**, which makes the assignment illegal. In the second assignment, the right operand must evaluate to an **int**. This evaluation is not possible with iPtr, which is an **int***. In the third assignment, the right operand needs to evaluate to an **int***. However, cPtr evaluates to **char***. Thus, none of the assignments met the C++ requirement that the right operand of an assignment evaluate to the same type as the left operand of an assignment.

Always define one object per statement

When defining a pointer object, some programmers juxtapose the indirection operator with the type name rather than the object name as in the following definition:

```
char* Ptr;
```

This form is appealing because it clearly identifies that the type being used is a pointer type. However, it can lead to misunderstandings. For example, consider the following statement:

```
char* s, t; // really char *s; char t
```

The preceding statement first creates an object s that is a pointer to a **char**. It then creates an object t that is a **char**. The different object types are the result of the right associativity of the indirection operator—even though the indirection operator is juxtaposed with the type **char**, it is still associated with object s. You should recall our earlier warning that objects should always be defined one per statement. Avoiding this type of error is a principal reason for that warning.

12.2.1

Addressing and indirection

C++ provides the unary *address* operator & so that the location of an object can be computed and used by a program. When the address operator is applied to an object in an expression, the value produced by the addressing operation is a pointer to that object. Suppose the following code segment has been executed.

```
int j = 1;
int *Ptr;
Ptr = &j;
```

The first definition initializes j to the value 1; the assignment statement sets Ptr to the address of the memory location for j. The following figure depicts the result of these actions.

The value of j can now be accessed directly through j *or* indirectly through pointer object Ptr. The indirect method requires the use of the indirection operator *. This operator is also known as the *dereferencing* operator.

When the indirection operator is used in an expression, the right operand must be a pointer object. The indirection operation computes the lvalue of the

object to which that pointer object points. For example, in the following insertion statement, the value 1 is displayed to the standard output stream.

```
cout << *Ptr << endl; // displaying object j
```

The value 1 is displayed because `*Ptr` is the object to which `Ptr` points.
Because `Ptr` points to the memory location where object `j` is stored, `*Ptr`
evaluates to value 1.

As noted in our initial discussion of lvalues, the left operand of the assignment operator can be any lvalue expression. This flexibility is demonstrated in
the following assignment:

```
*Ptr = 0;                    // modifying object j
```

The right operand is the value 0, the left operand is the expression `*Ptr`. The
expression `*Ptr` is an lvalue that refers to `j`. Therefore, this assignment operation indirectly modifies `j` so that it now has the value 0. A picture of memory
for objects `j` and `Ptr` is the following:

If the following two insertion statements are now executed, two zeros would be
inserted to the standard output stream.

```
cout << j<< endl;
cout << *Ptr << endl;
```

Like other objects, the definitions of pointer objects can include various
initialization expressions, as illustrated in the following code segment:

```
int m = 0;
int n = 1;
int *Ptr1 = &m;
int *Ptr2 = Ptr1;
int *Ptr3 = &n;
```

The first two definitions create and initialize **int** objects m and n. The next
three definitions create and initialize **int** * objects Ptr1, Ptr2, and Ptr3.

Pointer Ptr1 is initialized so that it points to m. Pointer Ptr2 is initialized
so that it is a copy of Ptr1's current value. Therefore, Ptr2 also points to m.
Finally, Ptr3 is initialized so that it points to n. A picture of the memory for
the five objects is the following:

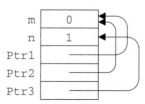

Suppose the following code segment is executed. What would be the changes in the various objects?

```
*Ptr1 = *Ptr3;
Ptr2 = Ptr3;
```

The right operand of the first assignment is the expression `*Ptr3`. Because `Ptr3` is a pointer to the memory location of n, expression `*Ptr3` evaluates to 1. The left operand of the first assignment is the expression `*Ptr1`. Because `Ptr1` is a pointer to the memory location of m, the expression `*Ptr1` is a legal lvalue expression referring to that value of m. Therefore, the first assignment indirectly modifies m so that it is a copy of n. A picture of the memory at this point is the following:

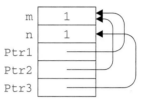

The second assignment in our code segment replaces the value of `Ptr2` with the value of `Ptr3`. Because `Ptr3` points to n, `Ptr2` now also points to n. The picture of the memory would now be the following:

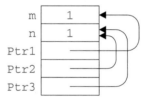

If a pointer object points to class-type objects then, by using the indirection and selection operators, individual members can be accessed. Because the selection operator has higher precedence, the indirection operator must be nested within parentheses.

```
Rational a(4,3);
Rational *aPtr = &a;
(*aPtr).Insert(cout); // invokes member Insert() of
                      // object *aPtr. Parentheses
                      // are necessary
```

Because this syntax is clumsy, C++ includes the indirect member selector operator `->` that combines indirection with selection. Thus, the following statement also displays the `Rational` object to which `aPtr` points.

```
aPtr->Insert(cout);
```

The indirection and indirect member selector operators are not tools for overcoming class access permissions. A nonpublic data member cannot be accessed by a client using either of these operators. For example, the following statements are illegal:

```
(*aPtr).NumeratorValue = 1; // illegal: member is
                            // private
aPtr->DenominatorValue = 2; // illegal: member is
                            // private
```

A pointer object whose value is the null address cannot be dereferenced. For example, the following code segment is illegal:

```
int *NullPtr = 0;
*NullPtr = 1; // illegal: NullPtr is not pointing to
              // a location of an int object
```

**Programming
Tip**

Pointer power

The ability to access and change the value of an object whose name is not part of the assignment statement is the characteristic that makes pointer objects so powerful and also so confusing. This capability is used most often by dynamic objects, which we consider in Chapter 13.

12.2.2

Pointers to pointers

C++ allows pointer types whose objects are pointers to pointers. C++ also allows pointer types whose objects are pointers to pointers to pointers, and so on. The following definition defines a pointer object `PtrPtr` that points to an **int*** object.

```
int **PtrPtr;
```

Each asterisk in a definition indicates another level of indirection. For example, the two asterisks in front of `PtrPtr` indicate a pointer to a pointer, and three asterisks would have indicated a pointer to a pointer to a pointer.
Suppose the following definitions are also in effect.

```
int i = 0;
int *Ptr= &i;
```

Then the following assignment is correct because `Ptr` is an **int***, which makes expression `&Ptr` evaluate to an **int****.

```
PtrPtr = &Ptr;
```

As the result of this assignment, the objects i, Ptr, and PtrPtr have the following relationship:

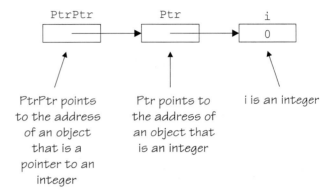

As noted previously, C++ considers two pointer objects to be of different types if the types of values to which they point are different. Therefore, the following assignment is illegal.

```
PtrPtr = Ptr;  // illegal: PtrPtr needs an int**
```

The assignment is illegal because the right operand is of type **int*** while PtrPtr expects a value of type **int****.

12.2.3

Pointers as parameters

Up to this point, our examples have been isolated code segments. We now consider a small program, Program 12.1, which invokes a **void** function IndirectSwap(). Function IndirectSwap() has two formal parameters Ptr1 and Ptr2. Both parameters are value parameters of type **char***.

When the program begins, objects a and b are initialized to 'y' and 'n', respectively. The following figure depicts the activation record of main() after executing the definitions of a and b.

main()		
	a	'y'
	b	'n'

The invocation of function IndirectSwap() in Program 12.1 is IndirectSwap(&a, &b). The actual parameters for this invocation are the values of the expressions &a and &b. Because expression &a is a pointer to a, value parameter Ptr1 points to a; and because expression &b is a pointer to b, value

Program 12.1

Demonstrates that pointers can be used to simulate reference parameters

```
// Program 12.1: Swapping objects using indirection
#include <iostream.h>
void IndirectSwap(char *Ptr1, char *Ptr2) {
    // swap the contents of the char objects to which
    // Ptr1 and Ptr2 point
    char c = *Ptr1;
    *Ptr1 = *Ptr2;
    *Ptr2 = c;
}
int main() {
    char a = 'y';
    char b = 'n';
    // pass the lvalues of a and b to IndirectSwap()
    IndirectSwap(&a, &b);
    // display the new values of a and b
    cout << a << b << endl;
    return 0;
}
```

parameter `Ptr2` points to b. An initial picture of the memory associated with this invocation of `IndirectSwap()` is the following:

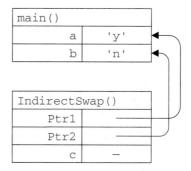

In function `IndirectSwap()`, local object c is initialized with the value of the expression `*Ptr1`. In particular, in this invocation of `IndirectSwap()`, because `Ptr1` points to object a of `main()` that has the value `'y'`, object c is initialized to `'y'`.

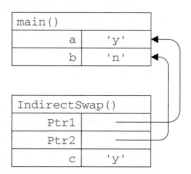

The two assignment statements in `IndirectSwap()` then modify the objects to which `Ptr1` and `Ptr2` point.

```
*Ptr1 = *Ptr2;
*Ptr2 = c;
```

Because `Ptr1` points to object a of `main()`, the first assignment in modifying the lvalue `*Ptr1` in fact modifies a. Thus, the assignment does not alter any of the values in the activation record of `IndirectSwap()`. The new value of a is the lvalue of `*Ptr2`. Because `Ptr2` points to object b from `main()`, this assignment in effect gives a the value `'n'`.

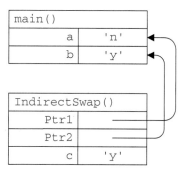

For the second assignment in `IndirectSwap()`, the left operand is `*Ptr2`. Because `Ptr2` points to object b of `main()`, this assignment in effect modifies b. Thus, this assignment, like the previous assignment, does not alter any of the values in the activation record of `IndirectSwap()` but again updates the contents of the activation record for `main()`. The new value of b is a copy of c, which is a `'y'`.

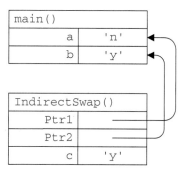

The execution of `IndirectSwap()` is completed with the second assignment, and the flow of control then returns to `main()`. Thus, the result of the invocation of `IndirectSwap()` is a swapping of the values of the objects to which the actual parameters point. Function `IndirectSwap()` is equivalent to function `Swap()` of Chapter 7.

C++ Language

12.3

CONSTANT POINTERS AND POINTERS TO CONSTANTS

The modifier **const** can also be applied in pointer definitions. Depending on where the modifier **const** is placed either the pointer is a constant or the contents of the location to which the pointer points are considered to be constant.

Suppose the following definitions are in effect.

```
char c1 = 'a';
char c2 = 'b';
```

Then the following code segment illustrates the three legal places in a pointer definition where the modifier **const** may be applied.

```
const char *Ptr1 = &c1;  // *Ptr1 is considered to
                         // be a constant; Ptr1 is
                         // not a constant
char const *Ptr2 = &c1;  // *Ptr2 is considered to
                         // be a constant; Ptr2 is
                         // not constant
char *const Ptr3 = &c1;  // Ptr3 is a constant;
                         // *Ptr3 is not constant
```

The modifier **const** can appear immediately before or after the type; the **const** can also appear after the unary operator *. According to the language definition, a type modifier can appear either before or after the type without changing the meaning of the definition. Therefore, the first two definitions in the preceding code segment define pointer objects with similar capabilities.

In the preceding discussion, we used the phrase *considered to be a constant*. For example, the phrase was used in conjunction with the definition of Ptr1. As a result of that particular pointer definition, the value of the object to which Ptr1 points cannot be changed through an assignment to *Ptr1. However, the value of c1—the object to which Ptr1 points—can still be changed through a direct assignment to c1.

```
*Ptr1 = 'A';    // illegal: *Ptr1 is a constant
c1 = 'A';       // legal: c1 is not a constant
```

A mnemonic to remember what is being defined to be constant is to read the definition backwards substituting *is a pointer to a* for the * in the definition. Thus, the definition of Ptr1 reads "Ptr1 is a pointer to a **char** constant," the definition of Ptr2 reads "Ptr2 is a pointer to a constant **char**," and the definition of Ptr3 reads "Ptr3 constant is a pointer to a **char**." While the last phrase is grammatically poor, this method should help you determine what is constant and what is not. For the preceding definitions, *Ptr1, *Ptr2, and Ptr3 are constants. As a result, the following statements are illegal.

```
*Ptr1 = 'A';    // illegal: *Ptr1 cannot be changed
*Ptr2 = 'B';    // illegal: *Ptr2 cannot be changed
Ptr3 = Ptr2;    // illegal:  Ptr3 cannot be changed
```

Because Ptr1, Ptr2, and *Ptr3 are not constants, the following statements are all legal.

```
Ptr1 = Ptr2;    // legal:  Ptr1 can be changed
Ptr2 = Ptr1;    // legal:  Ptr2 can be changed
*Ptr3 = 'C';    // legal: *Ptr3 can be changed
```

In the following definition, we define a constant pointer to a location whose contents are considered to be a constant.

```
const char *const Ptr4 = &c1;
```

As a result, the following assignments are illegal.

```
Ptr4 = &c2;     // illegal:  Ptr cannot be changed
*Ptr4 = 'D';    // illegal: *Ptr cannot be changed
```

The first assignment is illegal because it attempts to modify Ptr4. The second assignment is illegal because it attempts to change the contents to which Ptr4 points.

It is also illegal to assign a pointer to a constant to a pointer that this not pointing to a constant.

```
char *Ptr5 = Ptr4;    // illegal: potentially allows
                      // constant *Ptr4 to be modified
```

12.4

ARRAYS AND POINTERS

In C++, the name of an array is considered to be a constant pointer, that is, the name of an array is associated with a particular memory location and that association cannot be changed by statements in the program. In fact, the name of an array is associated with the memory location of the first element in the array. For example, consider the following six definitions:

```
int A[5];
int B[10];
int *Ptr1 = A;      // Ptr1 points to A[0]
int *Ptr2 = B;      // Ptr2 points to B[0]
int *Ptr3 = &B[0];  // Ptr3 points to B[0]
int *Ptr4 = &A[4];  // Ptr4 points to A[4]
```

The first two definitions create 5-element and 10-element **int** arrays A and B, respectively. The last four definitions create pointer objects of type **int***. Based on the preceding discussion, the initialization expression A for Ptr1 is equivalent to a pointer to the first element in array A. Similarly, the definition of Ptr2 initializes it to point to the first element of B. The definition of Ptr3 explicitly initializes it to also point to the first element of B. The definition of Ptr4 initializes it to point to the last element in array A.

The equality and relational operators are defined for pointers of the same type; therefore, given the preceding definitions, the comparisons in the following code segment are legal.

```
if (A == B)
    cout << "A and B: same values" << endl;
else
    cout << "A and B: different values" << endl;
if (Ptr1 == A)
    cout << "A and Ptr1: same values" << endl;
else
    cout << "A and Ptr1: different values" << endl;
if (Ptr2 != Ptr3)
    cout << "Ptr2 and Ptr3: different values"
      << endl;
else
    cout << "Ptr2 and Ptr3: same values" << endl;
if (Ptr1 < Ptr4)
    cout << "Ptr1 and Ptr4: Ptr1 is first" << endl;
else
    cout << "Ptr1 and Ptr4: Ptr1 is not first"
      << endl;
```

The output of the code segment is the following:

```
A and B: different values
A and Ptr1: same values
Ptr2 and Ptr3: same values
Ptr1 and Ptr4: Ptr1 is first
```

Note that the relational operators <, <=, >, and >= are defined only for pointers that point to the same array or to the object that occurs in memory immediately after the array.

The increment and decrement operators are defined for pointer objects. The effect of the increment operator ++ on a pointer object is to have the new address to which it points be the starting location of the object immediately after the object to which it previously pointed. This behavior is demonstrated

in the following code segment that displays the value 20 to output stream
`cout`.

```
int A[4] = {10, 20, 30, 40};
int *Ptr = A;
++Ptr;
cout << *Ptr << endl;
```

Suppose the following depicts the initial values in the memory associated
with the definitions of A and Ptr.

```
A[0]|    10    |
A[1]|    20    |
A[2]|    30    |
A[3]|    40    |
 Ptr|          |
```

After the increment of Ptr in the code segment, the memory associated with A
and Ptr would have the following depiction:

```
A[0]|    10    |
A[1]|    20    |
A[2]|    30    |
A[3]|    40    |
 Ptr|          |
```

The location of A[1] is the new value for Ptr because the pointer increment
operator updates its operand to point to the object immediately after the object
to which its operand previously pointed. Because A[1] is 20, *Ptr displays a
20 in the following insertion statement:

```
cout << *Ptr << endl;
```

The effect of the decrement operator -- on a pointer object is analogous to
the behavior of the increment operator. If a pointer object is decremented, the
new location to which it points is the object immediately before the object to
which it previously pointed. For example, suppose Ptr is now decremented as
in the following statement:

```
--Ptr;
```

The new value of Ptr would be the location of A[0].

```
A[0]|    10    |
A[1]|    20    |
A[2]|    30    |
A[3]|    40    |
 Ptr|          |
```

**Programmer
Alert**

Addition and subtraction operators are also defined for pointer objects. For example, the expression Ptr + i would be a pointer to the ith object beyond the object to which Ptr points. In this expression, i is called an *offset*. The contents of that offset address are given by the lvalue expression * (Ptr + i). Similarly, the expression Ptr - i is a pointer to the ith object prior to the object to which Ptr points. The contents of that offset address are given by the lvalue expression * (Ptr - i).

The following example demonstrates the use of the indirection and pointer arithmetic operators to display the contents of an array A.

```
int A[4]  = {10, 20, 30,40};
int *Ptr = A;
for (int i = 0; i < 4; ++i) {
   cout << *(Ptr+i) << endl;
}
```

To complete the correspondence between pointers and arrays, we observe that in C++ the expression * (Ptr+i) is equivalent to the expression Ptr[i]. Therefore, the contents of the array A can also be displayed using Ptr in the following manner:

```
for (int i = 0; i < 4; ++i) {
   cout << Ptr[i] << endl;
}
```

12.5

CHARACTER STRING PROCESSING

The iostream library includes definitions for the insertion and extraction operators when the right operands are **char*** objects.

The result of inserting a **char** pointer to an output stream is equivalent to displaying a **char** array whose first element is located at the address to which the **char*** object points. An example of this use of the insertion operator is contained in the following code segment:

```
char Text[6] = "Hello";
for (char *Ptr = Text; *Ptr != '\0'; ++Ptr) {
    cout << Ptr << endl;
}
```

The output of the code segment is

```
Hello
ello
llo
lo
o
```

For each iteration of the **for** statement, the string is displayed that starts at the current location to which Ptr points. Once Ptr points to the address that contains the null character, the test expression evaluates to false and the **for** statement is done.

When the right operand of an extraction operator is a **char*** object, the behavior is the same as that of an extraction target to a **char** array—by default leading white space is skipped and the next non-white-space string of characters is extracted. The characters in the extracted string—including a terminating null character—are assigned to the memory starting at the location to which the **char*** object points. For example, suppose the following definitions are in effect.

```
char Word[4];
char *WordPtr = Word;
```

If standard input contains

```
ab xyz
```

then the extraction

```
cin >> WordPtr;
```

would have the following effect (the dash again indicates that the object is uninitialized).

```
Word[0]      'a'  ◄
Word[1]      'b'
Word[2]      '\0'
Word[3]       —
WordPtr       —
```

Make sure the memory is there

It is important when using a **char** pointer in conjunction with an extraction that the pointer point to an array of **char** of sufficient length to store the extracted characters. The pointer is automatically assumed to be pointing to valid and sufficient memory. If it is not, then the effect of the extraction on your program is undefined.

The interchangeability of pointer and array notation is most obvious in the passing of character strings to functions. The following is a possible implementation of the string library function strlen().

```
// strlen() with s passed as a const array
int strlen(const char s[]) {
    for (int i = 0; s[i] != '\0'; ++i) {
        continue;
    }
    return i;
}
```

The function expects a character string terminated with a null character as its single parameter, and it returns the length of the string (excluding the terminating null character). The length of the string is determined by scanning the array for the terminating null character. The index of the null character is the length of the string (the characters in the string are array elements s[0] through s[i-1]).

The function strlen() can also be implemented in the following manner with the character string being passed via a pointer to its first character.

```
// strlen() with s passed as a pointer to constant
// characters
int strlen(const char *s) {
    for (int length = 0; *s != '\0'; ++s) {
        ++length;
    }
    return length;
}
```

The **const** declaration of the value parameter s indicates that the contents of the location to which s points are considered constant, that is, *s cannot be the target of an assignment. The length of the string is determined by incrementing a local **int** object length once for each non-null character in the string.

Updating s so that it points to the next character in the string is accomplished through a separate increment operation.

We now consider another implementation of function strlen(). This implementation combines the character comparison with a side effect that increments the pointer to the next character.

```
// strlen() with s passed as a pointer to constant
// characters. the incrementing of the pointer is
// done as a side effect of the test expression.
int strlen(const char *s) {
    for (int length = 0; *s++ != '\0'; ++length) {
        continue;
    }
    return length;
}
```

The test expression has the following interpretation: determine whether the **char** object to which s points is the null character and, as a side effect of that test, increment pointer s. This combination of evaluation and pointer increment is quite common in string-processing code. However, it is a matter of debate whether the terseness contributes to or detracts from its understanding.

We next consider an **int** function strcmp(). This function expects two strings as parameters and through its return value indicates whether the two strings are the same or whether the first occurs before the second lexicographically (dictionary order).

```
int strcmp(const char *s, const char *t) {
    // look for first difference or until *s is null
    while ((*s == *t) && (*s != '\0')) {
        ++s;
        ++t;
    }
    // return encoding difference
    return *s - *t;
}
```

The string parameters for strcmp() are s and t. Function strcmp() returns 0 if the strings are the same; returns a negative value if s occurs lexicographically before t; and returns a positive value if s occurs lexicographically after t.

The **while** loop in strcmp() iterates while the current characters to which s and t point are the same and while the current character to which s points is not the null character. (We do not need to explicitly check whether t is null because the existing terms in the **while** expression catch this condition.) When the loop terminates, we examine the current characters to which s and t point to determine the return value of the function. If the characters are the same, the return value, which is the difference *s - *t, will be 0. If the strings are different, then s and t will point to the first difference in the two strings. In this case, the expression *s - *t will be negative if s occurs lexicographically before t and positive if s occurs lexicographically after t.

12.6

COMMAND-LINE PARAMETERS TO A PROGRAM

Many operating systems (e.g., Unix and MS-DOS) provide command-line interpreters. These interpreters allow a user to type a command or program and then have the operating system execute it. For example, the following instruction uses the command chdir to changes the current directory to the directory code.

```
chdir code
```

In the instruction, the string code is a parameter to the command chdir. The command line consists of two strings chdir and code.

As another example, the following instruction runs the program cmd with the strings 123 and ab as its command-line parameters.

```
cmd 123 ab
```

C++ provides a method for creating programs that use command-line parameters. The command-line parameters are communicated to a program via its function main(). To make this communication straightforward, C++ requires that a program view a command line as a sequence of strings. The first string is the program name and the remaining strings are its parameters. For our second example, the three strings in order are cmd, 123, and ab.

To access the strings that compose the command line, C++ has an alternative parameter list declaration for main() that specifies two parameters. A prototype of main() using the alternative form is given below.

```
int main(int argc, char *argv[]);
```

The first parameter is an **int** value parameter. By convention, this parameter has the name argc. When the program is run, parameter argc is initialized automatically to be the number of strings that make up the command line. This number includes the program name in its count, so argc is the number of command-line parameters plus one for the program name. For our cmd example, argc is set to 3.

The second parameter in the alternative declaration is an array of **char** pointers. By convention, this array has the name argv. When the program is run, pointer argv[0] is automatically initialized to point to a character string that represents the program name, and pointers argv[1] through argv[argc-1] are automatically initialized to point to character strings that represent the individual command-line parameters to the program. This initialization is depicted for our cmd example in Figure 12.2.

It is important to remember that argc and argv are parameters to main(). As a result, they are not global objects. If other functions require the values of argc and argv during their execution, then argc and argv must be passed to those functions as parameters.

Figure 12.2

Correspondence of command-line parameters and function main( ) parameters argc and argv

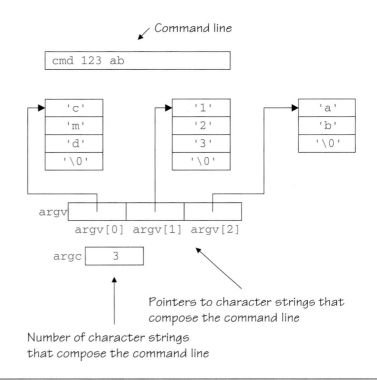

Program 12.2 is a simple program that displays its command-line parameters to the standard output stream. The command-line parameters passed to the program are iteratively displayed using a **for** loop that iterates once for each command-line parameter. An individual parameter is displayed using the insertion operator. As discussed in section 12.5 of this chapter, the insertion operator is overloaded for **char*** pointers, that is, the string being pointed to is displayed.

Program 12.2

Mimics operating system command echo

```
// Program 12.2: Mimics operating system command echo.
// The command-line parameters are displayed to the
// standard output stream (separated by spaces).
#include <iostream.h>
int main(int argc, char *argv[]) {
   for (int i = 1; i < argc; ++i) {
      // display argv[i]
      cout << argv[i] << " ";
   }
   cout << endl;
   return 0;
}
```

Program 12.3 also uses command-line parameters. This program expects that its parameters are filenames. Each parameter is used in turn to open an input file stream. The contents of the file stream are then displayed to the standard output stream. The program makes use of the file stream library `fstream.h`.

Program 12.3

Mimics operating system command type

```
// Program 12.3: Mimics operating system command type.
// Each of the command-line parameters is treated as a
// filename. The contents of the associated file are
// displayed to the standard output stream cout.
#include <iostream.h>
#include <fstream.h>
int main(int argc, char *argv[]) {
   for (int i = 1; i < argc; ++i) {
      // open file stream associated with i-th
      // command-line parameter
      ifstream fin(argv[i]);
      if (fin) {
         // argv[i] is a valid filename, so extract
         // and display the characters in the file
         char c;
         while (fin.get(c)) {
            cout << c;
         }
      }
      else {
         // argv[i] is not a valid filename, so
         // display and error message and terminate
         cerr << argv[0] << ": " << argv[i]
            << " not a valid file name" << endl;
         return 1;
      }
   }
   return 0;
}
```

Like Program 12.2, Program 12.3 has a **for** loop that controls the processing of the parameters. If the construction of the `ifstream` object `fin` is successful, then the stream is extracted character by character. As each character is extracted, it is displayed to the standard output stream. If the construction of `fin` is unsuccessful, an error message is displayed. The error message consists of the name of the program being executed along with an indication of which parameter was an invalid filename.

12.7

POINTERS TO FUNCTIONS

Besides allowing pointers to objects, C++ also allows pointers to functions. The primary use of a pointer to a function is as a parameter to another function. This use enables the function that employs the pointer to perform a variety of actions. Such an ability is important in non-object-oriented languages, however C++ also has the polymorphism mechanism that we consider in Chapter 15, which greatly reduces the need for function pointers.

Pointer to function types are true types. As such, an object that is a pointer to a function can be assigned. Also, the return type of a function can be a pointer to a function, and arrays of pointers to functions can be defined.

The definition of an object that is a pointer to a function must include the return type of the function and the types of the function's parameters (for readability names of the parameters can also be supplied). The following definition defines an object FuncPtr that is a pointer to an **int** function that requires a single **int** value parameter.

$$\texttt{int (*FuncPtr)(int c);}$$

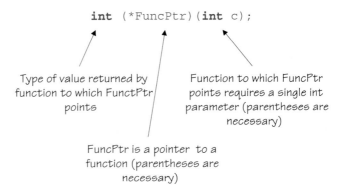

Type of value returned by function to which FunctPtr points

Function to which FuncPtr points requires a single int parameter (parentheses are necessary)

FuncPtr is a pointer to a function (parentheses are necessary)

Just as an array name is a pointer to its elements, a function name is a pointer to the code that comprises its actions. So the following assignment results in FuncPtr being a pointer to the **int** function toupper().

```
FuncPtr = toupper.
```

Program 12.4 demonstrates the use of pointers to functions. The program first prompts and extracts the name of a file. It then prompts and extracts whether the user wants the contents of the file to be displayed in uppercase or lowercase. A function Display() is then invoked. Function Display() expects two parameters: the first parameter fin is the input file stream; the second parameter ToFunc is a pointer to the function that will manipulate the characters in the input stream.

Functions toupper() and tolower() are used as the text manipulation function parameters in the invocations of Display() in main(). Functions toupper() and tolower() are defined in the ctype library, and although they are designed for character manipulation, their parameters and return types are defined to be **int**.

A syntax similar to its parameter declaration is used to invoke ToFunc in Display().

```
CurrentChar = (*ToFunc)(CurrentChar);
```

The parameter CurrentChar in the invocation contains the currently extracted character from the input stream. CurrentChar is modified to get the result of the function invocation. A simpler invocation syntax is permit-

Program 12.4

Demonstrates use of
function pointer as a
parameter

```
// Program 12.4: Displays a file in either upper- or
// lowercase depending upon a user request.
#include <fstream.h>
#include <ctype.h>
// Display(): display text stream using ToFunc
// modification
void Display(ifstream &fin, int (*ToFunc)(int c)) {
   // extract and display characters one-at-a-time
   char CurrentChar;
   while (fin.get(CurrentChar)){
      // modify current character using ToFunc
      CurrentChar = (*ToFunc)(CurrentChar);
      cout << CurrentChar;
   }
   return;
}
// main(): manage file stream display
int main() {
   const int MaxFileNameSize = 256;
   // prompt and extract the name of the file
   cout << "Enter name of file: " << flush;
   char FileName[MaxFileNameSize];
   cin >> FileName;
   // make sure a valid filename was provided
   ifstream fin(FileName);
   if (fin) {
      // we have valid file, so determine the action
      cout << "Display file in uppercase or "
       << "lowercase (u, l):" << flush;
      char reply;
      cin >> reply;
      // display file according to request
      if (reply == 'l')
         Display(fin, tolower);
      else if (reply == 'u')
         Display(fin, toupper);
      else {
         cerr << "Bad request" << endl;
         return 1;
      }
   }
   else { // process invalid filename
      cerr << "Invalid file name: " << FileName
       << endl;
      return 1;
   }
   return 0;
}
```

ted—the surrounding parentheses and the indirection operator can be omitted
as in the following invocation:

```
CurrentChar = ToFunc(CurrentChar);
```

However, the explicit indirection syntax is a clear clue to a reader of the code
that the actual function being invoked is not `ToFunc`.

**History of
Computing**

The Altair 8800

As chip fabrication technology improved, Intel produced ever more power-ful chips. In 1974, Intel introduced the 8080 microprocessor. The power of the 8080 rivaled some of the minicomputers being sold at that time. This fact was not lost on a number of inventors and electronics hobbyists. Edward Roberts owned a small company in Albuquerque, New Mexico, that sold hobby kits. With the introduction of the 8080, Roberts saw the opportunity to make and sell a home-computer kit. The kit was the cover story of the January 1975 issue of *Popular Electronics*. The machine was called the Altair 8800. Interestingly, the name Altair was used because a recent episode of the popular TV series *Star Trek* had mentioned the name as the destination of the *Enterprise*. It was also the name of the planet in the classic science fiction movie, *Forbidden Planet*.

It's safe to say that the appearance of the Altair 8800 on the cover of *Popular Electronics* (see Figure 12.3) gave a kick start to the personal com-puter revolution. The article inspired computer hobbyists all over the United States to begin working on computers and writing software to run on these machines. Several of these hobbyists stand out because they went on to found companies that helped shaped the computer industry in the late 1970s and the 1980s (e.g., Paul Allen and William Gates of Microsoft).

Figure 12.3

*The January 1975 cover
of* Popular Electronics
*featuring the Altair
8800*

12.8

POINTS TO REMEMBER

- Lvalues are expressions that represent objects that can be evaluated and modified.

- Rvalues are expressions that can only be evaluated.

- A pointer is an object whose value is the location of another object.

- There is a different pointer type for each type of object. There are even pointer types whose objects are pointers to other pointers.

- The location of an object can be computed using the address operator &.

- The literal 0 can be assigned to any pointer type object. In this context, the literal 0 is known as the null address.

- The value of the object at a given location can be computed using the indirection operator * on the location.

- The indirection operator produces an lvalue.

- The null address is not a location which can be dereferenced.

- The indirect member selector operator -> allows a particular member of object to be dereferenced.

- Pointer operators can be compared using the equality and relational operators.

- The increment and decrement operators are defined for pointer objects.

- When pointers are passed as value parameters, we can simulate reference parameters by using the indirection operator.

- An array name is viewed by C++ as constant pointer. This fact gives us flexibility in which notation to use when accessing and modifying the values in a list.

- Through the use of pointers, command-line parameters are communicated to programs.

- To access the command-line parameters, function main() must be defined to have two formal parameters. The first formal parameter is an **int** whose value is automatically initialized to be one more than the number of actual parameters to the command. The second formal parameter is an array of **char***. Each element of the array is a pointer to a character string. The first element points to the command itself. The other array elements point to the various actual parameters given to the command.

- By convention, the first formal parameter of main() has the name argc, and the second formal parameter of main() has the name argv.

- We can define objects that are pointers to functions. Such objects are typically used as function parameters. This type of parameter enables the function that uses it to have greater flexibility in accomplishing its task.

12.9

EXERCISES

12.1 What kind of values do pointer objects represent? Explain.

12.2 What is an lvalue? What is an rvalue?

12.3 What is the purpose of the address operator? What is the purpose of the indirection operator?

12.4 Can pointers of different types be assigned to one another? Explain.

12.5 What happens if a pointer object is incremented by one?

12.6 How are command-line parameters communicated to a program?

12.7 Give definitions that correspond to the following figure:

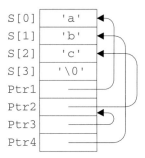

12.8 What is the only literal constant for pointer types? What is its purpose?

12.9 How are array names and pointer objects similar? How are they dissimilar?

12.10 Describe two ways for a function to declare a parameter A that represents a list of **float** values that cannot be modified.

12.11 Suppose Ptr is of type **int*** and i is of type **int**. Identify the problems in the following code segment:

```
Ptr = i;
i = Ptr;
i = &Ptr;
Ptr = Ptr + Ptr;
*i = Ptr;
&i = *Ptr;
```

12.12 Identify the lvalues and rvalues in the following code segment:

```
cin >> k;
i = 0;
A[A[3]] = 2*b;
```

12.13 Define objects for the following situations:

  a) A pointer P that can point to **double** objects.

  b) A pointer Q that can point to pointer objects that point to objects that point to **char** objects.

c) A pointer R that can point to a **bool** function that has two **int** reference parameters.

12.14 Define a pointer P that is initialized to point to the location of **int** object i. The definition should make it illegal to subsequently modify the value of P.

12.15 Define a pointer P that is initialized to point to the location of **int** object i. The definition should make it illegal to subsequently modify the value of i indirectly through P.

12.16 What is the output of the following code segment? Explain.

```
char A[] = "Patricia";
char *Ptr = A;
++Ptr;
cout << Ptr << endl;
Ptr += 2;
cout << Ptr << endl;
cout << --Ptr << endl;
```

12.17 What is the output of the following code segment? Explain.

```
char A[] = "Rust never sleeps";
char *Ptr;
for (Ptr = &A[16]; Ptr != A; Ptr -= 2) {
    cout << Ptr << endl;
    cout << *Ptr << endl;
}
```

12.18 What is syntactically wrong with the following code segment? Explain.

```
char A[] = "James";
char B[] = "Gertrude";
char *Ptr1 = &A[4];
char *Ptr2 = &B[5];
if (Ptr1 < Ptr2)
    cout << "Hello" << endl;
else
    cout << "Good bye" << endl;
```

12.19 Suppose the following command line is to be executed.

```
C:> play A-flat four beats
```

Also suppose that the definition of the function main() that implements the play command begins as follows:

```
int main(int argc, char *argv[]) { // ...
```

a) What does argc represent?

b) What does argv[0] represent?

c) What does argv[1] represent?

d) What does argv[argc-1] represent?

12.20 Suppose the following definitions are in effect.

```
char *cPtr;
char *sPtr[12];
char **cPtrPtr;
```

a) Is cPtr of type **char**? Explain.

b) Is sPtr a pointer to a **char** array with 12 elements? Explain.

c) Is the following assignment legal? Explain.

```
cPtrPtr = &cPtr;
```

12.21 Suppose the following definitions are in effect.

```
Rational A[10];
Rational B[10];
Rational C;
Rational *D;
```

Which of the following assignments are legal? Explain.

```
B = A;
C = A[1];
D = A;
D = &C;
```

12.22 Consider the following program fragment:

```
void f(int *iPtr) {
    *iPtr = 1;
}

int main() {
    int i = 0;
    f(&i);
    cout << i << endl;
    return 0;
}
```

a) Is the program syntactically correct? Explain.

b) Is the invocation f(&i) in function main() along with the definition of function f() a simulation of a reference parameter? Explain.

12.23 Under what conditions does the following statement make sense?

```
cout << **Ptr << endl;
```

12.24 Suppose the last parameter to a program is the name of a file to be used as input. Identify which code fragment(s) below defines and initializes a stream variable in the function main(), where main() has the following interface: **int** main (**int** argc, char *argv[]). Explain.

a) ifstream myin(argv[argc-1]);

b) ifstream myin(argv[argc]);

c) ifstream myin(argc[argv]);

d) ifstream myin(argv[0]);

12.25 Define a **void** function Sort() that expects three parameters. The first parameter is an **int** array A; the second parameter is an integer value n, and the third parameter LTE is a **bool** function that expects two integer parameters. Function Sort() sorts the list A using LTE to make the comparisons. When invoked, the actual parameter for LTE returns true if according to the comparison scheme, its first parameter is less than or equal to its second parameter.

12.26 Define a class `Item` that has two data members `Value` and `NextItem`, where `Value` is of type **int** and `NextItem` is of type `NextItem*`. The default constructor should initialize `Value` to 0 and `NextItem` to the null address. Define other constructors, inspectors, and mutators as you see fit.

12.27 Give a code segment that uses the class `Item` from Exercise 12.26 to define four `Item` objects a, b, c, and d. The code segment should also define two `Item*` objects `Front` and `Rear`. The values of these objects should correspond to the following representation.

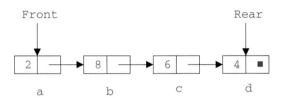

CHAPTER 13

Dynamic data types

Introduction

The solutions to many problems require that a significant amount of information be represented. C++ provides mechanisms for dynamically creating and managing new objects during the running of the program. This ability allows programs to be flexible and to represent arbitrarily sized problem instances. Dynamic objects are created using the **new** operator and are returned to the system using the **delete** operator. Access to a dynamically created object is through a pointer.

Key Concepts

- dynamic objects
- free store
- operators **new** and **delete**
- exception handling
- new library function `set_new_handler()`
- dangling pointers
- memory leak
- destructors
- copy constructor
- member assignment
- **this** pointer
- **friend** to a class

13.1

DYNAMIC OBJECTS

Based upon previous discussions, you should be able to use the indirection and address operators to manipulate pointers and the objects to which they point. You should also recognize that pointer notation can be used as alternative notation for manipulating arrays and that pointers are the mechanism by which C++ programs have access to command-line arguments. Although the alternative pointer notation and the access to command-line arguments are both important, these roles are not the main reasons that pointers are part of the C++ language. The major role of pointers is in the creation of dynamic objects. In particular, for objects whose memory needs vary during program execution.

Except for some global stream objects, such as `cout` and `cin`, and some global constants, the objects we have defined in our programs have generally been local objects. A local object comes into existence when its definition is executed, and it is automatically destroyed when its defining scope block has ended. Analogous rules govern the lifetime of a global object—a global object comes into existence when program execution begins (the start of the global scope), and it is automatically destroyed when the program terminates (the end of the global scope).

Dynamic objects are different from local and global objects in that they come into existence as the result of specific memory allocation requests by the program. The dynamic objects continue to exist until the program returns their memory through a specific deallocation request. Thus, the lifetime of a dynamic object is independent of its defining scope.

The memory used by a dynamic object is said to come from the free store. Conceptually, the *free store* is memory controlled by the operating system that can be broken up and allocated to a program as needed. The principal C++ method of acquiring free store memory is through the use of the unary operator **new**. When the dynamic objects from a given request are no longer needed, their memory is returned to the free store through the unary operator **delete**.

The operator **new** has three forms. The simplest form is a memory allocation request for a single object that expects the name of a type as the right operand to the **new** operator. If sufficient unallocated free store memory is available, the operation returns a pointer to a memory location of the proper size for that type. This form is used in the following code segment:

```
char *cptr;
cptr = new char; // cptr points to an uninitialized
                 // char object
```

The code segment first defines a **char*** object `cptr`. If free store memory is available, then the assignment statement in the code segment sets `cptr` to a **char** object memory location that was previously part of the free store. The memory for the **char** object is uninitialized because there are no constructors for fundamental type objects.

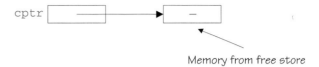

Memory from free store

If the type of object requested from the free store is a class type as in the following example, then the class default constructor is automatically invoked to initialize the newly allocated memory.

```
Rational *rptr;
rptr = new Rational; // rptr points to a Rational
                     // object representing 0/1
```

The execution of the assignment statement in the preceding code segment causes Rational pointer rptr to point to a dynamic Rational object representing the default value of 0/1.

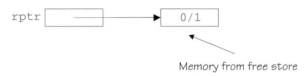

Memory from free store

Once a pointer has been successfully set with a location returned by a **new** request, the object at that location can be used like any other object of that type. In particular, it can be evaluated and manipulated.

In the following statement, the value of the dynamic object to which cptr points is set to the value of the next available input character.

```
cin >> *cptr;      // assign next input to the char
                   // object to which cptr points
```

Suppose the next available input is the character 'j'. After its extraction, memory would have the following depiction:

As a result, the following insertion statement displays a 'j' to cout.

```
cout << *cptr;     // display char object to which
                   // cptr points
```

A second form of the **new** operator not only requests a single dynamic object but also provides initialization for that object. The initializer value(s) are specified within parentheses, using commas to separate the initializers. In the following code segment, pointers `ip` and `rp` are defined along with initializers for the values to which they point.

```
int *ip;
ip = new int(256);          // ip points to dynamic
                            // object representing 256

cout << *ip << endl;
Rational *rp;
rp = new Rational (3, 4);   // rp points to dynamic
                            // object representing 3/4
```

If sufficient free store memory exists, then `ip` points to a dynamic **int** object that represents 256 and `rp` points to a dynamic `Rational` object that represents 3/4.

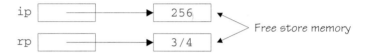

The third form of the **new** operator permits multiple dynamic objects to be requested in a single operation. This form expects that the right operand to the **new** operator is the name of a type along with a subscripted expression indicating the number of requested objects of that type. If sufficient, contiguous, unallocated free store memory is available, the operation returns a pointer to a block of dynamic memory sufficient to hold the requested number of objects. If the type of the requested dynamic objects is a class type, then the class default constructor is invoked automatically to initialize each of the requested objects. This form is used in the following code segment:

```
Rational *rlist;
rlist = new Rational[5];
```

In the preceding assignment statement, if the **new** operation is successful then `rlist` will point to the first object in a block of memory sufficient to hold five `Rational` objects.

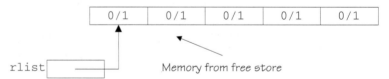

Because the memory is contiguous, pointer `rlist` can be viewed as a `Rational` array with five elements. Each of the dynamic objects is initialized with the `Rational` default constructor, that is, each of the five `Rational` objects initially represents the rational value 0/1.

Although the preceding `rlist` example uses a constant expression in requesting multiple dynamic objects, constant expressions are not a require-

C++ Language

New operation and exception handling

Our discussion of the **new** operation has not included what happens if a request for free store memory cannot be satisfied. In most existing C++ implementations, if the request cannot be satisfied then the operation produces 0, which corresponds to the null address. In the proposed standard, an exception is generated.

An *exception* is a program error that occurs during execution. If an *exception-handler* code segment has been defined for the exception, then flow of control is transferred to the handler when the exception occurs. If there is no handler, the program terminates when an exception occurs. Programmers often also develop exception detection and handling functions for arithmetic errors (e.g., division by 0), unexpected input, and improper array subscripting.

The C++ exception handling mechanism allows us to define different exception handlers for each kind of free store request that cannot be satisfied. Depending upon the application, this flexibility may prove useful. The proposed standard also provides a straightforward method to maintain traditional behavior where 0 is returned as the result of any unsatisfied **new** operation. In particular, the proposed standard includes the new library. This library defines a **void** function set_new_handler() that expects as its parameter a pointer to an exception handler function for the operator **new**. If the null address 0 is used as the actual parameter, then the traditional behavior of returning 0 for an unsatisfied **new** operation is in effect. Thus, by including the new library and by invoking set_new_handler(0), the code in this book, which assumes 0 is returned for an unsuccessful **new** operation, continues to work.

Implementing your own exception handlers is an involved process beyond the scope of this book. For additional information on this topic examine the draft of the proposed standard or advanced texts on object-oriented program design.

- Working Paper for the Draft Proposed International Standard for Information Systems—Programming Language C++, X3J16/96-0018 WG21/N0836, Washington: American National Standards Institute, 1996.

- M. D. Carroll and M. A. Ellis, *Designing and Coding Reusable C++*, Reading, MA: Addison-Wesley, 1995.

ment. For example, the next code segment determines the size of the free store request by extracting a value from cin.

```
cout << "Size of list: " << flush;
int ListSize;
cin >> ListSize;
int *values = new int[ListSize];
```

Memory acquired from the free store using either of the single object request forms can be returned to the free store by providing a pointer to that

Programming Tip

> ### One size does not fit all
> The ability to create what are effectively dynamic arrays, is very important for designing programs with great user flexibility. Lists can be the right size, neither too small to process user's desired input nor too large for the system to handle easily.

memory as the right operand of a **delete** operation. Such a return is demonstrated in the following code segment that returns the memory to which `cptr` points.

```
delete cptr;
```

A side effect of the **delete** operation is that the value of `cptr` becomes undefined.

Programmers need to be particularly careful if their code can contain multiple pointers to the same object because accessing a memory location that has been returned to the free store is illegal. For example, consider the following code segment:

```
char *ptr1 = new char('c');
char *ptr2 = ptr1;
delete ptr1;
cout << *ptr2; // undefined result -- ptr2 points
              // to returned free store memory
```

The segment begins by defining two **char*** pointers `ptr1` and `ptr2`. Pointer `ptr1` is initialized via a **new** operation to the location of a dynamic **char** object whose value is `'c'`. Pointer `ptr2` is initialized to point to that same object.

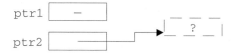

The **delete** statement that follows the two definitions returns the memory representing the `'c'` to the free store. As a result of that deletion, the value of `ptr1` becomes undefined. Another side effect of the deletion is that `ptr2` has become a *dangling pointer*—`ptr2` now points to an invalid memory location.

Accessing memory that has been returned to the free store produces undefined results.

Dynamic objects acquired using the **new** form that specifies the number of objects in the free store request must be returned as a group using a **delete** form that includes a pair of brackets between the keyword word **delete** and the pointer to memory being returned. After the deletion, the value of the pointer is undefined.

In the following statement, the **delete** operation returns to the free store the memory of the five Rational dynamic objects to which rlist points.

```
delete [] rlist;
```

If things go wrong

The effect of using a dangling pointer may not be immediately obvious. Therefore, when it is clear that a program using dynamic objects is misbehaving, you should reconsider the impact of each deletion on your data structures.

If the memory being returned to the free store represents class type objects and if a *destructor* for that class exists, then the destructor is automatically invoked on each of the object(s). A destructor is a member function that performs any necessary processing for the class object that is being destroyed. The classes we have defined in previous chapters (e.g., Rational and Deck) have not required such actions, so no destructors were defined for them. Destructors are normally necessary only for class objects with data members that are pointers to dynamic memory. They are required in such cases because it is the destructor that typically invokes the **delete** operation on those data members.

Consider the following code segment that in successive statements acquires dynamic storage and assigns the location of that storage to pointer p.

```
int *p;
p = new int;   // p points to dynamic memory
p = new int;   // p now points to different memory
```

When the first assignment statement is executed, free store memory is acquired and p points to it.

When the second assignment statement is executed, additional free store memory is acquired and p now points to it. The memory acquired in the previous assignment is now lost to the program.

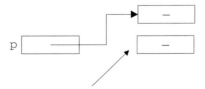

A memory leak has occurred. This locatio
cannot be accessed by the program.

The loss occurs because there is now no pointer object whose value is the location of the memory acquired in the first **new** operation. This loss is called a *memory leak*. In most C++ implementations, the loss will be in effect for the remainder of program execution. Memory leaks can seriously impact the ability of a program to complete its task—it may be the case that subsequent dynamic memory requests cannot be satisfied because of insufficient free store memory. For this reason, memory leaks should be avoided.

13.2

CONSTRUCTING A STRING TABLE

Many applications require the use of a data structure that represents a table of strings. For example, a compiler maintains a table of the identifiers found in the program being translated and a spell checker maintains a table of correctly spelled words to compare with the words in the document being examined.

One representation for a table of strings is a two-dimensional array of **char** elements. This data structure is used by function `PuzzleSearch()` of Listing 10.5 in its search for hidden names. The first subscript into the two-dimensional array is the index to a particular word; the second subscript is the index to the desired character of that word. This data structure requires that each row in the array be of the same size, where size is the length of the longest possible word to be represented. The row-length requirements of two-dimensional arrays make them wasteful of memory because average word length is typically much shorter than maximum word length.

An alternative data structure representation for a table of strings could use an array of **char*** pointers. An element of this array would be a pointer to a particular string. The memory reserved for a given string would be the number of characters in the string plus one for the terminating null character. The advantage of this representation is that it has minimal wasted space. An instance of the data structure is depicted in Figure 13.1. In the figure, elements of an array `Table` point to representations of various character strings.

We explore the basics of the string pointer table representation in the following problem:

> Display to standard output one copy of each string that appears in standard input, that is, if the same string appears multiple times in standard input, it is displayed only once to standard output. An example input is the following:

```
sixty seconds to a minute
sixty minutes to an hour
twenty-four hours to a day
```

For this input, the following output should occur.

```
sixty
seconds
to
a
minute
minutes
an
hour
twenty-four
hours
day
```

We assume that there will be no more than 100 unique strings in the input and that the longest string is at most 25 characters. (In Chapter 15, we consider a data structure, called a *linked list*, that allows the size of a list to change during program execution).

Figure 13.1

Representation of a list of words using an array of pointers to point to individual words

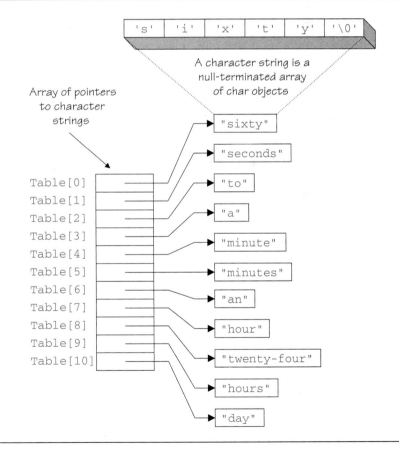

An algorithm to solve this problem follows.

Step 1.   Initialize an empty string table.

Step 2.   For each extracted input string do the following:

Step 2.1   Search the existing string table to determine whether the current extracted string is already present.

Step 2.2   If the current extracted string is not in the string table, add the string to the string table (if there is room).

Step 3.   For each string in the string table do the following:

Step 3.1   Display the string.

Step 4.   For each string in the string table do the following:

Step 4.1   Delete the string from the table.

Program 13.1 implements the preceding algorithm. The program does so by using the pointer array version of a string table. In addition to function `main()`, the program uses a function `TableSearch()` that examines the current string table to determine whether a given string is present.

To implement the first step of the algorithm, function `main()` defines several objects. The first object is a **char*** array `Table` with `MaxNbr-Strings` elements. This array is the basis of our string table. The elements of `Table` will point to the copies of the various input strings.

```
char *Table[MaxNbrStrings];
```

The second object is `NbrStrings`, which represents the number of strings currently in the string table. Because no strings are currently represented in the string table, `NbrStrings` is initialized to zero.

```
int NbrStrings = 0;
```

The processing of the second algorithm step requires that we have access to the current extracted string. This string is maintained in the **char** array `Buffer`.

```
char Buffer[MaxStringSize+1];
```

The size of `Buffer` is one more than constant `MaxStringSize`. This size enables `Buffer` to represent a string of length `MaxStringSize` along with a terminating null character.

Processing the current input string begins with function `Table-Search()`. The function determines whether the string is already represented by the string pointer table. If the input string is already represented, this new appearance of the string can be ignored.

`TableSearch()` expects three parameters. The first parameter `T` is the string pointer table; the second parameter `Size` is the number of entries in the table, and the third parameter `Key` is the string in question. If a copy of `Key` is in table `T`, the function returns the index of the string table array element that points to the copy; otherwise, the function returns `Size`. Because `TableSearch()` should change neither the pointers in the actual array nor the contents to which they point, `T` is declared as an array of constant pointers to constant **char** objects.

Program 13.1

A driver program that uses a table of string pointers

```cpp
// Program 13.1: Displays each input word once
#include <iostream.h>
#include <string.h>
const int MaxStringSize = 25;
const int MaxNbrStrings = 100;
int TableSearch(const char * const T[], int Size,
 const char Key[]); // prototype
int main() {
   // set-up empty string table
   char *Table[MaxNbrStrings];
   int NbrStrings = 0;
   // buffer to hold current extracted string
   char Buffer[MaxStringSize+1];
   // load the string table
   while (cin >> Buffer) {
      // got another string to check
      if (TableSearch(Table, NbrStrings, Buffer)
       == NbrStrings){ // need to add string to table
         if (NbrStrings < MaxNbrStrings) {
            // first reserve the space for the new word
            int n = strlen(Buffer) + 1;
            Table[NbrStrings] = new char[n];
            // check whether the space was acquired
            if (Table[NbrStrings] != 0) {
               // copy buffer into the new space
               strcpy(Table[NbrStrings], Buffer);
               // strings in Table has increased
               ++NbrStrings;
            }
            else // could not get the memory
               cerr << "Cannot store:" << Buffer << endl;
         }
         else { // table is full
            cerr << "No more strings allowed" << endl;
            break;
         }
      }
   }
   // print the list
   for (int i = 0; i < NbrStrings; ++i)
      cout << Table[i] << endl;
   // all done with the strings, so return the space
   for (int i = 0; i < NbrStrings; ++i)
      delete [] Table[i];
   // the program is done
   return 0;
}
// TableSearch(): search T to see if it contains Key
int TableSearch(const char * const T[], int Size,
 const char Key[]) {
   for (int i = 0; i < Size; ++i) {
      if (strcmp(T[i], Key) == 0) // found string
         return i;
   }
   // string key is not there
   return Size;
}
```

TableSearch() uses local object i as an index into array parameter T. It uses C-based string library function strcmp() to iteratively compare Key to the string to which array element T[i] points.

```
for (int i = 0; i < Size; ++i) {
    if (strcmp(T[i], Key) == 0) // found string
        return i;
}
// string key is not there
return Size;
```

If strcmp() returns 0, the strings are the same. In this case, the function returns i. If none of the Size array elements are equal to Key, then the function returns the value Size.

Function main() invokes TableSearch() in the test expression for an **if** statement. If expression (TableSearch(Table, NbrStrings, Buffer) == NbrStrings) is true, an attempt is made to add the string to the table data structure.

To add a string to the data structure, there must be an available element in Table that can be set to point to a copy of the input string. An element is available if the number of strings already pointed to by the table is less than the maximum number of permitted string pointers. Thus if test expression (NbrStrings < MaxNbrStrings) is true, an available element is in the table.

If there is an available table pointer, a free store request is made by main(). The request attempts to acquire sufficient dynamic memory to represent the current input string stored in Buffer. As part of this action, an object n is defined to represent the amount of dynamic memory needed—the amount is the length of the string plus one for the terminating null character.

```
int n = strlen(Buffer) + 1;
```

The length of the string is computed using standard C-based string library function strlen(). Operator **new** is then invoked requesting n **char** objects.

```
Table[NbrStrings] = new char[n];
```

The result is assigned to Table[NbrStrings]. This array element is used because it is the first available element in Table.

If the value assigned to Table[NbrStrings] is zero, then no free store memory is available to make a copy of the current input string. An error message is issued and the program continues. If instead, the value assigned to Table[NbrStrings] is nonzero, then the allocation request is successful and Table[NbrStrings] points to sufficient memory to make the copy. For this case, the copy is made using standard string library function strcpy().

```
strcpy(Table[NbrStrings], Buffer);
```

Once the copy is made, the string table data structure contains one more string. The addition requires that object NbrStrings be incremented by one.

```
++NbrStrings;
```

At this point, the processing of the current input string is completed and another extraction can be performed. Once there are no more input strings to extract, a **for** loop can implement the third step of the algorithm, displaying the strings in the table.

```
for (int i = 0; i < NbrStrings; ++i)
   cout << Table[i] << endl;
```

To accomplish the final step of the algorithm, function main() iteratively returns the dynamic memory to which the elements in Table point. The deletions are accomplished using a **for** statement.

```
for (int i = 0; i < NbrStrings; ++i)
   delete [] Table[i];
```

Each deletion returns the memory associated with a different free store allocation.

This completes our development and analysis of Program 13.1. In the exercises, we explore modifications to the program including the use of an ADT to represent and manipulate string tables.

13.3

AN ADT FOR VERY BIG NUMBERS

The existing integral types are limited with respect to the maximum integer we can represent. For example, if an **unsigned int** object uses 16 bits, then the maximum integer that we can represent is 65,535. (i.e., 2^{16} -1). Doubling the number of bits allows us to represent an integer on the order of 4,000,000,000. However, there are many applications where such numbers are far too small (e.g., computing national budgets and surpluses). Such applications required *extended-precision* arithmetic.

In this example, we consider an extended-precision representation of positive whole numbers where there is no predefined limit on the size of the number. Our ADT representation is called BigNum. Program 13.2 demonstrates the use of the BigNum ADT by calculating desired input requests. A sample run of the program is

```
Enter an expression: 1234567890 + 9876543210
1234567890 + 9876543210 = 11111111100
Enter an expression: 11291985 * 11281991
11291985 * 11281991 = 127396073142135
Enter an expression: 5121928 / 141932
5121928 / 141932 = 36
Enter an expression: 1000000000000001 - 2
1000000000000001 - 2 = 999999999999999
Enter an expression: ^Z
```

In terms of the requirements for a BigNum ADT, all of the usual arithmetic and relational operators should be applicable. We also require default

Program 13.2

A driver program that performs BigNum calculations

```
// Program 13.2: Demonstrate BigNum ADT
#include <iostream.h>
#include "bignum.h"
int main() {
   BigNum a;
   BigNum b;
   char op;
   cout << "Enter an expression: " << flush;
   while (cin >> a >> op >> b) {
      BigNum Result;
      switch (op) {
         case '+': Result = a + b; break;
         case '*': Result = a * b; break;
         case '-': Result = a - b; break;
         case '/': Result = a / b; break;
      }
      cout << a << " " << op << " " << b << " = "
       << Result << endl << endl;
      cout << "Enter an expression: " << flush;
   }
   return 0;
}
```

In terms of the requirements for a `BigNum` ADT, all of the usual arithmetic and relational operators should be applicable. We also require default and copy constructors. Finally, we require **int**-based and string-based constructors.

```
BigNum a;                              // default
BigNum b(a);                           // copy
BigNum c(3000);                        // int based
BigNum d("1234567890987654321");       // string based
```

The utility of the first three constructors is obvious. The fourth constructor seems odd—using a string to initialize a number—but it provides an easy way to define a number whose initial value can be arbitrarily large.

When representing an extended-precision number, we cannot store the number in a data member whose size is prespecified because some values could be too large for the data member to store. Thus the data members used to represent a `BigNum` value must have a dynamic component.

There are several ways to represent a `BigNum` value. In this implementation, we choose to represent a value using a dynamic array `Digits`. Each element of the array will store a different digit of the number. The least significant digit will be stored in the 0th element of the array, the next least significant digit will be stored in the 1th element of the array, and so on. Our representation will also have a data member `NumberDigits` that maintains the number of digits in the number. For example, the following definition constructs a `BigNum` with the internal representation depicted in Figure 13.2.

```
BigNum j(4301954);
```

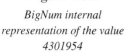

Figure 13.2

BigNum internal representation of the value 4301954

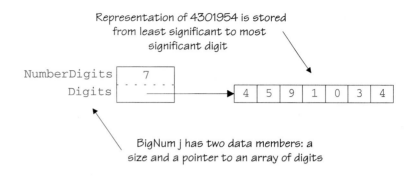

13.3.1

BigNum class definition

A copy of the header file for the bignum library is given in Listing 13.1. Table 13.1 provides a summary of the `BigNum` member functions. In the remainder of this section, we justify these member functions and the associated interface.

13.3.2

Member operators versus auxiliary operators

Performing an operation such as `BigNum` addition requires access to the individual digits in the representation. This access can be either direct reference and manipulation of the data members or indirect through inspector and mutator member functions.

```
Digits[3] = 5;    // direct mutation
SetDigit(3, 5);   // indirect mutation
```

Similarly, the insertion of a `BigNum` requires the inspection of the individual digits.

Based upon previous discussions of insertion operator overloading, you should recognize that it is inappropriate for `<<` to be a member function. If `<<` is made a member function, then the syntax of a `BigNum` insertion would reverse the normal position of the operands.

```
BigNum d(5000);
d << cout;    // form of insertion if << is a member
```

As you should recall, the operand reversal is necessary in this case because the object invoking the member is required by C++ to be the left operand. Because this syntax is unnatural with respect to the form of other insertions, we do not make the overloading of the insertion operator a member of the `BigNum` class. Instead, we make the insertion operator an auxiliary operator.

Listing 13.1

*Header file bignum.h
for the bignum library*

```
#ifndef BIGNUM_H
#define BIGNUM_H

#include <iostream.h>

class BigNum {
  public:
    // constructors
    BigNum();
    BigNum(int n);
    BigNum(const BigNum &n);
    BigNum(const char s[]);
    // destructor
    ~BigNum();
    // assignment operator
    BigNum& operator=(const BigNum &n);
    // facilitators
    BigNum Add(const BigNum &n) const;
    BigNum Multiply(const BigNum &n) const;
    BigNum Subtract(const BigNum &n) const;
    BigNum Divide(const BigNum &n) const;
    void Insert(ostream &sout) const;
    void Extract(ostream &sout) const;
    int Compare(const BigNum &n) const;
  protected:
    // inspectors
    int GetDigit(int i) const;
    int GetNumberDigits() const;
    // mutators
    void SetDigit(int i, int d);
    void SetNumberDigits(int n);
    void GetMemory(int n);
    void ResizeMemory(int n);
    void RemoveLeadingZeros();
    // facilitators
    BigNum LeftDigitShift(int i) const;
    BigNum Scale(int n) const;
  private:
    // data members
    int *Digits;
    int NumberDigits;
};

// auxiliary operators
BigNum operator+(const BigNum &m, const BigNum &n);
BigNum operator-(const BigNum &m, const BigNum &n);
BigNum operator*(const BigNum &m, const BigNum &n);
BigNum operator/(const BigNum &m, const BigNum &n);
bool operator<(const BigNum &m, const BigNum &n);
bool operator>(const BigNum &m, const BigNum &n);
bool operator==(const BigNum &m, const BigNum &n);
bool operator!=(const BigNum &m, const BigNum &n);
bool operator>=(const BigNum &m, const BigNum &n);
bool operator<=(const BigNum &m, const BigNum &n);
ostream& operator<<(ostream &sout, const BigNum &n);
istream& operator>>(istream &sin, BigNum &n);

#endif
```

Function	Purpose
BigNum()	Default constructor initializes representation to 0.
BigNum(**const** BigNum &n)	Copy constructor.
BigNum(**int** n)	Constructor using n as a basis.
BigNum(**const char** s[])	Constructor using a numeric string s as a basis.
~BigNum()	Destructor.
operator=(**const** BigNum &n)	Assignment operator.
Add(**const** BigNum &n)	Return the sum of the object and n.
Subtract(**const** BigNum &n)	Return the difference of the object and n.
Multiply(**const** BigNum &n)	Return the product of the object and n.
Divide(**const** BigNum &n)	Return the quotient of the object and n.
Insert(ostream &sout)	Display the object to stream sout.
Extract(istream &sin)	Extract a value from sin for the object.
Compare(**const** BigNum &n)	Compare object to n. If they are equal return 0; if n is the larger of the two objects, return -1; otherwise, return 1.
GetDigit(**int** i)	Return the value of the ith digit being represented.
SetDigit(**int** i, **int** n)	Set the ith digit being represented to n.
GetNumberDigits()	Return the number of digits in the object.
SetNumberDigits(**int** n)	Set the number of digits in the object to n.
GetMemory(**int** i)	Get sufficient memory to represent i digits.
ResizeMemory(**int** i)	Resize the object if necessary so that it can represent an i digit number.
LeftDigitShift(**int** i)	Shift the digits in the object left by i places and put zeros in the i least significant digits.
RemoveLeadingZeros()	Remove any extra leading zeros in the representation.
Scale(**int** n)	Return the product of the object and n.

There are several ways to enable an insertion operation. One method is to make the data members public. This scheme violates the information-hiding principle and subjects our representation to improper manipulations (e.g, an individual digit could be set to a nondigit value). This method is clearly undesirable and is therefore immediately rejected.

A second method to enable an insertion operation is to provide public inspector member functions that can return the size of the number and an individual digit in the number. Using these functions, we can display a BigNum number. We view this method as unsatisfactory because it offers an abstraction of a number that is inconsistent with other types of numbers.

A third method to enable an insertion operation is to declare operator << as a **friend** of the BigNum class. A **friend** of a class is given complete access to all members of its objects—regardless of whether they are public, protected, or private. A function, operator, or even another class can be made a **friend** of a class. To declare a function, operator, or class a **friend**, the function, operator, or class is prototyped using the modifier **friend** within the definition of the class in question.

```
class BigNum {
   // ...
   friend ostream& operator<<(ostream &sout,
    const BigNum &n); // << is a friend of BigNum
   // ...
};
```

The actual definition of the **friend** requires no special syntax. Thus, the following overloading of << can appear in the implementation file for BigNum.

```
ostream& operator<<(ostream &sout, const BigNum &n){
   for (int i = n.NumberDigits - 1; i >= 0; --i) {
      sout << n.Digits[i];
   }
   return sout;
}
```

Because it is a **friend** to the class BigNum, the definition of << can use the private data members to display the BigNum number.

Although the **friend** method provides some control over what function or operator manipulates the underlying representation, it still creates a major security hole with respect to information hiding. For this reason, a **friend** is used only as a last resort. In this case, we have another alternative, so we do not make << a **friend** of the class BigNum.

In our implementation, we define a public BigNum member function Insert() that expects a single ostream parameter. This member function practices information hiding and uses protected inspectors to display the Big-Num number. To provide the customary insertion operator interface, we use this function in an auxiliary overloading of the insertion operator for BigNum numbers. The two functions are defined in Listing 13.2.

For similar reasons, our BigNum interface also provides public member functions Add(), Subtract(), Multiply(), and Divide(). These member functions can be used in the definitions of BigNum arithmetic operators.

Listing 13.2

Insertion functions from bignum.cpp

```
// Insert(): facilitator for BigNum insertion
void BigNum::Insert(ostream &sout) const {
  for (int i = NumberDigits; i >= 1; --i) {
    sout << GetDigit(i);
  }
}

// auxiliary operator << for BigNums
ostream& operator<<(ostream &sout, const BigNum &n){
  n.Insert(sout);
  return sout;
}
```

The public `BigNum` member function `Compare()` can be used in the definition of the relational operators. Like the insertion operator, the `BigNum` arithmetic and relational operators are auxiliary library operators. Because the definitions of the auxiliary `BigNum` arithmetic operators are straightforward given the member functions, their definitions are left for the exercises.

Defining the `BigNum` arithmetic and relational operators as auxiliary operators (i.e., nonmembers of the `BigNum` class) offers another advantage. Consider the following code segment that defines `BigNum` objects a, b, and c.

```
BigNum a("999999999999999999");
BigNum b = a + 1;   // legal if + is member or
                    // auxiliary
BigNum c = 1 + a;   // legal only if + is auxiliary
```

First, suppose addition is defined to be a `BigNum` member operator with the right operand being a `BigNum`. Even though 1 is not a `BigNum`, the initialization of `BigNum` object b would be correctly performed because the compiler checks for a promotion method that converts an **int** into a `BigNum` and finds a `BigNum` constructor that expects a single **int** as a parameter. This constructor is applied to produce the proper parameter for the member operator.

Now consider the initialization of `BigNum` object c. The plus operator used in the expression 1 + a is not the `BigNum` member operator. (To be a member operator, the left operand must be part of the class.) Therefore, the only plus operators that are applicable are those defined for the fundamental types. As a result, there is no workable promotion process and the statement is illegal. Hence, we do not have the commutativity property that we expect with addition.

Now suppose that `BigNum` addition is defined to be an auxiliary operation. If either the expression a + 1 or the expression 1 + a is encountered, the auxiliary definition will be considered and promotion of the 1 to a `BigNum` makes the definition applicable. Hence, commutativity is in effect in this case. The availability of commutativity makes the auxiliary operator version the preferred strategy.

The rules for promotion are quite involved because they must cover cases where multiple promotions are possible or required. A complete specification of these rules may be found in a C++ reference manual (e.g., Ellis and Stroustrup).

13.3.3

Copy constructors, member assignment, and destructors

As noted in Chapter 9, C++ specifies that default versions of the copy constructor and the member assignment operator are automatically available to a class. The default versions perform memberwise copying where each source data member is copied in a bit-by-bit manner to the corresponding target data member. This bit-by-bit assignment is suitable for a simple ADT such as `Rational` or `Deck`. However, for sophisticated classes whose objects can acquire storage dynamically, the straightforward memberwise copying of data members can introduce storage conflicts.

Suppose there is no explicitly defined `BigNum` copy constructor. Let's consider what happens when the following code segment is executed with the default copy constructor in effect.

```
BigNum a("123456789");
BigNum b(a);
```

When `BigNum` object a is created, its data members are initialized from scratch. In particular, dynamic space is acquired to hold the various digits in the number. A comparable acquisition is not performed for object b. Because the default copy constructor is being supposed, the data members of object a are directly copied to object b. Under this scenario, objects a and b now share the same dynamic space for their `Digits` data members. This scenario is depicted in Figure 13.3.

Figure 13.3

Depicts the effect of memberwise copying of one BigNum to another

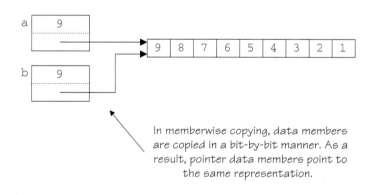

In memberwise copying, data members are copied in a bit-by-bit manner. As a result, pointer data members point to the same representation.

A change to either a or b affects the other. For example, suppose a was incremented by 1. Then a display of object b

```
cout << b << endl;
```

would output

```
1234567890
```

rather than its last assigned value of `123456789`.

Such side effects are not what a client would expect in the manipulation of numbers. Therefore, the default copy constructor cannot be used.

For similar reasons we cannot use the default member assignment operator—like the default copy constructor, it directly copies the data members of the right operand to the data members of the invoking object. Thus this memberwise copying also leads to side effects.

To avoid side effects in our ADT, we explicitly developed a BigNum copy constructor and member assignment operator. The use of dynamic space by a BigNum object requires that we also define a destructor that returns the acquired dynamic space when we are finished with the object. Therefore, our BigNum class definition contains a declaration of a copy constructor, assignment operator, and destructor.

```
// copy constructor
BigNum(const BigNum &n);
// assignment operator
BigNum& operator=(const BigNum &n);
// destructor
~BigNum();
```

The syntax of the destructor and member assignment declarations are different from previous declarations. The name of a class' destructor is always composed of a ~ followed by the class name. Thus ~BigNum() is the BigNum destructor. Like a constructor, a destructor does not have a return type.

The syntax for the member assignment is confusing at first glance—an assignment operator should have two operands, yet the declaration specifies only one operand. This syntax is used because the left operand is understood to be the object invoking the member operator. Therefore, only the right operand needs to be declared. The reason the assignment operation returns a value is so that larger expressions can be composed, as in the following code segment:

```
BigNum a(1);
BigNum b;
BigNum c;
c = b = a;
```

The assignment operator performs a reference return for reasons of efficiency—this way no copy needs to be made.

The remaining functions in our BigNum class definition are protected functions. These functions are used to inspect and mutate the data members so that the member functions in the public interface can be implemented using information-hiding principles. Although they are important, their declarations do not introduce new concepts. Their discussion is limited to Table 13.1 and to the next section where we consider BigNum implementation details.

Programming Alert

Gang of three

It is generally the case that when you need to define a class copy constructor, member assignment, or a destructor, it is appropriate and necessary to define the other two members. If such a requirement is not apparent, then reanalyze your design for inconsistencies.

13.3.4

Implementation of the BigNum constructors

Through use of the facilitator member functions, the default and copy constructors have straightforward implementations. The default value for a `Big-Num` is zero. This representation can be achieved by performing the following actions:

- Set the number of digits being represented to one.
- Acquire dynamic memory for a single digit.
- Set the acquired digit to zero.

As shown in Listing 13.3, these actions can be performed by invoking the proper member function.

Listing 13.3

BigNum default and copy constructors from bignum.cpp

```
// default BigNum constructor sets number to zero
BigNum::BigNum() {
   SetNumberDigits(1);
   GetMemory(1);
   SetDigit(1, 0);
}

// BigNum constructor from another BigNum
BigNum::BigNum(const BigNum &n) {
   SetNumberDigits(n.GetNumberDigits());
   GetMemory(GetNumberDigits());
   for (int i = 1; i <= GetNumberDigits(); ++i) {
      SetDigit(i, n.GetDigit(i));
   }
}
```

Note that requests to `SetDigit()` for setting a particular digit specify a digit location in the range 1 through `NumberDigits`. (`GetDigit()` expects a value in a similar range.)

The copy constructor is also given in Listing 13.3. Using its parameter, n, it performs actions comparable to the default constructor.

- Set the number of digits in the copy so that the copy has the same number of digits as n.
- Acquire dynamic memory to store the digits to be copied.
- Perform the actual copying of the digits of n.

The first two actions can be performed by invoking member functions.

```
SetNumberDigits(n.GetNumberDigits());
GetMemory(GetNumberDigits());
```

Once the memory has been acquired, it can be initialized using a **for** loop to copy the digits into the representation, digit by digit.

```
for (int i = 1; i <= GetNumberDigits(); ++i) {
   SetDigit(i, n.GetDigit(i));
}
```

We next consider how to implement the constructor that initializes a `Big-Num` using a numeric string parameter s. This implementation is given in Listing 13.4. Our working assumption is that the string is in decimal format. We consider other formats in the exercises.

Listing 13.4

BigNum constructor
using a numeric string
from bignum.cpp

```
// BigNum constructor that takes string of digits
BigNum::BigNum(const char s[]) {
   if (strlen(s) == 0) { // empty string is 0
      SetNumberDigits(1);
      GetMemory(1);
      SetDigit(1, 0);
   }
   else { // have nonempty string to process
      // process digits
      int nd = strlen(s);
      SetNumberDigits(nd);
      GetMemory(nd);
      for (int i = 0; i < nd; ++i) {
         if (isdigit(s[i])) { // digit
            SetDigit(nd - i, s[i] - '0');
         }
         else { // non-digit
            cerr << "Bad number: " << s << endl;
            exit(1);
         }
      }
      RemoveLeadingZeros();
   }
}
```

An examination of Listing 13.4 shows that the constructor uses an **if** statement to distinguish whether s is the empty string. An empty string is associated with the value zero. The actions in this case are therefore identical to actions of the default constructor.

If parameter s is nonempty, there is a nontrivial string to process. The number of characters in the string is then computed. This value, nd, should be the number of digits in the representation. Object nd is also used to specify the amount of dynamic memory to be acquired.

```
int nd = strlen(s);
SetNumberDigits(nd);
GetMemory(nd);
```

A **for** loop processes the characters in the string. The loop uses the ctype library function isdigit() to determine whether the current character is a digit. If the character is a digit, the equivalent numeric digit is copied into the appropriate position. (As noted previously, the number is stored internally by `BigNum` from least significant digit to most significant digit.)

```
for (int i = 0; i < nd; ++i) {
    if (isdigit(s[i])) { // digit
        SetDigit(nd - i, s[i] - '0');
    }
    else { // non-digit
        cerr << "Bad BigNum: " << s << endl;
        exit(1);
    }
}
```

The expression `s[i] - '0'` maps a digit-character value to the associated numeric value.

Once the string has been processed, some cleaning up is attempted.

```
RemoveLeadingZeros();
```

The cleaning up is attempted because the user may have included leading zeros as in the following declaration of `c`.

```
BigNum c("000000000001");
```

This completes our discussion of constructors. We leave it to the exercises to develop a `BigNum` constructor using an **int** value.

13.3.5

Inspectors and mutators

We now consider some of the other basic member functions of the `BigNum` class. These protected member functions are the means by which information hiding is practiced. The functions are given in Listing 13.5.

Listing 13.5

Basic member functions of the BigNum class from bignum.cpp

```
// GetNumberDigits(): set the size of the number
int BigNum::GetNumberDigits() const {
    return NumberDigits;
}

// SetNumberDigits(): set the size of the number
void BigNum::SetNumberDigits(int n) {
    assert (n > 0);
    NumberDigits = n;
}

// GetDigit(): return the desired digit value
int BigNum::GetDigit(int i) const {
    assert ((i > 0) && (i <= GetNumberDigits()));
    return Digits[i-1];
}

// SetDigit(): set desired digit to desired value
void BigNum::SetDigit(int i, int n) {
    assert((i > 0) && (i <= GetNumberDigits()));
    assert((n >= 0) && (n <= 9));
    Digits[i-1] = n;
}
```

As with our other ADTs, pairs of functions inspect and modify the various data members. These functions use `assert` statements to check our programming logic. If the other member functions have been designed correctly, these assertions should always be true.

Observe that the `GetDigit()` and `SetDigit()` member functions interpret the space pointed to by data member `Digits` as an array where the individual digits are stored such that the least significant digit is kept in `Digits[0]` and the most significant digit is kept in `Digits[NumberDigits-1]`. Therefore, a request to access the ith digit references `Digits[i-1]`.

13.3.6

Managing BigNum dynamic memory

The `BigNum` class has three member functions that perform dynamic memory requests. These members are `GetMemory()`, `ResizeMemory()`, and the destructor `~BigNum()`, and they are defined in Listing 13.6.

Listing 13.6

Member functions for managing dynamic memory from bignum.cpp

```cpp
// GetMemory(): get space for digits
void BigNum::GetMemory(int n) {
   assert(n > 0);
   Digits = new int [n];
   if (Digits == 0) {
      cerr << "Out of memory" << endl;
      exit(1);
   }
}

// Bignum destructor
BigNum::~BigNum() {
   delete [] Digits;
}

// ResizeMemory(): reset the space to hold the new
// desired number of digits
void BigNum::ResizeMemory(int n) {
   assert(n > 0);
   delete [] Digits;
   GetMemory(n);
}
```

As Table 13.1 indicates, the purpose of function `GetMemory()` is to acquire the requested amount of dynamic memory. The dynamic memory is assigned to the pointer `Digits`, which, as noted previously, is treated by the `BigNum` member functions as a dynamically sized array. The acquired memory is used to store the representations of the digits individually.

Function `GetMemory()` requires a single **int** parameter n, which is the number of **int** objects to be acquired. The function first asserts that the value of n is valid. If n is valid, the operator **new** is invoked.

```cpp
Digits = new int[n];
```

The function then determines whether `Digits` points to the null address. If `Digits` is null, the free store would not able to provide the dynamic memory.

In this case, an error message would be generated and the program would terminate. If `Digits` is not null, then function is finished because `Digits` points to the newly acquired memory.

The `BigNum` destructor `~BigNum()` is the second function defined in Listing 13.6. The only cleanup performed on a `BigNum` object going out of existence is the return of the dynamic memory to which its data member `Digits` points. This return to the free store is accomplished through a **delete** statement.

```
delete [] Digits;
```

During the lifetime of a `BigNum` object, the number being represented may change. In this implementation, the memory to which `Digits` points is exactly the right size for the number being represented. As the number being represented changes, the number of digits in the representation can also change. The purpose of function `ResizeMemory()` is to ensure that the exact amount of dynamic memory is available. Function `ResizeMemory()` has a single **int** parameter n, which represents the number of **int** objects to which `Digits` should point.

The implementation of `ResizeMemory()` in Listing 13.6 begins by asserting that a proper value for n has been passed.

```
assert(n > 0);
```

If n is greater than 0, the following actions are taken.

```
delete [] Digits;
GetMemory(n);
```

The **delete** makes the memory to which `Digits` currently points available to the system. At that point, it is safe to reset `Digits` through the use of `Get-Memory()`.

Observe that although we used the **delete** operator in the implementation of `ResizeMemory()`, we did not use the `BigNum` destructor to release the memory. According to the C++ proposed standard, a destructor processes an object that is going out of existence. This condition is not the case during resizing; in contrast the object is being modified.

13.3.7

Member assignment and the this pointer

The reassignment of an object requires three actions.

- Return existing dynamic memory.

- Acquire sufficient new dynamic memory.

- Copy the number of digits and the digits of the source object.

These actions can seemingly be accomplished in the following manner where object n is the BigNum parameter representing the right operand.

```
ResizeMemory(n.GetNumberDigits());
SetNumberDigits(n.GetNumberDigits());
for (int i = 1; i <= n.GetNumberDigits(); ++i) {
    SetDigit(i, n.GetDigit(i));
}
```

Suppose that the preceding code segment is the function body for our member assignment operator. What would happen if the following assignment was executed where object a was a BigNum?

```
a = a;
```

The assignment would make object a undefined! In this case, the left operand and right operand are the same object—parameter n of the member assignment operator is an alias for the object a. When ResizeMemory() performs its release of the dynamic memory controlled by a, we lose the ability for n, which is in fact also a, to reference that memory in the **for** loop. The invocation of SetDigit() in the **for** loop is merely copying the uninitialized space to itself.

We cannot dismiss this problem by saying that a programmer never has the need to write such a statement because the problem can also come about in a disguised manner. For example, the object in question can be passed multiple times as a parameter to some function or because the object is both a global object and a parameter.

A simple way to handle this aliasing problem is to perform the assignment if the two operands represent different objects. C++ provides a pointer to the invoking object that can be used for this purpose. The pointer is referenced using the keyword **this**. We can compare the value of **this** with &n, which is the location of n. If the locations are different, the invoking object is updated.

By using the indirection operator * in conjunction with **this** (i.e., *this), we have an expression that is suitable for the return value of the member assignment operator. The complete definition of the member assignment operator is given in Listing 13.7.

Listing 13.7

BigNum member assignment operator from bignum.cpp

```
// operator =: assignment for BigNum
BigNum& BigNum::operator=(const BigNum &n) {
    if (this != &n) {
        ResizeMemory(n.GetNumberDigits());
        SetNumberDigits(n.GetNumberDigits());
        for (int i = 1; i <= GetNumberDigits(); ++i) {
            SetDigit(i, n.GetDigit(i));
        }
    }
    return *this;
}
```

13.3.8

Member addition with the BigNum class

Listing 13.8 provides the definition of facilitator `Add()`. The function produces and returns a `BigNum Result` whose value is the sum of the invoking object and `BigNum n`.

Listing 13.8

BigNum member facilitator Add() from bignum.cpp

```
// Add(): facilitator for BigNum addition
BigNum BigNum::Add(const BigNum &n) const {
   BigNum Result;
   int nd; // maximum number of digits in sum
   if (GetNumberDigits() < n.GetNumberDigits())
      nd = n.GetNumberDigits() + 1;
   else
      nd = GetNumberDigits() + 1;
   Result.ResizeMemory(nd);
   Result.SetNumberDigits(nd);
   int Carry = 0;
   for (int i = 1; i <= nd; ++i) {
      int d1; // current digit of left operand
      int d2; // current digit of right operand
      if (i <= GetNumberDigits())
         d1 = GetDigit(i);
      else
         d1 = 0;
      if (i <= n.GetNumberDigits())
         d2 = n.GetDigit(i);
      else
         d2 = 0;
      Result.SetDigit(i, (d1 + d2 + Carry) % 10);
      Carry = (d1 + d2 + Carry) / 10;
   }
   Result.RemoveLeadingZeros();
   return Result;
}
```

After defining `Result`, function `Add()` defines an object `nd` to represent the maximum number of digits to be stored in `Result`. This value is at most one greater than the maximum number of digits used by either operand. Object `nd` is then used to reset `Result`'s representation. An object `Carry` is then defined that represents the carry associated with the previous digit calculation for `Result`. Because no such calculation has been performed, `Carry` is initialized to zero.

The major activity in `Add()` is the **for** loop, which iteratively sets the digits of `Result`. The setting of the ith digit begins by defining objects `d1` and `d2`. These objects are used to store the ith digits of the left and right operands. In determining the value of `d1`, `Add()` tests whether `i` is a valid index into `Digits`. If `i` is valid, the value of the corresponding digit is used to set `d1`. If `i` is not a valid index, then zero is used. The setting of `d2` is done in a similar manner. The settings are demonstrated in Figure 13.4.

Once `d1` and `d2` have been set, the ith digit of the sum can be computed. The sum digit is the result modulus 10 of adding `d1`, `d2`, and `Carry`. The new

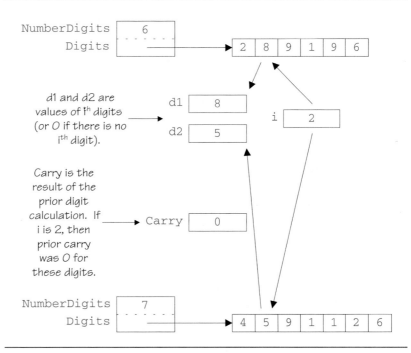

value of `Carry` can be determined by dividing the sum `d1 + d2 + Carry` by 10. The result will be either 0 or 1 depending whether the sum is greater than 10.

In the final iteration of the loop, `i` is greater than both `GetNumberDig-its()` and `n.GetNumberDigits()`. The purpose of this iteration is to deal with the remaining carry value.

Once all the digits in `Result` have been set, its member function `RemoveLeadingZeros()` is invoked to perform any necessary cleanup. Afterwards, `Result` is returned.

This completes our discussion of `BigNum` member function `Add()`.

13.3.9

Multiplication in the BigNum class

Implementing `BigNum` multiplication is straightforward given member functions `Scale()` and `LeftDigitShift()`. Function `Scale()` provides the ability to compute the product of a `BigNum` times an **int**. Function `Left-DigitShift()` provides the ability to insert zeros of least significance into a `BigNum` object. Using these two functions, we can compute the product of two `BigNum` objects by simulating the traditional multiplication process:

- Iteratively multiply the right operand by the current digit from the invoking left operand to produce a term.

- Shift the term by the appropriate number of zeros.

■ Add the shifted term to a running total whose final value will be the product.

The multiplication method is implemented in Listing 13.9. The code for `RemoveLeadingZeros()` and `Scale()` is given without comment in Listing 13.10. This completes our discussion of the `BigNum` ADT and our introduction to dynamic objects.

Listing 13.9

BigNum member Multiply() from bignum.cpp

```
// Multiply (): facilitator for BigNum multiplication
BigNum BigNum::Multiply(const BigNum &n) const {
   BigNum Product;
   for (int i = 1; i <= GetNumberDigits(); ++i) {
      BigNum Term = n.Scale(GetDigit(i));
      BigNum ShiftedTerm = Term.LeftDigitShift(i-1);
      Product = Product + ShiftedTerm;
   }
   return Product;
}
```

13.4

POINTS TO REMEMBER

■ Dynamic objects are created during program execution as the result of a specific request for memory.

■ Dynamic memory is said to come from the free store.

■ The major C++ memory allocation request mechanism is the **new** operator, which has three forms.

■ The most basic form of a **new** operation expects a type as the right operand for the operator. If sufficient free store memory is available for an object of that type, the location of a single dynamic object is returned. The dynamic object is initialized only if there is a default constructor for the type of that object.

■ A second form of a **new** operation supports the initialization of the dynamic object whose location is returned. The initialization is specified as an actual parameter list following the type of object to be allocated.

■ The third form of a **new** operation has a subscripted expression following the type of object(s) being requested. The expression represents the number of dynamic objects to be returned. If there is sufficient, contiguous free store memory, a pointer to a block that can hold the requested number of objects is returned. The objects in the block are initialized only if their type is a class type with a default constructor.

■ In most current C++ implementations, if a **new** operation cannot return the dynamic storage that is requested, then the null address (0) is returned. In the proposed C++ standard, an exception is instead issued.

Listing 13.10

BigNum member functions RemoveLeadingZeros() and Scale()

```
// RemoveLeadingZeros(): remove zeros in front of most
// most significant digit
void BigNum::RemoveLeadingZeros() {
   int nd = GetNumberDigits();
   while ((nd > 1) && (GetDigit(nd) == 0)) {
      --nd;
   }
   if (nd != GetNumberDigits()) {
      int *OldDigits = Digits;
      SetNumberDigits(nd);
      GetMemory(nd);
      for (int i = 1; i <= nd; ++i) {
         SetDigit(i, OldDigits[i-1]);
      }
      delete [] OldDigits;
   }
}

// Scale(): multiply the BigNum object by an int object
BigNum BigNum::Scale(int n) const {
   assert(n >= 0);
   if (n == 0)
      return 0;
   else if (n == 1)
      return *this;
   else {
      BigNum Product;
      int i = 0;
      while (n) {
         int Digit = n % 10;
         BigNum Term;
         Term.ResizeMemory(GetNumberDigits() + 1);
         Term.SetNumberDigits(GetNumberDigits() + 1);
         int Carry = 0;
         for (int j = 1; j <= GetNumberDigits(); ++j){
            int d = (Digit*GetDigit(j) + Carry) % 10;
            Carry = (Digit*GetDigit(j) + Carry) / 10;
            Term.SetDigit(j, d);
         }
         Term.SetDigit(Term.GetNumberDigits(),Carry);
         Term = Term.LeftDigitShift(i);
         Product = Product + Term;
         n = n / 10;
         ++i;
      }
      Product.RemoveLeadingZeros();
      return Product;
   }
}
```

- The proposed standard defines the new library that includes a function set_new_handler(). This function, when invoked with the null address as its parameter, causes the current **new** behavior to be in effect.

- Unlike local objects, dynamic objects can exist beyond the execution of the function in which they were created. A dynamic object exists until the **delete** operator makes a deallocation request.

History of Computing

The founding of Microsoft

Paul Allen and Bill Gates were computer whizzes that had become friends while attending high school in Seattle. Their deep fascination with computers had drawn them together. Gates, Allen, and a few other students formed a company that did programming. For kids in high school, they did quite well. In fact, they earned about $20,000 from a project that analyzed traffic data for local highway departments.

When the article on Edward Roberts' Altair 8800 appeared in *Popular Electronics* in 1974, Allen was working as a programmer for Honeywell in Boston and Gates was attending Harvard majoring in mathematics. When Allen saw the article, he immediately realized its significance. The Altair heralded a new generation of computing—personal computing. Allen rushed over to Harvard and found Gates. He convinced Gates that this was their big opportunity. The Altair would need software to be usable, and Allen proposed that they write a Basic interpreter for the machine. Basic was the language used by most hobbyists. Gates called Roberts in Albuquerque and told him that he and Allen had developed a Basic interpreter that could be adapted for the Altair. Roberts, who had already heard similar claims from several other people, told Gates that he would make a deal with the first person to demonstrate a working Basic interpreter.

Gates and Allen (see Figure 13.5) then began to write a interpreter for Basic that would run on the Altair. However, they had one serious problem—they didn't have an Altair. How were they going to develop software for a machine they didn't have? The solution was to write a program for one of the computers at Harvard that could mimic the actions of the 8800, the chip inside the Altair. They could then use this program to test their Basic. Allen worked on the simulator while Gates worked on Basic. At the end of February, a little less than eight weeks after they started, they had a Basic that they felt they could demonstrate to Roberts. Of course, neither knew whether the code would work at all on the Altair. Allen flew to Albuquerque with the software to do the demonstration. Amazingly, the software worked the first time.

Allen went to work for Ed Roberts improving the Basic interpreter to make it more marketable. Gates finished his sophomore year at Harvard, and then he joined Allen in Albuquerque. It was there, in 1975, that they formed a partnership they called Micro-soft. (The hyphen was eventually dropped.) Roberts, Allen, and Gates toured the country in a mobile home to demonstrate Roberts' Altair running Gates and Allen's Basic.

Microsoft was off to a good start with Basic, selling versions that ran on other computers to other companies. However, it was in 1980 that Microsoft's big break came. IBM had decided to enter the personal computer market. In a departure from typical IBM initiatives, IBM decided to get outside help in developing the software that would run on what is now known as the PC. They selected Microsoft to provide both the operating system and the Basic interpreter that would run on the PC. The operating system came to be known as MS-DOS, for Microsoft Disk Operating System. The IBM PC became incredibly popular and Microsoft grew rapidly.

In 1985 Microsoft released the very popular Windows operating system which has sold more than 10,000,000 copies since its introduction. Microsoft is now the undisputed giant of personal computer software, selling popular programs that run both on the PC and Apple's Macintosh computer.

Needless to say, Gates and Allen are extremely wealthy, each worth over a billion dollars. Allen left Microsoft in 1983 after he was diagnosed as having Hodgkin's disease. He has since recovered and is a major founder/investor in several smaller companies that do advanced software development. Bill Gates is the CEO of Microsoft and continues to be a major player in shaping and defining what computing will be like in the 90s and beyond.

Figure 13.5

Paul Allen and Bill Gates in 1975

- The objects acquired in a given **new** operation must be deallocated as a group.

- A dangling pointer is a pointer object that points to deallocated memory.

- A memory leak is dynamically acquired memory that has not been deallocated, but to which no pointer object points.

- A major use of dynamic objects is with ADTs. To implement their representations, many ADTs require data members that point to dynamic objects. In particular, this is true of the `BigNum` ADT.

- A destructor is a member function that is automatically invoked as an object goes out of existence.

- For class types with data members that point to dynamic objects, the destructor normally performs a **delete** operation returning the dynamic memory to which the data members point.

- Class objects that use dynamic memory must generally supply a copy constructor, destructor, and assignment operator. Otherwise, the default versions of the copy constructor and the member assignment operator are used. Such use can lead to unintended side effects.

- The keyword **this** can be used in a member function or operator body as a pointer to the object that performed the invocation. The **this** pointer is typically used in the implementations of the assignment operator for an ADT.

- A **friend** to a class is not a member of the class, but a **friend** can access all of the class's data members regardless of whether they are public, private, or protected. A **friend** can be a function, operator, or another class.

- To represent numbers of extended precision, classes must be developed. The fundamental types cannot do the job because they have fixed sizes for their representations.

13.5

EXERCISES

13.1   What is the scope of a dynamic object?

13.2   Describe the three forms of a **new** operation. Give an example of each form.

13.3   Describe the two forms of a **delete** operation. When is their use appropriate?

13.4   What is the free store?

13.5   What is a memory leak?

13.6   What is a dangling pointer?

13.7   What is a **friend**? What access rights does it have?

13.8   What does the keyword **this** represent? What does the expression *this represent?

13.9   What is the purpose of the invocation set_new_handler(0)?

13.10 Does BigNum need a destructor? What would happen if it did not have one?

13.11 Identify the mistakes in the following code segment:

```
char *p = new ('a');
char *q = new char('b');
char *r = new char('c');
char *s = new char [100] ('d');
char *t = *q;
char *u = r;
delete q;
*t = 'e';
```

13.12 Write a code segment that sets up a dynamic list of 100 `Rational` objects. Each of these dynamic objects is to represent 0/1.

13.13 Write a code segment that sets up a dynamic list of 100 `Rational` objects. Each of these objects is to represent 3/4.

13.14 Run the following two programs. Speculate on why they perform differently for most C++implementations.

```
#include <iostream.h>
int main() {
    long int counter = 0;
    int *ptr;
    do {
        ptr = new int;
        ++counter;
    } while (ptr);
    cout << counter << endl;
    return 0;
}
```

```
#include <iostream.h>
int main() {
    long int counter = 0;
    int *ptr;
    do {
        ptr = new int [1];
        ++counter;
    } while (ptr);
    cout << counter << endl;
    return 0;
}
```

13.15 Perform an experiment that determines the largest block of free store memory that can be allocated on your system. Report your results.

13.16 Does the following code segment represent an infinite loop? Why?

```
while (true) {
    int *p = new int;
    if (p == 0) {
        break;
    }
    delete p;
}
```

13.17 Design a class to implement a string table. The class should have at least two constructors. The default constructor creates a table with 10 entries. Another constructor would allow the number of entries in the table to be specified. The basic inspector functions would indicate whether a string is present in the table and what string is represented by a particular entry. The basic mutating functions would be adding and removing strings from the table. Is it necessary for the class to define a copy constructor, destructor, and member assignment? What should be done if the table is full and another string is to be added?

13.18 Design and implement the `BigNum` member function `Subtract()`.

13.19 Design and implement the `BigNum` member function `Divide()`.

13.20 Implement the auxiliary arithmetic operators for `BigNum` objects using the member facilitators.

13.21 Design and implement the `BigNum` member function `Compare()`.

13.22 Design and implement the `BigNum` member function `Extract()`.

13.23 Implement an auxiliary extraction operator `>>` for `BigNum` objects using the facilitator `Extract()` of the previous exercise.

13.24 Implement the auxiliary relational operators for `BigNum` objects. Should all of the operators directly invoke the member facilitator `Compare()`? Explain.

13.25 Redesign and reimplement the string-based `BigNum` constructor so that it accepts octal and hexadecimal strings.

13.26 Design and implement the constructor that creates a `BigNum` from an **int**. Hint: use an in-memory `ostrstream` object to convert the number to a string.

13.27 Design and implement increment and decrement operators for `BigNum` objects.

13.28 Design and implement a modulus operator for `BigNum` objects.

13.29 Design and implement the `+=`, `-=`, `*=`, and `/=` operators for `BigNum` objects.

13.30 Redesign and reimplement the `BigNum` member function `Multiply()` so that the product is produced by scaling the larger operand by the digits of the smaller operand.

13.31 Design and implement the `BigNum` member function `LeftDigit-Shift()`.

13.32 Redesign and reimplement the `BigNum` member function `ResizeMemory()` so that if the requested change in the number of digits is the same as the current number of digits, no action is taken.

13.33 Redesign and reimplement `BigNum` so that it can also handle negative numbers.

13.34 Design and implement a program that expects three parameters. The first and third parameters are to be used to construct `BigNum` objects. The second parameter is to be an arithmetic operator. The program should display to standard output the result of performing that operation on the two constructed `BigNum` objects.

13.35 Design and implement a class `IntArray`. The class is a simpler version of the standard class `vector`. Class `IntArray` is to represent objects that emulate arrays. An `IntArray` object when subscripted will produce the corresponding element. The overloading of the subscript operator should perform subscript checking. The default constructor allows a list with 10 elements to be represented. Another constructor should allow the number of elements in the list to be specified via an initialization parameter.

CHAPTER 14

Inheritance

Introduction

A key feature of an object-oriented language is inheritance. Inheritance is the ability to define new classes using existing classes as a basis. The new class inherits the attributes and behaviors of the classes on which it is based, and in addition, it can have attributes and behaviors that are specific to it. Inheritance is a powerful mechanism that provides a natural framework for producing software that is reliable, understandable, cost effective, adaptable, and reusable. In this chapter, we introduce C++'s inheritance mechanism by developing a class hierarchy for representing and displaying two-dimensional shapes. The resulting classes are used to refine and expand the kaleidoscope program developed in Chapter 8.

Key Concepts

- is-a relationship
- has-a relationship
- uses-a relationship
- base class
- derived class
- public inheritance
- private inheritance
- single inheritance
- multiple inheritance

14.1

OBJECT-ORIENTED DESIGN USING INHERITANCE

We are all familar with the concept of biological inheritance. All living things inherit characteristics from their ancestors. For example, whether we want to admit it or not, we have all inherited characteristics from our parents. These characteristics may have been unique to our parents, or perhaps our parents inherited the characteristic from their parents. The concept of inheritance can be used to design complex systems. It provides a way of organizing the components of the system into a hierarchical structure that helps us understand the system. In addition, it provides a framework for reusing code.

Typically, inheritance is used to organize abstractions in a top-down fashion from most general to least general. Figure 14.1 contains a hierarchical organization of different types of writing instruments.

For example, we see different types of pens: ballpoints, roller balls, felt tips, calligraphy pens, and fountain pens. These are all specific types of pens, and they inherit the distinguishing characteristic of a pen—they use ink. However, each type of pen has an attribute that is specific to it and distinguishes it from the other types. At the highest level of hierarchy of pens, the distinguishing characteristic is the mechanism used to put the ink on the paper. Using the notion of inheritance to create a hierarchy of abstractions certainly helps understand the relationships between the abstractions, but it can also help reduce the effort to create new and useful abstractions.

The relationship that we can use to help us create a hierarchy of abstractions based on inheritance is the *is-a* relationship. The is-a relationship specifies that one abstraction is a specialization of another. For example, a pen *is a* special kind of writing instrument. Similarly, a roller ball is a type of pen, which *is a* type of writing instrument. Notice that the is-a relationship is transitive (that is, a roller ball is a pen, a pen is a writing instrument, therefore a roller ball is a writing instrument), but it is not reflexive (that is, not all writing instruments are pens). Another way of expressing the is-a relationship is to say that a roller ball is a *kind of* pen, and a pen is a *kind of* writing instrument.

In addition to the is-a relationship that represents inheritance between abstractions, two other relationships between abstractions are commonly used in object-oriented design. One, which we have used quite a bit already, is called the *has-a* relationship. The has-a relationship says that some object is part of another. For example, a fountain pen has a nib and some pencils have an eraser. The has-a relationship implies containment. An automobile contains an engine, a battery, and a horn.

In Chapter 11 we introduced several abstractions that contained the `Card` abstraction. These abstractions used the has-a relationship. A `Hand` consists of an array of five cards. Thus, `Hand` has a `Card`. Similarly, a `Deck` is an array of 52 cards. Therefore, `Deck` has a `Card`. It is tempting to think that a `Card` abstraction has a suit and face. However, face and suit are not objects, but

Figure 14.1

*Writing instrument
hierarchy*

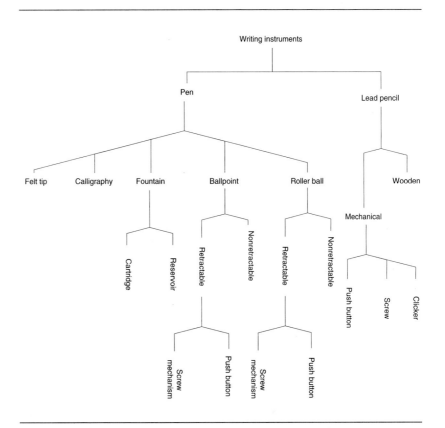

rather attributes of a card. We must always be careful to distinguish between the notions of attributes or characteristics and objects.

Another relationship between objects is the *uses-a* relationship. The uses-a relationship says that one object uses another object in some way. In object-oriented programming this relationship is typically realized by one object communicating with another via member functions. For example, suppose the operating system we are using has a clock object that maintains the current date and time. The clock object has member functions that return the current date and time. Other objects that need the date or time use the clock object by calling the appropriate member functions to fetch the current time or date.

14.2

REUSE VIA INHERITANCE

In Chapter 8 we used class RectangleShape to develop a program that simulated the images produced by a kaleidoscope. The patterns produced by the program were nice, but most kaleidoscopes use more than one shape of glass to produce the multicolored patterns. Suppose we wanted to enhance the kaleido-scope program so that it used additional shapes such as a circles and triangles.

One approach would be to create an additional class to represent a circle. Indeed, if we used the class `RectangleShape` as a model, this would not be too hard to do.

Listing 14.1 contains the declaration for our original `RectangleShape` class and the declaration for the new `CircleShape` class. Notice that the two definitions are very similiar. The two classes contain exactly the same member functions. Only the member function `SetSize()` differs slightly between the two classes. `RectangleShape` has two `float` parameters to `SetSize()`— `Length` and `Width`, while `CircleShape` has a single float parameter named `Diameter`. Similarly, the private data members of the two classes are identical except that `RectangleShape` stores its size attributes in `Length` and `Width`, while `CircleShape` uses `Diameter` to hold its size attribute.

Of course, we would also need to provide implementations of `Circle-Shape`'s member functions. Again, this would not be too hard to do because most of the code would be identical to that developed for `RectangleShape`. Only the member function `Draw()` would be very different. Thus, much com-monality exists between the two classes

So far, so good, but now suppose we wanted to have other shapes as well. For example, it might be nice to use triangles as well as rectangles and circles. Things start to get complicated and messy. We have a lot of code, some it simi-lar and some of it not. Furthermore, if we decide to add a new behavior or attribute to our shapes, it becomes harder because we must change all the shapes. We can reduce the complexity of both our design and implementation dramatically if we design our shape abstractions using inheritance. Using inheritance requires us to think about our design in a top-down fashion rather than bottom-up. That is, we need to think about the most general abstraction of a shape and build the more specific abstractions using the general ones as a basis.

Determining the most general abstraction, or base abstraction, for a hierar-chy of abstractions is one of the keys to a successful object-oriented design. Unfortunately, designing a flexible hierarchy of abstractions is quite difficult. It is all too easy to make the base abstraction too specific or not specific enough. If the base abstraction is too specific, the is-a relationship may not hold between the abstractions that we wish to create or derive from the base abstrac-tion because a derived abstraction inherits the attributes of its ancestors in the hierarchy. So, for example, if the base abstraction for a hierarchy of passenger vehicle types included an attribute for the number of wheels, all abstractions lower in the hierarchy inherit this attribute. Consequently, this abstraction could not be used to derive abstractions for vehicles without wheels such as ships, sleighs, or all-terrain vehicles that use treads.

If the base abstraction is not specific enough, the problem is that attributes and behaviors will needlessly be duplicated in the derived abstractions. For example, if the base abstraction for a hierarchy of passenger vehicles omits an

Listing 14.1

Declarations of RectangleShape and CircleShape classes

```cpp
class RectangleShape {
  public:
      RectangleShape(SimpleWindow &Window,
        float XCoord, float YCoord,
        const color Color,
        float Length, float Height);
      void Draw();
      color GetColor() const;
      void GetSize(float &Length, float &Height) const;
      void GetPosition(float &XCoord,
        float &YCoord) const;
      SimpleWindow &GetWindow() const;
      void SetColor(const color Color);
      void SetPosition(float XCoord, float YCoord);
      void SetSize(float Length, float Height);
  private:
      SimpleWindow &Window;
      float XCenter;
      float YCenter;
      color Color;
      float Length;
      float Height;

};
class CircleShape {
  public:
      CircleShape(SimpleWindow &Window,
        float XCoord, float YCoord,
        const color Color, float Diameter);
      void Draw();
      color GetColor() const;
      float GetSize() const;
      void GetPosition(float &XCoord,
        float &YCoord) const;
      SimpleWindow &GetWindow() const;
      void SetColor(const color Color);
      void SetPosition(float XCoord, float YCoord);
      void SetSize(float Diameter);
  private:
      SimpleWindow &Window;
      float XCenter;
      float YCenter;
      color Color;
      float Diameter;
};
```

attribute for the number of passengers, this attribute will have to be added to each kind of vehicle that is derived from that base abstraction.

14.3

A HIERARCHY OF SHAPES

To illustrate the development of an hierarchy of abstractions based on inheritance, we develop a class hierarchy for a set of window objects that consists of two-dimensional shapes and text labels. Using some of the two-dimensional shapes, we design and implement an enhanced kaleidoscope program. The first job is to decide what attributes and behaviors the base class should contain. Because of the way most windowing graphic systems work, the context or window that contains an object must be known in order to display it. Thus, an attribute of a window object is the window that contains it. Another attribute of any window object is its location or position in the window. Other attributes such as size, color, or how the object is drawn depend on the type of object and therefore should not be part of the base class. Of course, in addition to the attributes, we will need public member functions that set and manipulate these attributes. Figure 14.2 illustrates the window object abstraction, and Listing 14.2 contains the corresponding class declaration.

Figure 14.2
WindowObject abstraction

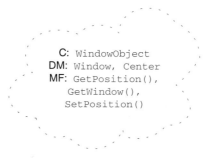

Listing 14.2

WindowObject class declaration from wobject.h

```
#ifndef WINDOWOBJECT_H
#define WINDOWOBJECT_H
#include "ezwin.h"
// WindowObject base class for objects that can be
// displayed in a window
class WindowObject {
    public:
        WindowObject(SimpleWindow &w, const Position &p);
        Position GetPosition() const;
        SimpleWindow &GetWindow() const;
        void SetPosition(const Position &p);
    private:
        SimpleWindow &Window;
        Position Center;
};
#endif
```

The WindowObject class contains two private member items: Center and Window are instances of the classes Position and SimpleWindow, which were introduced in Chapter 11. The data member Window is a reference object. Recall that once reference objects are set to refer to something, what they refer to cannot be changed; therefore once Window is set to refer to a particular SimpleWindow, it will always refer to that SimpleWindow. This rule makes sense because once a WindowObject is bound to a window, it does not make sense to make it move or appear in a different Window.

The implementation of `WindowObject` is simple and straightforward and is given in Listing 14.3. Notice that the constructor has no body and that the implementations of the member functions are single-line functions.

Listing 14.3

Implementation of WindowObject from wobject.cpp

```
#include "wobject.h"
WindowObject::WindowObject(SimpleWindow &w,
  const Position &p) : Window(w), Center(p) {
    // No code needed!
}
Position WindowObject::GetPosition() const {
    return Center;
}
SimpleWindow& WindowObject::GetWindow() const {
    return Window;
}
void WindowObject::SetPosition(const Position &p) {
    Center = p;
}
```

From this base abstraction, `WindowObject`, we can now derive abstractions for the two-dimensional shapes and text labels. Let's first concentrate on the two-dimensional shapes. The additional attribute that all two-dimensional shapes have is a color. So from the base abstraction `WindowObject`, we derive a new abstraction called `Shape` that has a color. Since `Shape` is derived from `WindowObject`, it inherits the data members (i.e., `Window` and `Center`), and the corresponding member functions (i.e., `GetPosition()`, `GetWindow()`, and `SetPosition()`) from `WindowObject`. Another way to think about the relationship between a base class and a derived class is that the base class provides a set of common services for all the classes derived from it. Thus, `WindowObject` provides the basic services necessary for all objects that will be displayed in a window.

At this point, we have one level of inheritance where `Shape` inherits the behaviors and attributes of `WindowObject`. As our previous discussions of inheritance have illustrated, inheritance can be multilevel. Using another level of inheritance, we can derive specific shape types from the class `Shape`. Three basic shapes that will be useful are rectangles, ellipses, and triangles. Each specific shape will have its own data members for storing the size of the shape because, of course, the size of each shape is specified somewhat differently. Figure 14.3 shows the data members related to size required for each shape type. Similarly, each derived shape will have its own draw member function because how a shape is rendered or drawn on the screen depends on what kind of shape it is.

Thus, `EllipseShape` has two data members that are specific to it. They are `Length` and `Height`, which specify the horizontal and vertical diameters of the ellipse. Similarly, `RectangleShape` has two data members, `Length` and `Width`, which are, as you know, the length and width of the rectangle. For the sake of simplicity, `TriangleShape` is an equilateral triangle where all sides have the same length. Consequently, `TriangleShape` has only one

Figure 14.3
*Shapes and their size
data members*

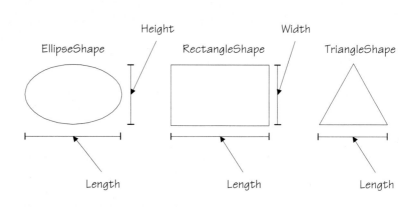

member—Length. Figure 14.4 illustrates our hierarchy of window objects thus far.

14.3.1

Declaring a derived class

To declare a derived class requires a simple addition to the syntax for declaring a class in order to specify the base class. The syntax for declaring a derived class is

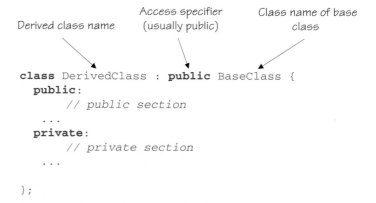

```
class DerivedClass : public BaseClass {
    public:
        // public section
    ...
    private:
        // private section
    ...

};
```

As noted, the access specifier is usually **public**, which says that the public members of the base class are public members of the derived class. This relationship is called *public inheritance*. We can also specify private and protected inheritance; these relationships are rarely used, and we will defer discussing them at this time.

Programming Tip

Inline member functions

Typically we have divided a class into two separate components—the interface to the class (.h file) and the implementation of the class. (.cpp file). For example, the interface to class WindowObject is contained in wobject.h, and the implementation is contained in wobject.cpp.

Generally, partitioning a class into an interface (.h file) and an implementation (.cpp file) is a good rule to follow. However, at times this rule needs to be broken. Sometimes, for the sake of efficiency, we need to include the implementation with the interface. In the following code, for example, we include the implementation of WindowObject in the .h file.

```cpp
class WindowObject {
  public:
      WindowObject(SimpleWindow &w,
       const Position &p);
      Position GetPosition() const;
      SimpleWindow &GetWindow() const;
      void SetPosition(const Position &p);
  private:
      SimpleWindow &Window;
      Position Center;
};
inline WindowObject::WindowObject(SimpleWindow &w,
 const Position &p) : Window(w), Center(p) {
 // No code needed!
}
inline Position WindowObject::GetPosition()
 const {
   return Center;
}
inline SimpleWindow& WindowObject::GetWindow()
 const {
   return Window;
}
inline void WindowObject::SetPosition(const
 Position &p) {
   Center = p;
}
```

In addition, the reserved word **inline** has been added to the definitions of constructor and member functions. Inline directs the compiler to replace a call to the function with the actual body of the function with the parameters substituted appropriately. This method avoids the overhead of a function call and for heavily used member functions can result in a significantly faster program. Inlining can also be obtained by defining the member functions in the class definition. However, this approach joins the interface and the implementation even more tightly, and we do not recommend it.

Figure 14.4

*Hierarchy of window
objects*

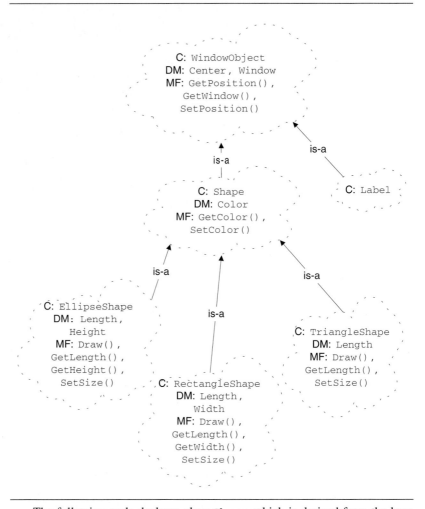

The following code declares class Shape which is derived from the base
class WindowObject.

```cpp
class Shape : public WindowObject {
    public:
        Shape(SimpleWindow &w, const Position &p,
         const color c = Red);
        color GetColor() const;
        void SetColor(const color c);
    private:
        color Color;
};
```

C++ programmers often read this as "Shape is a kind of WindowObject."

Other than the change to the first line, Shape's declaration follows our
standard technique for declaring a new class. It contains the constructors along
with the public member functions. The constructor for a shape has two

required parameters—the window that contains the shape and the location to draw the shape. The parameter for color is optional because a default value is provided.

In addition to its constructor, Shape has two public member functions. The inspector GetColor() retrieves the color of the shape, and the mutator SetColor() changes the color. Finally, Shape has one private data member, Color. This data member holds the color of the shape.

From the class shape, we can create the classes for the specific shapes. The following code declares RectangleShape, which is derived from Shape.

```
class RectangleShape : public Shape {
  public:
      RectangleShape(SimpleWindow &w,
        const Position &Center, const color c = Red,
        float Length = 1.0, float Width = 2.0);
      float GetLength() const;
      float GetWidth() const;
      void Draw();
      void SetSize(float Length, float Width);
  private:
      float Length;
      float Width;
};
```

In addition to its constructor, RectangleShape has four public member functions. Two inspectors retrieve the length and width of the rectangle, and SetSize() is a mutator for setting the length and width. Finally, the member function Draw() draws the rectangle. These member functions are specific to RectangleShape because their behavior (i.e., what they do) depends on the particular type of shape. For example, how a rectangle is drawn will be different from how an ellipse or triangle is drawn. Similarly, the parameters necessary to specify the size of a shape depend on the type of shape.

Finally, RectangleShape has two private data members, Length and Width. As in our original version of RectangleShape, these members hold the length and width of the rectangle.

Along with RectangleShape, we also want to create EllipseShape and TriangleShape abstractions. Their declarations are very similar to the RectangleShape's declaration. Listing 14.4 contains the declaration for the derived class EllipseShape.

We see that the declaration of EllipseShape is nearly identical to RectangleShape. In fact, the only differences are the names of the classes and the private member data. Of course, the implementation of the member function Draw() will be different.

Listing 14.5 contains the declaration of the class TriangleShape. Again, the declaration is similar to the other shapes. The public member section contains a constructor, a draw function, and a set size function. However, for the triangle shape, the private section contains one data member—the length of the sides of the triangle. We only need one side because we have limited ourselves to working with equilateral triangles.

Listing 14.4

Declaration of EllipseShape from ellipse.h

```
#ifndef ELLIPSESHAPE_H
#define ELLIPSESHAPE_H
#include "shape.h"
class EllipseShape : public Shape {
  public:
     EllipseShape(SimpleWindow &w,
       const Position &Center, const color c = Red,
       float Length = 1.0, float Height = 2.0)
     float GetLength() const;
     float GetHeight() const;
     void Draw();
     void SetSize(float Length, float Height);
  private:
     float Length;
     float Height;
};
#endif
```

Listing 14.5

Declaration of TriangleShape from triangle.h

```
#ifndef TRIANGLESHAPE_H
#define TRIANGLESHAPE_H
#include "shape.h"
class TriangleShape : public Shape {
  public:
     TriangleShape(SimpleWindow &w, const Position &p,
       const color c = Red, float Length = 1.0);
     float GetLength() const;
     void SetSize(float l);
     void Draw();
  private:
     float Length;
};
#endif
```

14.3.2

Implementing a derived class

As we have seen, declaring a derived class is not too different from declaring a base class. Similarly, the implementation of a derived class is not very different from the implementation of a base class. The key point to remember is that the derived class constructor essentially adds to a base class object the features needed to make that object into a derived class object, that is, a derived class is a specialization of the base class. Consequently, the constructor for the base class must be called to create a base class object before the constructor for the derived class can do its job. If you think about what inheritance means for a moment, this sequence makes sense. The base class object must exist before it can be turned into a derived class object.

To provide a convenient facility for creating an instance of the base class when an instance of the derived class is being created requires a small extension to how a constructor is specified. The syntax for the constructor of a derived class is

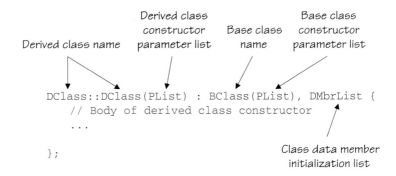

DClass::DClass(PList) : BClass(PList), DMbrList {
    // Body of derived class constructor
    ...

};

Notice that the first line includes a call to the base class constructor. For example, the implementation of the constructor for Shape is

```
Shape::Shape(SimpleWindow &w, const Position &p,
const color c) : WindowObject(w, p), Color(c) {
// no code needed!
}
```

This constructor specifies that when a Shape object is defined, the constructor for WindowObject should be called and the window and position parameters w and p should be passed to it so a WindowObject with those attributes can be created. The constructor for the base class is called before the body of the derived class constructor is executed. This sequence makes sense because the base object forms the basis for the derived object (we need the base object before we turn it into a derived object). After the base object is instantiated and it is turned into a derived object, the constructors for any data members that are on the data member initialization list are invoked. Shape's attribute Color is initialized in this way. The last step is to execute the code in the body of the constructor. In Shape's case, everything has been handled by the constructor of the base class and the constructor of the data attribute Color. Consequently, no code is needed.

Programming Tip

Using data member initialization lists

When implementing the constructor of a class there are two ways to initialized the data members. One way is to invoke the data member's mutator from within the body of the constructor. The other way is to invoke the constructor for the data member via the data member initialization list. This is the preferred method for initializing data members because it is more efficient. With the former method, the data member default constructor is invoked to construct an object with default values, and then the mutator is called to overwrite the default values with the initial values. Using the data member initialization list method, the data member is constructed with the appropriate initial values.

The constructors for the classes derived from Shape are similar. In these, however, the constructors for the specific shapes use the constructor for Shape, which in turn uses the constructor for WindowObject. For example, the implementation of the constructor for Rectangleshape is

```
RectangleShape::RectangleShape(SimpleWindow &window,
  const Position &Center, const color c, float l,
  float w) : Shape(window, Center, c),
Length(l), Width(w) {
    // no code needed!
}
```

This constructor specifies that when a RectangleShape object is defined, the constructor for Shape should be called and the window, position, and color parameters should be passed to it. The Shape constructor will, of course, use the WindowObject constructor to initialize the window and position data members.

For example, when the definition

```
RectangleShape Lawn(TWindow, LeftCorner, Green,
  2.5, 3.5);
```

is executed, the first action taken by the compiler is to invoke the Shape constructor with the arguments TWindow, LeftCorner, and Green. The implementation of Shape's constructor invokes WindowObject's constructor with the values for TWindow and LeftCorner. At this point a WindowObject is instantiated, the constructors for Window and Center are invoked, and the empty body of the WindowObject constructor is invoked. Then a Shape object is instantiated, and the constructor for Color is called to initialize it with the value c. Next the body of Shape's constructor is executed, which also required no code. Finally, a RectangleShape Lawn is instantiated, and the Length and Width constructors are called to initialize them. The last step is to invoke the body of RectangleShape's constructor. Again, no code is needed because the constructor of the parent class and the constructors for the data members have done all the work.

The constructors for the other derived classes are similar. The constructor for the ellipse shape is

```
EllipseShape::EllipseShape(SimpleWindow &w,
  const Position &Center, const color c, float l,
  float h) : Shape(w, Center, c),
Length(l), Height(h)   {
    // no code needed!
}
```

and the constructor for TriangleShape is

```
TriangleShape::TriangleShape(SimpleWindow &w,
  const Position &p, const color c, float l)
  : Shape(w, p, c), Length(l) {
    // no code needed!
}
```

The interesting thing to note about these constructors is that they are very short. If fact, we did not need to write any code for the body of the constructors! The reason is that we are able to use the code we developed for the parent class, `Shape`. While our classes are pretty simple, and the savings is not that great, you can imagine that if the classes were even a little bit more complex, the savings would be substantial.

The syntax for defining the implementation of the member functions of a derived class is identical to the syntax for defining the implementation of a base class. The syntax is

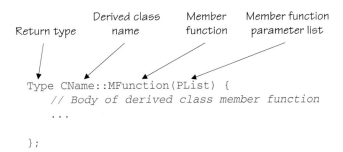

```
Type CName::MFunction(PList) {
    // Body of derived class member function
    ...

};
```

For example, the implementation of `RectangleShape`'s `SetSize()` member function is

```
void RectangleShape::SetSize(float l, float w) {
    Length = l;
    Width = w;
}
```

This mutator function just changes the value of `RectangleShape`'s size attributes, `Length` and `Width`.

Similarly, the implementation of the `Draw()` member function for `RectangleShape` is

```
void RectangleShape::Draw() {
    Position Center = GetPosition();
    float Length = GetLength();
    float Width = GetWidth();
    Position UpperLeft = Center
     + Position(-.5 * Length, -.5 * Width);
    Position LowerRight = Center
     + Position(.5 * Length, .5 * Width);
    GetWindow().RenderRectangle(UpperLeft,
     LowerRight, GetColor());
}
```

`RectangleShape`'s draw member function calls `RenderRectangle()`, which is a member function of the EzWindows class `SimpleWindow`. `RenderRectangle` paints the rectangle in the window. The parameters to this function are the coordinates of the upper-left and lower-right corners of the rectangle and the color to paint the rectangle. Because our abstraction of a rectangle contained the length and width of the rectangle in centimeters and the location of the center of the rectangle, `Draw()` has to compute coordinates of the upper-left and lower-right corners of the rectangle. This task is simple given the center of the rectangle and its length and width.

Other low-level member functions of the `SimpleWindow` class that we will use are `RenderEllipse()` and `RenderPolygon()`. `RenderEllipse()` is similar to `RenderRectangle()`. The parameters to it are the coordinates of the bounding box of the ellipse and the color of the ellipse. The bounding box is defined to be the rectangle that contains the ellipse. This relationship is illustrated in Figure 14.5.

Figure 14.5

Relationship of an ellipse to its bounding box

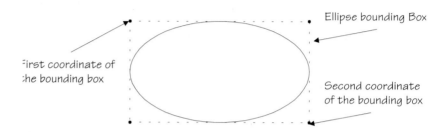

The implementation of `EllipseShape`'s `Draw()` function is similar to that of `RectangleShape`'s `Draw()`. The code is

```
void EllipseShape::Draw() {
    Position Center = GetPosition();
    float Length = GetLength();
    float Height = GetHeight();
    Position UpperLeft = Center
     + Position(-.5 * Length, -.5 * Height);
    Position LowerRight = Center
     + Position(.5 * Length, .5 * Height);
    GetWindow().RenderEllipse(UpperLeft, LowerRight,
     GetColor());
}
```

In a manner similar to `RectangleShape`'s draw function, the code creates `Position` objects for the coordinates of the bounding box using the center of the ellipse and the length and height of the ellipse.

The implementation of the `TriangleShape`'s draw member function is a bit more complicated. The low-level routine available for drawing a triangle is called `RenderPolygon`. This function requires three arguments. The first is an array of `Position` objects, or the locations of the vertices of the polygon to draw. The second argument is the number of vertices contained in the array, and the final argument is the color of the polygon. To do its job, `TriangleShape`'s draw function must compute the vertices of the triangle. Because we have restricted ourselves to equilateral triangles, the job is not too complicated.

The center of the triangle is located at the intersection of the three lines that bisect the angles at the vertices of the triangle. Figure 14.6 shows an equilateral triangle with the bisecting lines drawn. We assume that the center of the triangle is given by the position (x, y). From this diagram we can see that the position of vertex 1 is (x, y − r), vertex 2 is (x − b, y + a), and vertex 3 is (x + b, y + a). Of course, we know that b is ½ the length of the side of the triangle. Using the following basic trigonometric functions

$$\tan\theta = \frac{a}{b} \text{ and } \cos\theta = \frac{b}{c}$$

and the fact that θ is 30 degrees, we can compute the length of a and c. The equation for a is

$$a = \tan 30 \cdot b \text{ and substituting } \frac{l}{2} \text{ for b yields } a = \tan 30 \cdot \frac{l}{2}$$

Similarly, the equation for c is

$$c = \frac{b}{\cos 30} \text{ and substituting } \frac{l}{2} \text{ for b yields } c = \frac{l}{2 \cdot \cos 30}$$

Figure 14.6

A triangle, its center, and its vertices

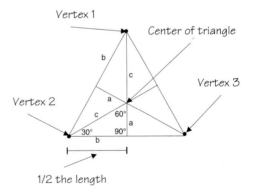

We can now write the code to compute the vertices of an equilateral triangle given its center and the length of its sides. However, one small detail remains. Recall from Chapter 5 that the argument to the trigonometric functions is the angle in radians. One degree is π ÷ 180 radians. The code for computing the lengths of the segments c and a is

```
const double Pi = 3.1415;
float c = Length / (2.0 * cos(30 * Pi / 180.0));
float a = tan(30 * Pi / 180.0) * .5 * Length;
```

With the length of these segments computed, we can create an array of positions to pass to RenderPolygon using the array initialization syntax introduced in Chapter 10. C++ permits an array of programmer-defined objects to be initialized just like primitive objects. The code for creating the necessary array of positions is

```
Position TrianglePoints[3] = {
   Center + Position(0, -c),
```

```
        Center + Position(-.5 * SideLength, a),
        Center + Position( .5 * SideLength, a) };
```

and we can now send a message to the window containing the triangle to render the rectangle. The call is

```
GetWindow().RenderPolygon(TrianglePoints, 3,
  GetColor());
```

The complete implementation of `TriangleShape`'s draw function is

```
void TriangleShape::Draw() {
    const float Pi = 3.1415;
    const Position Center = GetPosition();
    float SideLength = GetLength();

    // Compute c, the distance from center of the
    // triangle to the top vertex, and a, the
    // distance from the center to the base
    float c = SideLength / (2.0 * cos(30 * Pi
      / 180.0));
    float a = tan(30 * Pi / 180.0) * .5 * SideLength;

    // Create an array containing the positions of
    // the vertices of the triangle
    Position TrianglePoints[3] = {
     Center + Position(0, -c),
     Center + Position(-.5 * SideLength, a),
     Center + Position( .5 * SideLength, a) };

    // Draw the triangle
    GetWindow().RenderPolygon(TrianglePoints, 3,
      GetColor());
}
```

To check out our new classes, we should write a program that displays the three shapes in a window to ensure that our code is working properly. The program we will write will display the three shapes centered in a window and aligned along their bottoms. To display the shapes, we will use the EzWindows's `SimpleWindow` class. The global declaration of the window that will contain the shapes is

```
SimpleWindow TestWindow("TestShapes", 17.0, 7.0,
  Position(4.0, 4.0));
```

which will create a window called `TestWindow` with its upper-left corner located 4 centimeters from the left edge of the screen and 4 centimeters from the top of the screen. The window will be 17 centimeters wide and 7 centimeters high. `TestWindow` will be labeled "TestShapes."

Recall that the EzWindows API calls the function `ApiMain()` for any initial processing, and, for this simple program, `ApiMain()` will instantiate and draw the shapes. The code to create our shapes is quite simple. The entire routine is

```
int ApiMain() {
    TestWindow.Open();
    TriangleShape T(TestWindow, Position(3.5, 3.5),
      Red, 3.0);
    T.Draw();
```

```
RectangleShape R(TestWindow, Position(8.5, 3.5),
  Yellow, 3.0, 2.0);
R.Draw();
EllipseShape E(TestWindow, Position(13.5, 3.5),
  Green, 3.0, 2.0);
E.Draw();
return 0;
}
```

When EzWindows receives a message from the operating system that a window under its control should be closed, it calls ApiEnd() to do any cleanup. In our test program, the only cleanup is to close the window as shown in the following code:

```
int ApiEnd() {
    TestWindow.Close();
    return 0;
}
```

Figure 14.7 shows the resulting window. From this output, we can see that the new shapes appear to be implemented correctly. Of course, this simple test by no means constitutes an adequate testing of our shape class hierarchy. Much more thorough testing would be required in practice.

Figure 14.7

Displaying test shapes

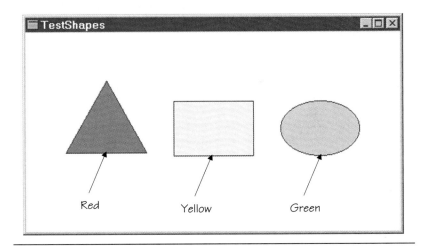

14.4

PROTECTED MEMBERS AND INHERITANCE

An important feature of C++ is its ability to control access to the members of a class. In our previous examples, we used the keywords **public** and **private** to control access to members of a class. The keyword **protected** signals a third level of access. In terms of a base class, protected members are like private members. They are accessible only by member functions of the class. To illustrate, consider the code

```
class SomeClass {
    public:
        void MemberFunction();
        int PublicData;
    protected:
        int ProtectedData;
    private:
        int PrivateData;
};
void SomeClass::MemberFunction() {
    PublicData = 1;      // access allowed
    ProtectedData = 2; // access allowed
    PrivateData = 3;    // access allowed
}
void NonMemberFunction() {
    SomeClass C;
    C.PublicData = 1;      // access allowed
    C.ProtectedData = 2;   // illegal
    C.PrivateData = 3;     // illegal
}
```

The member function `MemberFunction()` can access data members in all three sections. However, the nonmember function `NonMemberFunction()` can only access the member data in the public section. The data in the protected and private sections are not accessible.

Based on this example, you might wonder what the difference between protected and private membership is. The difference becomes apparent when a new class is publicly derived from a base class. Consider the following base and derived class declarations:

```
class BaseClass {
    public:
        int PublicData;
    protected:
        int ProtectedData;
    private:
        int PrivateData;
};
class DerivedClass : public BaseClass {
    public:
        void DerivedClassFunction();
    private:
    // Details omitted
};
```

The derived class member functions have access to the public and protected members of the base class, but not to the private members. `DerivedClass-Function()` illustrates a publicly derived member function's access to the members of the base class.

```
void DerivedClass::DerivedClassFunction() {
    PublicData = 1;      // access allowed
    ProtectedData = 2;   // access allowed
    PrivateData = 3;     // illegal
}
```

We should note that while we have used access to data members to illustrate C++'s protection mechanism, the protection mechanism applies to member functions as well.

The question arises as to when one should use protected members in designing a base class. This question has two answers. One answer we can give now; the other must be deferred until we can discuss protected and private inheritance in the next section.

In our hierarchy of shapes we did not use a protected section. The justification is that the derived shapes (e.g., RectangleShape or Triangle-shape) have access to their ancestor data members through inherited public inspector functions. This strategy works well, and it hides the representation of the ancestor class data members from the derived class. However, in some cases accessing inherited class member data through inspectors might be more expensive in terms of run time than accessing them directly. In cases where efficiency outweighs other design considerations, one might be able to justify the use of protected data. In this way, the member functions of the derived class could have direct access to the data held by the base class.

To illustrate, suppose we revised the declaration of the class WindowObject to be

```
class WindowObject {
   public:
        WindowObject(SimpleWindow &w,
         const Position &p);
        Position GetPosition() const;
        SimpleWindow &GetWindow() const;
        void SetPosition(const Position &p);
   protected:
        Position Center;
        SimpleWindow &Window;
};
```

and Shape to be

```
class Shape : public WindowObject {
   public:
        Shape(SimpleWindow &w, const Position &p,
         const color c = Red);
        color GetColor() const;
        void SetColor(const color c);
   protected:
        color Color;
};
```

That is, the member data are now declared in protected sections. This arrangement allows member functions of a class publicly derived from WindowObject and Shape to directly access this data. For example with these class declarations, RectangleShape's Draw member function could be implemented as

```
void RectangleShape::Draw() {
   Position UpperLeft = Center
     + Position(-.5 * Length, -.5 * Width);
   Position LowerRight = Center
```

```
        + Position(.5 * Length, .5 * Width);
      GetWindow().RenderRectangle(UpperLeft,
      LowerRight, GetColor());
   }
```

In this version the calls to the public inspector functions have been removed and Shape's data members are accessed directly. We generally avoid accessing data members directly since it makes the implementation of the class less flexible because changes to data members will affect all member functions, not just the inspectors.

14.5

CONTROLLING INHERITANCE

The second answer to why one might use a protected section has to do with the kind of inheritance that is used. Let's examine all three types of inheritance: public, private, and protected.

14.5.1

Public inheritance

In our previous examples of inheritance involving the Shape class, we used public inheritance. For example, the declaration of the RectangleShape was

```
class RectangleShape: public Shape {
   public:
      // details omitted
   private:
      // details omitted
};
```

This declaration specifies that the public members of Shape are public members of RectangleShape and permits users of RectangleShape objects to use Shape's public functions. For example, the following code

```
RectangleShape R(Window, P1);
R.SetColor(Green);    // Use member function of Shape
R.Draw();
```

works because Shape's SetColor member function is publicly available to users of RectangleShape. With public inheritance, the members of the derived class inherited from the base class have the same protection as they did in the base class. Public inheritance is almost always used in practice because it models the *is-a* relationship.

14.5.2

Private inheritance

To illustrate private inheritance consider the following revised declaration of `RectangleShape`.

```
class RectangleShape: private Shape {
    public:
        // details omitted
    protected:
        // details omitted
    private:
        // details omitted
};
```

The access specifier has been changed to **private**. With this declaration in effect, the code

```
RectangleShape R(Window, P1);
R.SetColor(Green);
R.Draw();
```

would be illegal. That is, users of `RectangleShape` are denied access to `Shape`'s public member functions because they are private members of `RectangleShape`. With private inheritance, the public and protected members of the base class become private members of the derived class. In effect, users of the derived class have no access to the facilities provided by the base class. Interestingly, the private members of the base class are inaccessible to the member functions of the derived class.

Private inheritance is used much less frequently than public inheritance. It is useful when the facilities of the base class are not part of the interface the user will see or the derived class will use. Private inheritance hides the base class from the user, and so it is possible to change the implementation of the base class or remove it all together without requiring any changes to the user of the interface. When an access specifier is not present in the declaration of a derived class, private inheritance is used. Because situations where the use of private inheritance is appropriate are rare and other methods can achieve the same effect, we will defer discussion of its use to more advanced textbooks.

14.5.3

Protected inheritance

With protected inheritance, public and protected members of the base class become protected members of the derived class, and private members of the base class become private members of the derived class. Protected inheritance is useful when the facilities or capabilities of the base class are useful in the implementation of the derived class, but are not part of the interface the user of the derived class will see. Protected inheritance is used even less frequently than private inheritance. Table 14.1 summarizes the effects of the three types of inheritance on the accessibility of the members of a derived class. The entry inaccessible indicates that the derived class has no access to the base class member.

Table 14.1

Types of inheritance and the resulting access they permit

Inheritance type	Base class member access	Derived class member access
`public`	`public`	`public`
	`protected`	`protected`
	`private`	*inaccessible*
`protected`	`public`	`protected`
	`protected`	`protected`
	`private`	*inaccessible*
`private`	`public`	`private`
	`protected`	`private`
	`private`	*inacessible*

14.6

MULTIPLE INHERITANCE

In our shape hierarchy thus far, we used single inheritance. That is, each derived class had a single parent. C++ also supports multiple inheritance. With multiple inheritance, a derived class can inherit from two or more base classes. The derived class inherits the attributes and behaviors of all parents.

To illustrate the concept of multiple inheritance, suppose we have been asked to redesign a bank's computerized accounts system to use object-oriented technology. We first design a base class called `Basic`. This class encapsulates the base set of attributes and actions for any account. Among other capabilities, such a class would certainly maintain a balance, keep a record of transactions, and provide the ability to print the transactions. From `BasicAccount`, we could derive specialized types of accounts. Some candidate account types might be: `Loan`, `Interest`, `Checking`, and `Brokerage`. Figure 14.8 shows our inheritance hierarchy thus far.

Figure 14.8

A basic account inheritance hierarchy

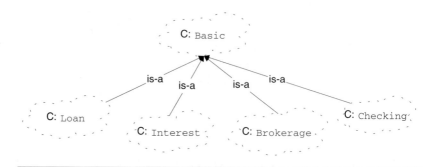

Now we also want to offer other types of accounts such as checking accounts that pay interest or brokerage accounts that allow checks to be written. These new types of accounts can be created using multiple inheritance. An

InterestChecking account can be created by deriving many of its capabilities and features from the Checking and Interest account types. Similarly, a BrokerageChecking account can be created from Checking and Brokerage accounts. The new inheritance hierarchy is shown in Figure 14.9.

Figure 14.9

Account hierarchy with mulitple inheritance

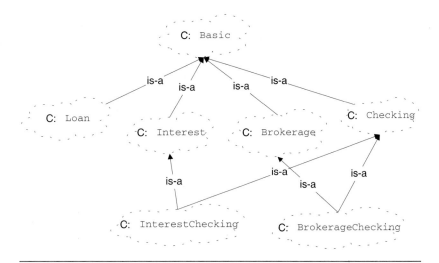

Multiple inheritance provides a way to create a new class that is the intersection of two existing classes. For example, an InterestChecking account can invoke all the public member functions of Interest and Checking accounts. Thus, an InterestChecking account is both an Interest account and a Checking account.

Multiple inheritance provides a powerful capability for creating new abstractions. This power is not without some peril. To illustrate both its power and some of its problems, let's use multiple inheritance to extend our hierarchy of window objects.

In our hierarchy (refer to Figure 14.4), a Label class that we have not yet developed was shown. Let's design and implement Label so we can use it to illustrate multiple inheritance. Recall the purpose of the label class was to provide the capability to place text objects in a window. Thus, one of the private data members of Label should be the text string. In addition, we need a data member that specifies the background color to use when we display the text. We could also include data members that specify the font, the size of the font, and the color of the text, but in the interest of simplicity, we defer these extensions for the exercises. In terms of behaviors, we will need mutators and inspectors for the private data members and a member function that causes the text to be written to the window. Thus, the class declaration of Label is

```
class Label : public WindowObject {
    public:
        Label(SimpleWindow &w, const Position &p,
            const string &Text,
            const color Color = White);
```

```
      color GetColor() const;
      void SetColor(const color c);
      void Display();
   private:
      color Color;
      string Text;
};
```

Listing 14.6 contains the implementation of `Label`. With few exceptions, the code is similar to the various shape classes we have implemented. `Label`'s constructor uses member data constructors to do all the work. Member function `Display()` is similar to the draw functions for the shape classes. It computes a bounding box required by `SimpleWindow` member function `RenderText` to paint the string in the correct position.

Listing 14.6

Implementation of class Label from label.cpp

```
#include <assert.h>
#include "label.h"
Label::Label(SimpleWindow &w, const Position &p,
 const string &t, const color c) : WindowObject(w, p),
 Text(t), Color(c) {
   // No code needed!
}
color Label::GetColor() const {
   return Color;
}
void Label::SetColor(const color c) {
   Color = c;
}
void Label::Display() {
   Position Center = GetPosition();
   Position UpperLeft = Center + Position(-2.0, -2.0);
   Position LowerRight = Center + Position(2.0, 2.0);
   GetWindow().RenderText(UpperLeft, LowerRight,
    Text.c_str(), GetColor());
}
```

`Label` gives us the ability to label objects on the screen. To illustrate its usefulness, let's modify our test program for displaying shapes so that the shapes are labeled with their class names. With `Label` available, this modification requires only a few additions to `ApiMain()`. After drawing a shape, we just need to instantiate a label object positioned under the shape and display it.

Listing 14.7 contains the revised `ApiMain()`. In addition to adding the labels, the test program has been parameterized so that it is easy to change the size of the window and have the size of the shapes scale accordingly. The code for `ApiEnd()` is unchanged. Figure 14.10 shows the window created when the revised program runs.

The window object `Label` is quite useful. We can use it to label shapes and print messages in windows. Label will also be useful if we want to create new types of shapes that contain labels. For instance, suppose we need to create a new type of shape for use on black and while monitors. Since the monitor is black and white, we need a way to indicate the color of the shape. We can do this by placing a label in the middle of the shape to indicate is color. Recall that the colors supported by EzWindows are white, red, yellow, green, blue,

Figure 14.10
Test shape display

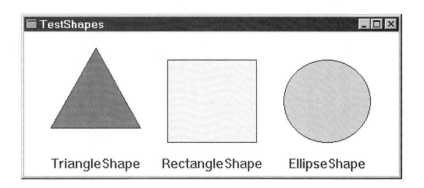

Listing 14.7
A test program for class Label

```
#include "label.h"
#include "triangle.h"
#include "rect.h"
#include "ellipse.h"
const float WindowWidth = 14.0;
const float WindowHeight = 3.0;
SimpleWindow TestWindow("TestShapes",
 WindowWidth, WindowHeight, Position(2.0, 2.0));
// ApiMain(): draw shapes and label them
int ApiMain() {
    // Put a one centimeter gap between ellipses and the
    // edge of the screen
    float ShapeWidth = (WindowWidth - 4.0) / 3.0;
    float ShapeHeight = WindowHeight - 2.0;

    Position ShapeCenter((ShapeWidth / 2.0) + 1.0,
     WindowHeight / 2.0);
    Position LabelCenter((ShapeWidth / 2.0) + 1.0,
     (WindowHeight / 2.0) + ShapeHeight / 2.0 + 0.75);

    TestWindow.Open();

    // Draw a triangle and label it
    TriangleShape T(TestWindow, ShapeCenter, Red,
     ShapeWidth);
    T.Draw();
    Label TLabel(TestWindow, LabelCenter,
     "Triangle", White);
    TLabel.Draw();

    // Draw a rectangle and label it
    ShapeCenter = ShapeCenter
     + Position(ShapeWidth + 1.0, 0.0);
    RectangleShape R(TestWindow, ShapeCenter, Yellow,
     ShapeWidth, ShapeHeight);
    R.Draw();
    LabelCenter = LabelCenter
     + Position(ShapeWidth + 1.0, 0.0);
    Label RLabel(TestWindow, LabelCenter,
     "Rectangle", White);
    RLabel.Draw();

    // Draw a ellipse and label it
    ShapeCenter = ShapeCenter
```

```
        + Position(ShapeWidth + 1.0, 0.0);
    EllipseShape E(TestWindow, ShapeCenter, Green,
      ShapeWidth, ShapeHeight);
    E.Draw();
    LabelCenter = LabelCenter
        + Position(ShapeWidth + 1.0, 0.0);
    Label ELabel(TestWindow, LabelCenter,
      "Ellipse", White);
    ELabel.Draw();

    return 0;
}
```

magenta, and cyan. Therefore, we can use the first letter of the color to label
the shape with its color. We want to create new types of shapes that have both
the properties of regular shapes and labels. To create these new types of
shapes, we make use of multiple inheritance. As you will see, it is the most
efficient and simple way to create these new types of shapes. Indeed, very little
new code needs to be written.

To illustrate the multiple inheritance, we will create a new object called
LabeledEllipseShape, which is derived from EllipseShape and
Label. Figure 14.11 shows the inheritance hierarchy. Labeled versions of the
other shapes can be created analogously and doing so is left as an exercise.

Figure 14.11

*The multiple
inheritance
relationship of
LabeledEllipseShape*

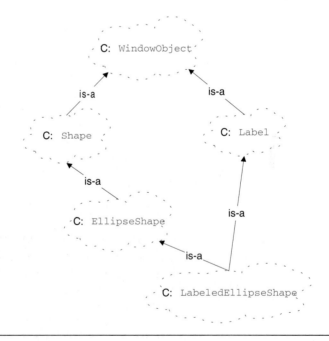

The syntax for declaring a class derived using multiple inheritance is

Derived class name

Comma-separated list of base classes

```
class DClass : public BClass, public BClass {
  public:
      // public section
  ...
  private:
      // private section
  ...

};
```

This syntax is similar to the one specifying a single inheritance, the only difference is that more than one class is being used as a basis for the new class.

The declaration for class `LabeledEllipseshape` is

```
class LabeledEllipseShape : public Label,
  public EllipseShape {
    public:
        LabeledEllipseShape(SimpleWindow &w,
          const Position &Center, const color c = Red,
          string Text = "R", float Length = 1.0,
          float Height = 2.0);
        void Draw();
};
```

The constructor for a `LabeledEllipseShape` specifies the window, the position of the shape, the color of the shape, the text to label it with, and the size of the ellipse to create. `Draw()` is the only public member function. It will, of course, display the ellispe in the window. The default text to label the ellipse is the first letter of the default color of the ellipse. Labeling the ellipse with its color is useful if the ellipse is used in a program that will be run on a computer with a monochrome monitor.

The implementation of `LabelEllipseShape` is equally simple. The code for its constructor is

```
LabeledEllipseShape::LabeledEllipseShape(
  SimpleWindow &w, const Position &Center,
  const color c, string t, float l, float h)
  : EllipseShape(w, Center, c, l, h),
  Label(w, Center, t, c)  {
    // no code needed!
}
```

We see that `LabeledEllipseShape`'s constructor calls the constructors for the two base classes to initialize the data members. They do all the work, and no code is required in the body of the constructor.

The implementation of `LabeledEllipseShape`'s `Draw()` member function brings to light some interesting issues. The code for it is

```
void LabeledEllipseShape::Draw() {
    EllipseShape::Draw();
    Label::Draw();
}
```

Notice the calls to the two `Draw()` member functions. When a new class is created via multiple inheritance, it inherits all the behaviors and capabilites of the base classes. Thus `LabeledEllipseShape` inherits a draw function from both `Label` and `EllipseShape`. This situation is called a *name ambiguity* because when `LabeledEllipseShape` refers to `Draw()`, it is not clear which one should be invoked. We can solve this problem by using the scope resolution operator to indicate which member we mean. Thus, to draw a `LabeledEllipseShape`, we call `EllipseShape`'s draw function to draw the ellipse and `Label`'s draw function to draw the label.

It is worth noting that since `EllipseShape` and `Label` were derived from the same class, `WindowObject`, and `LabelEllipseShape` is derived from `EllipseShape` and `Label`, `LabeledEllipseShape` has two instances of everything in a `WindowObject`. It has two `GetWindow()` member functions, two `GetPosition()` member functions, and two `SetPosition()` member functions. Similarly, it has two instances of the private member data `Center` and `Window`. In general, this duplication causes no problems, and if a particular member function must be invoked, the scope resolution operator can select the appropriate one.

As our `LabeledEllipseShape` example shows, multiple inheritance allows us to create new, powerful classes with a minimum of effort. Without writing very much new code, we created a new class with useful properties. The following code tests `LabeledEllipseShape`.

```
#include <assert.h>
#include "lellipse.h"
const float WindowWidth = 10.0;
const float WindowHeight = 3.0;
SimpleWindow TestWindow("TestShapes",
 WindowWidth, WindowHeight, Position(2.0, 2.0));
// ApiMain(): open the window, create and draw
// the shapes
int ApiMain() {
    // Put a 1 centimeter gap between ellipses
    // and the edge of the screen
    float EllipseLength = (WindowWidth - 4.0) / 3.0;
    float EllipseHeight = WindowHeight - 2.0;
    Position Center((EllipseLength / 2.0) + 1.0,
     WindowHeight / 2.0);
    TestWindow.Open();
    assert(TestWindow.GetStatus() == WindowOpen);

    LabeledEllipseShape E1(TestWindow, Center,
     Red, "R", EllipseLength, EllipseHeight);
    E1.Draw();

    Center = Center
     + Position(EllipseLength + 1.0, 0.0);
```

```
LabeledEllipseShape E2(TestWindow, Center,
  Green, "G", EllipseLength, EllipseHeight);
E2.Draw();

Center = Center
  + Position(EllipseLength + 1.0, 0.0);
LabeledEllipseShape E3(TestWindow, Center,
  Blue, "B", EllipseLength, EllipseHeight);
E3.Draw();

return 0;
}
```

It creates and displays three ellipses each of a different color. The ellipses are labeled with a single letter indicating their color as shown in Figure 14.12.

Figure 14.12
Labeled Ellipses

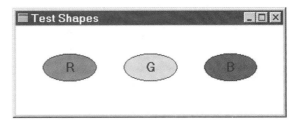

14.7

A PRETTIER KALEIDOSCOPE

Before moving on, we should put our new shape classes to work. Let's revise our original kaleidoscope program to make use of our new shapes. While we are at it, we should redesign the program to take advantage of the benefits of object-oriented design now that we have a better handle on creating and using classes.

A clear statement of what the program will do always helps in designing a program. From this statement, the abstractions necessary to construct the program can be determined. Here is the statement of what the kaleidoscope program should do.

The kaleidoscope program displays a kaleidoscope image in a window. The window should be a square 10 centimeters on a side, and it should be labeled "Kaleidoscope." The kaleidoscope image consists of the shapes circle, square, and triangle.

The kaleidoscope should be "turned" once a second so the image is updated. Each time the kaleidoscope is turned, four new shapes of the same type are added to the image. The centers of the shapes are located on the lines that bisect each quadrant. The shape and its size and color are determined randomly each turn. Shapes in diagonally opposite quadrants are the same color.

For the above problem statement, we will need abstractions for the window, the kaleidoscope image, and the shapes. For the abstraction for the window, we will use the `SimpleWindow` class introduced previously. We already have one of the shapes—the triangle, and can easily create the other two shapes, the square and circle, using inheritance. Figure 14.13 shows a possible extended hierarchy of shapes.

Figure 14.13

An extended hierarchy of shapes

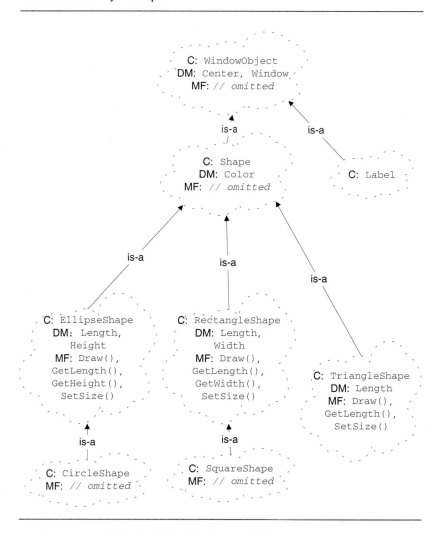

However, this hierarchy has a serious problem. Recall that a derived class inherits all the attributes and behaviors of its ancestors. Thus `CircleShape` inherits the public member functions `SetSize()` and `Draw()` from `EllipseShape`. Let's assume we have a constructor for `CircleShape` that is similar to the constructors for the other shapes we have implemented. For instance, we could write

```
Circle C(TWindow, Position(4.0, 4.0), Green, 2.0);
```

which instantiates a green circle with a diameter of 2 centimeters contained in `SimpleWindow TWindow`. The position of the circle is 4 centimeters from the top and left edges of the window. Unfortunately, we could then also legally write the code

```
C.SetSize(2.0, 1.0);
C.Draw()
```

which would not draw a circle but would draw an ellipse with a length of 2 centimeters and a height of 1 centimeter.

The problem is that an `EllipseShape` has a behavior or capability that a `CircleShape` should not have. A `CircleShape` is not an `EllipseShape`, and we should not try to derive a `CircleShape` from an `EllipseShape`, even though it is tempting to do so. The situation with `SquareShape` and `RectangleShape` is analogous. When defining a class hierarchy, we must examine the abstractions carefully to ensure that all of the capabilities or behaviors of the ancestor classes are appropriate for the descendant classes.

Instead of deriving `CircleShape` and `SquareShape` from `Ellipse-Shape` and `RectangleShape`, we should derive them from `Shape`. The declaration for the class `SquareShape` is

```
class SquareShape : public Shape {
   public:
      SquareShape(SimpleWindow &w,
       const Position &Center, const color c = Red,
       float Side = 1.0);
      float GetSideLength() const;
      void SetSize(float SideLength);
      void Draw();
   private:
      float SideLength;
};
```

and its implementation is

```
SquareShape::SquareShape(SimpleWindow &w,
 const Position &center, const color c, float s)
   : Shape(w, center, c), SideLength(s) {
 // no code needed!
}
```

The code for a circle is analogous. The complete code for `SquareShape` and `CircleShape` is contained in Listings 14.8 through 14.11.

The only abstraction left to design is the one for a kaleidoscope. The first question is, What attributes and actions should the kaleidoscope abstraction have? An attribute for all objects that are displayed in a window has been the window that the object is associated with. The kaleidoscope class is no different. It should contain a reference to the instance of the `SimpleWindow` that contains it. In addition to the window, the kaleidoscope class needs objects to represent the glass trinkets. We use our newly developed shape classes `CircleShape`, `SquareShape`, and `TriangleShape` to represent the trinkets.

Another obvious attribute of the kaleidoscope is the speed at which it should be turned. According to the problem statement, the kaleidoscope should

Listing 14.8

*Declaration of class
SquareShape from
square.h*

```
#ifndef SQUARESHAPE_H
#define SQUARESHAPE_H
#include "shape.h"
class SquareShape : public Shape {
   public:
      SquareShape(SimpleWindow &w,
       const Position &Center, const color c = Red,
       float Side = 1.0);
      float GetSideLength() const;
      void SetSize(float SideLength);
      void Draw();
   private:
      float SideLength;
};
#endif
```

Listing 14.9

*Implementation of
SquareShape from
square.cpp*

```
#include "square.h"
SquareShape::SquareShape(SimpleWindow &w,
 const Position &center, const color c, float s) :
 Shape(w, center, c), SideLength(s) {
   // No code needed!
}
float SquareShape::GetSideLength() const {
   return SideLength;
}
void SquareShape::Draw() {
   const Position Center = GetPosition();
   float SideLength = GetSideLength();

   Position UpperLeft = Center
    + Position(-.5 * SideLength, -.5 * SideLength);
   Position LowerRight = Center
    + Position(.5 * SideLength, .5 * SideLength);
   GetWindow().RenderRectangle(UpperLeft, LowerRight,
    GetColor());
}
void SquareShape::SetSize(float s) {
   SideLength = s;
}
```

Listing 14.10

*Declaration of class
CircleShape from
circle.h*

```
#ifndef CIRCLESHAPE_H
#define CIRCLESHAPE_H
#include "shape.h"
class CircleShape : public Shape {
   public:
      CircleShape(SimpleWindow &w,
       const Position &Center, const color c = Red,
       float Diameter = 1.0);
      float GetDiameter() const;
      void SetSize(float Diameter);
      void Draw();
   private:
      float Diameter;
};
#endif
```

Listing 14.11

*Implementation of
CircleShape from
circle.cpp*

```
#include "circle.h"
CircleShape::CircleShape(SimpleWindow &w,
 const Position &center, const color c, float d)
 : Shape(w, center, c), Diameter(d) {
    // no code needed!
}
float CircleShape::GetDiameter() const {
    return Diameter;
}
void CircleShape::Draw() {
    Position Center = GetPosition();
    float Diameter = GetDiameter();

    Position UpperLeft = Center
     + Position(-.5 * Diameter, -.5 * Diameter);
    Position LowerRight = Center
     + Position(.5 * Diameter, .5 * Diameter);
    GetWindow().RenderEllipse(UpperLeft, LowerRight,
     GetColor());
}
void CircleShape::SetSize(float d) {
    Diameter = d;
}
```

be updated once a second. We could hard-code this constant into the class, but our class will be more flexible if we make the turning speed one of the kaleidoscope's attributes. In this way, the value can be changed if desired.

Other not so obvious attributes of a kaleidoscope abstraction are the type of shapes it can contain and the number of shapes to draw on each turn of the kaleidoscope. Our goal is to capture all the characteristics of the kaleidoscope within the abstraction. As usual, the data attributes will be private members of the class.

Two attributes that are specifically not part of the abstraction are the size of the largest shape that can be created and the largest offset from the center of the window. The reason we have chosen not to make these attributes part of the class is that they depend on the size of the window that contains the kaleidoscope. If the window is large, then we can use larger shapes, but if the window is small, we certainly do not want to draw a shape that is larger than the window. It is tempting to say that these can be computed once and stored in the class, but remember a window can be resized. If this happens, we want the kaleidoscope to adjust what it does too. Consequently, these attributes are computed each time the kaleidoscope is turned just in case the window is resized.

To summarize, the attributes of a kaleidoscope thus far are

- A `SimpleWindow` for displaying the image.
- The shapes `CircleShape`, `SquareShape`, and `TriangleShape` to represent the glass trinkets.
- The speed to turn the kaleidoscope.

Like the kaleidoscope program we developed in Chapter 8, we need to pick the color for the trinket, the size of the trinket, and the offset from the center of the window to draw the trinket. In addition, we need to pick the type of shape to use for the trinket. We use the `Random` class developed in Chapter 9 to pick these values.

To pick the type of shape for the trinket and the color of the trinket, we include in the kaleidoscope abstraction two objects `RandomShape` and `RandomColor`, which are instances of class `Random`. When a shape type is needed, we will ask `RandomShape` to pick one randomly. Similarly when a color for a shape is needed, we will ask `RandomColor` to pick one randomly.

It is tempting to include instances of class `Random` to pick the size of the trinket and the offset from the center of the window to place the trinkets, but because these values depend on the size of the window different random distributions are required. Consequently, appropriate objects of class `Random` will be created each time we need to pick a shape size and an offset.

The actions for the kaleidoscope abstraction are somewhat harder to determine. Like our previous classes, we will want inspectors for the private data. Thus, `GetWindow` and `GetSpeed` member functions should be provided. Another action clearly needed is the "turn" action. When the kaleidoscope receives this message, four new shapes are created and added to the display. Because this message will be sent from the window class that contains the kaleidoscope, it should be a public member function so that it is accessible to the window class.

In addition to the constructor and `Turn()`, class `Kaleidoscope` will have one private member function. This utility function will compute the offset from the center of the window to draw the shapes. Since this capability will be needed only when `Turn()` is invoked, it is a private function. Figure 14.14 illustrates how the kaleidoscope objects interact.

Based on our design, we can now create a class declaration for a kaleidoscope abstraction. The declaration of class `Kaleidoscope` is

```
class Kaleidoscope {
   public:
      Kaleidoscope(SimpleWindow &w,
        int Speed = 1000);
      int GetSpeed();
      SimpleWindow &GetWindow() const;
      int Turn();
   private:
      // types and constants
      enum { ShapesPerTurn = 4,
       NumberOfShapeTypes = 3 };
      enum ShapeType { CircleType, SquareType,
       TriangleType };
      // member function
      float RandomOffset(int Range, float ShapeSize);
      // data members
      SimpleWindow &Window;
      int Speed;    // Speed in uSec to update image
      CircleShape CircleTrinket;
      SquareShape SquareTrinket;
      TriangleShape TriangleTrinket;
      Random RandomShape;
      Random RandomColor;
};
```

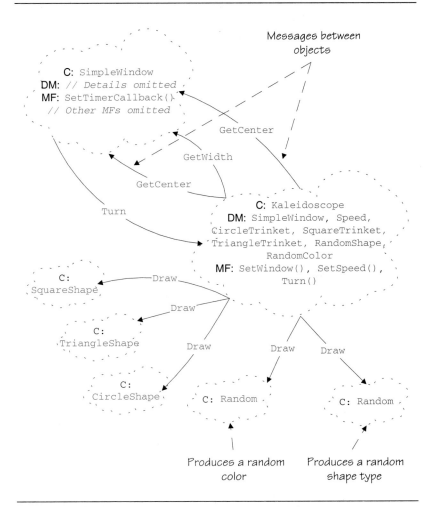

With few exceptions, the declaration is similar to the other classes we have defined. In order to encapsulate the constants ShapesPerTurn and Number-OfShapeTypes in the class declaration, we resort to a trick. We would like to define some private constants in the class declaration, but the current version of C++ does not allow initialized constants to be declared as part of a class. Instead, we can use an anonymous enumeration. The code

```
enum { ShapesPerTurn = 4, NumberOfShapes = 3 };
```

declares an enumeration that does not have a name. However, the members of the enumeration ShapesPerTurn and NumberOfShapes are defined and given the appropriate values. The member functions of Kaleidoscope can refer to these names as if they were constants.

Notice that the window for displaying the kaleidoscope and the shapes for representing the trinkets are data members of class Kaleidoscope. This models the has-a relationship. A kaleidoscope has a window and it has trinkets. In addition, we have encapsulated within class `Kaleidoscope` the objects for picking a shape color and a shape type.

Now that we have settled on what a kaleidoscope abstraction looks like, we can start on its implementation. Since most of the work is done by member function `Turn()`, let's focus on its implementation. The other member functions are so similar to our previous implementation that we do not discuss them further here. Their implementations are shown in Listing 14.12.

The redesigned kaleidoscope program, use the same method to produce the image as we used in our previous implementation. That is, when a `Kaleidoscope` object receives a turn message, it will draw four shapes one in each quadrant of the window. Shapes in diagonally opposite quadrants are the same color. The major functional difference between the `Turn()` member function and the kaleidoscope function in Chapter 8 is that `Turn()` randomly picks the type of shape to draw each time it is invoked.

In addition to the functional difference between the two versions of the program, we have some implementation differences. By using some of the constructs introduced in the preceding chapters, the implementation of the member function `Turn()` can be shortened.

Member function `Turn()` logically starts off like the earlier kaleidoscope function. It obtains the coordinates of the center of the window. However, with the introduction of class `Position` and the `SimpleWindow` class, we obtain the center of the window containing the image by calling `SimpleWindow`'s `GetCenter()` member function, which returns a `Position` object whose value is the center of the window that contains the image. The following code

```
// Get position of the center of the window
const Position CenterOfWindow =
  GetWindow().GetCenter();
```

does the job.

Another improvement to this version is that rather than use **const**s to specify the size of the largest shape and the largest offset from the center of the window, we can make these values a function of the window size. Consequently, the user can resize the window containing the kaleidoscope, and the sizes of the shapes and where they are drawn will be automatically adjusted. To achieve this added flexibility, member function `Turn()` simply asks `Window` how big it is and uses this value to compute the appropriate values. The corresponding code follows.

```
// The largest shape should be 1 centimeter
// smaller than 1/2 the size of the window
float MaxShapeSize =
  (GetWindow().GetWidth() / 2.0) - 1.0;
// The largest offset should be 1 centimeter
// smaller than 1/2 the size of the window
float MaxOffset
  = (GetWindow().GetWidth() / 2.0) - 1.0;
```

In the first version, the only shape was a square, so the straightforward approach was to instantiate the four squares and draw them. In this version, we

Listing 14.12

Implementation of Kaleidoscope from kaleido.cpp

```cpp
#include <assert.h>
#include <iostream.h>
#include "square.h"
#include "circle.h"
#include "triangle.h"
#include "random.h"
#include "kaleido.h"
// Kaleidoscope constructor
Kaleidoscope::Kaleidoscope(SimpleWindow &w, int s)
 : Window(w), Speed(s)
 CircleTrinket(w, Position(0,0)),
 SquareTrinket(w, Position(0,0)),
 TriangleTrinket(w, Position(0,0)),
 RandomColor(0, MaxColors - 1),
 RandomShape(0, NumberOfShapeTypes - 1) {
   assert(&w != NULL);
   RandomColor.Randomize();
   RandomShape.Randomize();
}
// GetSpeed(): return the speed
int Kaleidoscope::GetSpeed() {
   return Speed;
}
// GetWindow(): return the window that contains the
// kaleidoscope
SimpleWindow &Kaleidoscope::GetWindow() const {
   return Window;
}
// RandomOffset(): generate a random amount to offset a
//   square from the center of the window. Generate a
//   random offset in the
//   interval 0..Range-1 in .1 centimeter increments.
//   The offset generated must take into account
//   the size of the shape so the shapes do not
//   overlap at the center.
float Kaleidoscope::RandomOffset(int Range,
 float ShapeSize) {
   Random R(0, Range * 10);
   R.Randomize();
   float Offset = R.Draw() / 10.0;
   // if Offset is not large enough to keep
   // the shape from overlapping set the offset
   // to half the shape size
   if (Offset < ShapeSize / 2)
      Offset = ShapeSize / 2;
   return Offset;
}
```

can simplify the implementation if we take a different approach. We use data structures to hold the positions and colors of the shapes we will eventually draw. The advantage of this approach is that these attributes need to be created only once, since they are independent of the type of shape that we will draw.

The following code accomplishes the task of initializing the two arrays.

```cpp
color ShapeColor[] = {(color) RandomColor.Draw(),
 (color) RandomColor.Draw()};
```

```
// Generate a random size in the interval
// .1 to MaxShapeSize in .1 centimeter increments
// (i.e., 1, 1.1, 1.2, .....)
Random RandomShapeSize(10, MaxShapeSize * 10);
RandomShapeSize.Randomize();
float ShapeSize = RandomShapeSize.Draw() / 10.0;

// Compute and create the four positions to draw
// the shapes
float Offset = RandomOffset(MaxOffset, ShapeSize);
Position ShapeLocation[ShapesPerTurn] = {
 CenterOfWindow + Position( Offset, -Offset),
 CenterOfWindow + Position(-Offset, -Offset),
 CenterOfWindow + Position(-Offset,  Offset),
 CenterOfWindow + Position( Offset,  Offset)};
```

Array `ShapeColor` holds the two colors that the shapes will be. Array element `ShapeColor[0]` holds the color of the shape for quadrants 1 and 3, while array element `ShapeColor[1]` holds the color of the shape that will be drawn in quadrants 2 and 4. The object `RandomColor` of class `Random` produces the random color. Array `ShapeLocation` holds the positions to draw the four shapes. Array element `ShapeLocation[0]` is the location in quadrant 1, `ShapeLocation[0]` is the location in quadrant 2, and so on.

The last step is to pick a shape and to draw the four versions of it. To pick a shape, we use another `Random` object called `RandomShape`. It randomly picks one of the shape types defined in the enumeration `ShapeType` and returns it. The final step is to draw the required four shapes. The code to do this is

```
// Pick a shape to draw
ShapeType KindOfShape
  = (ShapeType) RandomShape.Draw();
if (KindOfShape == CircleType) {
   for (int i = 0; i < ShapesPerTurn; ++i) {
      CircleTrinket.SetPosition(ShapeLocation[i]);
      CircleTrinket.SetColor(ShapeColor[i % 2]);
      CircleTrinket.SetSize(ShapeSize);
      CircleTrinket.Draw();
   }
}
else if (KindOfShape == SquareType) {
   for (int i = 0; i < ShapesPerTurn; ++i) {
      SquareTrinket.SetPosition(ShapeLocation[i]);
      SquareTrinket.SetColor(ShapeColor[i % 2]);
      SquareTrinket.SetSize(ShapeSize);
      SquareTrinket.Draw();
   }
}
else if (KindOfShape == TriangleType) {
   for (int i = 0; i < ShapesPerTurn; ++i) {
      TriangleTrinket.SetPosition(
        ShapeLocation[i]);
      TriangleTrinket.SetColor(ShapeColor[i % 2]);
      TriangleTrinket.SetSize(ShapeSize);
      TriangleTrinket.Draw();
   }
}
```

Essentially, each branch of the if-then-else handles one of the shape types. Each branch loops ShapesPerTurn times, setting the attributes of the trinket drawing it. Listing 14.12 and Listing 14.13 contain the complete code for kaleido.cpp.

Listing 14.13

Implementation of Turn member function from kaleido.cpp

```
// Turn(): turn the kaleidoscope
int Kaleidoscope::Turn() {
   // Get logical coordinates of the center of the
   // window
   const Position CenterOfWindow =
   GetWindow().GetCenter();

   // The largest shape should be 1 centimeter
   // smaller than half the size of the window
   const float MaxShapeSize =
   (GetWindow().GetWidth() / 2.0) - 1.0;

   // The largest offset should be 1 centimeter
   // smaller than half the size of the window
   const float MaxOffset =
   (GetWindow().GetWidth() / 2.0) - 1.0;

   // Create four shapes, one in each quadrant. All
   // shapes are the same size. However, size is picked
   // randomly.
   // The colors of the shapes are also chosen randomly.
   // The shapes in diagonally opposite quadrants are
   // the same color.
   color ShapeColor[] = {(color) RandomColor.Draw(),
     (color) RandomColor.Draw()};

   // Generate a random size in the interval
   // .1 to MaxShapeSize in .1 centimeter increments
   // (i.e., 1, 1.1, 1.2, .....)
   Random RandomShapeSize(10, MaxShapeSize * 10);
   RandomShapeSize.Randomize();
   const float ShapeSize = RandomShapeSize.Draw()
    / 10.0;
   // Compute and create the four positions to draw
   // the shapes
   const float Offset
    = RandomOffset(MaxOffset, ShapeSize);
   const Position ShapeLocation[ShapesPerTurn] = {
    CenterOfWindow + Position( Offset, -Offset),
    CenterOfWindow + Position(-Offset, -Offset),
    CenterOfWindow + Position(-Offset,  Offset),
    CenterOfWindow + Position( Offset,  Offset)};

   // Pick a shape to draw
   const ShapeType KindOfShape
    = (ShapeType) RandomShape.Draw();
   if (KindOfShape == CircleType) {
      for (int i = 0; i < ShapesPerTurn; ++i) {
         CircleTrinket.SetPosition(ShapeLocation[i]);
         CircleTrinket.SetColor(ShapeColor[i % 2]);
         CircleTrinket.SetSize(ShapeSize);
         CircleTrinket.Draw();
      }
   }
   else if (KindOfShape == SquareType) {
```

```
      for (int i = 0; i < ShapesPerTurn; ++i) {
         SquareTrinket.SetPosition(ShapeLocation[i]);
         SquareTrinket.SetColor(ShapeColor[i % 2]);
         SquareTrinket.SetSize(ShapeSize);
         SquareTrinket.Draw();
      }
   }
   else if (KindOfShape == TriangleType) {
      for (int i = 0; i < ShapesPerTurn; ++i) {
         TriangleTrinket.SetPosition(ShapeLocation[i]);
         TriangleTrinket.SetColor(ShapeColor[i % 2]);
         TriangleTrinket.SetSize(ShapeSize);
         TriangleTrinket.Draw();
      }
   }
   return 1;
}
```

The only remaining part of the program is getting things going. We need to write `ApiMain()` and `ApiEnd()`. These functions will be contained in a separate module called `kmain.cpp`. Figure 14.15 shows the modules required to build the program.

Figure 14.15

Modules needed to build the kaleidoscope program

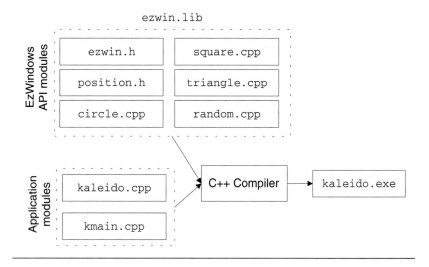

Both the `Kaleidoscope` object and the window where it is displayed are instantiated in the module `kmain.cpp`. Because these objects must persist throughout the execution of the program, they are global objects. The definitions of the objects are

```
SimpleWindow KWindow("Kaleidoscope", 10.0, 10.0,
   Position(2.0, 2.0));
Kaleidoscope KScope(KWindow, 1000);
```

The first creates a window named `KWindow` with the label "Kaleidoscope." The size of the window is 10 centimeters by 10 centimeters. The window is positioned with its upper-left corner 2 centimeters from the left edge of the screen and 2 centimeters down.

The second definition creates a `Kaleidoscope` object called `KScope`. It will be displayed in window `KWindow`. The kaleidoscope will be turned once every 1,000 milliseconds, or once a second.

The order of these definitions is important. The second one refers to the first. Fortunately, C++ executes global definitions in the order in which they appear in the source file.

The job of `ApiMain()` is to open `KWindow`, make the connection between `KWindow`'s timer, and start the timer. The code follows.

```
int DispatchTimerClick() {
    KScope.Turn();
    return 1;
}
// ApiMain(): begins program execution
int ApiMain() {
    KWindow.Open();
    // Tell KWindow to call function TimerClick
    // when the timer interrupts
    KWindow.SetTimerCallback(DispatchTimerClick);
    // Start the timer and have it interrupt
    // at the requested speed
    KWindow.StartTimer(KScope.GetSpeed());

    return 0;
}
```

For the most part the code is straightforward. The only step that needs explanation is the invocation of `KWindow`'s `SetTimerCallback` member function. We would have liked to set it up so that `KWindow` sent a turn message directly to `KScope`, for example

```
KWindow.SetTimerCallback(KScope.Turn);
```

Unfortunately, the type-checking rules of C++ prevent us from writing this statement. `SimpleWindow`'s `SetTimerCallback` function expects a pointer to a function that returns an integer. In other words, it expects something with the type `int (*)()`. The type of member function `Turn()` is `int (Kaleidoscope::*)()`. That is, the class that a function is a member of is part of its type. Thus, the parameter type expected by `SetTimerCallback` is not what is being passed. To get around this, we use a simple indirection. The function `KWindow` should call on a timer event is set to `DispatchTimerClick`, and this function calls `KScope`'s `Turn()` function.

Just before the program terminates, the routine `ApiEnd()` is called to do any necessary cleanup. For the kaleidoscope program, the only cleanup is to close `Kwindow` and return. Listing 14.14 contains the implementation of `ApiEnd()` and `ApiMain()`, as well as the definitions of `KWindow` and `KScope`.

Figure 14.16 shows our new kaleidoscope image after several turns. As you can see, the addition of the new shapes has made the image look much more like a real kaleidoscope image.

Listing 14.14

Implementation of kaleidoscope user interactions from kmain.cpp

```
#include "kaleido.h"
// Instantiate a  window to display the kaleidoscope
SimpleWindow KWindow("Kaleidoscope", 10.0, 10.0,
 Position(2.0, 2.0));
// Instantiate a kaleidoscope named Kscope that will
// turn once a second
Kaleidoscope KScope(KWindow, 1000);
// DispatchTimerClick(): call Kscope's turn function
int DispatchTimerClick() {
   KScope.Turn();

   return 1;
}
// ApiMain(): open the window, set up the call back,
// and start the timer
int ApiMain() {
   KWindow.Open();
   KWindow.SetTimerCallback(DispatchTimerClick);
   KWindow.StartTimer(KScope.GetSpeed());

   return 0;
}
// ApiEnd(): clean up by closing KWindow
int ApiEnd() {
   KWindow.Close();

   return 0;
}
```

Figure 14.16
Improved kaleidoscope image

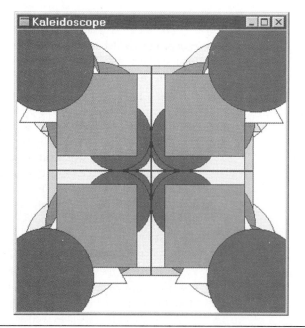

History of Computing

Emerging technologies

The 1990s have been characterized by the continued introduction of cheaper and faster computers every year. Today, a PC costing about $2,000 has 80 to 100 times the computational power of a PC that sold in the middle 80s for $5,000 or more. Experts agree that this rate of growth will continue. Because of this phenomenal increase in performance and drop in price, computers are being used for a variety of tasks that, even a few years ago, would have been unthinkable. Many cars have computers that control the engine as well as many of the instrument displays. We are beginning to see computers that have enough power to analyze and recognize human speech. Similarly, small "digital assistant" computers can recognize handwriting are beginning to appear. At this time, these devices are limited in their capabilities, but it is only a matter of time before we routinely communicate with computers via voice commands.

Today's computers all share the common characteristic of using electricity to operate. Some researchers believe that the way to achieve even greater speed is to use light instead of electricity. Indeed, researchers have built an optical replacement for the transistor called the *transphasor*. Some predict that an optical computer, if realized, could easily perform a trillion operations per second. Optical computers would have another advantage. Computers based on optical components could be much smaller than electronic computers because light beams can pass through themselves without interference, whereas computers based on electricity must use wires that cannot cross.

An even wilder and potentially revolutionary approach to building computers involves organic molecules. Currently, computer chips are constructed by placing tiny transistors on a chip of silicon. However, it is possible to build organic molecules that operate much like silicon transistors. Working at this molecular level promises even greater speed and smaller computers. Thus some experts predict that in the future, rather than building a computer from a silicon crystal, we will grow computers from vats of protein.

14.8

POINTS TO REMEMBER

- The relationship is-a indicates inheritance. For example, a car is a kind of vehicle. A border collie is a kind of dog.
- The is-a relationship is transitive. A Siamese cat is a type of cat, a cat is a mammal, therefore a Siamese cat is a mammal.
- The relationship has-a indicates containment. For example, a radio has a tuner. A car has an engine. Aggregate objects are constructed using containment.
- Both inheritance and containment are methods for software reuse.

- A new class that is created from an existing class using inheritance is called a derived class or subclass. The parent class is called the base class or superclass.

- When an object that is a instance of derived class is instantiated, the constructor for the base class is invoked before the body of the constructor for the derived class is invoked.

- When required for efficiency, the implementation of a class can be included with the declaration of the class in the .h file. The member functions can be declared inline, and the C++ compiler will replace calls to the member functions with the body of the function. This method avoids the overhead of calling a function and, for heavily used member functions, can significantly reduce the execution time of a program.

- Initializing data members of a class using a data member initialization list is more efficient than calling a mutator from the constructor.

- Destructors are called in reverse order from the constructor calls. Thus, the destructor for a derived class is called before the destructor of the base or superclass.

- With public inheritance, the public members of the base class are public members of the derived class. The private members of the base class are not accessible by the member functions of the derived class.

- With protected inheritance, public and protected members of the base class become private members of the derived class. The private members of the base class are not accessible to the member functions of the derived class.

- With multiple inheritance, a derived class inherits the attributes and behaviors of all parent classes.

- With private inheritance, public and protected members of the base class become private members of the derived class.

14.9

EXERCISES

14.1   Design a hierarchy of toys. The base class is a toy. Examples of possible specialized subclasses are stuffed toy, battery-powered toy, and mechanical toy. Constrain your hierarchy to use only single inheritance. Illustrate your hierarchy by drawing a diagram like the one in Figure 14.1.

14.2   Redo Exercise 14.1, to employ multiple inheritance.

14.3   Design an inheritance hierarchy for lights. For example, there are electric lights, combustible lights (kerosene latterns, propane latterns, etc.), and electroluminescent lights. Do not use multiple inheritance. Illustrate you hierarchy by drawing a diagram like the one in Figure 14.1.

14.4 Design a inheritance hierarchy for shoes. Do not use multiple inheritance. The first level of your hierarchy should be men's and women's shoes. Illustrate you hierarchy by drawing a diagram like the one in Figure 14.1.

14.5 Design an inheritance hierarchy of clocks. After you have designed the hierarchy, create classes for each type of clock. Your solution should be a figure like the one in Figure 14.13 and a set of class declarations. Do not implement the member functions of the classes.

14.6 Design an inheritance hierarchy for publications. After you have designed the hierarchy, create classes for each type of publication. Your solution should be a figure like the one in Figure 14.13 and a set of class declarations. Do not implement the member functions of the classes.

14.7 Design a hierarchy of computer printers. Use multiple inheritance in your hierarchy. Illustrate you hierarchy by drawing a diagram like the one in Figure 14.1. Some types of printers to consider in designing your hierarchy are laser, inkjet, impact, and dye sublimation.

14.8 Assume that class HoundDog is privately derived from class Dog. Indicate whether HoundDog object Blue declared in function main() can access the following members.

a) The private members of HoundDog.

b) The protected members of HoundDog.

c) The public member of HoundDog.

d) The private members of Dog.

e) The protected members of Dog.

f) The private members of Dog.

14.9 The code for the Kaleidoscope's Turn() function used a cascaded if-then-else statement to determine the type of shape to add to the display. A switch statement would be more natural. Modify the code to use a switch statement. Did your code work? What other changes did you have to make to the code in order to use a switch statement?

14.10 Modify the shape classes so that the shape has a default position. That is, it should be possible to declare a shape by only supplying the window that contains the shape. Before modifying the code, determine a good default position. Justify your answer.

14.11 Currently the location of a shape is given by the center of the shape. This method works well for many shapes, but some shapes do not have an easily defined center. Modify the hierarchy of shapes so that the position of a shape is specified by providing the upper-left corner of the bounding box. You must determine what the bounding box is for an equilateral triangle.

14.12 Design and implement labeled versions of the following existing shape classes:

a) RectangleShape

b) TriangleShape

c) `CircleShape`

d) `SquareShape`

14.13 Add the following shapes to the original shapes hierarchy.

a) Diamond

b) Pentagon

c) Hexagon

14.14 Create a class called `CylinderShape` for drawing a cylinder on the screen. Class `CylinderShape` should be derived from the class `Shape`. A cylinder can be rendered by drawing two ellipses and a rectangle. The following picture shows a cylinder that has been drawn using

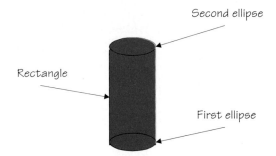

Second ellipse

Rectangle

First ellipse

this method. Illustrate the use of your `CylinderShape` by writing a program that accepts the dimensions of a cylinder, renders the cylinder and labels it with its volumes. Assume the dimensions of the cylinder are given in centimeters. Make sure you use the appropriate units of measure for the volume.

14.15 Create a class called `StarShape` for drawing stars in a window. Class `StarShape` should be derived from the class `Shape`. A star can be rendered using `SimpleWindow`'s `RenderPolygon` member function. A `StarShape` has the characteristics shown in the following diagram:

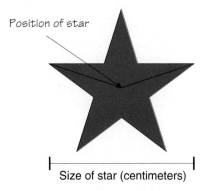

Position of star

Size of star (centimeters)

The position of a star is specified by giving the coordinates of its center. The size of a star is specified by giving the length (in centimeters) of the distance across the star. Demonstrate the use of `StarShape` by writing a program that draws six stars in a window. The stars should have the following colors: red, blue, green, yellow, cyan, and magenta.

14.16 Using `StarShape` and the other shapes we have developed, write a program that creates a `SimpleWindow` that contains an image of the American flag.

14.17 Modify the kaleidoscope program so that it has a separate control window. The control window contains the following buttons: quit, turn, run, and stop. When the mouse is clicked on the quit button, all windows close and the program terminates. When the turn button is clicked, the kaleidoscope is turns. If the kaleidoscope is in automatic mode, the turn button has no effect. When the run button is clicked, the kaleidoscope goes into automatic mode. In this mode, the image is automatically updated every second. If the kaleidoscope is already in automatic mode, this run button has no effect. When the stop button is clicked, the kaleidoscope goes into manual mode. In this mode, the image is updated only when the turn button is clicked. If the kaleidoscope is already in manual mode, the stop button has no effect.

14.18 Use the `Kaleidoscope` class to write a program that creates four kaleidoscopes. Position the kaleidoscopes in the four quadrants of the screen. Each kaleidoscope should turn at a different rate.

14.19 Redesign the kaleidoscope program so the class `Kaleidoscope` is derived from class `SimpleWindow`. Does this approach offer any advantages over the previous design? Explain why or why not. Implement your design.

14.20 The labeled rectangle shape (see Exercise 14.12) can serve as a basis for a button class. Design and implement a button class. The button class has the following properties. When the mouse is clicked inside the button, a user-defined function is called. Thus one of the data members of the button class should be a pointer to a function. Demonstrate your new button class by writing a program that implements a stop watch. The stop watch has two buttons—a start button and a stop button. When the start button is pushed, the current time is recorded. When the stop button is pushed, the elapsed time is displayed in the console window. Hint: You will need to implement a member function IsInside that works for a rectangular shape.

14.21 Write a program that simulates a slot machine. The window display should look like the following diagram. When the mouse is clicked on

Pull

the pull button the shapes spin for a period of time. The shapes consist of a red circle, a blue square, and a magenta triangle. When the shapes stop spinning, if two of the shapes are the same, the player wins $1. If all three shapes are the same, the player wins $20. If no shapes match, the player loses. Use an alert message to tell the player what happened.

Think carefully about how to design the spinning shapes. Does it make sense to consider using multiple inheritance? Before implementing the shapes, list the responsibilities, interactions, and attributes of the objects in your design.

14.22 Using inheritance, create a new type of shape. These shapes are shaded. For example, the following is a `ShadedRectangleShape`.

In addition to `ShadedRectangleShape`, create `ShadedEllipse-Shape` and `ShadedTriangleShape`. Your classes should allow the color of the shading to be specified by the client users of the shape. Write a program that demonstrates the use of the new shapes.

14.23 Using multiple inheritance, create a new type of shape. These shapes are shaded and labeled. For example, the following is a `LabeledShade-dRectangleShape`.

In addition to `LabeledShadedRectangleShape`, create `Labeled-ShadedEllipseShape` and `LabeledShadedTriangleShape`. Write a program that demonstrates the use of the new shapes.

CHAPTER 15

Templates and polymorphism

Introduction

Polymorphism is a language mechanism that permits the same code expression to invoke different functions depending upon the type of objects using the code. Name reuse in function overloading is a primitive form of polymorphism. In this chapter we explore other C++ methods for achieving polymorphism. The first method is through class and function templates. A template, when invoked with particular types and values, can generate a new function or class. All functions or classes generated from a given template will have the same name. The second method of achieving polymorphism is through virtual member functions. This method is sometimes called pure polymorphism. In an expression involving a virtual function invocation, the decision on which function to use is delayed until run time. The decision is then based on the type of object being referenced in the invocation.

Key Concepts

- function template
- class template
- container class
- linked list
- iterator class
- virtual function
- pure virtual function
- abstract base class
- virtually derived class

15.1

GENERIC ACTIONS AND TYPES

If we asked experts to list the necessary features of an object-oriented language, their replies would generally be the same. Their answers would surely state that the most important feature of an object-oriented language is its ability to allow both data and behavior to be encapsulated in a single object. Class and inheritance mechanisms would also appear in all the answers. These three features—objects, classes, and inheritance—are the core of object-oriented programming. If our experts were to agree on one more necessary language feature, it would likely be *polymorphism.*

A polymorphic function is a generic function that can act upon objects of different types. The action taken depends upon the types of the objects.

Function and operator overloading is sometimes considered a primitive form of polymorphism. With overloading we can *repeatedly* define functions or operators with the same name. For example, in previous chapters we overloaded the addition operator to work with both `Rational` and `BigNum` operands. As another example, we can overload the function `min()` for the various numeric types so that it returns the lesser value of its two parameters. With overloading, analogous behavior is not required but is expected.

One of the topics that we consider in this chapter is *templates.* A C++ template is exactly what the term indicates. It is a form that can generate a function or class once the particulars are supplied. In terms of language mechanisms, templates are akin to overloading—they offer a syntactic convenience that looks like polymorphism. In true polymorphism the choice of which function to execute is made during run time. The choice is made then because the exact nature of the object cannot be determined during compilation. True polymorphism is achieved in C++ using special member functions called *virtual functions.* This form of polymorphism is the other major topic of this chapter.

15.2

FUNCTION TEMPLATES

C++ has two kinds of templates—*class generators* and *function and operator generators.* The following code segment defines a template that can generate a family of functions, each of which is named `min()`.

```
template <class T> T min(const T &a, const T &b) {
   if (a < b)
      return a;
   else
      return b;
}
```

A function or operator template definition begins with the keyword **template**. Following this keyword is a template parameter list enclosed within angled brackets. The template parameter declarations are separated from each other by commas. There are two different kinds of template parameters: type and value. A type template parameter specifies a placeholder for a type. A value template parameter specifies a placeholder for a value. Following the template parameter list is a function description that uses the parameters.

The syntax for a value template parameter is the same as a function value parameter—it consists of a known type followed by an identifier name. We note that value template parameters are not typically used in function templates.

The syntax for a type template parameter in a function template consists of the keyword **class** followed by the identifier name of the template parameter.

Each template parameter must be used in the function description. In particular, the template parameters must be used in the signature of the function description. Each of the functions min() that can be generated from our template example has two constant reference parameters. The type of these two parameters and the return type are all the same and are determined by the actual type used for template parameter T. The actual type will be determined by a function invocation using that template name.

Suppose the following code segment appears in the same program as our min() template definition.

```
int Input1;
int Input2;
cin >> Input1 >> Input2;
cout << min(Input1, Input2) << endl;
```

A function min() is then automatically generated and invoked with two constant **int** reference parameters and an **int** return type.

```
int min(const int &a, const int &b) {
    if (a < b)
        return a;
    else
        return b;
}
```

Similarly, if the code segment

```
Rational x;
Rational y;
cin >> x >> y;
Rational z = min(x, y);
```

occurs, then the following function min() with two constant Rational reference parameters and a Rational return type is automatically generated and invoked.

```
Rational min(const Rational &a, const Rational &b){
    if (a < b)
        return a;
    else
        return b;
}
```

The test expression (a < b) is the interesting part of the min() template definition because the type of comparison varies with the template instantiation. The invocation min(Input1, Input2) causes an **int** comparison to be generated, and the invocation min(x, y) causes a Rational comparison to be generated. Such comparisons can be generated as the < operator is built-in for **int** objects and our definition of the rational library includes an auxiliary < operator.

The following invocation results in a *template instantiation failure.*

```
cout << min(7, 3.14); // illegal: parameter mismatch
```

Our min() template does not apply because the values 7 and 3.14 do not have the same type. For a function to be generated using the template, the compiler must be able to form an *exact* match with the template parameter description and the types of the actual parameters in the invocation. Conversions are not automatically tried in an attempt to generate a function.

A template instantiation failure can also result if actions specified within the template are not defined for objects of the type given in the invocation. For example, the invocation of min() in the following insertion results in an error.

```
cout << min(cout, cerr);   // illegal: streams cannot
                           // be used in this manner
```

Our template does not apply in part because the < operator is not defined for stream objects.

The usefulness of function templates is especially apparent in sorting. By implementing a sorting algorithm as a template, we can generate sorts for all types of arrays without any additional work on our part. The following code provides a template version of the InsertionSort() defined in Chapter 10.

```
template <class T>
  void InsertionSort(T A[], int n) {
    for (int i = 1; i < n; ++i) {
      if (A[i] < A[i-1]) {
        // some shifting is necessary
        T v = A[i];
        int j = i;
        do {
          A[j] = A[j-1];
          --j;
        } while ((j > 0) && (v < A[j-1]));
        A[j] = v;
      }
    }
  }
```

In the InsertionSort() template definition, the template parameter T is the type of the objects to be sorted. For this template, like the template for determining the minimum value, the < operator must be defined. Observe that the template parameter T is also used in the function body.

The use of a function template does not prevent a program from also having explicitly defined functions with the same name. Program 15.1 demonstrates this point.

Program 15.1

Demonstrates that an explicit function definition can override a template definition

```
#include <iostream.h>
template <class T> void f(T i) {
    cout << "template f(): " << i << endl;
}
void f(int i) {
    cout << "explicit f(): " << i << endl;
}
int main() {
    f(1.5);
    f(1);
    f('a');
    return 0;
}
```

Program 15.1 defines both a function template `f()` and an explicitly defined function `f()` with an **int** parameter. The output of the program is given below.

```
template f(): 1.5
explicit f(): 1
template f(): a
```

This example shows that if there is a choice of functions to invoke, an explicit definition takes precedence over a template definition.

15.3

CLASS TEMPLATES

The template mechanism can also be used for defining a *class template*. For a class template, the keyword **template** and the template parameter declarations precede the class description.

Like function templates, a class template can also have type and value template parameters. The type and value template parameters must be used in the declarations of the data members or in the signatures of the member functions.

To generate a class from a class template, you provide actual parameters for the template parameters. The actual parameters are provided after the template name within angled brackets. An actual type parameter must be a known type; an actual value parameter must be a constant whose value can be calculated during compilation.

The following simple example defines and uses a template class named TC. The class has two template parameters X and n. Template parameter X is a type template parameter; n is an **int** value template parameter.

```
template <class X, int n> class TC {
    public:
        TC();
        void Assign(X xvalue);
        // ...
    private:
        X ValueArray[n];
};
```

C++ Language

Standard template library for generic algorithms

The proposed C++ standard includes the standard template library (STL). This library in part defines a collection of template algorithms for basic data manipulation. The template algorithms include a variety of methods for searching, sorting, combining, copying, and rearranging lists.

The standard template library is available for downloading over the Internet from FTP site `butler.hpl.hp.com/stl`.

Template class TC<X,n> has a member function `Assign()` whose parameter xvalue has a type that is determined during class generation from the template. The template class TC<X,n> also has an array data member ValueArray whose type and size are determined during class generation.

The TC<X,n> template is used to generate two classes in the following definitions of objects A and B.

```
TC<char, 80> A;
TC<int, 125> B;
```

Object A is of type TC<**char**,80> and has a member function `Assign()` with a **char** parameter xvalue. The object also has a data member Value-Array, which is an array of 80 **char** elements. Object B is of type TC<**char**,80> and has a member function `Assign()` with an **int** parameter xvalue. The object also has a data member ValueArray, which is an array of 125 **int** elements.

15.4

A SIMPLE LIST CLASS USING A CLASS TEMPLATE

As discussed in Chapter 10, array types are not first-class types in C++—an array cannot be passed by value; it cannot be a return value for a function, and it cannot be the target of an assignment. In addition, the language neither provides a range checking capability to ensure that an index represents a proper subscript nor does it provide the ability to determine the number of elements in an array.

The programming limitations associated with array types are serious. However, these limitations can be overcome through the use of *container classes*. A container class is an ADT whose objects represent a collection of subobjects. The proposed C++ ANSI standard includes a rich set of container classes, and software vendors are happy to provide still others.

The choice of which container class to use depends upon your list-processing needs. In choosing a particular container class, a software engineer must examine the information to be represented and determine necessary container characteristics. Some of the questions that the engineer must ask when making the decision are the following:

- Is the maximum number of elements in the list known?
- Do the elements in the list all have the same type?
- Are the elements in the list to be ordered, and if so, how are the elements in the list to be ordered?
- Are the elements in the list to be referenced in a random or sequential manner?
- What is the required relative efficiency of inspecting, modifying, adding, and removing elements?
- Is the list associative, that is, can we use key values to determine other information regarding the list?

In this chapter, we next develop two container classes: an ADT with an arraylike interface and a ADT that supports dynamically sized lists whose elements are referenced in sequential order. Both of the ADTs require that all elements in a given collection be of the same type. Thus we will be creating *homogeneous* container classes. We will develop *heterogeneous* lists when we consider polymorphism through virtual functions.

In developing our arraylike container ADT, we have two major choices. We can explicitly develop a class ADT for each individual type for which we want listlike capabilities, or we can develop a single template class ADT. The latter alternative is clearly preferred.

Because our ADT interface is to resemble the standard array interface, access to elements will be through a member subscript operator. Other ADT capabilities include

- Passing a list ADT object using any of the parameter-passing styles.
- Using a list ADT object as either the source or target of an assignment.
- Passing an element of a list ADT object using any of the parameter-passing styles.
- Using an element of a list ADT object as either the source or target of an assignment.
- Providing access to the number of elements represented by a list ADT object.

The elements represented by one of our list ADT objects will be *type distinguishing* (i.e., a list object that represents a collection of **int** elements has a different type than a list object that represents a collection of **char** elements). We must also decide whether the number of elements being represented in a list is type distinguishing (e.g., does an object representing 10 **int** elements have a different type than an object representing 20 **int** elements). If the number of elements being represented is type distinguishing, then the number of elements being represented must be a value template parameter for the list ADT. If the number of elements being represented is not type distinguishing, then the number of elements being represented can be a parameter to the list constructor.

Listing 15.1 defines the interface for a class template named Bunch<T,n> where the number of elements being represented is type distin-

Listing 15.1

Definition of template class Bunch from bunch.h

```
template <class T, int n> class Bunch{
   public:
      // default constructor
      Bunch();
      // constructor initializes all elements to val
      Bunch(const T &val);
      // constructor initializes from standard array
      Bunch(const T A[n]);
      // inspector for number of elements in list
      int Size() const { return NumberValues; } ;
      // inspector for element of a constant list
      const T& operator[](int i) const;
      // inspector for element of nonconstant list
      T& operator[](int i);
   private:
      // data members
      T Values[n];        // list elements
      int NumberValues; // size of list
};
```

guishing. For example, the objects A and B defined in the following code segment have different types.

```
Bunch<int, 10> A; // represents 10 int elements
Bunch<int, 20> B; // represents 20 int elements
```

This difference means that unless we explicitly overload the assignment operator for each kind of assignment that we want to perform, then the assignment of B to A would not be legal.

```
A = B; // illegal: A and B have different types
```

Listing 15.2 defines a class template named Array where the number of elements being represented is not type distinguishing.

Thus the Array<int> objects C and D defined in the following code segment have the same type.

```
Array<int> C(10);           // represents 10 ints
Array<int> D(20);           // represents 20 ints
const Array<int> E(20, 0);  // represents 20 0s
```

Because C and D have the same type, we can assign them to each other (note that the semantics of the assignment have not yet been defined).

```
C = D; // legal: C and D have the same type
```

The definition for template Array<T> is more complicated than the definition for Bunch<T,n> because the data member Values for an Array<T> object is a pointer to dynamic space, while the data member Values for a Bunch<T,n> object is an array of n elements. Because an Array<T> object acquires dynamic space, the Array<T> class needs to define a copy constructor, assignment operator, and destructor. These members are not explicitly required for the Bunch<T,n> class because a Bunch<T,n> object does not acquire dynamic space—the copy constructor, assignment operator, and destructor provided automatically by the compiler will suffice.

Listing 15.2

*Definition of template
class Array from alist.h*

```
template <class T> class Array {
  public:
    // default constructor
    Array(int n = 10);
    // constructor initializes elements to given value
    Array(int n, const T &val);
    // constructor initializes from a standard array
    Array(const T A[], int n);
    // copy constructor
    Array(const Array<T> &A);
    // destructor
    ~Array();
    // inspector for size of the list
    int Size() const { return NumberValues; }
    // assignment operator
    Array<T> & operator=(const Array<T> &A);
    // inspector for element of a constant list
    const T& operator[](int i) const;
    // inspector for element of a nonconstant list
    T& operator[](int i);
  private:
    // data members
    T *Values;          // pointer to list elements
    int NumberValues;   // size of list
};
```

We believe client programming flexibility should be the basis for deciding which class—Bunch<T,n> or Array<T>—is the basis for our ADT. Therefore, our choice is to develop the class Array<T> where the number of list elements being represented is not type distinguishing. In the remainder of this section we consider how to implement some of the member functions and operators of the class Array<T>. The class Bunch<T,n> is left to the exercises.

The definition of the class Array<T> in Listing 15.2 overloads the subscript operator twice. The member subscript operator prototypes differ in their return type and use of the qualifier **const**. The qualifier is part of a member function signature. As such, when the compiler translates an invocation of the subscript operator on an Array<T> object, it will use context to determine which definition applies. The definition of the subscript operator using the qualifier **const** is invoked in situations where a **const** Array<T> object is inspected.

```
cout << E[2] << endl;
int i = E[6];
```

The subscript operator with the reference return type is used in situations where a non-**const** Array<T> object is being inspected or mutated, as shown in the invocations in the following statements:

```
C[9] = 17;
Swap(D[3], D[4]);
cin >> C[5];
cout << D[19];
```

Our definitions of the `Array<T>` member function templates begin in Listing 15.3. In particular, this listing provides the templates for some of the `Array<T>` constructors. The definitions show that the syntax for a template member function defined outside the class definition is quite cumbersome (the member `Size()` defined within the class definition does not suffer so). Observe that we define the member function templates in the same file as the class definition itself. These definitions cannot be placed in a separate file and linked to the client application because the definitions are templates for implementations rather than implementations themselves.

Listing 15.3

Array constructor templates from alist.h

```
// default constructor
template <class T> Array<T>::Array(int n) {
   assert(n > 0);
   NumberValues = n;
   Values = new T [n];
   assert(Values);
}
// constructor initializes elements to given value
template <class T>
Array<T>::Array(int n, const T &val) {
   assert(n > 0);
   NumberValues = n;
   Values = new T [n];
   assert(Values);
   for (int i = 0; i < n; ++i) {
      Values[i] = val;
   }
}
// constructor initializes from a standard array
template <class T>
Array<T>::Array(const T A[], int n) {
   assert(n > 0);
   NumberValues = n;
   Values = new T [n];
   assert(Values);
   for (int i = 0; i < n; ++i) {
      Values[i] = A[i];
   }
}
```

The default `Array<T>` constructor has one optional parameter that specifies the number of elements in the list to be represented (the class definition specifies that 10 is the default number). For pedagogical simplicity, we use `assert()` statements where checks need to be made.

The first of the two specialized `Array<T>` constructors has two parameters. The first parameter indicates the number of elements to be represented. The second parameter is the initial value for each of the elements. The second of the specialized constructors uses a standard C++ array of appropriate type to initialize the object.

The templates for the `Array<T>` copy constructor, destructor, and assignment operator are given in Listing 15.4. The implementations are all straight-

Listing 15.4

Array member and auxiliary functions and operators from alist.h

```
// copy constructor
template <class T> Array<T>::Array(const Array<T> &A) {
  NumberValues = A.Size();
  Values = new T [A.Size()];
  assert(Values);
  for (int i = 0; i < A.Size(); ++i)
    Values[i] = A[i];
}
// destructor
template <class T> Array<T>::~Array() {
  delete [] Values;
}
// assignment
template <class T>
 Array<T>& Array<T>::operator=(const Array<T> &A) {
  if (this != &A) {
     if (Size() != A.Size()) {
        delete [] Values;
        NumberValues = A.Size();
        Values = new T [A.Size()];
        assert(Values);
     }
     for (int i = 0; i < A.Size(); ++i)
        Values[i] = A[i];
  }
  return *this;
}

// inspector of the value of an individual element
template <class T>
 const T& Array<T>::operator[](int i) const {
  assert((i >= 0) && (i < Size()));
  return Values[i];
}

// inspector/mutator facilitator of individual element
template <class T>
 T& Array<T>::operator[](int i) {
  assert((i >= 0) && (i < Size()));
  return Values[i];
}

// template insertion operator for Array
template <class T>
 ostream& operator<<(ostream &sout, const Array<T> &A){
  sout << "[ ";
  for (int i = 0; i < A.Size(); ++i)
    sout << A[i] << " ";
  sout << "]";
  return sout;
}

// insertion operator for Array<char>
ostream& operator<<(ostream &sout, const Array<char>
&A) {
  for (int i = 0; i < A.Size(); ++i)
     sout << A[i];
  return sout;
}
```

forward. The only warranted explanation is that when an Array<T> copy is made, whether through construction or assignment, the operation is a *deep copy* (i.e., a separate list is made with each element individually copied), rather than a *shallow copy* where the copy operation merely duplicates the value of the pointer Values. With a deep copy, the source and target lists have identical but distinct representations. The Values data members point to different memory locations that contain the same values. (The class BigNum from Chapter 13 also performs a deep copy in its copy constructor and in the member assignment operator). In a shallow copy, the two lists share a single representation—the Values data members point to the same memory location.

The two overloadings of the subscript operator for **const** and non-**const** Array<T> objects are also given in Listing 15.4.

The insertion operator is twice overloaded in Listing 15.4. The first overloading is a template definition for Array<T> objects in general. The definition requires that the insertion operator be defined for the type of the elements represented in the list. The template version outputs the list within a pair of brackets. The individual elements in a list are separated by spaces. The second overloading of the insertion operator is specifically for Array<**char**> objects. This insertion definition displays the list in "string" style—the individual **char** elements of the list are concatenated together in the output stream.

The following test program demonstrates some of the capabilities of our Array<T> ADT.

```
#include <iostream.h>
int main() {
    Array<int> A(5, 0);   // A is five 0's
    const Array<int> B(8, 1); // B is eight 1's
    Array<char> C("hello", 5); // C is h, e, l, l, o
    cout << "A = " << A << endl;
    cout << "B = " << B << endl;
    cout << "C = " << C << endl;
    A = B;
    A[5] = 3;
    A[B[1]] = 2;
    cout << "A = " << A << endl;
    cout << "B = " << B << endl;
    cout << "C = " << C << endl;
    return 0;
}
```

The definitions of objects A and B specify both the number of elements and the initial value of those elements. The definition of object C invokes the specialized constructor that uses a standard array and a number of elements to perform the initialization. This constructor is invoked because C++ effectively treats a string as an array of constant **char** objects whose last element is the null character.

The following assignment statement from the test program makes A a distinct copy of B.

```
A = B;
```

The assignment

```
A[5] = 3;
```

makes use only of the non-**const** version of the member subscript operator. However, the assignment

```
A[B[1]] = 2;
```

makes use of both member subscript operators—the reference to B[1] uses the subscript operator for **const** Array objects, and the result of that operation (the value 3) is used as a parameter to the other subscript operator.

The output of a program run follows.

```
A = [ 0 0 0 0 0 ]
B = [ 1 1 1 1 1 1 1 1 ]
C = hello
A = [ 1 2 1 1 1 3 1 1 ]
B = [ 1 1 1 1 1 1 1 1 ]
C = hello
```

15.5

SEQUENTIAL LISTS

A major problem with an array-type list is that it cannot grow or shrink in size. With a standard array, the number of elements in the list is determined during its definition. An Array<T> object has more flexibility—through assignment, an Array<T> object can represent a different size list. However, during the assignment, the elements that were previously maintained are replaced. To overcome such size limitations, we now develop a template list ADT, named SeqList<T>, that permits elements to be both dynamically added and removed from the list.

The name SeqList<T> comes from the fact that the ADT is designed to offer *sequential* access to the elements in the list being represented. In such a list, the elements are ordered, and if the program can already access a particular element in the list, then the program can efficiently access the successive element in the list. Some implementations of a sequential list also have a method for efficiently accessing the preceding element.

Our implementation of the template SeqList<T> ADT will use a data structure known as a *singly linked list*. A singly linked list is a collection of elements where an individual element has two data members: one data member represents an individual list value, and the other data member is a pointer to the next subobject in the list. A null pointer value indicates the end of the list.

The following diagram depicts a linked list that represents the values 2, 8, 6, and 4. The arrows in the picture indicate the links from one subobject to another. The filled-in square in the last list item represents the null pointer value.

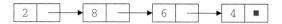

C++ Language

Standard template library for generic containers

In addition to providing generic algorithms, the proposed standard template library defines a collection of basic container classes for list representation. The representations differ in how the elements of the list can be accessed. Various container classes support random access of the elements, sequential access of the elements, and associative access of the elements. The standard container classes include vectors, lists, deques, sets, maps, stacks, and priority queues.

As the standard template library grows in availability and acceptance, many experts expect that the use of the standard container classes—especially the **vector** template class that provides arraylike capabilities—will gradually replace most client uses of arrays. The major reason for this migration is that the standard container classes are first-class types.

15.5.1

SeqItem class template

To implement a linked-list version of SeqList<T>, we will define an additional class template, named SeqItem<T> to represent individual elements of the linked list (i.e., a list value and its pointer to another element). The class template definition for SeqItem<T> is given in Listing 15.5.

Listing 15.5

*Class template SeqItem
from slist.h*

```
template <class T> class SeqItem{
   protected:
      // default constructor
      SeqItem(const T &Val, SeqItem *Succ)
       : ItemValue(Val), Successor(Succ) {
         // no code needed
      };
   private:
      T ItemValue;         // element value
      SeqItem *Successor; // pointer to next element
   friend class SeqList<T>;
   friend class SeqElement<T>;
};
```

Because client programmers will be provided access to elements in a SeqList<T> through other means, the definition of SeqItem<T> makes all member functions **protected** and all data members **private**. This qualification means that a client cannot directly define a SeqItem<T> object.

Because a SeqList<T> object requires access to the data members of a SeqItem<T> object, the class SeqList<T> is declared to be a **friend** class to SeqItem<T>. The template class SeqElement<T>, which will be discussed subsequently, is also a **friend** class to SeqItem<T>.

As appropriate for an element of a linked list, a SeqItem<T> object has two data members. The data member ItemValue represents a list value; the data member Successor points to the next element in the linked list.

```
T ItemValue;         // element value
SeqItem *Successor; // pointer to next element
```

The definition of the SeqItem<T> class includes the definition of its constructor.

```
SeqItem(const T &Val, SeqItem *Succ)
 : ItemValue(Val), Successor(Succ) {
   // no code needed
};
```

The constructor expects two values: a list value and a pointer to the remainder of the linked list.

The class template definition of SeqList<T> is given in Listing 15.6. The definition specifies a default constructor, a destructor, mutators to add and remove item(s) from the list, inspectors to provide the value of the first element in the list and the number of elements in the list, and a facilitator to display the elements in the list. A copy constructor and an assignment operator are also defined. However, the implementation of these two member functions is left to the exercises.

Listing 15.6

Class template SeqList
from slist.h

```
template <class T> class SeqList {
  public:
    // default constructor
    SeqList();
    // destructor
    ~SeqList();
    // mutator to add item to list
    void Add(const T &NewValue);
    // mutator to remove item from list
    T Remove();
    // mutator to remove all elements from list
    void RemoveAll();
    // inspector of first value in list
    T First() const;
    // inspector of number of elements in list
    int Size() const;
    // method to display list
    void Insert(ostream &sout) const;
    // copy constructor
    SeqList(const SeqList &T);
    // assignment
    SeqList& operator=(const SeqList &T);
  private:
    SeqItem<T> *Front;  // pointer to first element
    SeqItem<T> *Rear;   // pointer to last element
    int ListLength;     // number of elements
  friend class SeqElement<T>;
};
```

The definition for `SeqList` also specifies three data members. Data members `Front` and `Rear`, respectively, point to the `SeqItem<T>` objects representing the first and last elements in the linked list representation of the sequential list. The **int** data member `ListLength` represents the number of elements in the list.

15.5.2

SeqList member function basics

The member and auxiliary functions and operators for `SeqList<T>` are given in Listing 15.7. The constructor uses an initialization list to specify initial values for the data members. The pointers `Front` and `Rear` are both initialized to the null address, indicating the list is currently empty. Data member `ListLength` is initialized to zero to also reflect this list condition. The `SeqList<T>` destructor uses the member function `RemoveAll()` to accomplish its task. Discussion of `RemoveAll()` appears in section 15.5.4.

Inspector `Size()` accomplishes its task by simply returning the value of `ListLength`.

Inspector `First()` can accomplish its task only if the list is nonempty. If the list is nonempty, then data member `Front` is a pointer to the `SeqItem` object that represents the first element in the linked list. The expression `Front->ItemValue` represents the list value maintained there. If `Front`, `Rear`, and the linked list have the following depiction, then the value 2 would be returned by `First()`.

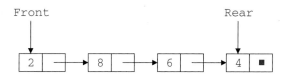

15.5.3

Insert() member function

The member function `Insert()` of Listing 15.7 allows for the easy overloading of the insertion operator. The function begins by defining a `SeqItem<T>` pointer `Ptr` that will be assigned iteratively the address of each `SeqItem` in the linked list.

```
SeqItem<T> *Ptr;
```

`Ptr` is set in the initialization statement of the **for** loop to the value of `Front`.

```
for (Ptr = Front; Ptr; Ptr = Ptr->Successor)
```

Listing 15.7

SeqList member functions from slist.h

```
// default SeqList constructor
template <class T> SeqList<T>::SeqList()
 : Front(0), Rear(0), ListLength(0) { // no code needed
}
// SeqList destructor
template <class T> SeqList<T>::~SeqList() {
   RemoveAll();
}
// Size(): return size of list
template<class T> int SeqList<T>::Size() const {
   return ListLength;
}
// Front(): return first element in list
template<class T> T SeqList<T>::First() const {
   assert(Size() != 0);
   return Front->ItemValue;
}
// Insert(): display list
template<class T>
void SeqList<T>::Insert(ostream &sout) const {
   SeqItem<T> *Ptr;
   for (Ptr = Front; Ptr; Ptr = Ptr->Successor)
      sout << " " << Ptr->ItemValue;
}
// Add(): add value to end of list
template<class T> void SeqList<T>::Add(const T &Val) {
   SeqItem<T> *Ptr = new SeqItem<T>(Val,0);
   assert(Ptr);
   if (Size() == 0)
      Front = Ptr;
   else
      Rear->Successor = Ptr;
   Rear = Ptr;
   ++ListLength;
}
// Remove(): remove value from front of the list
template<class T> T SeqList<T>::Remove() {
   assert(Front);
   SeqItem<T> *Ptr = Front->Successor;
   T ReturnValue = Front->ItemValue;
   delete Front;
   Front = Ptr;
   if (Front == 0)
      Rear = 0;
   --ListLength;
   return ReturnValue;
}
// RemoveAll(): purge list
template<class T> void SeqList<T>::RemoveAll() {
   SeqItem<T> *Ptr = Front;
   while ( Ptr ) {
      SeqItem<T> *Next = Ptr->Successor;
      delete Ptr;
      Ptr = Next;
   }
   Front = Rear = 0;
   ListLength = 0;
}
```

At this point, the involved objects have the following depiction:

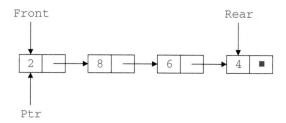

The **for** loop is iterated as long as the value of `Ptr` is not null. The body of the **for** loop consists of a single insertion statement.

```
sout << " " << Ptr->ItemValue;
```

The `ItemValue` (2) of the current `SeqItem<T>` to which `Ptr` points is inserted to the output stream. Afterwards, `Ptr` is updated in the post expression (`Ptr = Ptr->Successor`) of the **for** loop header. `Ptr`'s new value becomes the address of the next element in the linked list. The objects now have the following depiction:

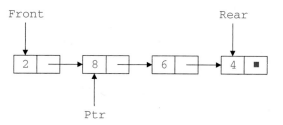

Because `Ptr` is not null, the loop is iterated again and an 8 is inserted to the output stream. `Ptr` is again updated. The objects now have the following depiction:

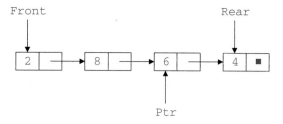

Ptr is still not null and the loop is reiterated causing a 6 to be inserted to the output stream. Ptr is updated once again. The objects now have the following depiction:

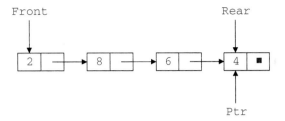

Ptr now points to the last element of the linked list. The loop body is reiterated one last time, and the value 4 is inserted to the output stream. The **for** loop post expression Ptr = Ptr->Successor causes Ptr to take on the null value. The test expression for the **for** loop then evaluates to zero and the loop is terminated.

15.5.4

Adding and removing elements

We now define the semantics of the Add() or Remove() member functions. The list semantics we use are the First-In-First-Out protocol (FIFO). This protocol adds new values at the end of the list and removes values from the front of the list. Data structures with this property are also known as *queues*.

In designing the Add() member function, we must consider two cases depending on whether the current list is empty. If the list is empty, the code for adding a value Val to the list should result in a linked list with the following depiction. As shown in the figure, Front and Rear are pointing to the same new object. The v represents the value added to the list.

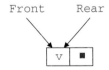

If the list is not empty, then the current first element in the list remains so. The previous end of list now becomes the second to last element in the list, and its Successor value must point to the new last element. The following figure depicts the result of such actions. In the figure, the filled-in circles represent previous values added to the list.

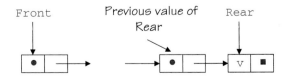

Observe that regardless of whether the list is empty or not, a new dynamic `SeqItem<T>` object must be acquired from the free store. The new object should be initialized using `Val` and the null pointer value. Also observe that once this new object has been linked to the old list, `Rear` should be assigned the address of this new object. These actions are performed in the following code segment, which is the body of member function `Add()` from Listing 15.7.

```
SeqItem<T> *Ptr = new SeqItem<T>(Val,0);
assert(Ptr);
if (Size() == 0)
    Front = Ptr;
else
    Rear->Successor = Ptr;
Rear = Ptr;
++ListLength;
```

Because member function `Remove()` of Listing 15.7 removes the first element of the list, there needs to be a first element. If this is the case, the function copies the values of `Front->Successor` and `Front->ItemValue` to temporary objects `Ptr` and `ReturnValue`, respectively.

```
assert(Front);
SeqItem<T> *Ptr = Front->Successor;
T ReturnValue = Front->ItemValue;
delete Front;
Front = Ptr;
```

The value of `Front->Successor` is remembered because it will be the value of `Front` after the current first element is deleted. The value of `Front->ItemValue` is remembered because it will be the return value for the function. Once these two objects have been copied, the **delete** operation on `Front` can be performed. Afterwards `Front` can be set to the remembered pointer value `Ptr`.

Deleting the first item can only affect the value of `Rear` if the linked list previously consisted of a single element. This condition can be easily tested by checking if the new value of `Front` is null. If it is null, `Rear` must also be set to the null address. The only other actions that must be performed are decrementing `ListLength` and returning the old value that headed the list.

```
if (Front == 0)
    Rear = 0;
--ListLength;
return ReturnValue;
```

Member function `RemoveAll()` of Listing 15.7 is similar to `Insert()` in that a `SeqItem*` object `Ptr` with an initial value of `Front` is used to iterate through the elements in the linked list.

```
SeqItem<T> *Ptr = Front;
```

The loop should iterate while `Ptr` points to an actual element in the list (i.e., it is not null). Within the body of the loop, a temporary pointer object `Next` remembers the next element of the linked list (`Ptr->Successor`). Once the current linked list item has been deleted, `Ptr` can be reset to `Next` to prepare for the next possible iteration of the loop.

```
while ( Ptr ) {
    SeqItem<T> *Next = Ptr->Successor;
    delete Ptr;
    Ptr = Next;
}
```

Once the loop is finished, to complete `RemoveAll()`, the three data members of the `SeqList<T>` object must be reset so that they reflect the representation of an empty list.

```
Front = Rear = 0;
ListLength = 0;
```

15.5.5

A small program using SeqList template class

The following program demonstrates most of the features of our `SeqList<T>` template class. It performs a mixture of additions and deletions to a list of integers.

```
#include<iostream.h>
#include "slist.h"
int main() {
    SeqList<int> P;
    cout << "List: (" << P << " )" << endl;
    for (int i = 1; i <= 5; ++i) {
        P.Add(i);
        cout << "List: (" << P << " )" << endl;
    }
    cout << "List: (" << P << " )" << endl;
    cout << "Removing: " << P.Remove() << endl;
    cout << "Removing: " << P.Remove() << endl;
    cout << "List: (" << P << " )" << endl;
    cout << "Removing all" << endl;
    P.RemoveAll();
    cout << "List: (" << P << " )" << endl;
    P.Add(1);
    cout << "List: (" << P << " )" << endl;
    return 0;
}
```

Note that the overloading of the insertion operator using member function `Insert()` is left to the exercises. The output of our example program is given below.

```
List: ( )
List: ( 1 )
List: ( 1 2 )
List: ( 1 2 3 )
List: ( 1 2 3 4 )
List: ( 1 2 3 4 5 )
List: ( 1 2 3 4 5 )
Removing: 1
Removing: 2
```

```
List: ( 3 4 5 )
Removing all
List: ( )
List: ( 1 )
```

15.5.6

A SeqList iterator class

An important list processing operation that is conspicuously absent in our example program is the individual referencing of elements in the list. We introduce this capability by supplying an *iterator* class template SeqElement that works in conjunction with SeqList and SeqItem. In general, an iterator class provides the means for individually accessing the elements of an associated container class. Depending upon the associated class, an iterator class may also provide the means to modify a referenced element. Our class SeqElement<T> provides both the ability to access and modify the elements of a list.

The definition of the SeqElement<T> class template is given in Listing 15.8.

The single constructor for the class SeqElement<T> requires a SeqList<T> object as its reference parameter L. At the end of the following code segment, an iterator a is defined using that constructor. The definition associates iterator a with the first element of list P.

```
SeqList<char> P;
P.Add('x');
P.Add('y');
P.Add('z');
SeqElement<char> a(P);
```

The SeqElement<T> iterator class provides an extensive set of capabilities. Two of the member capabilities are provided by overloading the operators ++ and (). The prefix version of the ++ operator is overloaded in the definition (to overload the postfix version, the keyword **void** is placed in the formal parameter declaration).

In our SeqElement<T> implementation, the grouping () operator is used to inspect the value of the element currently associated with the iterator. If the iterator is associated with an element that is not the last element in the list, then the ++ operator associates the iterator with the next element in the list. If instead, the iterator is associated with the last element in the list, then the ++ operator associates the iterator with no element in the list.

The code segment below uses the ++ and () operators to help display the first two elements of the previously defined list P.

```
cout << a() << endl;
++a;
cout << a() << endl;
```

Listing 15.8

*SeqElement class
template definition from
slist.h*

```
template <class T> class SeqElement {
  public:
    // default constructor
    SeqElement(SeqList<T> &L);
    // iterator operator for next element in list
    void operator++();
    // inspector for value of current element in list
    T operator()() const;
    // mutator for value of current element in list
    void operator=(const T &NewListValue);
    // method to determine if current element is first
    bool IsFirst() const;
    // method to determine if current element is last
    bool IsLast() const;
    // method to associate iterator with first element
    void ResetToFront();
    // cast to determine whether list is empty
    operator bool() const;
  private:
    SeqItem<T> *ItemPtr; // pointer to current element
    SeqList<T> &TheList; // list being iterated
    friend class SeqList<T>;
};
```

The output of the segment is

```
x
y
```

The assignment operator = is overloaded in SeqElement<T> to allow modification of the value of the element currently associated with the iterator. The assignment in the following code segment continues the use of the iterator a associated with the second element of list P. The member assignment operator of a is applied with an operand of 'w'.

```
a = 'w';
cout << "List: (" << P << " )" << endl;
```

The output of the segment is

```
List: ( x w z )
```

For client convenience, the iterator class also provides two **bool** facilitators IsFirst() and IsLast() that determine whether the iterator is currently associated respectively with the first and last elements of the list. So that the iterator can be reused, a member function ResetToFront() is supplied that associates the iterator with the first element of the list.

A cast member operator **bool** is also defined. The cast returns a true value if the iterator is associated with an actual element in the list; the cast returns a false value if the iterator is not currently associated with any element in the list. The existence of the cast permits an iterator to be used where a logical expression is expected (the conversion will be *automatically* attempted by the compiler). An example of where an automatic conversion is to occur appears in the test expression of the **while** statement in the following code segment:

```
a.ResetToFront();
while(a) {
    cout << "Element: " << a;
    if (a.IsFirst())
        cout << " first";
    if (a.IsLast())
        cout << " last";
    cout << endl;
    ++a;
}
```

The invocation of `a.ResetToFront()` prior to the loop resets the iterator to be associated with the element representing the `'x'` in our nonempty list. Because the test expression for a **while** loop expects a **bool** value and because we have defined such a conversion, the conversion is applied to the expression. Based on the behavior we have described for this conversion, the test expression will evaluate to true and the **while** body will be executed. Because a is presently associated with the first element in the list, the iteration will produce the following output:

```
Element: x first
```

The last statement in the body of the loop causes the iterator to be associated with the element representing `'w'`. The loop is again iterated to produce as its output

```
Element: w
```

The iteration also causes iterator a to be associated with the last element in the list that is representing the `'z'`. The loop is again iterated to produce as its output

```
Element: z last
```

The iteration also causes the iterator to lose its association with any particular element. When the test expression is evaluated this time, based upon the behavior we described for the conversion, the test expression will evaluate to false.

15.5.7

Implementation of the SeqElement iterator class

An implementation of the `SeqElement<T>` member functions and operators is given in Listing 15.9. The definitions of the various members are relatively straightforward.

The `SeqElement<T>` constructor sets both of its data members using an initialization list. Because an iterator is associated with a single list during its existence, data member `TheList` is declared to be a reference object of type `SeqList<T>&`. Once it is initialized with parameter `L`, the value of `TheList` cannot be changed during program execution. `ItemPtr`, the other SeqEle-

Listing 15.9

SeqElement member and auxiliary functions and operators from slist.h

```
// SeqElement(): constructor
template <class T>
 SeqElement<T>::SeqElement(SeqList<T> &L)
 :  ItemPtr(L.Front), TheList(L) {
   // no code needed
}
// ++: SeqElement() successor iterator
template <class T> void SeqElement<T>::operator++() {
   assert(ItemPtr != 0);
   ItemPtr = ItemPtr->Successor;
}
// (): SeqElement() data inspector
template <class T> T SeqElement<T>::operator()() const{
   assert(ItemPtr != 0);
   return ItemPtr->ItemValue;
}
// =: SeqElement() data mutator
template <class T> void SeqElement<T>::operator=(
 const T &NewListValue) {
   assert(ItemPtr != 0);
   ItemPtr->ItemValue = NewListValue;
}
// bool: indicates whether there is a list element
template <class T> void SeqElement<T>::operator bool()
 const {
   return ItemPtr != 0;
}
// IsFirst(): indicates whether first element
template <class T> bool SeqElement<T>::IsFirst() const{
   assert(ItemPtr != 0);
   return TheList.Front == ItemPtr;
}
// IsLast(): indicates whether last element
template <class T> bool SeqElement<T>::IsLast() const {
   assert(ItemPtr != 0);
   return ItemPtr->Successor == 0;
}
// ResetToFront(): associate with first element
template <class T> void SeqElement<T>::ResetToFront() {
   ItemPtr = TheList.Front;
}
// <<: overload insertions for list element
template <class T>ostream& operator<<(ostream &sout,
 const SeqElement<T> &a) {
   return sout << a();
}
```

ment<T> data member, is initialized to the value of the expression L.Front. If L is a nonempty list, then the constructed iterator object is associated with the first element in the list. If L is empty, then L.Front has the null value and the iterator is not currently associated with any element.

The **bool** conversion operator is one of the most straightforward of the SeqElement<T> members. The return value is computed by comparing ItemPtr to the null address. If the values are different, then the iterator is associated with an element in the list. If the values are the same, then the iterator is not associated with an element in the list.

The increment operator ++ for a SeqElement<T> iterator accomplishes its task by first asserting that the iterator is currently pointing to an actual element. If so, it is possible to evaluate the expression ItemPtr->Successor. The value of the expression is either the address of the next element in the list (if there is another element) or it is the null address (if the iterator is currently associated with the last element in the list). Either way the value of expression ItemPtr->Successor is now the correct value for ItemPtr. Because SeqElement<T> is a friend class of the SeqItem<T> class, the SeqItem<T> data member ItemPtr->Successor can be accessed by a SeqElement<T> member function.

Like the ++ operator, the operator () for a SeqElement<T> iterator first determines whether there is an associated element. If so, then the return value of the operation is the list value of the associated element, which is simply ItemPtr->ItemValue. Similarly, a determination of whether the iterator is associated with a list element is first made by the member assignment operator = before attempting to update ItemPtr->ItemValue with the value of operand NewListValue.

Member function IsFirst() is also meant to be invoked only if the iterator is associated with an element from the list. If so, then the address of the element to which the iterator is currently associated is compared to the address pointed to by the expression TheList->Front. If the addresses match, then the iterator is associated with the first element.

Member function IsLast() operates in a manner comparable to IsFirst(). In its comparison, IsLast() matches the address of the element to which the iterator is currently associated with the address pointed to by the expression TheList->Rear. If the addresses match, then the iterator is associated with the last element.

For client convenience, the insertion operator is overloaded for a SeqElement<T> iterator object. Its task is accomplished by simply inserting the value associated with the current element to output stream operand sout.

15.6

POLYMORPHISM

Suppose you want to develop a client program that manipulates figures using the various shapes designed in Chapter 14. You would probably like to have a collection of figure objects where each figure object is viewed as a list of the various shapes composing the figure being represented. In general, such a list would be a heterogeneous list—there could be for example, circles, rectangles, and triangles. In order to process a heterogeneous list, we need polymorphic capabilities.

What type of object can represent a collection of disparate shapes? Your first guess might be a simple Shape array because Shape is the base class for our various shapes. After all, a CircleShape is a Shape, a Rectangle-Shape is a Shape, and a TriangleShape is a Shape, and so on.

Suppose a window W and a position P have been previously defined as well as the objects S, R, T, and C that are given below.

```
SquareShape S(W, P, Blue, 1);
TriangleShape T(W, P, Red, 1);
RectangleShape R(W,P, Yellow, 3, 2);
CircleShape C(W, P, Yellow, 4);
```

Also suppose that an array A of Shape objects have been defined in the following manner:

```
Shape A[4] = {S, T, R, C}; // figure A is composed of
                           // four shapes
```

Can we display our figure A using the following loop?

```
for (int i = 0; i < 4; ++i) {
   A[i].Draw();
}
```

The answer is no because A is an array of Shape objects and there is no Shape::Draw() member function to invoke iteratively.

A next attempt might be to add a Draw() member function to the Shape class as in Listing 15.10 to act as a placeholder.

Listing 15.10

Shape definition with a placeholder Draw() function

```
class Shape : public WindowObject {
   public:
      Shape(SimpleWindow &w, const Position &p,
       const color c = Red);
      color GetColor() const;
      void SetColor(const color c);
      void Draw() { cout << GetColor(); };
   private:
      color Color;
};
```

Because a Shape object does not have a full specification, the only characteristic of the object that a Draw() function can express is an indication of its color. However, the **for** loop still does not work as desired—now the Shape::Draw() function is iteratively invoked. In particular, although S represents a SquareShape, A[0] is only a Shape. The initialization of A[0] using S did not assign all of the SquareShape properties to A[0], only the Shape members are copied.

Your next attempt in representing a figure might be to have A be an array of Shape pointers

```
Shape *A[4] = {&S, &T, &R, &C};
```

where, for example, based on the preceding definition, `A[0]` is a pointer to a `SquareShape` and `A[1]` is a pointer to a `TriangleShape`, and so on. The earlier **for** loop cannot be used because the elements of `A` are no longer `Shape` objects but pointers to `Shape` objects. Now consider the following **for** loop. Does this loop perform the desired actions of drawing the various `Shape` objects?

```
for (int i = 0; i < 4; ++i)
    A[i]->Draw();
```

The answer depends upon how base class `Shape` is defined. If the base class `Shape` for our derived shape classes is defined as in Listing 15.11, where the member function `Draw()` has the modifier **virtual** applied to it, then the new loop does work in the desired manner.

Listing 15.11

Shape class definition with a virtual Draw() function

```
class Shape : public WindowObject {
  public:
     Shape(SimpleWindow &w, const Position &p,
      const color c = Red);
     color GetColor() const;
     void SetColor(const color c);
     virtual void Draw();          // virtual function!
  private:
     color Color;
};
```

In the new loop, when i equals 0, member function `Square-Shape::Draw()` is invoked to process `A[0]`, and when i equals 1, member function `TriangleShape::Draw()` is invoked to process `A[1]`, and so on. *It is not the type of pointer that determines the invocation, but the type of object at the location to which the pointer refers!* The reason this implementation works is that the `Draw()` member function for base class `Shape` is a *virtual function.*

If a virtual function is invoked via either a dereferenced pointer or a reference object, then the actual function to be run is determined from the type of object that is stored at the memory location being accessed rather than the type of the pointer or reference object. The definition of the derived function *overrides* the definition of the base class version. In general, the determination of which virtual function to use cannot be made at compile time and must instead be made during run time. As a result, slightly more overhead is associated with the invocation of a virtual function than with a nonvirtual function.

15.7

VIRTUAL FUNCTION NUANCES

The invocation `A[i]->Draw()` in the **for** loop of the previous section represents our first true use of polymorphism—the invocation performs different actions depending upon the type of object being accessed. This polymorphic capability in dealing with its individual elements effectively makes `A` a hetero-

Programming
Tip

geneous collection. To see some of the subtleties involving virtual functions, suppose that the definitions of Listing 15.12 are in effect for the next several examples.

As a first example, try to determine the output of the following code segment:

```
A.Display();
B.Display();
C.Display();
Ptr = &A;
Ptr->Display();
Ptr = &B;
Ptr->Display();
Ptr = &C;
Ptr->Display();
```

The first three lines of output produced by the segment are

```
BaseClass Display
DerivedClass1 Display
DerivedClass2 Display
```

These output lines occur because objects A, B, and C are of type BaseClass, DerivedClass1, and DerivedClass2, respectively, and therefore invoke the Display() functions BaseClass::Display(), DerivedClass1::Display(), and DerivedClass2:Display().

The next three lines of output produced by the segment are

```
BaseClass Display
DerivedClass1 Display
DerivedClass2 Display
```

This output occurs because Ptr is a pointer to a BaseClass object that invokes the virtual member function Display() through dereferencing. The decision on which virtual function to invoke is made at run time where it is determined that Ptr in successive displays is pointing to memory where BaseClass, DerivedClass1, and DerivedClass2 objects are stored.

Listing 15.12

Some definitions for illustrating virtual function basics

```cpp
class BaseClass {
   public:
      BaseClass() { return; };
      virtual void Display() {
         cout << "BaseClass Display" << endl;
      };
      void Print() {
         cout << "BaseClass Print" << endl;
      };
};
class DerivedClass1 : public BaseClass {
   public:
      DerivedClass1() { return; };
      virtual void Display() {
         cout << "DerivedClass1 Display" << endl;
      };
      void Print() {
         cout << "DerivedClass1 Print" << endl;
      };
};
class DerivedClass2 : public BaseClass {
   public:
      DerivedClass2() { return; };
      virtual void Display() {
         cout << "DerivedClass2 Display" << endl;
      };
      void Print() {
         cout << "DerivedClass2 Print" << endl;
      };
};
class DerivedClass3 : public BaseClass {
   public:
      DerivedClass3() { return; };
      virtual void Display(int i) {
         cout << "DerivedClass3 Display " << i << endl;
      };
      void Print() {
         cout << "DerivedClass3 Print" << endl;
      };
};
void Output(BaseClass &R) {
   R.Display();
}

BaseClass A;
DerivedClass1 B;
DerivedClass2 C;
DerivedClass3 D;

BaseClass *Ptr;
```

Now suppose the following code segment is executed:

```cpp
A = B;
A.Display();
A = C;
A.Display();
```

The output produced by this segment is

```
BaseClass Display
BaseClass Display
```

This output occurs because A is a BaseClass. Therefore, the two assignments to A copy over only the BaseClass data members, which means that the Display() function remains the BaseClass one.

If function Output() of Listing 15.12 is invoked as below

```
Output(A);
Output(B);
Output(C);
```

then the output produced by the segment is

```
BaseClass Display
DerivedClass1 Display
DerivedClass2 Display
```

This output occurs because the parameter to Output() is a reference parameter. Thus the type of object at the memory location being referenced determines which virtual member function is invoked.

In still another use of the objects from Listing 15.12, consider the following code segment:

```
Ptr = &A;
Ptr->Print();
Ptr = &B;
Ptr->Print();
Ptr = &C;
Ptr->Print();
```

The output produced by the segment is

```
BaseClass Print
BaseClass Print
BaseClass Print
```

This output is produced because member function Print() is not virtual. Therefore, the decision on which member function to invoke is determined at compile time, which in turn causes the base class member function to be used.

Note that the Display() functions for the derived classes DerivedClass1 and DerivedClass2 would remain virtual even if they were not explicitly given the modifier **virtual** as the Display() function for BaseClass was given. The modifier is unnecessary because a member function of a derived class is automatically virtual if it has the same name and signature as a virtual base class member function. Although the modifier **virtual** is syntactically unnecessary in such cases, it is generally added to provide supporting information to a reader of the derived class definition.

Listing 15.12 also derives the class DerivedClass3 from BaseClass. DerivedClass3 defines a member function Display() with a signature different from the Display() of BaseClass. As such, the following statement would be illegal because the `BaseClass` member function `Display()` is hidden.

```
D.Display(); // illegal: Display() is hidden
```

However, the invocations of `Display()` in the following code segment are legal

```
D.Display(3);
D.BaseClass::Display();
Ptr = &D;
Ptr->Display();
```

and produce the following output:

```
DerivedClass3 Display 3
BaseClass Display
BaseClass Display
```

The first of the preceding invocations of `Display()` for obvious reasons calls the `Display()` of `DerivedClass3`. The second invocation uses the scope operator to explicitly call the `Display()` of `BaseClass`. Because a `DerivedClass3` object does not have a `Display()` member function with an empty parameter list and because a `DerivedClass3` object is a `Base-Class` object, the expression `Ptr->Display()` in its dereferencing of `BaseClass` pointer `Ptr` invokes the `Display()` of `BaseClass`.

Note that when overriding a base class member function, the derived class function cannot differ only in return type. The signatures of the two functions must be different.

Programming Tip

Assume reuse

When defining a class, unless you know it can never serve as a base class for a derived class, give the class a virtual destructor. For example, a `Shape` class could have a destructor with an empty function body. By making the destructor virtual, all derived destructors will also be virtual, and then whenever an object is deleted, the correct destructor will be invoked regardless of the context.

15.8

ABSTRACT BASE CLASSES

A virtual member function is a *pure virtual function* if it has no implementation. A pure virtual function is defined by assigning that function the null address within its class definition. For example, the class definition of `Shape` in Listing 15.13 makes its member function `Draw()` a pure virtual function. A class with a pure virtual function is known as an *abstract base class*.

Because an abstract base class does not have a complete implementation, attempting to define an object of an abstract base class type through construction is illegal. In particular, there can be no construction of an object of an

Listing 15.13

Shape class definition with a pure virtual Draw() function from vshape.h

```
class Shape : public WindowObject {
  public:
      Shape(SimpleWindow &w, const Position &p,
       const color c = Red);
      color GetColor() const;
      void SetColor(const color c);
      virtual void Draw() = 0; // pure virtual function!
  private:
      color Color;
};
```

abstract base class type in a definition nor as a return value nor as a value parameter. Thus, the declaration and prototypes below are illegal.

```
Shape S;            // illegal: no Shape definition
Shape f();          // illegal: no Shape return value
void f(Shape S);    // illegal: no Shape value
                    // parameter
```

Because no construction is needed, you may use an abstract base class as a reference. Therefore, the following declarations and prototypes using Shape are legal.

```
TriangleShape T(W, P, Red, 1);
Shape &R = T;       // T is a TriangleShape that is
                    // a Shape
Shape& F();         // can return a reference to an
                    // existing shape
void G(Shape &S);   // can pass an existing Shape as
                    // a reference
```

The main use of an abstract base class is to provide a standard interface for derived classes. An abstract base class describes the interface that derived classes must support. However, when appropriate, the abstract base class leaves the implementation of that functionality to the derived classes. For this reason, Draw() was made a pure virtual function in Listing 15.13—the drawing activities for specific shapes are left to the derived shape classes.

In the following example, we use the functionality of the abstract base class Shape to create and display a simple drawing of a house. The two functions that implement this activity are given in Program 15.2. The output of the program is given in Figure 15.1. The functions are named BuildHouse() and DrawFigure(). Both functions manipulate a sequential list object of type SeqList<Shape*>. A sequential list allows us to add as many as shapes as needed to represent the house.

Function BuildHouse() returns a pointer to a sequential list of type SeqList<Shape*>. Each element of that list is a pointer to a component shape of the drawing. Because both the shapes that compose the figure and the sequential list whose elements point to those shapes must exist after the completion of BuildHouse(), these objects are constructed by BuildHouse() using free store memory.

The house representation is quite simple—the elements in the sequential list point to only six shapes. The shapes are a frame for the house, a roof, a

Figure 15.1

*Dream house drawing
using BuildHouse()
and DrawFigure()*

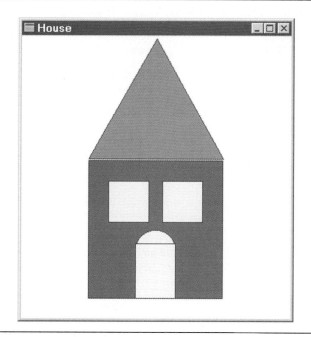

door, a skylight over the door, and two upstairs windows. The frame and windows are `SquareShape` objects; the roof is a `TriangleShape` object; the door is a `RectangleShape` object; and the skylight is a `CircleShape` object. The figure is composed in a manner that the door is drawn after the skylight. Because the upper part of the door overlaps the skylight, the skylight appears to be a semicircle.

The purpose of function `DrawFigure()` is to iteratively invoke the `Draw()` functions of the shapes to which the elements of F point. Function `DrawFigure()` uses an iterator `Part` of type `SeqElement<Shape*>` to accomplish this task. The body of the **for** loop that processes the various elements of list is

```
Part()->Draw();
```

The subexpression `Part()` refers to the list value currently associated with the iterator. This value is a pointer to one of the shapes in the figure. The dereferencing operator is then applied so that the `Draw()` member function can be invoked. Because `Shape` has a virtual `Draw()` function, the `Draw()` function of the derived class is invoked.

Program 15.2

House building and displaying from house.cpp

```
// Program 15.2: Display a dream house
#include "vshape.h"
#include "triangle.h"
#include "circle.h"
#include "rect.h"
#include "square.h"
#include "slist.h"

// prototypes
SeqList<Shape*>* BuildHouse(SimpleWindow &W);
void DrawFigure(SeqList<Shape*> *F);

// ApiMain(); manage building and display of house
int ApiMain() {
  SimpleWindow Window("House", 10, 10);
  Window.Open();
  SeqList<Shape*> *DreamHouse = BuildHouse(Window);
  DrawFigure(DreamHouse);
  return 0;
}

// BuildHouse(): use basic shapes to make a house
SeqList<Shape*>* BuildHouse(SimpleWindow &W) {
  // House composed of a list of parts
  SeqList<Shape*> *House = new SeqList<Shape*>;

  House->Add( // house has a square frame
    new SquareShape(W, Position(5, 7), Blue, 5)
  );

  House->Add( // house has a triangular roof
    new TriangleShape(W, Position(5, 3), Red, 5)
  );

  House->Add( // house has a skylight
    new CircleShape(W, Position(5, 7.75), Yellow, 1.5)
  );

  House->Add( // house has a door
    new RectangleShape(W, Position(5, 8.5), Yellow,
      1.5, 2)
  );

  House->Add( // house a left window
    new SquareShape(W, Position(4,6), Yellow, 1.5)
  );

  House->Add( // house has a right window
    new SquareShape(W, Position(6,6), Yellow, 1.5)
  );

  return House;
}

// DrawFigure(): draw shapes in list F
void DrawFigure(SeqList<Shape*> *F) {
  for (SeqElement<Shape*> Part(*F); Part; ++Part)
    Part()->Draw();
}
```

Functions `BuildHouse()` and `DrawFigure()` are used by `Api-Main()` in Program 15.2 to produce and display the object to which `Dream-House` points.

```
SeqList<Shape*> *DreamHouse = BuildHouse(Window);
DrawFigure(DreamHouse);
```

15.9

VIRTUAL MULTIPLE INHERITANCE

The modifier **virtual** can also be used in conjunction with class derivation. It is useful when a derived class inherits from the same base class multiple times. If the modifier is applied, then only one copy of each base class data member is inherited. To illustrate this behavior, we first define a class `BaseClass` with a data member `DataValue` of type **int** and two derived classes `DerivedClass1` and `DerivedClass2` from `BaseClass`.

```
class BaseClass {
    protected:
        int DataValue;
};
class DerivedClass1 : public BaseClass {
    // ...
};
class DerivedClass2 : public BaseClass {
    // ...
};
```

If a class `MultipleClass1` is derived from both `DerivedClass1` and `DerivedClass2` without using the modifier **virtual**, then objects of type `MultipleClass1` would have two distinct data members named `Data-Value`.

```
class MultipleClass1
  : public DerivedClass1, public DerivedClass2 {
    // ...
};
```

A `MultipleClass1` member function needs to use the resolution operator to distinguish between the two data members. The following insertion and extraction are legal because they are unambiguous references to specific `Dat-aValue` objects.

```
// inside a MultipleClass1 member function
cout << DerivedClass1::DataValue;  // unambiguous
cin >> DerivedClass2::DataValue;   // unambiguous
```

The following assignment statement is not legal in a `MultipleClass1` member function because there is no context to distinguish which `DataValue` is being referenced.

```
// inside a MultipleClass1 member function
DataValue = 1024;                          // ambiguous
```

To see the effect of the modifier **virtual** in a class derivation, suppose we define a class MultipleClass2, which is virtually derived from both DerivedClass3 and DerivedClass4 which are in turn virtually derived from BaseClass.

```
class DerivedClass3 : virtual public BaseClass {
    // ...
};
class DerivedClass4 : virtual public BaseClass {
    // ...
};
class MultipleClass2
  : virtual public DerivedClass1,
    virtual public DerivedClass2 {
    // ...
};
```

Inside a member function of MultipleClass2, we do not need to use the resolution operator to distinguish which DataValue is being referenced—the modifier **virtual** ensures that we have only one data member DataValue. The data member can be referenced directly or by using the resolution operator in conjunction with the base classes. Thus, the following insertion statements all display the same value.

```
// inside a MultipleClass2 member function
cout << DataValue << endl;
cout << BaseClass::DataValue << endl;
cout << DerivedClass1::DataValue << endl;
cout << DerivedClass1::DataValue << endl;
```

History of Computing

The information superhighway

While advances in computing will yield more computational power, advances in computer networking will bring that power into more and more homes. Vast amounts of information will be accessible via computer networks. For example, at our university, many of the works of Thomas Jefferson have been made available via the Internet or as it is sometimes known, the information superhighway. This electronic availability means that scholars all over the world can have access to this work without ever leaving their offices. In the course for which this textbook was written, every student has an electronic mail account (E-mail) and access to a bulletin board or newsgroup devoted to the class. If students have questions, they can send E-mail to the instructor rather than telephone or attempt to see the instructor in person. Usually, they receive a prompt answer to their question. In addition, as questions are answered, both the question and the answer are posted to the course newsgroup. Thus by reading articles in the newsgroup periodically, a student can benefit from questions asked by other students, much as if everyone were in the classroom. Inexpensive and fast communication will change the way we interact. How broad, inexpensive, high-speed access to information changes society is a matter of intense interest to both computer and social scientists. We definitely live in interesting times.

15.10

POINTS TO REMEMBER

- Polymorphism is a language mechanism that permits the same interface to invoke different functions or operators depending upon the type of objects using the interface.

- Name reuse in function overloading is a primitive form of polymorphism. Another method of achieving syntactic polymorphism is the use of function and class templates.

- A function template is a mechanism for generating a new function.

- A class template is a mechanism for generating a new class.

- A template parameter can be either a type or a value.

- The type template parameters in a function template definition can be used to specify the return type and parameter types of the generated function.

- All of the template parameters in a function template definition must be used in the function interface. The template parameters can also be used in the function body.

- The proposed C++ standard describes a standard template library that in part includes template versions of common computing tasks such as searching and sorting.

- All of the template parameters in a class template must be used in the definition of the class interface.

- Qualifiers are part of member function signatures. As a result, a compiler can distinguish in an invocation of an overloaded function whether the **const** or non-**const** member is being invoked. The **const** member is invoked for **const** objects, the non-**const** member is invoked for non-**const** objects.

- Class templates are particularly useful in the development of container class ADTs. A container ADT represents a list of objects.

- One major way of classifying container ADTs is by whether they efficiently support random access or only sequential access to the elements in the list.

- Through the use of class templates, we can develop a container class that represents lists in an arraylike manner. A major reason that such a container class is preferred to standard arrays is that the container class does not suffer array use limitations (e.g., a container class can be the return type of a function or be a value parameter).

- A linked list is a method for implementing a collection of values. A linked list represents the collection using a group of objects that have two components. One component maintains the list value being represented; the other component is one or more pointers to other objects in the list representation. One pointer that is normally present is a successor pointer that points to the next object in the representation.

- The standard template library defines a collection of common container classes for list representation. The representations differ in how the elements of the list can be accessed. Various container classes support random access of the elements, sequential access of the elements, and associative access of the elements.

- Often a container class will have an iterator class associated with it. The iterator class provides the means for iteratively accessing the various elements of the list.

- Conversion operators can be overloaded. A standard conversion operator to overload is **bool**. When the conversion is applied to the object of the specified type, the conversion can produce a value that indicates whether the object has a desired value. For example, in the SeqElement iterator class, the **bool** operator was overloaded to indicate whether the iterator object currently represented a valid element in the list.

- The C++ method of achieving true polymorphism is through virtual functions.

- A virtual function is required to be a member function.

- If a function of a derived class has the same name and type as a virtual function of its base class, then the member function of the derived class overrides the base class function.

- With a virtual function, the decision on which actual function is being invoked in an interface is delayed until run time. The decision will be based upon the type of object being accessed by a pointer or reference object, rather than by the type of the pointer or reference object.

- By declaring an array of pointers for a common base type, the array can be used to represent a heterogeneous list—the individual elements can point to objects of the different derived types from that base class.

- When a virtual function is invoked by dereferencing one of the elements in a heterogeneous list, the action to be taken can be specific to the derived type of the object to which the pointer refers. Such code will continue to work properly even if a new derived type is defined and one of its objects is added to the list.

- Destructors for a base class are typically virtual. That way, regardless of the context of the destruction, the appropriate destructor is invoked.

- A pure virtual function is a virtual function to which the pure specifier has been applied, i.e., it has been assigned the null address.

- A pure virtual function has no implementation.

- It is not possible to construct an object from a class with a pure virtual function because the construction cannot be completed.

- A class with a pure virtual function is an abstract base class.

- An abstract base class is used to describe the common interface of its derived classes. For example, because a common activity of shape manipulation is drawing the shape to the display, a virtual member function Draw() should be part of the shape common interface. Because only a derived shape has sufficient characteristics to be rendered to a display, the `Draw()` member should be a pure virtual function.

■ The modifier **virtual** can be used in conjunction with class derivation.

■ The modifier **virtual** is useful when a derived class inherits from the same base class multiple times. The modifier indicates that there should be only one copy of each data member from that base class. If the modifier is not present, then the normal rules of multiple inheritance apply, which means that each inherited class supplies a copy of the data member.

15.11
TO DELVE FURTHER

For further information on the standard template library consider the following references.

■ Working Paper for the Draft Proposed International Standard for Information Systems—Programming Language C++, X3J16/96-0018 WG21/N0836, Washington: American National Standards Institute, 1996.

■ D. R. Musser and A. Saini, *STL Tutorial and Reference Guide*, Reading, MA: Addison-Wesley, 1995.

■ P. J. Plauger, A. Stepanov, M. Lee, and D. R. Musser, *The Standard Template Library*, Englewood Cliffs, NJ: Prentice-Hall, 1996.

15.12
EXERCISES

15.1 Speculate why templates are not considered as important as virtual functions in terms of the object-oriented paradigm.

15.2 Discuss why templates as a language mechanism are considered to be closer to name reuse in function overloading than to pure polymorphism.

15.3 Identify and correct the error(s) in the following definition so that it is a valid template.

```
template <type S, type T, int n> S f(S A[n]) {
    S x;
    cin >> x;
    A[x] = x;
}
```

15.4 Why is the decision on which virtual function to invoke made at run time rather than compile time?

15.5 Implement a template version of a search function for determining whether an array contains a particular value. Will your template function work if you use the template container class `Array` as the template parameter type? Why?

15.6 Implement a template version of `QuickSort()`.

15.7 Design and implement a template function `min()` for finding the minimum value in a list represented by a `SeqList<T>` object.

15.8 Design and implement a template function `max()` for finding the maximum value in a list represented by a `SeqList<T>` object.

15.9 Design and implement a template function `Search()` for determining whether a given value appears in a list represented by a `SeqList<T>` object. If the given value is in the list, function `Search()` should return a `SeqElement<T>` iterator that is associated with an element with that value. If the given value is not in the list, function `Search()` should return a `SeqElement<T>` iterator that is not associated with any value in the list.

15.10 Design and implement a template function `Sort()` that sorts a list represented by a `SeqList<T>` object.

15.11 Redo the `Rational` class so that the type of the data members comes from a template type representing an integral value type. Test your implementation by trying the various standard integral types. Also test your implementation by using the `BigNum` ADT.

15.12 Implement the template class `Bunch<T,n>`.

15.13 Add a member function `Resize()` with a single **int** parameter n to the `Array<T>` ADT that alters the representation of the list being represented, so that the object now represents a list with n elements. An element from the old list being represented should remain represented if its index remains valid.

15.14 Redesign and reimplement the `Array<T>` ADT so that a client can specify a desired subscript interval. For example, the definition

```
Array<float> GNP(1990, 1999, 0);
```

represents an array of 10 elements. The first element has an index of 1990; the last element has an index of 1999. The elements are all initialized to 0.

15.15 No implementation of a copy constructor or a member assignment is specified for `SeqList<T>` ADT. What type of operations (if any) are performed by default? Why? Explicitly implement deep copy versions of the two member operations.

15.16 Modify the `SeqList<T>` ADT by including a member function `Insert()` that adds a new element to the beginning of the list.

15.17 Modify the `SeqList<T>` ADT by including a member function `Pop()` that removes the last element from the list.

15.18 Modify the `SeqList<T>` ADT by including a member operator `[]` whose integer operand i is an index into the list. The operator returns a reference to the ith element in the list being represented.

15.19 What is the output of the following code segment? Why?

```
SeqList<int> P;
P.Add(1);
P.Add(2);
P.Add(3);
SeqElement<int> a(P);
SeqElement<int> b(P);
++a;
++a;
a = b();
P.Insert(cout);
```

15.20 Why is the `SeqElement<T>` iterator functionality developed in a separate class rather than being part of the `SeqList<T>` class.

15.21 Redesign the `SeqElement<T>` iterator ADT so that member functions `InsertBefore()` and `InsertAfter()` are defined. These functions have a single parameter that represents a value to be added to the list. The functions respectively add this value to the list before and after the current element associated with the iterator object.

15.22 Modify `SeqElement<T>` to allow the element currently associated with an iterator to be deleted.

15.23 Reimplement `SeqList<T>` member function `Insert()` to make use of the iterator class `SeqElement<T>`.

15.24 Reimplement `SeqList<T>` member function `RemoveAll()` to make use of the iterator class `SeqElement<T>`.

15.25 Define a member addition operator for `SeqList<T>` objects. The result should append a copy of the elements represented by the right operand `SeqList<T>` to the end of the list of the invoking `SeqList` object.

15.26 Define a member subtraction operator for `SeqList<T>` objects. The result should remove all occurrences of the elements represented by the right operand `SeqList<T>` from the list of the invoking `SeqList<T>` object.

15.27 Overload the insertion operator for `SeqList<T>` objects by using the `SeqList<T>` member function `Insert()`.

15.28 Redesign and implement the `SeqList<T>` and `SeqItem<T>` ADTs so that the list being represented is *doubly linked*. The elements in a doubly-linked list have both successor and predecessor pointers. Also redesign and reimplement the iterator class `SeqElement<T>` to support forward and backward progression through the list.

15.29 Are the assertion statements for `SeqElement<T>` member functions `IsFirst()` and `IsLast()` appropriate; that is, should these members be like the **bool** conversion member?

15.30 Why is no check needed in the overloading of the insertion operator for a `SeqElement<T>` to make sure that the iterator is associated with an actual element?

15.31 What changes to `Array<T>` and `SeqList<T>` need to be made to make them appropriate base classes for inheritance?

15.32 Speculate why pure virtual functions are used rather than virtual functions that simply do an immediate return. Consider what would happen if a derived class did not have an overriding definition.

15.33 Which of the following activities are appropriate actions for inclusion as virtual functions in the abstract base class Shape? Why?

   a) Rotating.

   b) Repositioning.

   c) Scaling.

   d) Flipping.

   e) Setting a stipple pattern.

15.34 Which of the activities in the previous exercise are appropriate actions for inclusion as pure virtual functions in the abstract base class Shape? Why?

15.35 Design an abstract base class for the writing instrument hierarchy discussed in Chapter 14. Design derived classes for various types of writing instruments. Use insertion statements in your implementation to indicate the particular instrument property associated with the various member functions.

15.36 Design a hierarchy for vehicles. From the base class derive classes that organize vehicles by energy source—fossil fuel, solar, chemical, steam, electric, or nuclear; by use—commercial, individual, agricultural, or governmental; and by whether the vehicle is wheeled or nonwheeled. Further develop the hierarchy for classes for snowmobiles, school buses, and station wagons. Justify which functions are virtual or pure virtual.

15.37 Design a hierarchy for representing trees. Justify which functions are virtual or pure virtual.

15.38 Design a hierarchy for representing birds. Justify which functions are virtual or pure virtual.

15.39 Design a class Segment that makes use of the previously defined EzWindows class Position to specify the end points of a line. Redefine the shape hierarchy to describe the polygonal shapes using a list of Segment objects.

15.40 Design and develop a class CardIterator to be associated with the class Deck of Chapter 10. The class should have the following member functions:

   ■ A default constructor that initializes its value to a representation of the two of clubs.

   ■ A constructor that sets its value to a particular representation.

   ■ **bool** facilitators IsFirst() and IsLast() that indicate whether the current value is the first or last value in a canonical ordering of a deck of cards.

- An inspector `Current()` with a return type of `Card` that returns the value of the current card.
- A mutator `Next()` with a return type of `Card` that resets the value of the current card to the next card in the canonical ordering and then returns that value.

15.41 Write a function `BuildPerson()` similar to `BuildHouse()` that uses the abstract base class `Shape` and the various derived classes to construct a picture of a person. An example person is given below. Display your person using the function `DrawFigure()`.

CHAPTER 16

Software project — bug hunt!

Introduction

We are now ready to put some of the object-oriented skills we have learned to use. In this chapter we design and implement a program called Bug Hunt. The object of the game is eliminate bugs that scurry around inside a window. The bugs are eliminated by swatting them with the mouse. The implementation of the game will require the use of most of the object-oriented features of C++ we have covered including inheritance, virtual functions, and polymorphism. The implementation of the game will make heavy use of the EzWindows API.

Key Concepts

- encapsulation
- inheritance
- derived class
- virtual functions
- polymorphism
- object-oriented design

16.1

BUG HUNT

Bug Hunt is simple to play. A bug is scurrying around in a window. The object of the game is to get rid of the bug. A bug is eliminated by clicking the mouse when the sprite is positioned over a bug. Like bugs in programs, Bug Hunt bugs are hard to get rid of. The player has to click on a bug several times before it is eliminated. Once the player gets rid of a bug, another trickier bug appears. The game ends when there are no more bugs to get rid of. If the player misses a bug, the game starts over from the beginning.

Sounds simple enough, so let's begin with the high-level design of the game. The game consists of several objects. From the description above, it is obvious that a key object is a bug. In fact, this version of the game has two types of bugs—a slow bug that's easy to get rid of and a fast bug that's hard to eliminate. Inheritance will prove useful in realizing an implementation of the bugs. Another object is the window that contains the bugs. We will use the EzWindows class `SimpleWindow` to implement the window. Finally, we need an object that controls the play of the game, a game controller. It sets up the game, maintains the state of the game, and controls the game as it progresses. Figure 16.1 illustrates some aspects of the high-level design of the program.

Using EzWindows, the game controller receives both mouse-click events and timer-tick events from the window. On a mouse-click event, the game controller sends a message to the bug to see if it is pointed at. If so, the bug records the hit. If the bug has been hit enough times, it dies. When a bug dies, the game controller removes the bug and advances the game to the next stage. If the mouse click is not pointing at the bug, then the game controller starts the game over from the beginning.

On timer-tick events, the game controller tells the bug to move. If the timer-tick events occur fast enough, the bug appears to scurry around within the window. Of course, how the bug moves is part of the implementation of the bug, and the game controller need not know or understand how that is done.

Our program will consist of three modules. The module `bug.cpp` will contain the code that relates to the implementation of the bugs. The module `control.cpp` will contain the implementation of the game controller, and `bughunt.cpp` will contain the start-up and cleanup code for the program (i.e., `ApiMain()` and `ApiEnd()`). Each module will have a corresponding `.h` file that contains the interface to the module. Of course, the program will be linked with the EzWindows API library code.

Since Bug Hunt centers around the behavior of the bug, let's begin with it.

Figure 16.1

*High-level design of
Bug Hunt*

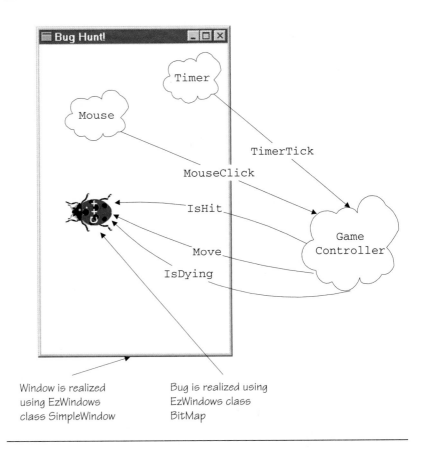

Window is realized
using EzWindows
class SimpleWindow

Bug is realized using
EzWindows class
BitMap

16.2

BASE CLASS BUG

Because the game requires different types of bugs, it makes sense to consider using inheritance. The basic idea is to have a base class with all the common behaviors required by a bug and to create specialized versions of bugs (i.e., with different behaviors) via inheritance. As shown in Figure 16.2, two types of bugs will be derived from the base class Bug—SlowBug and FastBug. The difference between a SlowBug and a FastBug is how they move.

From the perspective of the game controller, the interface to the two types of bugs should be the same. So let's begin our design by considering the behaviors or methods that a bug needs from the perspective of the game controller. As Figure 16.1 shows, the game controller needs to be able to ask a bug if the bug was hit, it needs to be able to make a bug move, and it needs to find out if the bug is dying. In addition, the game controller needs to be able to create and kill bugs as the game progresses.

Figure 16.2
FastBug and SlowBug are derived from Bug

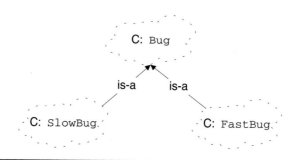

To summarize, the public interface for Bug should include

- Move—Bug moves to next location in the window.
- IsHit—Bug determines if the supplied window coordinates are within it. If so, it updates the count of hits it has taken and it returns true; otherwise, it returns false.
- IsDying—Bug returns true if it the number of hits taken is equal to or greater than the number of hits required to kill it.
- Create—Bug is created and drawn in the window.
- Kill—Bug is removed from the window.

What attributes should Bug have? Because a Bug is displayed in an EzWindows SimpleWindow, it should contain a reference to the window that contains it to facilitate its display. In addition, it should have a position within the window. A Bug will also contain an EzWindows BitMap so an image for a bug can be displayed. To simulate a bug moving in a window, we will use four bitmap images. Each image corresponds to the direction the bug is moving (Figure 16.3). Because we want to simulate the erratic movements of a bug, Bug has an attribute that is the probability that the bug will change direction. Other attributes are the direction the bug is currently moving, the number of mouse hits the bug has taken so far, and the number of mouse hits required to kill the bug.

To summarize, the attributes of Bug should include

- Window—the window that contains the bug.
- Bmp—an array of four bitmaps that correspond to the direction the bug is moving.
- HitsTaken—the number of mouse-click hits the bug has taken so far.
- HitsRequired—the number of mouse-click hits the bug can take before it is killed.
- DirectionChangeProbability—the likelihood that the bug will change direction.
- CurrentDirection—the direction (up, down, left, or right) that the bug is moving.
- CurrentPosition—the current location of the bug.

Figure 16.3

Bitmaps used to simulate moving bug

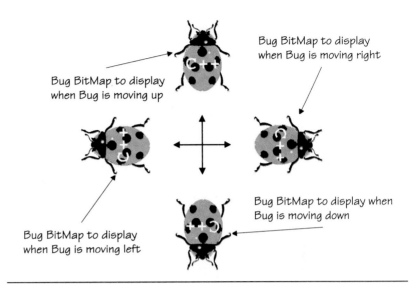

Bug BitMap to display when Bug is moving up

Bug BitMap to display when Bug is moving right

Bug BitMap to display when Bug is moving left

Bug BitMap to display when Bug is moving down

An important implementation question is how to make the bug appear to move in the window. A simple technique for making a screen object appear to move is to erase the bitmap image of the object and then redraw it at its new position. This technique is illustrated in Figure 16.4. If the erase/redraw operations are done frequently enough and the new position is not too far from the original position, the image will appear to move. This technique works reasonably well if there are not too many objects and they are not moving too fast. If smoother, faster motion is required, other slightly more complicated techniques can be used. For Bug Hunt, however, the simple technique just outlined is acceptable.

Figure 16.4

Simulating motion by erasing and redrawing

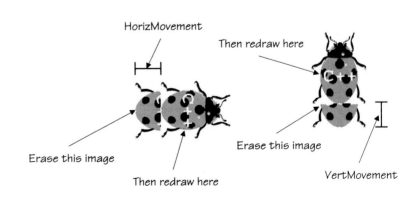

HorizMovement

Then redraw here

Erase this image

Then redraw here

Erase this image

VertMovement

Class `Bug` will also contain two data members, `HorizMovement` and `VertMovement`. These will hold, respectively, the amount to move the bitmap image horizontally and vertically to simulate motion.

Of course, in addition to the public member functions, class `Bug` needs inspectors and mutators. Because these will be used only by class `Bug` and the classes derived from `Bug`, they are not part of the public interface for `Bug`. To make these member functions inaccessible to users of `Bug`, yet make them accessible to classes derived from `Bug`, these methods are declared in the protected section. Thus, `Bug` has a public interface and a protected one. The data members of `Bug` are still in a private section, and the derived classes must use the inspectors and mutators provided in the protected section to access them. Listing 16.1 contains the declaration for `Bug`.

Listing 16.1

Declaration of class Bug from bug.h

```
#ifndef BUG_H
#define BUG_H
#include "bitmap.h"
#include "random.h"
//
// class for a simple bug
//
enum Direction {Up, Down, Left, Right };

class Bug {
    public:
        Bug(SimpleWindow &w, int HitsNeeded = 3,
          int DirectionChangeProbability = 50);
        int IsHit(const Position &MousePosition);
        int IsDying();
        void Create();
        void Kill();
        virtual void Move() = 0;
    protected:
        // Bug inspectors
        SimpleWindow &GetWindow() const;
        Position GetPosition() const;
        Direction GetDirection() const;
        float GetHorizMovement() const;
        float GetVertMovement() const;
        int GetDirectionChangeProbability() const;
        BitMap &GetBmp(const Direction &d);
        const BitMap &GetBmp(const Direction &d)
          const;
        // Bug mutators
        void SetWindow(SimpleWindow &w);
        void SetDirection(const Direction &d);
        void SetHorizMovement(float h);
        void SetVertMovement(float v);
        void Draw();
        void Erase();
        void SetPosition(const Position &p);
        void ChangeDirection();
        Position NewPosition() const;
        Random GeneratePercentage;
    private:
        // Data members
```

```
       SimpleWindow &Window;
       BitMap Bmp[4];
       float HorizMovement;
       float VertMovement;
       int HitsRequired;
       int HitsTaken;
       int DirectionChangeProbability;
       Direction CurrentDirection;
       Position CurrentPosition;
};
#endif
```

Preceding the declaration of Bug in Listing 16.1 is the declaration of an **enum** that gives symbolic names to the four directions. Using an enumeration instead of numbers to encode the direction of a bug helps make the program more readable and understandable.

Bug is an abstract base class because public member function Move() is a pure virtual function. We made it a pure virtual function because it's only use will be to realize implementations of "real" bugs. These bugs will differ in how they move. Making Bug a pure virtual function ensures that an object of type Bug can never be instantiated.

Most of the member functions of Bug are short and simple. Listing 16.2 contains the implementation of the member functions of class Bug.

Listing 16.2

Constructor and member functions of class Bug from bug.cpp

```
// Bug(): constructor for a bug
Bug::Bug(SimpleWindow &w, int h, int p) :
 Window(w), HitsRequired(h), HitsTaken(0),
 GeneratePercentage(1, 100),
 DirectionChangeProbability(p) {
   GeneratePercentage.Randomize();
}
void Bug::Create() {
   HitsTaken = 0;
   Draw();
}
void Bug::Kill() {
   Erase();
}
// Hit(): return true if mouse is inside bug
// and update hit taken count
bool Bug::IsHit(const Position &MousePosn) {
   if (GetBmp(GetDirection()).IsInside(MousePosn)) {
      ++HitsTaken;
      return true;
   }
   else
      return false;
}
// IsDying: is the bug dying
bool Bug::IsDying() {
   return HitsTaken >= HitsRequired;
}
// inspectors
SimpleWindow& Bug::GetWindow() const {
   return Window;
```

```
                }
                Position Bug::GetPosition() const {
                   return CurrentPosition;
                }
                Direction Bug::GetDirection() const {
                   return CurrentDirection;
                };
                float Bug::GetHorizMovement() const {
                      return HorizMovement;
                   };
                float Bug::GetVertMovement() const {
                      return VertMovement;
                }
                int Bug::GetDirectionChangeProbability() const {
                   return DirectionChangeProbability;
                }
                BitMap &Bug::GetBmp(const Direction &d) {
                   return Bmp[d];
                }
                const BitMap &Bug::GetBmp(const Direction &d) const {
                   return Bmp[d];
                }
                // mutators
                void Bug::SetWindow(SimpleWindow &w) {
                   Window = w;
                }
                void Bug::SetDirection(const Direction &d) {
                   CurrentDirection = d;
                };
                void Bug::SetHorizMovement(float h) {
                   HorizMovement = h;
                }
                void Bug::SetVertMovement(float v) {
                   VertMovement = v;
                }
                // facilitators
                void Bug::Draw() {
                   GetBmp(GetDirection()).Draw();
                }
                void Bug::Erase() {
                   GetBmp(GetDirection()).Erase();
                }
                void Bug::ChangeDirection() {
                   Random R(Up, Right);
                   R.Randomize();
                   SetDirection((Direction ) R.Draw());
                }
                // SetPosition(): set position for all bug bitmaps
                void Bug::SetPosition(const Position &p) {
                   for (Direction d = Up; d <= Right;
                    d = (Direction) (d + 1))
                      Bmp[d].SetPosition(p);
                   CurrentPosition = p;
                }
                // NewPosition(): compute a new position for a bug
                Position Bug::NewPosition() const {
                   if (GetDirection() == Left)
                      return GetPosition()
```

```
      + Position(-GetHorizMovement(), 0);
  else if (GetDirection() == Right)
     return GetPosition()
       + Position(GetHorizMovement(), 0);
  else if (GetDirection() == Up)
     return GetPosition()
       + Position(0, -GetVertMovement());
  else
     return GetPosition()
       + Position(0, GetVertMovement());
}
```

The implementation of Bug's constructor is

```
Bug::Bug(SimpleWindow &w, int h, int p) :
 Window(w), HitsRequired(h), HitsTaken(0),
 GeneratePercentage(1, 100),
 DirectionChangeProbability(p) {
    GeneratePercentage.Randomize();
}
```

The constructor initializes several of Bug's data members. It initializes the Window data member with the reference to the SimpleWindow that will contain the bug. It initializes HitsRequired to the number of hits the bug can take before being killed, and it initializes HitsTaken to 0. The data member initialization list also sets up object GeneratePercentage so it will produce a uniform distribution of integers between 1 and 100. This will be used to randomly change the direction a bug is moving. Finally, the data member DirectionChangeProbability is initialized. This attribute controls how often a bug changes directions.

The public member functions Create() and Kill() call the protected member functions Draw() and Erase(). In addition, Create() sets the data member HitsTaken to 0 so that when a bug is created it starts out without having any hits. The implementations of these public member functions are

```
void Bug::Create() {
    HitsTaken = 0;
    Draw();
}
void Bug::Kill() {
    Erase();
};
```

The implementation of Bug's protected member function Draw() gets the current direction the bug is moving and invokes the BitMap::Draw() function for the appropriate bit map. Its implementation is

```
void Bug::Draw() {
    GetBmp(GetDirection()).Draw();
};
```

The code for `Bug::Erase()` is similar except that the function `Bit-Map::Erase()` is called instead.

```
void Bug::Erase() {
    GetBmp(GetDirection()).Erase();
};
```

The member function `SetPosition()` sets a bug's position, but it also sets the position of the four bitmaps that contain the images of the bug going in each of the four directions. Updating the bitmap positions whenever `Bug::MyPosition` is updated ensures all the bitmaps are positioned consistently. The code for `SetPosition()` is

```
void Bug::SetPosition(const Position &p) {
    for (Direction d = Up; d <= Right;
     d = (Direction) (d + 1))
        Bmp[d].SetPosition(p);
    CurrentPosition = p;
}
```

The code calls `BitMap::SetPosition()` for each of the four bitmap images and then updates `Bug::CurrentPosition`.

The member function `NewPosition()` computes and returns the next position for the bug. It does this by looking at the direction the bug is moving and computes a new position by adding the proper movement distance to the current x- or y-coordinate of the bug depending on the direction the bug is moving. Its implementation is

```
Position Bug::NewPosition() const {
    if (GetDirection() == Left)
        return GetPosition()
            + Position(-GetHorizMovement(), 0);
    else if (GetDirection() == Right)
        return GetPosition()
            + Position(GetHorizMovement(), 0);
    else if (GetDirection() == Up)
        return GetPosition()
            + Position(0, -GetVertMovement());
    else
        return GetPosition()
            + Position(0, GetVertMovement());
}
```

The function uses the protected inspectors `GetHorizMovement()` and `GetVertMovement()` to obtain the proper distance to move the bug in either the x or y direction.

16.2.1

Derived class SlowBug

From `Bug`, we can create different types of bugs, that is, bugs that move differently. They may look different too, but that's not essential. The Bug Hunt game starts off with a light blue, big, slow bug that doesn't change directions very often (see Figure 16.5). The class declaration of SlowBug is

```
class SlowBug : public Bug {
   public:
      SlowBug(SimpleWindow &w, int HitsNeeded = 4,
         int DirectionChange = 10);
      void Move();
};
```

That is, SlowBug is a kind of Bug, and it inherits all the properties and behaviors of Bug. SlowBug's constructor, by default, sets the number of hits necessary to kill a slow bug to four. SlowBug has its own move function. This function will define the behavior of a slow bug. The declaration of class SlowBug follows declaration of class Bug in file bug.h.

Figure 16.5

Slow and fast bugs and the corresponding bitmap files

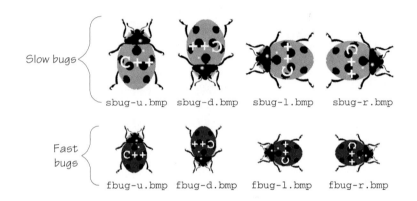

Slow bugs {
sbug-u.bmp sbug-d.bmp sbug-l.bmp sbug-r.bmp

Fast bugs {
fbug-u.bmp fbug-d.bmp fbug-l.bmp fbug-r.bmp

The implementation of SlowBug's constructor, unlike that of Bug, does quite a bit of work. In particular, it loads the bitmaps that will be used to display the bug in the game window. Listing 16.3 contains the implementation of SlowBug's constructor.

Listing 16.3

Implementation of SlowBug constructor from bug.cpp

```
SlowBug::SlowBug(SimpleWindow &w, int h, int p) :
Bug(w, h, p) {
   // Load the bit maps for the bug going in the
   // four directions
   string BitMapFiles[] = {
      "sbug-u.bmp",
      "sbug-d.bmp",
      "sbug-l.bmp",
      "sbug-r.bmp"
   };
   for (Direction d = Up; d <= Right;
    d = (Direction) (d + 1)) {
      GetBmp(d).SetWindow(GetWindow());
      GetBmp(d).Load(BitMapFiles[d]);
      assert(GetBmp(d).GetStatus() == BitMapOkay);
   }
   // Set the distance to move the bug in the
```

```
     // horizontal and vertical direction
     // The distance is based on the size of the bitmap.
     SetHorizMovement(GetBmp(Right).GetWidth() / 10.0);
     SetVertMovement(GetBmp(Up).GetHeight() / 10.0);
     // Initially make it go right
     SetDirection(Right);
     SetPosition(Position(3.0, 3.0));
}
```

The first part of the code loads the bitmaps that depict the bug moving in each of the four directions (see Figure 16.5). The second section of code computes how much to move the bug on each timer tick. Both a horizontal and vertical distance to move are computed. The distance to move is based on the size of the bitmap. Here, a `SlowBug` will move 1/10th the size of the bitmap that is being rendered each interval. The last two lines of the constructor set the initial direction (right) and the initial position (3 centimeters from the left edge of the window and 3 centimeters from the top edge of the window).

The job of `SlowBug::Move()` is to make the bug move in a particular way. A slow bug has the following behavior. When a slow bug hits the side of the window, it turns and goes in the opposite direction. A slow bug randomly changes direction about 10 percent of the time.

The beginning of `SlowBug::Move()` is

```
     Erase();
     // Randomly change directions
     if (GeneratePercentage.Draw()
      < GetDirectionChangeProbability())
        ChangeDirection();
     SetPosition(NewPosition());
     Draw();
```

The first step is to erase the currently displayed bitmap. The next step is to determine if the direction should be changed. Using the `GeneratePercentage` object a random number between 1 and 100 is drawn. If the number drawn is less than `DirectionChangeProbability`, then `ChangeDirection()` is called to randomly pick a new direction and the bug is set to go in that direction. See Listing 16.2 for the implementation of member function `ChangeDirection()`. Otherwise, the bug continues in its current direction. Once the direction is determined, a new position is computed and the bug is redrawn at its new location.

The next step of `Move()` is to determine if the bug, on its next move, is going to go through the side of the window. If it will, the bug is turned to go in the opposite direction. The code for accomplishing this is

```
     Direction BugDirection = GetDirection();
     float BugX = GetPosition().GetXDistance();
     float BugXSize = GetBmp(GetDirection()).GetWidth();
     float BugY = GetPosition().GetYDistance();
     float BugYSize
      = GetBmp(GetDirection()).GetHeight();
     // Decide if it needs to turn around
     if (BugDirection == Right
      && BugX + BugXSize + GetHorizMovement()
```

```
      >= GetWindow().GetWidth())
         SetDirection(Left);
   else if (BugDirection == Left
      && BugX - GetHorizMovement() <= 0.0)
         SetDirection(Right);
   else if (BugDirection == Down
      && BugY + BugYSize + GetVertMovement()
      >= GetWindow().GetHeight())
         SetDirection(Up);
   else if (BugDirection == Up
      && BugY - GetVertMovement() <= 0.0)
         SetDirection(Down);
```

The first block of code obtains some needed information about the bug. It obtains the current direction of the bug, the x-coordinate and the y-coordinate of the position of the bug, and the height and width of the bitmap being displayed.

Using this information, the code determines if the bug is about to hit a window edge. For example, if the bug is moving to the right and the right edge of the bitmap plus the amount it can move horizontally extend past the right edge of the window, the bug is turned to the left. (Recall that all coordinates as well as the size of the window are in centimeters.) Figure 16.6 illustrates the calculation. Similar calculations are performed for the three other directions.

Figure 16.6
Determining if a bug is about go through the side of the window

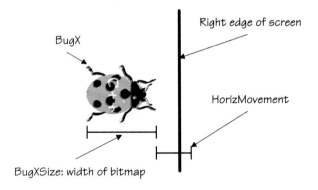

16.2.2

Derived class FastBug

Using base class Bug, we also want to create a fast bug that behaves differently from SlowBug. The declaration of class FastBug is very similar to that of SlowBug.

```
class FastBug : public Bug {
   public:
      FastBug(SimpleWindow &w, int HitsNeeded = 3,
         int DirectionChangeProbability = 20);
      void Move();
};
```

Because a `FastBug` is smaller than a `SlowBug`, it takes only three hits to kill it. However, it changes directions more often. The constructor for `FastBug` is also similar to `SlowBug`'s constructor. Listing 16.4 contains the implementation of `FastBug::FastBug()`.

Listing 16.4

Implementation of FastBug constructor from bug.cpp

```
FastBug::FastBug(SimpleWindow &w, int h, int p) :
 Bug(w, h, p) {
    // Load the four bitmaps for the bug to go in
    // four directions
    string BitMapFiles[] = {
       "fbug-u.bmp",
       "fbug-d.bmp",
       "fbug-l.bmp",
       "fbug-r.bmp"
    };
    for (Direction d = Up; d <= Right;
     d = (Direction) (d + 1)) {
       GetBmp(d).SetWindow(GetWindow());
       GetBmp(d).Load(BitMapFiles[d]);
       assert(GetBmp(d).GetStatus() == BitMapOkay);
    }
    // Set the distance to move the bug in the horizontal
    // and vertical directions. The distance is based
    // on the size of the bitmap. This should be a larger
    // distance than for a slow bug, so it moves faster
    SetHorizMovement(GetBmp(Right).GetWidth() / 5.0);
    SetVertMovement(GetBmp(Up).GetHeight() / 5.0);
    // Initially make it go down
    SetDirection(Down);
    SetPosition(Position(6.0, 2.0));
}
```

The differences between `FastBug`'s constructor and `SlowBug`'s constructor are that a different set of images are loaded, `HorizMovement` and `VertMovement` are computed differently, and the initial direction and position are set differently. The key difference, however, is that `HorizMovement` and `VertMovement` are larger in `FastBug`, relative to the size of the bitmap, than they were in `SlowBug`. Consequently, a `FastBug` appears to move faster than a `SlowBug`.

The implementation of `FastBug::Move()` is very different from the `SlowBug::Move()`. This is, of course, because we want `FastBug` to behave differently. We want it to move faster and be able to move through the window walls to the other side. Some computer scientists might call this a Heisenbug. In fact, if the only difference between a `FastBug` and a `SlowBug` had been the speed at which they move, we would not have needed a new class. This one difference could have been handled by setting the attributes of a generic bug to the proper values (i.e., loading the proper bitmaps and setting `HorizMovement` and `VertMovement` appropriately).

The first part of the implementation of `FastBug::Move()` is similar to that of `SlowBug`. The code is

```
void FastBug::Move() {
    Erase();
```

```
// Change directions randomly
if (GeneratePercentage.Draw()
 < GetDirectionChangeProbability())
   ChangeDirection();
SetPosition(NewPosition());
Draw();
```

The second part of the implementation determines what the bug should do when the side of the window is hit. Unlike the slow bug, which just reverses direction when it hits the edge of the window, a fast bug "tunnels" through and appears on the other side of the window moving in the same direction. The code that implements this behavior is

```
// Get bug position and its size
Direction BugDirection = GetDirection();
float BugX = GetPosition().GetXDistance();
float BugXSize = GetBmp(GetDirection()).GetWidth();
float BugY = GetPosition().GetYDistance();
float BugYSize
 = GetBmp(GetDirection()).GetHeight();
// Decide if bug pops through at the opposite side
if (BugDirection == Right
 && BugX + BugXSize + GetHorizMovement()
 >= GetWindow().GetWidth()) {
   Erase();
   SetPosition(Position(1,
    GetPosition().GetYDistance())));
   Draw();
}
else if (BugDirection == Left
 && BugX - GetHorizMovement() <= 0.0) {
   Erase();
   SetPosition(
    Position(GetWindow().GetWidth() - BugXSize,
    GetPosition().GetYDistance())));
   Draw();
}
else if (BugDirection == Down
 && BugY + BugYSize >= GetWindow().GetHeight()) {
   Erase();
   SetPosition(
    Position(GetPosition().GetXDistance(), 0.0));
   Draw();
}
else if (BugDirection == Up
 && BugY - GetVertMovement() <= 0.0) {
   Erase();
   SetPosition(
    Position(GetPosition().GetXDistance(),
    GetWindow().GetHeight() - BugYSize));
   Draw();
}
```

The logic for determining if the bug is at one of the four edges of the window is exactly the same as the code in SlowBug::Move(). The difference is what happens. For a fast bug, the current image is erased, and the bug is drawn at the opposite screen edge. The direction it is moving remains the same.

The similarity of the logic in the move functions of `SlowBug` and `FastBug` suggests that we can simplify the code by writing utility functions for determining if a bug is at one of the window edges. To be usable by both classes, these functions should be members of the base class `Bug`. The following member functions are added to the protected section of class `Bug`: `AtRightEdge()`, `AtLeftEdge()`, `AtBottomEdge()`, `AtTopEdge()`. These functions return true if the bug is at the corresponding edge and false otherwise. The implementations of these protected member functions are

```
// AtRightEdge(): determine if bug is at right edge
// of the window
int Bug::AtRightEdge() const {
    return (GetPosition().GetXDistance()
    + GetBmp(GetDirection()).GetWidth()
    + GetHorizMovement() >= GetWindow().GetWidth());
}
// AtLeftEdge(): determine if bug is at left edge of
// the window
int Bug::AtLeftEdge() const {
    return (GetPosition().GetXDistance()
    - GetHorizMovement() <= 0.0);
}
// AtBottomEdge(): determine if bug is at bottom
// edge the of window
int Bug::AtBottomEdge() const {
    return (GetPosition().GetYDistance()
    + GetBmp(GetDirection()).GetHeight()
    + GetVertMovement() >= GetWindow().GetHeight());
}
// AtTopEdge(): determine if bug is at top edge
// of window
int Bug::AtTopEdge() const {
    return (GetPosition().GetYDistance() -
    GetVertMovement() <= 0.0);
}
```

Using these functions for `FastBug::Move()`, the revised code for determining if a bug should "tunnel" through the edge of the window is

```
if (BugDirection == Right && AtRightEdge()) {
    Erase();
    SetPosition(Position(0.0,
     GetPosition().GetYDistance())));
    Draw();
}
else if (BugDirection == Left && AtLeftEdge()) {
    Erase();
    SetPosition(
     Position(GetWindow().GetWidth() - BugXSize,
     GetPosition().GetYDistance())));
    Draw();
}
else if (BugDirection == Down && AtBottomEdge()) {
    Erase();
    SetPosition(
     Position(GetPosition().GetXDistance(), 0.0));
    Draw();
```

```
    }
    else if (BugDirection == Up && AtTopEdge()) {
        Erase();
        SetPosition(
         Position(GetPosition().GetXDistance(),
         GetWindow().GetHeight() - BugYSize));
        Draw();
    }
```

The analogous code for `SlowBug::Move()` would also be shorter and cleaner.

Now that we have our bugs implemented, we can begin the design and implementation of the game controller.

16.3

CLASS GAMECONTROLLER

The job of the game controller is to control the play of the game. It needs to maintain the state of the game as it progresses and handle both mouse-click events and timer-tick events. The public interface to the game controller should include

- `Reset`—put the game back in its initial state.

- `Play`—start the game.

- `MouseClick`—handle a mouse-click event.

- `TimerTick`—handle a timer tick.

In addition to these public member functions, the game controller includes the following private data members:

- `GameWindow`—a pointer to the `SimpleWindow` for the game.

- `Level`—the current level of the game.

- `Status`—the status of the game.

- `KindOfBug`—an array that points to the different bug types used in the game.

Listing 16.5 contains the declaration of the class `GameController`. The code contains two enumerations. The first enumeration defines the levels of play. This version of Bug Hunt has two levels of play. At the first level a slow bug is hunted, and in the second level a fast bug is hunted. The second enumeration defines the various stages or status of the game. For example, the enumeration member `SettingUp` indicates that the game is being initialized and is not ready for play. Similarly, the status `Playing` indicates a game is in progress and that mouse-click events and timer-tick events should be handled appropriately. The constant `NumberOfBugTypes` defines how many different types of bugs the game supports. As the comment notes, this constant should correspond to the number of levels of the game.

Listing 16.5

Declaration of class GameController in bughunt.h

```
#ifndef BWINDOW_H
#define BWINDOW_H
#include "bug.h"

enum GameLevel { Slow, Fast, Done };
enum GameStatus {GameWon, Playing, GameLost,
 SettingUp };

// Speed of game (i.e. timer interval)
const int GameSpeed = 100;
// Types of bugs; this should match the number of
// game levels (Slow + Fast = 2)
const int NumberOfBugTypes = 2;

class GameController {
   public:
      GameController(string Title = "Bug Hunt!",
       const Position &WinPosition = Position(3.0, 3.0),
       const float WindLength = 14.0,
       const float WinHeight = 10.0),
      ~GameController();
      SimpleWindow *GetWindow();
      void Reset();
      void Play(const GameLevel Level);
      int MouseClick(const Position &MousePosition);
      int TimerTick();
   private:
      void BugHit();
      GameLevel CurrentLevel() const;
      Bug *CurrentBug() const ;
      SimpleWindow *GameWindow;
      GameLevel Level;
      GameStatus Status;
      Bug *KindOfBug[NumberOfBugTypes];
};
#endif
```

The `GameController` constructor allocates all the game objects. This includes the window and the bugs. In addition, it initializes the data members `Level` and `Status`. Its implementation is

```
GameController::GameController(string Title,
 const Position &WinPosition, float WinLength,
 float WinHeight) : Level(Slow),
 Status(SettingUp) {
   // Create a window and open it
   GameWindow = new SimpleWindow(Title.c_str(),
    WinLength, WinHeight, WinPosition);
   GetWindow()->Open();

   // Create the bugs. Note this must
   // be done AFTER the window is opened
   // because initialization of the bugs depends on
   // having a window.
   KindOfBug[Slow] = new SlowBug(*GetWindow());
   // Create a fast bug
   KindOfBug[Fast] = new FastBug(*GetWindow());
}
```

Notice that the code contains an important comment—the bugs must be constructed after the window is opened. This sequence is required because when a `Bug` is constructed, its bitmaps are initialized which requires knowing the `SimpleWindow` object that will contain it.

Class `GameController` has a destructor whose function is to deallocate the objects that have been dynamically allocated. These objects include the window and the bugs. Thus, `GameController::~GameController()` simply deletes these objects. Its implementation is

```
GameController::~GameController() {
    // Get rid of the bugs and the window
    delete KindOfBug[Slow];
    delete KindOfBug[Fast];
    delete GameWindow;
}
```

The public member function `Reset()` simply sets the game back to the beginning level and is used when a player misses a bug. The game starts over from the beginning. The code for `Reset()` is

```
void GameController::Reset() {
    Status = SettingUp;
    Level = Slow;
    CurrentBug()->Create();
}
```

Member function `Play()` is equally simple. Its implementation is

```
void GameController::Play(const GameLevel l) {
    Level = l;
    Status = Playing;
    GetWindow()->StartTimer(GameSpeed);
}
```

`Play()` sets the level, changes the status to playing, and starts the timer so that the current bug can be moved.

Most of the control of the game centers on handling mouse-click events and timer-tick events. On a mouse click, we must check to see if the game is in progress, and if so, if the current bug is hit. If it is hit, the member function `BugHit()` is called to update the status of the game. The status of the game is checked to see if the game has been won. If so, a `SimpleWindow` alert box pops up with a winning message.

If the game is in progress, but the player missed the bug, the timer is stopped, a message is displayed, the current bug is killed, and the game starts over. Listing 16.6 contains the code for `GameController::Mouse-Click()`.

The code for `GameController::TimerTick()` is also contained in Listing 16.6. It sends a message to the current bug telling it to move. Notice that C++ support of polymorphism makes this code both natural and simple. The appropriate `Move()` is automatically called depending on the current type of bug.

Listing 16.6

Implementation of MouseClick and TimerTick from file control.cpp

```cpp
// MouseClick() check to see if they hit the bug
// if so, update the status of the game
int GameController::MouseClick(const Position
 &MousePosition) {
    // Only pay attention to the mouse if game
    // is in progress
    if (Status == Playing
     && CurrentBug()->IsHit(MousePosition)) {
        BugHit();
        // They won the game!
        // Let them know and start over
        if (Status == GameWon) {
            GetWindow()->StopTimer();
            GetWindow()->Message("You Won!");
            Reset();
            Play(Slow);
        }
    }
    else {
        // They missed the bug
        // Let them know and start over
        GetWindow()->StopTimer();
        GetWindow()->Message("You Missed!");
        CurrentBug()->Kill();
        Reset();
        Play(Slow);
    }
    return 1;
}
// TimerTick(): move the bug
int GameController::TimerTick() {
    CurrentBug()->Move();
    return 1;
}
```

The final `GameController` member function to discuss is the private member function `BugHit()`. Its implementation is

```cpp
// BugHit(): player hit the bug
void GameController::BugHit() {
    // Determine if bug is dying. If so, kill it
    // and determine if the game is over.
    // If the game is not over advance to
    // the next level of play
    if (CurrentBug()->IsDying()) {
        CurrentBug()->Kill();
        Level = (GameLevel) (Level + 1);
        if (Level == Done)
            Status = GameWon;
        else
            // Create the new faster bug
            CurrentBug()->Create();
    }
}
```

It determines if the current bug is dying. If so, the bug is killed, the current hit count is reset, and the game advances to the next level. If there is no next level, the status of the game is set to GameWon; otherwise, the next kind of bug is created.

16.4

BUG HUNT

The only remaining piece of the program is the code that creates a game and sets up the callbacks. This code is contained in Listing 16.7. Function Api-Main() creates a game called BugHunt. Both the mouse and timer callbacks are set up and play is started at level Slow. ApiEnd(), which is called when the program is sent a terminating message, deletes the game. This action, of course, invokes the destructor for GameController, which deletes the bugs and the window.

Listing 16.7

Functions to set up callbacks and start and terminate the game from bughunt.cpp

```
#include "bughunt.h"
GameController *BugHunt;

// TimerCallback(): on a timer tick call BugHunt's
// timer-tick handler
int TimerCallback(void) {
    BugHunt->TimerTick();

    return 1;
}
// MouseCallback -- on a mouse click call BugHunt's
// mouse-click handler
int MouseCallback(const Position &MousePosition) {
    BugHunt->MouseClick(MousePosition);

    return 1;
}
// ApiMain(): allocate the game controller, set up
// the callbacks, and start the game
int ApiMain() {
    BugHunt = new GameController();
    (BugHunt->GetWindow())->
     SetTimerCallback(TimerCallback);
    (BugHunt->GetWindow())->
     SetMouseClickCallback(MouseCallback);
    BugHunt->Play(Slow);

    return 0;
}
// ApiEnd(): destroy the game
int ApiEnd() {
    delete BugHunt;

    return 0;
}
```

This completes the design and implementation of Bug Hunt. As we mentioned at the beginning of the chapter, the implementation of Bug Hunt consists of three modules (bug.cpp, control.cpp, and bughunt.cpp), their interfaces (bug.h, control.h, and bughunt.h), and the EzWindows API

History of Computing

Parallel computing and the grand challenges

The standard model of computing is do to things in a serial fashion. Each computation is done in sequence with one computation being completed before starting the next one. In parallel computing, the idea is to do as many computations in parallel as possible. Of course, to do so requires several computer chips that can work together. Just as five people can clean a house quicker than one person working alone, many computers working together on a single problem can reach a solution faster than a single computer.

Of course, the problem with parallel computing is that when the number of computers working on a problem becomes very large, it becomes difficult to partition and coordinate the work to be done. Imagine the difficulties you might have if 100 people showed up to help you clean your house! You'd have a hard time keeping them busy and not getting in each other's way.

As with any new technology, problems are to be expected. Researchers are making great strides in parallel computing. As a way of focusing the efforts to develop usable parallel systems, scientists and engineers have identified a list of important problems. These problems have been dubbed the "Grand Challenge" problems. These are fundamental problems in science and engineering, with broad economic and scientific impact, whose solution can be advanced by applying high performance computing techniques and resources. Many of these problems involve using the computer to model a complex system. Examples include modeling of the weather so accurate, long-term weather forecasting becomes a reality, modeling of geological activity so that forecasting of earthquakes is possible, and modeling of environmental effects on ecosystems so that any negative impact can be predicted and avoided or minimized.

Other Grand Challenge problems involve what is popularly called virtual reality. *Virtual reality* is using the computer to create an artificial environment that is indistinguishable from reality. If this makes you think of the HoloDeck in the television series *Star Trek: The Next Generation*, you've got exactly the right idea. Primitive virtual reality systems are already in use. Most airplane pilots learn to fly a new aircraft by flying a simulator of the aircraft. This type of simulator is very realistic, and it is a much cheaper and safer to learn to fly a new plane by starting in a simulator, rather than starting out in the real plane. Work is underway to develop similar techniques so that surgeons can be trained in delicate procedures. While these systems are primitive in comparison to the Enterprise's HoloDeck, advances in computing, display and sensor technology, and computer graphics will no doubt expand the uses of virtual reality systems.

library. The complete and final code is contained on the program disk. The design of Bug Hunt exemplifies the design of many games. The controller coordinates the play of the game and is responsible for keeping up with the state of the game. The start up code sets up the interface between the player and the game by arranging for the mouse clicks to be handled by the appropriate parts of the program. This model can be used to develop many fun and interesting games. Some possibilities are described in the exercises.

16.5

POINTS TO REMEMBER

- Do not be afraid of rewriting code to make the code shorter and more understandable. The time spent redesigning code will pay for itself later.

- Inheritance provides a natural way to reuse code. In Bug Hunt, the code for the base class `Bug` is used by the derived classes `SlowBug` and `FastBug`. If new bugs are added to the game, they too can use the code developed for the base class.

- Containment is a way to build complex objects out of other objects. In Bug Hunt, the `GameController` class is built using containment. A game contains a window (i.e., a `SimpleWindow`) and different kinds of bugs (i.e., array `KindOfBug`).

- Encapsulation is a way of building software where details about an object are hidden from the users of the object. The game controller in Bug Hunt uses the class `Bug`. How a bug is represented and how it moves is encapsulated in the class `Bug`. The game controller does not know how a bug is represented or how it moves. It knows only knows that it can ask a `Bug` to move by calling its public member function `Move()`.

- Polymorphism provides the ability to write code that manipulates objects related by inheritance without regard to the specific kind of object being manipulated. In Bug Hunt, the game controller can manipulate a bug without regard to whether it is a fast bug or a slow bug. For example, the member function `Move()` is a polymorphic function. Through the magic of polymorphism, when the game controller tells a bug to move, the `Move()` function appropriate for the type of bug being manipulated is called.

16.6

EXERCISES

16.1 In Bug Hunt, two enumerations, `GameLevel` and `GameStatus`, are defined in `control.h`. These should really be encapsulated in class `GameController`. Make the modifications to the Bug Hunt code so that these enumerations are encapsulated in class `GameController`. Document the changes you make by including comments at the beginning of each module that outline the change, who made them, and when they were changed.

16.2   Modify Bug Hunt so that it includes a new type of bug called, Warp-Bug. A warp bug occasionally goes into hyperspace and disappears for an interval. It returns at a random location in the window. A warp bug requires two hits to be killed. The new Bug Hunt will have three levels of play.

16.3   One of the deficiencies of Bug Hunt is that players get no feedback when the mouse is clicked unless they miss the bug or the bug is finally killed. Think of a scheme for providing feedback when the player hits a bug. Modify Bug Hunt to implement your scheme.

16.4   Most bugs run faster when you hit them. Modify Bug Hunt so that when a bug is swatted, it moves faster.

16.5   Modify Bug Hunt so that if the player misses a bug, another bug appears. The number of bugs in a window should not exceed three. Observe what happens when several bugs are in the window. Explain why this happens.

16.6   Modify Bug Hunt to include a timer. If all the bugs are not killed in a set time period, the player loses the game.

16.7   Modify Bug Hunt to include a timer. When a player kills all the bugs, record the time (in seconds) it took that player to kill all the bugs. Store the scores in a file and display them at the end of the game.

16.8   Design and implement a new game called Balloons. In this game, a balloon appears at the bottom of the window and begins floating to the top. The player must "pop" the balloon before it reaches the top of the window. If the balloon reaches the top, the player loses and the game starts from the beginning. As play progresses, balloons that move differently appear. At each level, the balloons behave in a way that makes them harder to pop than the balloons at the previous level.

APPENDIX A

Tables

O n successive pages two tables are provided. The first table lists the ASCII character set. The second table describes the C++ operator precedence rules.

A.1

ASCII CHARACTER SET

Code	Char.	Name	Code	Char.	Code	Char.	Code	Char.
0	^@	NUL	32	SP	64	@	96	`
1	^A	SOH	33	!	65	A	97	a
2	^B	STX	34	"	66	B	98	b
3	^C	ETX	35	#	67	C	99	c
4	^D	^EOT	36	$	68	D	100	d
5	^E	ENQ	37	%	69	E	101	e
6	^F	ACK	38	&	70	F	102	f
7	^G	BEL	39	'	71	G	103	g
8	^H	BS	40	(	72	H	104	h
9	^I	TAB	41	)	73	I	105	i
10	^J	LF	42	*	74	J	106	j
11	^K	VT	43	+	75	K	107	k
12	^L	FF	44	,	76	L	108	l
13	^M	CR	45	-	77	M	109	m
14	^N	SO	46	.	78	N	110	n
15	^O	SI	47	/	79	O	111	o
16	^P	DLE	48	0	80	P	112	p
17	^Q	DC1	49	1	81	Q	113	q
18	^R	DC2	50	2	82	R	114	r
19	^S	DC3	51	3	83	S	115	s
20	^T	DC4	52	4	84	T	116	t
21	^U	NAK	53	5	85	U	117	u
22	^V	SYN	54	6	86	V	118	v
23	^W	ETB	55	7	87	W	119	w
24	^X	CAN	56	8	88	X	120	x
25	^Y	EM	57	9	89	Y	121	y
26	^Z	SUB	58	:	90	Z	122	z
27	^[	ESC	59	;	91	[	123	{
28	^\	FS	60	<	92	\	124		
29	^]	GS	61	=	93	]	125	}
30	^^	RS	62	>	94	^	126	~
31	^_	US	63	?	95	_	127	DEL

A.2

OPERATOR PRECEDENCE

The following table summarizes the precedence of the C++ operators. Operators with equal precedence are separated from operators of lesser precedence by horizontal lines

Operator	Description	Category	Association
( )	function call	postfix	left
[ ]	subscript	postfix	left
. ->	selection, indirect selection	postfix	left
::	scope resolution	postfix	left
++ --	increment, decrement	postfix	right
! ~	logical not, bitwise not	unary	right
+ -	arithmetic plus, negation	unary	right
++ --	increment, decrement	prefix	right
& *	address, indirection	unary	right
sizeof	size	unary	right
( )	cast	unary	right
new delete	allocate, free	unary	right
.*	member selection	postfix	left
->*	member pointer selection	postfix	left
* / %	multiplicative	binary	left
+ -	additive	binary	left
<< >>	shift	binary	left
< <= > >=	ordering	binary	left
== !=	equality	binary	left
&	bitwise and	binary	left
^	bitwise xor	binary	left
|	bitwise or	binary	left
&&	logical and	binary	left
||	logical or	binary	left
? :	conditional	ternary	right
= *= /= %= += -= <<= >>= &= ^= |=	assignment	binary	right
throw	exception	unary	right
,	sequential evaluation	binary	left

APPENDIX B

Standard libraries

The proposed C++ standard includes an extensive collection of libraries. Some of the libraries were originally C libraries: assert, ctype, errno, float, limits, locale, math, setjmp, signal, stdarg, stddef, stdio, stdlib, string, and time. Other libraries are proposed specifically for C++. The proposed libraries are algorithm, bitset, complex, deque, exception, fstream, functional, iomanip, ios, iosfwd, iostream, istream, iterator, limits, list, locale, map, memory, new, numeric, ostream, queue, set, sstream, stack, stdexcept, streambuf, string, typeinfo, utility, valarray, and vector.

In the proposed standard, access to a C++ standard library does not require use of a header suffix. For example, the following statement includes the iostream library.

```
#include <iostream>
```

Similarly, access to a C-derived standard library does not require the use of a header suffix. However, a C library name will be preceded by a 'c' to indicate its origin. For example, the following statement includes the C assert macro library.

```
#include <cassert>
```

It is expected that for a reasonable time most compilers will allow the libraries to be included with or without the header suffix. The versions that use the header suffix will likely add the declarations to the global scope while the versions without the suffix will add their definitions to the std namespace (see Appendix D for a namespace discussion).

The discussion in the next sections presents a limited selection of functions, types, macros, and objects from some of the C and C++ libraries. For a more complete discussion of these libraries, the following language definition and reference materials are a good source.

- M. A. Ellis and B. Stroustrup, *The Annotated C++ Reference Manual*, Reading, MA: Addison-Wesley, 1990.
- Working Paper for the Draft Proposed International Standard for Information Systems—Programming Language C++, X3J16/96-0018 WG21/N0836, Washington: American National Standards Institute, 1996.
- P. J. Plauger, *The Standard C Library*, Englewood Cliffs, NJ: Prentice-Hall, 1992.

B.1

IOSTREAM LIBRARY

The iostream library and hierarchy has been discussed and used throughout the text. Besides defining the insertion and extraction operators and manipulators, and the global stream objects `cin`, `cout`, `cerr`, and `clog`, the library also provides access to `ios`, `istream`, and `ostream` member functions. The `istream` member functions include:

`int istream::get()`

> If the input stream contains additional data, the function extracts and returns the next character; otherwise, it returns EOF.

`istream& istream::get(char &c)`

> If the input stream contains additional data, the function extracts and assigns the next character to `c`; otherwise, the effect on `c` is undefined. A reference to `*this` (the invoking object) is returned.

`istream& istream::get(char s[], int n,`
`  char delim = '\n')`

> Extracts characters from the input stream and assigns them to `s` until one of the following conditions occurs: `n-1` characters have been extracted, there are no more characters to extract, or the next character to be extracted has the value `delim`. If the lattermost condition occurs, the delimiter is not extracted. A null terminating character is placed after the last extracted value copied to `s`. A reference to `*this` is returned.

`istream& istream::getline(char s[], int n,`
`  char delim = '\n')`

> Extracts characters from the input stream and assigns them to `s` until one of the following conditions occurs: `n-1` characters have been extracted, there are no more characters to extract, or the next character to be extracted is the delimiter character. If the lattermost condition occurs, the delimiter is also extracted but not assigned to `s`. A null terminating character is placed after the last extracted value copied to `s`. A reference to `*this` is returned.

`int istream::peek()`

> If the input stream contains additional data, the function returns the next character to be extracted; otherwise, it returns EOF.

```
istream& istream::pushback(char c)
```
> Character c is pushed back to the input stream. It will be the next character to be extracted. A reference to `*this` is returned.

The iostream library also provides access to an ios member function that some programmers use to detect end-of-file on an input stream.

```
int ios::eof()
```
> Returns a nonzero value if end-of-file has been reached on the stream; otherwise, the function returns zero.

The iostream library also provides two ostream member functions that are analogous to `get()` and `getline()`.

```
ostream& ostream::put(char c)
```
> Inserts the character c to the output stream. A reference to `*this` is returned.

```
ostream& ostream::write(const char s[], int n)
```
> Inserts n characters from s to the output stream. Null characters are considered valid. A reference to `*this` is returned.

The iostream library also provides another ostream member functions that sometimes proves useful.

```
ostream& ostream::flush()
```
> Forces any insertion operators that have not yet completed to be completed. A reference to `*this` is returned.

B.2
STDLIB LIBRARY

The stdlib library is a miscellaneous collection of types, functions, and macro definitions. The major type declared in this library is the integral type `size_t`. Some of the more commonly-used functions in this library are:

```
int abs(int n)
```
> Returns the absolute value of n.

```
double atof(const char s[])
```
> Returns a **double** representation of the number represented by string s. If the string is non-numeric, the value of the function is undefined.

```
int atoi(const char s[]
```
> Returns a **int** representation of the number represented by string s. If the string is non-numeric, the value of the function is undefined.

```
long int atol(const char s[])
```
> Returns a **long int** representation of the number represented by string s. If the string is non-numeric, the value of the function is undefined.

```
void exit(int status)
```
> The program terminates with a return value of status.

```
void free(void *ptr)
```
> Gives the memory to which ptr points back to the free store.

```
void* malloc(size_t size)
```
Returns a pointer to size bytes of now-allocated free store memory. If there is insufficient free store memory, 0 is returned.

```
int rand()
```
Returns a pseudo-random integer in the range 0 to RAND_MAX. The default seed value to generate the sequence is 1.

```
void srand(unsigned int val)
```
Sets the seed for the pseudo-random number generator to val.

```
int system(const char s[])
```
The string s is passed to operating system to be run by its command processor. An integer value that is system-dependent is returned.

B.3

TIME LIBRARY

The time library is a collection of types, functions, and macro definitions for manipulating calendar and program time. The major types declared in this library are clock_t, time_t, and tm. Types clock_t and time_t are integral types. Type tm is a **struct** type (a **class** type with all members being public) with the following definition:

```
struct tm {
    int tm_sec;    // seconds after the current minute
    int tm_min;    // minutes after the current hour
    int tm_mday;   // day of month
    int tm_mon;    // month of year
    int tm_year;   // years since 1900
    int tm_wday;   // days since Sunday
    int tm_yday;   // days since January 1
    int tm_isdst;  // flag indicating whether Daylight
                   // Savings Time is in effect.
                   // Positive value means in effect.
                   // Zero value means not in effect.
                   // Negative value means unknown.
};
```

The functions in this library deal with *calendar time*, which represents the current date and date using the Gregorian calendar, and *local time*, which is a calendar time for an implementation-dependent specific time zone. Some of the functions included in this library are:

```
clock_t clock()
```
Returns a clock_t value that when divided by CLOCKS_PER_SEC is an approximation of the number of seconds of processor time used by the program so far.

```
double difftime(time_t t1, time_t t2)
```
Returns a **double** value that is the difference between times t1 and t2.

```
time_t mktime(tm *tptr)
```
> Returns a `time_t` representation of the calendar time of the local time represented by object `*tptr`. Object `*tptr` is also modified to represent a calendar time.

```
time_t time(time_t *tptr)
```
> Computes returns a `time_t` representation of the current calendar time. If `tptr` is non-null, then `*tptr` is also set to the current calendar time.

char* asctime(**const** tm *tptr)
> Returns a pointer to a character string that is a representation of the tm object `*tptr`.

tm* localtime(**const** time_t *tptr)
> Returns a pointer to a local-time `tm` representation of the calendar time represented by `*tptr`.

B.4
STRING LIBRARY

The C-based string library provides string handling functions. It also defines the integral type `size_t` and the NULL macro. Some of the functions are:

char* strcat(**char** *t, **char** *s)
> Appends a copy of string `s` including its terminating null character at the end of the target string `s`. The copying begins by replacing the null character that terminates `t`. The function returns `t`.

char* strncat(**char** *t, **char** *s, size_t n)
> Appends a copy of the first n characters of string at the end of the target string `t`. If the length of the string `s` is less than n, the appending ends with a copy of the null character that terminates `s`. The copy begins by replacing the null character that terminates `t`. The function returns `t`.

int strcmp(**char** *t, **char** *s)
> Makes a lexicographical comparison of string `s` to string `t`. If the strings are equal then the function returns 0; if `s` occurs before `t` lexicographically, the function returns a negative value; otherwise, the function returns a positive value.

int strcmp(**char** *t, **char** *s, size_t n)
> Makes a lexicographical comparison of the first n characters of string `s` to string `t` (if either of strings is less than n characters long, the comparison is based on the length of the shorter string). If the characters of s and t being compared are equal, then the function returns 0; if the characters of s occur lexicographically before the characters of `t`, then the function returns a negative value; otherwise, the function returns a positive value.

```
char* strcpy(char *t, char *s)
```
Copies the source string s to the destination string t, including the null character which terminates s. The function returns t.

```
char* strncpy(char *t, char *s, size_t n)
```
Copies the first n characters of source string s to the destination string t. If the length of s is less than n, null characters are used for padding. The function returns t.

```
size_t strlen(const char *s)
```
Returns the number of characters that precede the null character which terminate s.

```
char* strstr(const char *t, const char *s)
```
If string s has zero length, then the function returns t; if string s is not a substring of string t, then the function returns NULL; otherwise, the function returns a pointer to the first occurrence of a copy of string s in string t.

```
char* strchr(const char *t, int c)
```
If character c is not a character in string t, then the function returns NULL; otherwise, the function returns a pointer to the first occurrence of the character c in string t.

```
char* strrchr(const char *t, int c)
```
If character c is not a character in string t, then the function returns NULL; otherwise, the function returns a pointer to the last occurrence of the character c in string t.

APPENDIX C

Standard classes

The proposed C++ standard defines over 100 standard classes and structs. The discussion in this appendix is limited to a partial coverage of two important classes. For information regarding the standard classes consider the following reference materials.

- M. A. Ellis and B. Stroustrup, *The Annotated C++ Reference Manual*, Reading, MA: Addison-Wesley, 1990.
- Working Paper for the Draft Proposed International Standard for Information Systems—Programming Language C++, X3J16/96-0018 WG21/N0836, Washington: American National Standards Institute, 1996.
- D. R. Musser and A. Saini, *STL Tutorial and Reference Guide*, Reading, MA: Addison-Wesley 1995.
- P. J. Plauger, A. Stepanov, M. Lee, and D. R. Musser, *The Standard Template Library*, Englewood Cliffs, NJ: Prentice-Hall, 1996.

C.1

CLASS VECTOR<T>

The template abstract data type vector<T> supports objects that can represent a list of elements using an array-like notation. It is expected that objects of this class, the ValArray class, and the string class of the following section will eventually replace most uses of conventional arrays and character strings. Our presentation of class template vector is simplified in that an optional template parameter regarding memory allocation is ignored.

The following list describes selected vector<T> member functions and operators. In the description, size_type is an integral unsigned type, iterator is a random access iterator, reference is a type that is convertible to T&, and const_reference is a type that is convertible to **const** T&. These types are declared in the class definition for vector<T>.

`vector::vector()`
> The default constructor creates a vector of zero length.

`vector::vector(const T &V)`
> The copy constructor creates a vector that is a duplicate of vector V.

`vector::vector(size_type n, const T &val = T())`
> Explicit constructor creates a vector of length n with each element initialized to `val`.

`vector::~vector()`
> The destructor releases any dynamic memory for the vector.

`vector<T> vector::operator =(const vector<T> &V)`
> The member assignment operator makes the vector a duplicate of vector V. The modified vector is returned.

`vector::operator [](size_type i)`
> Returns a reference to element `i` of the vector.

`vector::operator [](size_type i) const`
> Returns a constant reference to element `i` of the vector.

`size_type vector::size() const`
> Returns the numbers of elements in the vector.

`bool vector::empty() const`
> Returns true if there are no elements in the vector; otherwise, it returns false.

`iterator vector::begin()`
> Returns an iterator that points to the first element of the vector.

`iterator vector::end()`
> Returns an iterator that points to immediately beyond the last element of the vector.

`reference vector::front()`
> Returns a reference to the first element of the vector.

`const_reference vector::front() const`
> Returns a constant reference to the first element of the vector.

`reference vector::back()`
> Returns a reference to the last element of the vector.

`const_reference vector::back() const`
> Returns a constant reference to the last element of the vector.

`vector::insert(iterator pos, const T &val = T())`
> Inserts a copy of `val` at position `pos` of the vector and returns the position of the copy into the vector.

`vector::erase(iterator pos)`
> Removes the element of the vector at position `pos`.

`void vector::pop_back()`
> Removes the last element of the object

`void vector::push_back(const T &val)`
> Inserts a copy of `val` after the last element of the object.

`void vector::resize(size_type s, T val = T())`
> If s is greater than the number of elements in the vector, then the number of elements is increased to s; the new elements are added after the existing elements; and the initial value of the new elements is

val. If s is less than the number of elements in the vector, then the number of elements is decreased to s by removing current elements from the end of the vector. If s is equal to the number of elements in the vector, then no action is taken.

void vector::swap(vector<T> &V)

The current vector and vector V swap values.

C.2

CLASS STRING

In the proposed standard, the class string is an instantiated version of the template class basic_string.

    typedef basic_string<**char**> string;

This abstract data type supports objects that can represent a sequence of characters (the sequences may be of arbitrary length). During program execution a string object can represent different sequences of varying length. The following describes selected string member and auxiliary functions and operators. Some of the member functions make use of the unsigned integral type size_type that is defined within the class definition of string. An integral constant npos is also defined in the class. The constant has a value that lies outside of the interval 0 ... *n*-1, where *n* is the number of characters in the string being represented.

string::string()

Default constructor initializes to represent empty string.

string::string(**const char** s[])

Initializes an object to represent a copy of the **char** array s representation of a string sequence.

size_type string::length() **const**

Returns the length of the string.

size_type string::size() **const**

Returns the length of the string.

const char* string::c_str() **const**

Returns a pointer to the initial element of a **char** array whose elements are a copy of the string being represented. A null character terminates the copy.

const char* string::data() **const**

Returns a pointer to the initial element of a **char** array whose elements are copy of the string being represented. A null character terminates the copy.

char operator [](size_type i) **const**

If i is less than size(), the function returns a copy to i-th character being represented by the string; otherwise, an exception is thrown.

```
reference operator [](size_type i)
```
If i is less than size(), the function returns a reference to i-th character being represented; otherwise, an exception is thrown. The type reference is a **typedef** class defined in the class string that is convertible to **char**&.

int string::compare(**const** string &s, size_type n) **const**

Compares the current string starting at its position n with string s. If the compared portions are the same, then the function returns 0; if the current string-compared portion occurs first lexicographically, then a negative value is returned; otherwise, a positive value is returned.

```
string& string::append(char c)
```
Adds a copy of character c to the end of the current string. The modified current string is returned (*this).

```
string& string::append(const string &s)
```
Adds a copy of string s at the end of the current string. The modified current string is returned (*this).

```
string& string::erase(size_type n, size_type m)
```
Characters from position n through m are removed from the string. A reference to the modified string is returned (*this).

```
string& string::insert(size_type n, const string &s)
```
Inserts a copy of string s between positions n and n+1 of the current string. The modified current string is returned (*this).

```
size_type string::find(const string &s,
  size_type n) const
```
Searches leftward in the current string for the substring s, with the search beginning at position n. If substring is found, the function returns the starting position of the first-found occurrence of the substring. If the substring is not found, the constant npos is returned.

```
size_type string::rfind(const string &s, size_type
n) const
```
Searches rightward in the current string for the substring s with the search beginning at position n. If substring is found, the function returns the starting position of the first-found occurrence of the substring. If the substring is not found, the constant npos is returned.

The library also overloads the insertion, extraction and relational operators.

```
istream& operator >>(istream &sin, string &s)
```
Extracts the next non-whitespace string from input stream sin and assigns it to s. It returns a reference to sin.

```
ostream operator <<(ostream &sout, string &s)
```
Inserts string s to the output stream sout. It returns a reference to sout.

```
bool operator ==(const string &s, const string &t)
```
Returns s.compare(t) == 0.

```
bool operator !=(const string &s, const string &t)
```
Returns s.compare(t) != 0.

```
bool operator <(const string &s, const string &t)
    Returns s.compare(t) < 0.
bool operator <=(const string &s, const string &t)
    Returns s.compare(t) <= 0.
bool operator >(const string &s, const string &t)
    Returns s.compare(t) > 0.
bool operator >=(const string &s, const string &t)
    Returns s.compare(t) >= 0.
```

APPENDIX D

Namespaces

C++ recognizes several different scopes, or, more properly, *namespaces*. For example, there is a local namespace whose elements (e.g., classes, functions, objects) are limited to the block in which they are declared. The other primary namespaces are the global namespace, and the various class namespaces. Within a given namespace, and subject to the rules of overloading, the element names are unique. The proposed C++ standard includes the **namespace** and **using** mechanisms that allow other namespaces to be defined and referenced. Inside a namespace, a collection of classes, functions, objects, types, and other namespaces can be declared. Namespaces are particularly useful for client applications that must be able to distinguish between various overloaded classes and functions.

D.1

NAMESPACE DEFINITIONS

In developing an application, it is often the case that multiple libraries are required. Because these libraries may come from different sources, they may define classes or functions with the same name.

Suppose there is a library lib1 with header file `lib1.h` containing the following:

```
#ifndef LIB1_H
#define LIB1_H
class SimpleWindow {
    // EzWindows window representation ...
};
#endif
```

Similarly, suppose there is a library lib2 with a header file `lib2.h` containing the following:

```
#ifndef LIB2_H
#define LIB2_H
class SimpleWindow {
    // basic house window representation ...
};
#endif
```

Both lib1 and lib2 define `SimpleWindow` classes. What happens if a client application attempts to use both classes in the same program file, as in the following code segment?

```
#include "lib1.h"
#include "lib2.h"
void BuildHouse() {
    SimpleWindow FigureWindow; // lib1 or lib2?
    SimpleWindow StormWindow;  // lib1 or lib2?
    // process objects ...
}
```

Function `BuildHouse()` will not compile because of the ambiguity of which `SimpleWindow` class to use in the definitions of `FigureWindow` and `StormWindow`. If libraries lib1 and lib2 had instead been developed using the namespace mechanism, we could individually specify which `SimpleWindow` class to use as in the following code segment that redefines `BuildHouse()`.

```
#include "lib1.h"
#include "lib2.h"
void BuildHouse() {
    lib2::SimpleWindow FigureWindow; // lib1
    lib1::SimpleWindow StormWindow;  // lib2
    // process objects ...
}
```

Thus, namespaces create virtual packages whose elements can be fully specified to prevent name ambiguity.

The basic syntax for defining a namespace is quite simple.

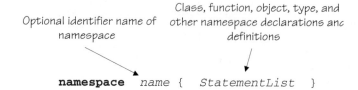

Optional identifier name of namespace

Class, function, object, type, and other namespace declarations and definitions

namespace *name* { *StatementList* }

To enable the modified version of function `BuildHouse()` to use both `SimpleWindow` classes, we redefine the header file for library lib1 using a namespace `lib1`.

```
#ifndef LIB1_H
#define LIB1_H
namespace lib1 {
   class SimpleWindow {
       // EzWindows window representation ...
   };
}
#endif
```

And we redefine similarly the header file for library lib2 so that it uses a namespace `lib2`.

```
#ifndef LIB2_H
#define LIB2_H
namespace lib2 {
   class SimpleWindow {
       // basic house window representation ...
   };
}
#endif
```

The name of a namespace is typically a variation on its header file name. To ensure namespace name uniqueness, software suppliers of a library sometimes include their name as part of the namespace name.

```
namespace FantasticFunctionsClassyClassesLib {
   // namespace definition
}
```

A client can avoid using an unwieldy name by using a namespace alias.

```
namespace Lib = FantasticFunctionsClassyClassesLib;
```

As the example suggests, a namespace alias has the following syntax.

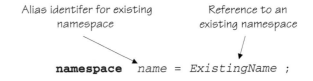

A namespace is not required to have a name. Such a namespace is an *anonymous namespace*. When an anonymous namespace is used, it is defined typically at the beginning of the translation unit (program file). The elements in an anonymous namespace can only be referenced in that same translation unit. The elements of an anonymous namespace are part of the global namespace for the translation unit in which the namespace occurs. This fact means that elements of an anonymous namespace can be referenced using their names without any additional namespace syntax. In the following example, an object MaxSize is defined in the anonymous space and then used within function f() in the definition of an array s.

```
namespace {
    const int MaxSize = 256;
}
void f() {
    int s[MaxSize];
    // process s ...
}
```

A namespace can have additional definitions and declarations added to it. Also, namespace definitions can be nested. For example, the following code segment first defines a namespace A that contains a function f(). A function g() is then defined. A namespace B is then defined that contains a function h(), and a namespace C which contains a function i(). Namespace A is then modified to also include a function j().

```
namespace A {
    void f();
}
void g() {
    // can use namespace A's f()
    // cannot use any component of namespace B
    // cannot use namespace A's g()
}
namespace B {
    void h();
    namespace C {
        void i();
    }
}
namespace A {
    void j();
}
```

Function g() in the preceding example cannot use the components of namespace B because they are not declared when g() is translated. For a similar reason, g() cannot use function j() of namespace A.

D.2

USING NAMESPACES

The **using** statement is often used in conjunction with namespaces. This statement is a mechanism for indicating which declaration is to be in effect. There are two forms of the **using** statement.

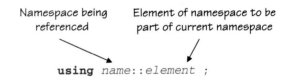

Namespace whose elements are to be
part of current namespace

    using namespace *name* ;

Namespace being
referenced

Element of namespace to be
part of current namespace

    using *name*::*element* ;

Suppose the following definitions are in effect.

```
namespace A {
    void f() {
        cout << "f(): from namespace A" << endl;
    }
    void g() {
        cout << "g(): from namespace A" << endl;
    }
}
namespace B {
    void f() {
        cout << "f(): from namespace B" << endl;
    }
    namespace C {
        void f() {
            cout << "f(): from namespace C" << endl;
        }
    }
}
void g() {
    cout << "g(): from global namespace" << endl;
}
```

What happens if the following example code segment is executed?

```
g();
A::f();
B::f();
B::C::f();
using namespace A;
f();
```

The result is the following output.

```
g(): from global namespace
f(): from namespace A
f(): from namespace B
f(): from namespace C
f(): from namespace A
```

There is no ambiguity regarding function `g()` in the example because non-namespace definitions take precedence. The invocation `A::f()` in the example is unambiguous because it is fully qualified using the scope resolution operator. The invocation `B::f()` is also unambiguous because the other function `f()` declared within the inner namespace `C` requires additional qualification to be referenced. The invocation `B::C::f()` is similarly unambiguous because it is fully qualified using the scope resolution operator.

The **using** statement in the example indicates that the definitions in namespace A are to be part of the current namespace.

```
using namespace A;
```

As there is no ambiguity with existing functions in the namespace, no qualification is needed in the invocation of `f()` following the **using** statement. However, the statement below would not compile.

```
g();
```

An ambiguity would exist here because there are two function named `g()` with the same signature in the current namespace. By using the scope resolution operator we can distinguish between these two functions.

```
::g();    // g() from global namespace
A::g();   // g() from namespace A
```

If in the example we had used the component namespace C of namespace B rather than namespace A as in the following code segment:

```
g();
A::f();
B::f();
B::C::f();
using namespace B::C;
f();
```

then the final invocation in this segment produces as its output:

```
f(): from namespace C
```

This output occurs because the definitions in C now take equal precedence with other names in the current namespace.

In the next code segment we define a namespace `constants` that contains several object definitions.

```
namespace constants {
    const double pi = 3.141592;
    const double e  = 2.718281;
    const double c  = 299792.4;
}
```

The **using** statement in this next segment provides access only to `pi` from namespace `constants`.

```
using constants::pi;
double r;
cout << "Circle radius: " << flush;
cin >> r;
double c = 2*pi*r;
cout << "Circumference of circle with radius " << r
 << ": " << c << endl;
```

As a result, the definition of object c does not introduce any syntactic ambiguity.

D.3

STD NAMESPACE

The proposed C++ standard specifies a standard namespace `std`. This namespace contains declarations of the various standard classes and libraries.

APPENDIX E

EzWindows API

The following is a summary of the EzWindows API types, classes, and capabilities.

E.1

ENUMERATED TYPES

The EzWindows API defines three enumerated types: `color`, `WindowStatus`, and `BitMapStatus`.

Enumerated type `color` provides symbolic names for the possible colors that can be displayed in a `SimpleWindow`.

```
enum color {White, Red, Green, Blue, Yellow, Cyan,
   Magenta};
```

Enumeration type `WindowStatus` defines the possible states for a `SimpleWindow` object

```
enum WindowStatus {WindowClosed, WindowOpen,
   WindowFailure};
```

where

- `WindowClosed` indicates an unopened window. Objects cannot be displayed in a window with this status.
- `WindowOpen` indicates an opened window. Objects can be displayed in a window with this status.
- `WindowFailure` indicates a failure state. Objects cannot be displayed in a window with this status.

Enumeration type `BitMapStatus` defines the possible states of a `Bit-Map` object

```
enum BitMapStatus {NoBitMap, BitMapOkay, NoWindow};
```

where

- `NoBitMap` indicates there is no bitmap to be displayed.
- `BitMapOkay` indicates there is a bitmap to display and an associated window.
- `NoWindow` indicates there is no associated window with the bitmap.

E.2

COORDINATE SYSTEM

Figure E.1 illustrates the EzWindows coordinate system. The origin is the upper-left corner of the screen. All coordinates are expressed as centimeters

Figure E.1

The EzWindows coordinate system

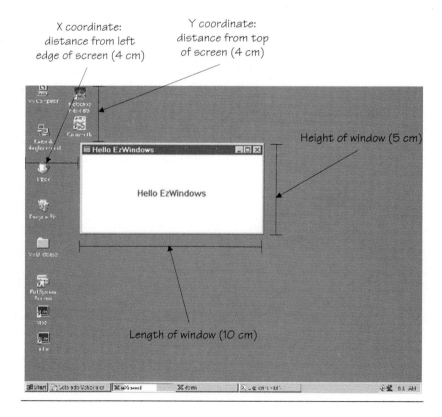

from the origin. The unit of measure for the size of EzWindows objects is also centimeters.

Some EzWindows API functions use a bounding box to specify the size of an object. For example, the following diagram illustrates the bounding box for an ellipse.

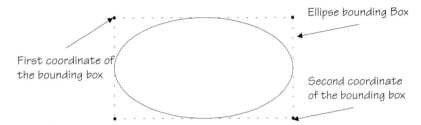

A bounding box is specified by giving the EzWindows coordinates of the upper-left and lower-right corners of a rectangle that bounds the shape.

E.3

CLASS SIMPLEWINDOW

The class `SimpleWindow` allows objects that represent simple window displays to be defined and manipulated. The class provides 10 public members functions that are described below.

```
SimpleWindow::SimpleWindow(char *t = "Untitled",
   float w = 8.0, float h = 8.0,
   const Position &p = Position(3.0,3.0))
```

Creates a `SimpleWindow` for displaying graphical objects. Parameter `t` is a pointer to the character string to be displayed in the title bar of the window. The default title is `"Untitled"`. Parameter `w` is the width of the window in centimeters. The default width is 8 centimeters. Parameter `h` is the height of the window in centimeters. The default height is 8 centimeters. Parameter `p` is the position of the window. The first coordinate is the distance in centimeters from the left edge of the screen. The second coordinate is the distance in centimeters from the top edge of the screen. The default position is 0, 0, which is the upper left-hand corner of the screen.

```
WindowStatus SimpleWindow::SimpleWindow::Open()
```

Makes window appear on display and be enabled for displaying objects. The function returns a `WindowStatus` value that represents the state of the window.

```
WindowStatus SimpleWindow::GetStatus()
```

Returns a `WindowStatus` value that represents the state of the window.

`Position SimpleWindow::GetCenter()`

Gets the location of the center of the window. The function returns a `Position` value that represents the logical coordinates of the center of the window, which are measured in centimeters from the left and top edges of the window.

float `SimpleWindow::GetWidth()`

Return the width of the window in centimeters.

float `SimpleWindow::GetHeight()`

Return the height of the window in centimeters.

float `SimpleWindow::GetXPosition()`

Return the x-coordinate of the position of the window.

float `SimpleWindow::GetYPosition()`

Return the y-coordinate of the position of the window.

`WindowStatus SimpleWindow::Close()`

Closes the window and makes it disappear. The return value is `WindowClosed`.

void `SimpleWindow::Erase(Position &UpperLeft,`
  float `Width,` **float** `Height)`

Erases a rectangular region. The upper-left corner of the rectangle is specified by the `Position UpperLeft`. A rectangle `Width` centimeters wide and `Height` centimeters high is erased.

void `SimpleWindow::RenderRectangle(`
  `Position &UpperLeft,`
  `Position &LowerRight, color Color)`

Draw a rectangle. The bounding box is specified by the coordinates `UpperLeft` and `LowerRight`. The rectangle is filled with color `Color`.

void `SimpleWindow::RenderEllipse(`
  `Position &UpperLeft,`
  `Position &LowerRight, color Color)`

Draw an ellipse. The bounding box is specified by the parameters `UpperLeft` and `LowerRight`. The ellipse is filled with color `Color`.

void `SimpleWindow::RenderPolygon(`
  `Position PolyPoints[],`
  int `NPoints, color Color)`

Draw a closed polygon. The points of the polygon are held in the array `PolyPoints`. The parameter `NPoints` is the number of points in the polygon. The polygon is filled with color `Color`.

void `SimpleWindow::RenderText(`
  const `Position &UpperLeft,`
  const `Position &LowerRight,`
  char `*Msg = "Message",`
  `color BackGroundColor = White)`

Displays a text string in a window. Parameter `UpperLeft` is the position of the upper left-hand corner of the bounding box for the text message. The default position is (0, 0), or the upper-left corner of the window. Parameter `LowerRight` is the position of the lower right-hand corner of the bounding box for the text message. The default position is (1,1). Parameter `Msg` is a pointer to a character string to be displayed in the window. The default message is `"Message"`. Parameter `BackGroundColor` is the background color for the text.

void `SimpleWindow::SetMouseClickCallback(`
`MouseClickCallbackFunction f)`

Registers a callback for a mouse click. Function `f()` will be called when a mouse click occurs in the window. Function `f()` must be declared to take a single parameter of type **const** `Position &`, and it should return an **int.** The return value of `f()` indicates whether the event was handled successfully. A value of 1 is to indicate success and a value of 0 is to indicate that an error occurred.

void `SimpleWindow::SetTimerCallback(`
`TimerTickCallbackFunction f)`

Registers a callback for a timer tick. Function `f()` will be called when a timer tick occurs. The function `f()` must be declared to take no parameters, and it should return an **int.** The return value of `f()` indicates whether the event was handled successfully. A value of 1 is to indicate success, and a value of 0 is to indicate an error occurred.

void `SimpleWindow::SetRefreshCallback(`
`RefreshCallbackFunction f)`

Registers a callback for a refresh message. Function `f()` will be called when the window receives a refresh event. The function `f()` must be declared to take no parameters, and it should return an int. The return value of `f()` indicates whether the event was handled successfully. A value of 1 is to indicate success, and a value of 0 is to indicate an error occurred.

void `SimpleWindow::SetQuitCallback(`
`QuitCallbackFunction f)`

Registers a callback for a quit message. Function `f()` will be called when the window receives a quit event. The function `f()` must be declared to take no parameters, and it should return an int. The return value of `f()` indicates whether the event was handled successfully. A value of 1 is to indicate success, and a value of 0 is to indicate an error occurred.

int `SimpleWindow::StartTimer(`**int** `Interval)`

Starts timer running. Parameter `Interval` is the number of milliseconds between timer events. The return value indicates whether the timer was successfully started. A return value of 1 indicates success, and a return value of 0 indicates the timer could not be set up.

void `SimpleWindow::StopTimer()`

Turns timer off.

void `SimpleWindow::Message(`**char** `*Msg)`

Pops up an alert window with a message. The parameter `Msg` is a pointer to the character string that should be displayed in the alert window.

E.4

CLASS WINDOWOBJECT

Class `WindowObject` is the base class for class `Shape`.

`WindowObject(SimpleWindow &w, ` **const** ` Position &p)`
> Creates a `WindowObject` that is centered at position p in window w.

`Position WindowObject::GetPosition() ` **const**
> Returns the position of the window object.

`SimpleWindow WindowObject::GetWindow() ` **const**
> Returns the window containing the `WindowObject`.

void ` WindowObject::SetPosition(` **const** ` Position &p)`
> Sets the position of the `WindowObject` to p.

E.5

CLASS SHAPE

Class `Shape` is the base class for classes `CircleShape`, `EllipseShape`, `RectangleShape`, and `TriangleShape`:

`Shape::Shape(SimpleWindow &w, ` **const** ` Position &p,`
`  ` **const** ` color c = Red)`
> Creates a `Shape` object that is centered at position p in window w. The color of the object is c which by default is the value `Red`.

`color Shape::GetColor() ` **const**
> Returns the color of the object.

void ` Shape::SetColor(` **const** ` color c)`
> Sets the color of the object to c.

E.6

CLASS ELLIPSESHAPE

Class `EllipseShape` is derived publicly from class `Shape`. Class `EllipseShape` has the following public member functions:

`EllipseShape::EllipseShape(SimpleWindow &w,`
`  ` **const** ` Position &p, ` **const** ` color c = Red,`
`  ` **float** ` len = 1, ` **float** ` h = 2)`
> Creates an `EllipseShape` object to represent an ellipse. The ellipse is centered at position p in window w. The ellipse has color c, which by default is the value `Red`. The ellipse has length `len` and height h. The default values of parameters `len` and h are 1 and 2 respectively. Parameters `len` and h both represent centimeter values.

float ` EllipseShape::GetLength() ` **const**
> Returns the length of the object in centimeters.

float ` EllipseShape::GetHeight() ` **const**
> Returns the height of the object in centimeters.

void EllipseShape::SetSize(**float** len, **float** hght)

Sets the length of the ellipse to len and the height of the ellipse to hght. Parameters len and hght both represent centimeter values.

void EllipseShape::Draw()

Displays the ellipse to its associated window.

E.7

CLASS CIRCLESHAPE

Class CircleShape is derived publicly from class Shape. Class CircleShape has the following public member functions:

CircleShape::CircleShape(SimpleWindow &w,
  const Position &p, **const** color c = Red,
  float d = 1)

Creates a CircleShape object to represent a circle. The circle is centered at position p in window w. The circle has color c, which by default is the value Red. The circle has diameter d. The default value of d is 1. Parameter d represents a centimeter value.

float CircleShape::GetDiameter() **const**

Returns the diameter of the circle.

void CircleShape::SetSize(**float** d)

Sets the diameter of the circle to d. Parameter d represents a centimeter value.

void CircleShape::Draw()

Displays the circle to its associated window.

E.8

CLASS RECTANGLESHAPE

Class RectangleShape is derived publicly from class Shape. Class RectangleShape has the following public member functions:

RectangleShape::RectangleShape(SimpleWindow &w,
  const Position &p, **const** color c = Red,
  float len = 1, **float** wid = 2)

Creates a RectangleShape object to represent a rectangle. The rectangle is centered at position p in window w. The rectangle has color c, which by default is the value Red. The length of the rectangle is len. The width of the rectangle is wid. The default values of len and wid are 1 and 2 respectively. Parameters len and wid represent centimeter values.

```
RectangleShape::RectangleShape(SimpleWindow &w,
    float xpos, float ypos, const color c = Red,
    float len = 1, float wid = 2)
```
Creates a `RectangleShape` object to represent a rectangle. The rectangle is centered at `Position(xpos,ypos)` in window w. The rectangle has color c, which by default is the value `Red`. The length of the rectangle is `len`. The width of the rectangle is `wid`. The default values of `len` and `wid` are 1 and 2 respectively. Parameters `len` and `wid` represent centimeter values.

float `RectangleShape::GetLength()` **const**
Returns the length of the rectangle in centimeters.

float `RectangleShape::GetWidth()` **const**
Returns the width of the rectangle in centimeters.

void `RectangleShape::SetSize(`**float** `len,` **float** `wid)`
Sets the length of the rectangle to `len` and the width of the rectangle to `wid`. Parameters `len` and `wid` both represent centimeter values.

void `RectangleShape::Draw()` **const**
Displays the rectangle to its associated window.

E.9
CLASS TRIANGLESHAPE

Class `TriangleShape` is derived publicly from class `Shape`. Class `TriangleShape` has the following public member functions:

```
TriangleShape::TriangleShape(SimpleWindow &w,
    const Position &p, const color c = Red,
    float len = 1)
```
Creates a `TriangleShape` object to represent an equilateral triangle. The triangle is centered at position p in window w. The triangle has color c, which by default is the value `Red`. The length of a side of the triangle is `len`. The default value of `len` is 1. Parameter `len` represents a centimeter value.

float `TriangleShape::GetLength()` **const**
Returns the length of a side of the triangle in centimeters.

void `TriangleShape::SetSize(`**float** `len)`
Sets the length of a side of the triangle to `len`. Parameter `len` represents a centimeter value.

void `TriangleShape::Draw()`
Displays the triangle to its associated window.

E.10
CLASS LABEL

Class `Label` has the following public member functions:

```
Label::Label(SimpleWindow &w, const Position &p,
  const string &Text, const color Color = White)
```
Creates a `Label` object to represent a text message. The message is centered at position p in window w. The message has background color c, which by default is the value `White`. (The foreground color is `Black`.)

```
Label::Label(SimpleWindow &w, float XCoord,
  float YCoord, const string &Text,
  const color Color = White)
```
Creates a `Label` object to represent a text message. The message is centered at position (`XCoord`, `YCoord`) in window w. The message has background color c, which by default is the value `White`. (The foreground color is `Black`.)

```
Label::Label(SimpleWindow &w, const Position &p,
  const char *Text, const color Color = White)
```
Creates a `Label` object to represent a text message. The message is centered at position p in window w. The message has background color c, which by default is the value `White`. (The foreground color is `Black`.)

```
Label::Label(SimpleWindow &w, float XCoord,
  float YCoord, const char *Text,
  const color Color = White)
```
Creates a `Label` object to represent a text message. The message is centered at position (`XCoord`, `YCoord`) in window w. The message has background color c, which by default is the value `White`. (The foreground color is `Black`.)

```
color Label::GetColor() const
```
Returns the background color of the label.

```
void Label::SetColor(const color c)
```
Sets the background color of the label to c.

```
void Label::Draw()
```
Displays the label to its associated window.

E.11

CLASS BITMAP

Class `BitMap` has the following public member functions:

```
BitMap::BitMap(SimpleWindow &w)
```
Creates a `BitMap` object with `BitMapStatus NoBitMap`. The object is associated with window w.

```
BitMap::BitMap(SimpleWindow *w)
```
Creates a `BitMap` object with `BitMapStatus NoBitMap`. The object is associated with window pointed to by w.

```
BitMap::BitMap()
```
Creates a `BitMap` object with `BitMapStatus NoBitMap`. The object is not associated with any window.

`BitMapStatus BitMap::Load(string Filename)`

The file whose name is pointed to by string `Filename` is used to set the bitmap. If the file contains a valid bitmap, the status of the object is set to `BitMapOkay`; otherwise, the status of the object is set to `NoBitMap`.

`BitMapStatus BitMap::Load(`**char** `*Filename)`

The file whose name is pointed to by character string `Filename` is used to set the bitmap. If the file contains a valid bitmap, the status of the object is set to `BitMapOkay`; otherwise, the status of the object is set to `NoBitMap`.

void `BitMap::SetWindow(SimpleWindow &w)`

Associates the bitmap with window w. The `BitMapStatus` of the bitmap is set to `NoBitMap`.

int `BitMap::Draw()`

Attempts to display the bitmap object to the associated window. The `BitMapStatus` of the object must be `BitMapOkay` for display to be successful. If the bitmap is displayed, the function returns 1; otherwise, the function returns 0.

int `BitMap::Erase()`

Overwrites the bitmap on the display by drawing a white rectangle of the same size.

int `BitMap::IsInside(`**const** `Position &p)` **const**

If position p lies within the bitmap, the function returns 1; otherwise, the function returns 0.

`BitMapStatus BitMap::GetStatus()` **const**

Returns the current `BitMapStatus` value associated with the object.

float `BitMap::GetXPosition()` **const**

Returns the distance from the upper left corner of the bitmap to the left edge of the associated window. The distance is in centimeters.

float `BitMap::GetYPosition()` **const**

Returns the distance from the upper left corner of the bitmap to the top edge of the associated window. The distance is in centimeters.

float `BitMap::GetWidth()` **const**

Returns the width of the bitmap in centimeters.

float `BitMap::GetHeight()` **const**

Returns the height of the bitmap in centimeters.

void `BitMap::SetPosition(`**const** `Position &p)`

Sets the position of the bitmap to p.

`Position BitMap::GetPosition()` **const**

Returns the position of the upper left corner of the bitmap.

E.12
MISCELLANEOUS FUNCTIONS

long `GetMilliseconds()`

Returns the value of a timer that is ticking continuously. The resolution of the timer is milliseconds.

void `Terminate()`

Sends a terminate message to the EzWindows window manager.

Index

A

Abacus, 24

Abnormal program termination, 225

Abstract base class, 637, 668–669, 675, 679–680, 687

Abstract data type, 363–366, 369, 379–380, 383–384, 390, 406–410, 412–414, 451–452, 456–458, 461–463, 467, 563, 570–571, 580, 583–584, 642–643, 645, 648–649, 674, 677–678, 715, 717

Abstraction, 28, 42

Access function (see Inspector)

Access specifier, 594, 609

Accessor (see Inspector)

Activation record, 204–206, 232, 240–241, 243, 245–246, 271–272, 282, 377, 443, 529, 531

`Add()`

    `BigNum`, 578

    `Matrix`, 446

    `Rational`, 381

Address, 523, 546

Address operator, 521, 525, 546–547

ADT (see Abstract data type)

Algorithm, 41

Allen, Paul, 582

Altair 8800, 545

Ambiguity

    `else`, 151

    name, 616, 722

Analytical Engine, 188

Anonymous

    `enum`, 623

    namespace, 723–724

ANSI, 642

`ApiEnd()`, 483

`ApiMain()`, 127

Apple I, 517

Apple II, 517

Application programmer interface (API), 475–476

Architecture, 59

`argc` and `argv`, 540, 546

Arithmetic

    operators, 75–78, 110

    overflow, 77–78

Array

    assignment, 421, 469, 522, 549, 644, 646, 648–649

    base type, 419, 430, 444, 469–471, 675

    declaration, 427, 540, 724

    default constructor, 419, 444, 469

    indexing, 417

    initialization, 418, 444, 603

P

Parameter

    actual, 202–206

    array, 427, 444

    command line, 521, 540–541, 546–547

    constant reference, 294

    constant value, 242

    correspondence, 240

    default, 296, 317, 342, 369, 379, 385, 412, 426, 646

    list, 201, 281

    passing, 197, 243, 279, 332

    reference, 260, 279–283, 285–288, 291, 293, 311, 315–316, 325, 332, 335, 367, 373, 376–377, 381, 410, 413, 427–428, 430, 444, 469–470, 473, 546, 548–549, 639, 658, 667

    stream, 200, 289–290, 296, 426, 543

    value, 202–206, 240–247

`Part`, 352

`Partition()`, 438

Pascal, Blaise, 128

Pass by

    reference, 281–282, 288, 294, 311, 316, 428, 469

    value, 205, 234, 280–281, 283, 311, 315–316, 642

PDP-8, 407

Persistent manipulator, 215–219

`PickOrder()`, 504, 510–511

Pixel, 12

`Play()`

    `GameController`, 699

    `SimonGame`, 504, 510–511

Pointer

    constant, 532–533, 546–547

    null, 523, 546

    to constant, 532–533, 546–547

    to function, 543

    to object, 521–523, 525, 527–528, 544, 546–547, 550, 575, 577, 580–581, 652, 656, 662, 668, 675

    to pointer, 528

`Poker`, 451, 462–463, 465, 474, 519

Polymorphism, 37–38, 42, 542, 637–638, 643, 662–664, 674–676, 681, 699, 703

`Position`, 479

`pow()`, 227

`Power()`, 267

Precedence, 47, 144, 153, 191, 705, 707

Preprocessor, 49, 91, 197, 207–210, 229, 232, 260, 301, 370, 385

Preprocessor directive, 49, 91, 207, 209–210

`PrintList()`, 429

`PrintSessionResults()`, 354

Private

    inheritance, 587, 607, 609, 632

    section, 331, 337, 356, 358, 372, 375, 385, 409–410, 452, 511, 597, 606, 686

Program

    command-line parameter, 521, 540–541, 546–547

    return value, 159, 225

Promotion, 227, 382–383, 569

Prompt, 51

`PromptAndRead()`, 248

Protected

    inheritance, 594, 605–607, 609, 632–633

    section, 371, 374–375, 394, 409, 606–608, 686, 696

Prototyping, 201

Pseudorandom number, 301–302, 304–305, 318, 363, 383–387, 389–390, 410, 413, 461, 712

Public

    inheritance, 587, 594, 608–609, 632

    section, 331, 337, 356, 358, 371–372, 409, 597, 606

Pure virtual function, 637, 668–669, 675–676, 687